Northamptonshire

Corby, Daventry, Kettering, Northampton, Wellingborough

First published in 1999 by

Philip's, a division of
Octopus Publishing Group Ltd
2-4 Heron Quays, London E14 4JP

Third edition 2007
First impression 2007
NHPCA

ISBN-10 0-540-09097-2 (pocket)
ISBN-13 978-0-540-09097-6 (pocket)

Printed by Toppan, China

Contents

II **List of mobile speed cameras**

III **Key to map symbols**

IV **Key to map pages**

VI **Route Planning**

X **Administrative and Postcode boundaries**

1 **Street maps** at 2⅔ inches to 1 mile

240 **Index** of towns, villages, streets, hospitals, industrial estates, railway stations, schools, shopping centres, universities and places of interest

Digital Data

The exceptionally high-quality mapping found in this atlas is available as digital data in TIFF format, which is easily convertible to other bitmapped (raster) image formats.

The index is also available in digital form as a standard database table. It contains all the details found in the printed index together with the National Grid reference for the map square in which each entry is named.

For further information and to discuss your requirements, please contact james.mann@philips-maps.co.uk

Mobile speed cameras

The vast majority of speed cameras used on Britain's roads are operated by safety camera partnerships. These comprise local authorities, the police, Her Majesty's Court Service (HMCS) and the Highways Agency.

This table lists the sites where each safety camera partnership may enforce speed limits through the use of mobile cameras or detectors. These are usually set up on the roadside or a bridge spanning the road and operated by a police or civilian enforcement officer. The speed limit at each site (if available) is shown in red type, followed by the approximate location in black type.

In addition to the routes below, mobile speed enforcement can also take place in local areas of concern requested by residents or as determined by the Police.

A5
- 60 DIRFT to County Boundary
- 60 Norton/Whilton Crossroads
- 30/40 Towcester Racecourse to A43

A6
- 60 Burton Latimer Bypass

A14
- 70 Kelmarsh
- 70 Kelmarsh Junctions 7-10

A43
- 60 Laxton Turn to A47 Duddington
- 60 Mawsley to A14 Junc 8 (inc Mawsley Spur)
- 70 Towcester to M1 Junc 15a

A45
- 60 M1 Junc 16 to Weedon
- 60 Stanwick to Raunds

A361
- 60 Byfield to Chipping Warden

A422
- 60 Brackley West to A43

A428
- 60 East Haddon
- 30/60 Great Houghton to Yardley Hastings

A508
- 30 Northampton, Plough Gyratory
- 30 Northampton, St Georges Avenue to Holly Lodge Rd
- 30 Northampton, St Peters Way to St Georges Avenue
- 30/60 Stoke Bruerne to A5
- 70 Wootton Flyover to M1 Junc 15

A509
- 60 Wellingborough to Isham

A605
- 40/60 Thrapston to Warmington

A4256
- 30 Daventry, Eastern Way

A4500
- 40/60 Great Billing to Earls Barton
- 30 Northampton, Abington Park to York Rd
- 30 Northampton, Park Avenue to Booth Lane South
- 30 Northampton, Weedon Rd to Duston Rd

A5076
- 40 Mere Way
- 40 Northampton, Great Billing Way South

A5193
- 30/40 Wellingborough, London Rd

A6003
- 50/60 Kettering to Corby

A6014
- 40/60 Corby, Oakley Rd

B569
- 50 Irchester to Rushden

B576
- 60 Desborough to Rothwell

B4038
- 30/60 Kilsby, Rugby Rd

B4525
- 40/60 Welsh Lane

B5385
- 60 Watford to West Haddon

Unclassified
- 30 Brackmills Industrial Estate
- 30 Northampton, Grange Rd

Key to map symbols

- **Motorway** with junction number
- **Primary route** – dual/single carriageway
- **A road** – dual/single carriageway
- **B road** – dual/single carriageway
- **Minor road** – dual/single carriageway
- **Other minor road** – dual/single carriageway
- **Road under construction**
- **Tunnel, covered road**
- **Speed cameras - single, multiple**
- **Rural track, private road or narrow road in urban area**
- **Gate or obstruction to traffic** (restrictions may not apply at all times or to all vehicles)
- **Path, bridleway, byway open to all traffic, road used as a public path**
- **Pedestrianised area**
- DY7 **Postcode boundaries**
- **County and unitary authority boundaries**
- **Railway, tunnel, railway under construction**
- **Tramway, tramway under construction**
- **Miniature railway**
- Walsall **Railway station**
- **Private railway station**
- South Shields **Metro station**
- **Tram stop, tram stop under construction**
- **Bus, coach station**
- **Ambulance station**
- **Coastguard station**
- **Fire station**
- **Police station**
- **Accident and Emergency entrance to hospital**
- **Hospital**
- **Place of worship**
- **Information Centre** (open all year)
- **Shopping Centre**
- **Parking**
- P&R **Park and Ride**
- PO **Post Office**
- **Camping site**
- **Caravan site**
- **Golf course**
- **Picnic site**
- Prim Sch **Important buildings, schools, colleges, universities and hospitals**
- **Built up area**
- **Woods**
- River Medway **Water name**
- **River, weir, stream**
- **Canal, lock, tunnel**
- **Water**
- **Tidal water**
- Church **Non-Roman antiquity**
- ROMAN FORT **Roman antiquity**
- 87 58 **Adjoining page indicators**

Acad	**Academy**	Inst	**Institute**	Recn Gd	**Recreation Ground**
Allot Gdns	**Allotments**	Ct	**Law Court**	Resr	**Reservoir**
Cemy	**Cemetery**	L Ctr	**Leisure Centre**	Ret Pk	**Retail Park**
C Ctr	**Civic Centre**	LC	**Level Crossing**	Sch	**School**
CH	**Club House**	Liby	**Library**	Sh Ctr	**Shopping Centre**
Coll	**College**	Mkt	**Market**	TH	**Town Hall/House**
Crem	**Crematorium**	Meml	**Memorial**	Trad Est	**Trading Estate**
Ent	**Enterprise**	Mon	**Monument**	Univ	**University**
Ex H	**Exhibition Hall**	Mus	**Museum**	W Twr	**Water Tower**
Ind Est	**Industrial Estate**	Obsy	**Observatory**	Wks	**Works**
IRB Sta	**Inshore Rescue Boat Station**	Pal	**Royal Palace**	YH	**Youth Hostel**
		PH	**Public House**		

■ The small numbers around the edges of the maps identify the 1 kilometre National Grid lines

■ The dark grey border on the inside edge of some pages indicates that the mapping does not continue onto the adjacent page

The scale of the maps on the pages numbered in blue is 4.2 cm to 1 km • 2⅔ inches to 1 mile • 1: 23810

0 ¼ ½ ¾ 1 mile

0 250 m 500 m 750 m 1 kilometre

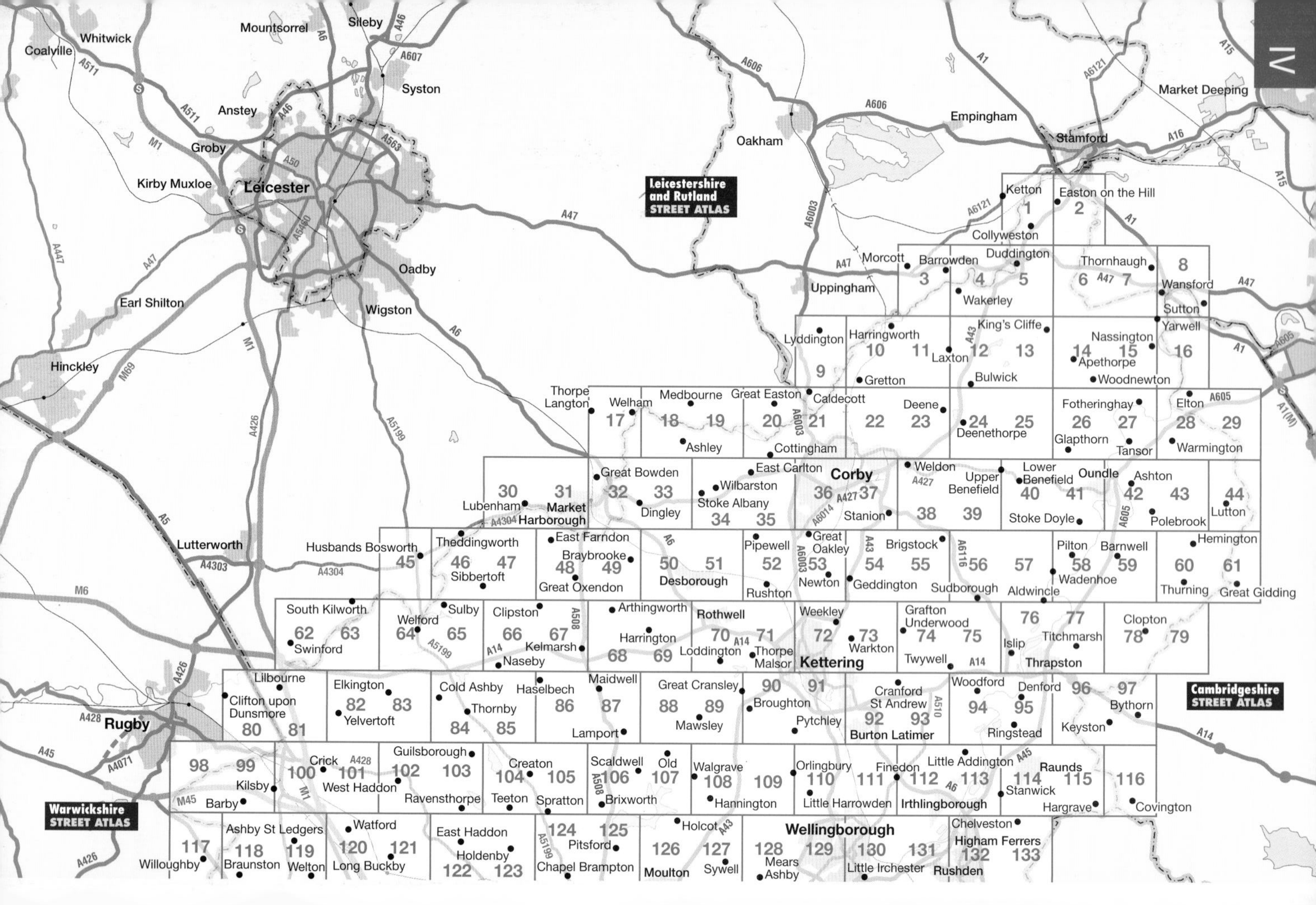
Leicestershire and Rutland STREET ATLAS
Cambridgeshire STREET ATLAS
Warwickshire STREET ATLAS
Leicester
Coalville
Whitwick
Mountsorrel
Sileby
Syston
Anstey
Groby
Kirby Muxloe
Oadby
Wigston
Earl Shilton
Hinckley
Lutterworth
Rugby
Oakham
Empingham
Stamford
Market Deeping
Uppingham
Corby
Kettering
Wellingborough
Market Harborough
Desborough
Rothwell
Oundle
Thrapston
Burton Latimer
Irthlingborough
Raunds
Higham Ferrers
Rushden
Moulton
1 Ketton
2 Easton on the Hill
Collyweston
3 Morcott Barrowden
4 5 Duddington Wakerley
6 7 Thornhaugh
8 Wansford Sutton
9 Lyddington
10 11 Harringworth Gretton
12 13 Laxton King's Cliffe Bulwick
14 15 Nassington Apethorpe Woodnewton
16 Yarwell
17 Thorpe Langton Welham
18 19 Medbourne Ashley
20 21 Great Easton Caldecott Cottingham
22 23 Deene
24 25 Deenethorpe
26 27 Fotheringhay Glapthorn Tansor
28 29 Elton Warmington
30 31 Lubenham
32 33 Great Bowden Dingley
34 35 Wilbarston Stoke Albany East Carlton
36 37 Stanion
38 39 Weldon Upper Benefield
40 41 Lower Benefield Stoke Doyle
42 43 Ashton Polebrook
44 Lutton
45 Husbands Bosworth
46 47 Theddingworth Sibbertoft
48 49 East Farndon Braybrooke Great Oxendon
50 51
52 Pipewell Rushton
53 Great Oakley Newton
54 55 Brigstock Geddington
56 57 Sudborough Aldwincle
58 59 Pilton Barnwell Wadenhoe
60 61 Hemington Thurning Great Gidding
62 63 South Kilworth Swinford
64 65 Welford Sulby
66 67 Clipston Kelmarsh Naseby
68 69 Arthingworth Harrington
70 71 Loddington Thorpe Malsor
72 73 Weekley Warkton
74 75 Grafton Underwood Twywell
76 77 Islip Titchmarsh
78 79 Clopton
80 81 Lilbourne Clifton upon Dunsmore
82 83 Elkington Yelvertoft
84 85 Cold Ashby Thornby
86 Haselbech
87 Maidwell Lamport
88 89 Great Cransley Mawsley
90 91 Broughton Pytchley
92 93 Cranford St Andrew
94 95 Woodford Denford Ringstead
96 97 Bythorn Keyston
98 99 Kilsby Barby
100 101 Crick West Haddon
102 103 Guilsborough Ravensthorpe
104 105 Creaton Teeton Spratton
106 107 Scaldwell Old Brixworth
108 109 Walgrave Hannington
110 111 Orlingbury Little Harrowden
112 113 Finedon Little Addington
114 115 Stanwick Hargrave
116 Covington
117 Willoughby
118 119 Ashby St Ledgers Braunston Welton
120 121 Watford Long Buckby
122 123 East Haddon Holdenby
124 125 Pitsford Chapel Brampton
126 127 Holcot Sywell
128 129 Mears Ashby
130 131 Little Irchester
132 133 Chelveston
A1 A1(M) A5 A6 A14 A15 A16 A43 A45 A46 A47 A50 A426 A427 A428 A447 A508 A510 A511 A563 A605 A606 A607 A4071 A4303 A4304 A5199 A5460 A6003 A6014 A6116 A6121 M1 M6 M45 M69

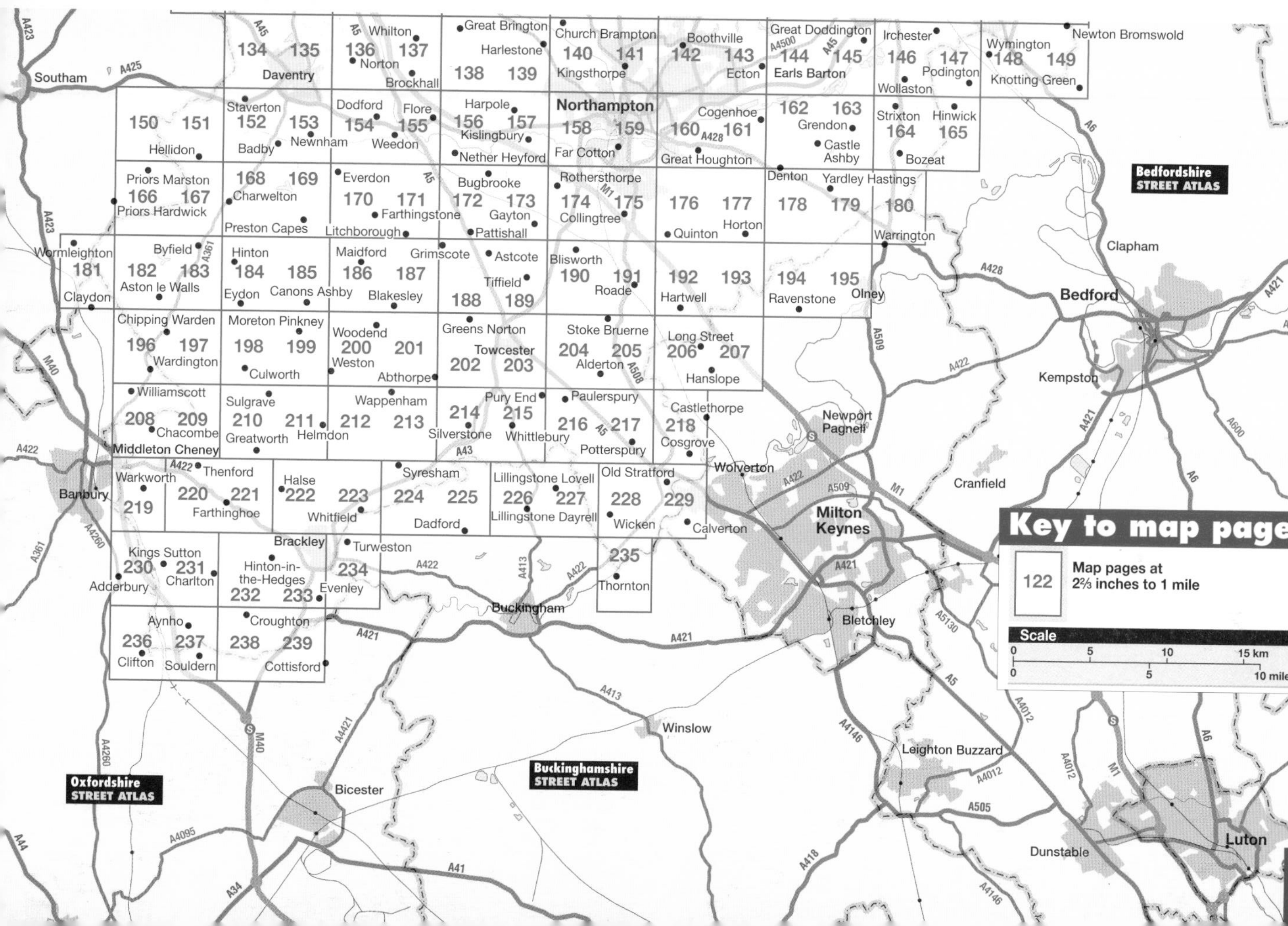

Key to map pages

122 Map pages at 2⅔ inches to 1 mile

Scale
0 5 10 15 km
0 5 10 miles

134 135 Daventry A45
136 137 Whilton Norton Brockhall A5
Great Brington Harlestone 138 139
Church Brampton 140 141 Kingsthorpe
Boothville 142 143 Ecton
Great Doddington A4500 144 A45 145 Earls Barton
Irchester 146 147 Wollaston Podington
Wymington 148 149 Newton Bromswold Knotting Green

150 151 Hellidon
Staverton 152 153 Badby Newnham
Dodford 154 Flore 155 Weedon
Harpole 156 157 Kislingbury Nether Heyford
Northampton 158 159 Far Cotton
160 A428 161 Cogenhoe Great Houghton
162 163 Grendon Castle Ashby
Strixton 164 Hinwick 165 Bozeat

Priors Marston 166 167 Priors Hardwick
168 169 Charwelton Preston Capes
Everdon 170 171 Farthingstone Litchborough A5
Bugbrooke 172 173 Gayton Pattishall
Rothersthorpe 174 M1 175 Collingtree
176 177 Quinton Horton
Denton 178 179 Yardley Hastings
180 Warrington

Wormleighton 181 Claydon
Byfield A361 182 183 Aston le Walls
Hinton 184 185 Eydon Canons Ashby
Maidford 186 187 Grimscote Blakesley
Astcote Tiffield 188 189
Blisworth 190 191 Roade
192 193 Hartwell
194 195 Ravenstone Olney

Chipping Warden 196 197 Wardington
Moreton Pinkney 198 199 Culworth
Woodend 200 201 Weston Abthorpe
Greens Norton Towcester 202 203
Stoke Bruerne 204 205 Alderton A508
Long Street 206 207 Hanslope

Williamscott 208 209 Chacombe Middleton Cheney
Sulgrave 210 211 Greatworth Helmdon
Wappenham 212 213
214 Pury End 215 Silverstone Whittlebury A43
Paulerspury 216 A5 217 Potterspury
Castlethorpe 218 Cosgrove

Warkworth 219 A422
Thenford 220 221 Farthinghoe
Halse 222 223 Whitfield
Syresham 224 225 Dadford
Lillingstone Lovell 226 227 Lillingstone Dayrell
Old Stratford 228 229 Wicken Calverton

Kings Sutton 230 231 Adderbury Charlton
Brackley Hinton-in-the-Hedges 232 233 Turweston 234 Evenley
235 Thornton

Aynho 236 237 Clifton Souldern
Croughton 238 239 Cottisford

Southam Banbury Buckingham Wolverton Newport Pagnell Milton Keynes Bletchley Winslow Leighton Buzzard Bicester Dunstable Luton Bedford Kempston Clapham Cranfield

Bedfordshire STREET ATLAS
Buckinghamshire STREET ATLAS
Oxfordshire STREET ATLAS

A423 A425 A422 M40 A361 A4260 A4095 A34 A44 A41 A4421 A421 A413 A422 A509 A428 A6 A603 A600 A421 M1 A5130 A5 A4146 A418 A4012 A505

Route planning

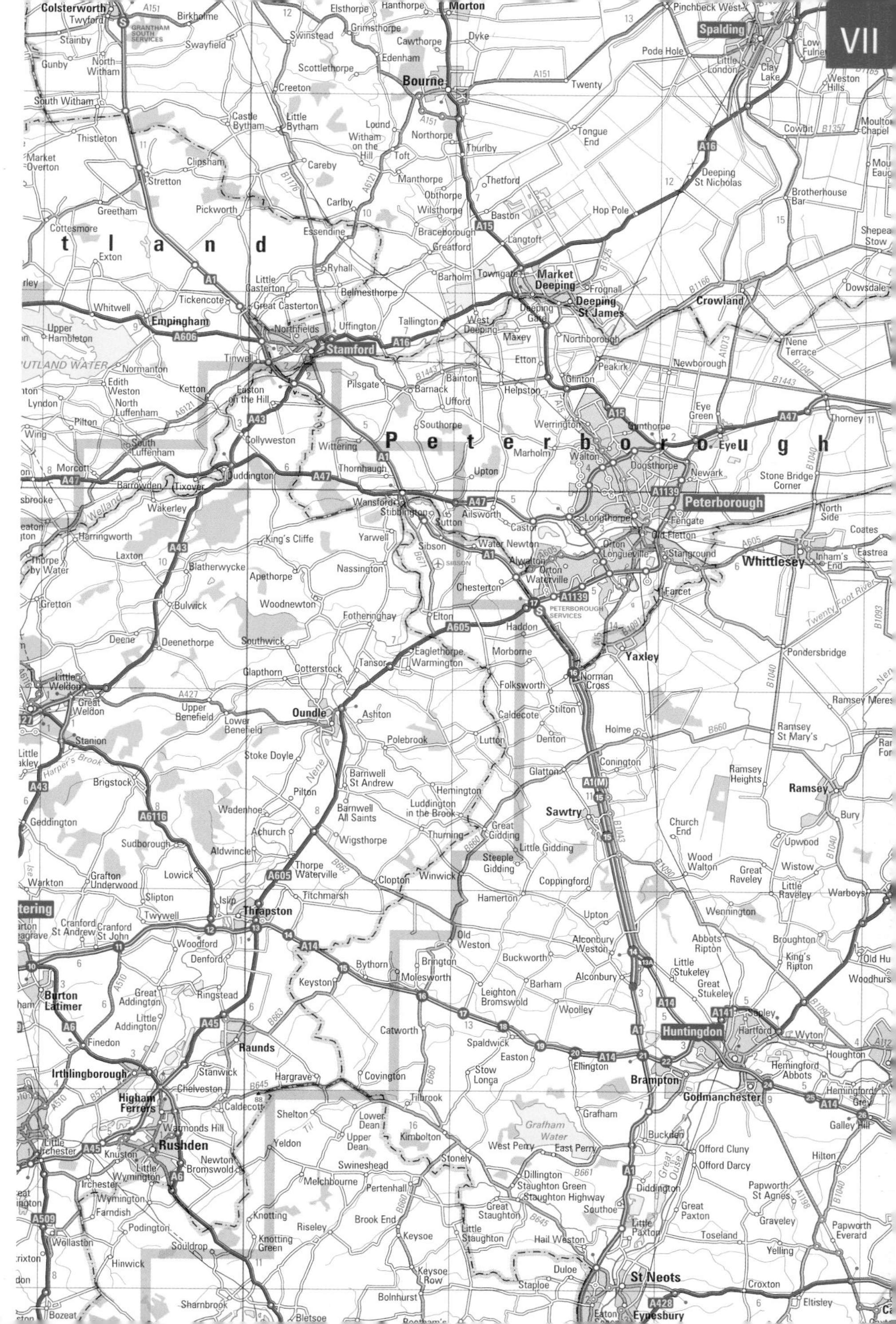
Colsterworth
Twyford
Birkholme
Stainby
Swayfield
Gunby
North Witham
South Witham
Castle Bytham
Little Bytham
Thistleton
Market Overton
Clipsham
Stretton
Greetham
Pickworth
Cottesmore
Exton
Whitwell
Tickencote
Empingham
Upper Hambleton
RUTLAND WATER
Normanton
Edith Weston
Ketton
North Luffenham
Lyndon
Pilton
Wing
South Luffenham
Morcott
Barrowden
Tixover
Duddington
Collyweston
Easton on the Hill
Tinwell
Wakerley
Harringworth
Laxton
Thorpe by Water
Gretton
Blatherwycke
Bulwick
Deene
Deenethorpe
Little Weldon
Great Weldon
Stanion
Little Oakley
Harper's Brook
Brigstock
Geddington
Sudborough
Warkton
Grafton Underwood
Lowick
Slipton
Twywell
Cranford St Andrew
Cranford St John
Kettering
Burton Latimer
Great Addington
Little Addington
Finedon
Irthlingborough
Higham Ferrers
Rushden
Knuston
Little Irchester
Irchester
Little Wymington
Wymington
Farndish
Podington
Wollaston
Hinwick
Bozeat
Sharnbrook
Souldrop
Knotting
Knotting Green
Riseley
Newton Bromswold
Chelveston
Caldecott
Stanwick
Raunds
Ringstead
Denford
Woodford
Islip
Thrapston
Titchmarsh
Aldwincle
Wadenhoe
Achurch
Thorpe Waterville
Pilton
Stoke Doyle
Oundle
Ashton
Lower Benefield
Upper Benefield
Glapthorn
Cotterstock
Southwick
Woodnewton
Apethorpe
King's Cliffe
Nassington
Fotheringhay
Tansor
Elton
Eaglethorpe, Warmington
Polebrook
Barnwell St Andrew
Barnwell All Saints
Luddington in the Brook
Hemington
Wigsthorpe
Clopton
Thurning
Winwick
Great Gidding
Little Gidding
Steeple Gidding
Lutton
Caldecote
Denton
Folksworth
Stilton
Norman Cross
Morborne
Haddon
Yaxley
Glatton
Conington
Holme
Sawtry
Coppingford
Hamerton
Upton
Old Weston
Brington
Bythorn
Keyston
Molesworth
Catworth
Covington
Hargrave
Shelton
Lower Dean
Upper Dean
Yeldon
Tilbrook
Kimbolton
Stonely
Swineshead
Melchbourne
Pertenhall
Brook End
Keysoe
Keysoe Row
Bolnhurst
Bletsoe
Little Staughton
Great Staughton
Staploe
Duloe
Hail Weston
Southoe
Dillington
Staughton Green
Staughton Highway
West Perry
East Perry
Grafham Water
Grafham
Buckden
Diddington
Little Paxton
Great Paxton
St Neots
Eynesbury
Eaton Socon
Toseland
Offord Cluny
Offord Darcy
Graveley
Yelling
Croxton
Eltisley
Papworth St Agnes
Papworth Everard
Hilton
Godmanchester
Huntingdon
Brampton
Ellington
Easton
Spaldwick
Stow Longa
Leighton Bromswold
Buckworth
Barham
Woolley
Alconbury
Alconbury Weston
Little Stukeley
Great Stukeley
Abbots Ripton
Kings Ripton
Broughton
Hartford
Sapley
Wyton
Houghton
Hemingford Abbots
Hemingford Grey
Galley Hill
Wennington
Wood Walton
Great Raveley
Little Raveley
Church End
Upwood
Wistow
Warboys
Bury
Ramsey
Ramsey Heights
Ramsey St Mary's
Ramsey Mereside
Pondersbridge
Twenty Foot River
Whittlesey
Inham's End
Eastrea
Coates
North Side
Stone Bridge Corner
Thorney
Eye
Eye Green
Newark
Fengate
Peterborough
PETERBOROUGH SERVICES
Stanground
Farcet
Old Fletton
Orton Longueville
Orton Waterville
Alwalton
Chesterton
Water Newton
Castor
Ailsworth
Sutton
Sibson
SIBSON
Stibbington
Wansford
Yarwell
Longthorpe
Dogsthorpe
Walton
Werrington
Gunthorpe
Marholm
Upton
Thornhaugh
Wittering
Southorpe
Ufford
Barnack
Bainton
Helpston
Pilsgate
Stamford
Northfields
Uffington
Tallington
West Deeping
Maxey
Etton
Glinton
Northborough
Peakirk
Newborough
Deeping Gate
Deeping St James
Market Deeping
Frognall
Towngate
Barholm
Belmesthorpe
Great Casterton
Little Casterton
Ryhall
Essendine
Greatford
Braceborough
Langtoft
Baston
Wilsthorpe
Obthorpe
Manthorpe
Carlby
Careby
Toft
Witham on the Hill
Lound
Northorpe
Thurlby
Thetford
Creeton
Scottlethorpe
Edenham
Swinstead
Grimsthorpe
Elsthorpe
Hanthorpe
Morton
Cawthorpe
Dyke
Bourne
Twenty
Tongue End
Hop Pole
Deeping St Nicholas
Crowland
Nene Terrace
Dowsdale
Shepeau Stow
Brotherhouse Bar
Cowbit
Moulton Chapel
Weston Hills
Clay Lake
Little London
Spalding
Low Fulney
Pode Hole
Pinchbeck West
GRANTHAM SOUTH SERVICES
Rutland
Peterborough
A1
A1(M)
A6
A14
A15
A16
A43
A45
A47
A151
A428
A509
A605
A606
A1073
A1139
A6116
Welland
Nene
Great Ouse
Isle
Til

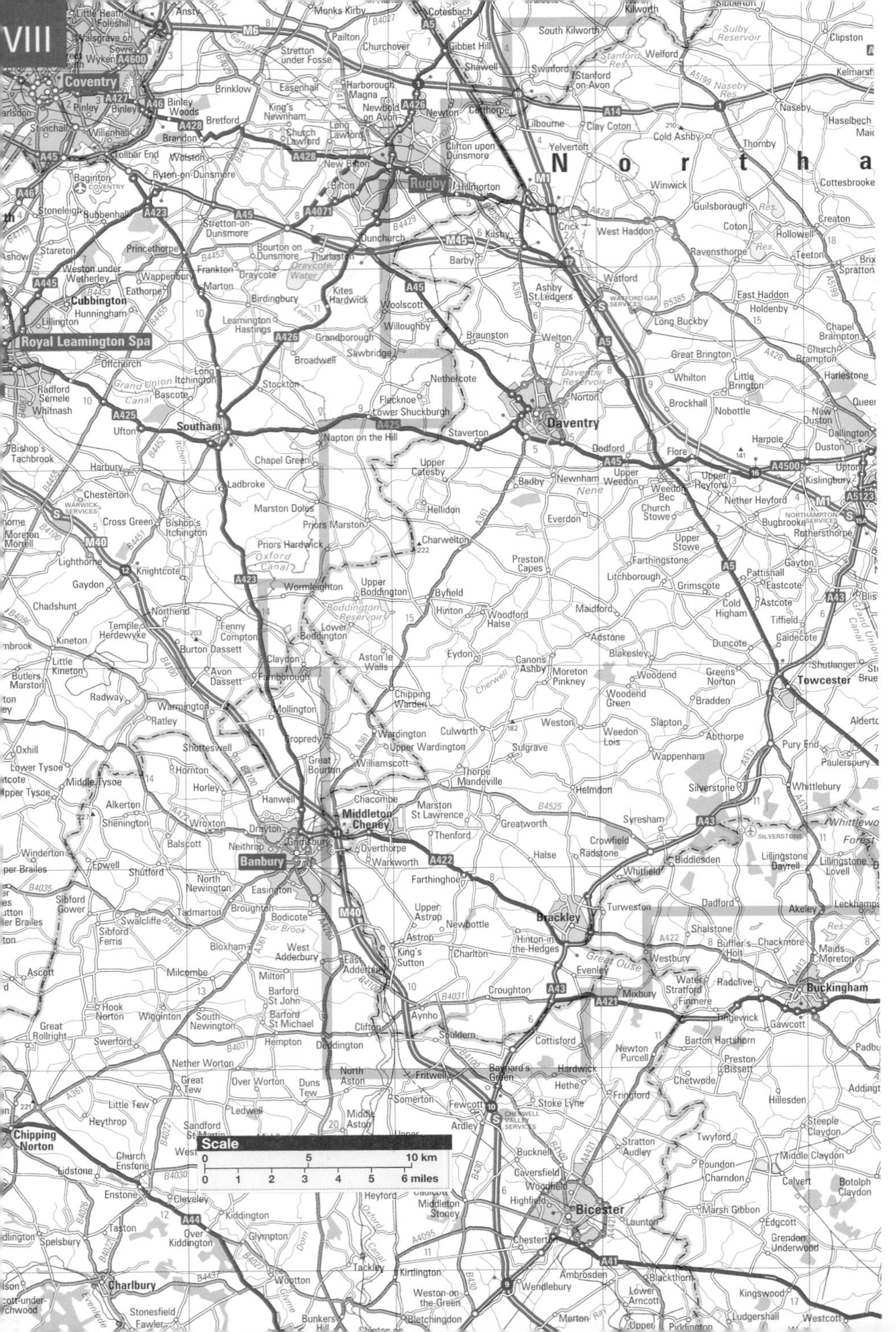
Coventry
Royal Leamington Spa
Rugby
Daventry
Southam
Banbury
Middleton Cheney
Brackley
Towcester
Buckingham
Bicester
Chipping Norton
Charlbury
N o r t h a
Scale
0
5
10 km
0
1
2
3
4
5
6 miles
Little Heath
Foleshill
Walsgrave on Sowe
Wyken
Ansty
Monks Kirby
Cotesbach
Pailton
Stretton under Fosse
Churchover
Gibbet Hill
Shawell
South Kilworth
Welford
Sulby Reservoir
Clipston
Kelmarsh
Stanford on Avon
Swinford
Naseby
Haselbech
Binley
Binley Woods
Brinklow
Easenhall
Harborough Magna
King's Newnham
Newbold on Avon
Newton
Catthorpe
Lilbourne
Clay Coton
Cold Ashby
Thornby
Bretford
Brandon
Church Lawford
Long Lawford
Clifton upon Dunsmore
Yelvertoft
Willenhall
Stivichall
Tollbar End
Wolston
Ryton-on-Dunsmore
New Bilton
Bilton
Hillmorton
Winwick
Cottesbrooke
Baginton
Coventry
Stoneleigh
Bubbenhall
Stretton-on-Dunsmore
Dunchurch
Kilsby
Crick
West Haddon
Guilsborough
Coton
Hollowell
Creaton
Stareton
Princethorpe
Frankton
Bourton on Dunsmore
Thurlaston
Draycote Water
Barby
Ravensthorpe
Teeton
Spratton
Weston under Wetherley
Wappenbury
Marton
Draycote
Kites Hardwick
Woolscott
Ashby St Ledgers
Watford
Watford Gap Services
East Haddon
Holdenby
Cubbington
Eathorpe
Hunningham
Birdingbury
Lillington
Leamington Hastings
Willoughby
Braunston
Welton
Long Buckby
Chapel Brampton
Church Brampton
Grandborough
Sawbridge
Broadwell
Great Brington
Offchurch
Long Itchington
Grand Union Canal
Nethercote
Daventry Reservoir
Whilton
Little Brington
Harlestone
Radford Semele
Whitnash
Bascote
Stockton
Flecknoe
Lower Shuckburgh
Norton
Brockhall
Nobottle
New Duston
Ufton
Napton on the Hill
Staverton
Dodford
Harpole
Duston
Dallington
Bishop's Tachbrook
Chapel Green
Upper Catesby
Newnham
Upper Weedon
Flore
Upper Heyford
Kislingbury
Upton
Harbury
Ladbroke
Badby
Weedon Bec
Nether Heyford
Chesterton
Warwick Services
Marston Doles
Hellidon
Everdon
Church Stowe
Bugbrooke
Northampton Services
Cross Green
Bishop's Itchington
Priors Marston
Upper Stowe
Rothersthorpe
Moreton Morrell
Priors Hardwick
Charwelton
Preston Capes
Farthingstone
Gayton
Lighthorne
Knightcote
Oxford Canal
Litchborough
Pattishall
Eastcote
Gaydon
Wormleighton
Upper Boddington
Byfield
Grimscote
Chadshunt
Northend
Boddington Reservoir
Hinton
Woodford Halse
Maidford
Cold Higham
Astcote
Tiffield
Temple Herdewyke
Fenny Compton
Lower Boddington
Adstone
Caldecote
Kineton
Burton Dassett
Aston le Walls
Duncote
Blakesley
Little Kineton
Claydon
Eydon
Canons Ashby
Moreton Pinkney
Greens Norton
Shutlanger
Butlers Marston
Avon Dassett
Farnborough
Woodend
Radway
Chipping Warden
Woodend Green
Bradden
Warmington
Mollington
Ratley
Wardington
Culworth
Weston
Slapton
Weedon Lois
Abthorpe
Oxhill
Shotteswell
Cropredy
Upper Wardington
Sulgrave
Wappenham
Pury End
Lower Tysoe
Hornton
Great Bourton
Williamscott
Thorpe Mandeville
Paulerspury
Middle Tysoe
Horley
Helmdon
Silverstone
Whittlebury
Upper Tysoe
Alkerton
Hanwell
Chacombe
Marston St Lawrence
Shenington
Wroxton
Drayton
Greatworth
Syresham
Balscott
Neithrop
Grimsbury
Thenford
Overthorpe
Crowfield
Winderton
Epwell
Warkworth
Halse
Radstone
Biddlesden
Lillingstone Dayrell
Lillingstone Lovell
Whittlewood Forest
Shutford
North Newington
Farthinghoe
Whitfield
Easington
Upper Astrop
Turweston
Dadford
Akeley
Sibford Gower
Tadmarton
Broughton
Bodicote
Sor Brook
Newbottle
Swalcliffe
Sibford Ferris
Astrop
Hinton-in-the-Hedges
Shalstone
Buffler's Holt
Chackmore
Maids Moreton
Bloxham
West Adderbury
King's Sutton
Charlton
Great Ouse
Westbury
East Adderbury
Evenley
Water Stratford
Radclive
Ascott
Milcombe
Milton
Barford St John
Croughton
Mixbury
Finmere
Hook Norton
Wigginton
South Newington
Barford St Michael
Aynho
Tingewick
Gawcott
Great Rollright
Swerford
Hempton
Deddington
Clifton
Souldern
Cottisford
Barton Hartshorn
Newton Purcell
Preston Bissett
Padbury
Nether Worton
Great Tew
Over Worton
Duns Tew
North Aston
Fritwell
Baynard's Green
Hardwick
Hethe
Chetwode
Little Tew
Ledwell
Somerton
Fewcott
Stoke Lyne
Fringford
Hillesden
Heythrop
Sandford St Martin
Middle Aston
Ardley
Cherwell Valley Services
Steeple Claydon
Twyford
Stratton Audley
Church Enstone
Bucknell
Poundon
Middle Claydon
Lidstone
Enstone
Caversfield
Charndon
Calvert
Botolph Claydon
Cleveley
Heyford
Middleton Stoney
Woodfield
Highfield
Kiddington
Launton
Marsh Gibbon
Edgcott
Taston
Over Kiddington
Glympton
Chesterton
Grendon Underwood
Spelsbury
Tackley
Kirtlington
Ambrosden
Blackthorn
Wootton
Wendlebury
Lower Arncott
Kingswood
Stonesfield
Fawler
Weston-on-the-Green
Bletchingdon
Bunkers Hill
Merton
Ludgershall
Westcott
Piddington
Cherwell
Nene
Avon
Leam
Itchen
Glyme
Dorn
Evenlode
M6
M1
M40
M45
A5
A14
A45
A46
A423
A425
A426
A428
A4071
A4600
A427
A445
A361
A422
A43
A421
A4421
A41
A44
A4500
A5123
A413
A5199
A4260
B4100
B4027
B4429
B4453
B4455
B4452
B4451
B4086
B4035
B4031
B4030
B4022
B4026
B4027
B4437
B430
B4525
B5385
A4095
222
203
182
141
227
221
210
Silverstone

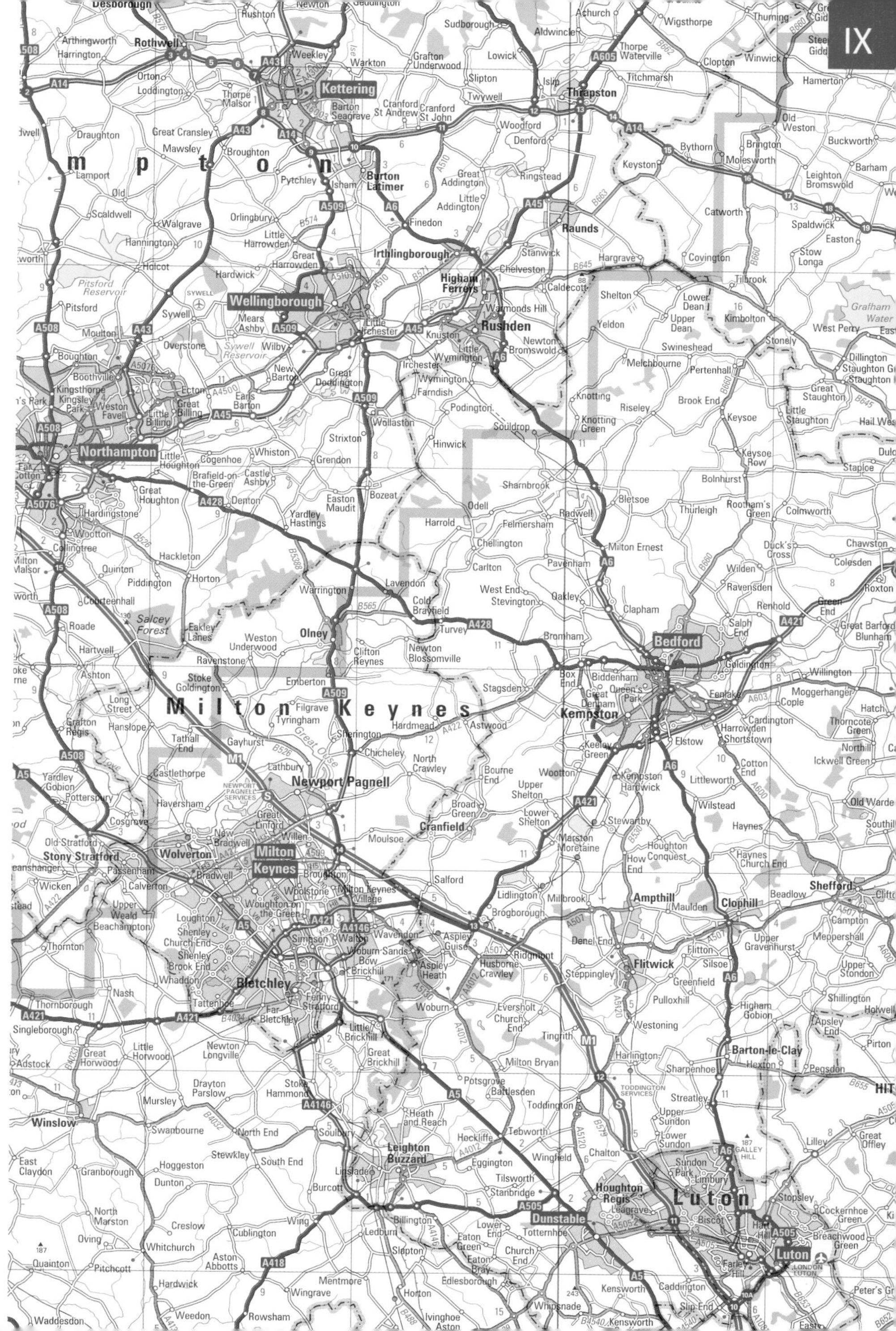
Desborough
Rushton
Newton
Geddington
Sudborough
Achurch
Aldwincle
Wigsthorpe
Thurning
Arthingworth
Harrington
Rothwell
Weekley
Warkton
Grafton Underwood
Lowick
Thorpe Waterville
Clopton
Winwick
Orton
Loddington
Thorpe Malsor
Kettering
Slipton
Islip
Titchmarsh
Thrapston
Hamerton
Barton Seagrave
Cranford St Andrew
Cranford St John
Twywell
Woodford
Denford
Old Weston
Draughton
Great Cransley
Mawsley
Broughton
Burton Latimer
Isham
Pytchley
Great Addington
Little Addington
Ringstead
Keyston
Bythorn
Brington
Molesworth
Buckworth
Barham
Leighton Bromswold
Lamport
Old
Scaldwell
Walgrave
Orlingbury
Finedon
Raunds
Catworth
Spaldwick
Easton
Hannington
Little Harrowden
Great Harrowden
Irthlingborough
Stanwick
Hargrave
Covington
Stow Longa
Holcot
Hardwick
Higham Ferrers
Chelveston
Caldecott
Tilbrook
Pitsford Reservoir
Sywell
Wellingborough
Shelton
Lower Dean
Upper Dean
Kimbolton
Grafham Water
Pitsford
Mears Ashby
Wilby
Little Irchester
Rushden
Newton Bromswold
Yelden
Swineshead
West Perry
Moulton
Overstone
Sywell Reservoir
Knuston
Little
Wymington
Irchester
Melchbourne
Pertenhall
Stonely
Dillington
Staughton Green
Staughton
Boughton
Boothville
Kingsthorpe
Kingsley Park
Weston Favell
Ecton
New Barton
Great Doddington
Earls Barton
Farndish
Knotting
Riseley
Brook End
Great Staughton
Little Billing
Great Billing
Podington
Wollaston
Souldrop
Knotting Green
Keysoe
Little Staughton
Hail Weston
Northampton
Whiston
Strixton
Hinwick
Little Houghton
Cogenhoe
Grendon
Keysoe Row
Far Cotton
Brafield-on-the-Green
Castle Ashby
Sharnbrook
Bolnhurst
Staploe
Great Houghton
Hardingstone
Denton
Easton Maudit
Bozeat
Odell
Bletsoe
Thurleigh
Roothams Green
Colmworth
Yardley Hastings
Harrold
Radwell
Felmersham
Wootton
Collingtree
Hackleton
Chellington
Milton Ernest
Duck's Cross
Chawston
Colesden
Milton Malsor
Quinton
Horton
Carlton
Pavenham
Wilden
Ravensden
Piddington
Warrington
Lavendon
West End
Stevington
Oakley
Roxton
Courteenhall
Cold Brayfield
Clapham
Renhold
Green End
Roade
Salcey Forest
Eakley Lanes
Weston Underwood
Olney
Turvey
Bromham
Salph End
Great Barford
Blunham
Hartwell
Ravenstone
Clifton Reynes
Newton Blossomville
Bedford
Goldington
Ashton
Stoke Goldington
Emberton
Stagsden
Box End
Biddenham
Queen's Park
Great Denham
Kempston
Fenlake
Willington
Moggerhanger
Cople
Long Street
Milton Keynes
Filgrave
Tyringham
Hatch
Grafton Regis
Hanslope
Tathall End
Gayhurst
Sherington
Hardmead
Astwood
Cardington
Harrowden
Shortstown
Thorncote Green
Great Ouse
Chicheley
North Crawley
Keeley Green
Elstow
Northill
Castlethorpe
Lathbury
Bourne End
Wootton
Kempston Hardwick
Cotton End
Ickwell Green
Yardley Gobion
Potterspury
Newport Pagnell
Upper Shelton
Littleworth
Haversham
Great Linford
Broad Green
Lower Shelton
Stewartby
Wilstead
Old Warden
Cosgrove
New Bradwell
Willen
Cranfield
Marston Moretaine
Haynes
Southill
Old Stratford
Stony Stratford
Wolverton
Moulsoe
Houghton Conquest
How End
Haynes Church End
Passenham
Bradwell
Broughton
Salford
Wicken
Calverton
Woolstone
Milton Keynes Village
Lidlington
Millbrook
Ampthill
Maulden
Clophill
Beadlow
Shefford
Upper Weald
Woughton on the Green
Brogborough
Campton
Beachampton
Loughton
Wavendon
Aspley Guise
Denel End
Flitwick
Flitton
Upper Gravenhurst
Meppershall
Thornton
Shenley Church End
Simpson
Walton
Woburn Sands
Husborne Crawley
Ridgmont
Silsoe
Upper Stondon
Shenley Brook End
Bow Brickhill
Aspley Heath
Steppingley
Greenfield
Whaddon
Bletchley
Woburn
Pulloxhill
Shillington
Nash
Tattenhoe
Fenny Stratford
Eversholt
Church End
Higham Gobion
Holwell
Thornborough
Far Bletchley
Westoning
Apsley End
Singleborough
Little Horwood
Little Brickhill
Tingrith
Great Horwood
Newton Longville
Great Brickhill
Harlington
Barton-le-Clay
Pirton
Adstock
Milton Bryan
Sharpenhoe
Hexton
Pegsdon
Drayton Parslow
Potsgrove
Battlesden
Toddington
Stoke Hammond
Streatley
Mursley
Toddington Services
Winslow
Swanbourne
North End
Soulbury
Heath and Reach
Upper Sundon
Lower Sundon
Stewkley
Hockliffe
Tebworth
Lilley
Great Offley
East Claydon
Granborough
Hoggeston
South End
Leighton Buzzard
Wingfield
Chalton
Galley Hill
Dunton
Linslade
Eggington
Sundon Park
Limbury
Tilsworth
Burcott
Stanbridge
Houghton Regis
Luton
Stopsley
Cockernhoe Green
North Marston
Wing
Billington
Dunstable
Leagrave
Biscot
Creslow
Cublington
Ledburn
Eaton Green
Lower End
Totternhoe
Hart Hill
Breachwood Green
Oving
Whitchurch
Slapton
Church End
Quainton
Pitchcott
Aston Abbotts
Eaton Bray
Farley Hill
London Luton
Hardwick
Mentmore
Edlesborough
Kensworth
Caddington
Peter's Green
Wingrave
Horton
Whipsnade
Slip End
Waddesdon
Weedon
Rowsham
Ivinghoe Aston
Kensworth
A14
A43
A6
A509
A45
A508
A5076
A428
A4500
A421
A422
A5
M1
A4146
A505
A418
A4012
A507
A5120
A603
A600
A605
A510
A6003
A5130
B660
B645
B663
B662
B574
B571
B526
B5388
B565
B530
B579
B4032
B4033
B4034
B488
B655
B4540
B653

Major administrative and
Postcode boundaries
County and unitary authority boundaries
District boundaries
Postcode boundaries
Area covered by this atlas
Scale
0 5 10 15 km
0 5 10 miles
SK TF
SK
SP
TF
TL
SP TL
Lincolnshire
Rutland
City of Peterborough
Leicestershire
Warwickshire
Cambridgeshire
Bedfordshire
Milton Keynes
Oxfordshire
Buckinghamshire
Herts
Luton
Northamptonshire
Corby
Kettering
East Northamptonshire
Daventry
Wellingborough
Northampton
South Northamptonshire
Easton on the Hill
PE9
LE15
Wansford
PE6
PE5
Wakerley
Lyddington
King's Cliffe
NN17
Deene
PE7
Warmington
Corby
Market Harborough
LE16
Wilbarston
Great Oakley
NN18
PE8
Oundle
Brigstock
Braybrooke
Desborough
Rothwell
LE17
Welford
NN16
Kettering
NN15
Thrapston
PE28
Woodford
Maidwell
Yelvertoft
CV21
CV22
Burton Latimer
Guilsborough
NN6
Raunds
NN9
CV23
Barby
Brixworth
Irthlingborough
Higham Ferrers
Wellingborough
NN8
Moulton
Rushden
NN10
NN2
NN3
Daventry
Wollaston
NN29
Harpole
NN5
NN1
Northampton
CV47
NN11
Bugbrooke
NN4
Bozeat
Hackleton
NN7
Byfield
Roade
MK46
MK16
Towcester
MK19
Culworth
NN12
Silverstone
OX17
Syresham
Cosgrove
MK12
OX16
Stony Stratford
MK11
Farthinghoe
MK18
Brackley
King's Sutton
NN13
Croughton
MK17
OX15
OX27
OX25

A B C D E F

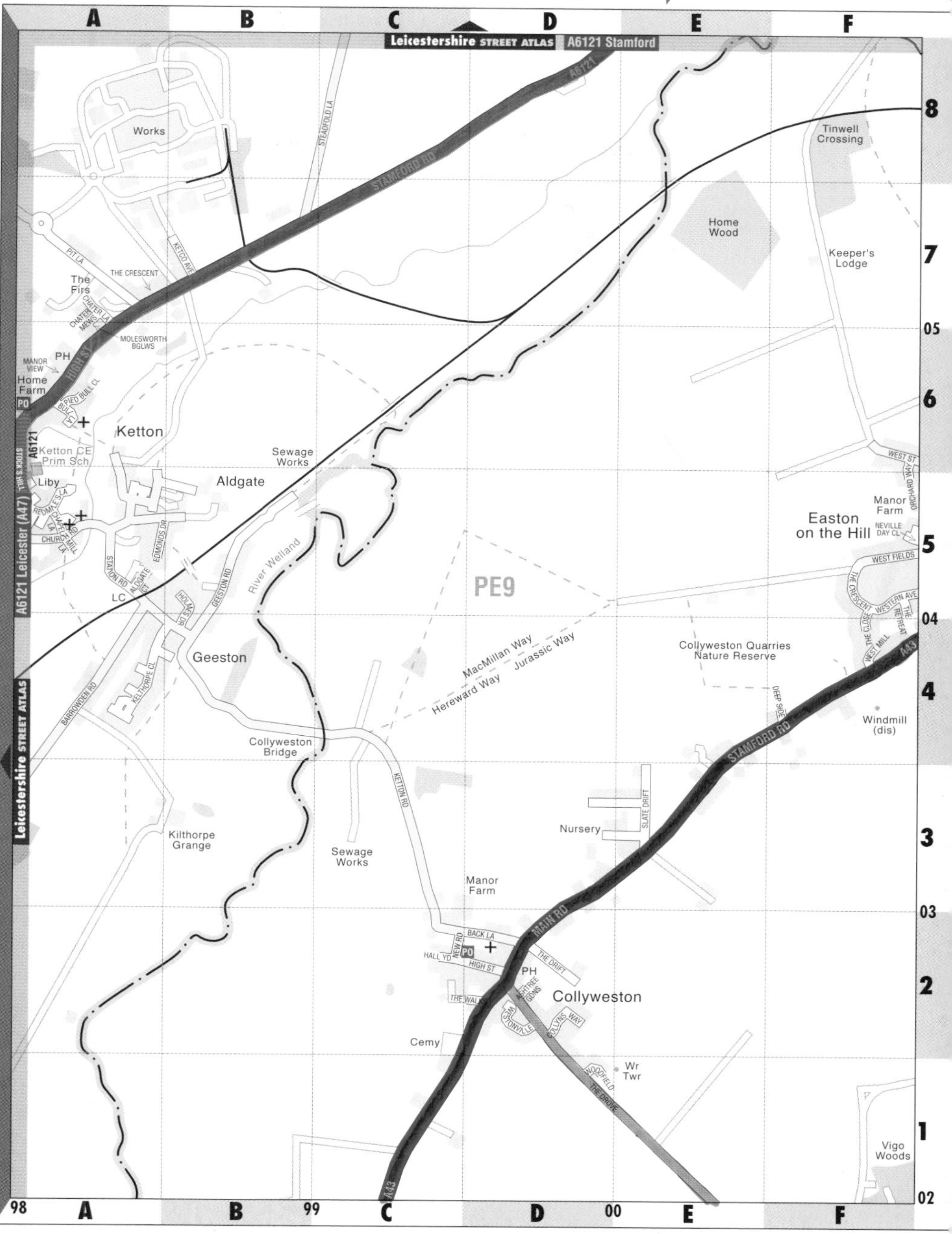

Works
STAMFORD RD
STEADFOLD LA
A6121
PIT LA
THE CRESCENT
KETCO AVE
The Firs
CHATER LA
CHATER MEWS
MOLESWORTH BGLWS
MANOR VIEW
PH
HIGH ST
Home Farm
PO
PIED BULL CL
BULL LA
Ketton
Ketton CE Prim Sch
STOCK'S HILL
A6121
Liby
REDMILES LA
CHAPEL LA
CHURCH LA
MILL LA
STATION RD
EDMONDS DR
ALDGATE CT
Aldgate
Sewage Works
GEESTON RD
River Welland
LC
HOLMES DR
Geeston
KELTHORPE CL
BARROWDEN RD
A6121 Leicester (A47)
Leicestershire STREET ATLAS
Collyweston Bridge
Kilthorpe Grange
Sewage Works
KETTON RD
Tinwell Crossing
Home Wood
Keeper's Lodge
PE9
MacMillan Way
Hereward Way
Jurassic Way
WEST ST
ORCHARD WAY
Manor Farm
Easton on the Hill
NEVILLE DAY CL
WEST FIELDS
THE CRESCENT
WESTERN AVE
THE RETREAT
THE CLOSE
WEST MILL
A43
Collyweston Quarries Nature Reserve
DEEP SIDE
STAMFORD RD
Windmill (dis)
SLATE DRIFT
Nursery
Manor Farm
MAIN RD
BACK LA
NEW RD
PO
HALL YD
HIGH ST
THE DRIFT
PH
ASHTREE GDNS
THE WALK
WESTONVILLE
COLLYNS WAY
Collyweston
Cemy
WOODFIELD
THE DROVE
Wr Twr
Vigo Woods
A43

8 7 05 6 5 04 4 3 03 2 1 02

98 A B 99 C D 00 E F

5
2

1

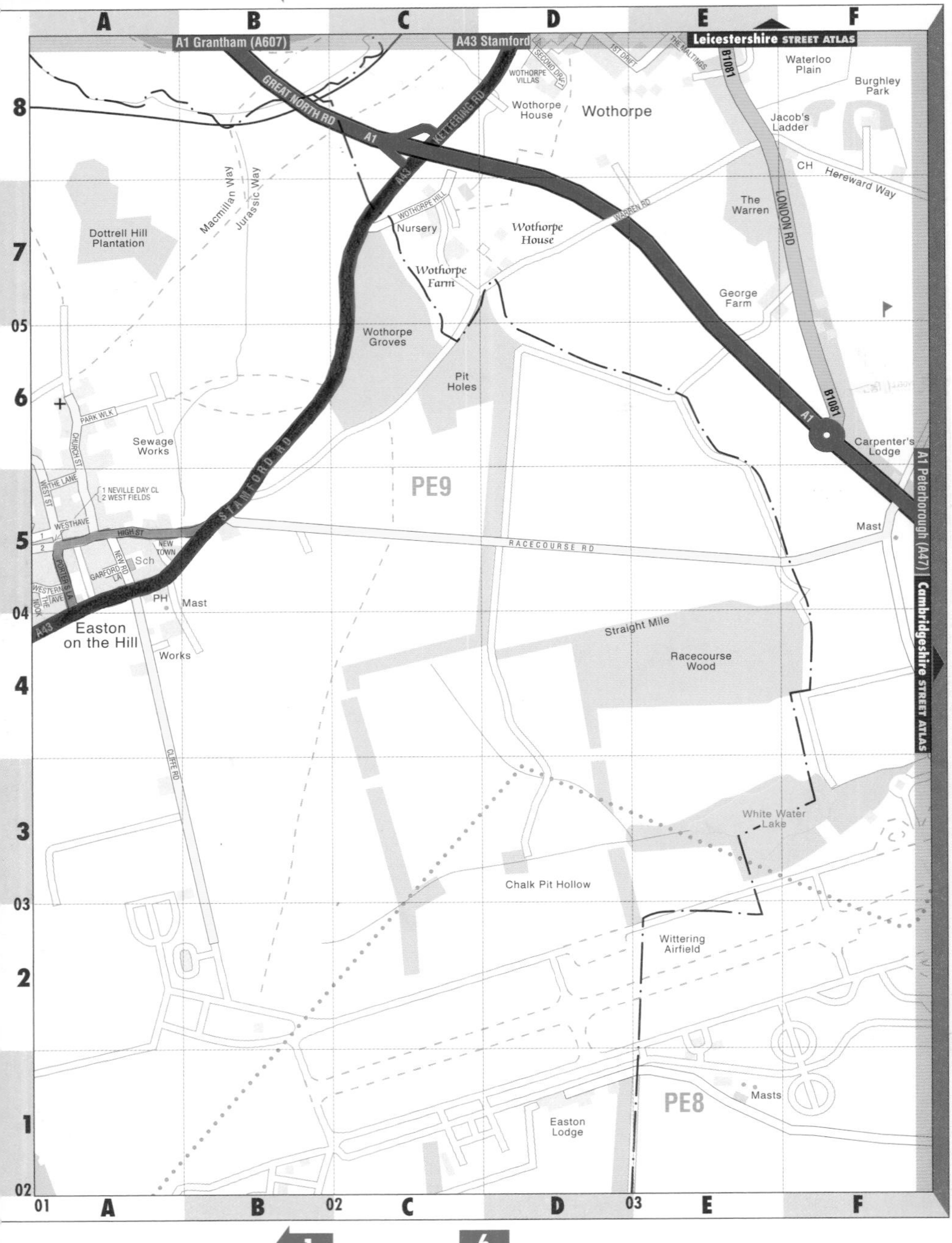
A
B
C
D
E
F
A1 Grantham (A607)
A43 Stamford
Leicestershire STREET ATLAS
A1 Peterborough (A47)
Cambridgeshire STREET ATLAS
8
7
05
6
5
04
4
3
03
2
1
02
01
02
03
GREAT NORTH RD
KETTERING RD
SECOND DRIFT
1ST DRIFT
THE MALTINGS
WOTHORPE VILLAS
Wothorpe House
Wothorpe
B1081
Waterloo Plain
Burghley Park
Jacob's Ladder
CH
Hereward Way
The Warren
LONDON RD
A1
A43
Macmillan Way
Jurassic Way
Dottrell Hill Plantation
WOTHORPE HILL
Nursery
Wothorpe House
WARREN RD
Wothorpe Farm
George Farm
Wothorpe Groves
Pit Holes
PARK WLK
CHURCH ST
Sewage Works
STAMFORD RD
Carpenter's Lodge
THE LANE
WEST ST
1 NEVILLE DAY CL
2 WEST FIELDS
PE9
WESTHAVE
HIGH ST
Mast
RACECOURSE RD
NEW TOWN
NEW RD
Sch
GARFORD LA
PORTER'S LA
WESTERN AVE
THE NOOK
PH
Mast
Easton on the Hill
Works
Straight Mile
Racecourse Wood
CLIFFE RD
White Water Lake
Chalk Pit Hollow
Wittering Airfield
PE8
Masts
Easton Lodge
01
A
B
02
C
D
03
E
F

1
6

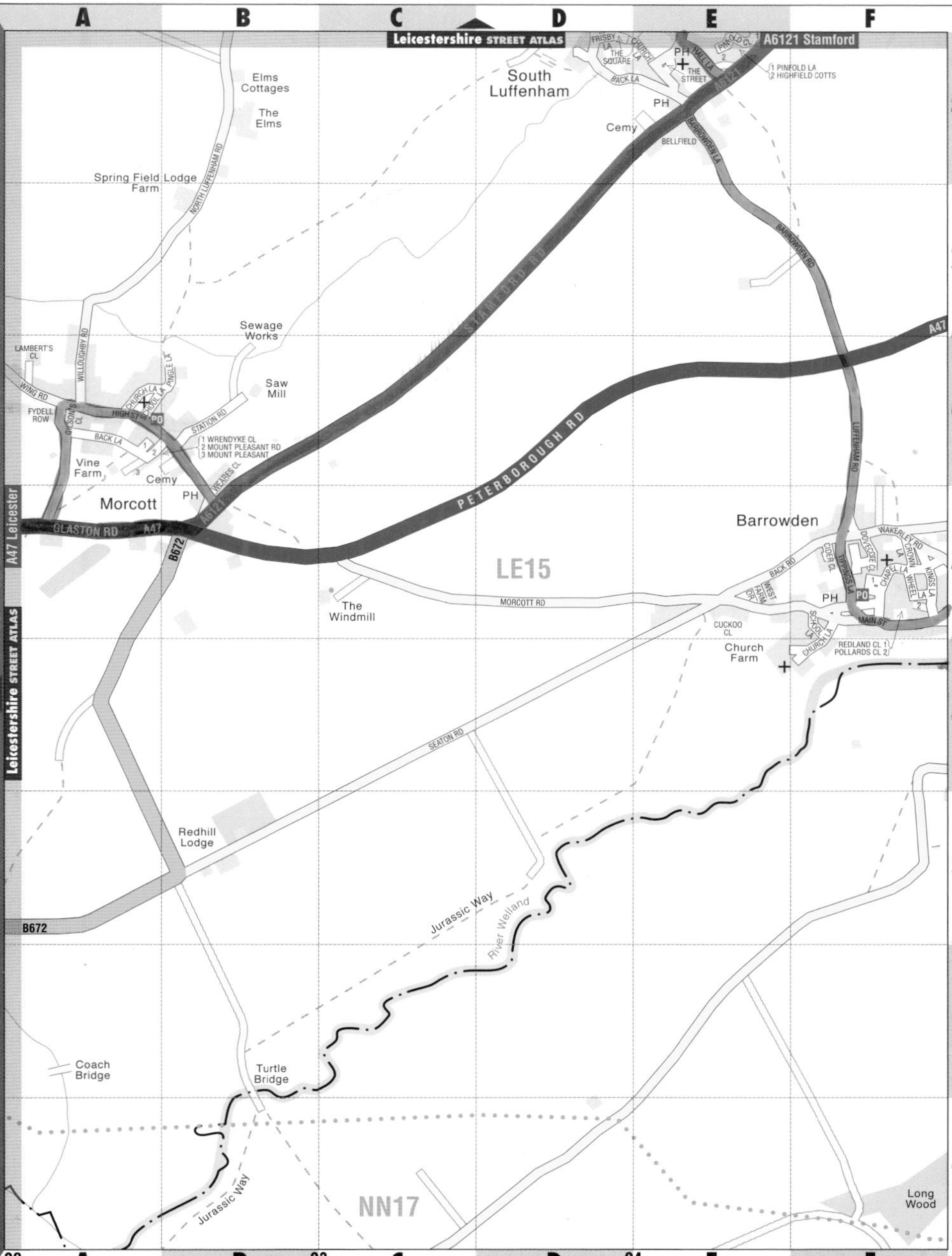

A B C D E F
Leicestershire STREET ATLAS
A6121 Stamford
South Luffenham
Elms Cottages
The Elms
Spring Field Lodge Farm
NORTH LUFFENHAM RD
STAMFORD RD
BARROWDEN LA
BARROWDEN RD
Sewage Works
Saw Mill
LAMBERT'S CL
WILLOUGHBY RD
WING RD
FYDELL ROW
HIGH ST
CHURCH LA
SCHOOL LA
PINGLE LA
BACK LA
STATION RD
1 WRENDYKE CL
2 MOUNT PLEASANT RD
3 MOUNT PLEASANT
Vine Farm
Cemy
Morcott
PH
PO
WEARES CL
GLASTON RD
A47
A6121
B672
PETERBOROUGH RD
LUFFENHAM RD
Barrowden
LE15
The Windmill
MORCOTT RD
BACK RD
WEST FARM DR
CIDER CL
TIPPINGS LA
DOVECOTE CL
WAKERLEY RD
CROWN LA
CHAPEL LA
WHEEL LA
KINGS LA
MAIN ST
SCHOOL LA
CHURCH LA
CUCKOO CL
Church Farm
REDLAND CL 1
POLLARDS CL 2
1 PINFOLD LA
2 HIGHFIELD COTTS
FRISBY LA
THE SQUARE
CHURCH LA
HALL LA
PINFOLD CL
THE STREET
BELLFIELD
SEATON RD
Redhill Lodge
Jurassic Way
River Welland
Coach Bridge
Turtle Bridge
NN17
Long Wood
A47 Leicester
Leicestershire STREET ATLAS
8 7 01 6 5 00 4 3 99 2 1 98
92 A B 93 C D 94 E F

3

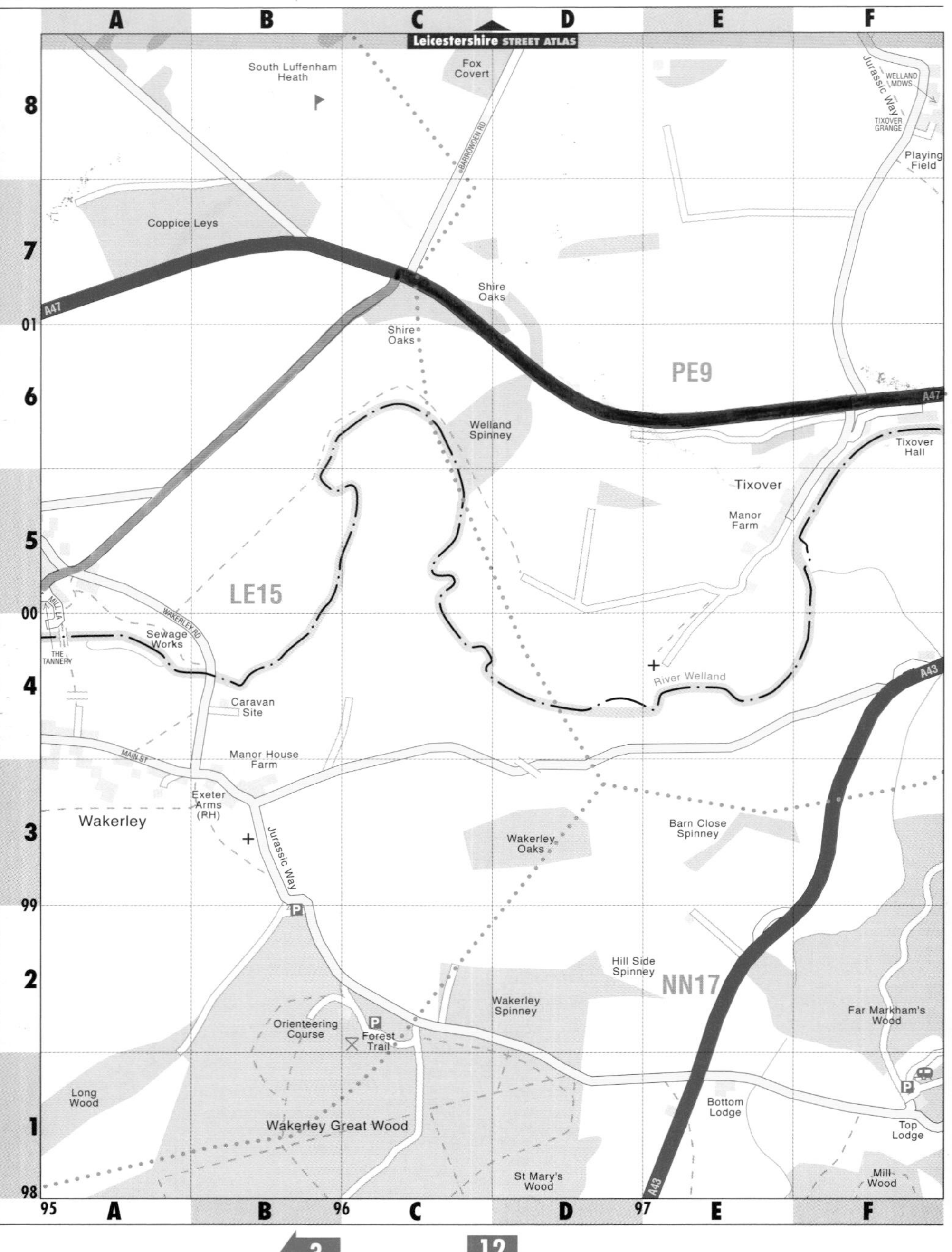
A
B
C
D
E
F
Leicestershire STREET ATLAS
South Luffenham Heath
Fox Covert
BARROWDEN RD
Jurassic Way
WELLAND MDWS
TIXOVER GRANGE
Playing Field
Coppice Leys
Shire Oaks
Shire Oaks
A47
PE9
A47
Welland Spinney
Tixover Hall
Tixover
Manor Farm
LE15
MILL LA
WAKERLEY RD
Sewage Works
THE TANNERY
River Welland
A43
Caravan Site
MAIN ST
Manor House Farm
Exeter Arms (PH)
Wakerley
Jurassic Way
Wakerley Oaks
Barn Close Spinney
Hill Side Spinney
NN17
Wakerley Spinney
Far Markham's Wood
Orienteering Course
Forest Trail
Long Wood
Bottom Lodge
Top Lodge
Wakerley Great Wood
St Mary's Wood
Mill Wood
A43
8
7
01
6
5
00
4
3
99
2
1
98
95
96
97

3

12

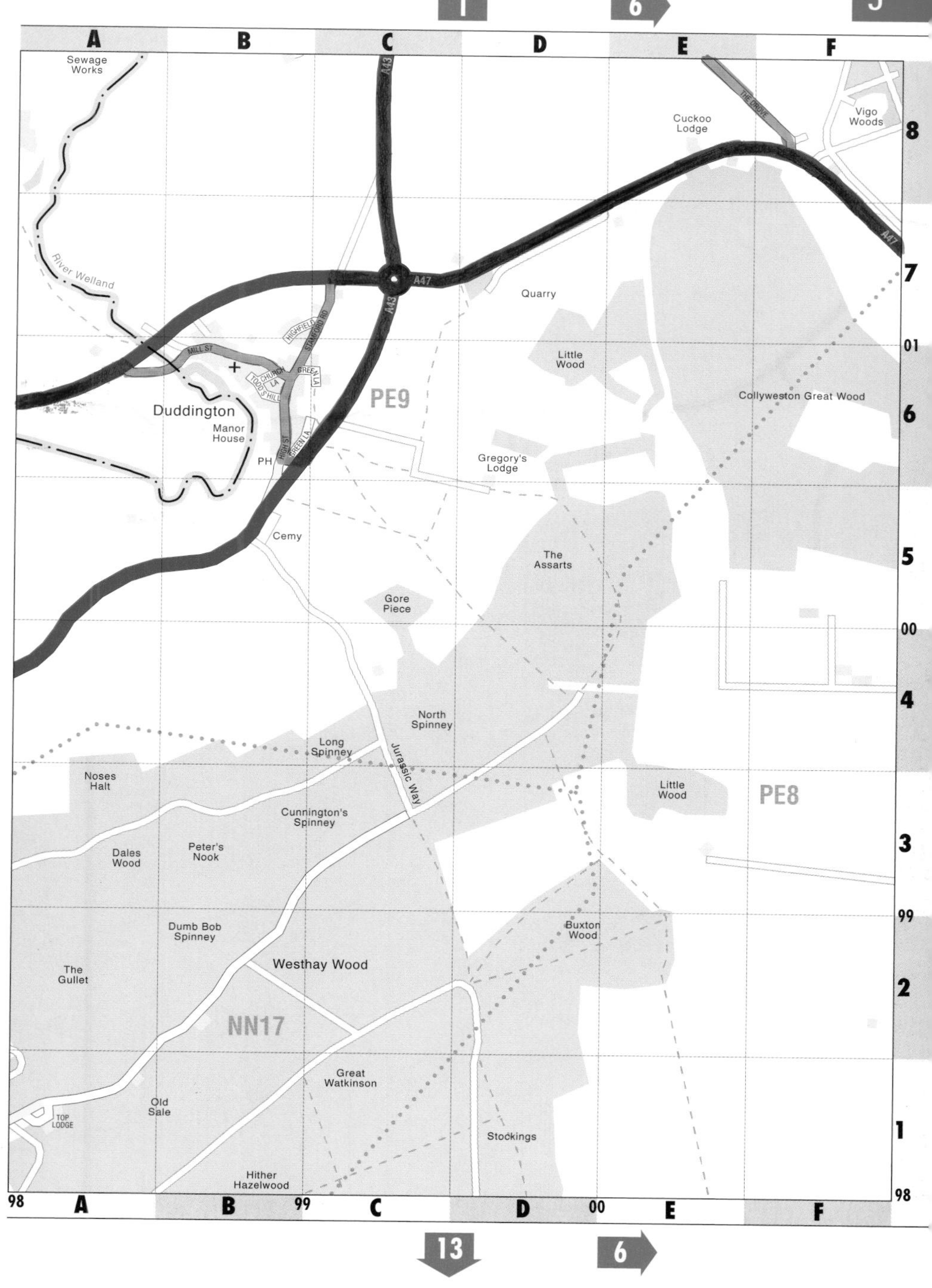
A
B
C
D
E
F
Sewage Works
A43
THE DROVE
Cuckoo Lodge
Vigo Woods
8
A47
River Welland
A47
7
Quarry
A43
HIGHFIELD
STAMFORD RD
MILL ST
CHURCH LA
GREEN LA
TODD'S HILL
01
Little Wood
PE9
Duddington
Collyweston Great Wood
6
Manor House
HIGH ST
GREEN LA
PH
Gregory's Lodge
Cemy
The Assarts
5
Gore Piece
00
4
North Spinney
Long Spinney
Jurassic Way
Noses Halt
Little Wood
PE8
Cunnington's Spinney
Dales Wood
Peter's Nook
3
99
Dumb Bob Spinney
Buxton Wood
The Gullet
Westhay Wood
2
NN17
Great Watkinson
Old Sale
TOP LODGE
1
Stockings
Hither Hazelwood
98
98
A
B
99
C
D
00
E
F

5
2

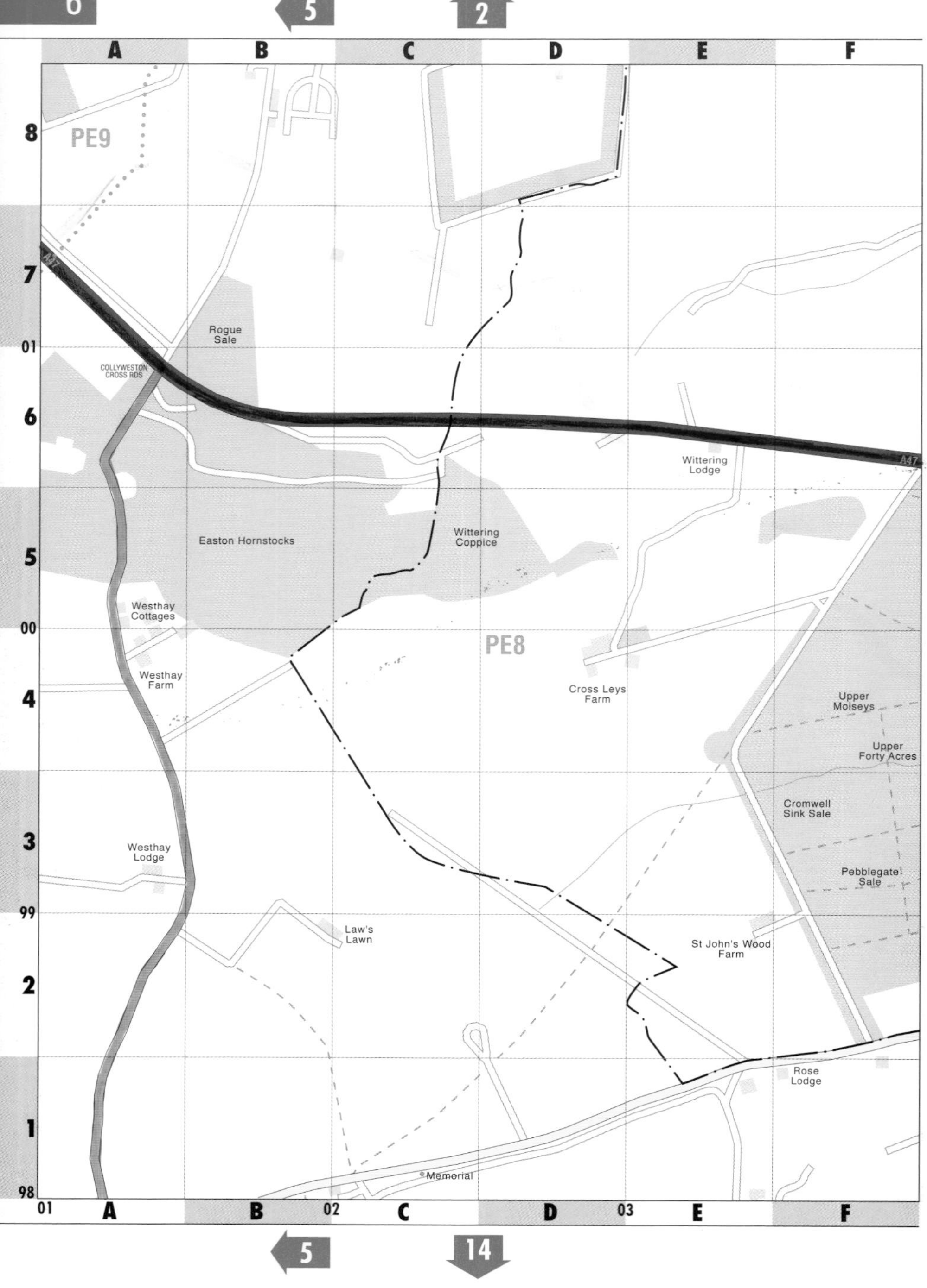
A
B
C
D
E
F
8
PE9
7
A47
01
Rogue
Sale
COLLYWESTON
CROSS RDS
6
A47
Wittering
Lodge
Easton Hornstocks
Wittering
Coppice
5
Westhay
Cottages
00
PE8
Westhay
Farm
Cross Leys
Farm
4
Upper
Moiseys
Upper
Forty Acres
Cromwell
Sink Sale
3
Westhay
Lodge
Pebblegate
Sale
99
Law's
Lawn
St John's Wood
Farm
2
Rose
Lodge
1
Memorial
98
01
A
B
02
C
D
03
E
F

5
14

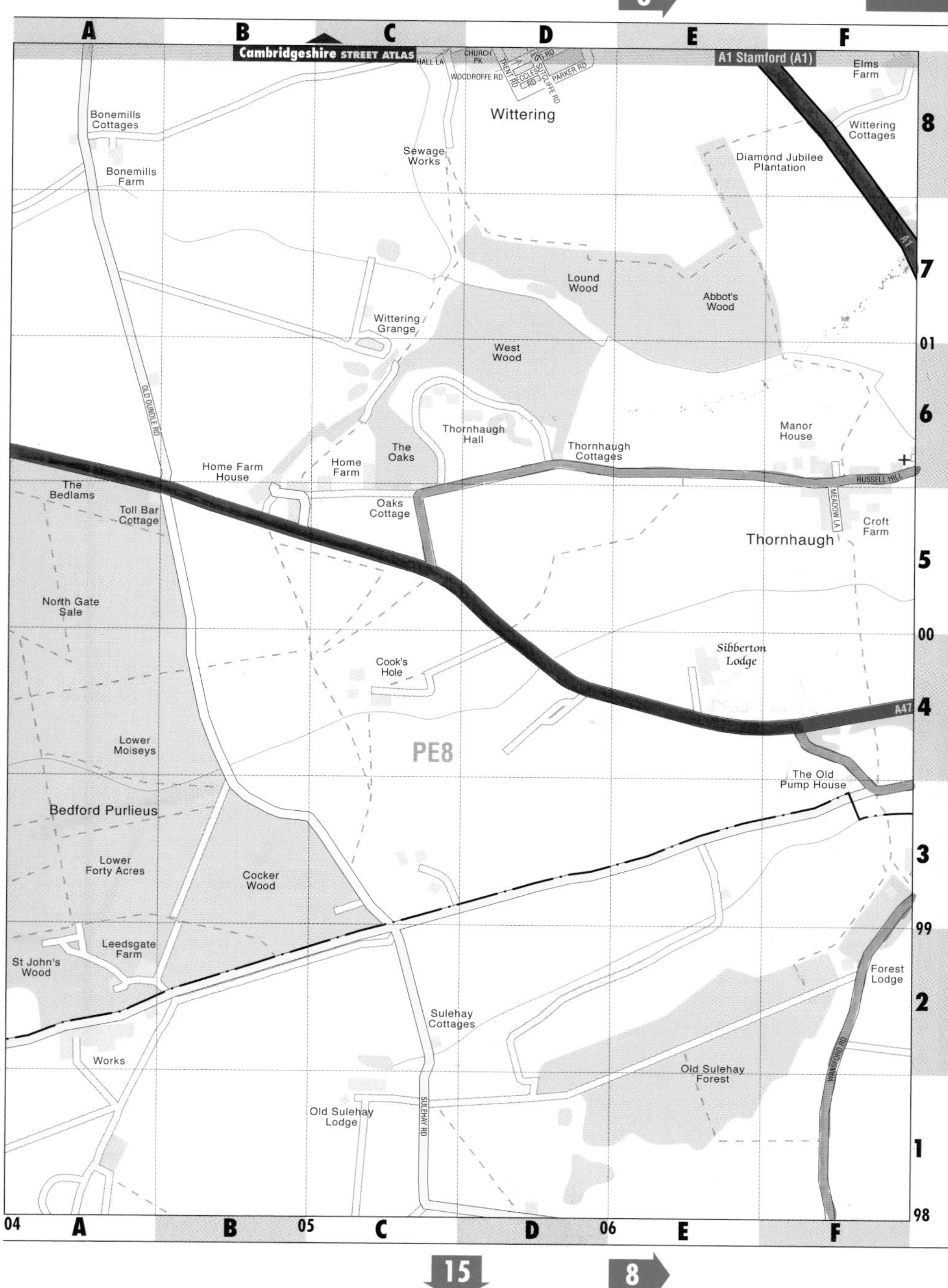
A
B
C
D
E
F
Cambridgeshire STREET ATLAS
A1 Stamford (A1)
HALL LA
CHURCH PK
WOODROFFE RD
TRENT RD
ECCLES RD
PARKER RD
Elms Farm
Wittering
Bonemills Cottages
Bonemills Farm
Wittering Cottages
Diamond Jubilee Plantation
Sewage Works
Lound Wood
Abbot's Wood
Wittering Grange
West Wood
OLD OUNDLE RD
Thornhaugh Hall
The Oaks
Home Farm
Home Farm House
Thornhaugh Cottages
Manor House
RUSSELL HILL
MEADOW LA
The Bedlams
Toll Bar Cottage
Oaks Cottage
Croft Farm
Thornhaugh
North Gate Sale
Cook's Hole
Sibberton Lodge
A47
A1
Lower Moiseys
PE8
The Old Pump House
Bedford Purlieus
Lower Forty Acres
Cocker Wood
Leedsgate Farm
St John's Wood
Forest Lodge
Sulehay Cottages
Works
Old Sulehay Forest
WANSFORD RD
SULEHAY RD
Old Sulehay Lodge
8
7
01
6
5
00
4
3
99
2
1
98
04
05
06

7

A B C D E F
Cambridgeshire STREET ATLAS
Nature Reserve
Lady Wood
Deardon Wood
Southorpe Bottom
Gazley Lodge
PE9
Beech Spinney
Wall Spinney
Crow Spinney
Sutton Wood
Research Centre
A1
Sacrewell Lodge
Jubilee Spinney
PE6
SUTTON HEATH RD
OLD RECTORY DR
RUSSELL HILL
WINDGATE WAY
Hereward Way
Sacrewell Farm & Country Centre
Mill House
Top Field Spinney
Hell Corner
THACKERS CL
OLD NORTH RD
PE8
Black Swan Hill
A6118
A47
Heath House
ROBINS WOOD
ROBINS FIELD
BLACK SWAN SPINNEY
SWAN
Wansford
Mast
Nene Way
River Nene
PE5
OLD NORTH RD
THE STABLES
OLD LEICESTER RD
NENE CL
PETERBOROUGH RD
Deep Springs
A47 Peterborough
YARWELL RD
WANSFORD RD
BRIDGE END
The Bungalow
THE DRIFT
Wansford Bridge
Hotel
LONDON RD
PH
PO
A6118
B671
CHAPEL ST
GREAT NORTH RD
Sutton
NENE WAY
Manor Farm
Stibbington Hall
OLD GREAT NORTH RD
ROMAN DR
CHURCH LA
MANOR RD
LOVERS LA
GRAEME RD
The Grange
Bunkers Hill
Stibbington
Stibbington House
Field Studies Centre
Manor Farm
Nene Way
ELTON RD
Sewage Farm
OLD GREAT NORTH RD
NEW LA
Depot
Ship End Pits
Nene Valley Railway
B671
Toll Bar Spinney
A1
8
7
01
6
5
00
4
3
99
2
1
98
07
08
09

7

16

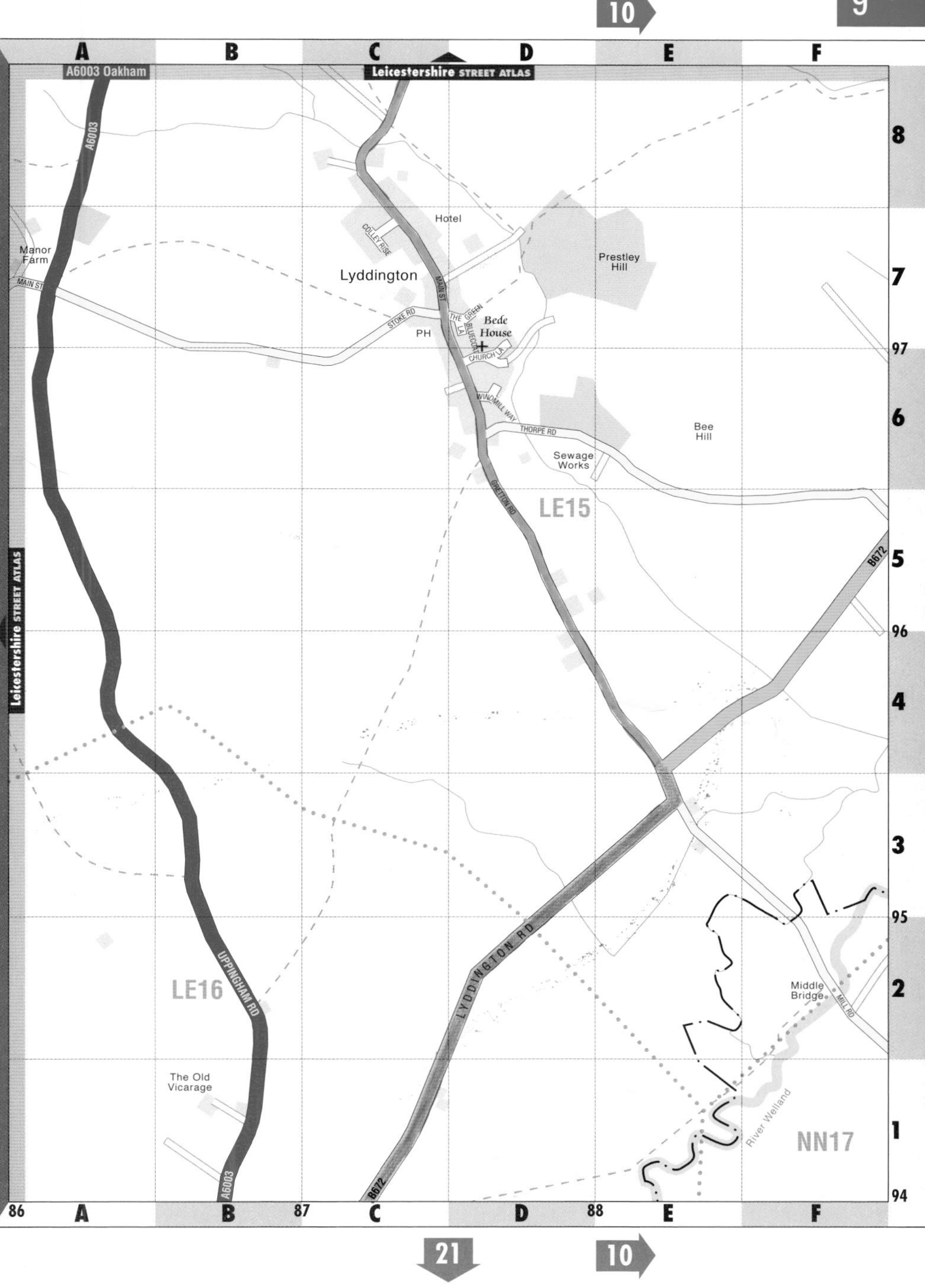
10
A
B
C
D
E
F
A6003 Oakham
Leicestershire STREET ATLAS
A6003
8
Hotel
COLLEY RISE
Manor Farm
MAIN ST
Lyddington
Prestley Hill
7
MAIN ST
STOKE RD
THE GREEN
Bede House
PH
CHURCH LA
97
WINDMILL WAY
THORPE RD
Bee Hill
6
Sewage Works
GRETTON RD
LE15
B672
5
96
4
3
95
UPPINGHAM RD
LYDDINGTON RD
LE16
Middle Bridge
MILL RD
2
The Old Vicarage
River Welland
1
NN17
A6003
B672
94
86
87
88
21
10

9

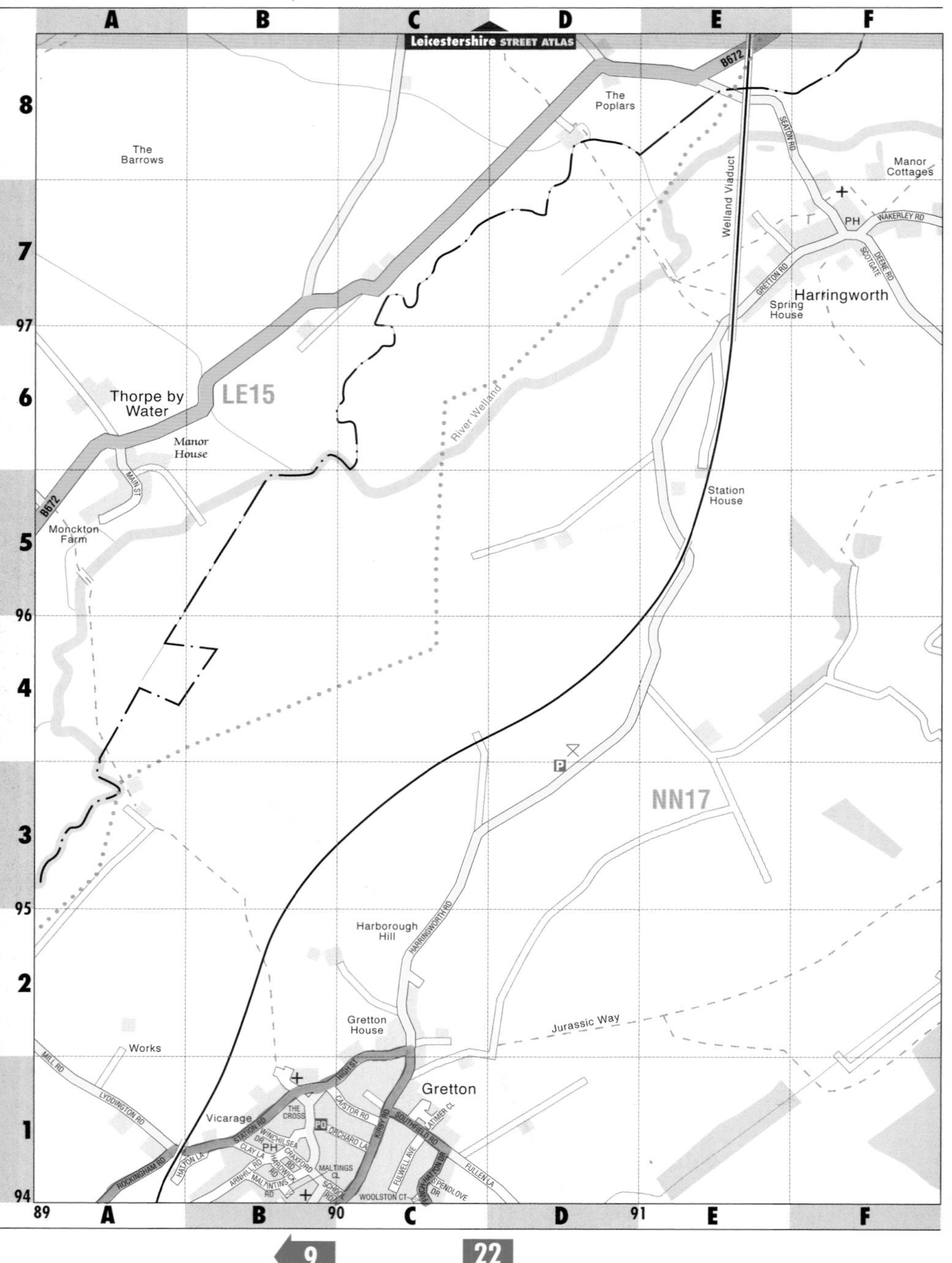
A
B
C
D
E
F
Leicestershire STREET ATLAS
B672
The Poplars
8
The Barrows
Manor Cottages
Welland Viaduct
SEATON RD
PH
WAKERLEY RD
7
SCOTGATE
DEENE RD
GRETTON RD
Harringworth
Spring House
97
6
Thorpe by Water
LE15
River Welland
Manor House
MAIN ST
Station House
5
Moncton Farm
96
4
P
NN17
3
95
Harborough Hill
HARRINGWORTH RD
2
Jurassic Way
Gretton House
Works
MILL RD
LYDDINGTON RD
HIGH ST
Gretton
Vicarage
THE CROSS
CAISTOR RD
PO
STATION RD
ORCHARD LA
KIRBY RD
SOUTHFIELD RD
LATIMER CL
1
WINCHILSEA DR
PH
CLAY LA
CRAXFORD RD
HARDWICK RD
ROCKINGHAM RD
HATTON LA
ARNHILL RD
MALTINGS CL
MALTINTINS RD
SCHOOL RD
FULWELL AVE
FINCH-HATTON DR
SPENDLOVE DR
FULLEN LA
WOOLSTON CT
94
89
90
91

9

22

3
12

A
B
C
D
E
F
River Welland
Airfield
(disused)
8
The
Bungalows
Quarry
WAKERLEY RD
Shotley
Short
Wood
Greenwood
Sale
7
Wood
Hollow
97
Town Wood
Farm
Town
Wood
6
HORSE LA
Memorial
5
NN17
Rose
Farm
Jurassic Way
PO
Laxton
96
Spanhoe
Farm
4
Spanhoe
Wood
Harringworth
Lodge
DEENE RD
The
Warren
3
95
Lodge
Coppice
Household
Coppice
Hollow
Wood
2
Dryleas
Wood
Geese
Wood
Ferrels
Wood
1
RED LODGE RD
Red Lodge
Farm
94
92
93
94

23
12

11 4

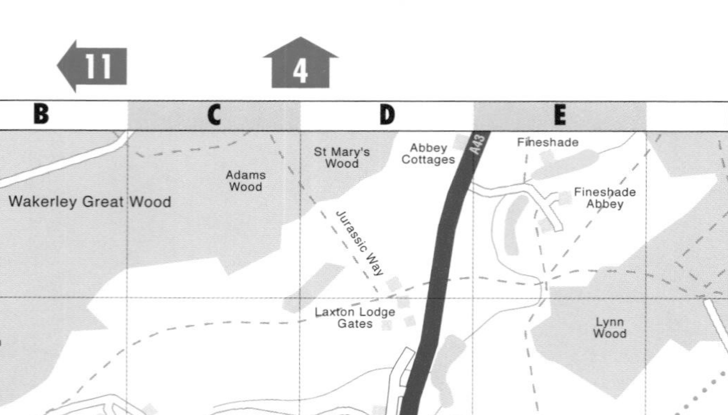
A
B
C
D
E
F
8
7
97
6
5
96
4
3
95
2
1
94
Wakerley Great Wood
Adams Wood
St Mary's Wood
Abbey Cottages
A43
Fineshade
Fineshade Abbey
Mill Wood
Jurassic Way
Laxton Lodge Gates
Laxton Wood
Lynn Wood
Laxton Hall
Home Farm
Gaussen Bushes
Park Bushes
Mill Planting
Laxton Park
Laxton Park House
Blatherwycke Lake
Townhill Plantation
Laxton
NN17
Blatherwycke Park Farm
Hill Top Farm
PE8
Glebe Farm
Blatherwycke
Keepers Cottage
New Lodge
Willow Brook
Bantrup Bushes
Cadge Wood
Bulwick
RED LODGE RD
MILLIES LA
Cookes Bushes
Bulwick Hall
PH
PO
A43
95
A
B
96
C
D
97
E
F

11 24

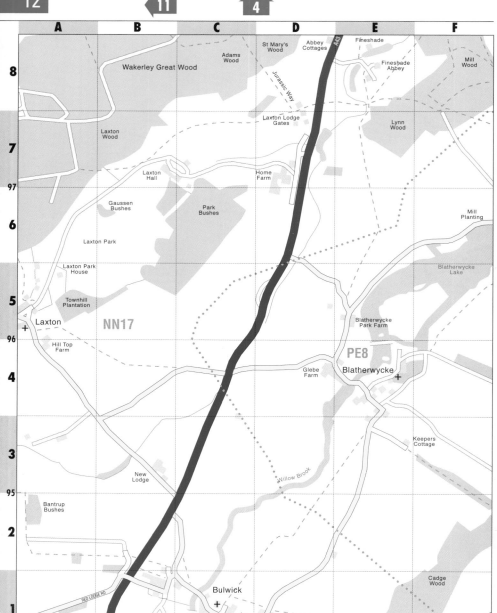

5
14

A
B
C
D
E
F
Far Hazelwood
Hither Hazelwood
Little Watkinson
Hollow Wood
NN17
Far Miers
Jurassic Way
Westhay Wood
Hither Miers
WOOD LA
King's Cliffe
L Ctr
KINGSMEAD
WALKERS FIELD
DAKIN CL
RD
STATION
HOWARDS MDW
DALESWOOD RISE
MILLWOOD WAY
FINESHADE CL
WILLOW LA
KING'S FOREST
PARK ST
THE DOVECOTE
WOOD RD
FOREST APP
RATE'S LA
King's Cliffe Endowed Prim Sch
MAZEWOOD GATE
WEST ST
PH
BLATHERWYCKE RD
CHURCH WALK
PO
HALL YD
LAWS LA
BRIDGE ST
ORCHARD LA
MOREHAY LA
Cemy
Britain Sale
Kit Spinney
Willow Brook
Alders Farm
PE8
Calvey Wood
The Spa (Chalybeate)
Spa Farm Cottages
Spa Farm
Brickhill Pond
Briary Wood
Tomlin Wood
Hostage Wood
Crayley Wood
Morehay Lawn
NN17
Bushey Wood
8
7
97
6
5
96
4
3
95
2
1
94
98
99
00

25
14

13
6

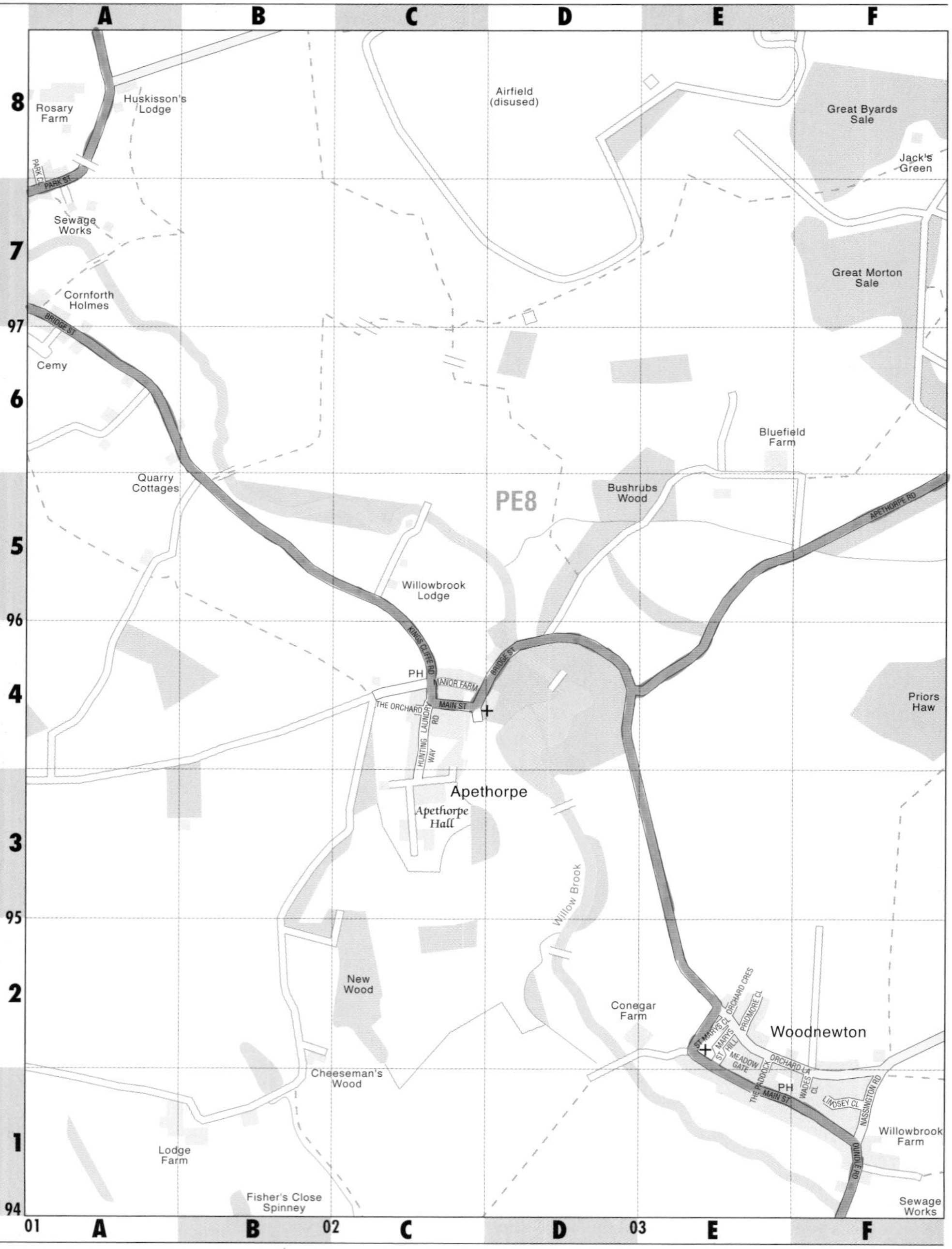

A B C D E F

8 Rosary Farm
Huskisson's Lodge
Airfield (disused)
Great Byards Sale
Jack's Green
PARK CL
PARK ST
7 Sewage Works
Great Morton Sale
Cornforth Holmes
97 BRIDGE ST
Cemy
6 Bluefield Farm
Quarry Cottages
PE8
Bushrubs Wood
APETHORPE RD
5 Willowbrook Lodge
96 KINGS CLIFFE RD
BRIDGE ST
PH
MANOR FARM
4 THE ORCHARD
MAIN ST
LAUNDRY RD
HUNTING WAY
Priors Haw
Apethorpe
Apethorpe Hall
3
Willow Brook
95
New Wood
2 Conegar Farm
ORCHARD CRES
PRIMROSE CL
ST MARYS CL
ST MARYS HILL
Woodnewton
MEADOW GATE
ORCHARD LA
THE PADDOCK
PH
WADES CL
MAIN ST
LINDSEY CL
NASSINGTON RD
Cheeseman's Wood
1 Lodge Farm
Willowbrook Farm
QUNDLE RD
Fisher's Close Spinney
Sewage Works
94

01 A B 02 C D 03 E F

13
26

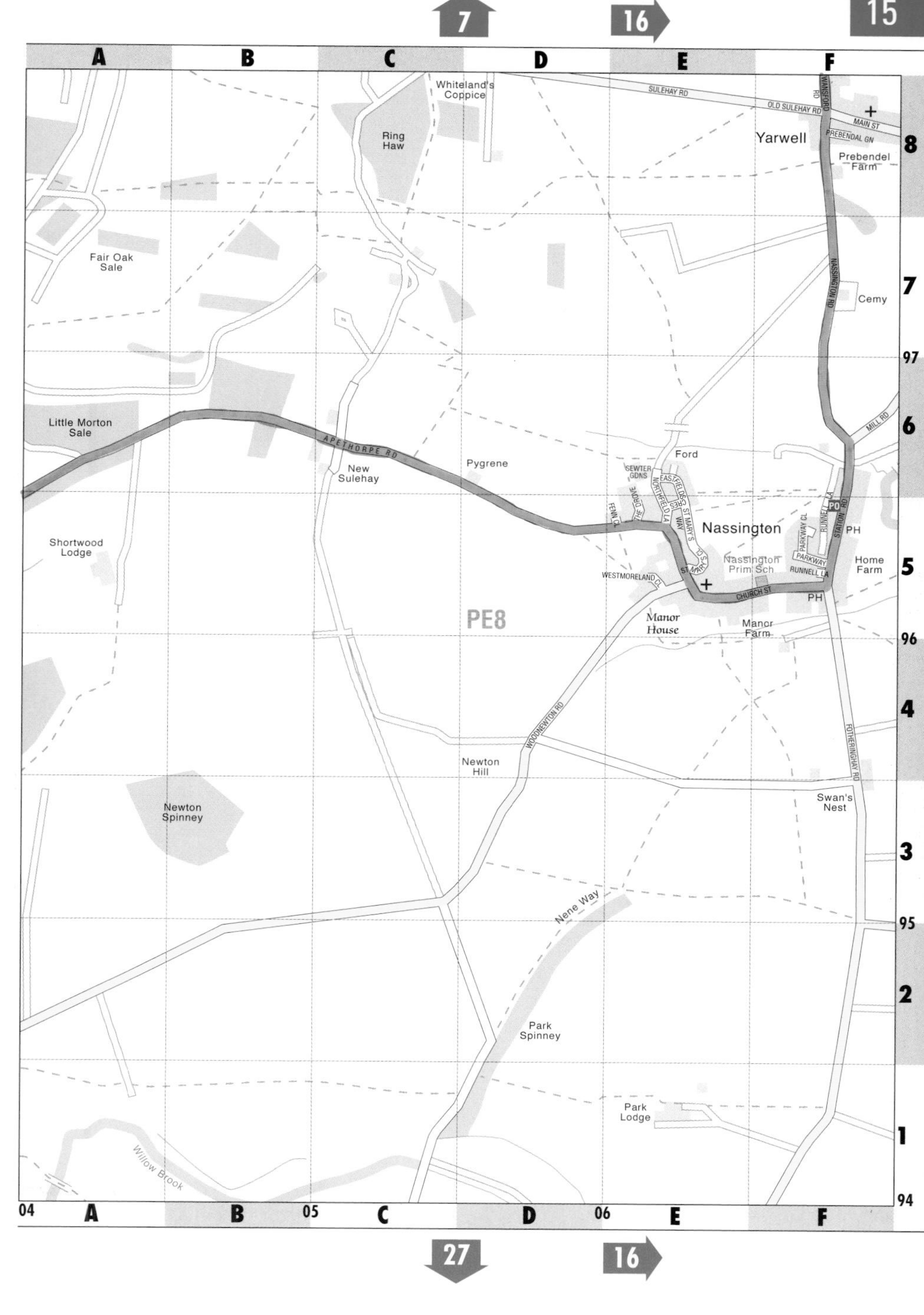
7
16
A
B
C
D
E
F
Whiteland's Coppice
Ring Haw
SULEHAY RD
OLD SULEHAY RD
WANSFORD RD
MAIN ST
PREBENDAL GN
Yarwell
Prebendel Farm
Fair Oak Sale
NASSINGTON RD
Cemy
Little Morton Sale
APETHORPE RD
New Sulehay
Pygrene
Ford
MILL RD
SEWTER GDNS
EASTFIELD
NORTHFIELD LA
THE DROVE
FENN CL
ST MARY'S WAY
ST MARY'S CL
Nassington
PO
RUNNELL LA
STATION RD
PARKWAY CL
PARKWAY
PH
Home Farm
Shortwood Lodge
Nassington Prim Sch
WESTMORELAND CL
CHURCH ST
PE8
Manor House
Manor Farm
WOODNEWTON RD
FOTHERINGHAY RD
Newton Hill
Swan's Nest
Newton Spinney
Nene Way
Park Spinney
Park Lodge
Willow Brook
8
7
97
6
5
96
4
3
95
2
1
94
04
05
06
27
16

15

8

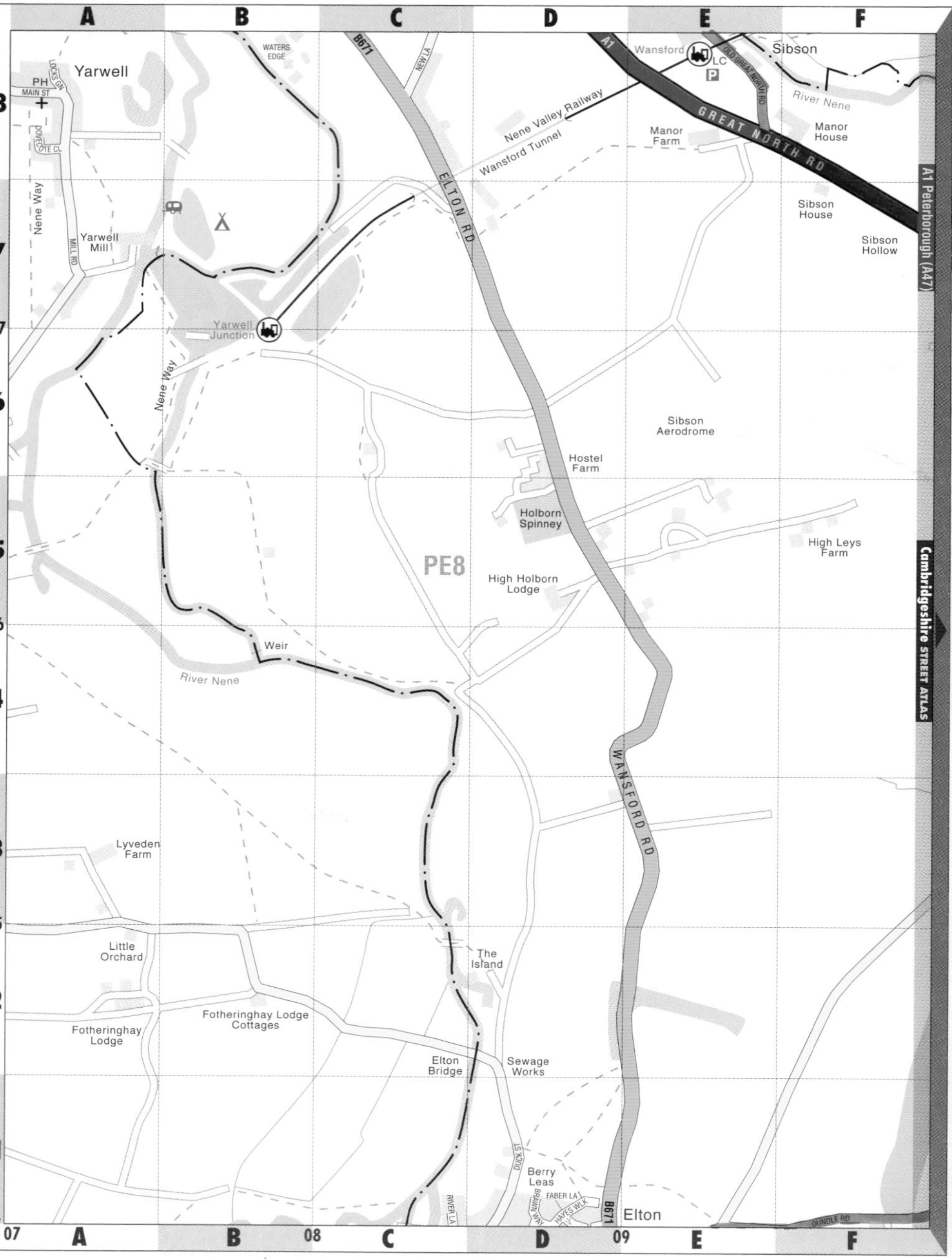

A B C D E F
8 7 97 6 5 96 4 3 95 2 1 94
07 08 09
Yarwell
PH
MAIN ST
LOCKS GN
DOVECOTE CL
Nene Way
MILL RD
Yarwell Mill
WATERS EDGE
B671
NEW LA
Nene Valley Railway
Wansford Tunnel
ELTON RD
A1
Wansford
LC
OLD GREAT NORTH RD
Sibson
River Nene
Manor Farm
Manor House
GREAT NORTH RD
Sibson House
Sibson Hollow
A1 Peterborough (A47)
Yarwell Junction
Nene Way
Sibson Aerodrome
Hostel Farm
Holborn Spinney
High Leys Farm
PE8
High Holborn Lodge
Cambridgeshire STREET ATLAS
Weir
River Nene
WANSFORD RD
Lyveden Farm
Little Orchard
The Island
Fotheringhay Lodge Cottages
Fotheringhay Lodge
Elton Bridge
Sewage Works
DUCK ST
Berry Leas
FABER LA
BRAMWAY
HAYES WLK
RIVER LA
B671
Elton
DUNDLE RD
15
28

18

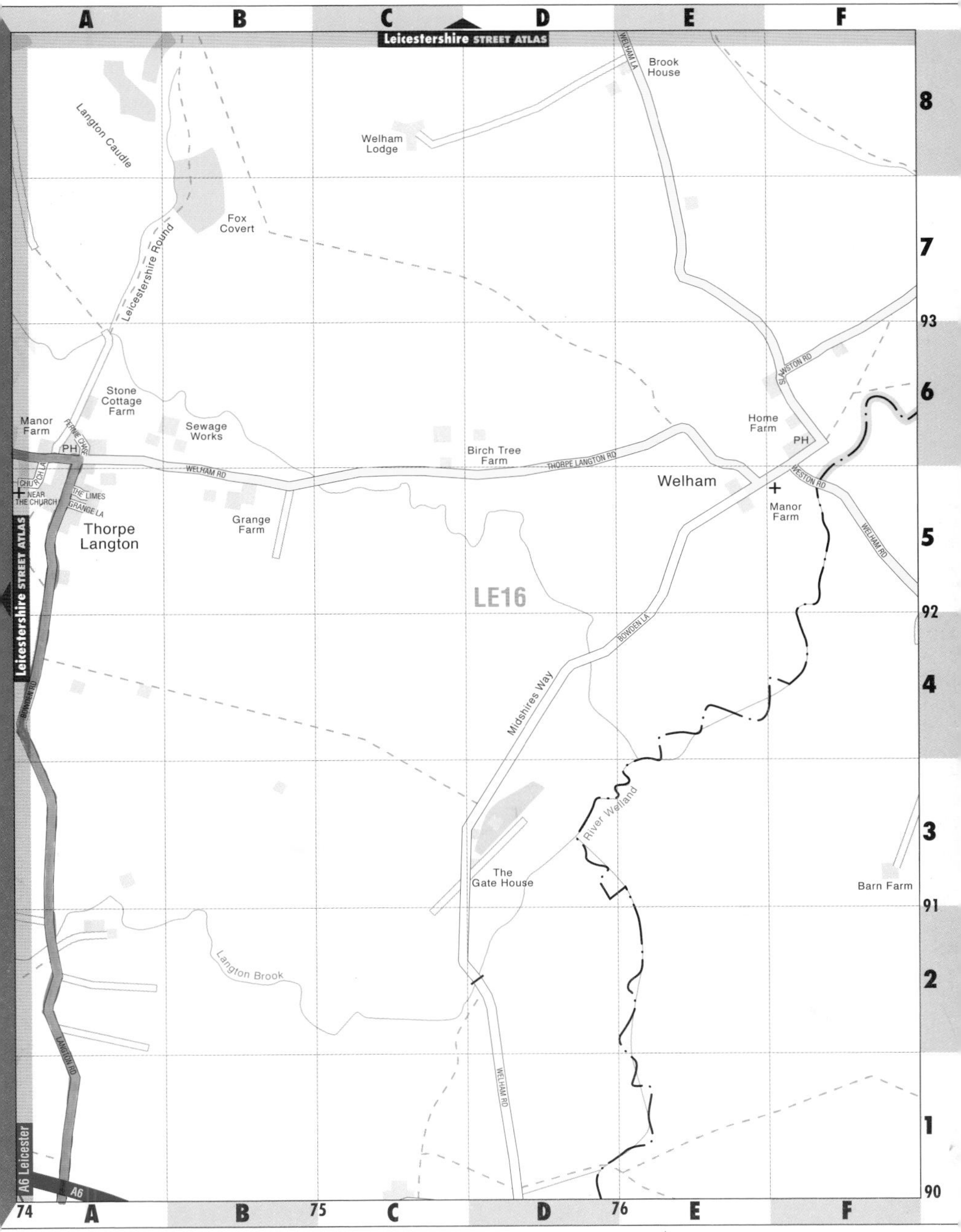

A B C D E F
Leicestershire STREET ATLAS
Brook House
Welham Lodge
Langton Caudle
Fox Covert
Leicestershire Round
WELHAM LA
Stone Cottage Farm
Manor Farm
Sewage Works
PH
FERNIE CHASE
CHURCH LA
NEAR THE CHURCH
THE LIMES
GRANGE LA
Thorpe Langton
Grange Farm
WELHAM RD
Birch Tree Farm
THORPE LANGTON RD
Home Farm
PH
SLAWSTON RD
Welham
Manor Farm
WESTON RD
WELHAM RD
LE16
BOWDEN LA
Midshires Way
BOWDEN RD
River Welland
The Gate House
Barn Farm
Langton Brook
LANGTON RD
WELHAM RD
A6 Leicester
A6
8 7 93 6 5 92 4 3 91 2 1 90
74 75 76

32

18

17

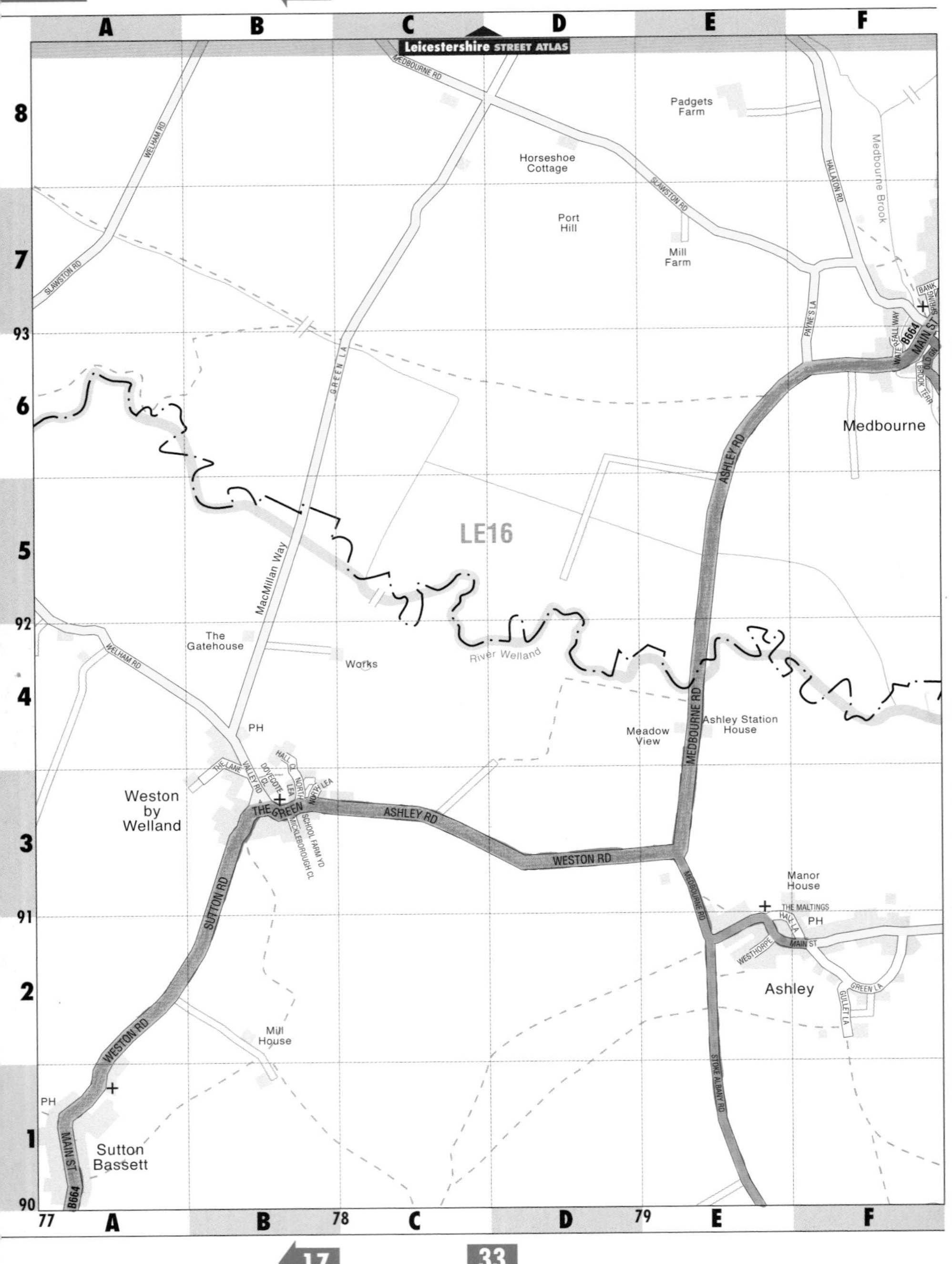
Leicestershire STREET ATLAS
A
B
C
D
E
F
8
7
93
6
5
92
4
3
91
2
1
90
77
78
79
MEDBOURNE RD
Padgets Farm
WELHAM RD
Horseshoe Cottage
Medbourne Brook
HALLATON RD
SLAWSTON RD
Port Hill
Mill Farm
SLAWSTON RD
PAYNE'S LA
BANK
SPRING
WATERFALL WAY
B664
MAIN ST
OLD GR
BROOK TERR
GREEN LA
Medbourne
ASHLEY RD
LE16
MacMillan Way
The Gatehouse
WELHAM RD
Works
River Welland
PH
Meadow View
Ashley Station House
MEDBOURNE RD
HALL CL
THE LANE
VALLEY RD
DOVECOTE CL
NORTH LEA
NORTH LEA
Weston by Welland
THE GREEN
ASHLEY RD
SCHOOL FARM YD
MICKLEBOROUGH CL
WESTON RD
SUTTON RD
Manor House
MEDBOURNE RD
THE MALTINGS
HALL LA
PH
WESTHORPE
MAIN ST
GREEN LA
Ashley
GULLET LA
Mill House
WESTON RD
STOKE ALBANY RD
PH
MAIN ST
Sutton Bassett
B664

17

33

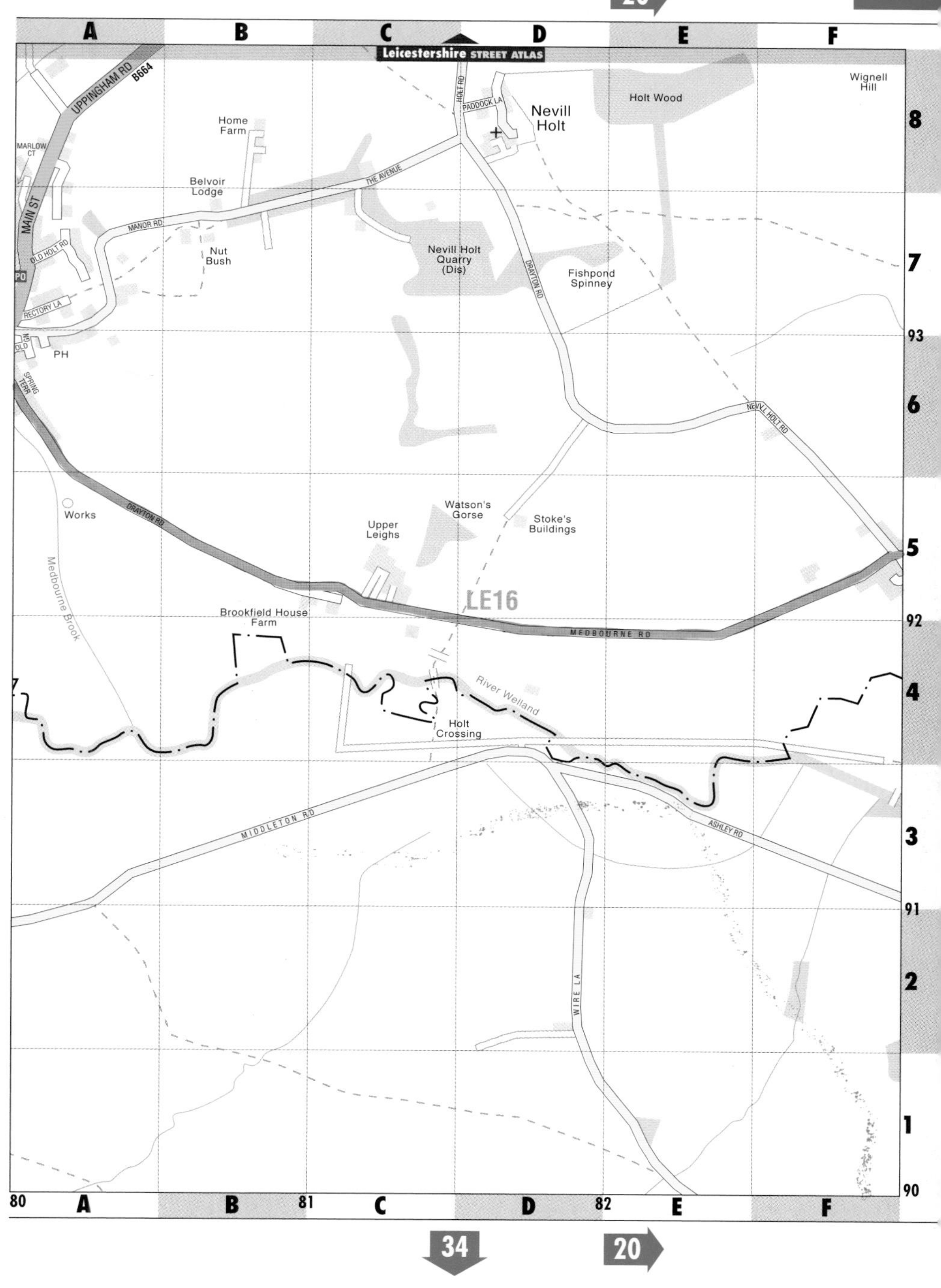
20
A
B
C
D
E
F
Leicestershire STREET ATLAS
UPPINGHAM RD
B664
HOLT RD
PADDOCK LA
Nevill Holt
Holt Wood
Wignell Hill
Home Farm
MARLOW CT
Belvoir Lodge
THE AVENUE
MAIN ST
MANOR RD
Nut Bush
OLD HOLT RD
Nevill Holt Quarry (Dis)
DRAYTON RD
Fishpond Spinney
PO
RECTORY LA
PH
SPRING TERR
NEVILL HOLT RD
Works
DRAYTON RD
Watson's Gorse
Stoke's Buildings
Upper Leighs
Medbourne Brook
LE16
Brookfield House Farm
MEDBOURNE RD
River Welland
Holt Crossing
MIDDLETON RD
ASHLEY RD
WIRE LA
8
7
93
6
5
92
4
3
91
2
1
90
80
81
82
34
20

19

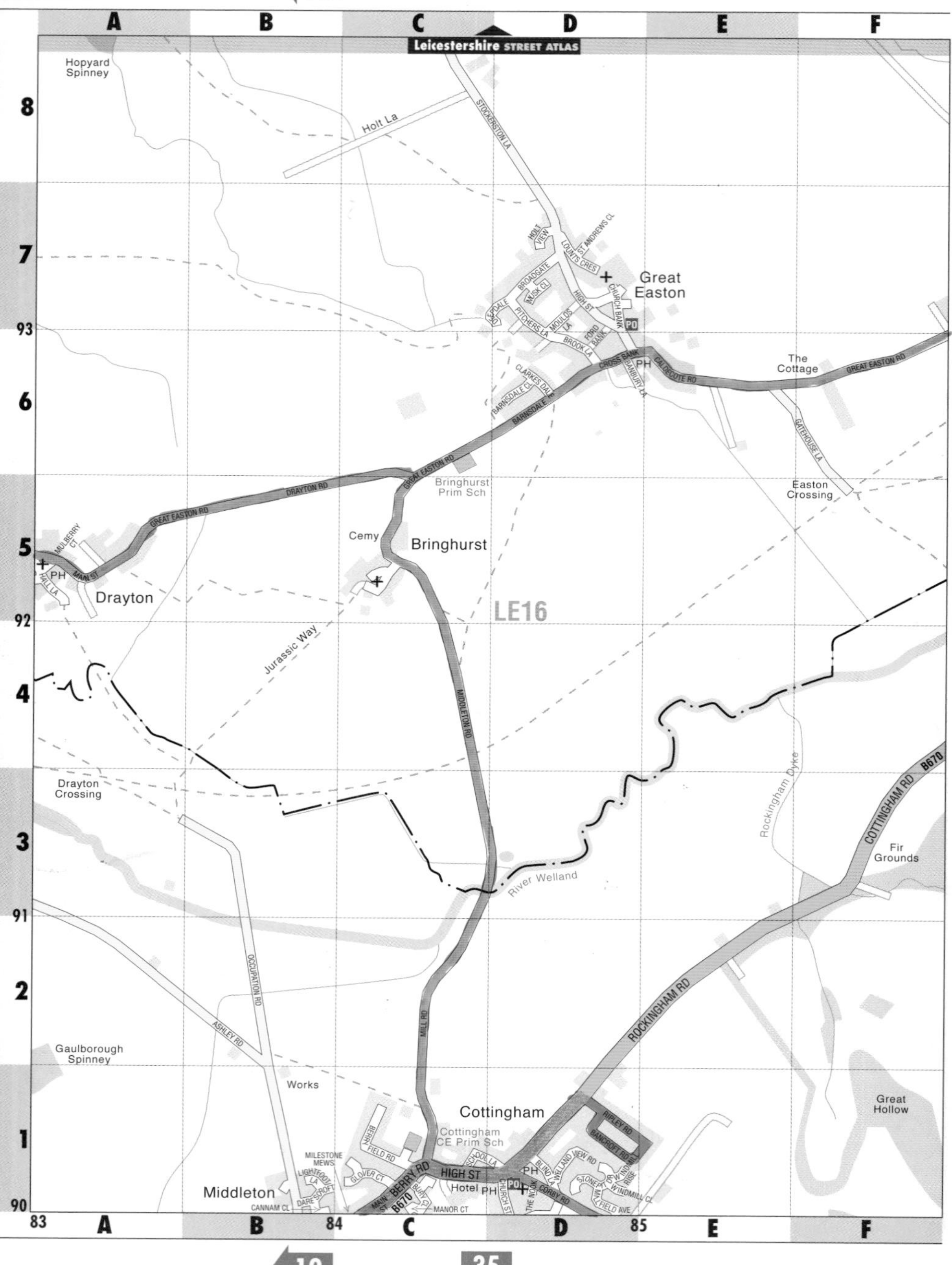
Leicestershire STREET ATLAS
A
B
C
D
E
F
8
7
93
6
5
92
4
3
91
2
1
90
83
84
85
Hopyard Spinney
Holt La
Stockerston La
Great Easton
The Cottage
Great Easton Rd
Caldecote Rd
Cross Bank
PH
PO
Gatehouse La
Easton Crossing
Bringhurst Prim Sch
Great Easton Rd
Drayton Rd
Cemy
Bringhurst
Drayton
LE16
Jurassic Way
Middleton Rd
Drayton Crossing
River Welland
Rockingham Dyke
Cottingham Rd
B670
Fir Grounds
Occupation Rd
Ashley Rd
Mill Rd
Rockingham Rd
Gaulborough Spinney
Works
Cottingham
Cottingham CE Prim Sch
Great Hollow
Middleton
High St
Berry Rd
Hotel
Ripley Rd
Bancroft Rd
Corby Rd
Cannam Cl
Manor Ct
Milestone Mews

19
35

9
22

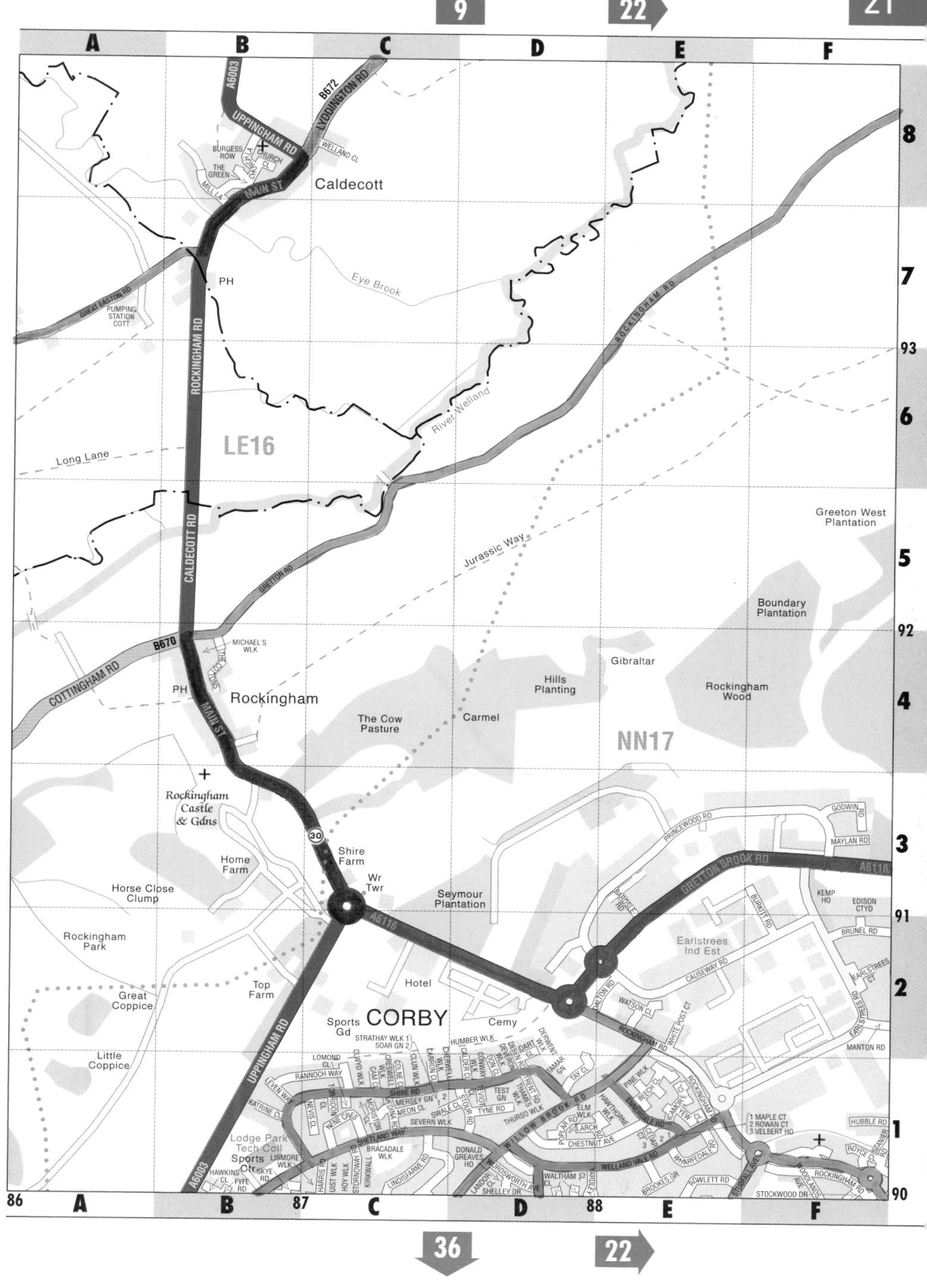
A
B
C
D
E
F
8
7
93
6
5
92
4
3
91
2
1
90
86
87
88
A6003
B672
UPPINGHAM RD
LYDDINGTON RD
BURGESS ROW
CHURCH CL
THE GREEN
MILL LA
MAIN ST
WELLAND CL
Caldecott
PH
Eye Brook
GREAT EASTON RD
PUMPING STATION COTT
ROCKINGHAM RD
River Welland
LE16
Long Lane
CALDECOTT RD
Greeton West Plantation
Jurassic Way
GRETTON RD
Boundary Plantation
B670
MICHAEL'S WLK
COTTINGHAM RD
PH
Rockingham
MAIN ST
Hills Planting
Gibraltar
Rockingham Wood
The Cow Pasture
Carmel
NN17
Rockingham Castle & Gdns
PRINCEWOOD RD
GODWIN RD
MAYLAN RD
30
Home Farm
Shire Farm
Wr Twr
GRETTON BROOK RD
A6116
Horse Close Clump
Seymour Plantation
KEMP HO
EDISON CTYD
A6116
BRUNEL RD
Rockingham Park
Earlstrees Ind Est
CAUSEWAY RD
EARLSTREES CT
Great Coppice
Top Farm
Hotel
WATSON CL
CORBY
Sports Gd
Cemy
ROCKINGHAM RD
WHITE POST CT
UPPINGHAM RD
EARLSTREES RD
MANTON RD
Little Coppice
RANNOCH WAY
SHIRE RD
TYNE RD
SEVERN WLK
WILLOW BROOK RD
ELM WLK
HAWTHORNE WLK
EMERDALE RD
PINE WLK
CHESTNUT AVE
1 MAPLE CT
2 ROWAN CT
3 VELBERT HO
HUBBLE RD
Lodge Park Tech Coll
Sports Ctr
SHETLAND WAY
BRACADALE WLK
DONALD GREAVES HO
WELLAND VALE RD
WALTHAM CL
BROOKES GR
ROWLETT RD
STOCKWOOD DR
ROCKINGHAM RD
ROYCE CL
A6003
HAWKINS CL
FYFE RD
SKYE RD
LISMORE WLK
HARRIS RD
UIST WLK
HOY WLK
STORNOWAY RD
KIRKWALL
LINDISFARNE RD
SHELLEY DR
86
A
B
87
C
D
88
E
F
90

36
22

21
10

A
B
C
D
E
F
8
7
93
6
5
92
4
3
91
2
1
90
89
90
91
ROCKINGHAM RD
NORTHERN CL
WELLAND CL
KIRBY RD
Wr Twr
Gretton Prim Sch
STAFFORD RD
FINCH-HATTON DR
Jurassic Way
South Lodge
FULLEN LA
Kirby Hall Farm
CORBY RD
Greeton East Plantation
NN17
Keepers Lodge Farm
Kirby Lodge
KIRBY LA
Corby Tunnel
Brookfield Plantation
Forest Nursery
Rockingham Motor Speedway
GRETTON BROOK RD
Factory
GRETTON RD
Greeton Brook Plantation
Weldon Lodge
A6116
MITCHELL RD
BRUNEL RD
Willowbrook East Ind Est
FLEMING RD
ALEXANDER CT
BRUNEL CT
PHOENIX PARKWAY
HERITAGE WAY
SHELTON RD
SHELTON CT
PYWELL CT
Earlstrees Ind Est
PRIORS CT 1
ADELAIDE HO 2
MELBOURNE HO 3
PERTH HO 4
DARWIN HO 5
CANBERRA HO 6
ARNSLEY RD 7
SONDES RD
PYWELL RD
BIRCHINGTON RD
MANTON RD
CORBY
STEEL RD
MACADAM RD
STOCKBRIDGE RD
MARCONI CTYD
RUTHERFORD CT
BAIRD RD
PRIESTLEY CT
BARON CT
SALLOW RD
VENTURE CL
Corby Gate Bsns Pk
Weldon North Ind Est
CAVENDISH CTYD
ARKWRIGHT RD
CURVER WAY
Enterprise Ind Pk
HUBBLE RD
STANIER RD
CRICK CL
PARSONS GR
GENNER RD
GAYDON HO
HUNTERS RD
BRAKEY RD
CORBY GATE
PRIORS HAW RD
LISTER CL
JAMES WATT AVE
STEPHENSON WAY
NEWTON GR
PEN GREEN LA
DARWIN RD
BOYLE RD
DARWIN RD
A6116

21
37

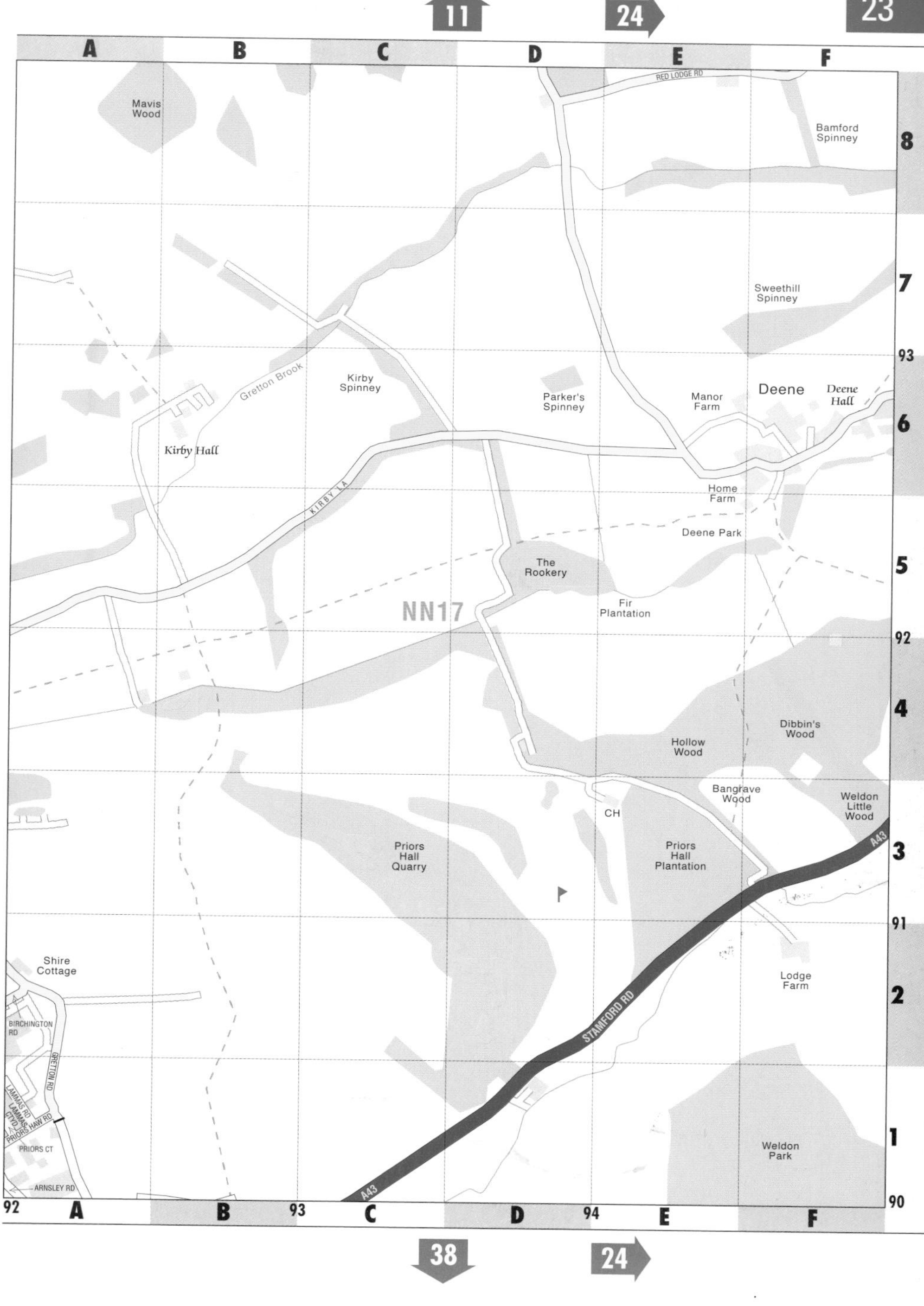
11
24
A
B
C
D
E
F
RED LODGE RD
Mavis Wood
Bamford Spinney
8
7
Sweethill Spinney
93
Gretton Brook
Kirby Spinney
Parker's Spinney
Manor Farm
Deene
Deene Hall
6
Kirby Hall
KIRBY LA
Home Farm
Deene Park
The Rookery
5
NN17
Fir Plantation
92
4
Dibbin's Wood
Hollow Wood
Bangrave Wood
Weldon Little Wood
CH
Priors Hall Quarry
Priors Hall Plantation
A43
3
91
Shire Cottage
Lodge Farm
2
STAMFORD RD
BIRCHINGTON RD
GRETTON RD
LAMMAS RD
LAMMAS CTYD
PRIORS HAW RD
PRIORS CT
ARNSLEY RD
1
Weldon Park
A43
92
93
94
90
38
24

23
12

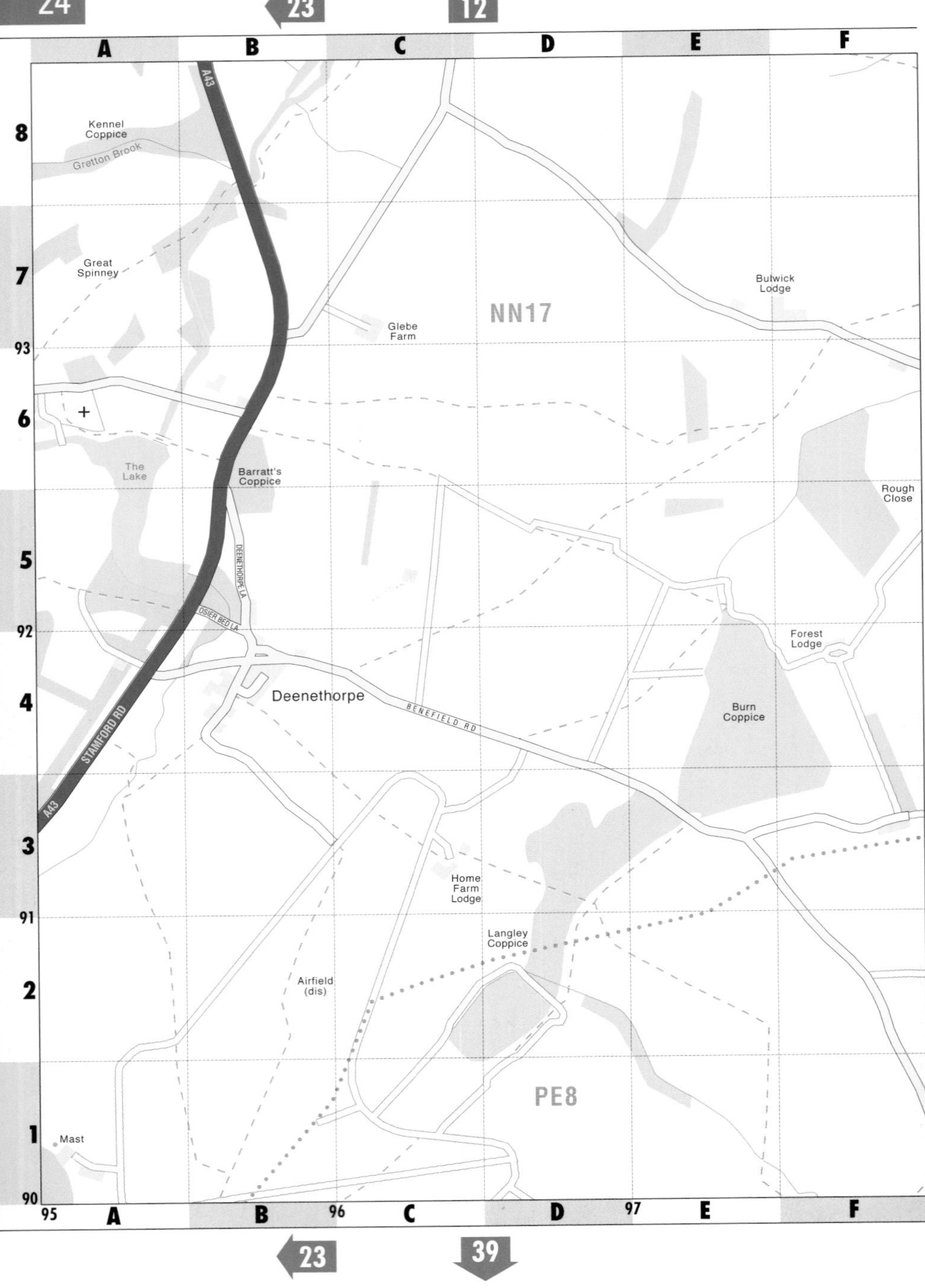
A
B
C
D
E
F
8
7
93
6
5
92
4
3
91
2
1
90
95
96
97
A43
Kennel Coppice
Gretton Brook
Great Spinney
Glebe Farm
NN17
Bulwick Lodge
The Lake
Barratt's Coppice
DEENETHORPE LA
OSIER BED LA
Rough Close
Forest Lodge
Deenethorpe
BENEFIELD RD
Burn Coppice
STAMFORD RD
Home Farm Lodge
Langley Coppice
Airfield (dis)
PE8
Mast

23
39

13
26

A
B
C
D
E
F
Holey Brookes
8
Boar's Head Cottage
Blackmore Thick Farm
7
Boar's Head Farm
NN17
Shire Hill Lodge
93
Stone Hill
6
Great Old Sale
Little Old Sale
New Hall
5
Frere Hill Wood
Crossway Hand Farm
Vicarage Farm
Frere Hill
92
Crossway Hand Cottages
4
Wymond Hill
PE8
Tottenhoe Lodge
3
91
Westwood Lodge
Provost Lodge
2
Glapthorn Cow Pasture
Sandy Forth Lodge
1
90
98
99
00

40
26

25
14

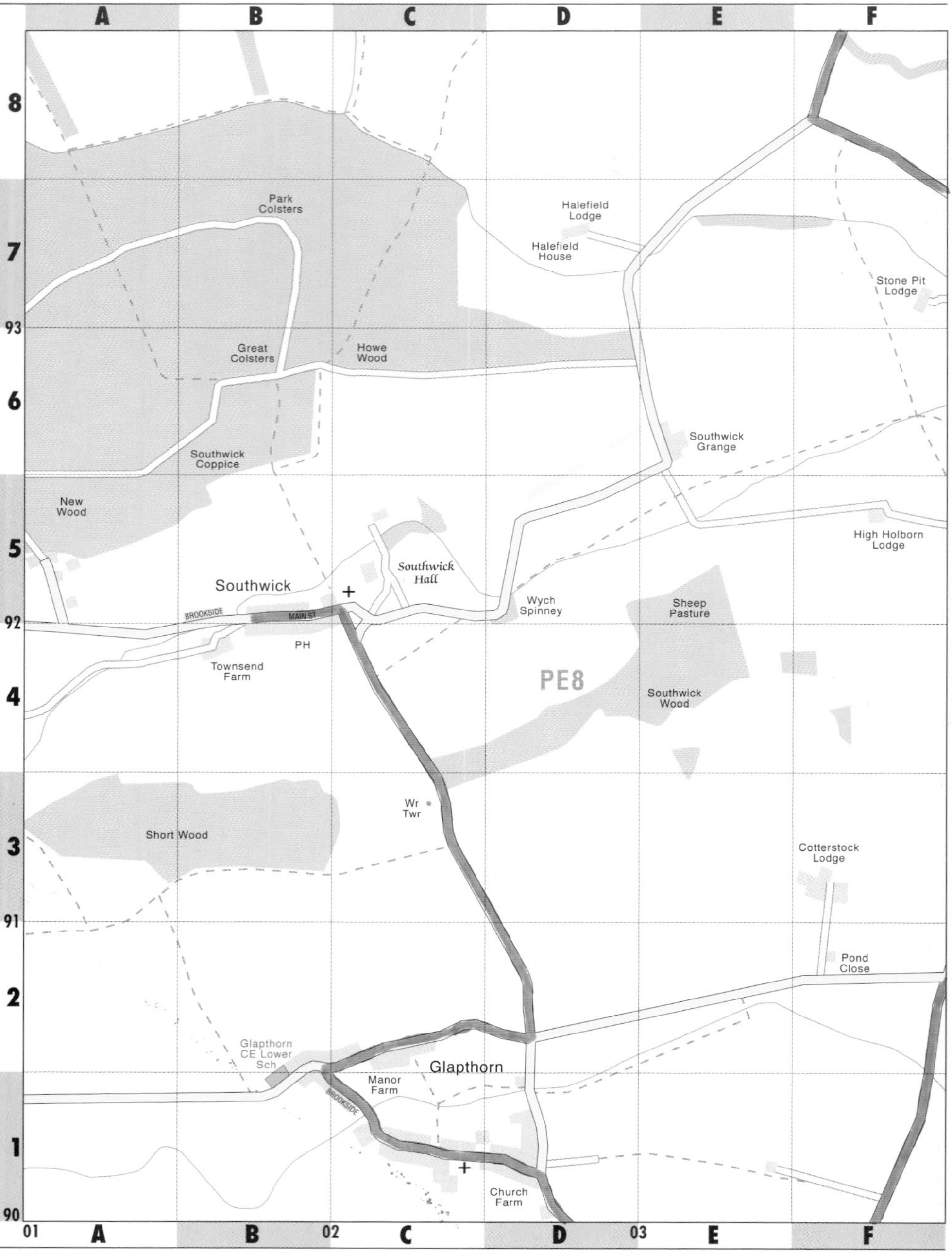

A B C D E F
8
7
93
6
5
92
4
3
91
2
1
90
01 02 03
Park Colsters
Halefield Lodge
Halefield House
Stone Pit Lodge
Great Colsters
Howe Wood
Southwick Grange
Southwick Coppice
New Wood
High Holborn Lodge
Southwick Hall
Southwick
Wych Spinney
Sheep Pasture
BROOKSIDE
MAIN ST
PH
Townsend Farm
PE8
Southwick Wood
Wr Twr
Short Wood
Cotterstock Lodge
Pond Close
Glapthorn CE Lower Sch
Glapthorn
Manor Farm
BROOKSIDE
Church Farm

25
41

15
28

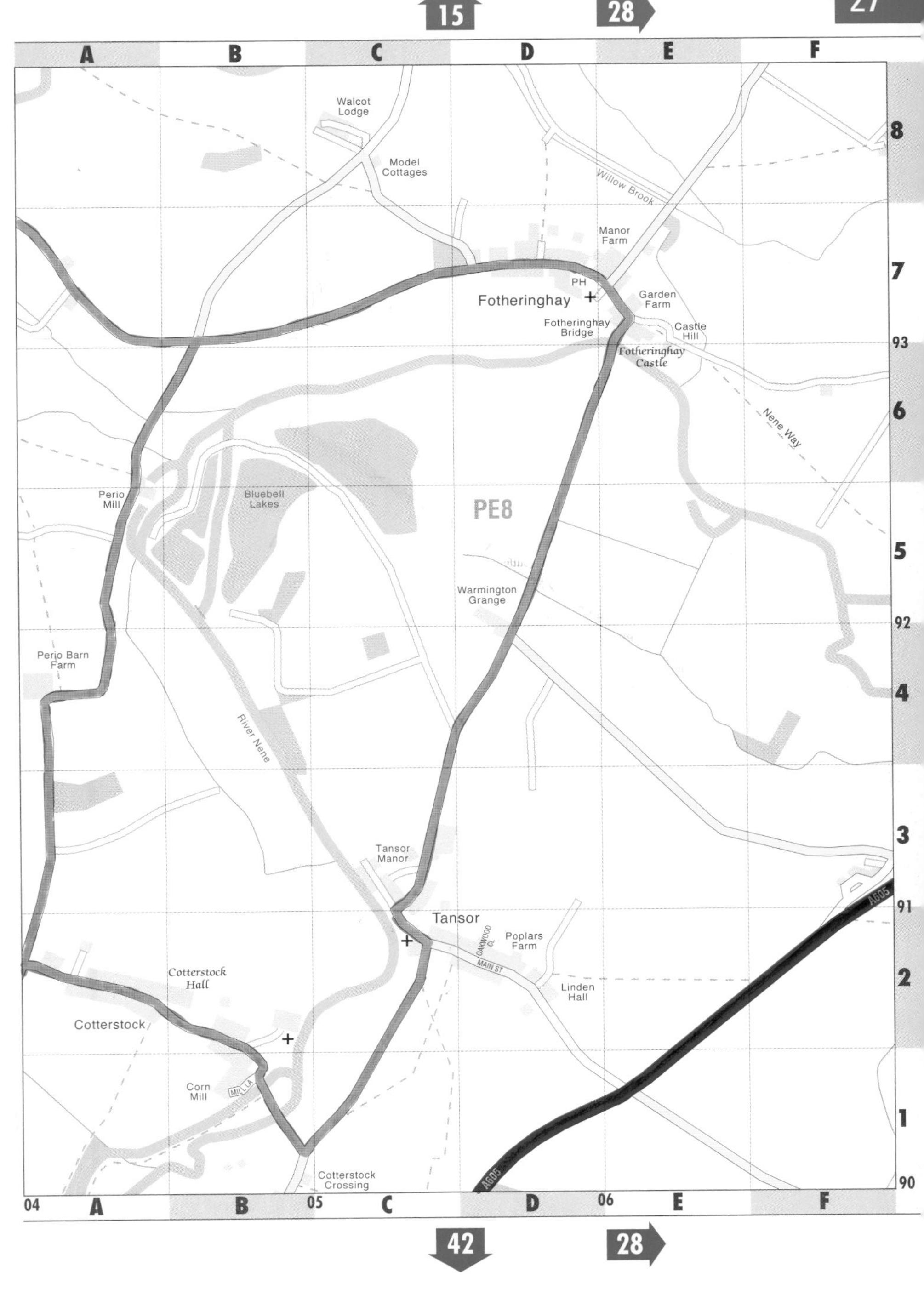
A
B
C
D
E
F
Walcot Lodge
Model Cottages
Willow Brook
Manor Farm
PH
Fotheringhay
Garden Farm
Fotheringhay Bridge
Castle Hill
Fotheringhay Castle
Nene Way
Perio Mill
Bluebell Lakes
PE8
Warmington Grange
Perio Barn Farm
River Nene
Tansor Manor
Tansor
OAKWOOD CL
Poplars Farm
MAIN ST
Linden Hall
Cotterstock Hall
Cotterstock
Corn Mill
MILL LA
Cotterstock Crossing
A605
8
7
93
6
5
92
4
3
91
2
1
90
04
05
06

42
28

27 16

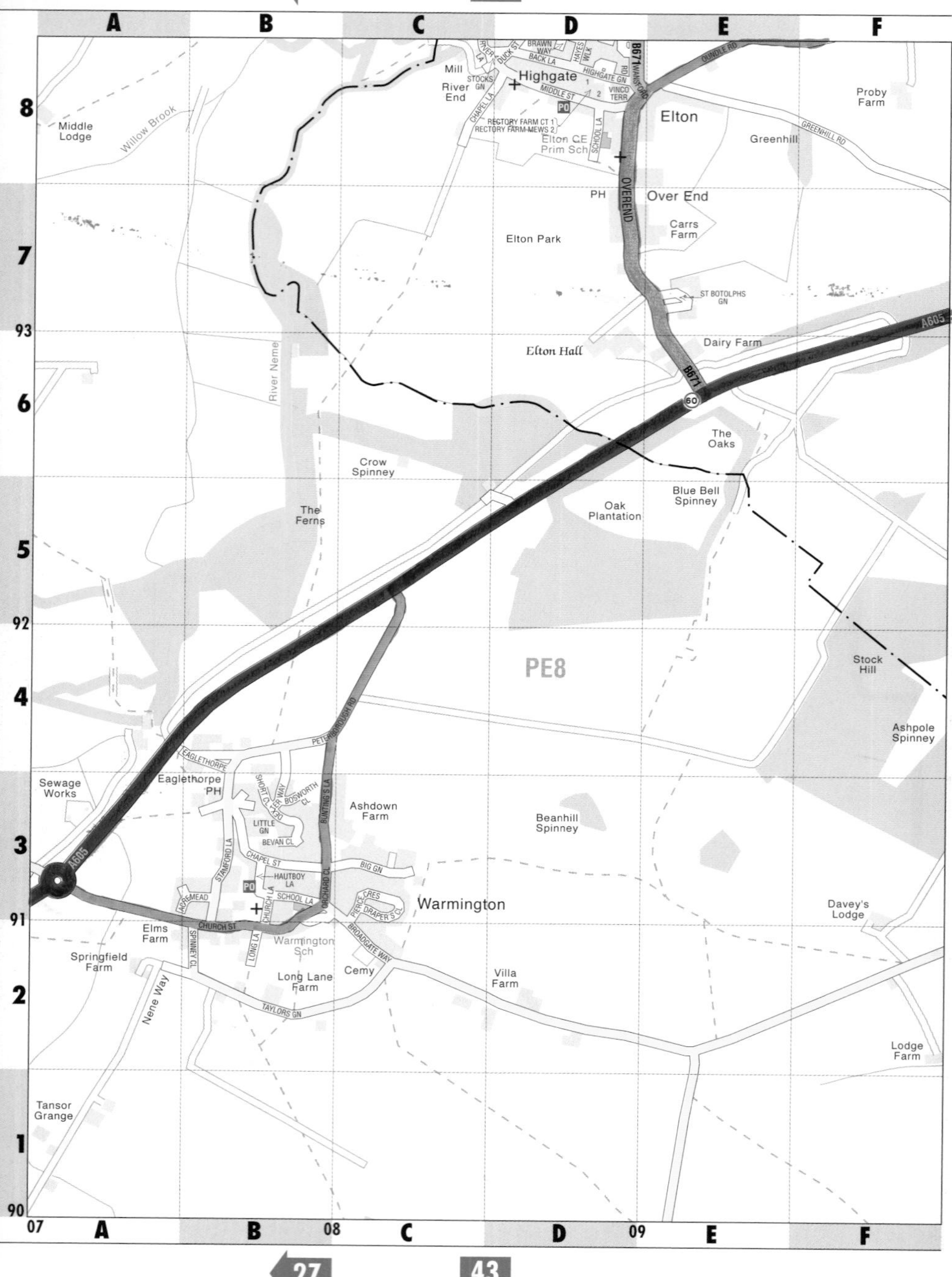
A
B
C
D
E
F
8
7
93
6
5
92
4
3
91
2
1
90
07
08
09
Highgate
Mill
River End
Elton
Proby Farm
Middle Lodge
Willow Brook
Greenhill
GREENHILL RD
OUNDLE RD
Elton CE Prim Sch
PH
Over End
OVEREND
Carrs Farm
Elton Park
ST BOTOLPHS GN
Elton Hall
Dairy Farm
A605
B671
River Nene
The Oaks
Crow Spinney
Blue Bell Spinney
Oak Plantation
The Ferns
PE8
Stock Hill
Ashpole Spinney
PETERBOROUGH RD
EAGLETHORPE
Eaglethorpe
PH
Sewage Works
Ashdown Farm
Beanhill Spinney
BUNTING'S LA
BOSWORTH CL
LITTLE GN
BEVAN CL
CHAPEL ST
BIG GN
HAUTBOY LA
SCHOOL LA
STAMFORD LA
ORCHARD CL
PIERCE CRES
DRAPER'S CL
Warmington
Davey's Lodge
CHURCH ST
Elms Farm
Warmington Sch
BROADGATE WAY
Springfield Farm
SPINNEY CL
LONG LA
Long Lane Farm
Cemy
Villa Farm
TAYLORS GN
Nene Way
Lodge Farm
Tansor Grange
PO
RECTORY FARM CT 1
RECTORY FARM MEWS 2
MIDDLE ST
BACK LA
HIGHGATE GN
SCHOOL LA
CHAPEL LA
STOCKS GN
DUCK ST
VINCO TERR
60

27 43

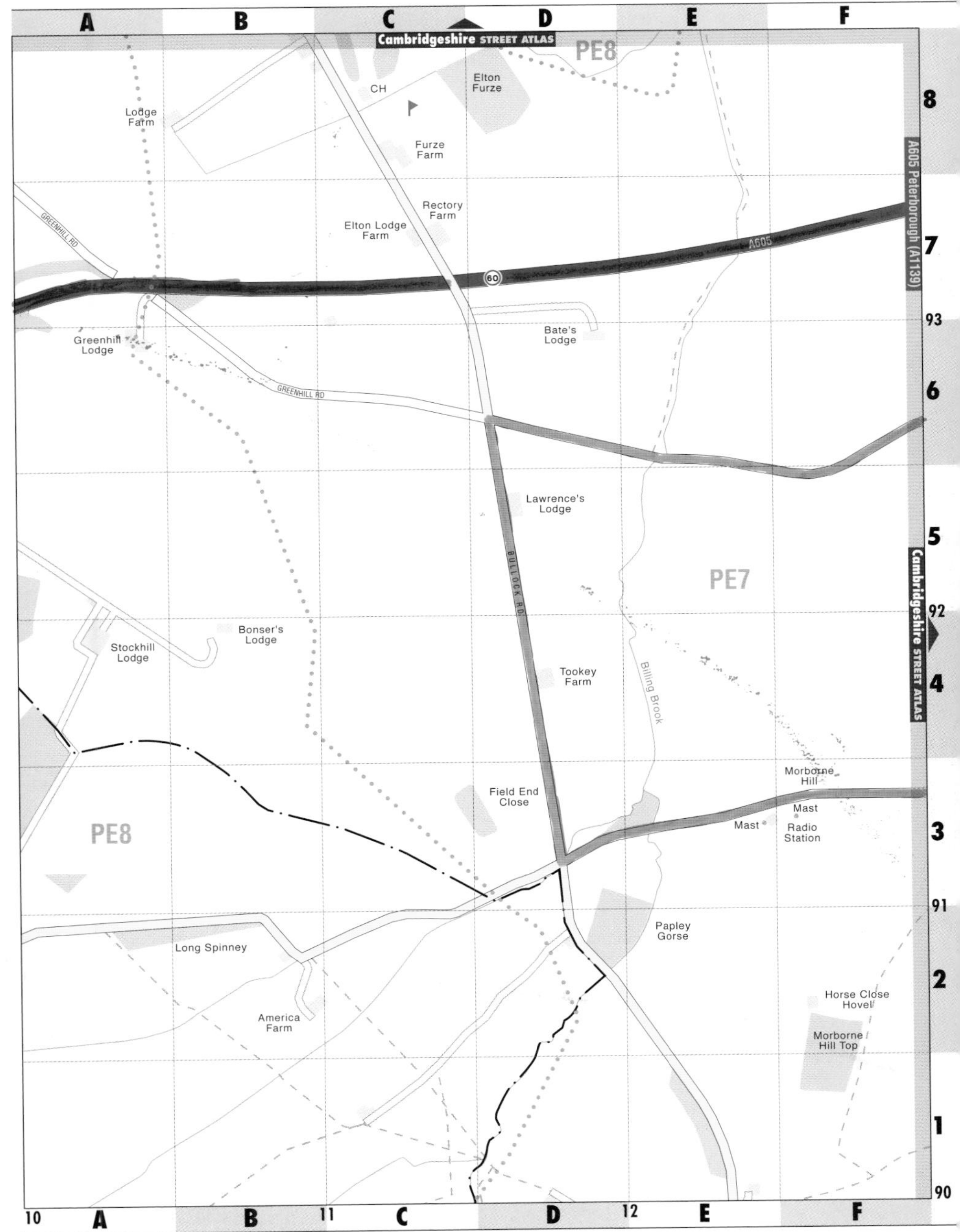
A
B
C
D
E
F
Cambridgeshire STREET ATLAS
PE8
Elton Furze
CH
Lodge Farm
Furze Farm
Rectory Farm
Elton Lodge Farm
GREENHILL RD
A605
60
A605 Peterborough (A1139)
8
7
93
6
5
92
4
3
91
2
1
90
Greenhill Lodge
Bate's Lodge
GREENHILL RD
Lawrence's Lodge
BULLOCK RD
PE7
Cambridgeshire STREET ATLAS
Bonser's Lodge
Stockhill Lodge
Tookey Farm
Billing Brook
Morborne Hill
Field End Close
Mast
Mast
Radio Station
PE8
Papley Gorse
Long Spinney
Horse Close Hovel
America Farm
Morborne Hill Top
10
11
12

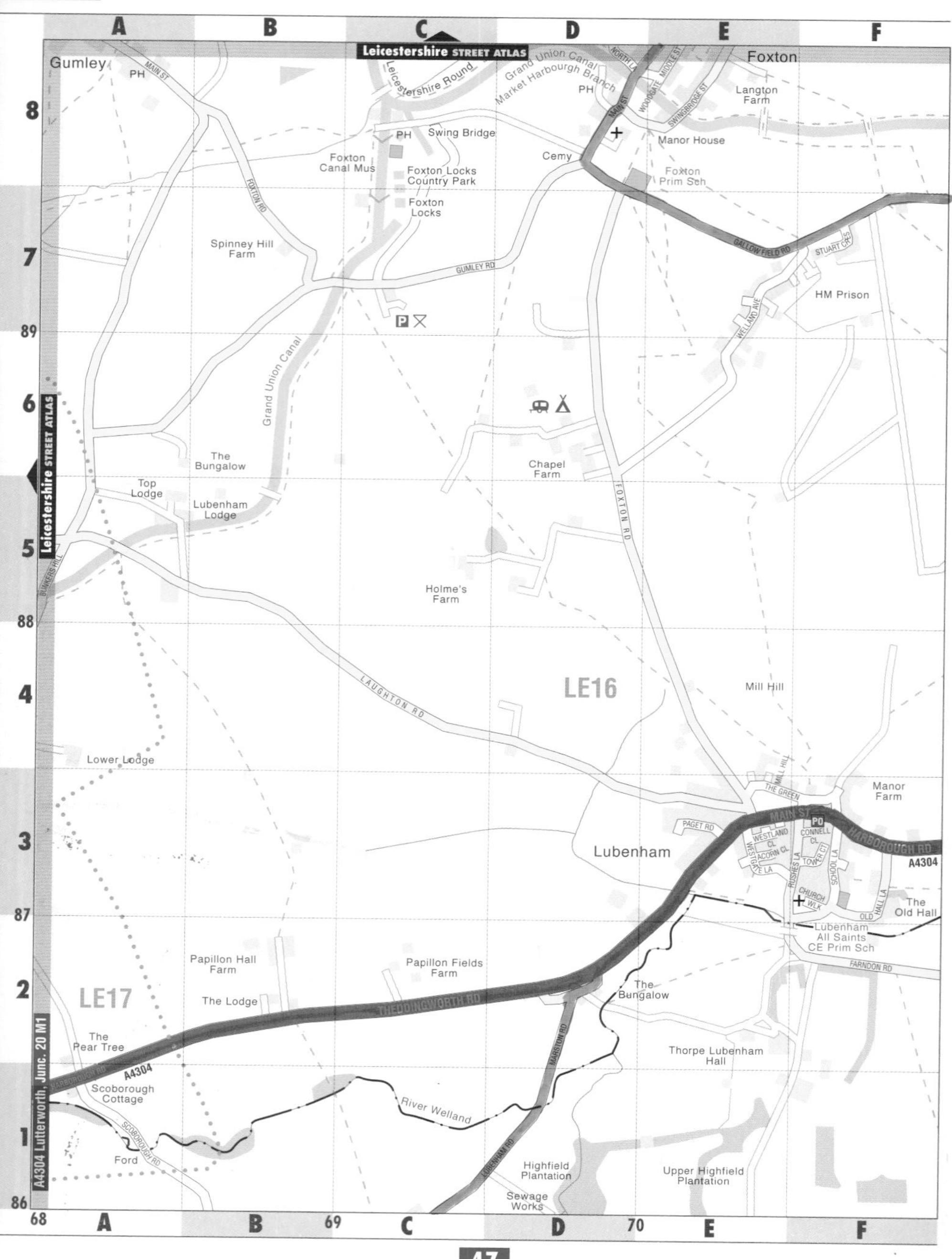
Leicestershire STREET ATLAS
Gumley
PH
MAIN ST
Leicestershire Round
Grand Union Canal
Market Harbourgh Branch
Foxton
Langton Farm
PH
Swing Bridge
Foxton Canal Mus
Foxton Locks Country Park
Foxton Locks
Cemy
Manor House
Foxton Prim Sch
FOXTON RD
Spinney Hill Farm
GUMLEY RD
GALLOW FIELD RD
STUART CRES
HM Prison
WELLAND AVE
Grand Union Canal
The Bungalow
Chapel Farm
Top Lodge
Lubenham Lodge
BUNKERS HILL
Holme's Farm
LE16
LAUGHTON RD
Mill Hill
Lower Lodge
MILL HILL
THE GREEN
Manor Farm
MAIN ST
PAGET RD
HARBOROUGH RD
A4304
Lubenham
WESTLAND CL
CONNELL CL
ACORN CL
TOWER CT
RUSHES LA
SCHOOL LA
CHURCH WLK
OLD HALL LA
The Old Hall
Lubenham All Saints CE Prim Sch
FARNDON RD
Papillon Hall Farm
Papillon Fields Farm
LE17
The Lodge
THEDDINGWORTH RD
The Bungalow
MARSTON RD
The Pear Tree
HARBOROUGH RD
A4304
Scoborough Cottage
Thorpe Lubenham Hall
River Welland
SCOBOROUGH RD
Ford
Highfield Plantation
Upper Highfield Plantation
Sewage Works
LUBENHAM RD
A4304 Lutterworth, Junc. 20 M1
A B C D E F
8 7 89 6 5 88 4 3 87 2 1 86
68 69 70

47

32

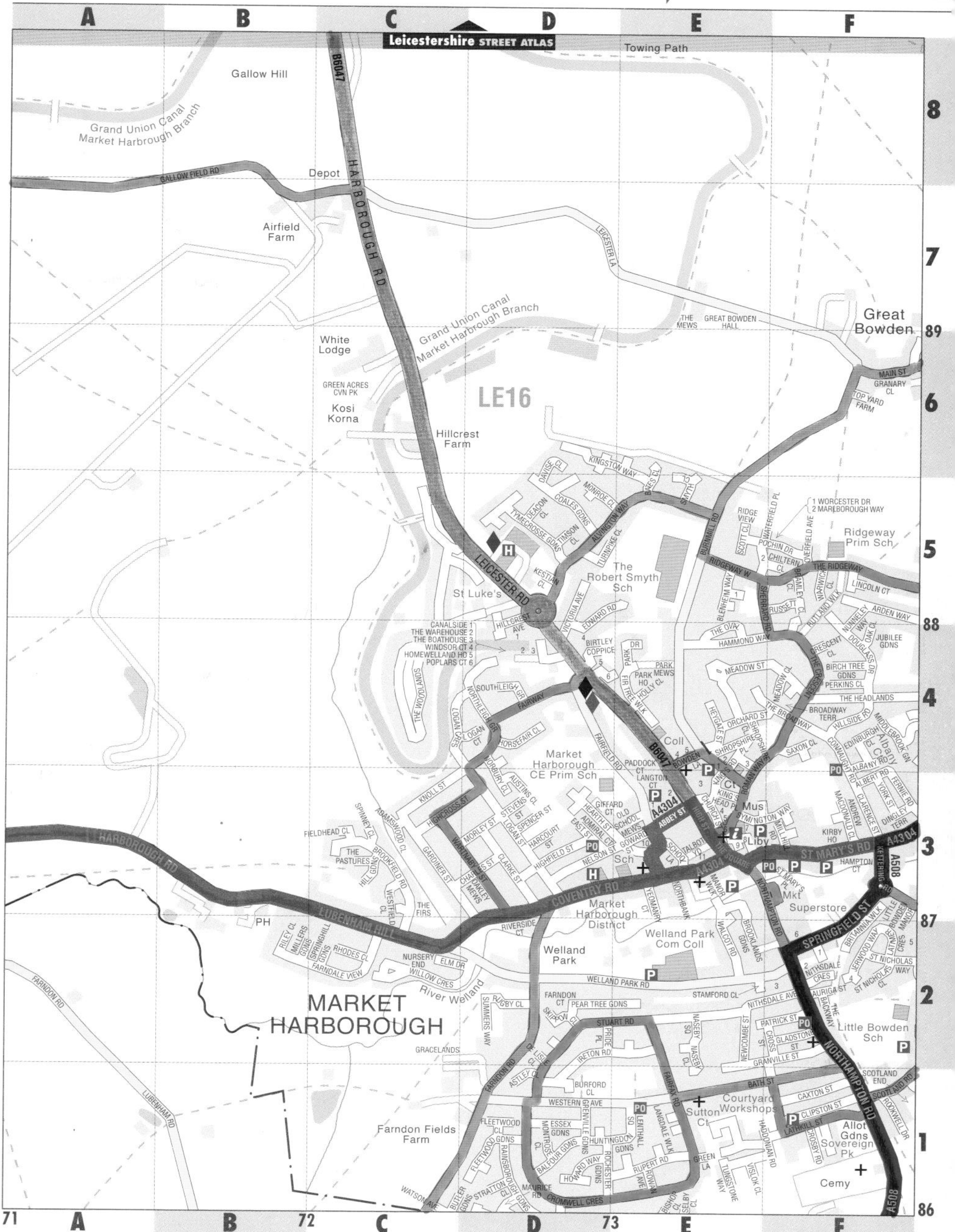

A B C D E F

Leicestershire STREET ATLAS

Towing Path

Gallow Hill

B6047

8

Grand Union Canal
Market Harbrough Branch

GALLOW FIELD RD

Depot

HARBOROUGH RD

Airfield
Farm

LEICESTER LA

7

Grand Union Canal
Market Harbrough Branch

THE MEWS

GREAT BOWDEN HALL

Great
Bowden

89

White
Lodge

GREEN ACRES
CVN PK

MAIN ST

GRANARY CL

TOP YARD FARM

LE16

6

Kosi
Korna

Hillcrest
Farm

KINGSTON WAY

DAVISE CL

MONROE CL

BATES CL

SMYTH CL

DEACON CL

COALES GDNS

TYMECROSSE GDNS

TIMSON CL

ALVINGTON WAY

TURNPIKE CL

BURNMILL RD

RIDGE VIEW

SCOTT CL

WATERFIELD PL

1 WORCESTER DR
2 MARLBOROUGH WAY

OVERFIELD AVE

POCHIN DR

CHILTERN

Ridgeway
Prim Sch

5

LEICESTER RD

KESTIAN CL

The
Robert Smyth
Sch

RIDGEWAY W

THE RIDGEWAY

BLENHEIM WAY

SHERRARD RD

BRAMLEY CL

WARWICK CL

LINCOLN CT

RUSSETT CL

RUTLAND WLK

ARDEN WAY

NUNNELEY WAY

OAK CL

St Luke's

VICTORIA AVE

EDWARD RD

88

CANALSIDE 1
THE WAREHOUSE 2
THE BOATHOUSE 3
WINDSOR CT 4
HOMEWELLAND HO 5
POPLARS CT 6

HILLCREST AVE

BIRTLEY COPPICE

PARK DR

THE OVAL

HAMMOND WAY

CRESCENT CL

DOUGLASS DR

JUBILEE GDNS

THE WOODLANDS

PARK MEWS

PARK HO

FIR TREE WLK

HOLLY CL

MEADOW ST

MEADOW CL

THE CRESCENT

BIRCH TREE GDNS

PERKINS CL

SOUTHLEIGH GR

NORTHLEIGH GR

FAIRWAY

HEYGATE ST

ORCHARD ST

SHROPSHIRE CL

THE BROADWAY

THE HEADLANDS

BROADWAY TERR

4

LOGAN CRES

LOGAN CT

HORSEFAIR CL

Coll

SHROPSHIRE PL

WILLSIDE RD

EDINBURGH WAY

MIDDLEBROOK GN

Albany Ct

Market
Harborough
CE Prim Sch

FAIRFIELD RD

PADDOCK CT

LANGTON CT

BOWDEN LA

ROMAN WAY

SAXON CL

CONNAUGHT RD

ALBANY RD

KNOLL ST

NORBURY CL

AUSTINS CL

B6047

KING ST

Ct

ALBERT RD

YORK ST

FERNIE RD

HIGHCROSS ST

STEVENS ST

SPENCER ST

GIFFARD CT

HEARTH ST

A4304

ABBEY ST

HIGH ST

HEAD

CHURCH ST

Mus

SYMINGTON WAY

MACDONALD CL

ANDREW CL

CLARENCE ST

DINGLEY TERR

SPINNEY CL

ADAMSWOOD CL

FIELDHEAD CL

HARBOROUGH RD

MORLEY ST

LOGAN ST

HARCOURT ST

ADMIRAL CT

EAST ST

OLD SCHOOL MEWS

GOWARD

Liby

MILL HILL

KIRBY HO

A4304

3

THE PASTURES

HILL GDNS

BROOKFIELD RD

GARDINER ST

WARTNABY ST

CHAPMAN ST

CLARKE ST

HIGHFIELD ST

NELSON ST

Sch

TALBOT YD

SCHOOL LA

THE SQUARE

ST MARY'S RD

HAMPTON CT

KETTERING RD

A508

WESTFIELD

OAKLEY MEWS

COVENTRY RD

A4304

NORTHBANK

MANOR WALK

ST MARY'S PL

Mkt

Superstore

SPRINGFIELD ST

LITTLE BOWDEN

MANOR

THE FIRS

Market
Harborough
District

YEOMANRY CT

NORTHAMPTON RD

87

PH

RILEY CL

MILLERS GDNS

SPRINGHILL

RHODES CL

FARNDALE VIEW

LUBENHAM HILL

RIVERSIDE CT

Welland
Park

Welland Park
Com Coll

WALCOT RD

BROOKLANDS GDNS

BRITANNIA WLK

JERWOOD WAY

LATHAM CRES

ST NICHOLAS CL

ST NICHOLAS WAY

NURSERY END

ELM DR

WILLOW CRES

River Welland

WELLAND PARK RD

NITHSDALE CRES

FARNDON RD

MARKET
HARBOROUGH

FARNDON CT

PEAR TREE GDNS

STAMFORD CL

NITHSDALE AVE

AURIGA ST

THE BACKWAY

2

RUGBY CL

SKIPTON CL

SUMMERS WAY

STUART RD

PRIDE PL

NASEBY SQ

NEWCOMBE ST

PATRICK ST

CROSS ST

GLADSTONE ST

Little Bowden
Sch

GRACELANDS

IRETON RD

NASEBY CL

GRANVILLE ST

NORTHAMPTON RD

LUBENHAM RD

CARLISLE

ASTLEY CL

FARNDON RD

BURFORD CL

FAIRFAX RD

BATH ST

SCOTLAND END

SCOTLAND RD

CAXTON ST

WESTERN AVE

GRENVILLE GDNS

Courtyard
Workshops

Sutton
Ct

LENTHALL SQ

CLIPSTON ST

ROCKWELL DR

FLEETWOOD GDNS

ESSEX GDNS

HUNTINGDON GDNS

LANGDALE WLK

HADDONIAN RD

LATHKILL ST

CROSBY RD

Allot
Gdns

Sovereign
Pk

Farndon Fields
Farm

1

FLEETWOOD GDNS

RAINSBOROUGH GDNS

MONTROSE CL

BALFOUR GDNS

HOWARD WAY

ROCHESTER GDNS

RUPERT RD

ROWAN AVE

GREEN LA

TUNGSTONE WAY

VISLOK CL

Cemy

WATSON AVE

BUTLER GDNS

STRATTON CL

MAURICE RD

CROMWELL CRES

BISHOP CL

SELBY CL

A508

86

71 A B 72 C D 73 E F

48

32

E3
1 ANGEL ST
2 ANGEL CT
3 ST MARTINS YD
4 ALDWINKLES YD
5 MILLER'S YD
6 CHURCH SQ
7 FOX YD
8 ADAM AND EVE ST
9 FACTORY LA
10 THE MALTINGS
11 PLOUGHMANS YD

E4
1 DODDRIDGE RD
2 KING'S CT
3 ASHFIELD RD
4 MATTHEW CLARKE HO
5 GODDARD CT

F2
1 SPRINGFIELD CT
2 MARSHALL CT
3 WELLAND CT
4 OAKLANDS PK
5 CHURCH WLK
6 THE OLD COFFEE MILLS

31
17

A B C D E F

A B C D E F

31
49

18
34

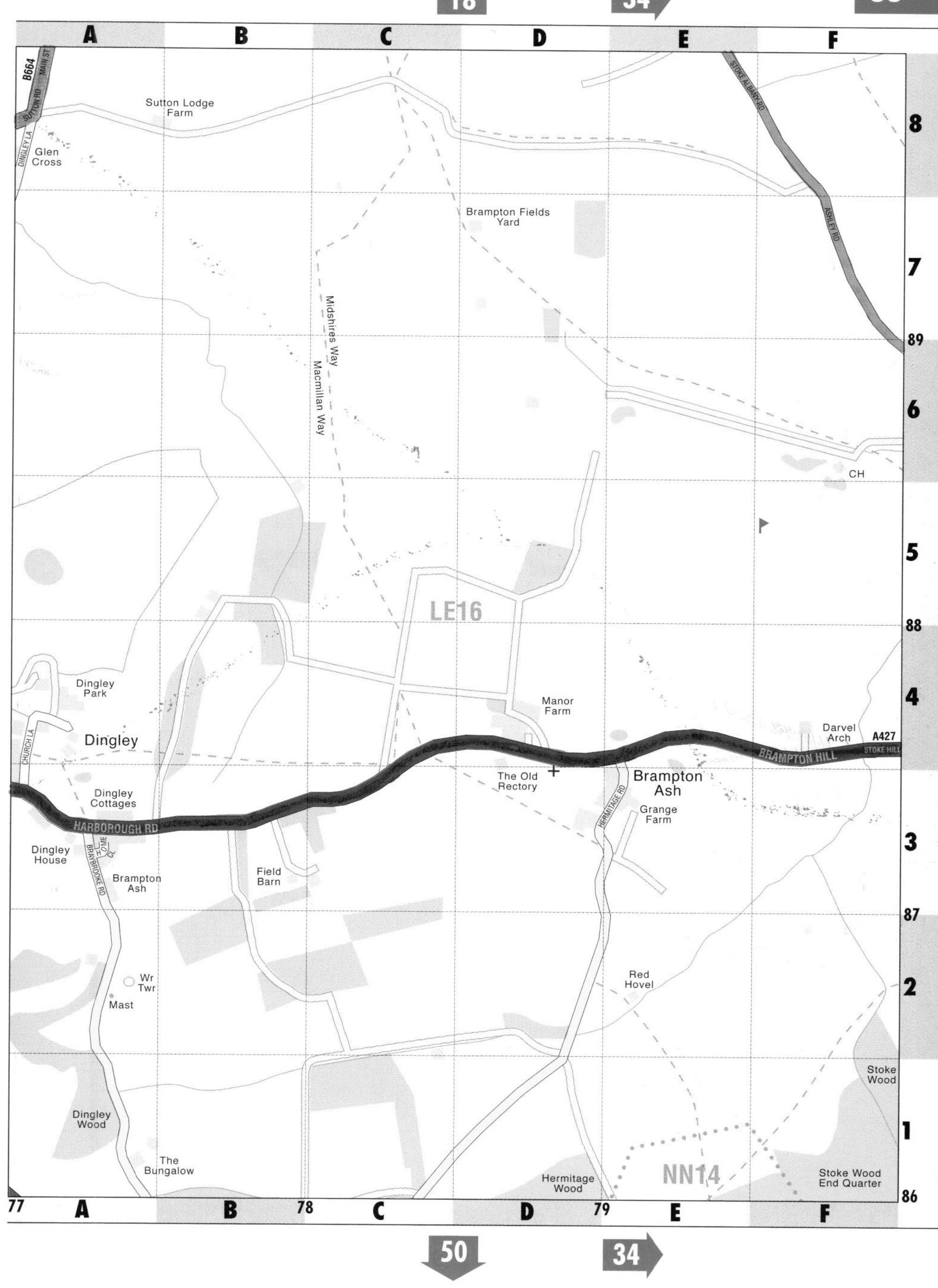
B664
MAIN ST
SUTTON RD
DINGLEY LA
Sutton Lodge Farm
Glen Cross
STOKE ALBANY RD
ASHLEY RD
Brampton Fields Yard
Midshires Way
Macmillan Way
CH
LE16
Dingley Park
Dingley
CHURCH LA
Manor Farm
Darvel Arch
A427
STOKE HILL
BRAMPTON HILL
The Old Rectory
Brampton Ash
HERMITAGE RD
Grange Farm
Dingley Cottages
HARBOROUGH RD
Dingley House
BRAYBROOKE RD
Brampton Ash
Field Barn
Wr Twr
Mast
Red Hovel
Stoke Wood
Dingley Wood
The Bungalow
Hermitage Wood
NN14
Stoke Wood End Quarter
A
B
C
D
E
F
8
7
89
6
5
88
4
3
87
2
1
86
77
78
79

50
34

33
19

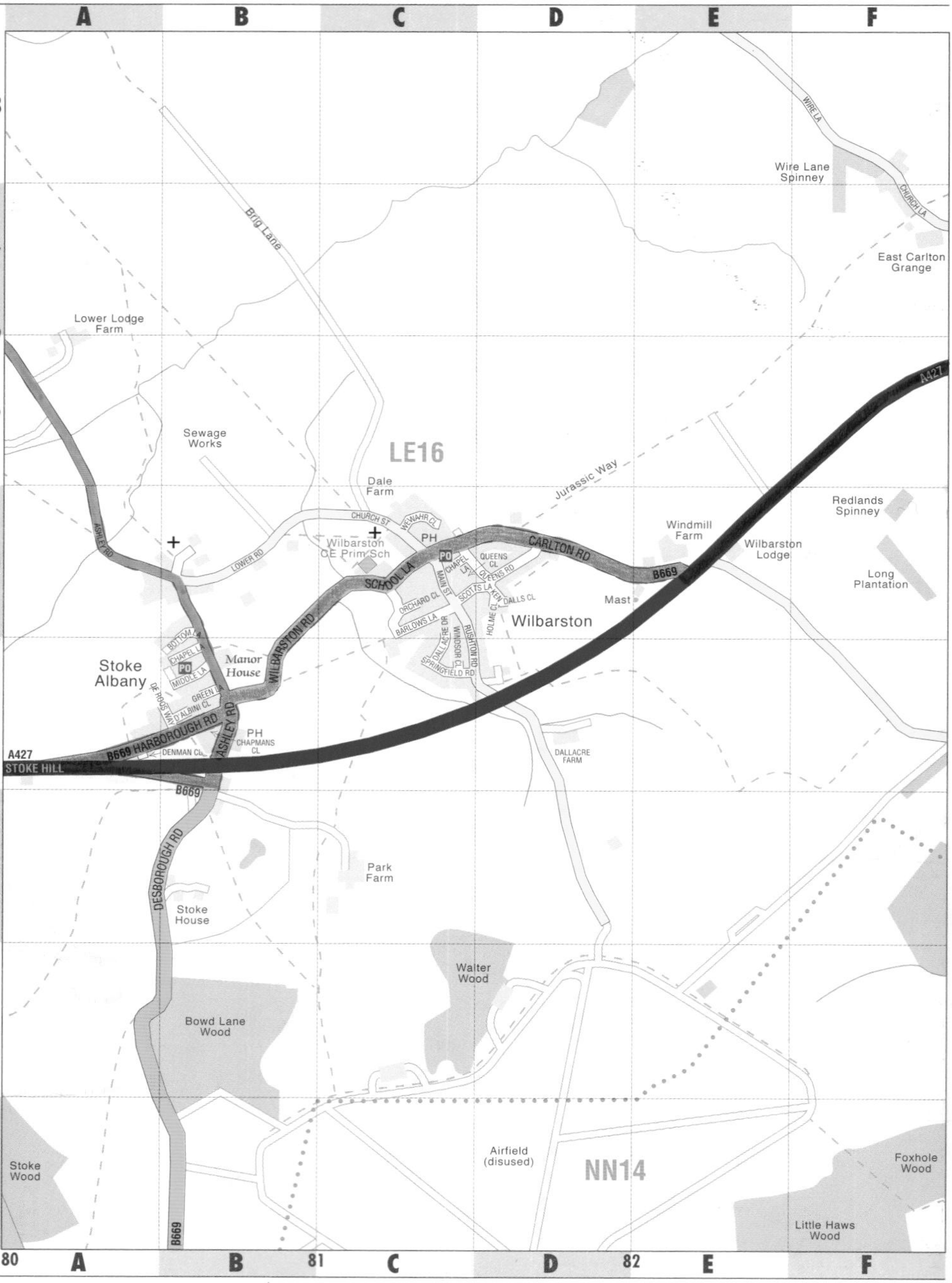

A B C D E F
8 7 89 6 5 88 4 3 87 2 1 86
Brig Lane
WIRE LA
Wire Lane Spinney
CHURCH LA
East Carlton Grange
Lower Lodge Farm
A427
Sewage Works
LE16
Jurassic Way
Dale Farm
ASHLEY RD
CHURCH ST
WELNAHR CL
PH
Wilbarston CE Prim Sch
PO
LOWER RD
SCHOOL LA
CARLTON RD
QUEENS CL
QUEENS RD
CHAPEL LA
MAIN ST
Windmill Farm
Redlands Spinney
Wilbarston Lodge
Long Plantation
B669
Mast
ORCHARD CL
SCOTTS LA
KEN DALLS CL
HOLME CL
Wilbarston
BARLOWS LA
DALLACRE DR
WINDSOR CL
RUSHTON RD
SPRINGFIELD RD
BOTTOM LA
CHAPEL LA
MIDDLE LA
Stoke Albany
Manor House
WILBARSTON RD
DE ROOS WAY
GREEN LA
D'ALBINI CL
HARBOROUGH RD
ASHLEY RD
PH
CHAPMANS CL
DALLACRE FARM
A427
STOKE HILL
B669
DENMAN CL
DESBOROUGH RD
Park Farm
Stoke House
Walter Wood
Bowd Lane Wood
Airfield (disused)
NN14
Stoke Wood
Foxhole Wood
Little Haws Wood
B669
80 A B 81 C D 82 E F

33
51

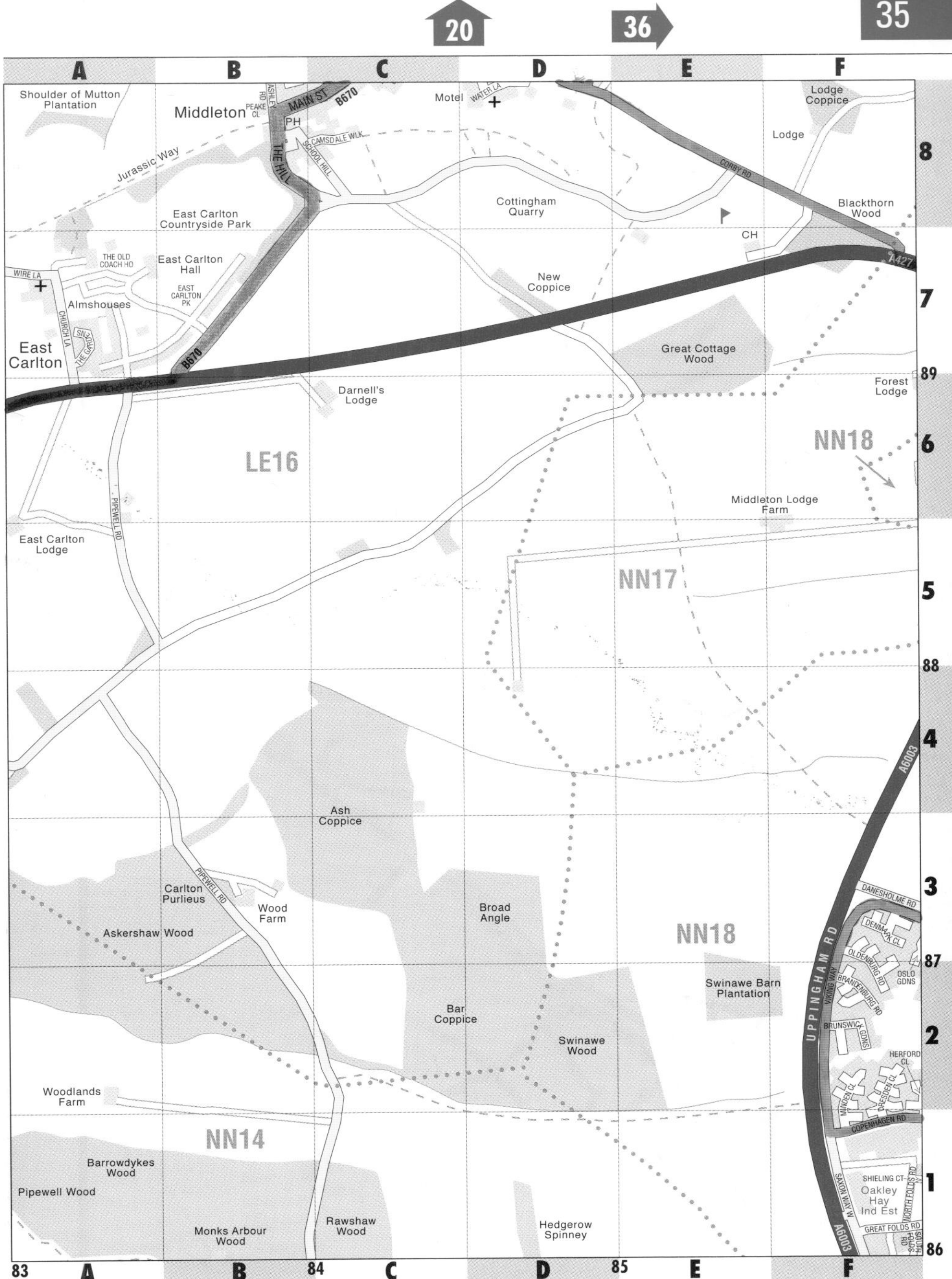
20
36
A B C D E F
Shoulder of Mutton Plantation
Middleton
MAIN ST
B670
Motel
WATER LA
Lodge Coppice
Lodge
Jurassic Way
THE HILL
CAMSDALE WLK
SCHOOL HILL
CORBY RD
Cottingham Quarry
Blackthorn Wood
East Carlton Countryside Park
CH
WIRE LA
THE OLD COACH HO
East Carlton Hall
EAST CARLTON PK
New Coppice
A427
Almshouses
CHURCH LA
East Carlton
Great Cottage Wood
Darnell's Lodge
Forest Lodge
LE16
NN18
PIPEWELL RD
Middleton Lodge Farm
East Carlton Lodge
NN17
Ash Coppice
A6003
Carlton Purlieus
Wood Farm
Broad Angle
Askershaw Wood
NN18
DANESHOLME RD
UPPINGHAM RD
VIKING WAY
OSLO GDNS
Swinawe Barn Plantation
Bar Coppice
BRUNSWICK GDNS
Swinawe Wood
HERFORD CL
Woodlands Farm
COPENHAGEN RD
NN14
Barrowdykes Wood
Pipewell Wood
SHIELING CT
Oakley Hay Ind Est
Monks Arbour Wood
Rawshaw Wood
Hedgerow Spinney
GREAT FOLDS RD
8
7
89
6
5
88
4
3
87
2
1
86
83
84
85
52
36

35
21

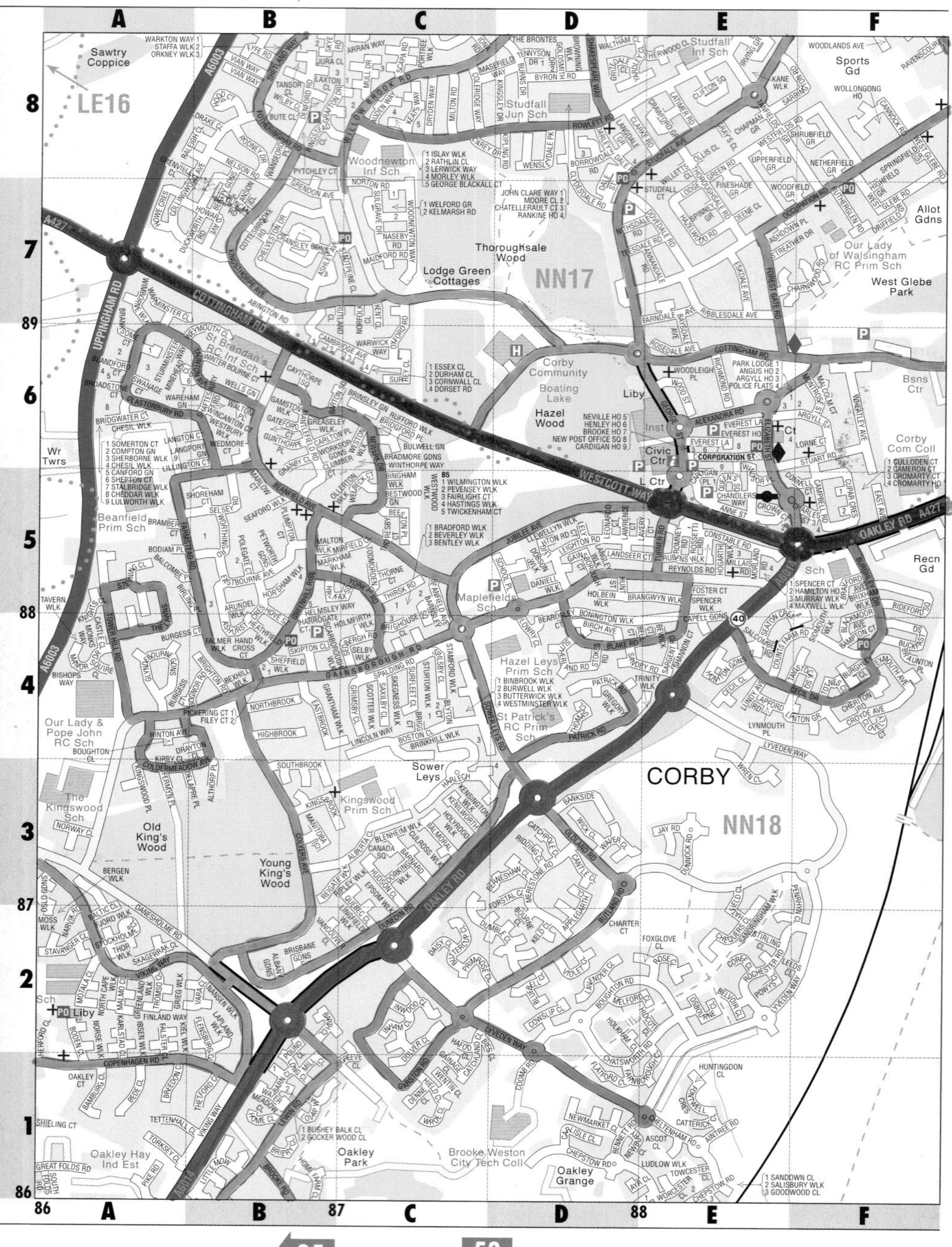
A
B
C
D
E
F
8
7
89
6
5
88
4
3
87
2
1
86
86
87
88
Sawtry Coppice
LE16
NN17
NN18
CORBY
Studfall Inf Sch
Studfall Jun Sch
Sports Gd
Woodnewton Inf Sch
Thoroughsale Wood
Lodge Green Cottages
Our Lady of Walsingham RC Prim Sch
West Glebe Park
Allot Gdns
St Brendan's RC Inf Sch
Corby Community
Boating Lake
Hazel Wood
Liby
Inst
Civic Ctr
L Ctr
Bsns Ctr
Corby Com Coll
Wr Twrs
Beanfield Prim Sch
Maplefields Sch
Hazel Leys Prim Sch
St Patrick's RC Prim Sch
Recn Gd
Sch
Our Lady & Pope John RC Sch
The Kingswood Sch
Old King's Wood
Young King's Wood
Kingswood Prim Sch
Sower Leys
Oakley Hay Ind Est
Oakley Park
Brooke Weston City Tech Coll
Oakley Grange
A6003
A427
A6014
COTTINGHAM RD
UPPINGHAM RD
WESTCOTT WAY
OAKLEY RD
ROCKINGHAM RD
GAINSBOROUGH RD
BEANFIELD AVE
WILLOW BROOK RD
OCCUPATION RD
STUDFALL AVE
JUBILEE AVE
ELIZABETH ST
CORPORATION ST
ALEXANDRA RD
LYVEDEN WAY
COPENHAGEN RD
VIKING WAY
OLDLAND RD
COLDERMEADOW AVE
COLYERS AVE

35
53

22
38

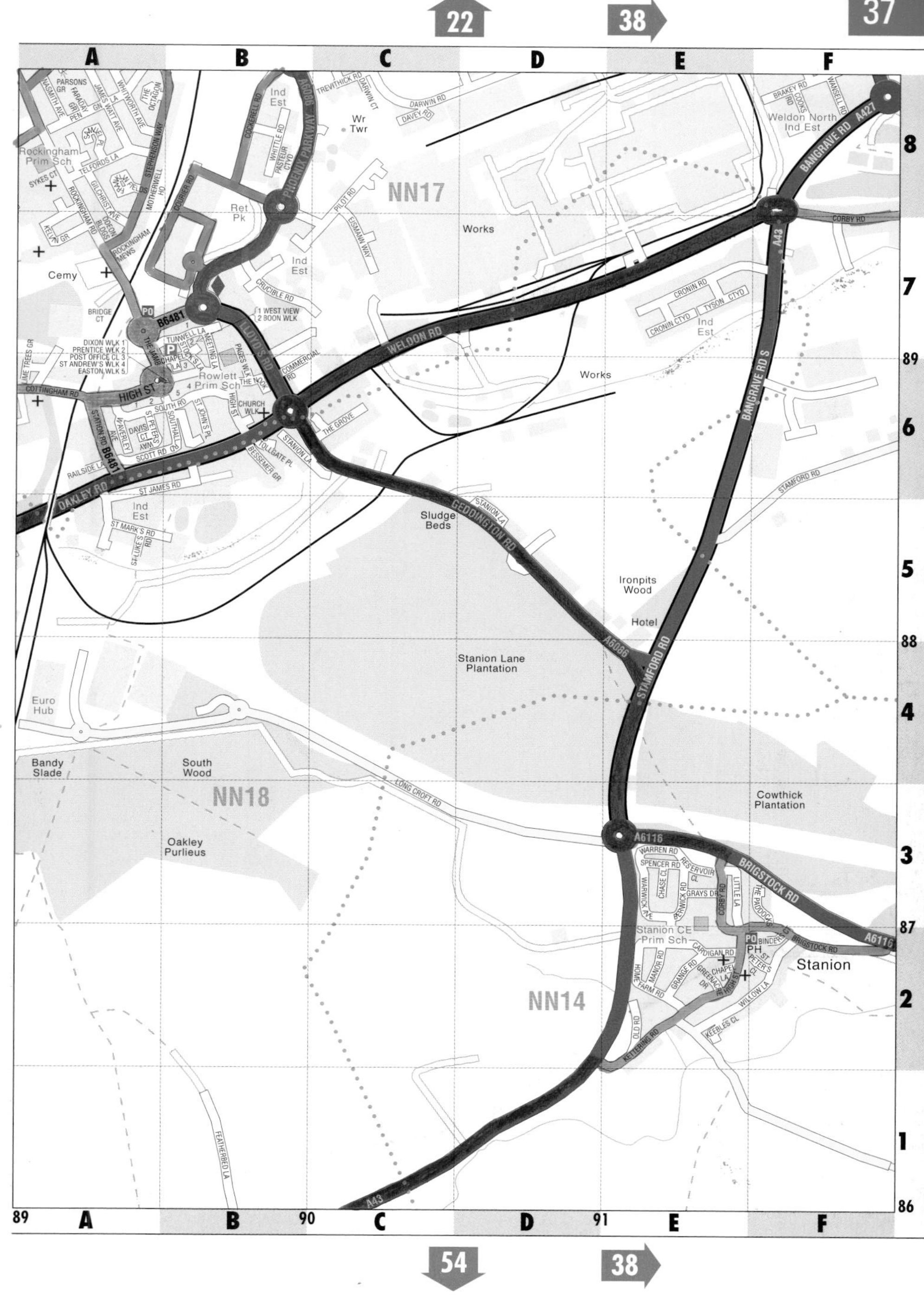
A
B
C
D
E
F
8
7
89
6
5
88
4
3
87
2
1
86
89
90
91
PARSONS GR
NASMITH AVE
FARADAY GR
JAMES WATT AVE
WHITWORTH AVE
THE OCTAGON
STEPHENSON WAY
Rockingham Prim Sch
TELFORDS LA
SYKES CT
MOTHERWELL RD
ROCKINGHAM RD
GILCHRIST AVE
BODON RD
KELVIN GR
ROCKINGHAM MEWS
Cemy
BRIDGE CT
PO
B6481
DIXON WLK 1
PRENTICE WLK 2
POST OFFICE CL 3
ST ANDREW'S WLK 4
EASTON WLK 5
LIME TREES GR
COTTINGHAM RD
HIGH ST
THE JAMB
TUNWELL LA
MEETING LA
CHAPEL LA
Rowlett Prim Sch
SOUTH RD
ST JOHN'S PL
WAVERLEY AVE
DAVIS CT
ST PETERS WAY
SOUTHALL RD
SCOTT RD
STATION RD
RAILSIDE LA
OAKLEY RD
ST JAMES RD
Ind Est
ST MARK'S RD
ST LUKE'S RD
COCKERELL RD
Ind Est
WHITTLE RD
PASTEUR CTYD
PHOENIX PARKWAY
A6086
COURIER RD
Ret Pk
CRUCIBLE RD
1 WEST VIEW
2 BOON WLK
LLOYDS RD
PAGES WLK
THE NOOK
COMMERCIAL RD
CHURCH WLK
HIGH ST
THE GROVE
STANION LA
TOLLGATE PL
BESSEMER GR
TREVITHICK RD
DARWIN CT
DARWIN RD
DAVEY RD
Wr Twr
PILOT RD
EISMANN WAY
Ind Est
NN17
Works
WELDON RD
BRAKEY RD
COOKS RD
WANSELL RD
Weldon North Ind Est
A427
BANGRAVE RD
CORBY RD
A43
CRONIN RD
TYSON CTYD
CRONIN CTYD
Ind Est
Works
BANGRAVE RD S
STAMFORD RD
Sludge Beds
STANION LA
GEDDINGTON RD
Ironpits Wood
Hotel
A6086
Stanion Lane Plantation
STAMFORD RD
Euro Hub
Bandy Slade
South Wood
NN18
LONG CROFT RD
Oakley Purlieus
Cowthick Plantation
A6116
WARREN RD
SPENCER RD
RESERVOIR CL
CHASE CL
WARWICK AVE
BERWICK RD
GRAYS DR
CORBY RD
LITTLE LA
THE PADDOCKS
BRIGSTOCK RD
Stanion CE Prim Sch
PO
BINDER CL
BRIGSTOCK RD
A6116
CARDIGAN RD
PH
ST PETER'S CL
Stanion
MANOR RD
HOME FARM RD
GRANGE RD
GREENACRE DR
CHAPEL LA
HIGH ST
WILLOW LA
KEEBLES CL
OLD RD
KETTERING RD
NN14
FEATHERBED LA
A43

54
38

37
23

A
B
C
D
E
F
8
7
89
6
5
88
4
3
87
2
1
86
92
93
94
A427
A43
Ind Est
LARRATT RD
WALNUT CL
HALL'S CL
CHAPEL RD
Ind Est
BRANSON MEWS
DEENESIDE
ROMAN CL
PH
STAMFORD RD A427
Weldon
Weldon CE Prim Sch
CORBY RD
HILLSIDE CRES
KETTERING RD
CHURCH ST
Manor House
Allot Gdns
THE ASHES
CRICKETERS GN
DEENE END
EAST CL
WOODLANDS RD
SPINNEY RD
WOODSIDE PK
Weldon Stone Quarry
STAMFORD RD
Weldon Park
Mast
OUNDLE RD
PE8
NN17
Upper Laundimer Wood
Harry's Park Wood
Harry's Wood
Middle Laundimer Wood
NN14
Meadow Leys
Bushylawn Lodge
Nether Laundimer Wood
Old Dry Hills
Old Dry Bushes
A6116
BRIGSTOCK RD
Works
STANION RD
Brigstock Camp
OLD DRY LA
Red Piece
Stanion Lodge
Maltley Farm

37
55

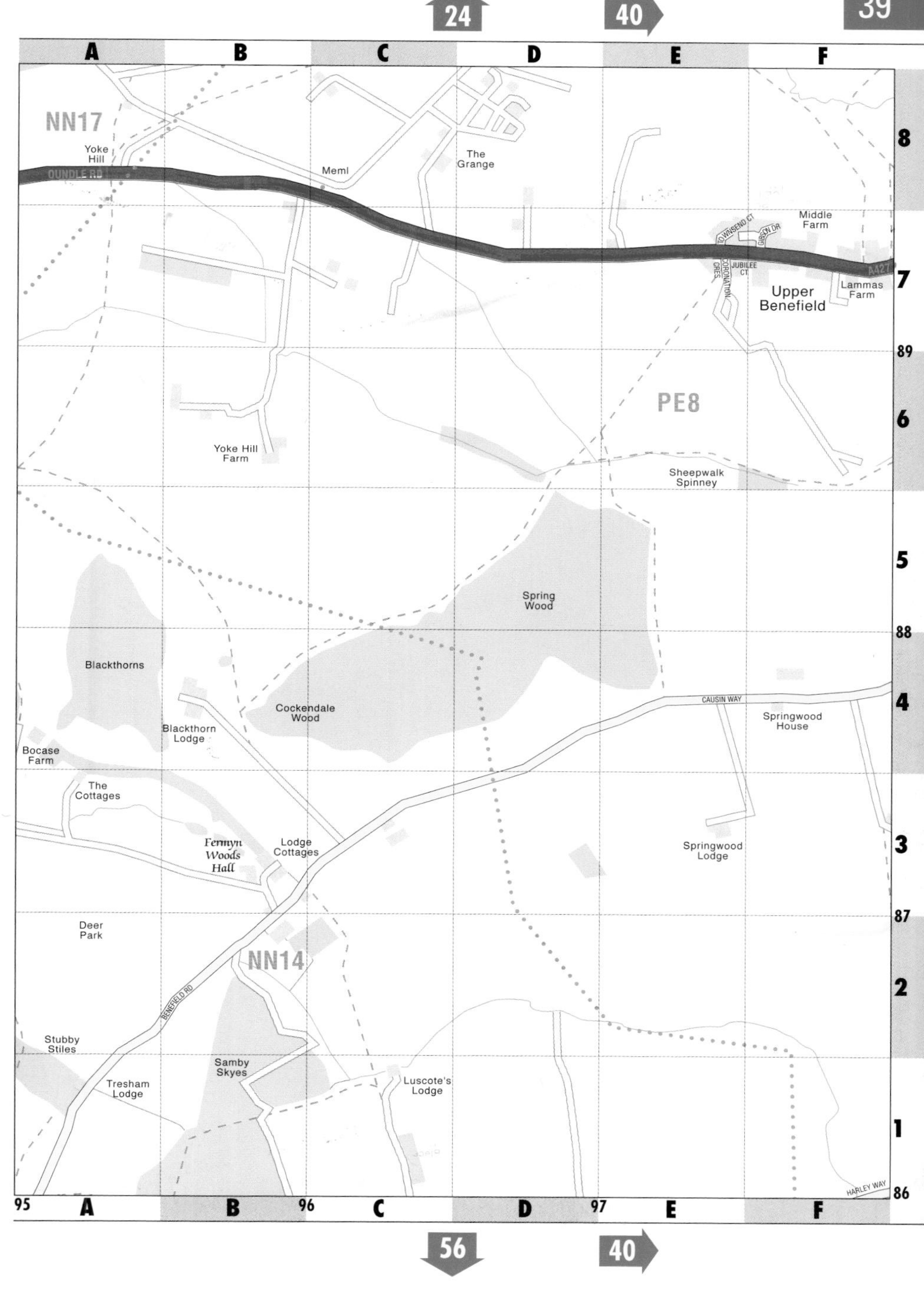
24
40
A
B
C
D
E
F
NN17
Yoke Hill
OUNDLE RD
Meml
The Grange
Middle Farm
TOWNSEND CT
GIBSON DR
CORONATION CRES
JUBILEE CT
A427
Upper Benefield
Lammas Farm
8
7
89
PE8
6
Yoke Hill Farm
Sheepwalk Spinney
5
Spring Wood
88
Blackthorns
CAUSIN WAY
4
Cockendale Wood
Blackthorn Lodge
Springwood House
Bocase Farm
The Cottages
3
Fermyn Woods Hall
Lodge Cottages
Springwood Lodge
87
Deer Park
NN14
2
BENEFIELD RD
Stubby Stiles
Samby Skyes
Tresham Lodge
Luscote's Lodge
1
HARLEY WAY
86
95
96
97
56
40

39
25

A
B
C
D
E
F
8
7
89
6
5
88
4
3
87
2
1
86
98
99
00
Hill Farm
Nethertown Farm
A427
Wheatsheaf Hotel
Brook Farm
Bird's Grave
Well Coppice
Crow Coppice
Banhaw Farm
Rectory Farm
CAUSIN WAY
Lower Benefield
PE8
Chesterfield Lodge
Silley Coppice
Brickyard Cottage
Churchfield Farm
Churchfield Coppice
Banhaw Wood
Churchfield Cottages
Banhaw Lodge
HARLEY WAY
Stoke Wood
Ridge Leys Plantation
Winning Foot Hill
Bearshank Wood
Stoke Coppice
P

39
57

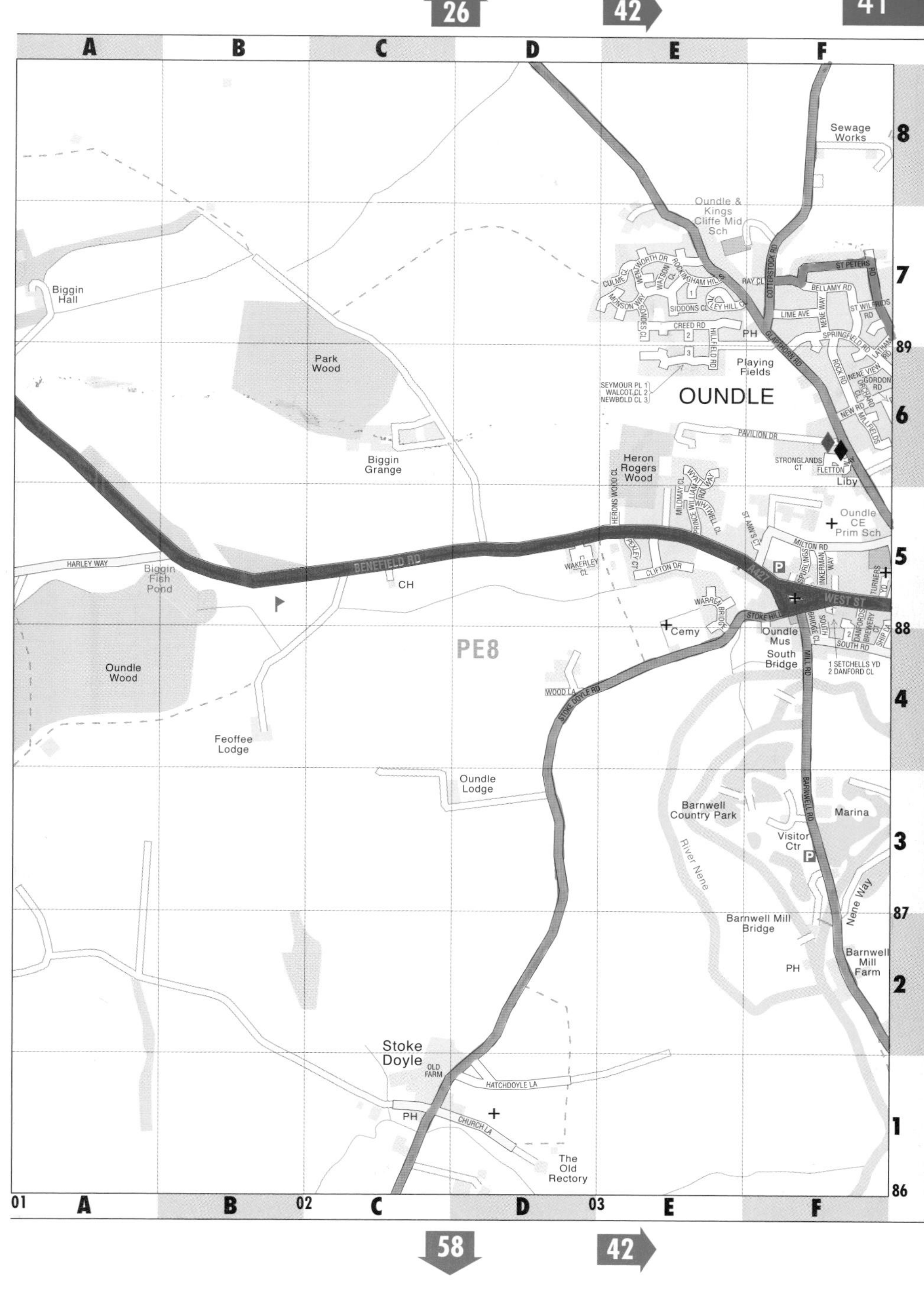
26
42
A
B
C
D
E
F
8
7
89
6
5
88
4
3
87
2
1
86
01
02
03
Sewage Works
Oundle & Kings Cliffe Mid Sch
Biggin Hall
Park Wood
OUNDLE
Playing Fields
PH
Heron Rogers Wood
Biggin Grange
Liby
Oundle CE Prim Sch
HARLEY WAY
Biggin Fish Pond
BENEFIELD RD
CH
WEST ST
A427
Cemy
Oundle Mus
South Bridge
PE8
Oundle Wood
Feoffee Lodge
Oundle Lodge
Barnwell Country Park
Marina
Visitor Ctr
River Nene
Nene Way
Barnwell Mill Bridge
Barnwell Mill Farm
Stoke Doyle
OLD FARM
HATCHDOYLE LA
CHURCH LA
The Old Rectory
STOKE DOYLE RD
WOOD LA
MILL RD
BARNWELL RD
SEYMOUR PL 1
WALCOT CL 2
NEWBOLD CL 3
1 SETCHELLS YD
2 DANFORD CL
58
42

41
27

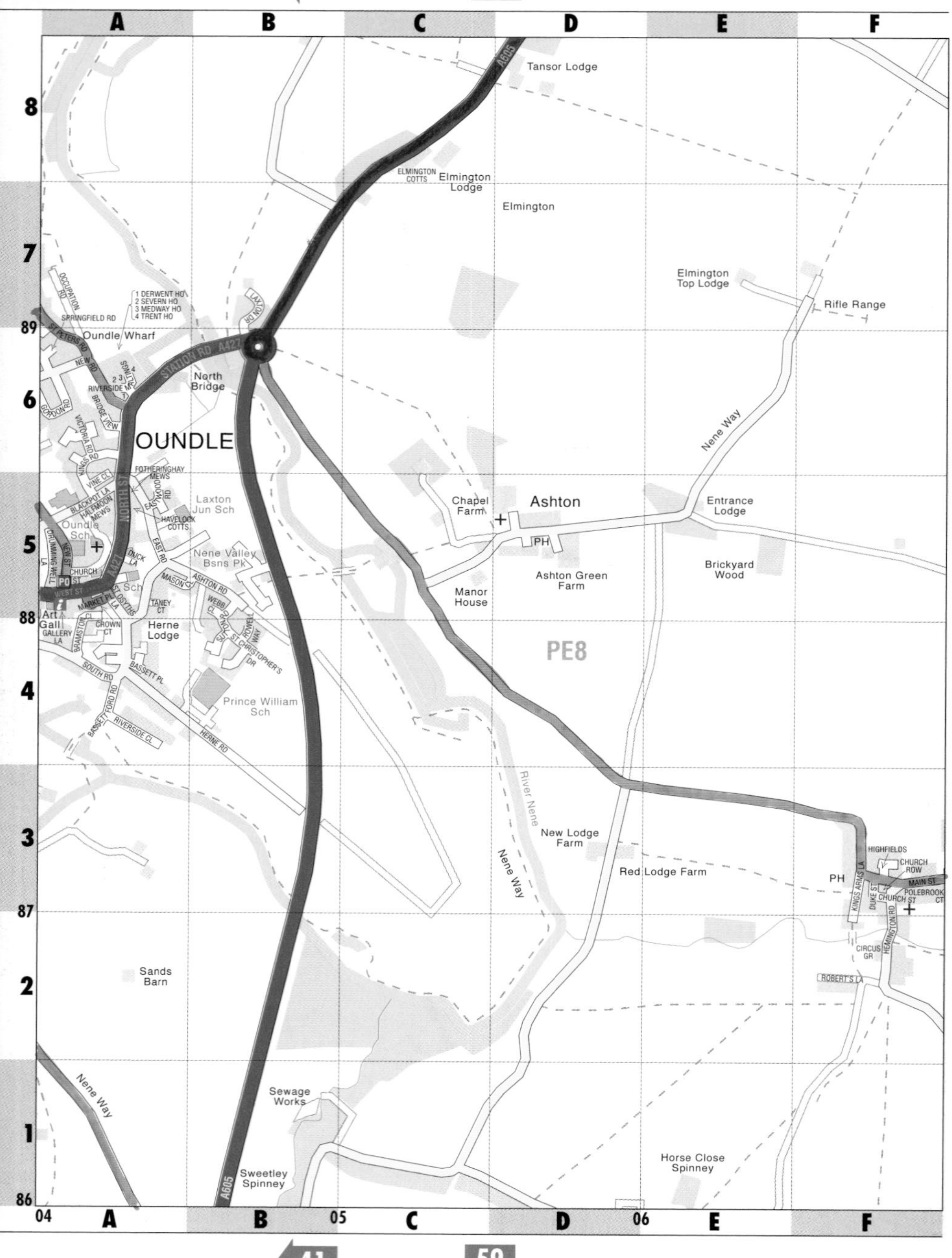
A
B
C
D
E
F
8
7
89
6
5
88
4
3
87
2
1
86
04
05
06
Tansor Lodge
A605
ELMINGTON COTTS
Elmington Lodge
Elmington
Elmington Top Lodge
Rifle Range
OCCUPATION RD
SPRINGFIELD RD
1 DERWENT HO
2 SEVERN HO
3 MEDWAY HO
4 TRENT HO
LAXTON DR
Oundle Wharf
ST PETERS RD
NEW RD
STATION RD
A427
North Bridge
RIVERSIDE
MALTINGS
BRIDGE VIEW
GORDON RD
VICTORIA RD
OUNDLE
Nene Way
FOTHERINGHAY MEWS
VINE CL
BLACKPOT LA
HALFMOON MEWS
NORTH ST
EASTWOOD RD
Laxton Jun Sch
Chapel Farm
Ashton
Entrance Lodge
HAVELOCK COTTS
Oundle Sch
PH
Brickyard Wood
Nene Valley Bsns Pk
DRUMMING WELL LA
NEW ST
CHURCH
DUCK LA
EAST RD
ASHTON RD
MASON CL
Ashton Green Farm
Manor House
PO
WEST ST
Sch
MARKET PL
ST OSYTHS LA
TANEY CT
WEBB CL
ROWELL WAY
Art Gall
GALLERY LA
BRAMSTON CL
CROWN CT
Herne Lodge
ST CHRISTOPHER'S DR
PE8
SOUTH RD
BASSETT PL
BASSETT FORD RD
Prince William Sch
RIVERSIDE CL
HERNE RD
River Nene
New Lodge Farm
Nene Way
Red Lodge Farm
HIGHFIELDS
CHURCH ROW
PH
MAIN ST
KINGS ARMS LA
DUKE ST
CHURCH ST
POLEBROOK CT
HEMINGTON RD
CIRCUS GR
ROBERT'S LA
Sands Barn
Nene Way
Sewage Works
Horse Close Spinney
Sweetley Spinney
A605

41
59

28
44
A
B
C
D
E
F
Rectory Farm
Tansor Wold Farm
Tansor Wold
Miriam's Cover
Stamford Hovels
Stamford Cover
Toll Bar Gate
The Gorse
Warmington Spinney Plantation
PE8
Ashton Wold Farm
West Lodge
Ashton Wold House
Greenhouse Corner
Ashton Wold
The Common
Lutton Hovels
Water Gap Field
Allard's Home
Polebrook
Lake Fields
Bluestone Covert
Lutton Road Cottages
FERGUSON'S CL
MORGANS CL
MAIN ST
HALL GDNS
Polebrook CE Prim Sch
LUTTON RD
Polebrook Airfield Nature Reserve
Polebrook Lodge
Rectory Farm
Airfield (disused)
8
7
89
6
5
88
4
3
87
2
1
86
07
08
09
60
44

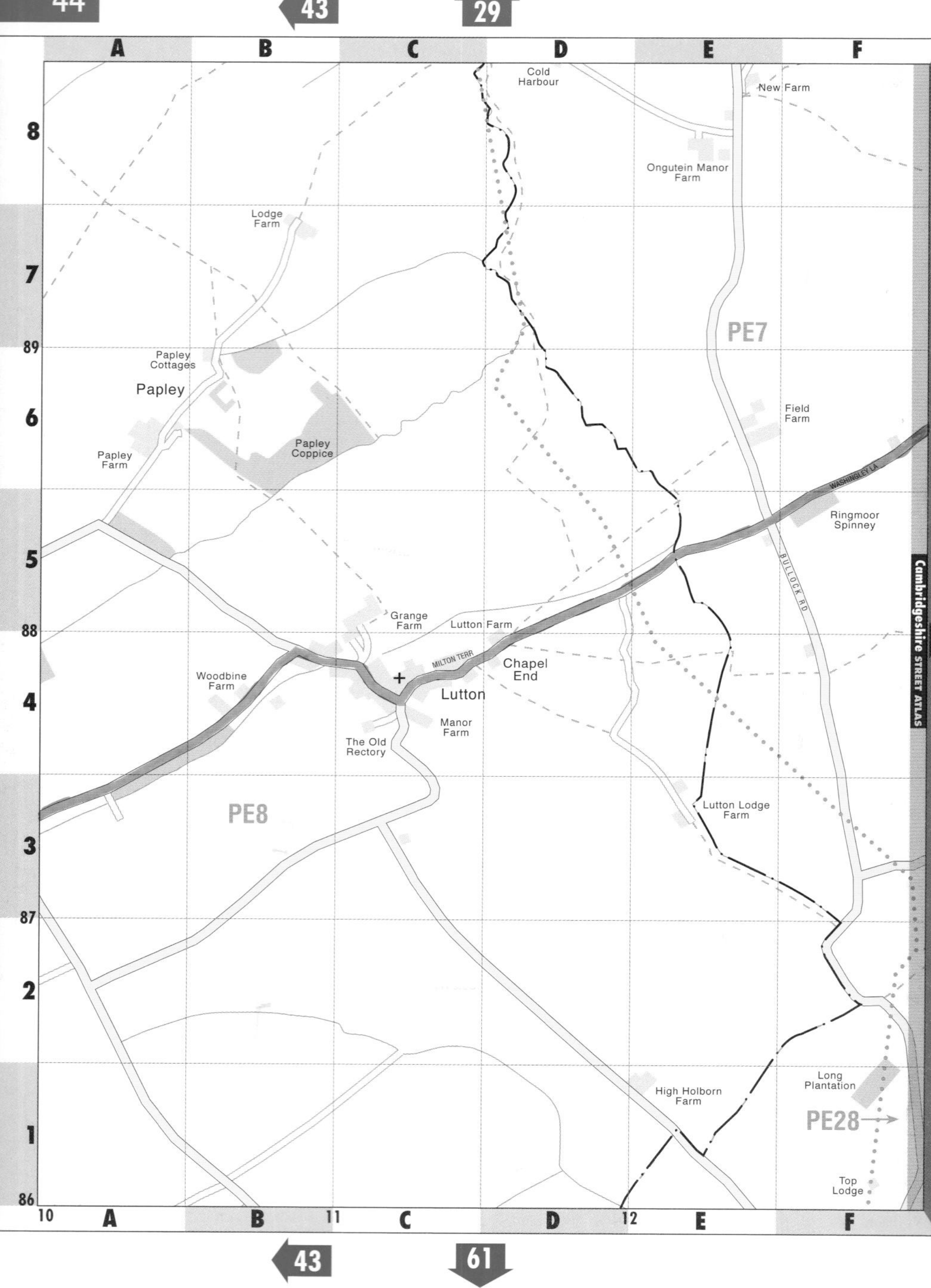
43
29
A
B
C
D
E
F
Cold Harbour
New Farm
Ongutein Manor Farm
Lodge Farm
PE7
Papley Cottages
Papley
Papley Farm
Papley Coppice
Field Farm
WASHINGLEY LA
Ringmoor Spinney
BULLOCK RD
Grange Farm
Lutton Farm
MILTON TERR
Chapel End
Woodbine Farm
Lutton
Manor Farm
The Old Rectory
Lutton Lodge Farm
PE8
High Holborn Farm
Long Plantation
PE28
Top Lodge
8
7
89
6
5
88
4
3
87
2
1
86
10
11
12
Cambridgeshire STREET ATLAS
43
61

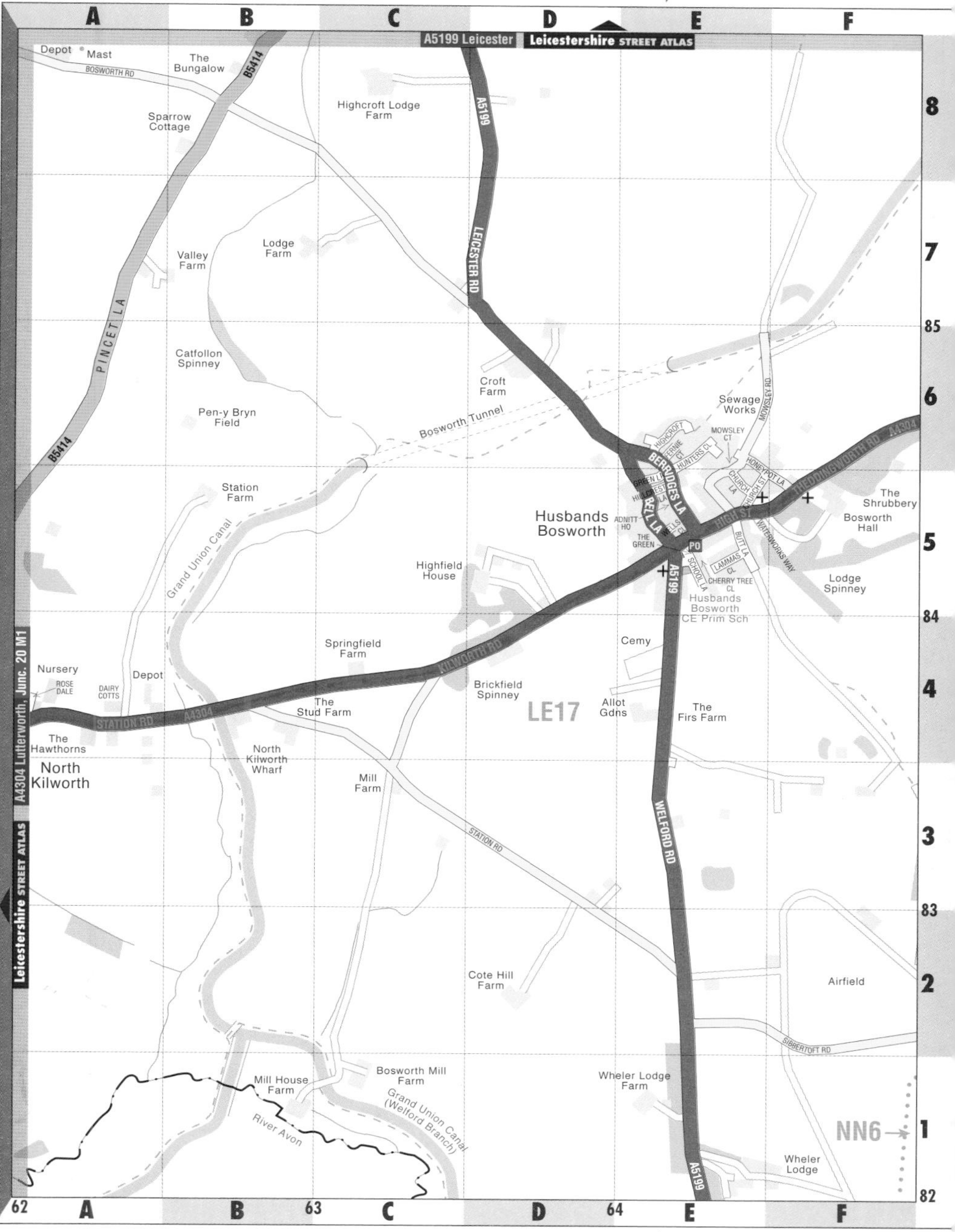

46

A B C D E F

A5199 Leicester

Leicestershire STREET ATLAS

Depot
Mast
BOSWORTH RD
The Bungalow
B5414
Sparrow Cottage
Highcroft Lodge Farm
A5199
8

Valley Farm
Lodge Farm
LEICESTER RD
7
PINCET LA
Catfollon Spinney
85
Croft Farm
Pen-y Bryn Field
Bosworth Tunnel
Sewage Works
MOWSLEY RD
6
B5414
HIGHCROFT
FERNIE CT
HUNTERS CL
MOWSLEY CT
BERRIDGES LA
HONEYPOT LA
GREEN LA
HILLCREST LA
BELL LA
CHURCH LA
CHURCH ST
THEDDINGWORTH RD
A4304
Station Farm
The Shrubbery
Husbands Bosworth
ADNITT HO
THE GREEN
WELLS CL
HIGH ST
BUTT LA
Bosworth Hall
WATERWORKS WAY
5
PO
Grand Union Canal
Highfield House
SCHOOL LA
LAMMAS CL
CHERRY TREE CL
A5199
Lodge Spinney
Husbands Bosworth CE Prim Sch
84
Cemy
Springfield Farm
KILWORTH RD
Nursery
ROSE DALE
DAIRY COTTS
Depot
Brickfield Spinney
4
The Stud Farm
Allot Gdns
LE17
The Firs Farm
STATION RD
A4304
The Hawthorns
North Kilworth
North Kilworth Wharf
Mill Farm
WELFORD RD
STATION RD
3

A4304 Lutterworth, Junc. 20 M1

Leicestershire STREET ATLAS

83
Cote Hill Farm
Airfield
2
SIBBERTOFT RD
Mill House Farm
Bosworth Mill Farm
Wheler Lodge Farm
Grand Union Canal (Welford Branch)
River Avon
NN6
1
A5199
Wheler Lodge
82

62 A B 63 C D 64 E F

64
46

45

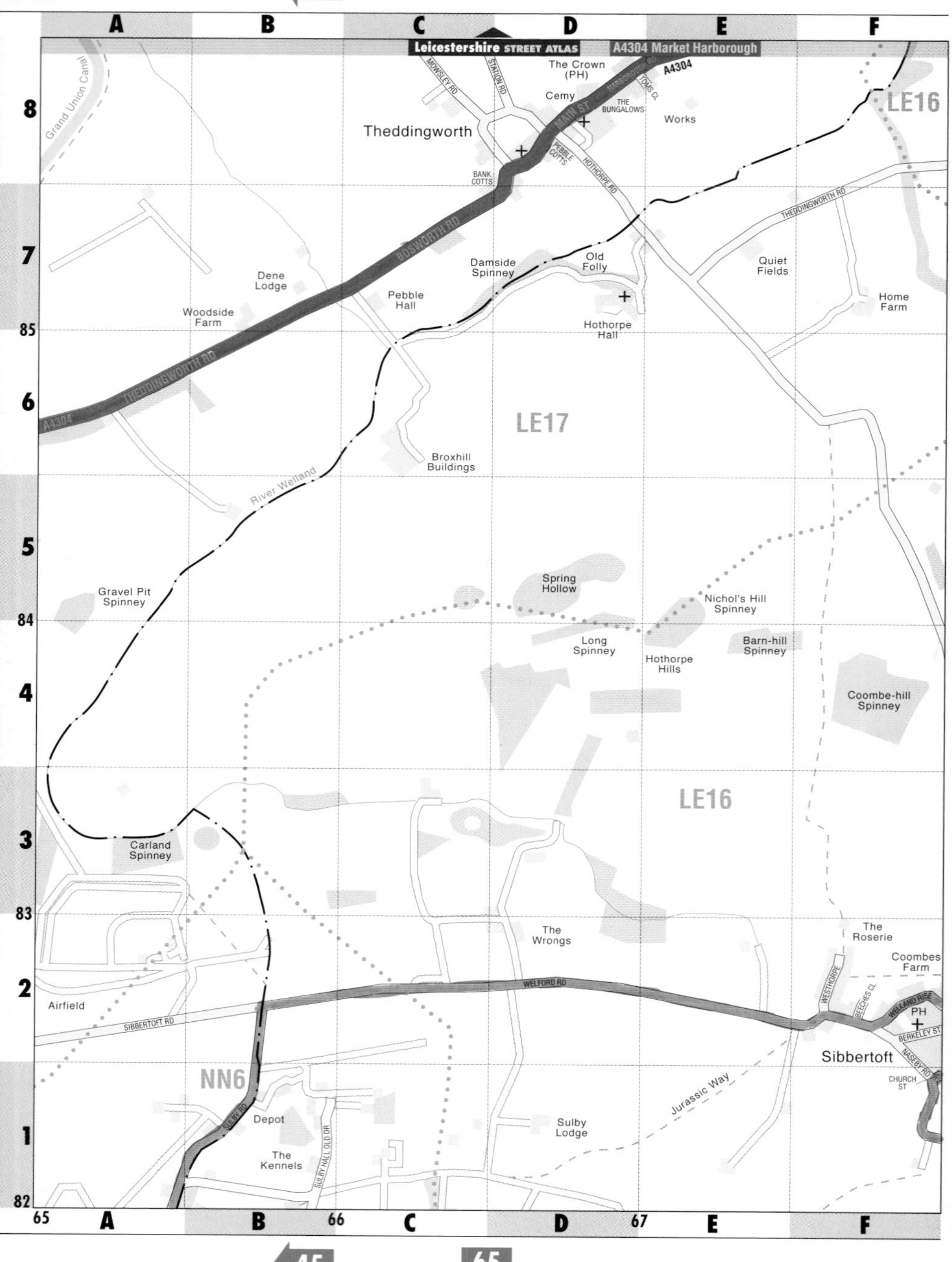
A
B
C
D
E
F
Leicestershire STREET ATLAS
A4304 Market Harborough
A4304
Grand Union Canal
Theddingworth
The Crown (PH)
Cemy
Works
LE16
MOWSLEY RD
STATION RD
MAIN ST
HARBOROUGH RD
TOMS CL
THE BUNGALOWS
PEBBLE COTTS
HOTHORPE RD
BANK COTTS
THEDDINGWORTH RD
BOSWORTH RD
Damside Spinney
Old Folly
Quiet Fields
Home Farm
Dene Lodge
Pebble Hall
Woodside Farm
Hothorpe Hall
THEDDINGWORTH RD
A4304
LE17
Broxhill Buildings
River Welland
Spring Hollow
Gravel Pit Spinney
Nichol's Hill Spinney
Long Spinney
Hothorpe Hills
Barn-hill Spinney
Coombe-hill Spinney
LE16
Carland Spinney
The Wrongs
The Roserie
Coombes Farm
WELFORD RD
WESTHORPE
BEECHES CL
WELLAND RISE
PH
BERKELEY ST
Airfield
SIBBERTOFT RD
Sibbertoft
NASEBY RD
CHURCH ST
NN6
Jurassic Way
SULBY RD
Depot
Sulby Lodge
The Kennels
SULBY HALL OLD DR
8
7
85
6
5
84
4
3
83
2
1
82
65
66
67

45
65

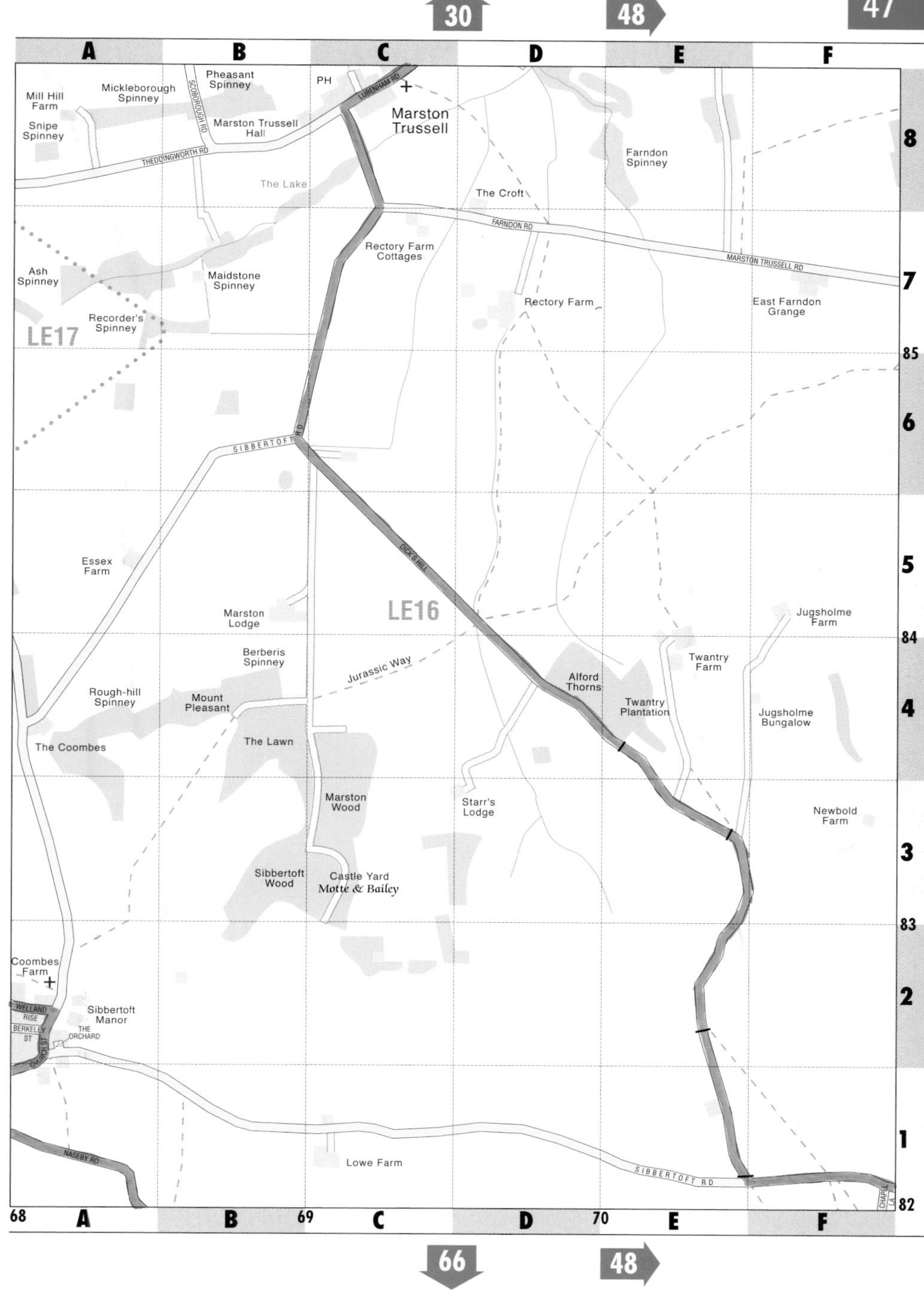
30
48
A
B
C
D
E
F
Mill Hill Farm
Mickleborough Spinney
Pheasant Spinney
SCOBOROUGH RD
PH
LUBENHAM RD
Marston Trussell
Snipe Spinney
Marston Trussell Hall
THEDDINGWORTH RD
Farndon Spinney
8
The Lake
The Croft
FARNDON RD
Rectory Farm Cottages
MARSTON TRUSSELL RD
Ash Spinney
Maidstone Spinney
7
Rectory Farm
East Farndon Grange
Recorder's Spinney
LE17
85
6
SIBBERTOFT RD
DICK'S HILL
Essex Farm
5
Marston Lodge
LE16
Jugsholme Farm
84
Berberis Spinney
Twantry Farm
Jurassic Way
Alford Thorns
Rough-hill Spinney
Mount Pleasant
Twantry Plantation
Jugsholme Bungalow
4
The Coombes
The Lawn
Marston Wood
Starr's Lodge
Newbold Farm
3
Sibbertoft Wood
Castle Yard
Motte & Bailey
83
Coombes Farm
2
WELLAND RISE
Sibbertoft Manor
BERKELEY ST
THE ORCHARD
CHURCH ST
1
NASEBY RD
Lowe Farm
SIBBERTOFT RD
CHAPEL LA
82
68
69
70
66
48

47 31

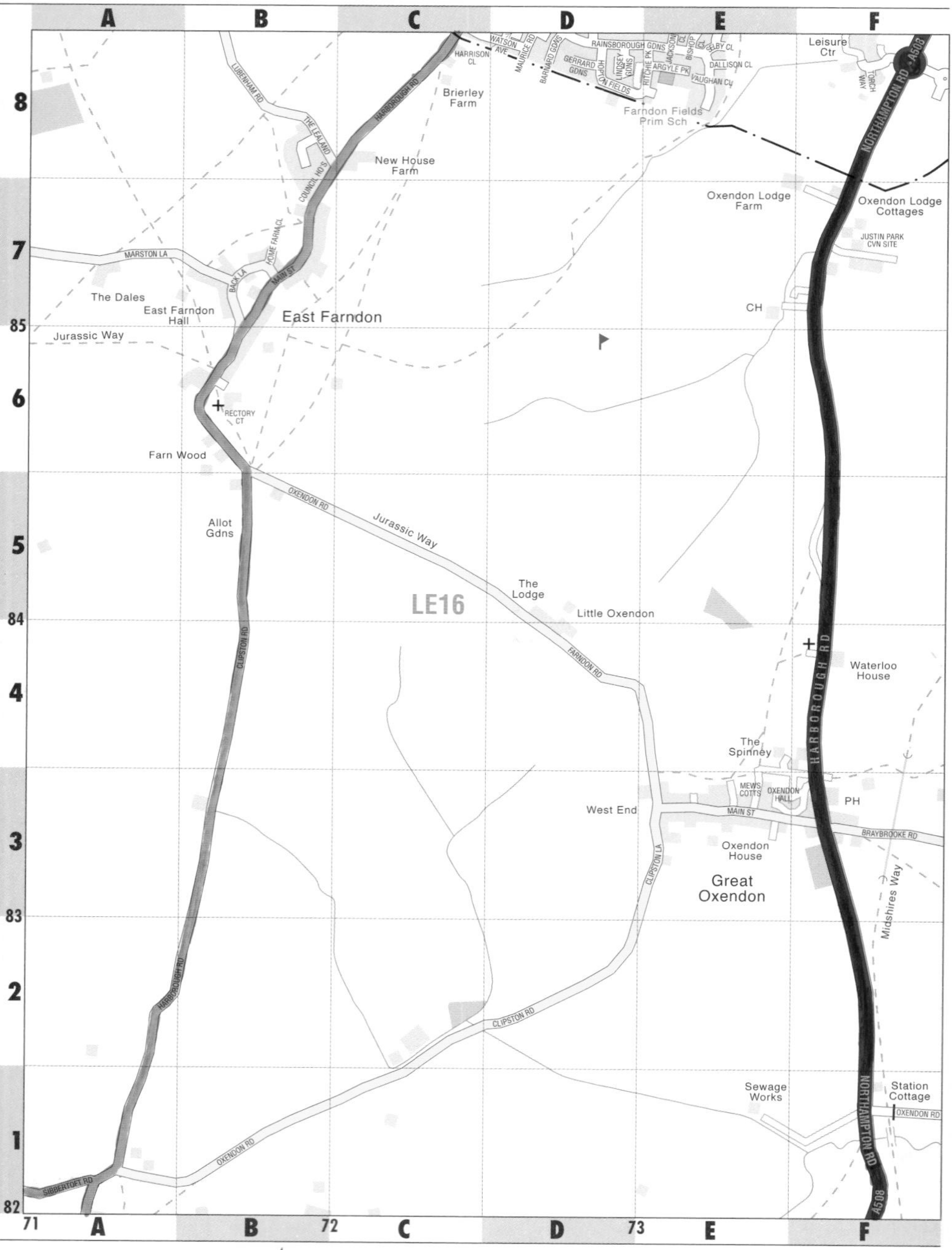

A B C D E F
8 7 85 6 5 84 4 3 83 2 1 82
71 72 73
Leisure Ctr
HARRISON CL
WATSON AVE
MAURICE RD
BARNARD GDNS
GERRARD GDNS
HOPTON FIELDS
RAINSBOROUGH GDNS
LINDSEY GDNS
RITCHIE PK
JACKSON CL
ARGYLE PK
BISHOP CL
SELBY CL
DALLISON CL
VAUGHAN CL
TORCH WAY
NORTHAMPTON RD
A508
LUBENHAM RD
HARBOROUGH RD
Brierley Farm
Farndon Fields Prim Sch
THE LEALAND
COUNCIL HO'S
New House Farm
Oxendon Lodge Farm
Oxendon Lodge Cottages
JUSTIN PARK CVN SITE
MARSTON LA
HOME FARM CL
BACK LA
MAIN ST
The Dales
East Farndon Hall
East Farndon
CH
Jurassic Way
RECTORY CT
Farn Wood
OXENDON RD
Jurassic Way
Allot Gdns
The Lodge
LE16
Little Oxendon
CLIPSTON RD
FARNDON RD
HARBOROUGH RD
Waterloo House
The Spinney
MEWS COTTS
OXENDON HALL
PH
West End
MAIN ST
BRAYBROOKE RD
Oxendon House
CLIPSTON LA
Great Oxendon
Midshires Way
HARBOROUGH RD
CLIPSTON RD
Sewage Works
Station Cottage
NORTHAMPTON RD
OXENDON RD
OXENDON RD
SIBBERTOFT RD
A508

47 67

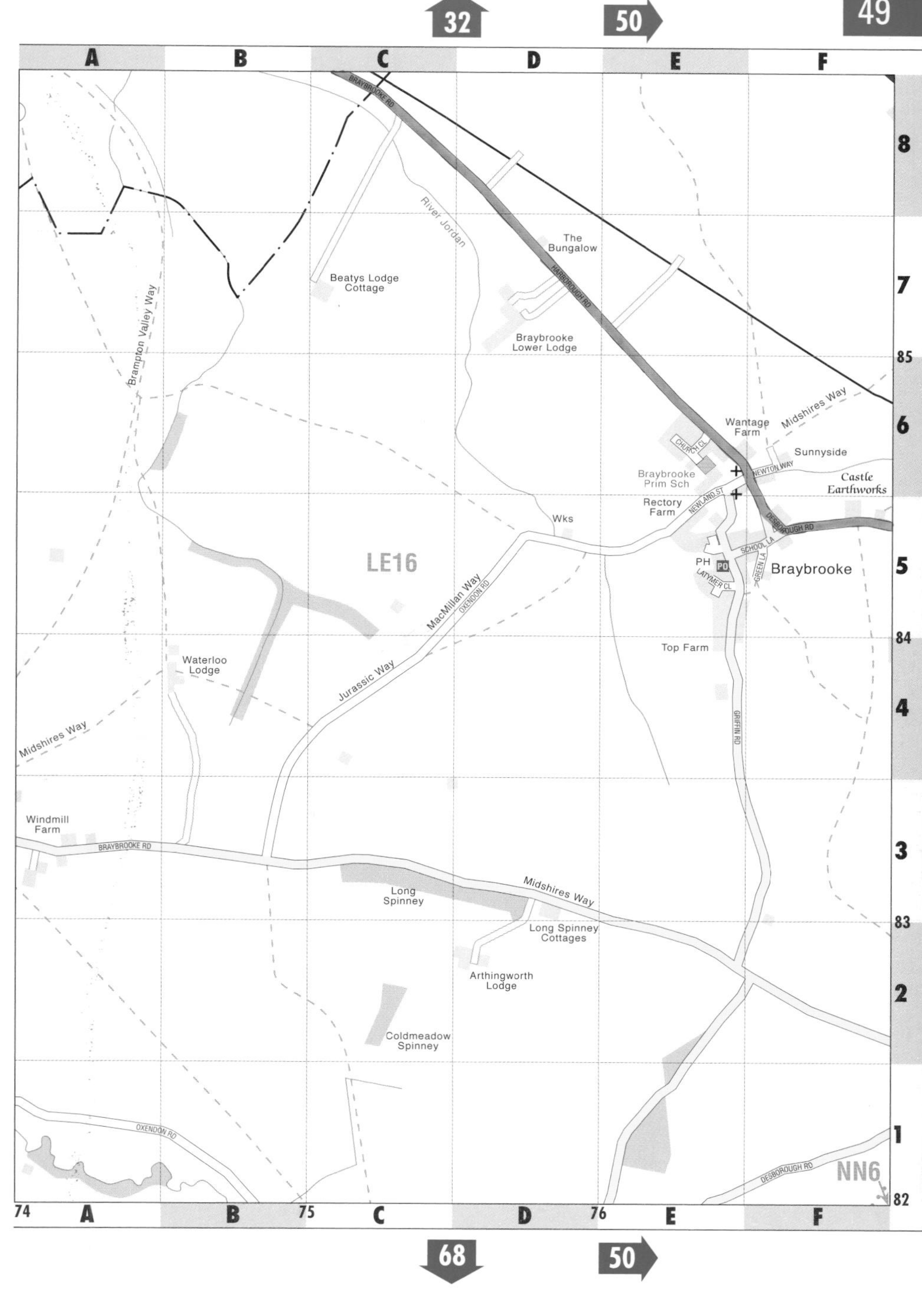
32
50
A
B
C
D
E
F
8
7
85
6
5
84
4
3
83
2
1
82
74
75
76
68
BRAYBROOKE RD
River Jordan
The Bungalow
HARBOROUGH RD
Beatys Lodge Cottage
Brampton Valley Way
Braybrooke Lower Lodge
Midshires Way
Wantage Farm
Sunnyside
CHURCH CL
NEWTON WAY
Braybrooke Prim Sch
Castle Earthworks
Rectory Farm
NEWLAND ST
Wks
DESBOROUGH RD
SCHOOL LA
LE16
PH
PO
GREEN LA
Braybrooke
LATYMER CL
MacMillan Way
OXENDON RD
Top Farm
Waterloo Lodge
Jurassic Way
GRIFFIN RD
Midshires Way
Windmill Farm
BRAYBROOKE RD
Midshires Way
Long Spinney
Long Spinney Cottages
Arthingworth Lodge
Coldmeadow Spinney
OXENDON RD
DESBOROUGH RD
NN6

49
33

Commons Farm
Hermitage Wood
Birch Quarter
LE16
Rogues Quarter
Brampton Wood
Pond Quarter
Tires Quarter
Hermitage Cottages
The Hermitage
B576
HARBOROUGH RD
Midshires Way
Jurassic Way
Midshires Way
Macmillan Way
Hotel
Glebe Cottage
BRAMPTON WOOD LA
Eckland Lodge Farm
Garden Ctr
Eckland Lodge Bsns Pk
Dob Hall Farm
Park Hill Farm
Factory
B669
STOKE RD
The Grange
The Bungalow
Smallholding
Wyndie Rydge Farm
LE16
NN14
A6
Lodge Farm
Humfrey's Lodge
ASHFORD LEA 1
BIRCHVALE CT 2
EDALE GN 3
HEATHCOTE GR 4
TIDESWELL CL 5
CHELMORTON VALE 6
HATHERSAGE CL 7
DOVEDALE GR 8
HOWDEN GN 9
Wr Twr
BRAYBROOKE RD
HILLTOP AVE
HILLTOP CL
BRIDGE RD
ASH GR
PEVREL PL
OAKHAM CL
RUTLAND CT
Upper Lodge
ARTHINGWORTH RD
THE RIDINGS
LANGDALE
Loatlands Prim Sch
HARRINGTON RD
Lodge Farm
GREEN LA
CYPRESS CL
COALPORT CL
MEISSEN AVE
NEVILLE WAY
ADDISON RD
ALEXANDRA RD
OAK TREE CL
AYNSLEY CL
DOULTON CL
WEDGWOOD CL
MINTON CL
ORCHARD CL
PRINCE RUPERT AVE
ROYAL GDNS
WOODWELL HILL
FEDERATION AVE
Monkfield Coll
PIONEER AVE
WINDSOR AVE
DESBOROUGH RD
NN6
Loatland Lodge Farm
A
B
C
D
E
F
8
7
85
6
5
84
4
3
83
2
1
82
77
78
79

49
69

34
52

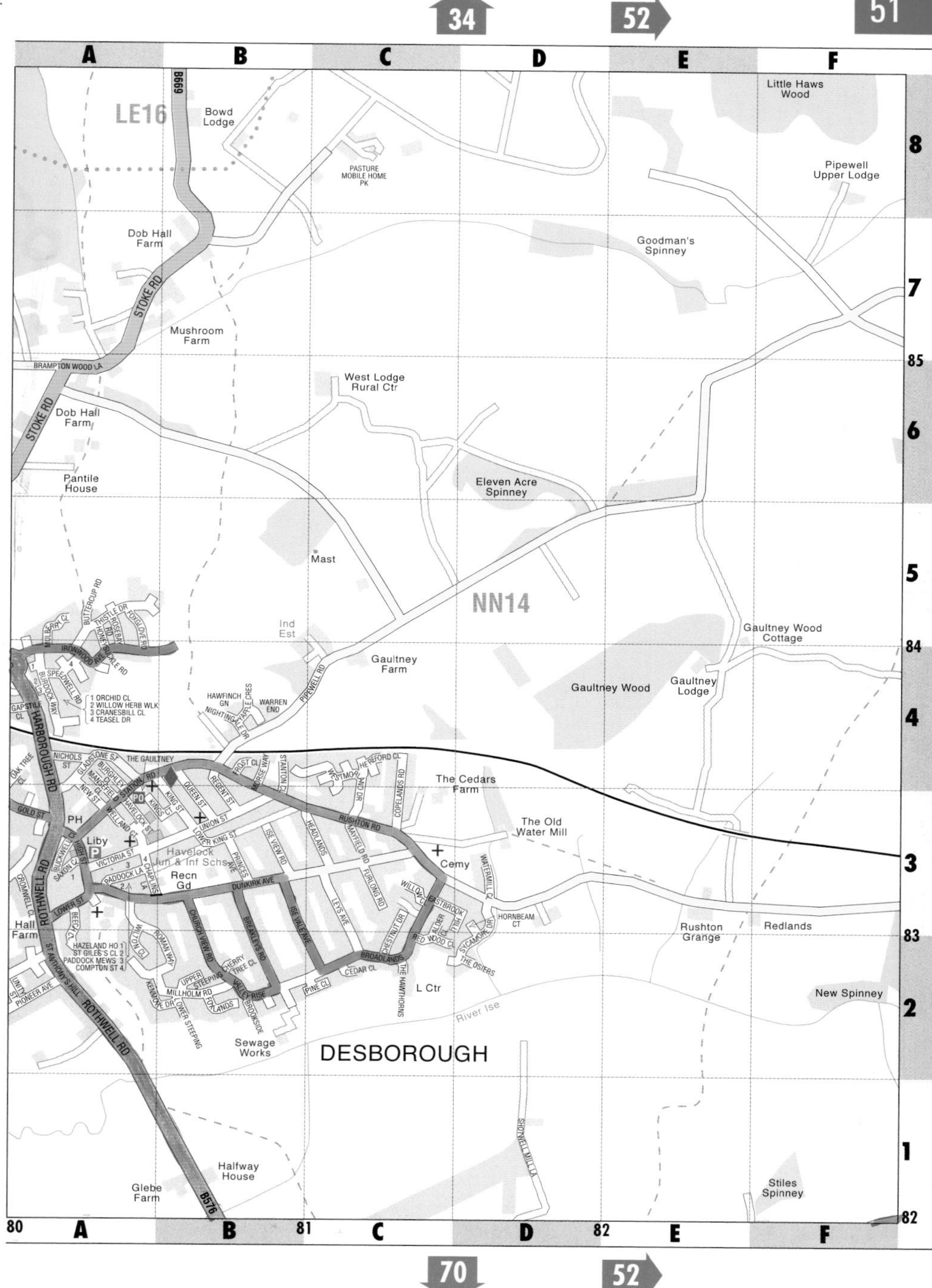
A
B
C
D
E
F
LE16
B669
Bowd Lodge
PASTURE MOBILE HOME PK
Little Haws Wood
Pipewell Upper Lodge
Dob Hall Farm
Goodman's Spinney
STOKE RD
Mushroom Farm
BRAMPTON WOOD LA
West Lodge Rural Ctr
Dob Hall Farm
Pantile House
Eleven Acre Spinney
Mast
NN14
Ind Est
Gaultney Farm
PIPEWELL RD
Gaultney Wood Cottage
Gaultney Wood
Gaultney Lodge
IRONWOOD AVE
HARBOROUGH RD
1 ORCHID CL
2 WILLOW HERB WLK
3 CRANESBILL CL
4 TEASEL DR
HAWFINCH GN
WARREN END
NIGHTINGALE DR
THE GAULTNEY
The Cedars Farm
The Old Water Mill
RUSHTON RD
PH
Liby
Havelock Jun & Inf Schs
Recn Gd
DUNKIRK AVE
Cemy
HORNBEAM CT
Rushton Grange
Redlands
ROTHWELL RD
Hall Farm
HAZELAND HO 1
ST GILES'S CL 2
PADDOCK MEWS 3
COMPTON ST 4
L Ctr
New Spinney
River Ise
Sewage Works
DESBOROUGH
SHOTWELL MILL LA
Halfway House
Glebe Farm
B576
Stiles Spinney
8
7
85
6
5
84
4
3
83
2
1
82
80
81
82

70
52

51
35

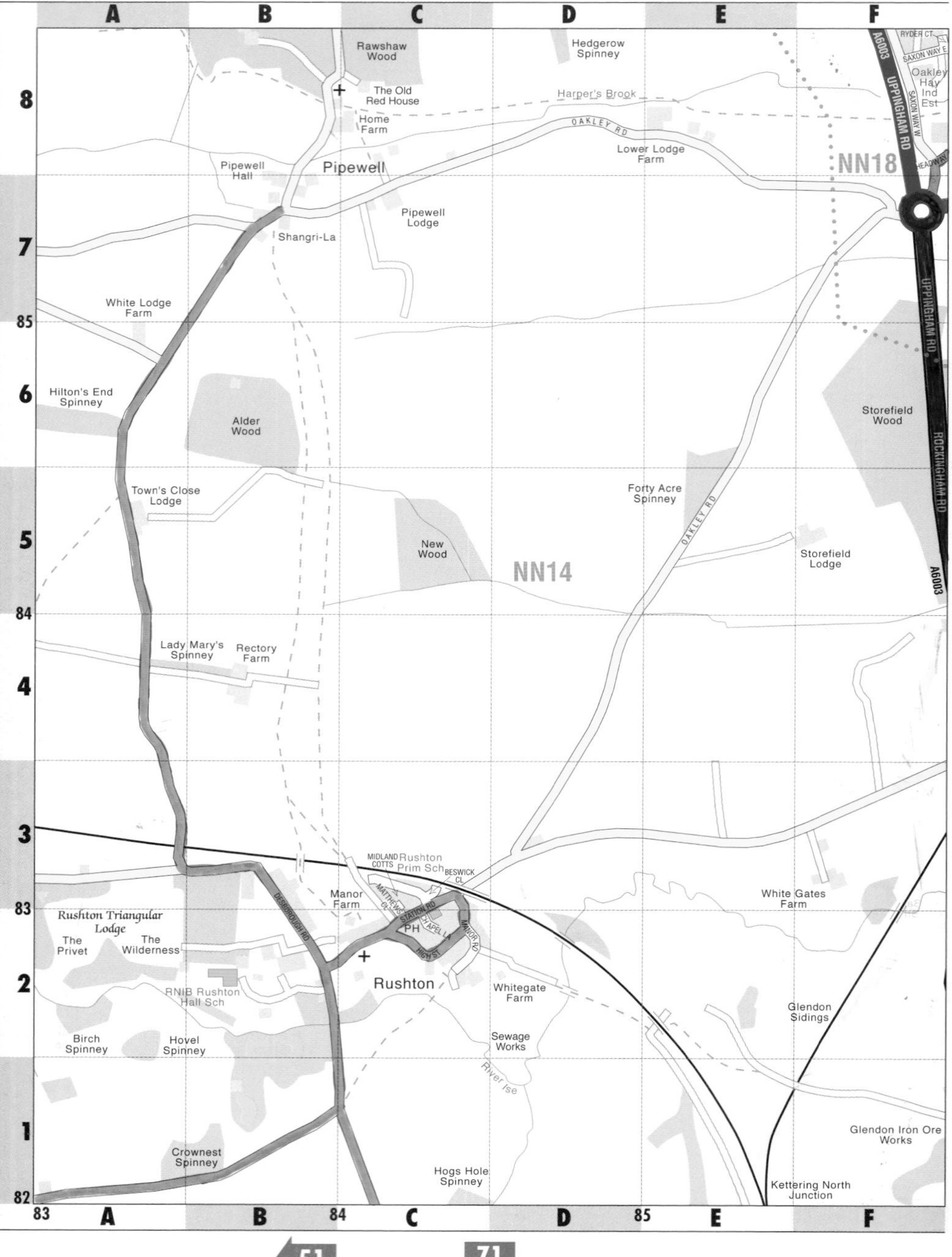
A
B
C
D
E
F
8
7
85
6
5
84
4
3
83
2
1
82
83
84
85
Rawshaw Wood
Hedgerow Spinney
The Old Red House
Home Farm
Harper's Brook
OAKLEY RD
Lower Lodge Farm
Pipewell Hall
Pipewell
Pipewell Lodge
Shangri-La
NN18
RYDER CT
SAXON WAY E
SAXON WAY W
Oakley Hay Ind Est
HEADWAY
A6003
UPPINGHAM RD
ROCKINGHAM RD
White Lodge Farm
Hilton's End Spinney
Alder Wood
Storefield Wood
Town's Close Lodge
Forty Acre Spinney
New Wood
NN14
Storefield Lodge
Lady Mary's Spinney
Rectory Farm
MIDLAND COTTS
Rushton Prim Sch
BESWICK CL
Manor Farm
MATTHEWS CL
STATION RD
CHAPEL LA
MANOR RD
HIGH ST
PH
DESBOROUGH RD
White Gates Farm
Rushton Triangular Lodge
The Privet
The Wilderness
Rushton
RNIB Rushton Hall Sch
Whitegate Farm
Glendon Sidings
Birch Spinney
Hovel Spinney
Sewage Works
River Ise
Glendon Iron Ore Works
Crownest Spinney
Hogs Hole Spinney
Kettering North Junction

51
71

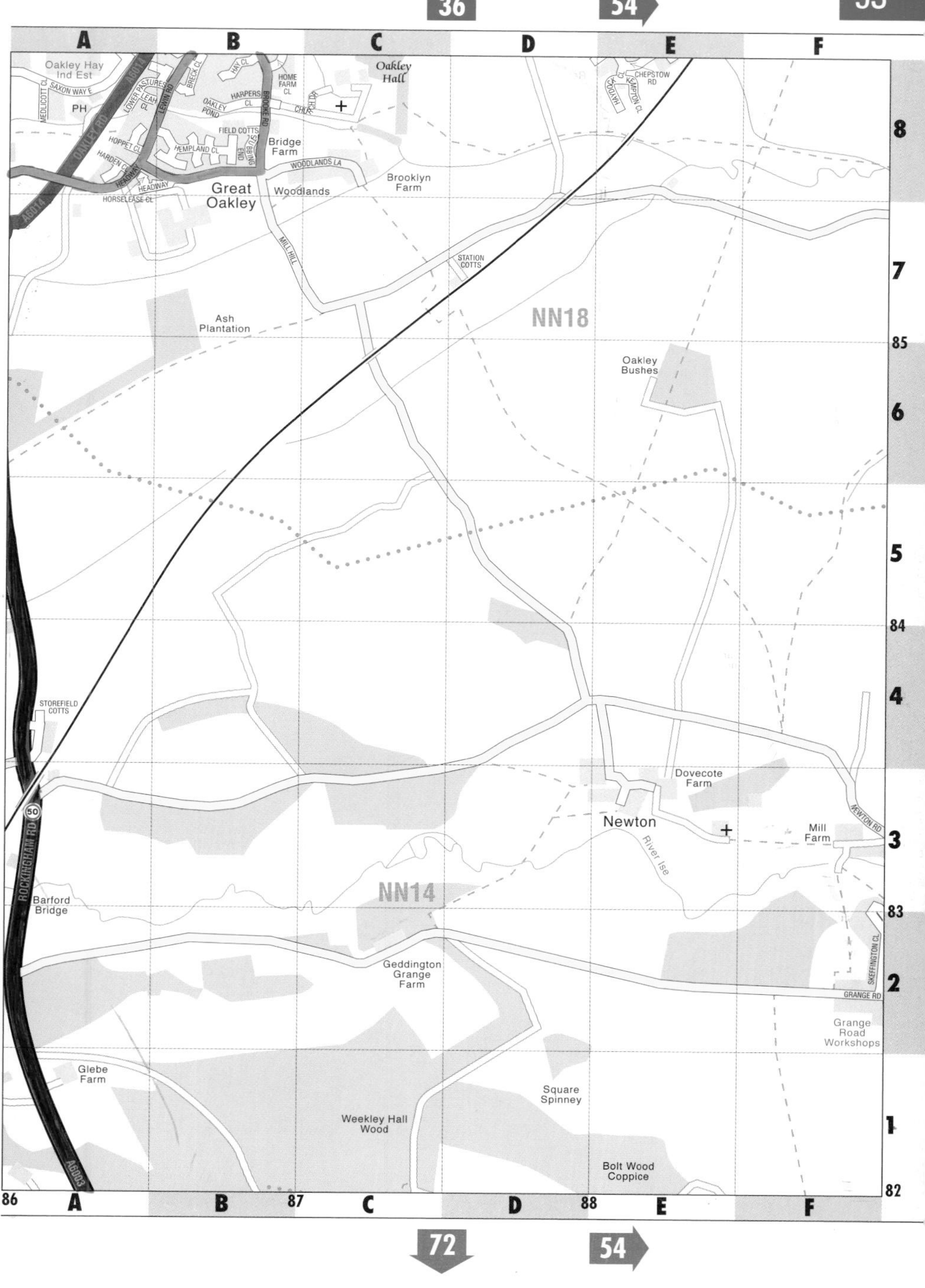
A
B
C
D
E
F
Oakley Hay
Ind Est
SAXON WAY E
MEDLICOTT CL
PH
A6014
OAKLEY RD
LOWER PASTURES
LEAH CL
LENNIN RD
BRECK CL
HAY CL
HOME FARM CL
HARPERS CL
OAKLEY POND
BROOKE RD
CHURCH
Oakley Hall
HAYDOCK CL
CHEPSTOW RD
KEMPTON CL
FIELD COTTS
HOPPET CL
HEMPLAND CL
STUBBING END
Bridge Farm
HARDEN CL
HEADWAY
WOODLANDS LA
Great Oakley
Woodlands
Brooklyn Farm
HORSELEASE CL
MILL HILL
STATION COTTS
NN18
Ash Plantation
Oakley Bushes
STOREFIELD COTTS
Dovecote Farm
Newton
River Ise
Mill Farm
NEWTON RD
50
ROCKINGHAM RD
NN14
Barford Bridge
SKEFFINGTON CL
Geddington Grange Farm
GRANGE RD
Grange Road Workshops
Glebe Farm
Square Spinney
Weekley Hall Wood
Bolt Wood Coppice
A6003
8
7
85
6
5
84
4
3
83
2
1
82
86
87
88

53
37

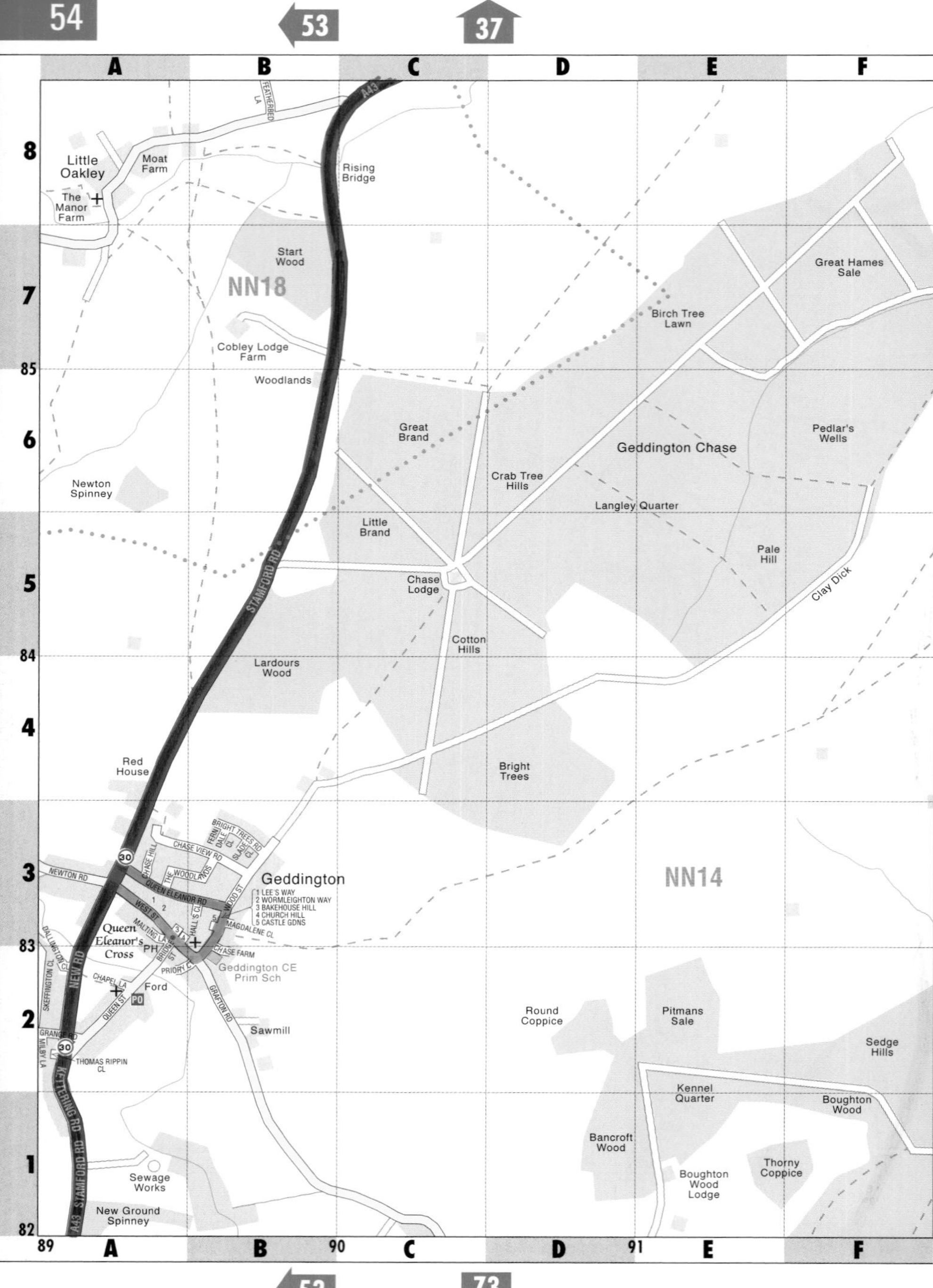
A
B
C
D
E
F
8
7
85
6
5
84
4
3
83
2
1
82
89
90
91
FEATHERBED LA
A43
Little Oakley
Moat Farm
Rising Bridge
The Manor Farm
Start Wood
NN18
Great Hames Sale
Birch Tree Lawn
Cobley Lodge Farm
Woodlands
Great Brand
Pedlar's Wells
Geddington Chase
Crab Tree Hills
Newton Spinney
Langley Quarter
Little Brand
Pale Hill
STAMFORD RD
Chase Lodge
Clay Dick
Cotton Hills
Lardours Wood
Bright Trees
Red House
CHASE VIEW RD
CHASE HILL
BRIGHT TREES RD
FERN DALE CL
SLADE CL
THE WOODLANDS
NEWTON RD
Geddington
NN14
QUEEN ELEANOR RD
WOOD ST
1 LEE'S WAY
2 WORMLEIGHTON WAY
3 BAKEHOUSE HILL
4 CHURCH HILL
5 CASTLE GDNS
WEST ST
HALL'S CL
MAGDALENE CL
MALTING LA
DALLINGTON CL
Queen Eleanor's Cross
PH
BRIDGE ST
CHASE FARM
PRIORY CL
Geddington CE Prim Sch
NEW RD
CHAPEL LA
SKEFFINGTON CL
Ford
PO
QUEEN ST
GRAFTON RD
Round Coppice
Pitmans Sale
Sawmill
Sedge Hills
GRANGE RD
MILBY LA
30
THOMAS RIPPIN CL
KETTERING RD
Kennel Quarter
Boughton Wood
Bancroft Wood
Thorny Coppice
Sewage Works
Boughton Wood Lodge
New Ground Spinney
STAMFORD RD

53
73

38
56
A
B
C
D
E
F
8
7
85
6
5
84
4
3
83
2
1
82
92
93
94
Harpers Brook
Playing Field
Brigstock
The Manor House
Sch
PH
PO
DUSTHILL RD
STANION RD
NEWTOWN
OLD DRY LA
FERMYN CL
WOODYARD CL
BACK LA
FARM CL
HIGH ST
BRIDGE ST
LATHAM ST
MILL LA
CHURCH ST
CAUSIN CL
KENNEL HILL
STABLE HILL
THE SYKE
BENEFIELD RD
A6116
1 WOODLANDS MEWS
2 WOODLANDS CL
3 HALL HILL
MONTERLY GATE
LYVEDEN RD
MAUNTLEY AVE
SANDLANDS AVE
SUDBOROUGH RD
SANDLANDS CL
HARPER'S CT
PARK WLK
BELLS CL
SWAN AVE
Chase Farm
Park Farm
Sewage Works
NN14
Bullymore's Lodge
Old Lodge Farm
GRAFTON RD
Park Cottages
Hillside Farm
Breakhill Cottage
Long Sale
Fox Earth
Roadside Quarter
Barn Quarter
Old Head Wood
Stevenson's Quarter
Great Bull Sedge
Schich's Corner
Snapes Wood
74
56

55
39

A
B
C
D
E
F
8
7
85
6
5
84
4
3
83
2
1
82
95
96
97
BENEFIELD RD
Mounterley Wood
HARLEY WAY
Luscote Lodge
Harley Way Lodge
Stephen Oak Riding
Cherry Lap
Sling's Nook
A6116
Royal Coppice
Fermyn Woods
PE8
Fermyn Woods Country Park
LYVEDEN RD
BARNARD'S WAY
Tresham Coppice
Lady Wood Head
Assart's Coppice
SUDBOROUGH RD
Lady Wood
Manor Farm
Sudborough Green Lodge
Souther Wood
SUDBOROUGH RD
Cat's Head Wood
NN14
Catshead Farm
Green Side Wood
Titchmarsh Wood
Green Lodge
Harper's Brook
Belle Vue
Snapes Lodge
Snapes Wood
Sudborough
Grange Farm
PH
MAIN ST
BREWERY YD
SLIPTON LA
A6116

55
75

40
58
A
B
C
D
E
F
Lyveden Manor
Bearshank Wood
Pilton Lodge
8
Lyveden New Bield
PE8
7
Coppice Lodge
85
Lilford Wood
New Plantation
Lady Wood
Wadenhoe Little Wood
6
Wadenhoe Lodge
Wadenhoe Great Wood
5
Souther Wood
84
WADENHOE LA
4
Experimental Plantation
Aldwincle Lodge
Green Side Wood
3
Little Wood
83
2
Nene Way
River Nene
NN14
WADENHOE RD
1
Aldwincle
MAIN ST
Recn Gd
Oxen Wood
CROSS LA
FULLERS CL
82
98
99
00
76
58

57
41

A
B
C
D
E
F
8
7
85
6
5
84
4
3
83
2
1
82
01
02
03
Manor House
Great Ground Spinney
PE8
Pilton Lodge Farm
Petty Fields Plantation
Lilford Lodge Farm
Pilton Grange
Manor House
River Nene
Pilton
Boat Houses
Lilford Hall
Lilford Park
Wr Twr
Lilford Woods
Lilford Bridge
Lilford Home Farm
WADENHOE LA
THE GREEN
Meml
GLEBE CT
PILTON RD
MAIN ST
PO
Wadenhoe
Wadenhoe House
Lilford
OAKLEE CL
CHURCH ST
MILL LA
PH
The Linches
A605
Sudden's Plantation
P
Nene Way
Ratling Irons Plantation
Achurch
B662
Rectory Farm
River Nene
NN14
A605
B662

57
77

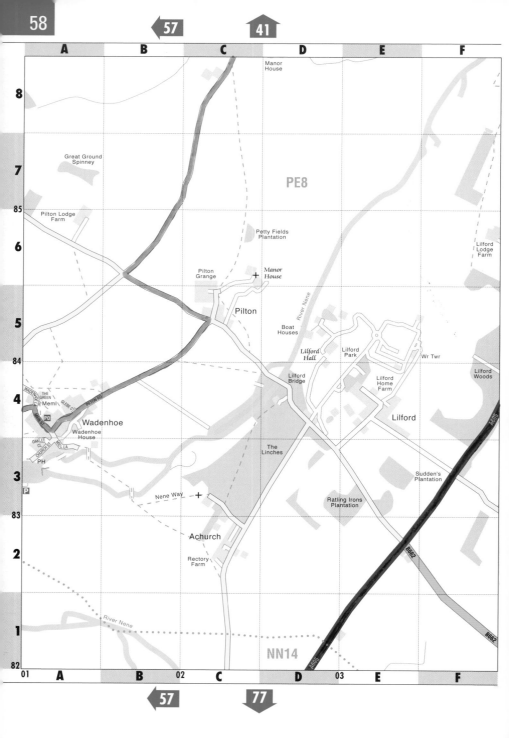

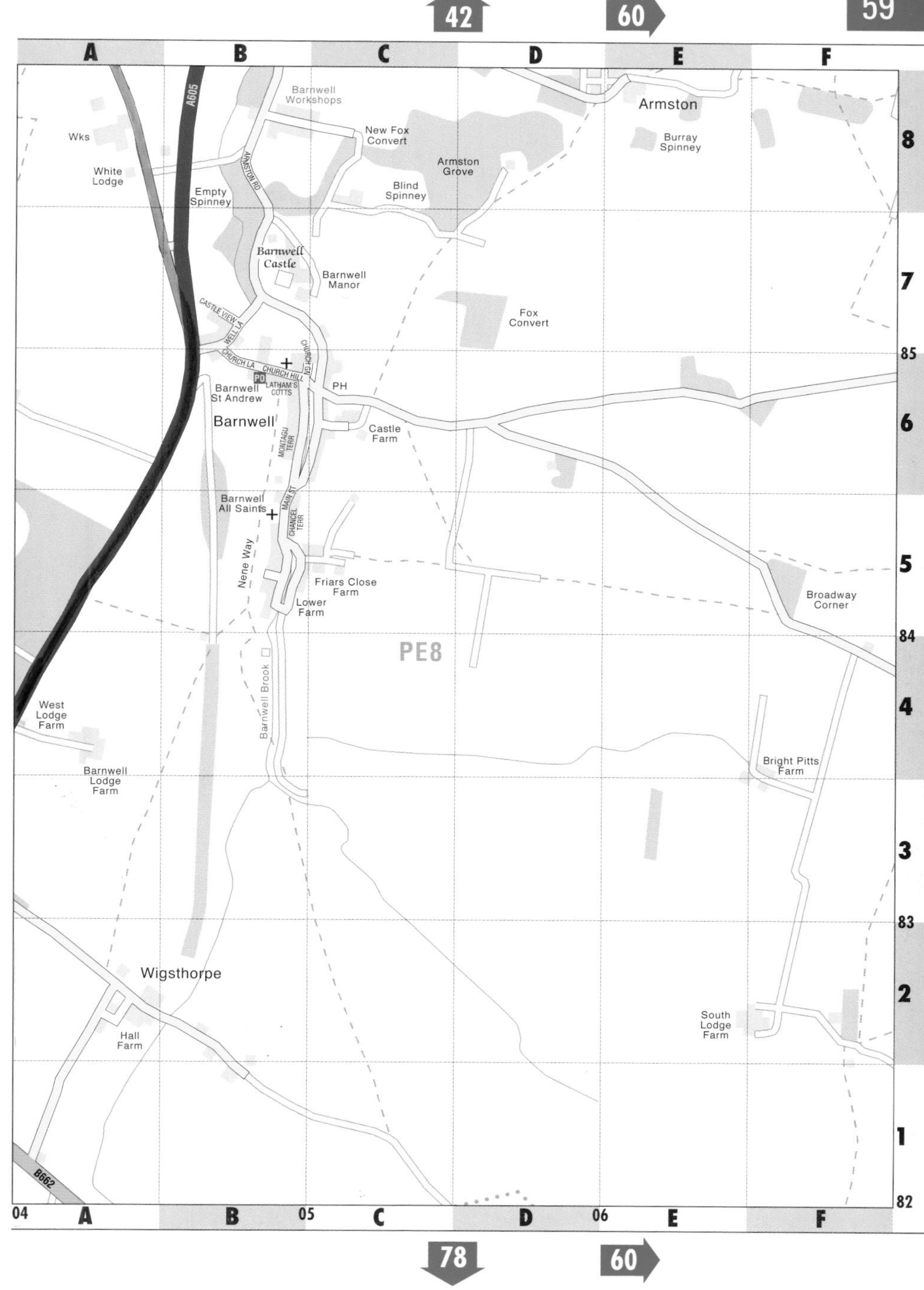
42
60
A
B
C
D
E
F
A605
Barnwell Workshops
Armston
Wks
New Fox Convert
Burray Spinney
White Lodge
Armston Grove
Empty Spinney
ARMSTON RD
Blind Spinney
Barnwell Castle
Barnwell Manor
CASTLE VIEW
WELL LA
Fox Convert
CHURCH GN
CHURCH LA
CHURCH HILL
PO
LATHAM'S COTTS
PH
Barnwell St Andrew
Barnwell
MONTAGU TERR
Castle Farm
Barnwell All Saints
MAIN ST
CHANCEL TERR
Nene Way
Friars Close Farm
Lower Farm
Broadway Corner
PE8
Barnwell Brook
West Lodge Farm
Bright Pitts Farm
Barnwell Lodge Farm
Wigsthorpe
Hall Farm
South Lodge Farm
B662
8
7
85
6
5
84
4
3
83
2
1
82
04
05
06
78
60

59
43

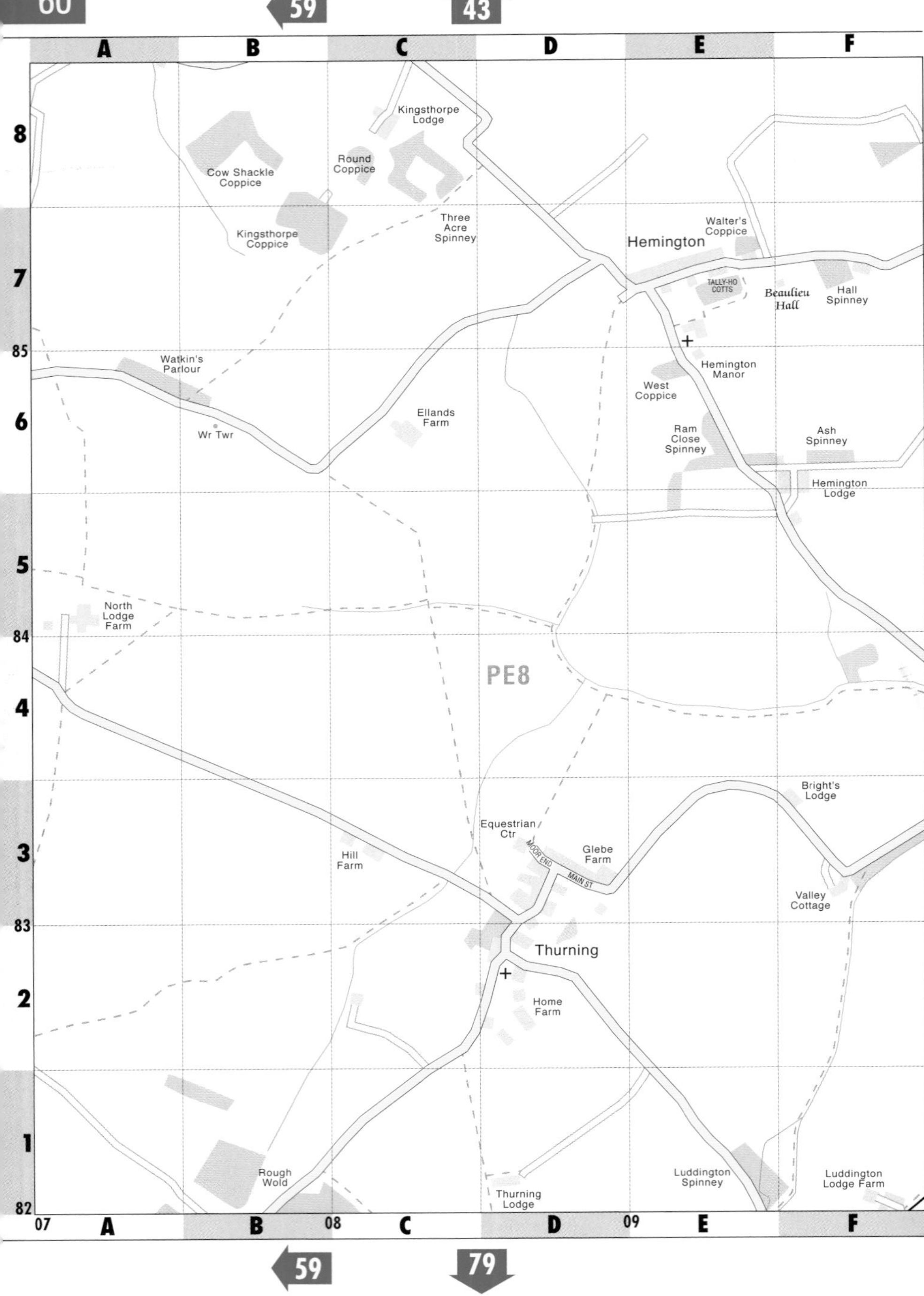
A
B
C
D
E
F
8
7
85
6
5
84
4
3
83
2
1
82
07
08
09
Kingsthorpe Lodge
Cow Shackle Coppice
Round Coppice
Kingsthorpe Coppice
Three Acre Spinney
Walter's Coppice
Hemington
TALLY-HO COTTS
Beaulieu Hall
Hall Spinney
Hemington Manor
West Coppice
Watkin's Parlour
Wr Twr
Ellands Farm
Ram Close Spinney
Ash Spinney
Hemington Lodge
North Lodge Farm
PE8
Bright's Lodge
Equestrian Ctr
MOOR END
MAIN ST
Glebe Farm
Hill Farm
Valley Cottage
Thurning
Home Farm
Rough Wold
Luddington Spinney
Luddington Lodge Farm
Thurning Lodge

59
79

44

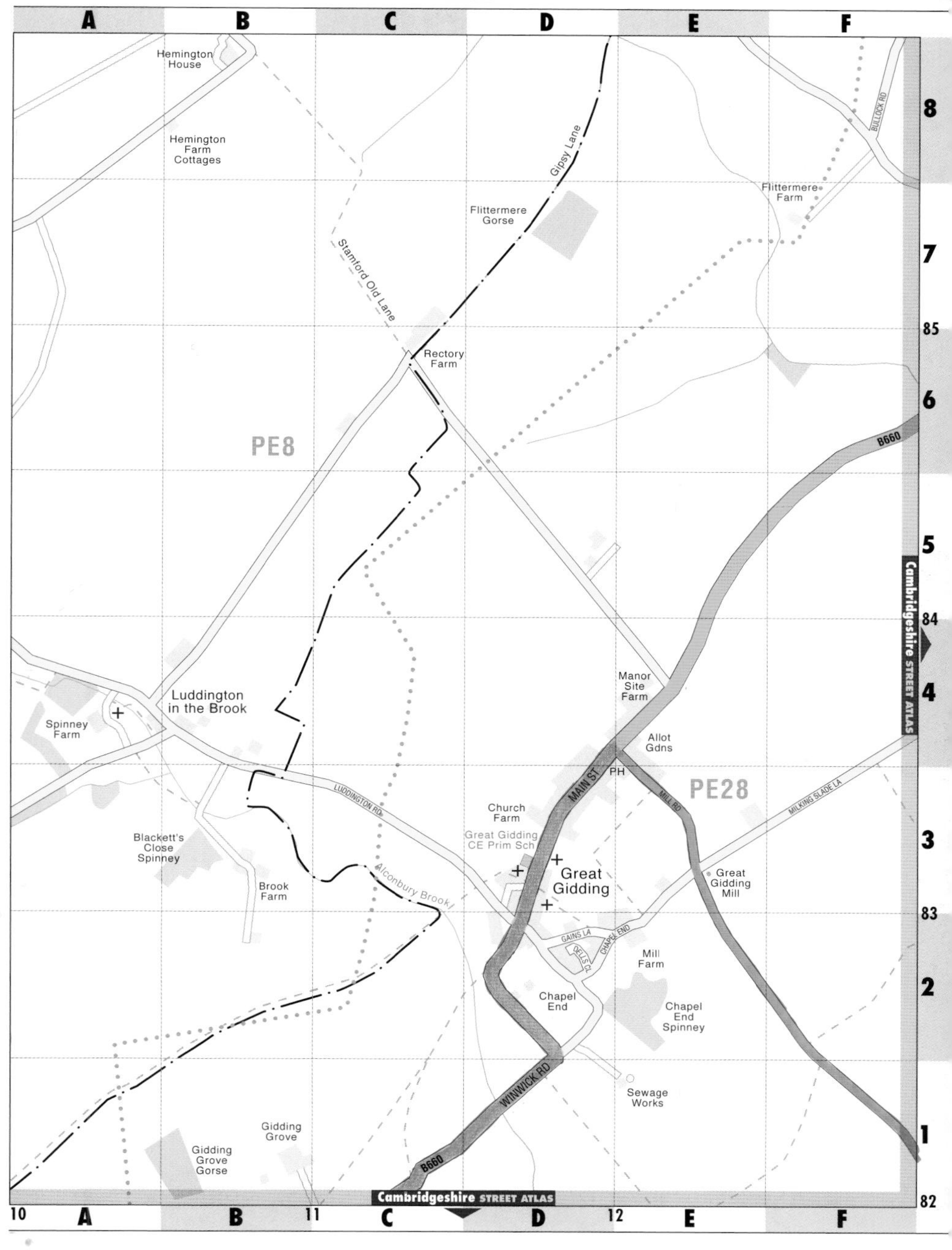
A
B
C
D
E
F
8
7
85
6
5
84
4
3
83
2
1
82
10
11
12
Hemington House
Hemington Farm Cottages
Gipsy Lane
BULLOCK RD
Flittermere Farm
Flittermere Gorse
Stamford Old Lane
Rectory Farm
PE8
B660
Cambridgeshire STREET ATLAS
Manor Site Farm
Luddington in the Brook
Spinney Farm
Allot Gdns
PH
MAIN ST
MILL RD
PE28
MILKING SLADE LA
LUDDINGTON RD
Church Farm
Blackett's Close Spinney
Great Gidding CE Prim Sch
Alconbury Brook
Great Gidding
Great Gidding Mill
Brook Farm
GAINS LA
CHAPEL END
DELLS CL
Mill Farm
Chapel End
Chapel End Spinney
WINWICK RD
Sewage Works
Gidding Grove
Gidding Grove Gorse
B660
Cambridgeshire STREET ATLAS

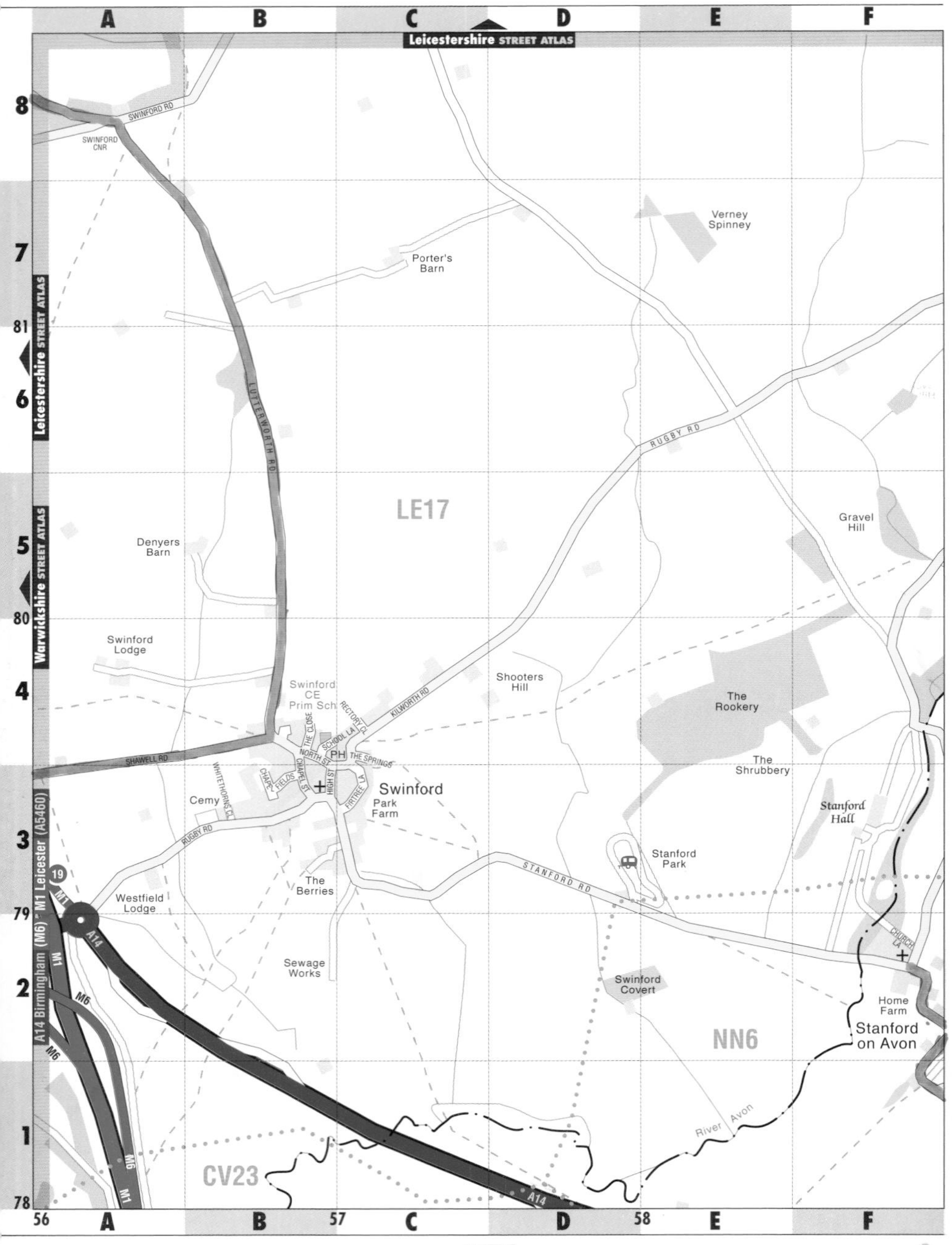
A
B
C
D
E
F
Leicestershire STREET ATLAS
8
7
81
6
5
80
4
3
79
2
1
78
Leicestershire STREET ATLAS
Warwickshire STREET ATLAS
SWINFORD RD
SWINFORD CNR
Porter's Barn
Verney Spinney
LUTTERWORTH RD
RUGBY RD
LE17
Gravel Hill
Denyers Barn
Swinford Lodge
Shooters Hill
Swinford CE Prim Sch
RECTORY CL
KILWORTH RD
THE CLOSE
SCHOOL LA
NORTH ST
PH
THE SPRINGS
SHAWELL RD
The Rookery
The Shrubbery
WHITETHORNS CL
CHAPEL FIELDS
CHAPEL ST
HIGH ST
FIRTREE LA
Swinford
Park Farm
Cemy
Stanford Hall
A14 Birmingham (M6) M1 Leicester (A5460)
19
RUGBY RD
Stanford Park
STANFORD RD
The Berries
Westfield Lodge
M1
A14
CHURCH LA
M6
Sewage Works
Swinford Covert
Home Farm
Stanford on Avon
NN6
River Avon
CV23
A14
M6
M1
56
57
58

81

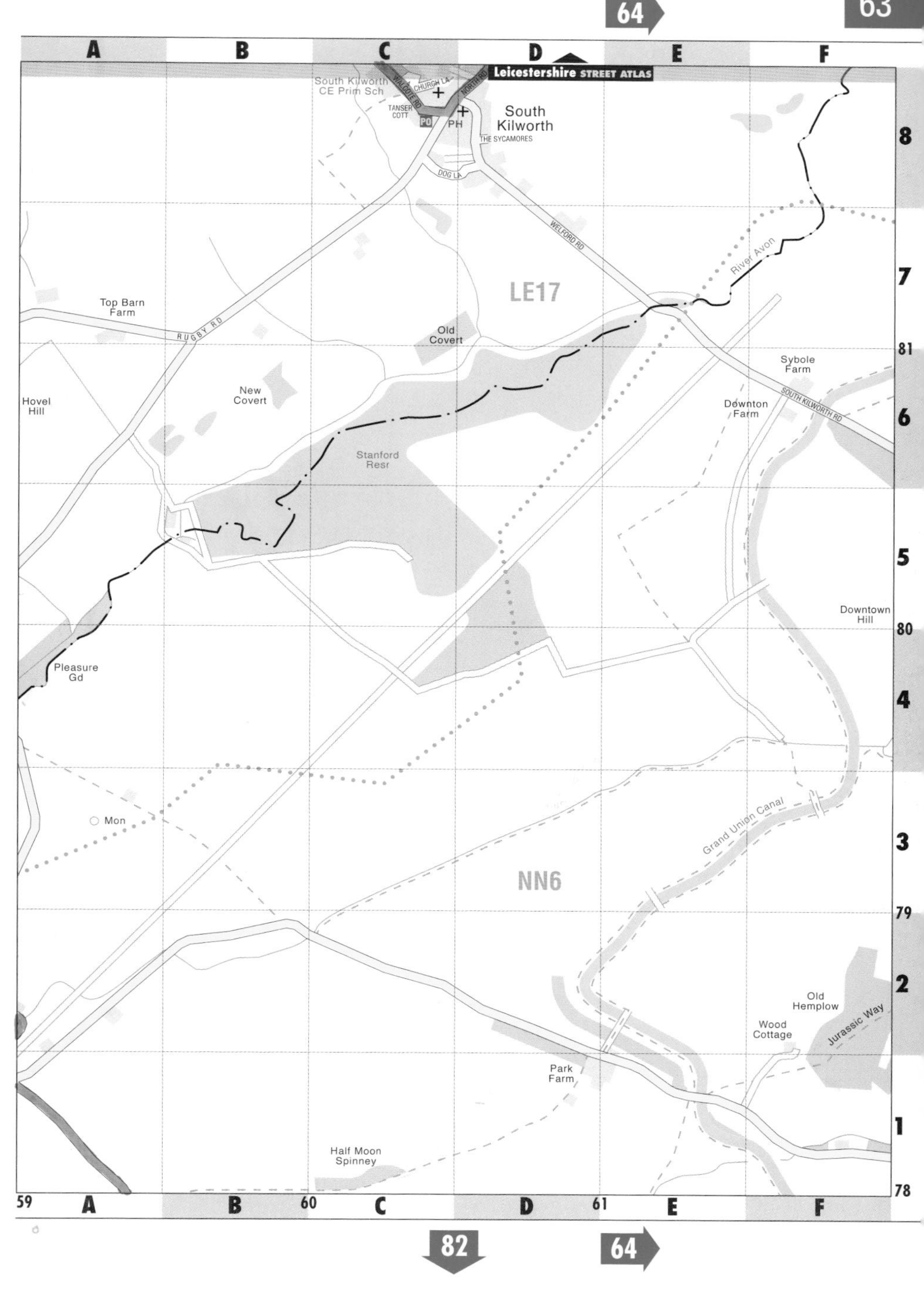
64
A
B
C
D
E
F
Leicestershire STREET ATLAS
South Kilworth CE Prim Sch
CHURCH LA
WALCOTE RD
NORTH RD
TANSER COTT
PO
PH
South Kilworth
THE SYCAMORES
DOG LA
WELFORD RD
LE17
Top Barn Farm
RUGBY RD
Old Covert
New Covert
Hovel Hill
Stanford Resr
River Avon
Sybole Farm
SOUTH KILWORTH RD
Downton Farm
Downtown Hill
Pleasure Gd
Mon
Grand Union Canal
NN6
Old Hemplow
Wood Cottage
Jurassic Way
Park Farm
Half Moon Spinney
8
7
81
6
5
80
4
3
79
2
1
78
59
60
61
82
64

63
45

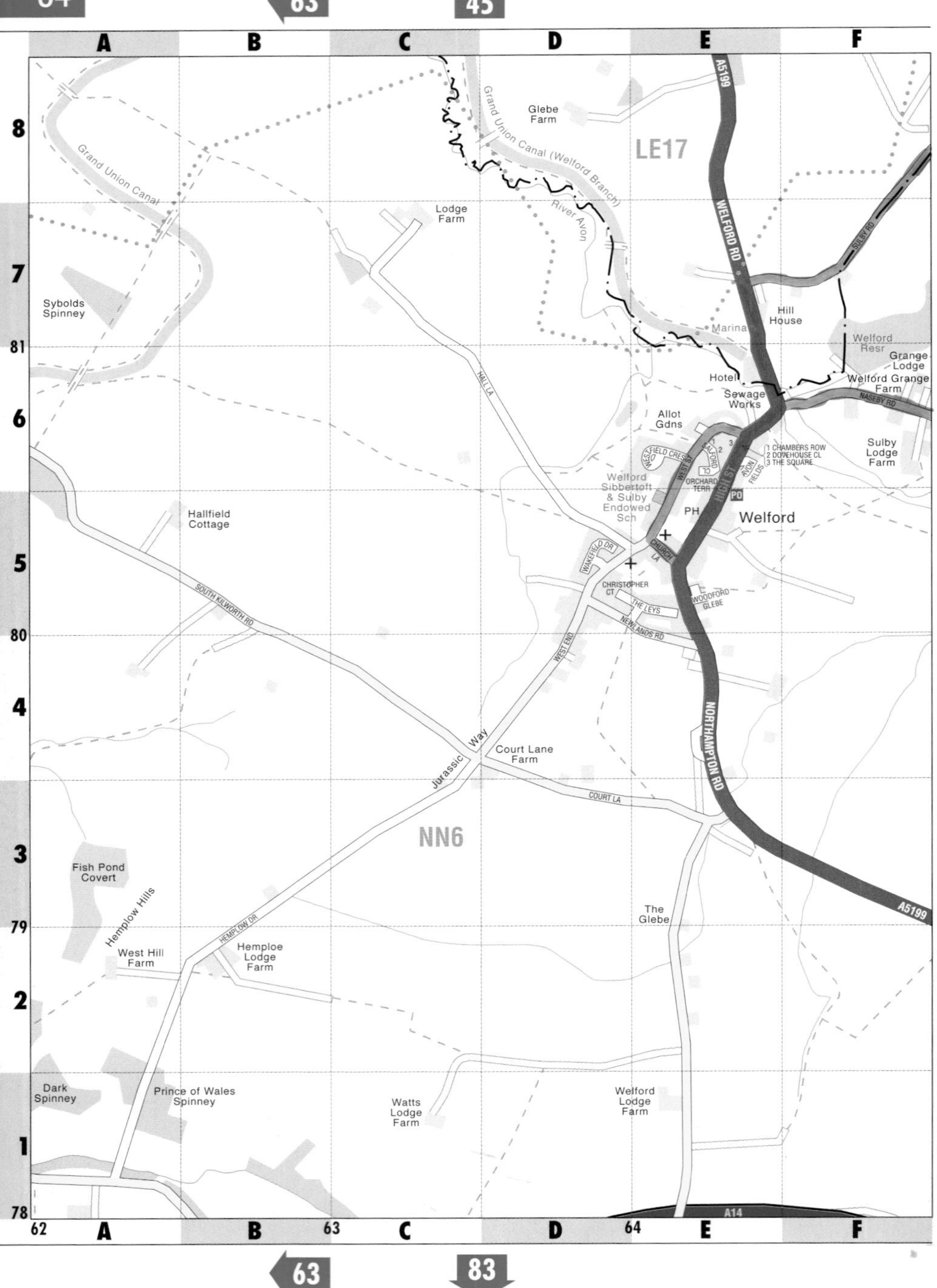
A B C D E F
8
7
81
6
5
80
4
3
79
2
1
78
62 63 64
Glebe Farm
Grand Union Canal (Welford Branch)
LE17
A5199
Grand Union Canal
Lodge Farm
River Avon
WELFORD RD
SULBY RD
Sybolds Spinney
Hill House
Marina
Welford Resr
Grange Lodge
Hotel
Welford Grange Farm
Sewage Works
NASEBY RD
HALL LA
Allot Gdns
WEST FIELD CRES
SALFORD CL
WEST ST
HIGH ST
1 CHAMBERS ROW
2 DOVEHOUSE CL
3 THE SQUARE
Sulby Lodge Farm
ORCHARD TERR
FIELDS
PO
Welford Sibbertoft & Sulby Endowed Sch
PH
Welford
Hallfield Cottage
WAKEFIELD DR
CHURCH LA
CHRISTOPHER CT
WOODFORD GLEBE
THE LEYS
SOUTH KILWORTH RD
NEWLANDS RD
WEST END
NORTHAMPTON RD
Jurassic Way
Court Lane Farm
COURT LA
NN6
Fish Pond Covert
Hemplow Hills
The Glebe
A5199
HEMPLOW DR
West Hill Farm
Hemploe Lodge Farm
Dark Spinney
Prince of Wales Spinney
Watts Lodge Farm
Welford Lodge Farm
A14

63
83

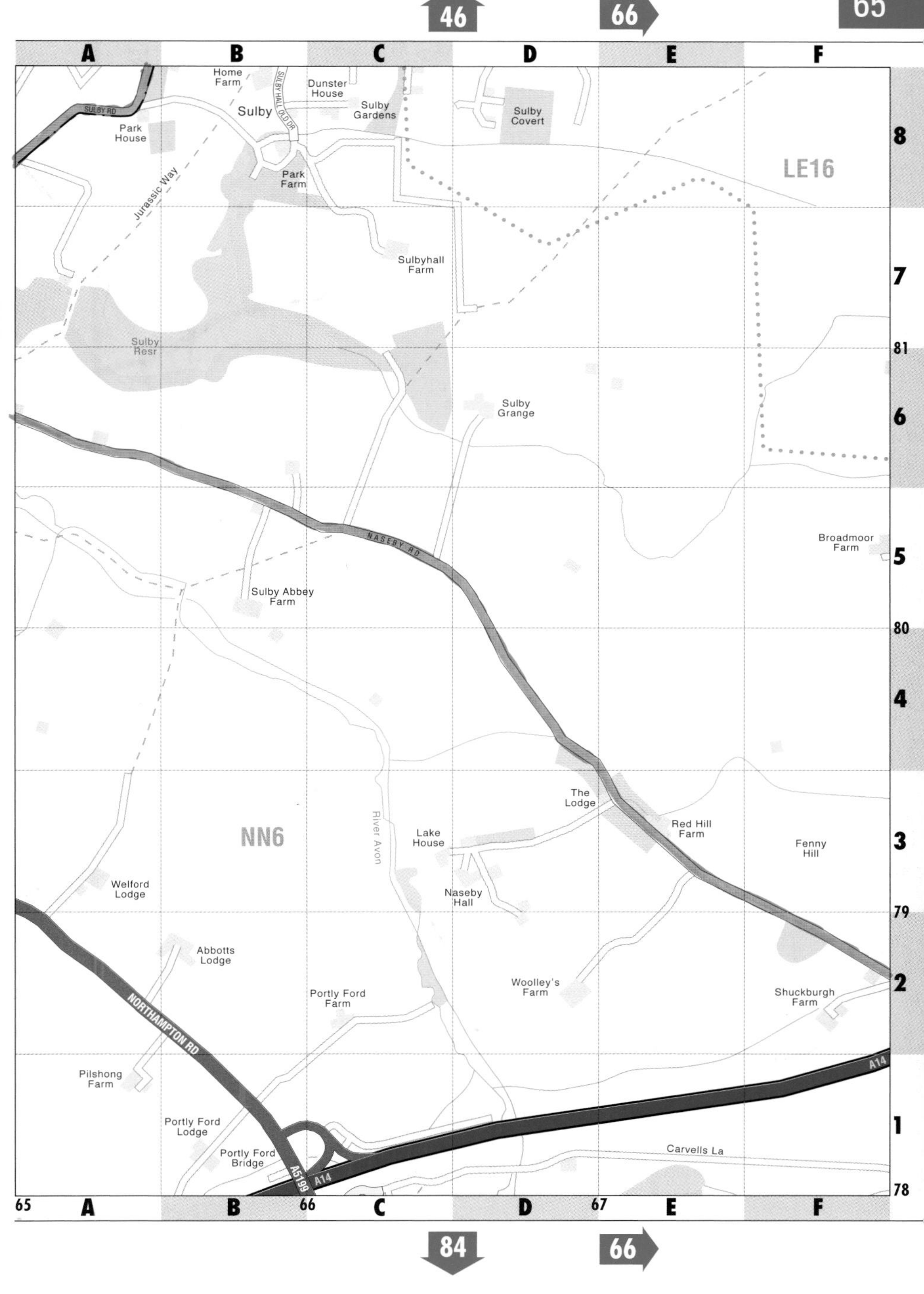
46
66
A
B
C
D
E
F
Home Farm
Dunster House
Sulby
SULBY HALL OLD DR
Sulby Gardens
Sulby Covert
SULBY RD
Park House
Park Farm
LE16
Jurassic Way
Sulbyhall Farm
Sulby Resr
Sulby Grange
NASEBY RD
Broadmoor Farm
Sulby Abbey Farm
River Avon
The Lodge
Red Hill Farm
NN6
Lake House
Fenny Hill
Welford Lodge
Naseby Hall
Abbotts Lodge
NORTHAMPTON RD
Woolley's Farm
Portly Ford Farm
Shuckburgh Farm
Pilshong Farm
A14
Portly Ford Lodge
Carvells La
Portly Ford Bridge
A5199
8
7
81
6
5
80
4
3
79
2
1
78
65
66
67
84
66

65
47
A 
B
C
D
E
F
8
7
81
6
5
80
4
3
79
2
1
78
NASEBY RD
The Paddocks
The Old Manse
Clipston
CHAPEL LA
NOBOLD CT
PEG'S LA
GOLD ST
The Chestnuts
NARECROFT
NASEBY RD
Longhold Lodge
LE16
Prince Rupert's Farm
Dust Hill
Long Hold Spinney
Dust Hill Farm
The Plantation
Mon
Naseby Covert
Paisnell Spinney
Naseby Field
Mill Hill
New-House Farm
A14
NN6
Mill Hill Farm
Mast
A14
Clothill Spinney
Obelisk
HALL CL
Naseby
PH
NEWLANDS
CHURCH ST
HIGH ST
Naseby CE Prim Sch
Carvells La
68
69
70
65
85

48
68

A
B
C
D
E
F
Newbold Farm
Playing Field
PH
NETHER GN
THE GREEN
HARBOROUGH RD
NASEBY RD
HIGH ST
CHURCH CL
CHURCH LA
BASSETT WAY
Clipston Endowed Prim Sch
WESKERS CL
KELMARSH RD
Sewage Works
Kelmarsh Field Farm
Wormslade Farm
Kelmarsh Field Farm
Midshires Way
Macmillan Way
A508
8
7
LE16
81
Lodge Ground Spinney
6
HARBOROUGH RD
Grasslands Farm
5
Shipley Wood
Hill Top Farm
80
Clipston Grange
Shipley Wood
4
Kelmarsh Hall
Wilderness Farm
Hall Farm
MAIN RD
Kelmarsh
3
HARRINGTON RD
The Dales
Church Spinney
79
2
Tallyho Covert
River Ise
Rectory Farm
40
A14
NN6
Scotland Wood
A508
1
78
71
72
73

86
68

67
49

Arthingworth
DESBOROUGH RD
OXENDON RD
Manor House
BRAYBROOKE RD
PO
HALL CL
HOME FARM GR
CHURCH FARM WAY
PH
INN YARD CT
SUNNY BANK
KELMARSH RD
Sidom's Ford
Arthingworth Lodge
LE16
River Ise
Clark's Spinney
Warren Hill Farm
Langborough Wood
PH
Rabbithill Spinney
Midshires Way
Warren Hill
Midshires Way
Macmillan Way
Far Hill
Sunderland Wood
New Covert
Tunnels
Wheatfield Lodge Farm
Top Lodge
NN6
Warth Lodge
Johnson's Covert
A14
Aviation Mus
Blue Covert
Sewage Works
A14
Cobdell
Green Lane Crossing
Scotland Wood Farm
Draughton Lodge
A508

67
87

50
70

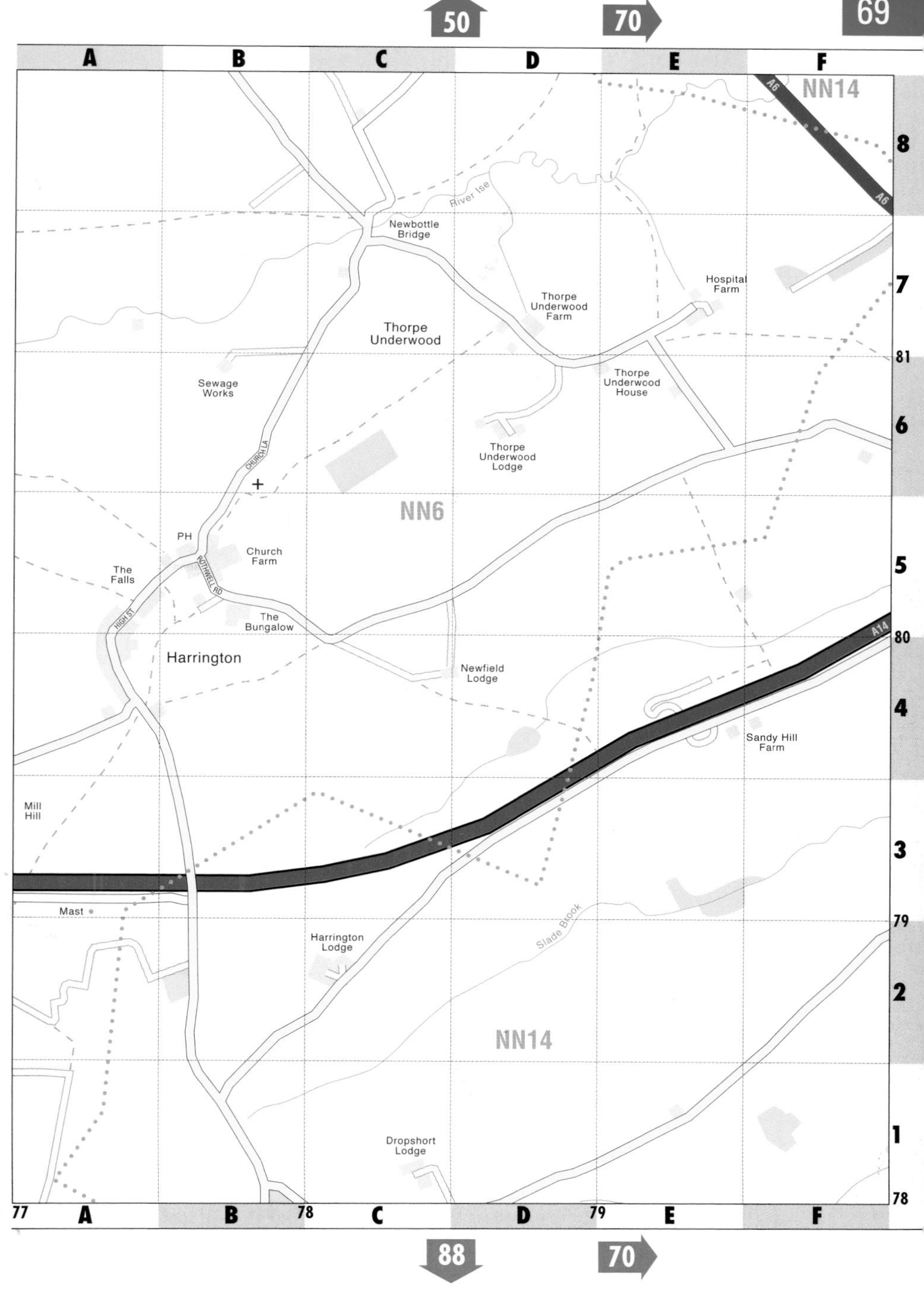
A
B
C
D
E
F
NN14
A6
8
River Ise
Newbottle
Bridge
Hospital
Farm
7
Thorpe
Underwood
Farm
Thorpe
Underwood
81
Sewage
Works
Thorpe
Underwood
House
6
Thorpe
Underwood
Lodge
CHURCH LA
NN6
PH
Church
Farm
5
The
Falls
ROTHWELL RD
The
Bungalow
HIGH ST
A14
80
Harrington
Newfield
Lodge
4
Sandy Hill
Farm
Mill
Hill
3
Mast
79
Harrington
Lodge
Slade Brook
2
NN14
1
Dropshort
Lodge
78
77
78
79

88
70

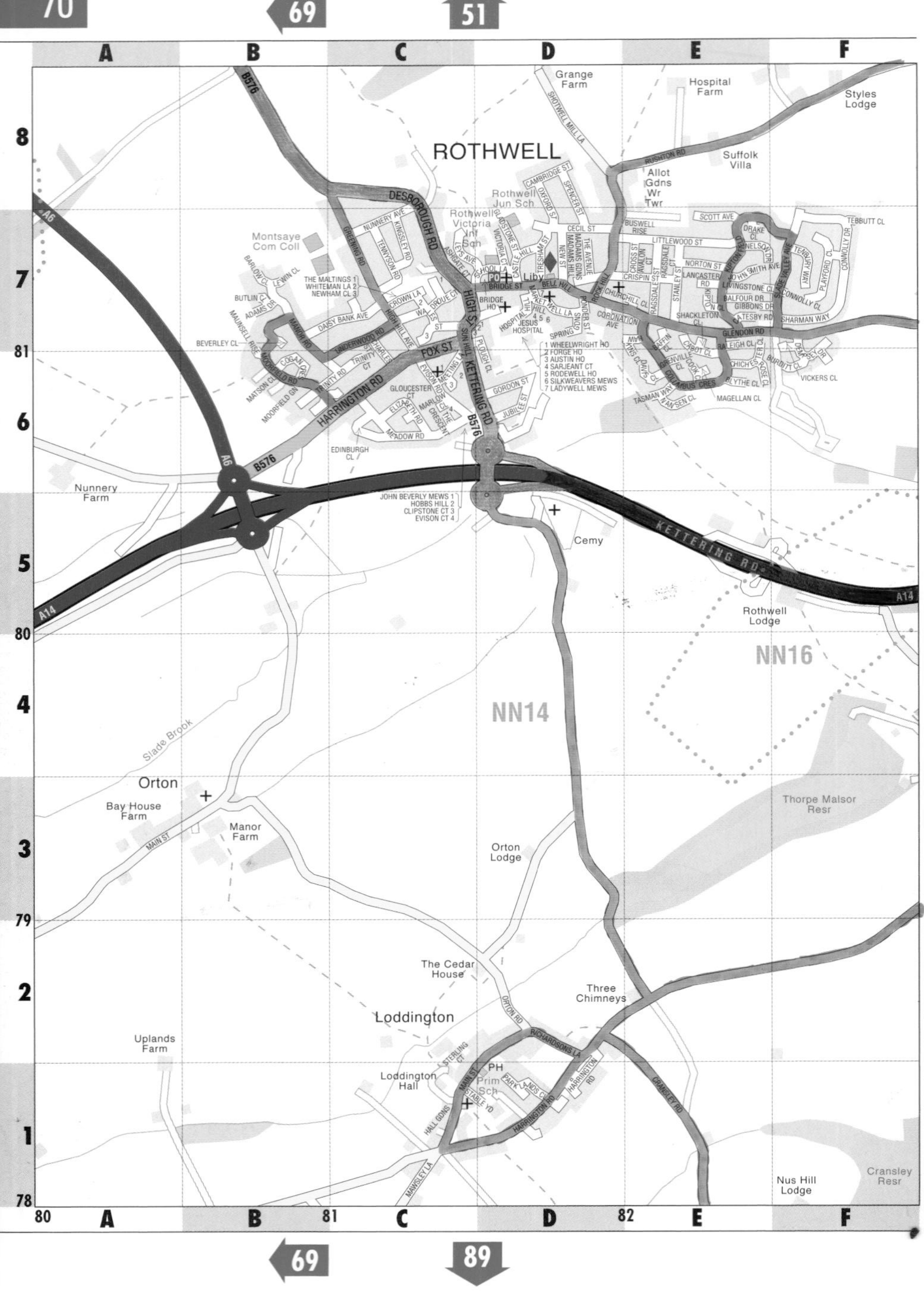
69
51
A
B
C
D
E
F
8
7
81
6
5
80
4
3
79
2
1
78
ROTHWELL
Grange Farm
Hospital Farm
Styles Lodge
Suffolk Villa
Allot Gdns
Wr Twr
Montsaye Com Coll
Rothwell Jun Sch
Rothwell Victoria Inf Sch
Liby
PO
Nunnery Farm
Cemy
Rothwell Lodge
NN16
NN14
KETTERING RD
A14
A6
B576
DESBOROUGH RD
HARRINGTON RD
KETTERING RD
HIGH ST
FOX ST
BRIDGE ST
GLENDON RD
RUSHTON RD
SHOTWELL MILL LA
THE MALTINGS 1
WHITEMAN LA 2
NEWHAM CL 3
1 WHEELWRIGHT HO
2 FORGE HO
3 AUSTIN HO
4 SARJEANT CT
5 RODEWELL HO
6 SILKWEAVERS MEWS
7 LADYWELL MEWS
JOHN BEVERLY MEWS 1
HOBBS HILL 2
CLIPSTONE CT 3
EVISON CT 4
EDINBURGH CL
JESUS HOSPITAL
VICKERS CL
MAGELLAN CL
TEBBUTT CL
SCOTT AVE
CECIL ST
LITTLEWOOD ST
SHARMAN WAY
Slade Brook
Orton
Bay House Farm
Manor Farm
MAIN ST
Orton Lodge
Thorpe Malsor Resr
The Cedar House
Three Chimneys
Loddington
Uplands Farm
Loddington Hall
PH
Prim Sch
ORTON RD
RICHARDSONS LA
HARRINGTON RD
CRANSLEY RD
MAWSLEY LA
HALL GDNS
Nus Hill Lodge
Cransley Resr
80
81
82

69
89

52 72

Glenn Spinney
GLENDON RD
Glendon Hall Cottages
Glendon Hall
NN14
Oddstones
Bunkers Hill Farm
Glen Hill Farm
Woodfield Farm
New Wood
Glendon Wood
Brookside Spinney
Slade Brook
Hill Spinnies
Rothwell Lodge Farm
VIOLET LA
Middle Lodge
Top Lodge
Rothwell Grange Farm
ROTHWELL GRANGE COTTS
ROTHWELL GRANGE CT
KETTERING RD
The Woodland
Rothwell Grange
Sewage Works
ROTHWELL RD
Wyatt's Plantation
Glebe Farm
Pottedbrig Spinney
GLEN BAULK RD
Potted Brig
A43
Motel
Crem
A4300
NN16
Thorpe Malsor
Allot Gdns
THE SQUARE
SHORT LA
CHURCH WAY
Thorpe Malsor Hall
NN14
Brooklands Farm
Breakmill Spinney
Northfield Farm
EAGLE LA
NORTHFIELD RD
Brocks Spinney
Cransley Resr
Bottom Lodge Homestead
Bottom Lodge Farm
A14
Wren Spinney Com Specl Sch
NN15
FURNACE LA
TELFORD WAY
HENSON CL
Vernon Ct
Henson Pk
Adam Bsns Ctr
TORRIDGE CL
LINNELL WAY
RILEY RD
WYNDHAM WAY
HENSON WAY
Ind Est
TELFORD WAY
ENTERPRISE CL
Kingsthorne Distribution Pk
ROBINSON WAY
Centre 2000
BARTLEY DR
ROBINSON CL
A6 Bsns Ctr
BARON AVE
Ind Est
KETTERING
WINTERBURN CT
WARREN HILL
B5323
HAWESWATER RD
GARRARD WAY
BUSHACRE
Express Pk
POPPY FIELDS
ROTHWELL RD
A4300
LANGSETT CL 1
CARSINGTON CL 2
LADYBOWER CL 3
THIRLMERE CL 4
THIRLMERE FLATS 5
BUTTERMERE CL
NASEBY HO
ULLSWATER RD
MAWSLEY CRES
Kettering General
GIPSY LA
CONISTON RD
WINDERMERE RD
DERWENT CRES
GRASMERE RD
BOWHILL
WESTOVER RD
Prim Sch
B5323
WESTHILL DR
WESTHILL CL
A6013
WESTWAY
WEST FURLONG
NORTHAMPTON RD
HALL LA
Prep Sch
GREENFIELD AVE

90 72

71
53

Weekley Hall Wood
Cid Wood
NN14
Glendon Lodge
Weekley Hall Farm
Burdyke
Upper Farm
Weekley
NN16
Allot Gdns
Well Cottage
Montagu Sch
One Acre House
Kettering Town FC
Recn Gd
Park Jun Sch
Superstore
Cunliffe Rd Ind Est
Northfield Point
Avondale Jun & Inf Schs
Allot Gdns
KETTERING
The Bsns Exchange
Superstore
The Mall Newlands Ctr
Ind Est
Prim Sch
Allot Gdns
NN15
Cemy
Mus Liby
Ise Com Coll
Henry Gotch Prim Sch
Kingsley Sch
Recn Gd
Kettering
St Mary's
River Ise

B1
1 HAZELWOOD CT
2 OAKTREE CT
3 PICCADILLY BLDGS

B2
1 MARTHA WALLIS CT
2 CAREY HO
3 WADCROFT
4 BELLFOUNDRY LA
5 WALKER'S LA
6 MEADOW CT
7 NEW BLDGS
8 WESTFIELD HO
9 GOADBY'S YD
10 MARKET STREET MEWS
11 BRIDEWELL LA
12 LAHNSTEIN CT
13 CROWN APARTMENTS
14 CRISPIN PL
15 MEETING LA
16 EBENEZER PL
17 BRITISH LA
18 LEATHERLAND CT
19 ANGEL YD
20 DALKEITH AVE
21 BRIDEWELL HO

71

C2
1 ARTHUR'S WAY
2 GLOUCESTER CL
3 ALBERT ST
4 TUDOR CT
5 MILL ROAD PAS
6 NEWMAN ST
7 GLADSTONE CT
8 CHANNING ST
9 HARCOURT ST

91

C2
10 VICTORIA CT
11 CHAPMANS CT
12 ST PETER'S MEWS

C3
1 Wellington Wks
2 WELDON ST
3 VERMONT STANDING
4 THE COURTYARD

C4
1 WOODLANDS CT
2 BLOSSOM CT
3 MILL GREENE CT
4 HAVELOCK HO

54
74
A
B
C
D
E
F
STAMFORD RD A43
Porters Lodge
Keeper's Lodge
Boughton Park
Boughton House
Grafton Strip
Warkton Common
The Wilderness
Star Pond
Boughton Home Farm
Acreland Farm
Wilderness Spinney
Meml
River Ise
NN16
NN14
Moorfield Farm
Warkton
PO
Fedwells Farm
Cinquefoil Lodge
Warkton Lodge
WARKTON LA
NN15
ST BARTHOLOMEW'S CL
ST CATHARINE'S RD
ST CHRISTOPHER'S CL
ST JOSEPH'S CL
ST PHILIP'S CL
ST BARNABAS CL
ST STEPHEN'S RD
ST SAVIOUR'S RD
ST ANNE'S RD
ST FRANCIS' CL
ST MATTHEW'S RD
DEEBLE RD
ST CHAD'S CL
ST GILES' CL
1 ST SIMON'S CL
2 ST AUGUSTINE'S CL
3 ST ALBAN'S CL
4 ST MARK'S CL
The Poplars
8
7
81
6
5
80
4
3
79
2
1
78
89
90
91
92
74

73 55

A
B
C
D
E
F
8
7
81
6
5
80
4
3
79
2
1
78
92
93
94
Round Green
Long Lown Wood
Grafton Park Wood
Ekens' Copse
Freer Wood
Little Green Wood
Park Lodge
Keeper's Cottage
Sale Hill Wood
Grafton Park Farm
PO
Grafton Underwood
Whitehouse Farm
The Manor House
NN14
Kirtley Barn
Kirtley Coppice
Sewage Works
Cranford Wood
Glebe Farm
Bushy Covert
SLIPTON LA
GORDON TERR
HIGH ST
THE HOMESTEAD

73 93

56
76
A
B
C
D
E
F
8
7
81
6
5
80
4
3
79
2
1
78
95
96
97
94
76
Glebe Farm
A6116
Round Lown Wood
New Lodge
Harper's Brook
Slipton Lodge
SUDBOROUGH RD
MAIN ST
MILL LA
PH
ROBB'S LA
ALDWINCLE RD
Alley Farm
MORDAUNT CL
DRAYTON RD
WOODFORD LA
Lowick
NN14
Drayton Park
Drayton Dairy Farm
Drayton House
Home Farm
Lady Grove
Colpman's Farm
CHURCH LA
Slipton
PH
SLIPTON LA
Huxloe Lodge
Islip Lodge
Manor Farm
HIGH ST
THE GREEN
PANTERS LA
Twywell
LOWER ST
PH
KETTERING RD
Ind Est
A14
KETTERING RD

75
57

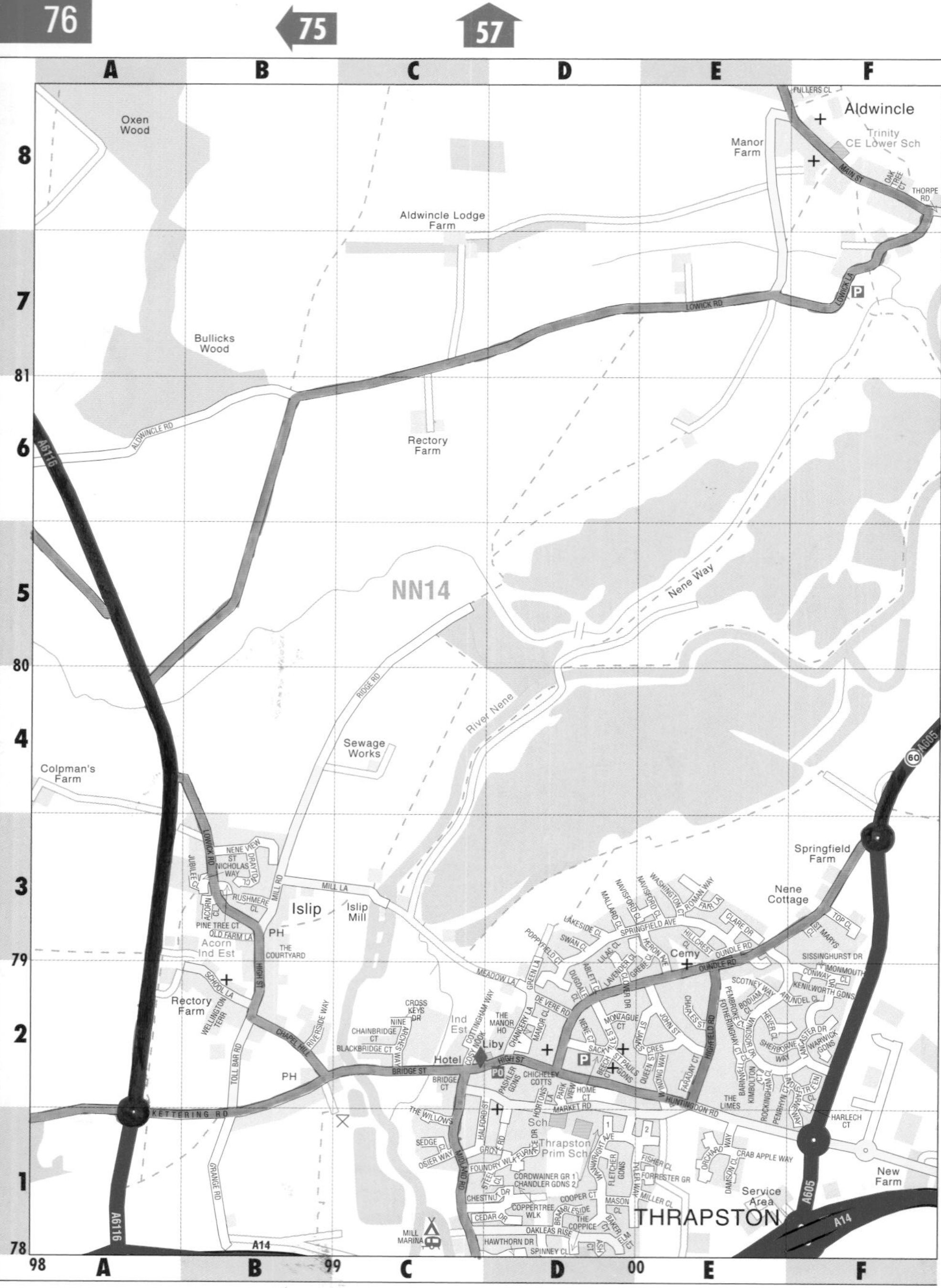
A
B
C
D
E
F
8
7
81
6
5
80
4
3
79
2
1
78
98
99
00
Oxen Wood
Aldwincle
Trinity CE Lower Sch
Manor Farm
FULLERS CL
MAIN ST
OAK TREE CT
THORPE RD
Aldwincle Lodge Farm
LOWICK RD
LOWICK LA
Bullicks Wood
ALDWINCLE RD
A6116
Rectory Farm
NN14
Nene Way
River Nene
RIDGE RD
Sewage Works
Colpman's Farm
A605
Springfield Farm
Nene Cottage
LOWICK RD
NENE VIEW
ST NICHOLAS WAY
DRAYTON CL
JUBILEE CL
RUSHMERE CL
ACORN CL
MILL RD
MILL LA
Islip
Islip Mill
PINE TREE CT
OLD FARM LA
PH
Acorn Ind Est
THE COURTYARD
SCHOOL LA
Rectory Farm
WELLINGTON TERR
HIGH ST
CHAPEL HILL
RIVERSIDE WAY
TOLL BAR RD
PH
KETTERING RD
GRANGE RD
A14
CROSS KEYS DR
NINE ARCHES WAY
CHAINBRIDGE CT
BLACKBRIDGE CT
BRIDGE ST
BRIDGE CT
Hotel
Liby
Ind Est
COTTINGHAM WAY
THE MANOR HO
MEADOW LA
GREEN LA
CHANCERY LA
MANOR CL
DE VERE RD
HIGH ST
PO
PASHLER GDNS
CHICHELEY COTTS
HORTONS LA
PARK VIEW
HOME CT
MARKET RD
THE WILLOWS
HALFORD ST
SEDGE CL
OSIER WAY
Sch
Thrapston Prim Sch
FOUNDRY WLK
CORDWAINER GR
CHANDLER GDNS
COOPER CT
COPPERTREE WLK
CEDAR DR
CHESTNUT DR
MIDLAND RD
OAKLEAS RISE
HAWTHORN DR
SPINNEY CL
THE COPPICE
MILL MARINA
WASHINGTON CT
ROMAN WAY
FAR LA
NAVISFORD CL
MALLARD CL
LAKESIDE CL
SPRINGFIELD AVE
SWAN CL
POPPYFIELD CL
HILLCREST
CLARE DR
OUNDLE RD
Cemy
LILAC CL
LAVENDER CL
HERON AVE
DUGDALE CL
CLOVER DR
MONTAGUE CT
JOHN ST
CHARLES ST
HIGHFIELD RD
QUEEN ST
ST PAULS
ST JAMES
CRES
WINNING WAY
FARADAY CT
HUNTINGDON RD
FOTHERINGHAY CT
PEMBROKE CT
SCOTNEY WAY
BODIAM CL
HEVER CL
WINDSOR DR
KIMBOLTON CT
ROCKINGHAM CL
PENHRYN CL
SHERBORNE WAY
LANCASTER DR
WARWICK GDNS
KENILWORTH GDNS
ARUNDEL CL
CONWAY CL
MONMOUTH
SISSINGHURST DR
TOP CL
ST MARYS
THE LIMES
HARLECH CT
ORCHARD WAY
CRAB APPLE WAY
DAMSON CL
FISHER CL
FORRESTER GR
TYLER WAY
MILLER CL
MASON CL
BAKER CL
ELM CT
FLETCHER GDNS
WAINWRIGHT AVE
THRAPSTON
Service Area
A605
A14
New Farm
60

75
95

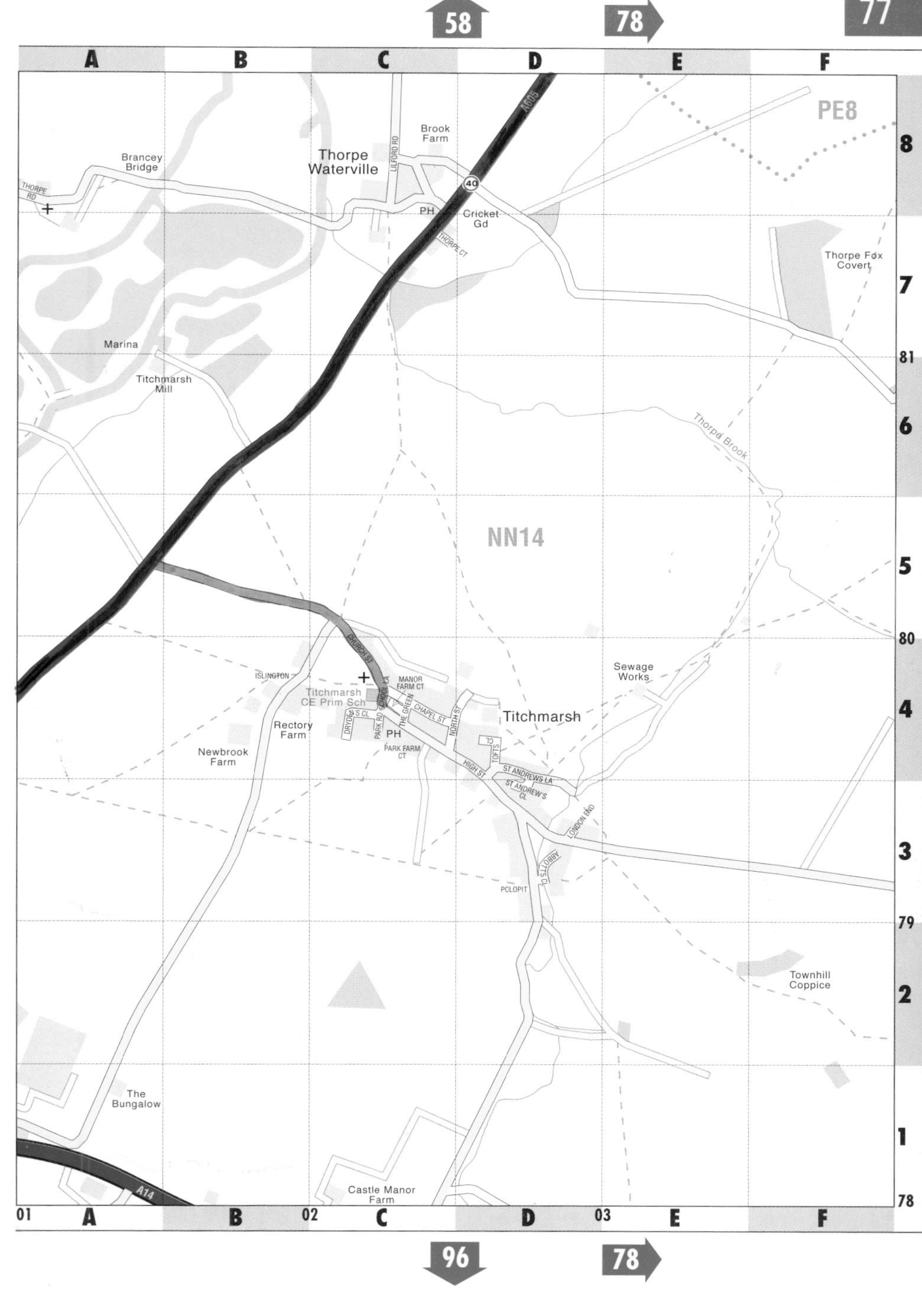
58
78
A
B
C
D
E
F
PE8
Brook Farm
Brancey Bridge
Thorpe Waterville
LILFORD RD
A605
40
THORPE RD
PH
Cricket Gd
THORPE CT
Thorpe Fox Covert
Marina
Titchmarsh Mill
Thorpe Brook
NN14
Sewage Works
ISLINGTON
CHURCH ST
MANOR FARM CT
SCHOOL LA
THE GREEN
CHAPEL ST
NORTH ST
Titchmarsh CE Prim Sch
Titchmarsh
DRYDEN'S CL
PARK RD
PH
Rectory Farm
Newbrook Farm
PARK FARM CT
TOFTS CL
HIGH ST
ST ANDREWS LA
ST ANDREW'S CL
LONDON END
ABBOTTS CL
PCLOPIT
Townhill Coppice
The Bungalow
A14
Castle Manor Farm
8
7
81
6
5
80
4
3
79
2
1
78
01
02
03
96
78

77
59

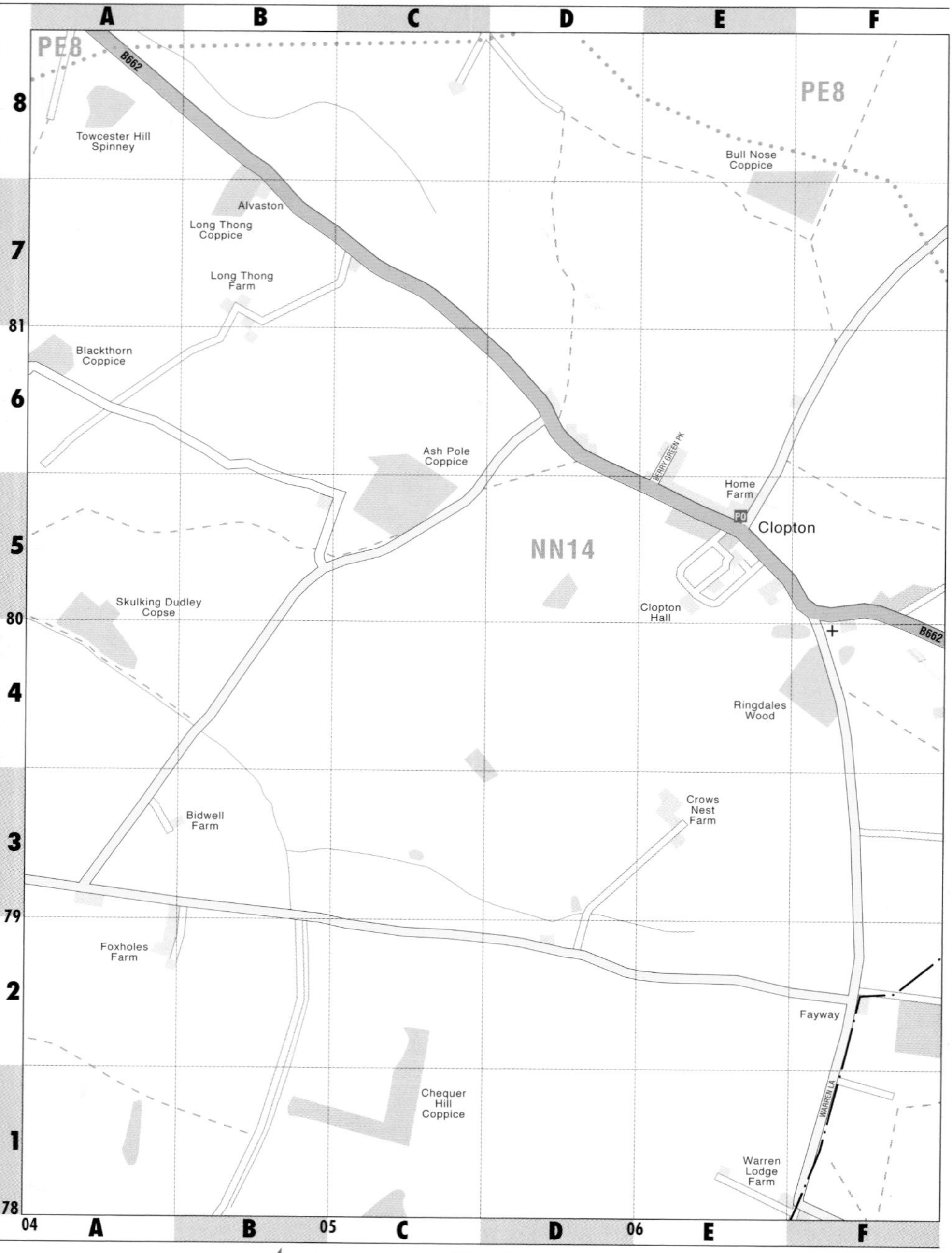

A B C D E F

8
7
81
6
5
80
4
3
79
2
1
78

PE8
B662
Towcester Hill Spinney
Alvaston
Long Thong Coppice
Long Thong Farm
Blackthorn Coppice
Bull Nose Coppice
Ash Pole Coppice
BERRY GREEN PK
Home Farm
PO
Clopton
NN14
Skulking Dudley Copse
Clopton Hall
B662
Ringdales Wood
Bidwell Farm
Crows Nest Farm
Foxholes Farm
Fayway
Chequer Hill Coppice
WARREN LA
Warren Lodge Farm

04 A B 05 C D 06 E F

77
97

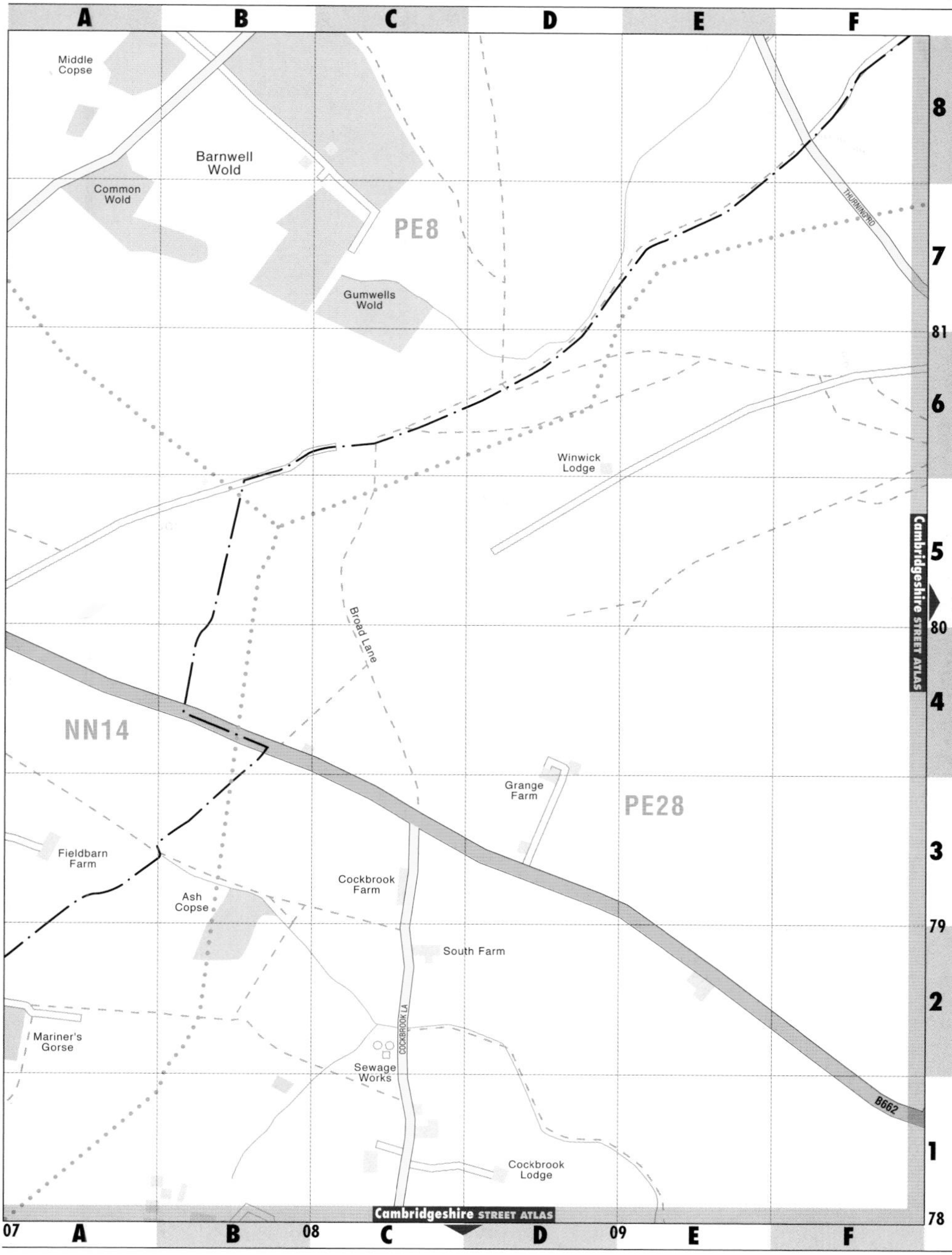

60

A B C D E F

8
7
81
6
5
80
4
3
79
2
1
78

Middle Copse
Barnwell Wold
Common Wold
PE8
Gumwells Wold
THURNING RD
Winwick Lodge
Broad Lane
NN14
Grange Farm
PE28
Fieldbarn Farm
Ash Copse
Cockbrook Farm
South Farm
COCKBROOK LA
Mariner's Gorse
Sewage Works
B662
Cockbrook Lodge

Cambridgeshire STREET ATLAS
Cambridgeshire STREET ATLAS

07 A B 08 C D 09 E F

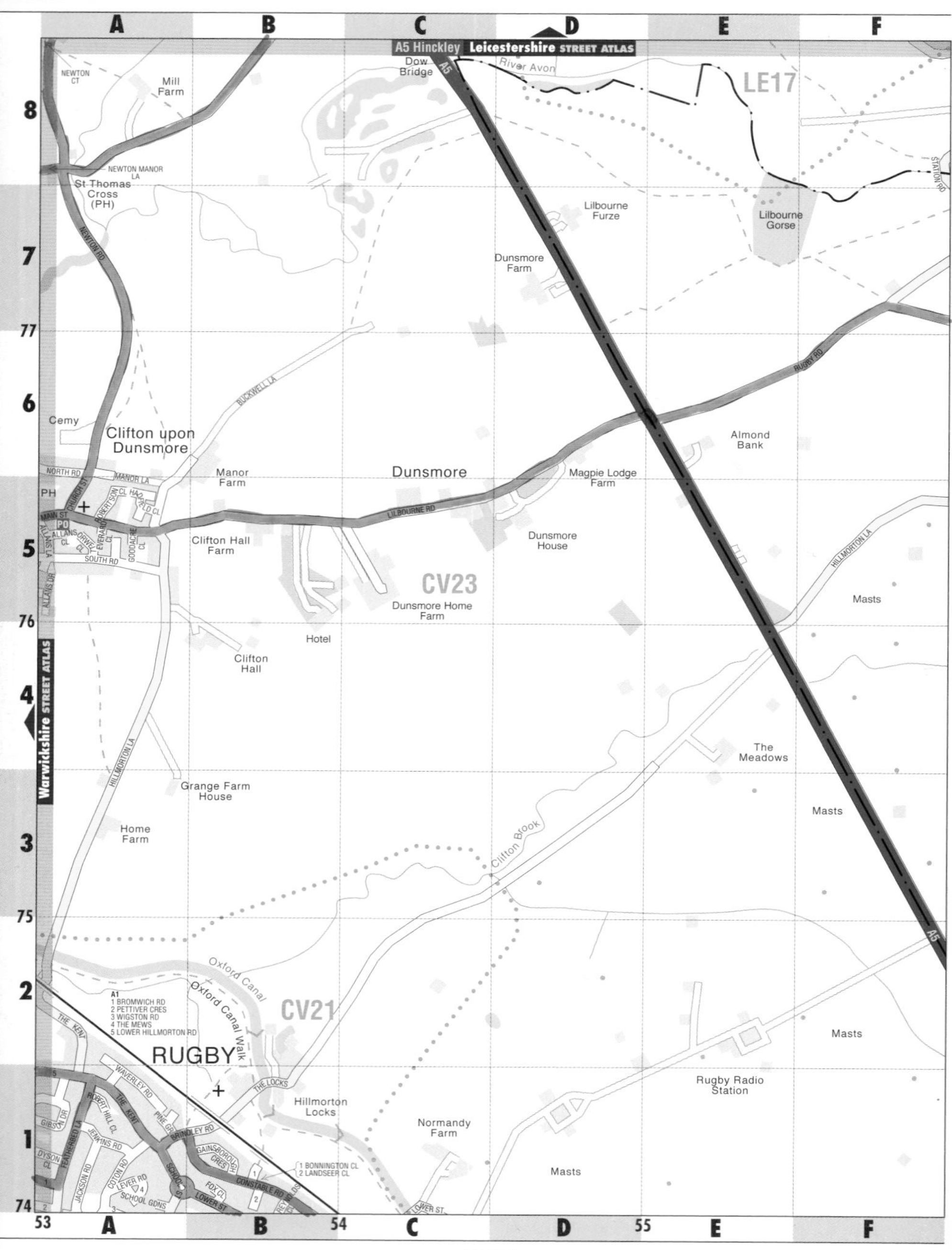
A5 Hinckley
Leicestershire STREET ATLAS
Warwickshire STREET ATLAS
LE17
CV23
CV21
Dow Bridge
River Avon
Newton Ct
Mill Farm
Newton Manor La
St Thomas Cross (PH)
Newton Rd
Lilbourne Furze
Lilbourne Gorse
Station Rd
Dunsmore Farm
Rugby Rd
Buckwell La
Cemy
Clifton upon Dunsmore
North Rd
Manor La
Manor Farm
Dunsmore
Magpie Lodge Farm
Almond Bank
PH
Church St
Main St
PO
Allans Cl
Allans La
Allans Dr
Orwell Cl
Everard Cl
Robertson Cl
Goodacre Cl
South Rd
Lilbourne Rd
Clifton Hall Farm
Dunsmore House
Hillmorton La
Masts
Dunsmore Home Farm
Hotel
Clifton Hall
The Meadows
Grange Farm House
Home Farm
Clifton Brook
A5
Oxford Canal
Oxford Canal Walk
A1
1 BROMWICH RD
2 PETTIVER CRES
3 WIGSTON RD
4 THE MEWS
5 LOWER HILLMORTON RD
The Kent
RUGBY
Waverley Rd
Robert Hill Cl
Pine Gr
Brindley Rd
The Locks
Hillmorton Locks
Gibson Dr
Featherbed La
Jenkins Rd
Dyson Cl
Jackson Rd
Coton Rd
Lever Rd
School Gdns
Gainsborough Cres
Fox Cl
Constable Rd
Lower St
1 BONNINGTON CL
2 LANDSEER CL
Normandy Farm
Rugby Radio Station
A B C D E F
8 7 6 5 4 3 2 1
77 76 75 74
53 54 55

62 82

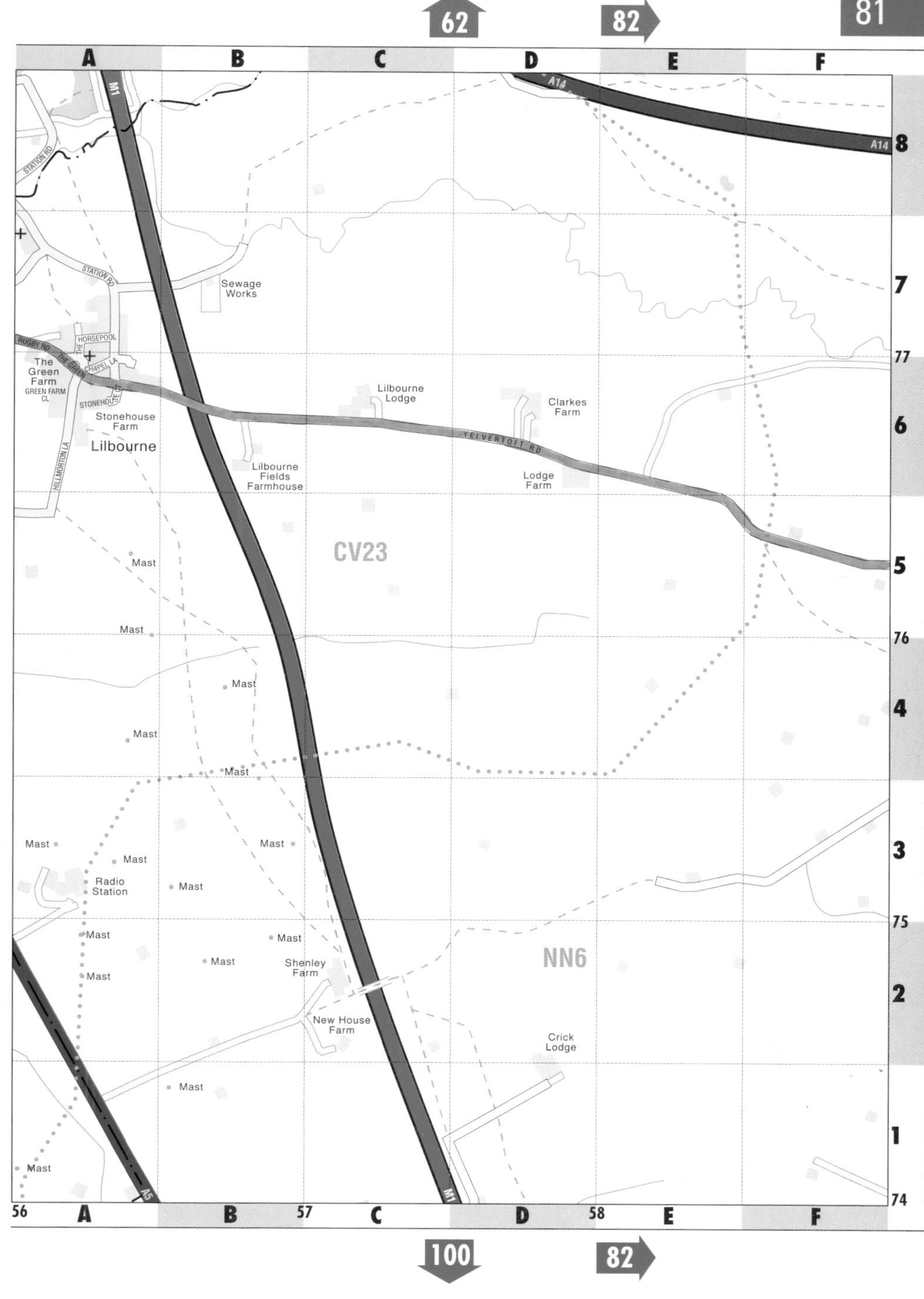

A B C D E F
M1
A14
STATION RD
Sewage Works
RUGBY RD
THE GREEN
THE HORSEPOOL
CHAPEL LA
The Green Farm
GREEN FARM CL
STONEHOUSE CT
Stonehouse Farm
Lilbourne
HILLMORTON LA
Lilbourne Lodge
Clarkes Farm
YELVERTOFT RD
Lilbourne Fields Farmhouse
Lodge Farm
CV23
Mast
Radio Station
Shenley Farm
New House Farm
NN6
Crick Lodge
A5
8
7
77
6
5
76
4
3
75
2
1
74
56
57
58

100 82

81
63

A
B
C
D
E
F
8
7
77
6
5
76
4
3
75
2
1
74
59
60
61
Stanford Mear
A14
Pages Lodge Farm
Jurassic Way
Manor Farm
Manor Farm
Rectory Farm
Clay Coton
Willow Farm Cottages
Blackdown Farm
Buffs Farm
Elkington Farm Cottage
THE PADDOCKS
YELVERTOFT RD
Yelvertoft Fieldside Covert
Mountain Barn
Sewage Works
BROOKSIDE CL 1
ORCHARD CL 2
BROOKSIDE MEWS 3
NN6
Hall
Yelvertoft Prim Sch
TARRYS END
SCHOOL LA
ASHWELLS LA
BRIDGEND
ELKINGTON RD
Yelvertoft
Glebe Farm
HILLMORTON LA
SCHOOL CL
KINGS LA
SWINNERTONS LA
ELKINS CL
MERRYCOT LA
KIRKHAMS CL
Grand Union Canal
Winwick Manor Farm
HIGH ST
PH
STYLES PL
WARDS LA
PO
Cemy
Grand Union Canal
CRICK RD
Flint Hill Farm
New House Farm
Winwick Grange

81
101

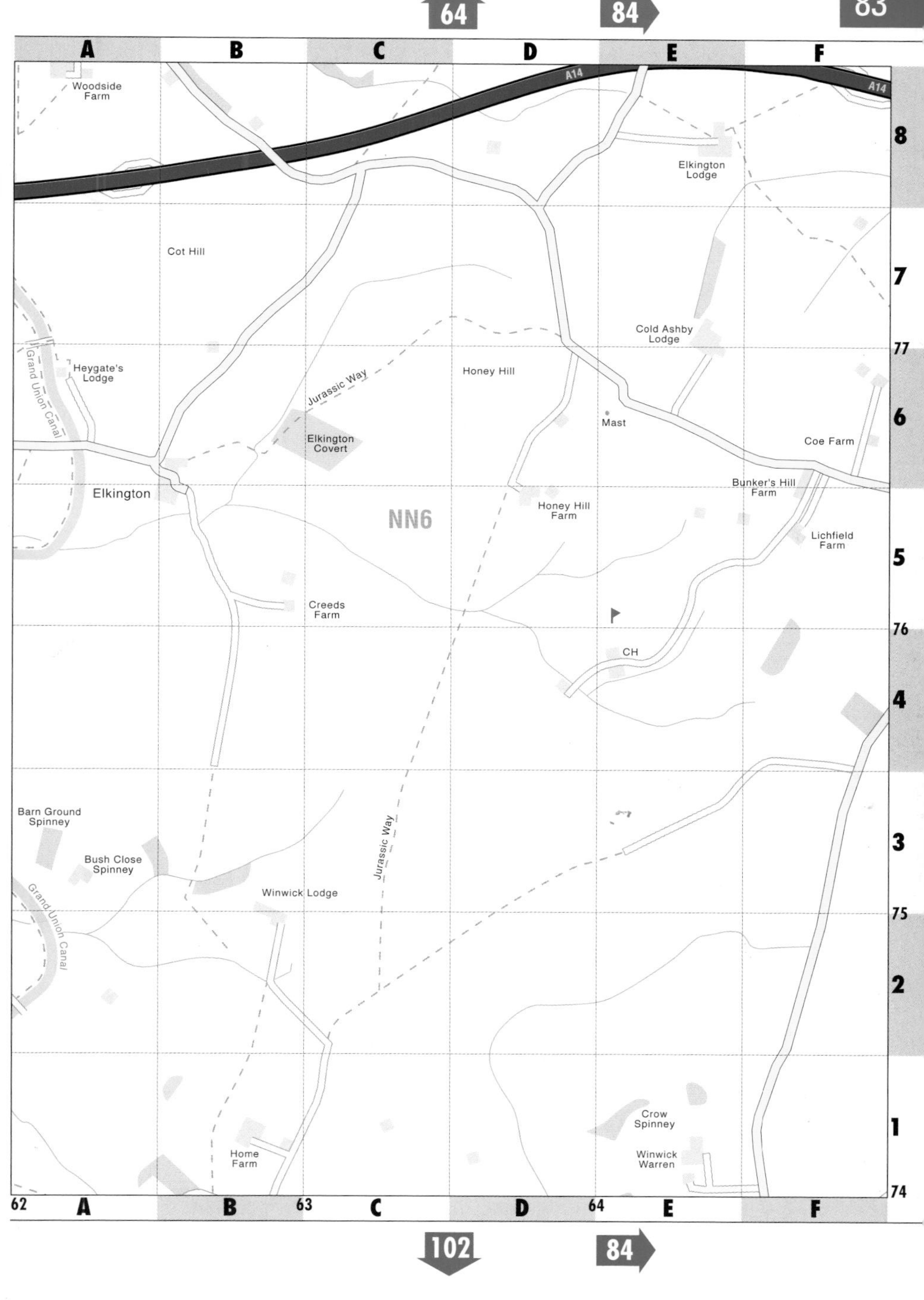
64
84
A
B
C
D
E
F
A14
A14
Woodside Farm
8
Elkington Lodge
Cot Hill
7
Cold Ashby Lodge
77
Heygate's Lodge
Grand Union Canal
Jurassic Way
Honey Hill
Mast
6
Elkington Covert
Coe Farm
Elkington
Bunker's Hill Farm
Honey Hill Farm
NN6
Lichfield Farm
5
Creeds Farm
76
CH
4
Barn Ground Spinney
3
Bush Close Spinney
Jurassic Way
Grand Union Canal
Winwick Lodge
75
2
Crow Spinney
1
Home Farm
Winwick Warren
74
62
63
64
102
84

83
65

A
B
C
D
E
F
8
7
77
6
5
76
4
3
75
2
1
74
65
66
67
A14
A5199
Naseby
Resr
Fulbrook
Farm
Reservoir
Farm
STANFORD RD
STANFORD CL
BRIDLE LA
WEST HADDON RD
MAIN ST
CRABTREE LA
CHURCH LA
PH
PARK
SPINNEY CL
THORNBY RD
NN6
Lodge Farm
Cold Ashby
Park
Spinney
Thornby
Hall
PH
COLD ASHBY RD
NASEBY RD
ST HELENS
CL
CHURCH
LA
STONE HOUSE
MEWS
Thornby House
Farm
Thornby
Doebank
Spinney
Lovells
Lodge
Firetail
Covert
Firetail
Thornby
Grange
Grange
Farm
Rabbit
Spinney
Nortoft
Lodge
Ashbylane
Farm
West Lodge

83
103

66
86

A
B
C
D
E
F
Reservoir Farm
SCHOOL LA
CHURCH ST
GYNWELL
HIGH ST
KNIGHTS HILL
BAKEHOUSE RISE
PO
PH
FAIRFAX RISE
SKIPPONS CT
NUTCOTE
THORNBY RD
CATTON CL
Naseby
Cromwell Farm
Brankley Farm
Hospital Farm
NASEBY RD
Naseby Battle & Farm Mus
Oak Farm
The Grange Farm
Purser's Hills
NN6
Vale Farm
New Covert
Old Covert
Stubb Purlieu
Calender Farm
Cott Hill Spinney
Cottesbrooke Park
Hanwell Spinney
A5199
Foalfoot Spinney
8
7
77
6
5
76
4
3
75
2
1
74
68
69
70

104
86

85
67

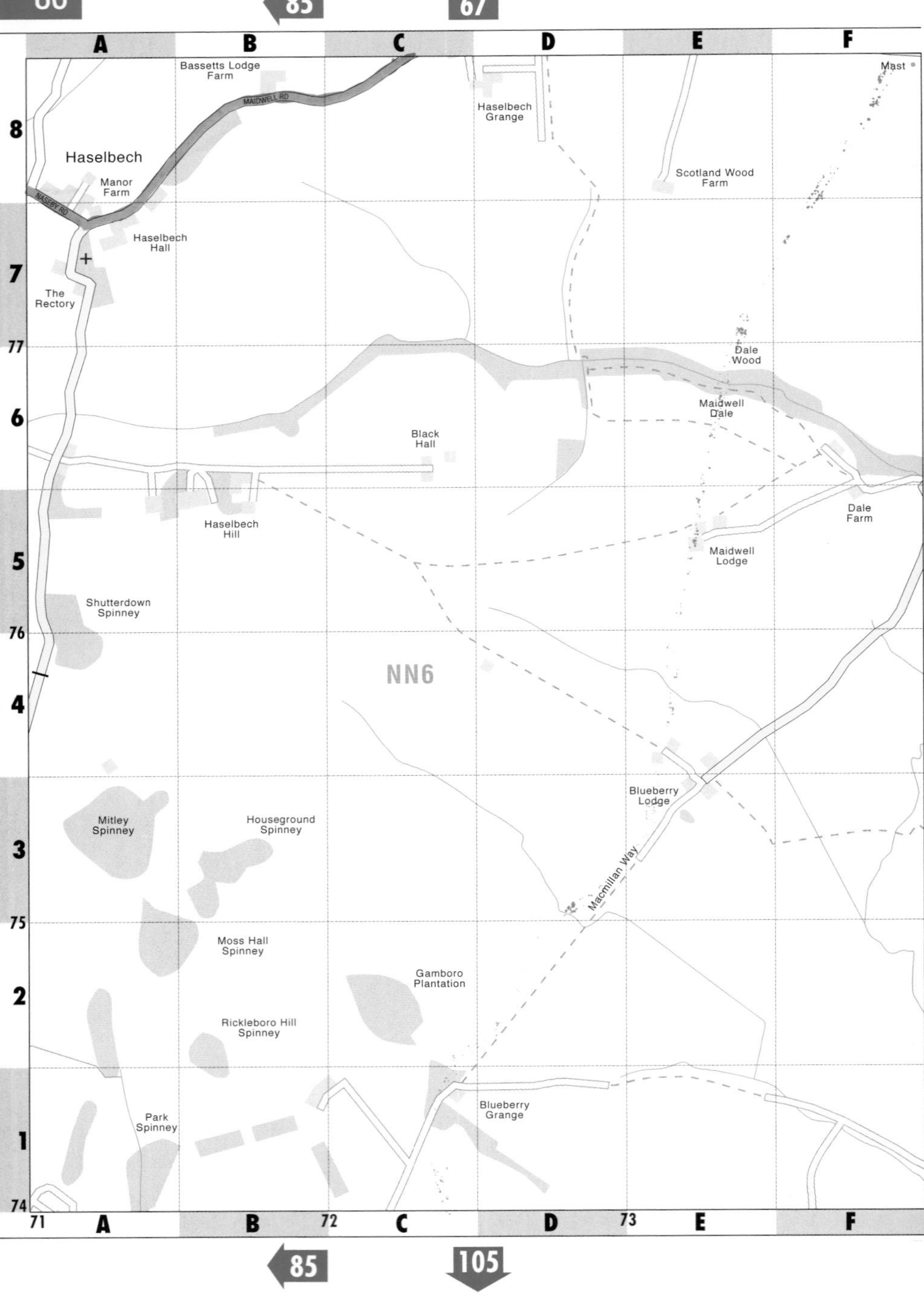
A
B
C
D
E
F
8
7
77
6
5
76
4
3
75
2
1
74
71
72
73
Bassetts Lodge Farm
MAIDWELL RD
Haselbech Grange
Mast
Haselbech
Manor Farm
NASEBY RD
Scotland Wood Farm
Haselbech Hall
The Rectory
Dale Wood
Maidwell Dale
Black Hall
Haselbech Hill
Dale Farm
Maidwell Lodge
Shutterdown Spinney
NN6
Blueberry Lodge
Mitley Spinney
Houseground Spinney
Macmillan Way
Moss Hall Spinney
Gamboro Plantation
Rickleboro Hill Spinney
Blueberry Grange
Park Spinney

85
105

68
88

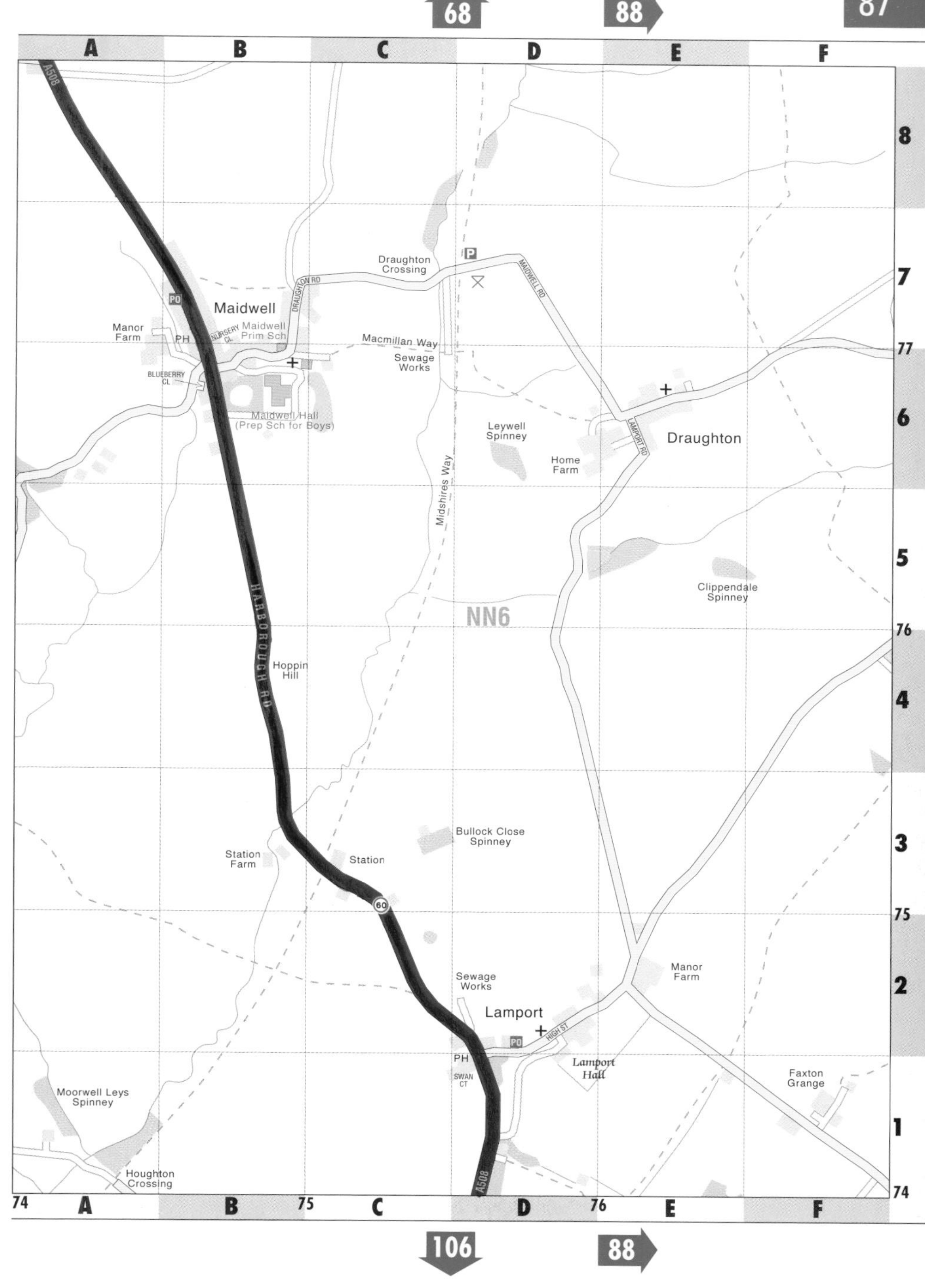
A
B
C
D
E
F
8
7
77
6
5
76
4
3
75
2
1
74
A508
Maidwell
PO
PH
Manor
Farm
NURSERY CL
Maidwell
Prim Sch
BLUEBERRY CL
Maidwell Hall
(Prep Sch for Boys)
DRAUGHTON RD
Draughton
Crossing
P
MAIDWELL RD
Macmillan Way
Sewage
Works
Leywell
Spinney
Home
Farm
LAMPORT RD
Draughton
Midshires Way
Clippendale
Spinney
NN6
HARBOROUGH RD
Hoppin
Hill
Bullock Close
Spinney
Station
Farm
Station
60
Sewage
Works
Lamport
Manor
Farm
HIGH ST
PO
PH
SWAN CT
Lamport
Hall
Faxton
Grange
Moorwell Leys
Spinney
Houghton
Crossing
A508
74
A
B
75
C
D
76
E
F

106
88

87
69

A
B
C
D
E
F
8
7
77
6
5
76
4
3
75
2
1
74
77
78
79
Foxhall Cottages
Loddington Lodge
Meml
Faxton Corner
Airfield (disused)
NN14
Bullock's Penn Spinney
Stonegrove Spinney
Loddington Coppice Farm
Loddington Coppice
Mawsley Wood
Short Wood
Claridge Spinney
Kites Hall Farm
Shortwood House
NN6
Faxton
Old Lodge
NN14
MILL LA

87
107

70
90

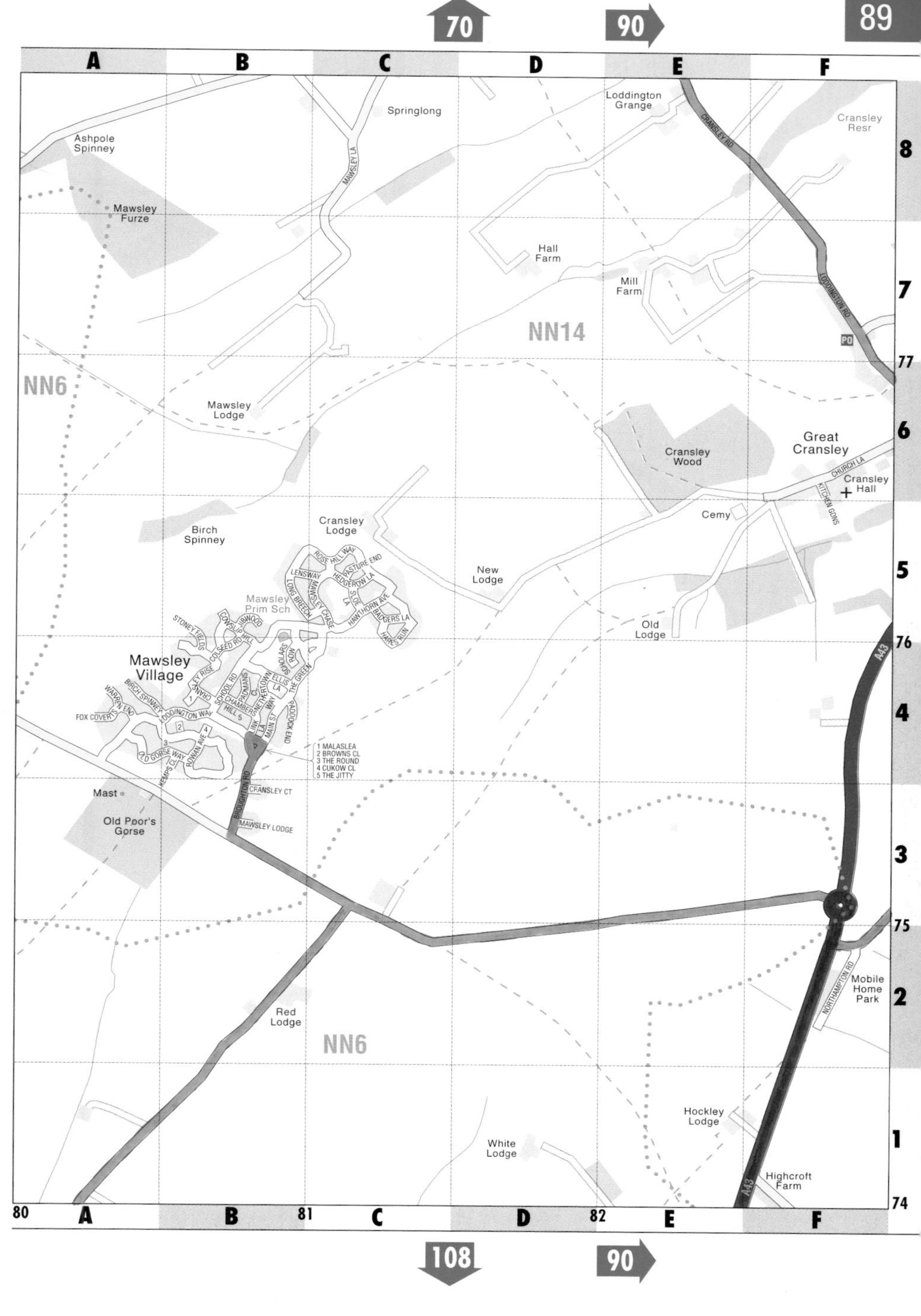
A
B
C
D
E
F
Springlong
Loddington Grange
Cransley Resr
Ashpole Spinney
Mawsley Furze
MAWSLEY LA
CRANSLEY RD
Hall Farm
Mill Farm
NN14
LODDINGTON RD
PO
NN6
Mawsley Lodge
Cransley Wood
Great Cransley
CHURCH LA
Cransley Hall
KITCHEN GDNS
Cemy
Birch Spinney
Cransley Lodge
New Lodge
Old Lodge
Mawsley Prim Sch
Mawsley Village
A43
1 MALASLEA
2 BROWNS CL
3 THE ROUND
4 CUKOW CL
5 THE JITTY
Mast
Old Poor's Gorse
BROUGHTON RD
CRANSLEY CT
MAWSLEY LODGE
NORTHAMPTON RD
Mobile Home Park
Red Lodge
NN6
Hockley Lodge
White Lodge
Highcroft Farm
8
7
77
6
5
76
4
3
75
2
1
74
80
81
82

108
90

89 71

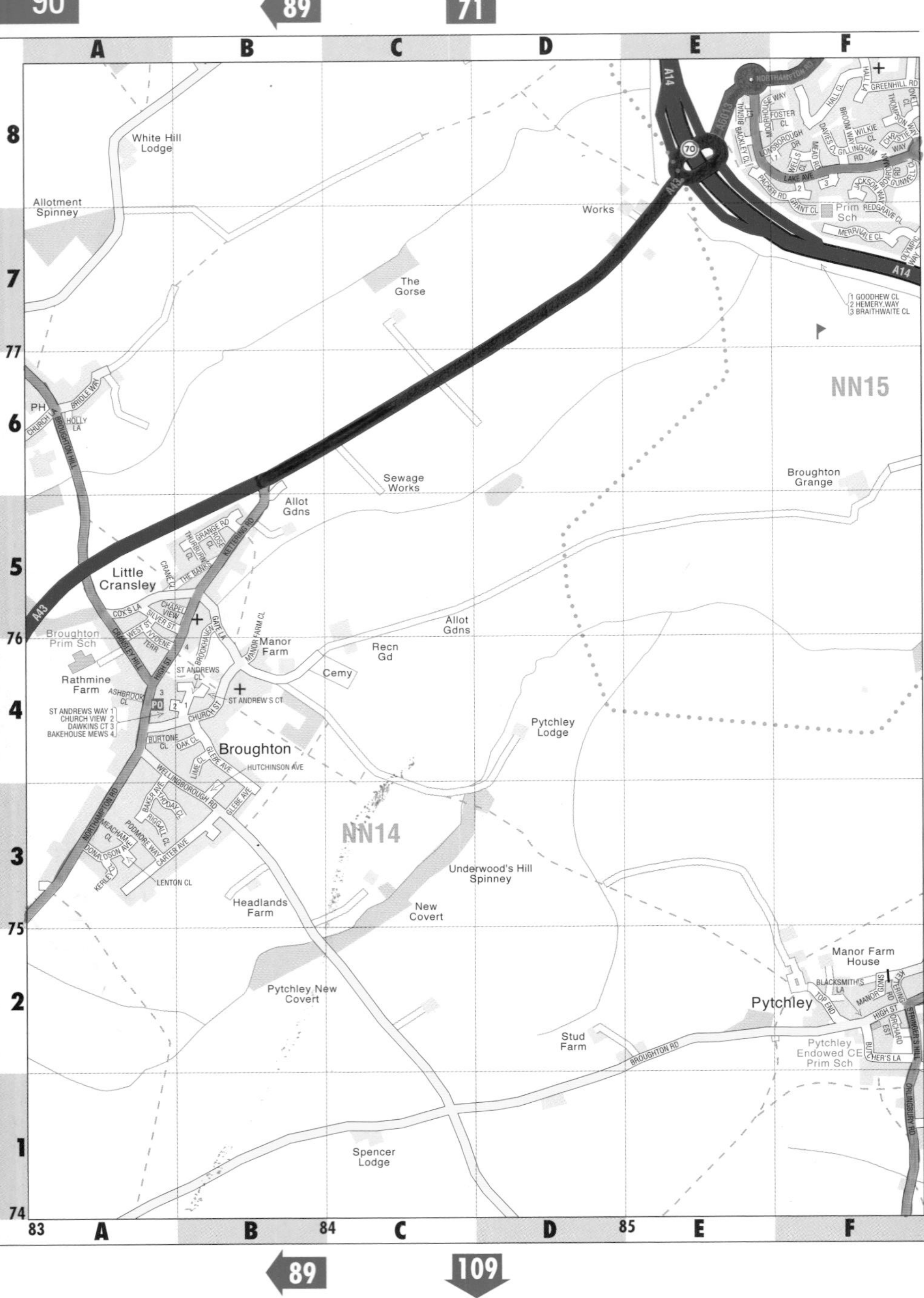

A B C D E F
8 7 77 6 5 76 4 3 75 2 1 74
83 84 85
White Hill Lodge
Allotment Spinney
Works
The Gorse
NN15
Sewage Works
Broughton Grange
Allot Gdns
Little Cransley
Broughton Prim Sch
Rathmine Farm
Manor Farm
Recn Gd
Cemy
Allot Gdns
Pytchley Lodge
Broughton
NN14
Underwood's Hill Spinney
New Covert
Headlands Farm
Pytchley New Covert
Manor Farm House
Pytchley
Pytchley Endowed CE Prim Sch
Stud Farm
Spencer Lodge
A14
A43
A6013
70
Prim Sch
1 GOODHEW CL
2 HEMERY WAY
3 BRAITHWAITE CL
ST ANDREWS WAY 1
CHURCH VIEW 2
DAWKINS CT 3
BAKEHOUSE MEWS 4
PH
PO
BROUGHTON RD
NORTHAMPTON RD
WELLINGBOROUGH RD
KETTERING RD
CRANSLEY HILL
BROUGHTON HILL
HIGH ST
CHURCH ST
ORLINGBURY RD
STRINGER'S HILL

89 109

72
92

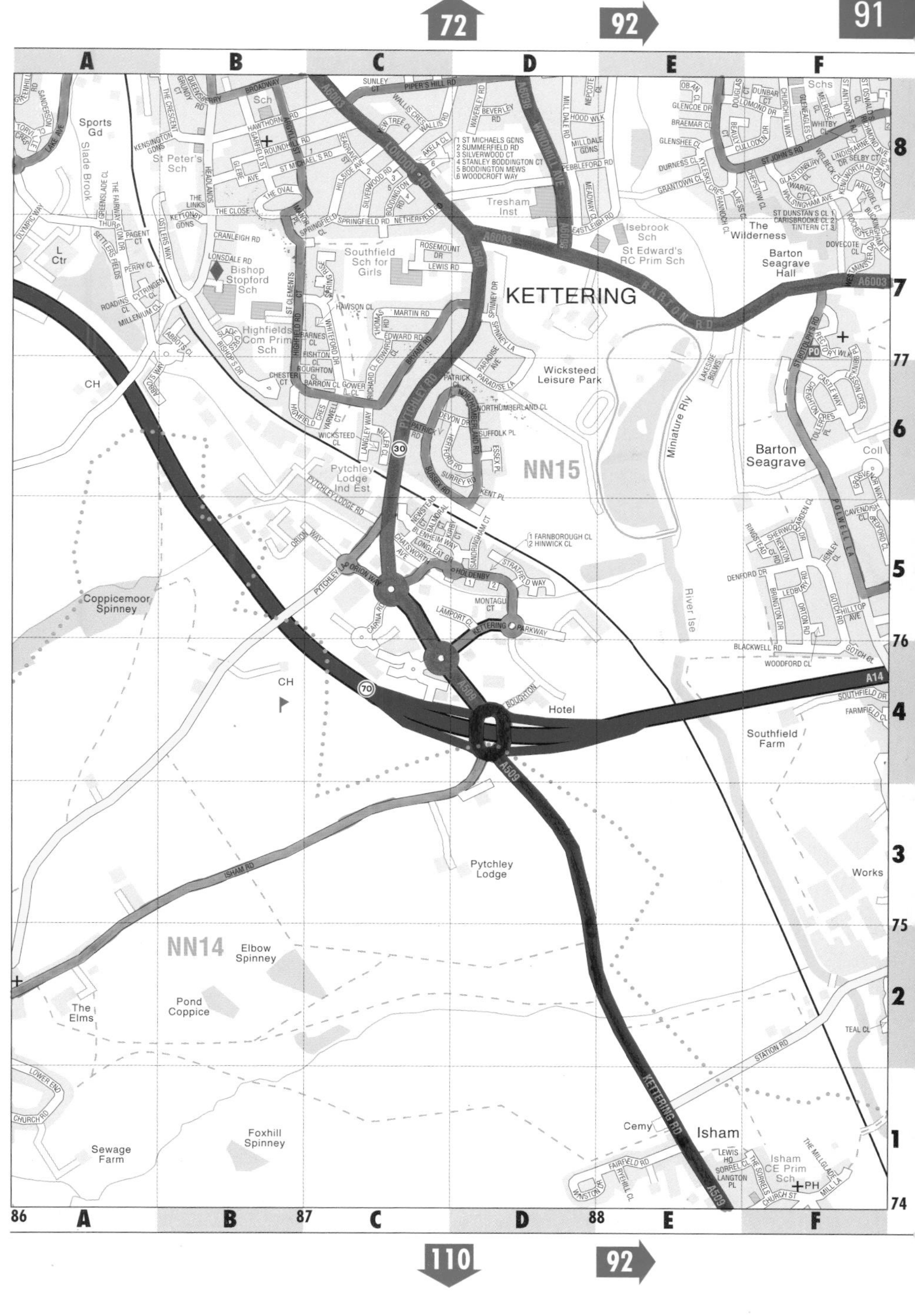
KETTERING
NN15
NN14
Sports Gd
Slade Brook
St Peter's Sch
Bishop Stopford Sch
Highfields Com Prim Sch
Southfield Sch for Girls
Tresham Inst
Isebrook Sch
St Edward's RC Prim Sch
The Wilderness
Barton Seagrave Hall
Wicksteed Leisure Park
Miniature Rly
Barton Seagrave
Coll
Pytchley Lodge Ind Est
River Ise
Coppicemoor Spinney
CH
L Ctr
Hotel
Southfield Farm
Pytchley Lodge
Works
Elbow Spinney
The Elms
Pond Coppice
Foxhill Spinney
Sewage Farm
Cemy
Isham
Isham CE Prim Sch
PH
PO
Schs
A6003
A6003
A509
A6003
A14
A509
KETTERING RD
ISHAM RD
STATION RD
BARTON RD
LONDON RD
WINDMILL AVE
PYTCHLEY RD
POLWELL LA
1 ST MICHAELS GDNS
2 SUMMERFIELD RD
3 SILVERWOOD CT
4 STANLEY BODDINGTON CT
5 BODDINGTON MEWS
6 WOODCROFT WAY
1 FARNBOROUGH CL
2 HINWICK CL
ST DUNSTAN'S CL 1
CARISBROOKE CL 2
TINTERN CT 3
A B C D E F
8 7 6 5 4 3 2 1
77 76 75 74
86 87 88

110
92

91
73

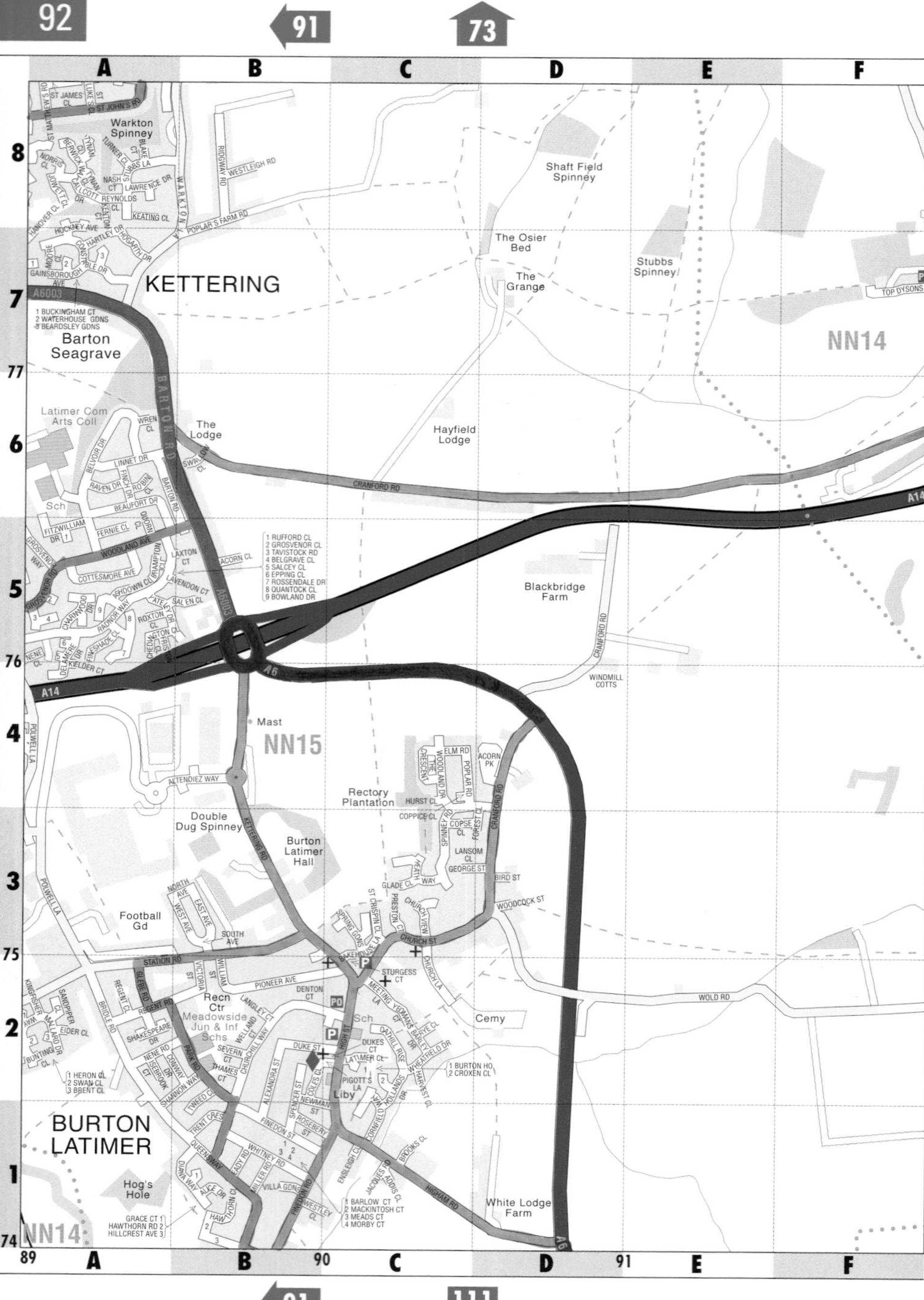
A
B
C
D
E
F
8
7
77
6
5
76
4
3
75
2
1
74
89
90
91
ST JAMES CL
ST JOHN'S RD
Warkton Spinney
WESTLEIGH RD
RIDGWAY RD
WARKTON LA
POPLAR'S FARM RD
KEATING CL
Shaft Field Spinney
The Osier Bed
The Grange
Stubbs Spinney
KETTERING
A6003
1 BUCKINGHAM CT
2 WATERHOUSE GDNS
3 BEARDSLEY GDNS
Barton Seagrave
TOP DYSONS
NN14
Latimer Com Arts Coll
The Lodge
Hayfield Lodge
BARTON RD
CRANFORD RD
A14
Sch
1 RUFFORD CL
2 GROSVENOR CL
3 TAVISTOCK RD
4 BELGRAVE CL
5 SALCEY CL
6 EPPING CL
7 ROSSENDALE DR
8 QUANTOCK CL
9 BOWLAND DR
ACORN CL
WOODLAND AVE
COTTESMORE AVE
Blackbridge Farm
WINDMILL COTTS
A6
Mast
NN15
ALTENDIEZ WAY
Rectory Plantation
Double Dug Spinney
KETTERING RD
Burton Latimer Hall
ELM RD
POPLAR RD
ACORN PK
HURST CL
COPPICE CL
COPSE CL
LANSOM CL
GEORGE ST
BIRD ST
WOODCOCK ST
Football Gd
CHURCH ST
STATION RD
PIONEER AVE
STURGESS CT
WOLD RD
Recn Ctr
Meadowside Jun & Inf Schs
Sch
Cemy
HIGH ST
1 HERON CL
2 SWAN CL
3 BRENT CL
1 BURTON HO
2 CROXEN CL
Liby
BURTON LATIMER
FINEDON ST
FINEDON RD
HIGHAM RD
Hog's Hole
White Lodge Farm
GRACE CT 1
HAWTHORN RD 2
HILLCREST AVE 3
1 BARLOW CT
2 MACKINTOSH CT
3 MEADS CT
4 MORBY CT

91
111

74
94

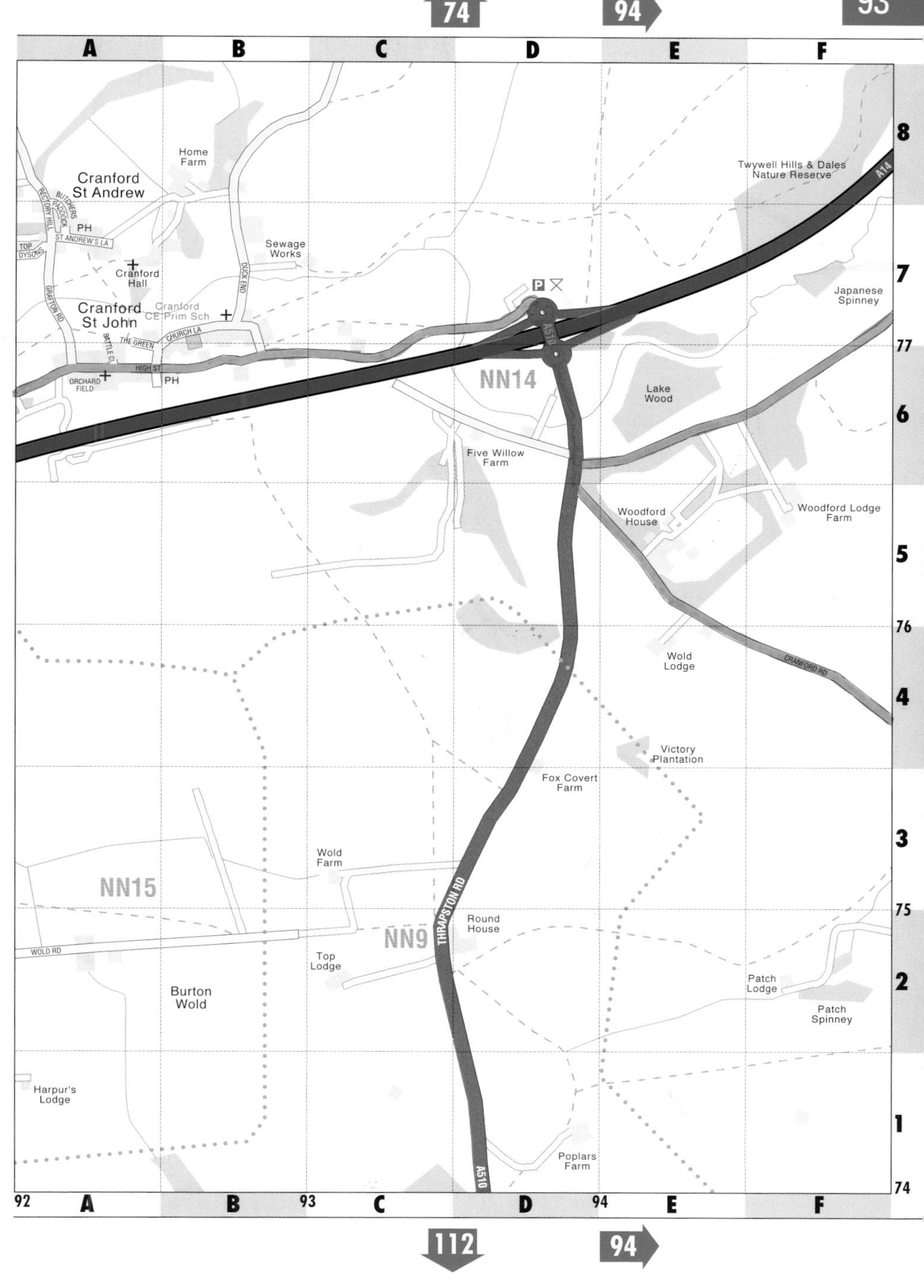
A
B
C
D
E
F
8
7
77
6
5
76
4
3
75
2
1
74
92
93
94
Cranford St Andrew
Home Farm
RECTORY HILL
BUTCHERS PADDOCK
PH
ST ANDREW'S LA
TOP DYSONS
Sewage Works
Cranford Hall
DUCK END
GRAFTON RD
Cranford St John
Cranford CE Prim Sch
BATTLE CL
THE GREEN
CHURCH LA
HIGH ST
ORCHARD FIELD
PH
A14
A510
Twywell Hills & Dales Nature Reserve
Japanese Spinney
NN14
Lake Wood
Five Willow Farm
Woodford House
Woodford Lodge Farm
Wold Lodge
CRANFORD RD
Victory Plantation
Fox Covert Farm
Wold Farm
NN15
THRAPSTON RD
Round House
NN9
WOLD RD
Top Lodge
Burton Wold
Patch Lodge
Patch Spinney
Harpur's Lodge
Poplars Farm
A510

112
94

93
75

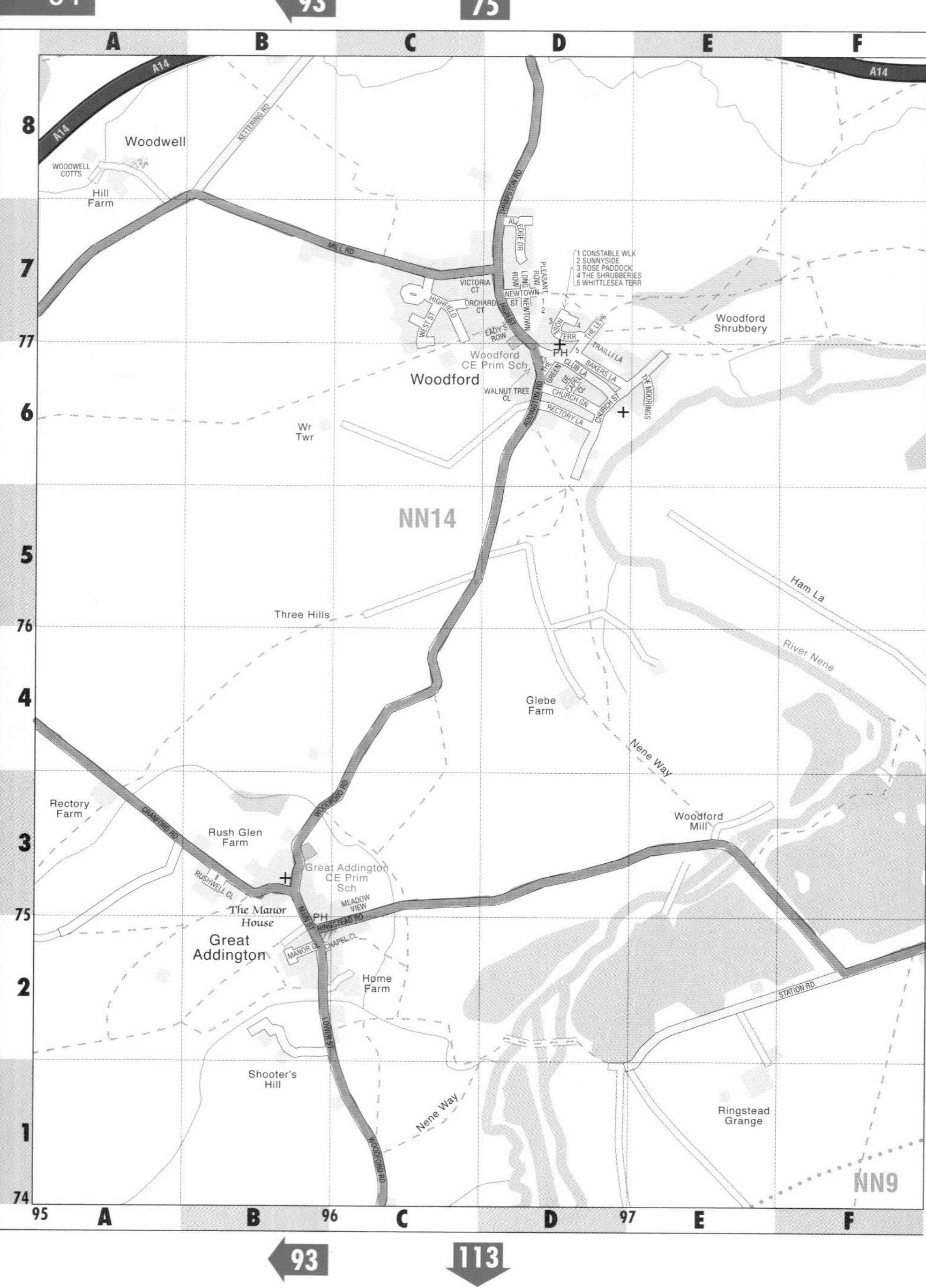
A
B
C
D
E
F
8
7
77
6
5
76
4
3
75
2
1
74
95
96
97
A14
Woodwell
WOODWELL COTTS
Hill Farm
KETTERING RD
MILL RD
THRAPSTON RD
ALEDGE DR
1 CONSTABLE WLK
2 SUNNYSIDE
3 ROSE PADDOCK
4 THE SHRUBBERIES
5 WHITTLESEA TERR
PLEASANT ROW
LONG ROW
VICTORIA CT
NEWTOWN
ST
ORCHARD CT
HIGHFIELD
WEST ST
HIGH ST
EADY'S ROW
ROSE TERR
THE LEYS
PH
TRAILLI LA
Woodford Shrubbery
Woodford CE Prim Sch
Woodford
THE GREEN
CLUB LA
BAKERS LA
DE CAPELL CL
CHURCH GN
WALNUT TREE CL
ADDINGTON RD
RECTORY LA
CHURCH ST
THE MOORINGS
Wr Twr
NN14
Ham La
Three Hills
River Nene
Glebe Farm
Nene Way
Rectory Farm
Rush Glen Farm
WOODFORD RD
GRANFORD RD
Woodford Mill
Great Addington CE Prim Sch
RUSHWELL CL
The Manor House
MEADOW VIEW
MAIN ST
RINGSTEAD RD
Great Addington
MANOR CL
CHAPEL CL
Home Farm
STATION RD
LOWER ST
Shooter's Hill
Ringstead Grange
NN9

93
113

76
96

A
B
C
D
E
F
A6116
A14
A45
HAWTHORN DR
MIDLAND RD
DENFORD RD
8
Woodford Grange
7
77
Nene Way
River Nene
6
Westfield Spinney
MEADOW LA
HIGH ST
PEG'S LA
FREEMAN'S LA
CHAPEL LA
DUCK END
SPINNEY RISE
CHILD'S ST
CHURCH LA
SCHOOL LA
PH
FRONT ST
BROWN'S LA
RIVERVIEW GDNS
Rose Hill Farm
Brawn's Spinney
Denford
RINGSTEAD RD
5
NN14
Newleys Farm
Vicarage Spinney
76
4
Allot Gdns
Tithe Farm
HAM LA
Brigg's Lodge Farm
Ringstead
NEWELL RD
BROOK WLK 1
THE GROVE 2
BRAMBLE CL 3
CHURCH WLK 4
PEACOCK DR
BURNELL CL
GREENBANK TERR
BATES AVE
NORTHFIELD AVE
BACK LA
PO
BRAYBROOKE CL
MOUNTBATTEN DR
ORCHARD CL
Ringstead Farm
3
Football Gd
BONSOR GDNS
CARLOW RD
HIGH ST
CHERRY ST
ROSEBERY ST
GLADSTONE ST
MEADOW CL
PH
CARLOW ST
TITHE CL
CHAPEL ST
CHURCH ST
PH
SPENCER ST
POUND CL
Raunds Lodge Farm
Kinewell Lake Nature Trail
KINEWELL CL
MIDDLEFIELD CL
P
Ringstead CE Prim Sch
75
STATION RD
KINGFISHER CL
Cemy
2
NN9
1
Blotts Barn
BROOKS RD
A45
74
98
99
00

114
96

95
77

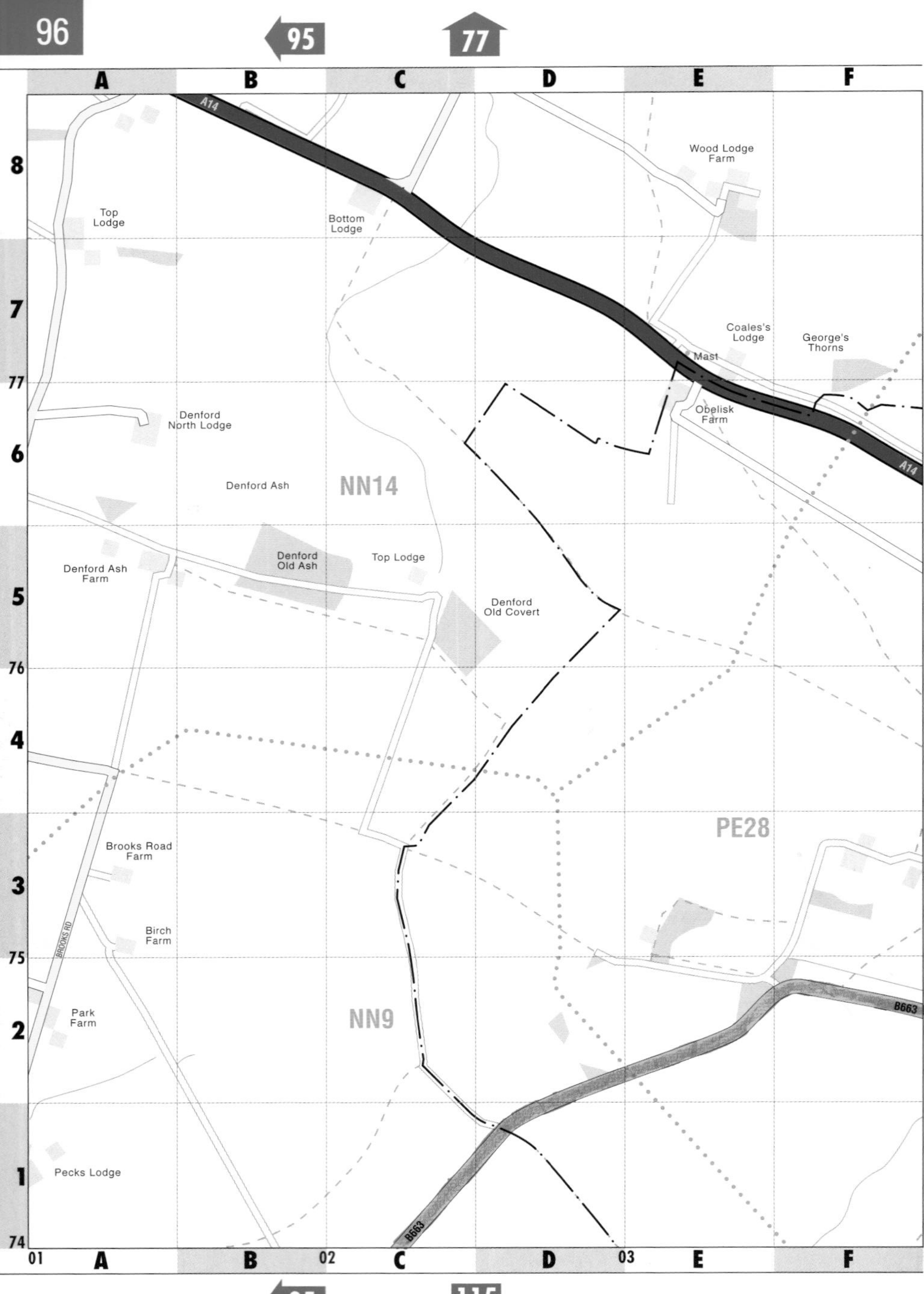
A
B
C
D
E
F
8
7
77
6
5
76
4
3
75
2
1
74
01
02
03
A14
Wood Lodge Farm
Top Lodge
Bottom Lodge
Coales's Lodge
George's Thorns
Mast
Obelisk Farm
Denford North Lodge
Denford Ash
NN14
Denford Ash Farm
Denford Old Ash
Top Lodge
Denford Old Covert
PE28
Brooks Road Farm
Birch Farm
BROOKS RD
Park Farm
NN9
B663
Pecks Lodge

95
115

78

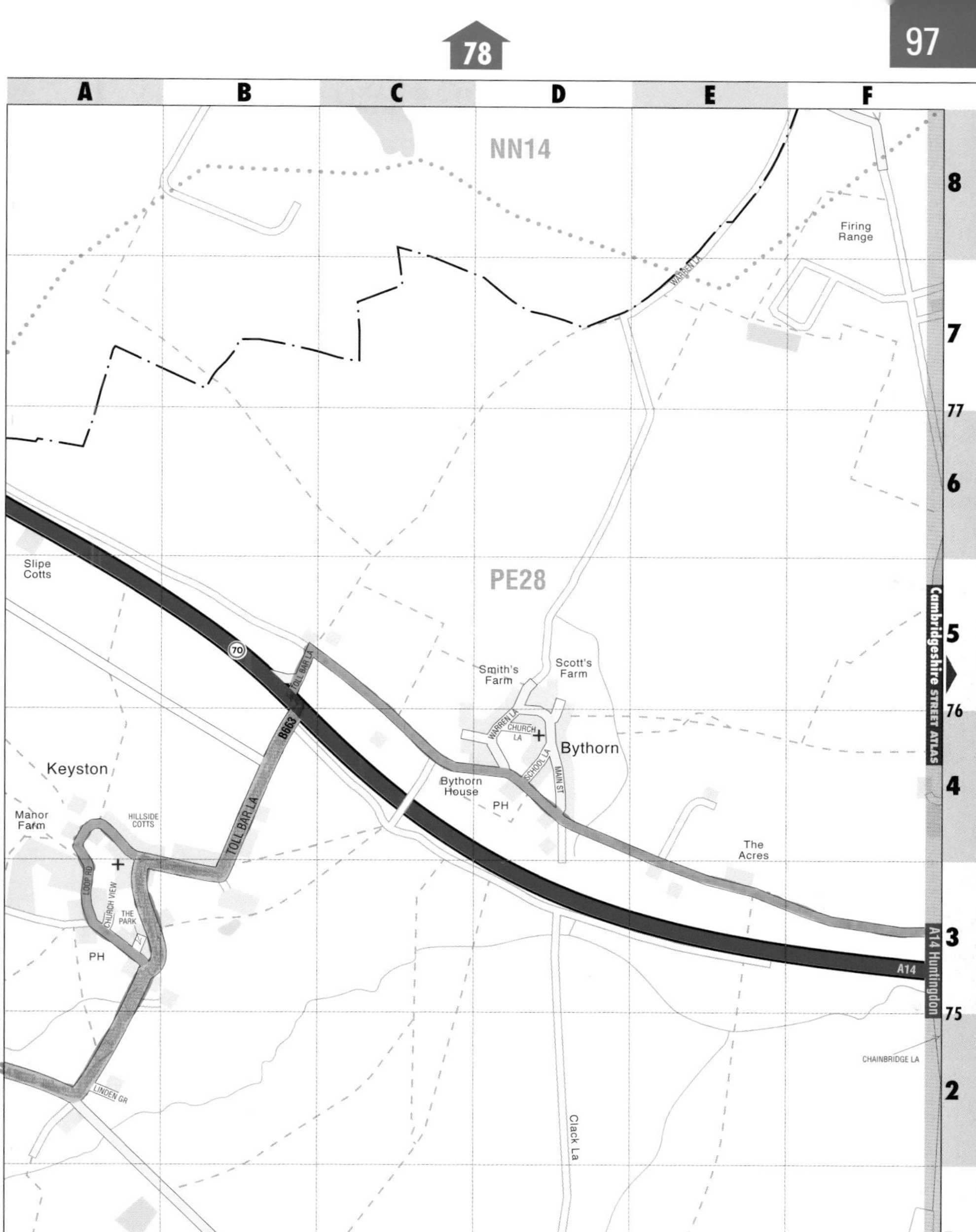

A
B
C
D
E
F
NN14
8
Firing Range
WARREN LA
7
77
6
Slipe Cotts
PE28
5
70
Smith's Farm
Scott's Farm
TOLL BAR LA
76
WARREN LA
CHURCH LA
B663
Bythorn
SCHOOL LA
MAIN ST
Keyston
Bythorn House
4
Manor Farm
HILLSIDE COTTS
PH
TOLL BAR LA
The Acres
LOOP RD
CHURCH VIEW
THE PARK
3
PH
A14
75
CHAINBRIDGE LA
2
LINDEN GR
Clack La
1
CHAINBRIDGE LA
Crow's Nest Hill
74
04
05
06
Cambridgeshire STREET ATLAS
A14 Huntingdon

116

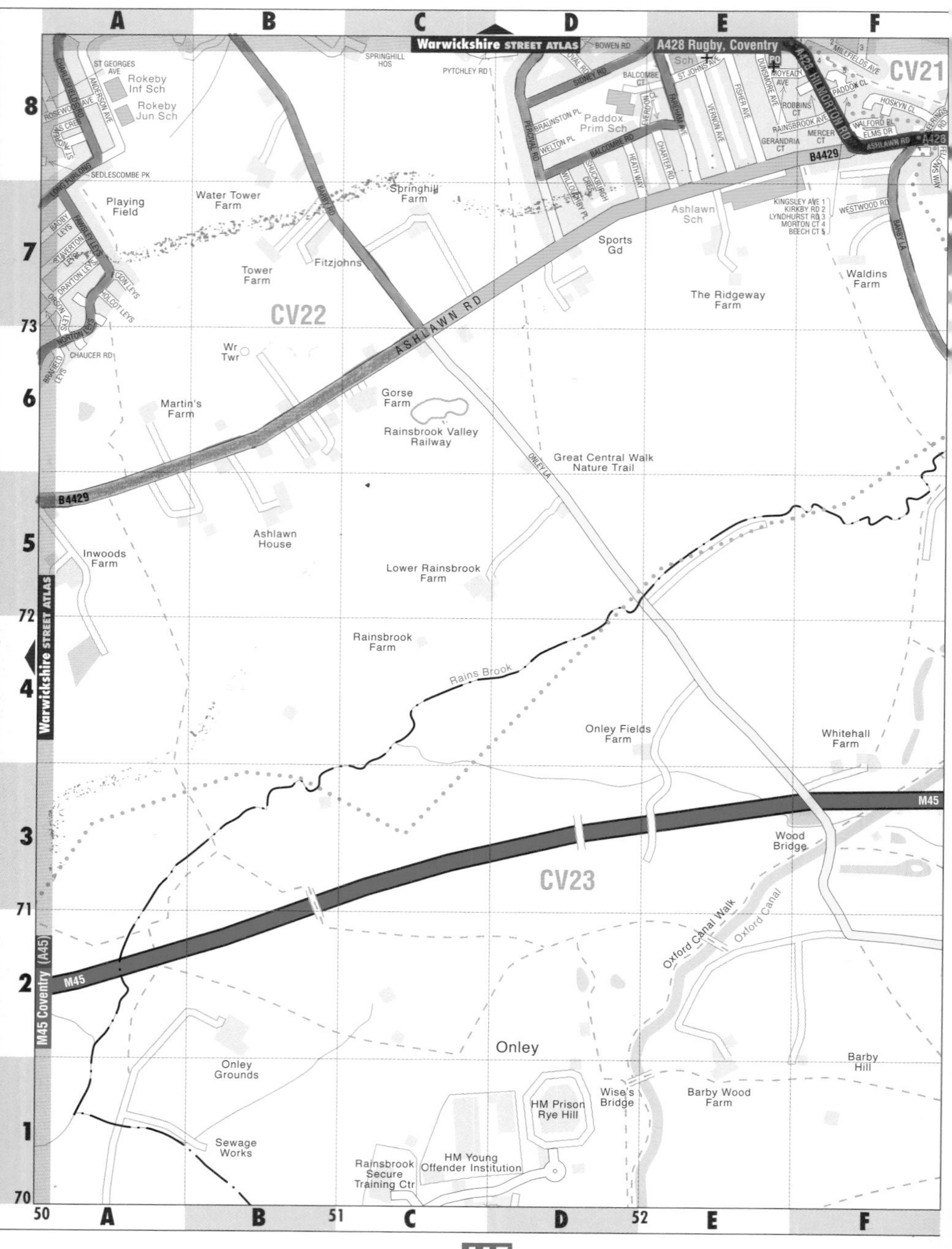

Warwickshire STREET ATLAS
A428 Rugby, Coventry
CV21
CV22
CV23
Rokeby Inf Sch
Rokeby Jun Sch
Paddox Prim Sch
Ashlawn Sch
Playing Field
Water Tower Farm
Springhill Farm
Tower Farm
Fitzjohns
Sports Gd
The Ridgeway Farm
Waldins Farm
ASHLAWN RD
B4429
Wr Twr
Martin's Farm
Gorse Farm
Rainsbrook Valley Railway
Great Central Walk Nature Trail
ONLEY LA
Ashlawn House
Inwoods Farm
Lower Rainsbrook Farm
Rainsbrook Farm
Rains Brook
Onley Fields Farm
Whitehall Farm
M45
Wood Bridge
Oxford Canal Walk
Oxford Canal
Onley
Onley Grounds
Barby Hill
Wise's Bridge
HM Prison Rye Hill
Barby Wood Farm
Sewage Works
HM Young Offender Institution
Rainsbrook Secure Training Ctr
M45 Coventry (A45)

117

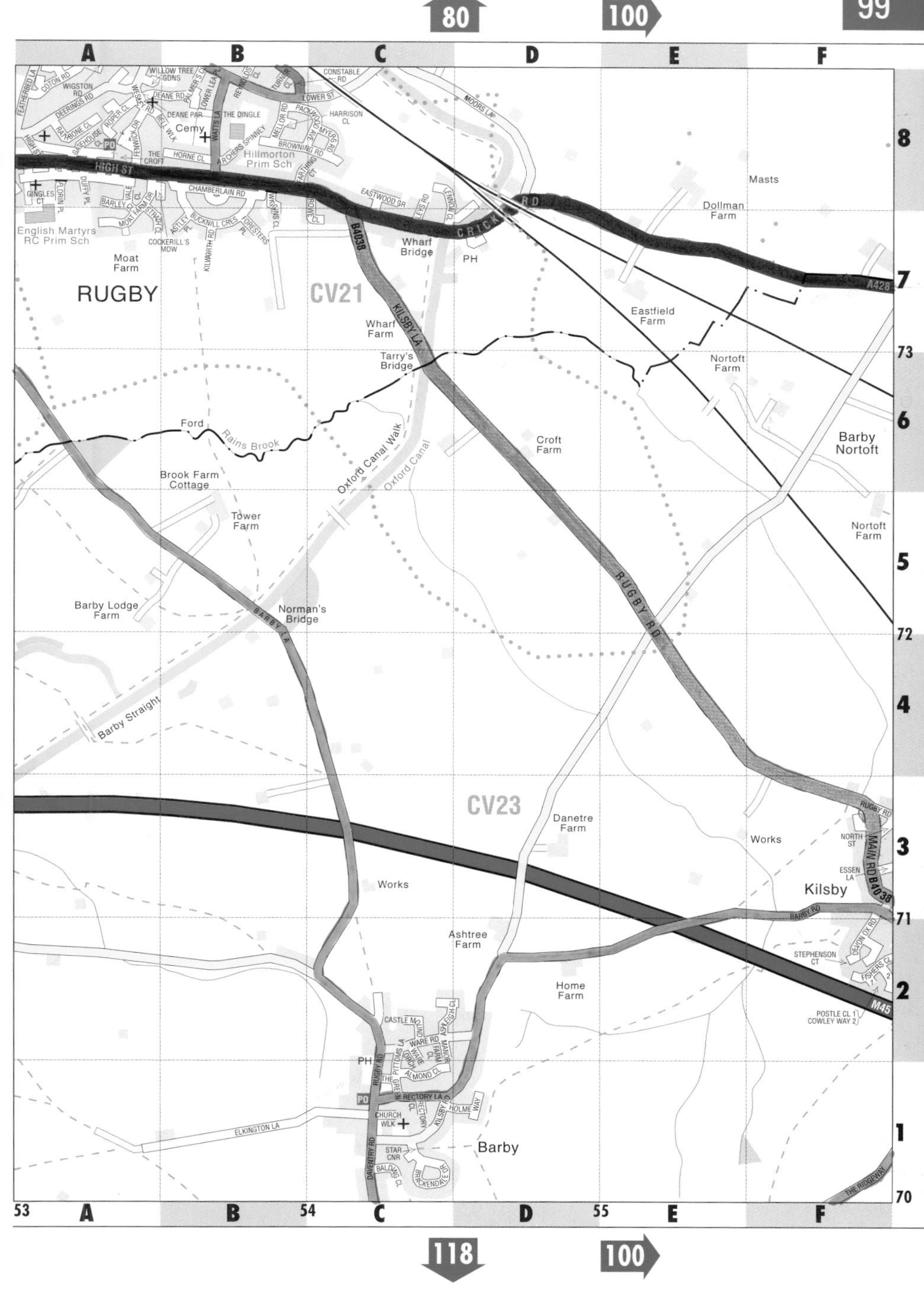
80
100
A
B
C
D
E
F
RUGBY
CV21
CV23
HIGH ST
CRICK RD
A428
B4038
KILSBY LA
RUGBY RD
BARBY LA
M45
Hillmorton Prim Sch
English Martyrs RC Prim Sch
Moat Farm
Wharf Bridge
Wharf Farm
Tarry's Bridge
PH
Masts
Dollman Farm
Eastfield Farm
Nortoft Farm
Barby Nortoft
Croft Farm
Ford
Rains Brook
Oxford Canal Walk
Oxford Canal
Brook Farm Cottage
Tower Farm
Barby Lodge Farm
Norman's Bridge
Barby Straight
Danetre Farm
Works
Kilsby
Ashtree Farm
Home Farm
Barby
ELKINGTON LA
DAVENTRY RD
RECTORY LA
CHURCH WLK
STAR CNR
CASTLE MOUND
ALMOND CL
HOLME WAY
BALDWIN CL
BRACKENDALE DR
MAIN RD
NORTH ST
ESSEN LA
BARBY RD
STEPHENSON CT
POSTLE CL 1
COWLEY WAY 2
THE RIDGEWAY
Cemy
CHAMBERLAIN RD
EASTWOOD GR
WILLOW TREE GDNS
CONSTABLE RD
LOWER ST
HARRISON CL
THE DINGLE
MOORS LA
8
7
73
6
5
72
4
3
71
2
1
70
53
54
55
118
100

99
81

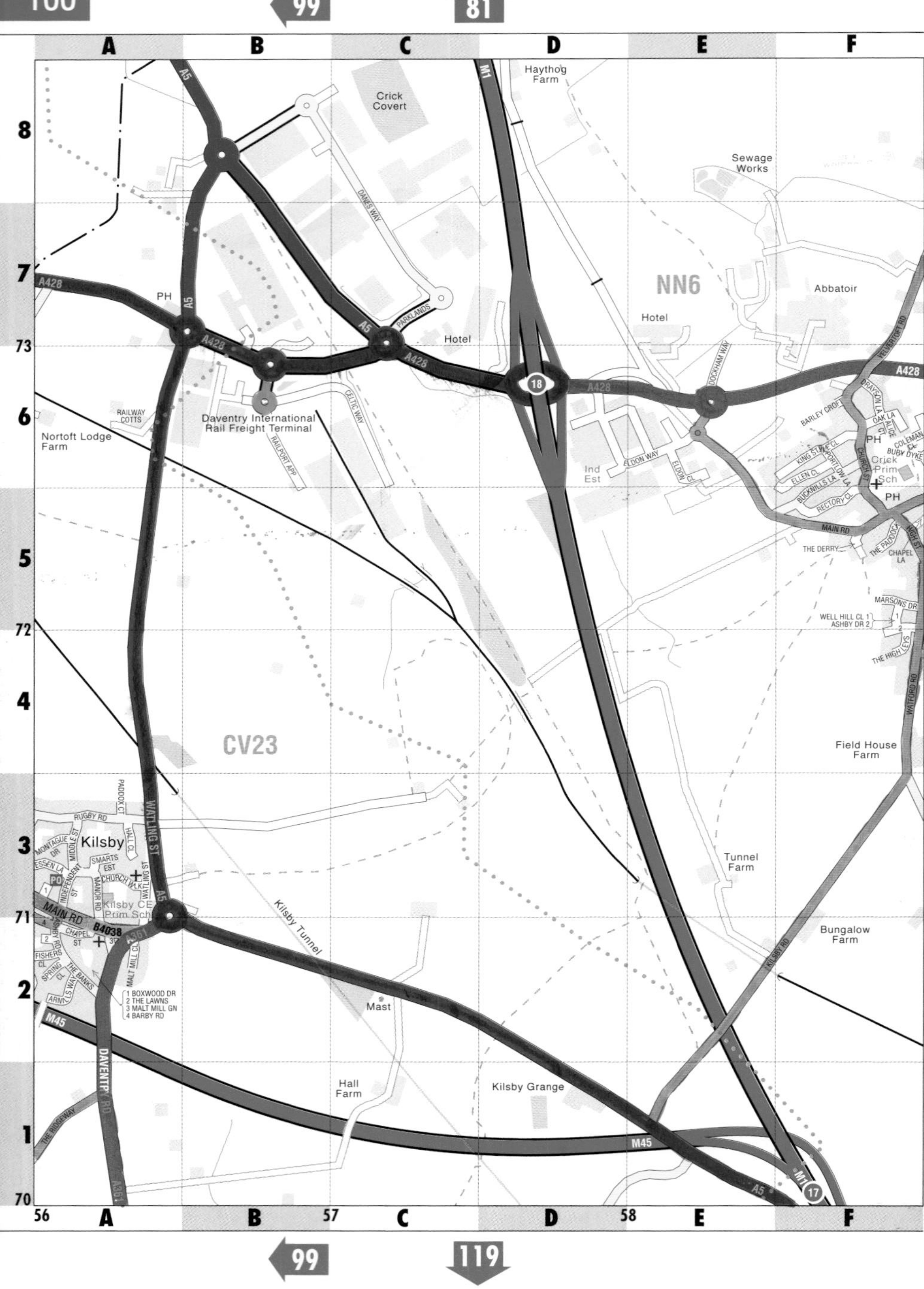
A
B
C
D
E
F
8
7
73
6
5
72
4
3
71
2
1
70
56
57
58
Haythog Farm
Crick Covert
Sewage Works
DANES WAY
NN6
Abbatoir
Hotel
PH
PARKLANDS
Hotel
A428
A5
M1
18
DOCKHAM WAY
YELVERTOFT RD
RAILWAY COTTS
Daventry International Rail Freight Terminal
CELTIC WAY
RAILPORT APP
Nortoft Lodge Farm
ELDON WAY
ELDON CL
Ind Est
BARLEY CROFT
OAK LA
ALICE CL
COLEMAN CL
BUBY DYKE
KING ST
ELLEN CL
BUCKNILLS LA
RECTORY CL
CHURCH ST
Crick Prim Sch
PH
MAIN RD
THE DERRY
THE PADDOCK
HIGH ST
CHAPEL LA
MARSONS DR
WELL HILL CL 1
ASHBY DR 2
THE HIGH LEYS
WATFORD RD
CV23
Field House Farm
PADDOCK CT
RUGBY RD
WATLING ST
Kilsby
MONTAGUE DR
MIDDLE ST
SMARTS EST
HALL CL
INDEPENDENT ST
MANOR RD
CHURCH WALK
Kilsby CE Prim Sch
MAIN RD
B4038
CHAPEL ST
FISHERS CL
SPRING CL
THE BANKS
MALT MILL CL
A361
1 BOXWOOD DR
2 THE LAWNS
3 MALT MILL GN
4 BARBY RD
Kilsby Tunnel
Tunnel Farm
Bungalow Farm
KILSBY RD
Mast
M45
DAVENTRY RD
Hall Farm
Kilsby Grange
THE RIDGEWAY
17

99
119

82
102

120
102

101
83

101
121

84
104

122
104

103
85

103
123

86
106
A
B
C
D
E
F
8
7
73
6
5
72
4
3
71
2
1
70
71
72
73
Cottesbrooke Hall
Cottesbrooke Hall Gdns
COTTESBROOKE GRANGE
MAIN ST
OLD SCHOOL COTTS
STATION RD
Home Farm
Beck Dairy
Pitmorehill Spinney
Gullivers
Macmillan Way
Creaton Covert
Badge Lodge
NN6
Sewage Works
BRIXWORTH RD
Corn Mill
Glebe Farm
STATION RD
Creaton Grange Farm
GROOMS LA
Little Creaton
Sewage Works
Matts Cottages
Midshires Way
Folly Farm
SPRATTON RD
WELFORD RD
Spratton Hall Sch
SMITH ST
ERSKIN WOOD
Spratton CE Prim Sch
Cemy
BRIXWORTH RD
Ash Tree Farm
HIGH ST
SCHOOL RD
MANOR RD
STARVOLD CL
SANDHILLS
PH
PO
OLDE HALL CL
BAKERS LA 1
HAYNES LA 2
THE PIECE 3
BLACKTHORN CL 4
GORSE RD
GLEBELANDS
ST LUKES CL
CHURCH RD
YEW TREE LA
CHURCH LA
Spratton
124
106

105
87

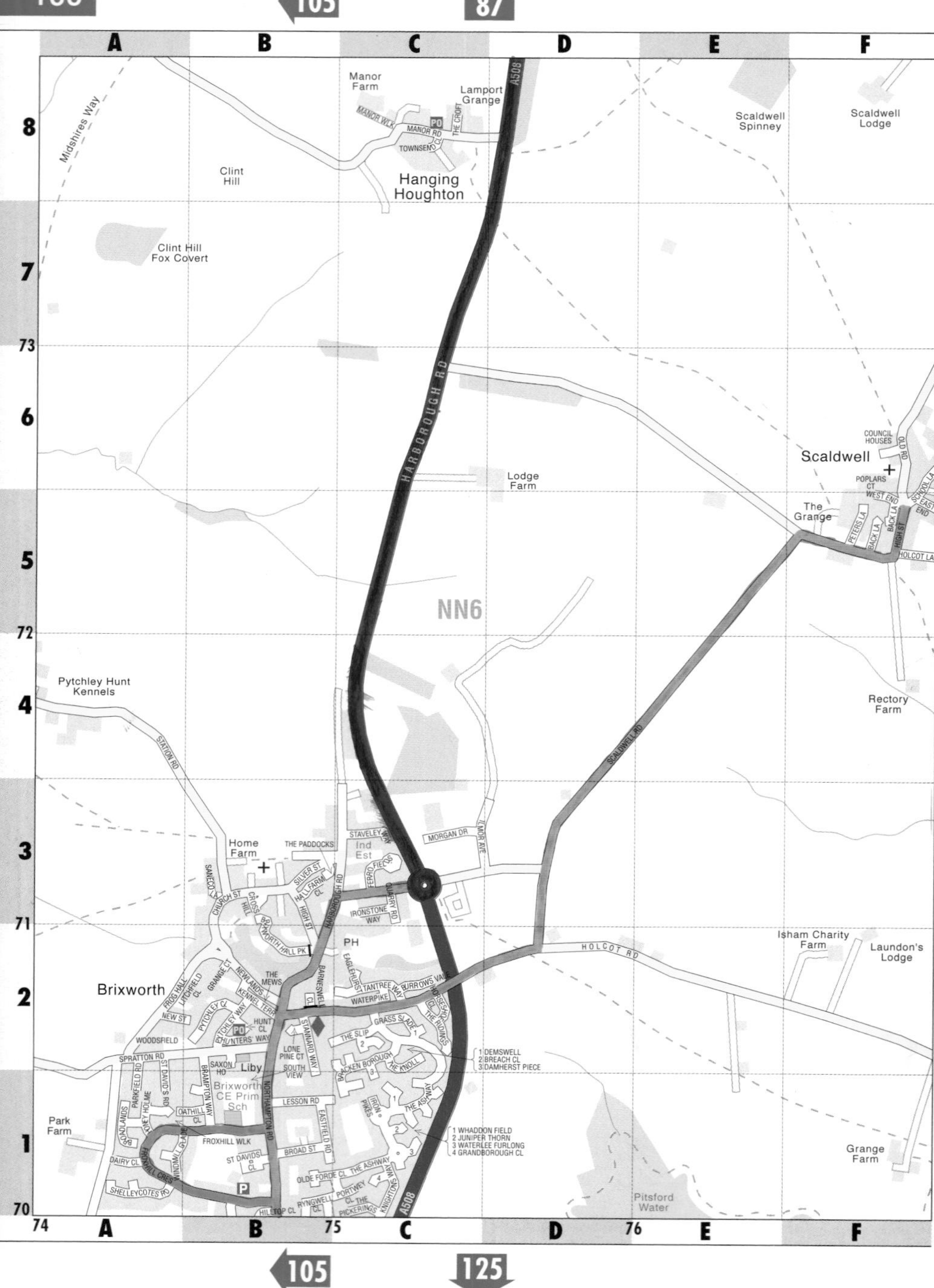

105
125

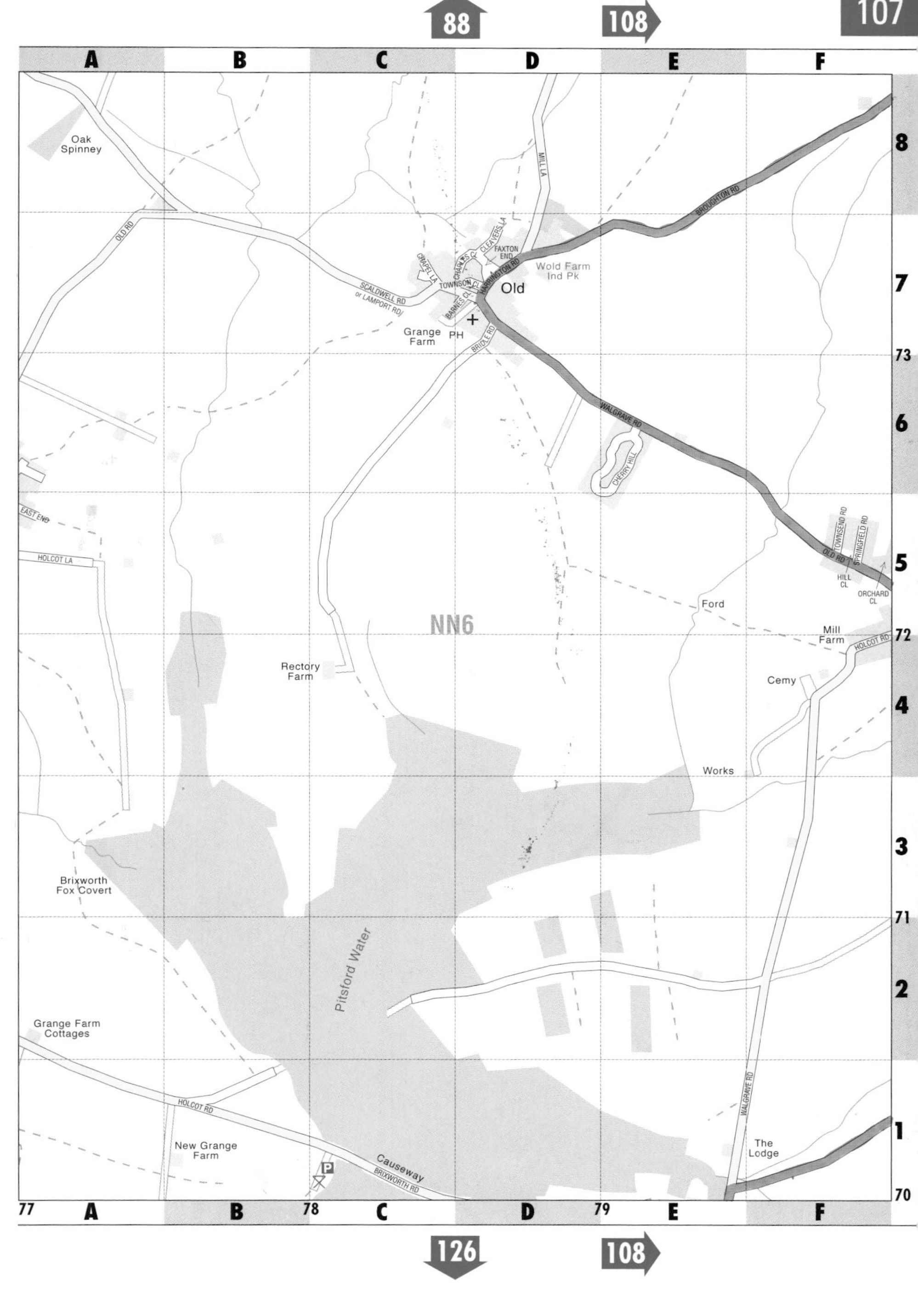

88
108
A
B
C
D
E
F
8
7
73
6
5
72
4
3
71
2
1
70
Oak Spinney
OLD RD
MILL LA
BROUGHTON RD
CLEAVERS LA
FAXTON END
HARRINGTON RD
Wold Farm Ind Pk
CHAPEL LA
TOWNSON
BARNES CL
SCALDWELL RD or LAMPORT RD
Old
Grange Farm
PH
BRIDLE RD
WALGRAVE RD
CHERRY HILL
EAST END
HOLCOT LA
TOWNSEND RD
SPRINGFIELD RD
OLD RD
HILL CL
ORCHARD CL
Ford
NN6
Mill Farm
HOLCOT RD
Rectory Farm
Cemy
Works
Brixworth Fox Covert
Pitsford Water
Grange Farm Cottages
HOLCOT RD
New Grange Farm
P
Causeway
BRIXWORTH RD
WALGRAVE RD
The Lodge
77
78
79
126
108

107
89

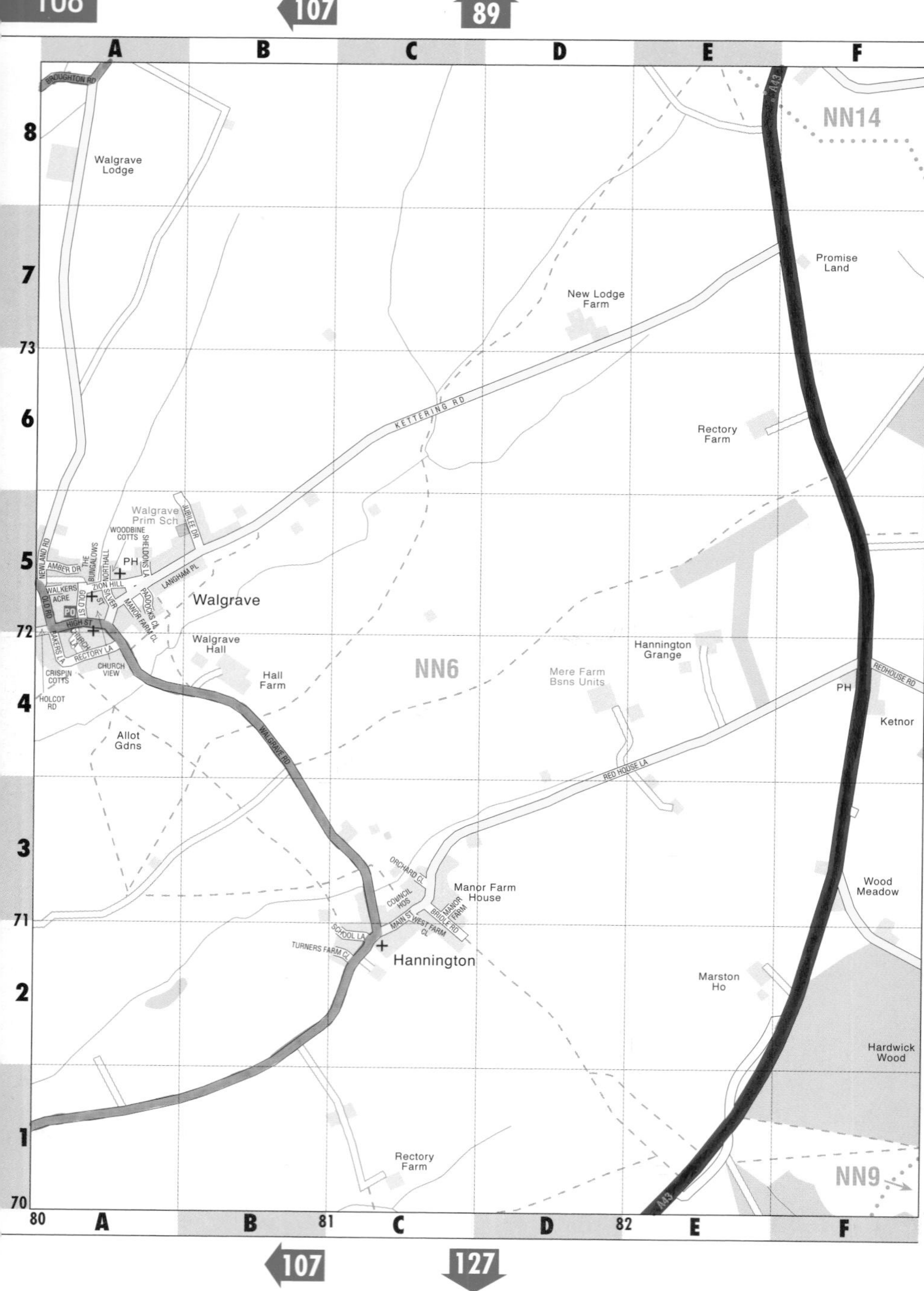

107
127

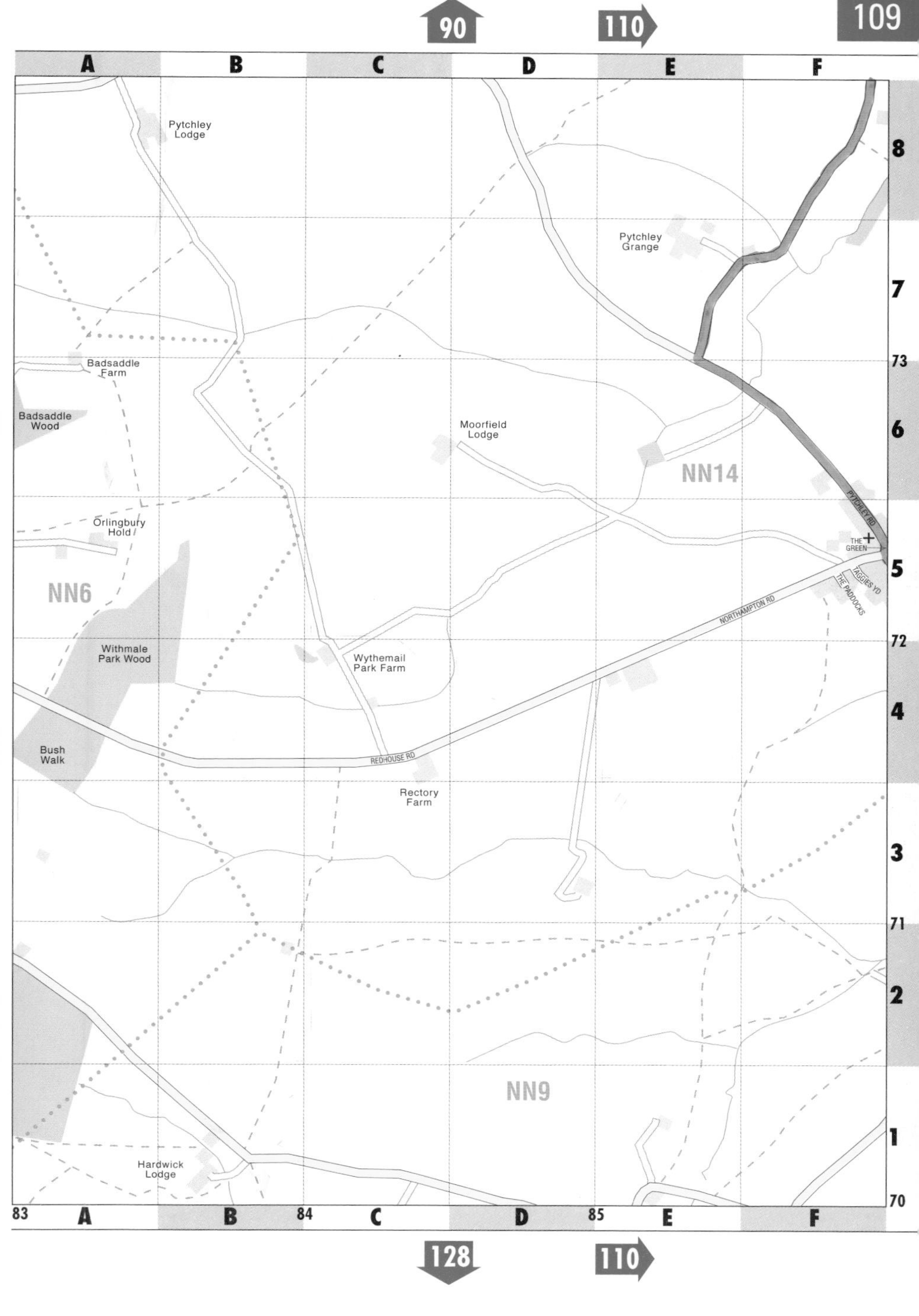
90
110
A
B
C
D
E
F
Pytchley Lodge
Pytchley Grange
Badsaddle Farm
Badsaddle Wood
Moorfield Lodge
NN14
PYTCHLEY RD
THE GREEN
AGGIES YD
THE PADDOCKS
Orlingbury Hold
NN6
NORTHAMPTON RD
Withmale Park Wood
Wythemail Park Farm
REDHOUSE RD
Bush Walk
Rectory Farm
NN9
Hardwick Lodge
8
7
73
6
5
72
4
3
71
2
1
70
83
84
85
128
110

109
91

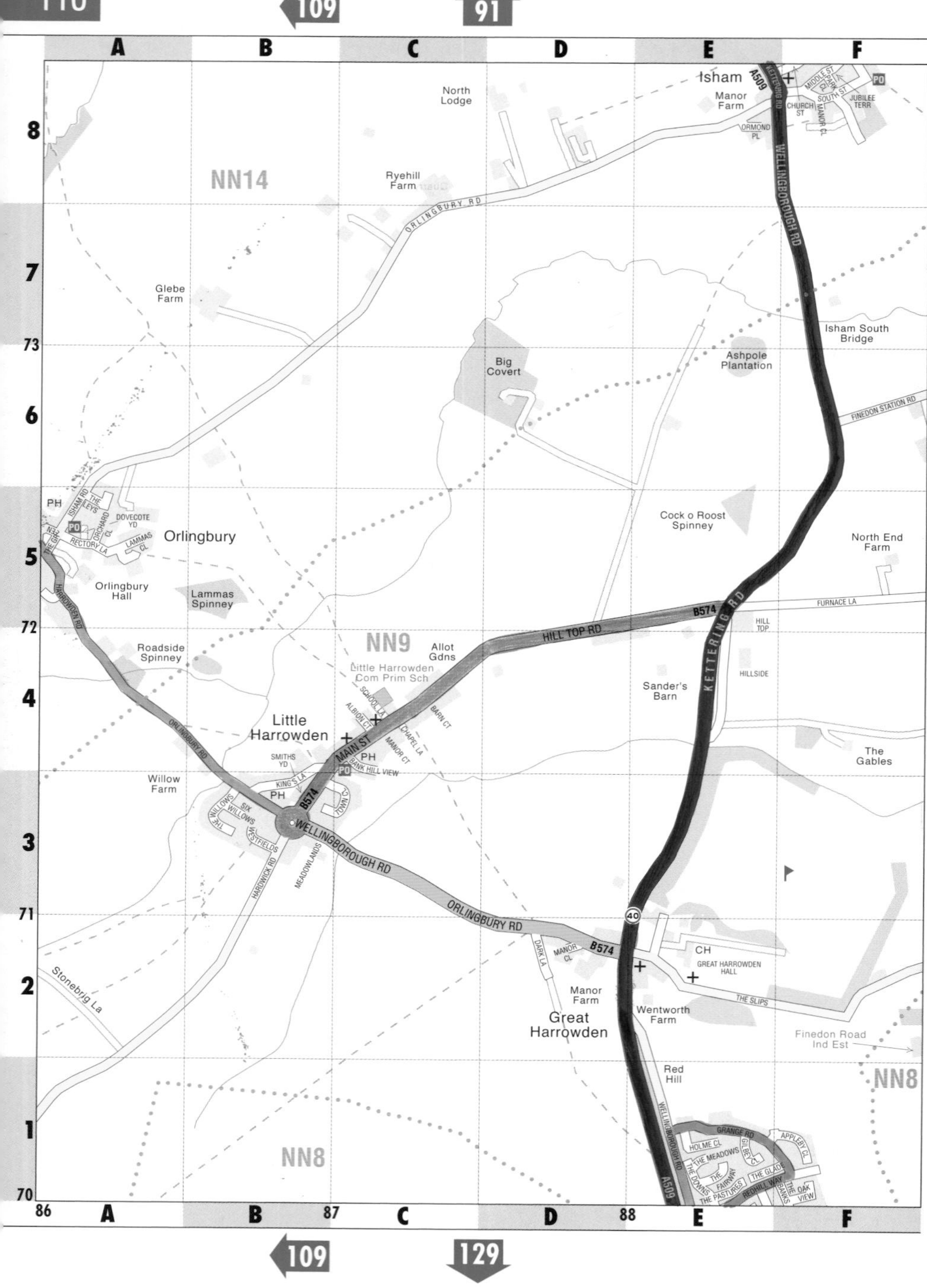

109
129

92
112
A
B
C
D
E
F
NN14
NN15
HILLCREST AVE
THE RUSHES
RIVERVIEW
FINEDON RD
Buccleuch Farm
Quarry (dis)
Barnfield Lodge Farm
Quarry (dis)
A6
Black Lodge
Isebrook Bridge
FINEDON STATION RD
BURTON RD
Quarry (dis)
Sewage Works
STATION RD
Furnace Lane Ind Est
Westfield Lodge
River Ise
1 ST MARY'S AVE
2 BERRY GREEN CT
3 ST MARY'S CT
4 APPLETREE CT
5 WATERLOW BRIDGE
6 THE WELLS
Cemy
FURNACE COTTS
FURNACE LA
Debdale Grove
TH
Liby
Sch
TINGDENE RD
ORCHARD RD
ORCHARD TERR
HIGH ST
WELL ST
CHURCH ST
AVENUE RD
BERRY GREEN RD
FINEDON HALL
CHURCH HILL
MACKWORTH DR
HOLLY WLK
DOLBEN CL
REGENT ST
BELL HILL
IVY LA
L Ctr
PO
CROMER RD
MILNER RD
SUMMERLEE RD
EWENFIELD RD
KENMUIR RD
HALL DR
GROVE WAY
NN9
Finedon
WELLINGBOROUGH RD
1 SUMMERLEE MEWS
2 PARKERS TERR
3 IRONSTONE CT
4 MACKWORTH GN
Allot Gdns
Eleanor's Wood
HARROWDEN RD
THE SLIPS
Great Harrowden Lodge
Hillside Farm
RYEBURY HILL
Quarry (dis)
BRADFIELD RD
VAUX RD
YELDON CT
Sports Gd
Finedon Road Ind Est
SANDERS RD
Works
BRIDLE CL
STEWARTS RD
STANTON CL
BENTLEY CT
PATERSON RD
A510
NN8
Works
Ryebury Farm
SIDEGATE LA
Carrol Spring Farm
8
7
73
6
5
72
4
3
71
2
1
70
89
90
91
130
112

111
93

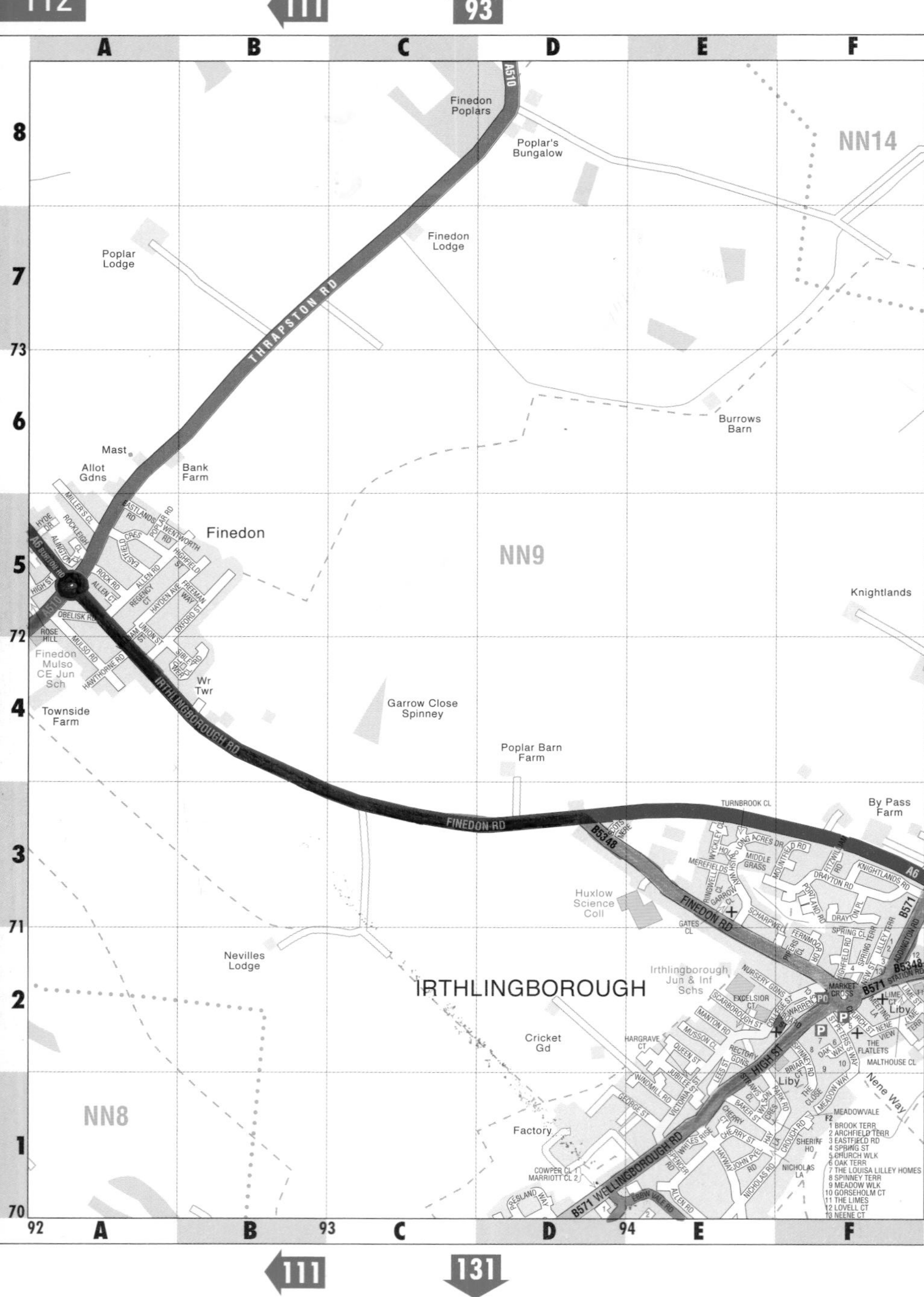

111
131

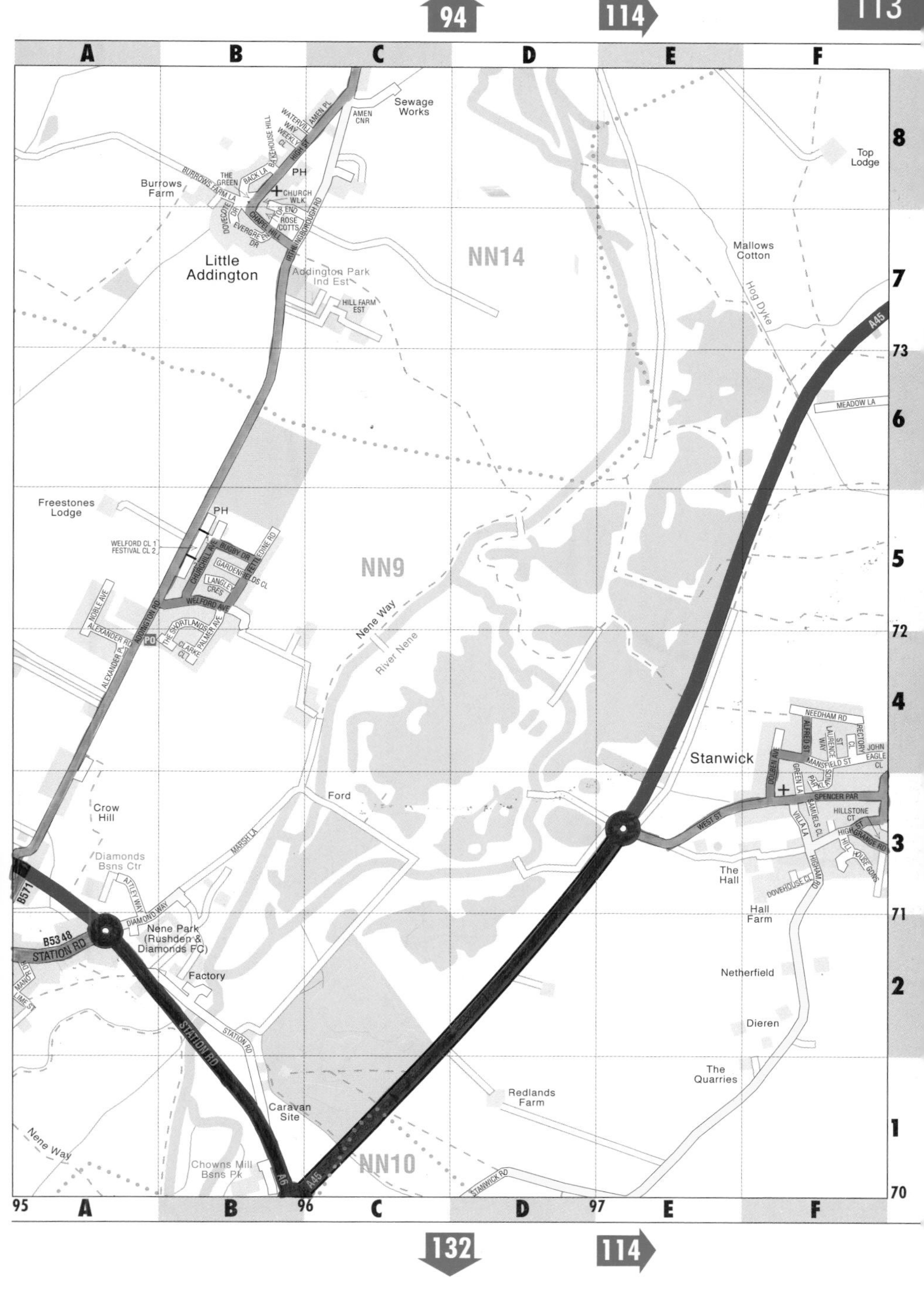
113
94
114
A
B
C
D
E
F
8
7
6
5
4
3
2
1
73
72
71
70
95
96
97
Sewage Works
AMEN CNR
AMEN PL
WATERVILLE WAY
WEEKLY CL
HIGH ST
BAKEHOUSE HILL
PH
THE GREEN
BACK LA
Burrows Farm
BURROWS FARM LA
CHURCH WLK
TOP END
ROSE COTTS
DOVECOTE DR
CHAPEL HILL
EVERGREEN DR
IRTHLINGBOROUGH RD
Little Addington
Addington Park Ind Est
HILL FARM EST
NN14
Mallows Cotton
Hog Dyke
Top Lodge
A45
MEADOW LA
Freestones Lodge
PH
WELFORD CL 1
FESTIVAL CL 2
CHURCHILL AVE
RUGBY DR
FETTLEDINE RD
GARDENFIELDS CL
LANGLEY CRES
WELFORD AVE
NN9
NOBLE AVE
ALEXANDER RD
ALEXANDER PL
ADDINGTON RD
PO
THE SHORTLANDS
PALMER AVE
CLARKE CL
Nene Way
River Nene
NEEDHAM RD
ALFRED ST
LAURENCE WAY
ST
RECTORY CL
JOHN EAGLE CL
Stanwick
DOLBEN AVE
GREEN LA
MANSFIELD ST
PARK LA
SPENCER PAR
HILLSTONE CT
WEST ST
SAMUELS CL
VILLA LA
HIGH ST
GRANGE RD
HIGHAM RD
HILL HOUSE GDNS
DOVEHOUSE CL
The Hall
Hall Farm
Ford
Crow Hill
MARSH LA
Diamonds Bsns Ctr
ATTLEY WAY
DIAMOND WAY
B571
B5348
STATION RD
Nene Park (Rushden & Diamonds FC)
Factory
LIME ST
Netherfield
Dieren
The Quarries
Redlands Farm
Caravan Site
Nene Way
Chowns Mill Bsns Pk
A6
A45
NN10
STANWICK RD
132
114

113
95

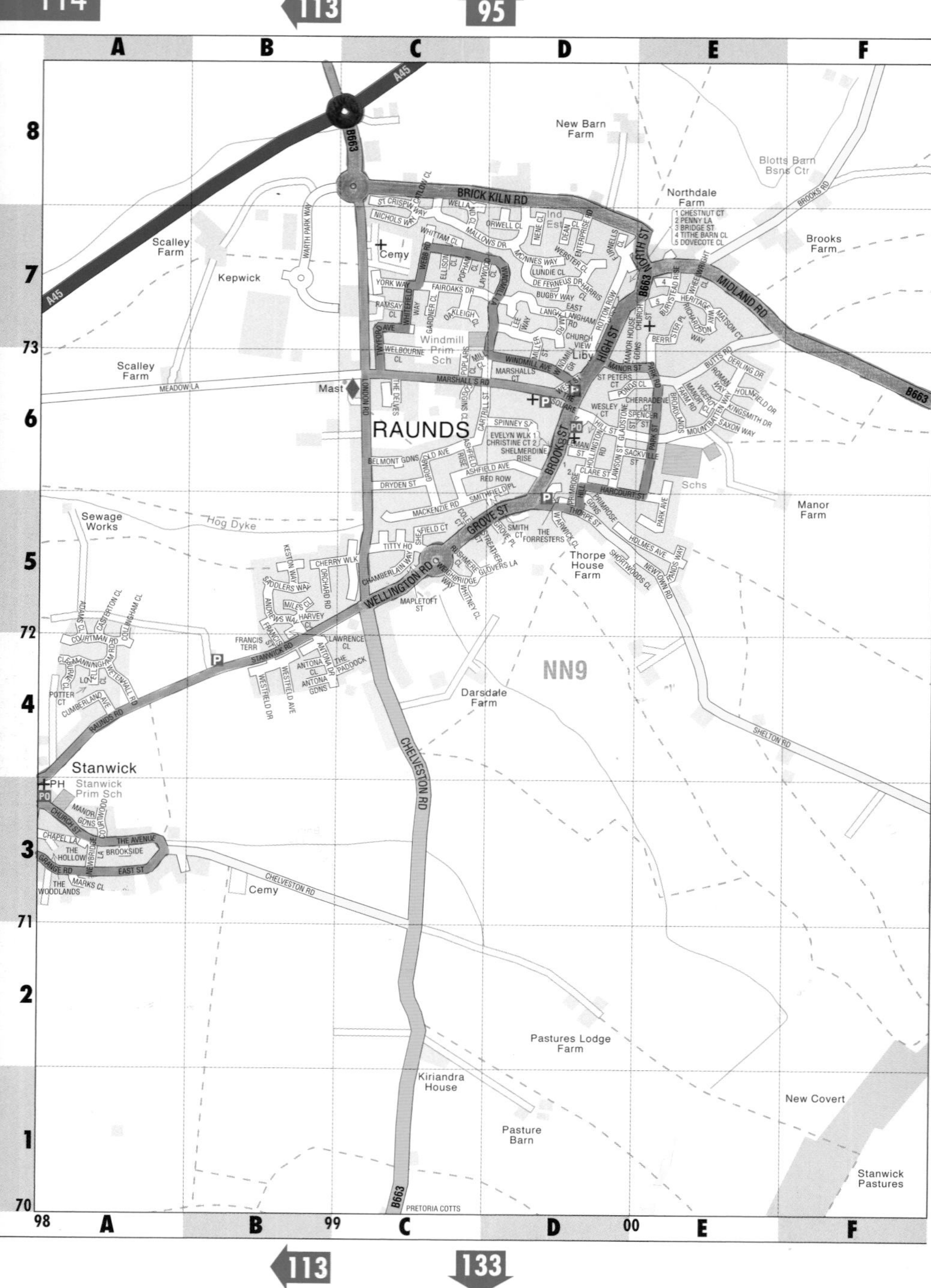

113
133

96
116

A
B
C
D
E
F
8
7
73
6
5
72
4
3
71
2
1
70
01
02
03
Napleton Lodge Farm
Station House
Inn
Napleton Cottage
Raunds Plantation
STATION RD
B663
Friendly Lodge
PE28
Old Meadow
Railway Lodge
Raunds Grange
NN9
Black Lodge
Red Lodge
Mere Farm
SHELTON RD
BROOK ST
Bottom Farm
Hillstone House
Rose Cottage
The Gables
Top Farm
CHURCH ST
NAGS HEAD LA
PH
ELM CL
Hargrave
CHURCH RD
PO
Hargrave Riding Centre
New England Farm
Grange Farm
The Grove
Hargrave Hall
B645
Mill View Farm
PE28
Bedfordshire STREET ATLAS

116

115
97

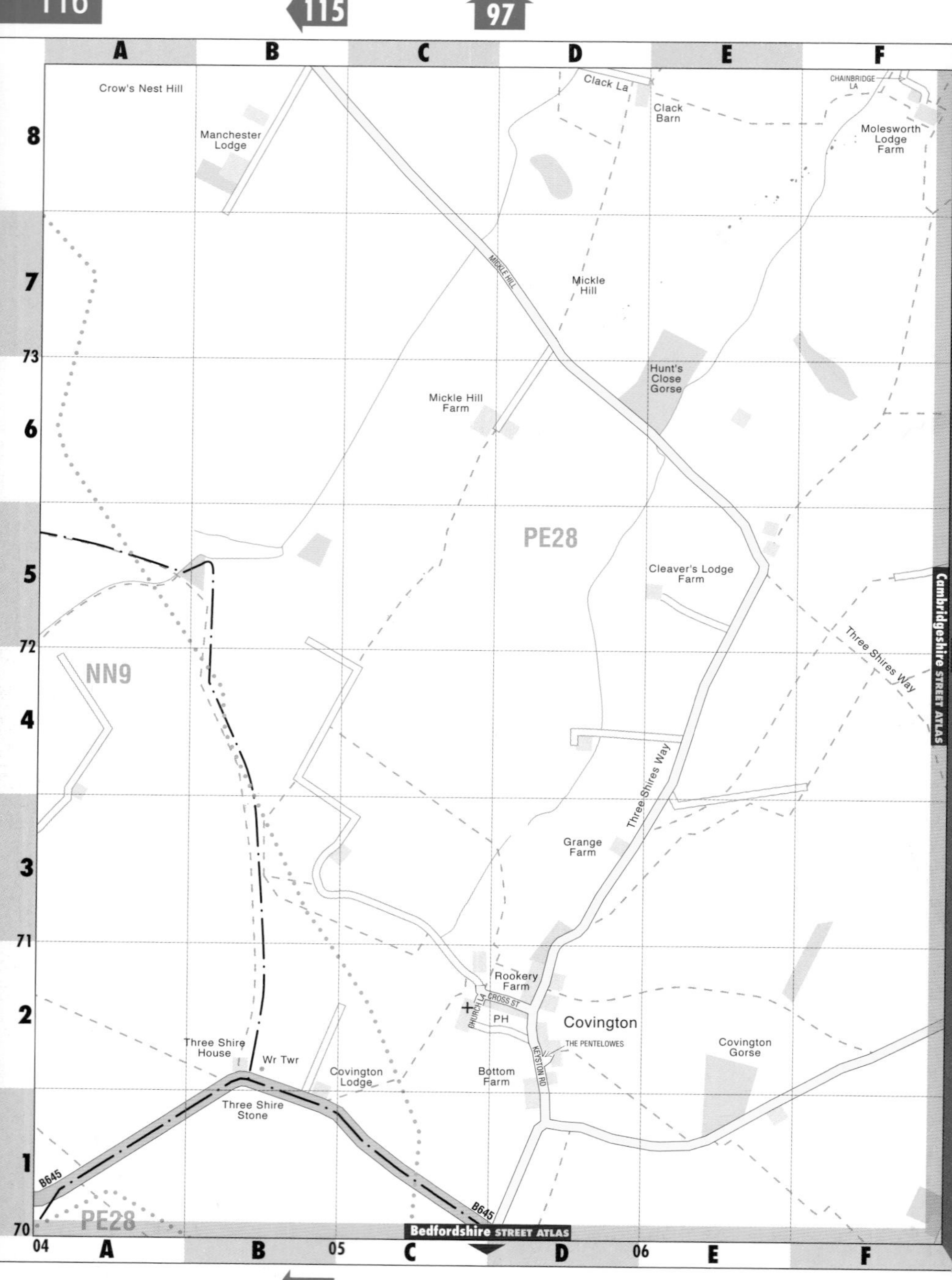
A
B
C
D
E
F
8
7
73
6
5
72
4
3
71
2
1
70
04
05
06
Crow's Nest Hill
Manchester Lodge
Clack La
Clack Barn
CHAINBRIDGE LA
Molesworth Lodge Farm
MICKLE HILL
Mickle Hill
Hunt's Close Gorse
Mickle Hill Farm
PE28
Cleaver's Lodge Farm
Three Shires Way
NN9
Three Shires Way
Grange Farm
Rookery Farm
CHURCH LA
CROSS ST
PH
Covington
THE PENTELOWES
KEYSTON RD
Covington Gorse
Three Shire House
Wr Twr
Covington Lodge
Bottom Farm
Three Shire Stone
B645
B645
PE28
Bedfordshire STREET ATLAS
Cambridgeshire STREET ATLAS

115

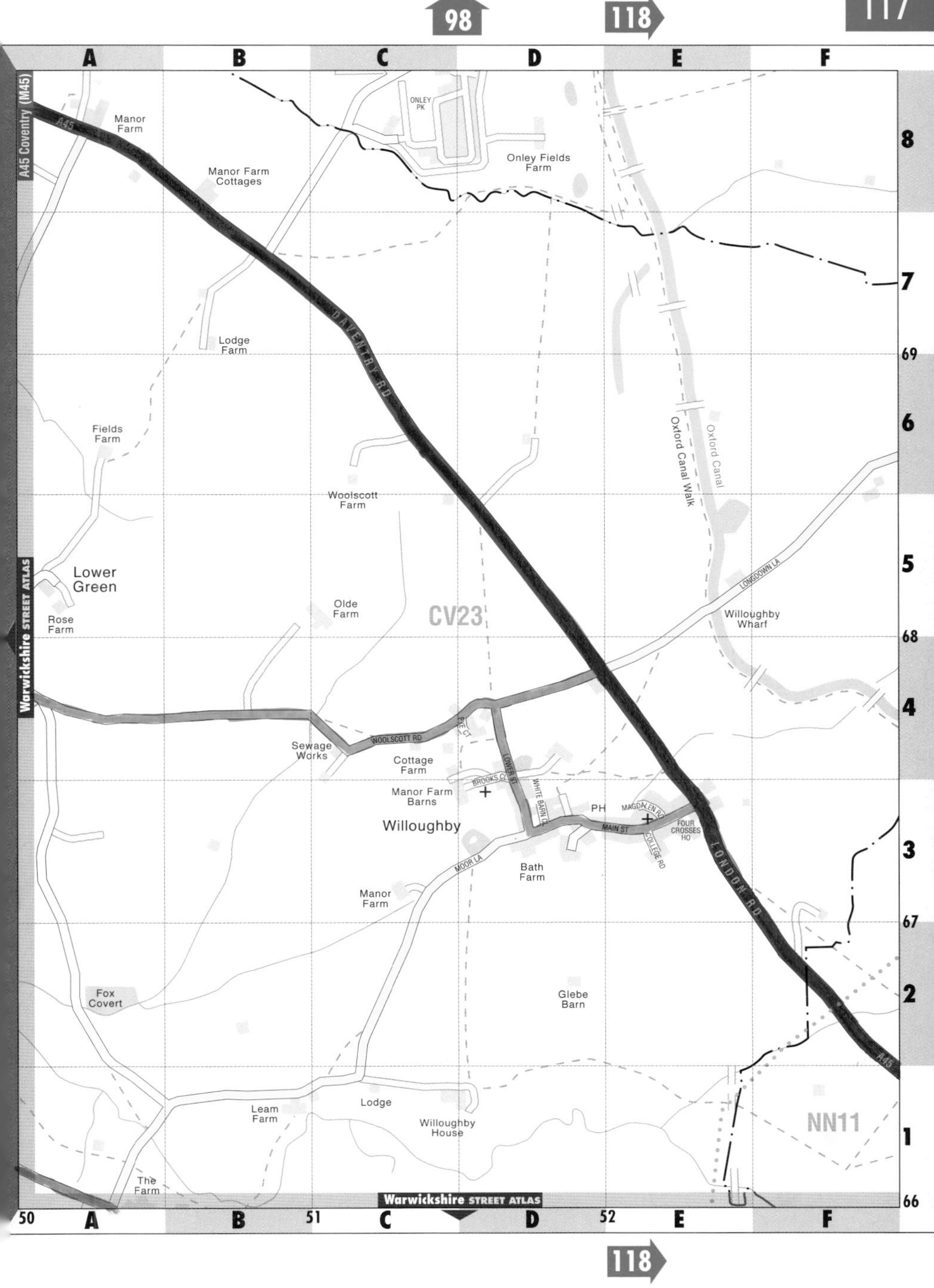
98
118
A
B
C
D
E
F
8
7
69
6
5
68
4
3
67
2
1
66
50
51
52
A45 Coventry (M45)
Warwickshire STREET ATLAS
A45
Manor Farm
Manor Farm Cottages
ONLEY PK
Onley Fields Farm
Lodge Farm
DAVENTRY RD
Fields Farm
Woolscott Farm
Oxford Canal Walk
Oxford Canal
Lower Green
Rose Farm
Olde Farm
CV23
LONGDOWN LA
Willoughby Wharf
Sewage Works
WOOLSCOTT RD
RYE CT
Cottage Farm
LOWER ST
BROOKS CL
WHITE BARN CL
Manor Farm Barns
PH
MAGDALEN RD
FOUR CROSSES HO
MAIN ST
COLLEGE RD
Willoughby
MOOR LA
LONDON RD
Bath Farm
Manor Farm
Fox Covert
Glebe Barn
Lodge
Leam Farm
Willoughby House
NN11
The Farm
Warwickshire STREET ATLAS
118

117
99

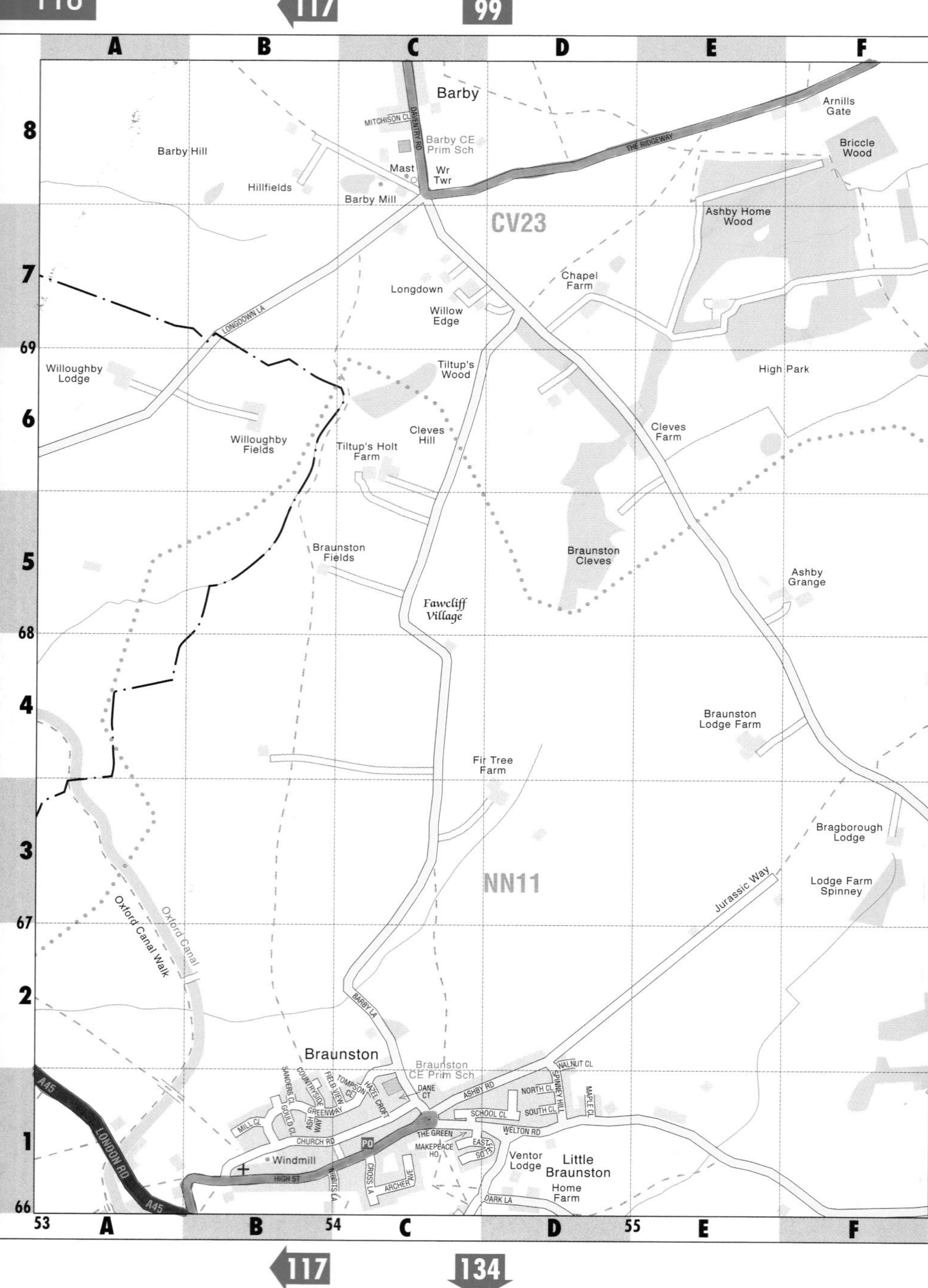

117
134

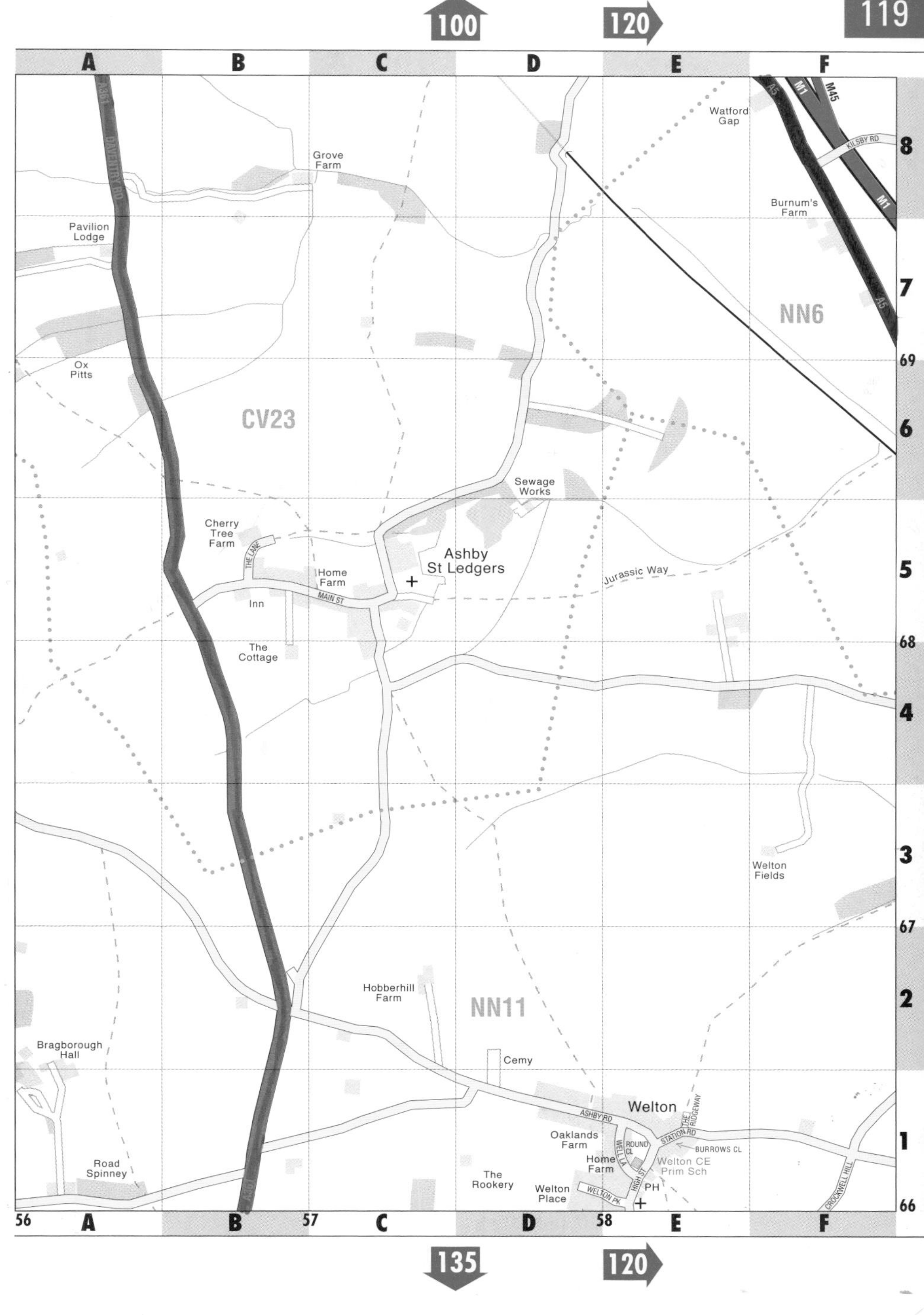
100
120
A
B
C
D
E
F
A361
DAVENTRY RD
Grove
Farm
Watford
Gap
M1
M45
A5
KILSBY RD
8
Pavilion
Lodge
Burnum's
Farm
7
NN6
Ox
Pitts
69
CV23
6
Sewage
Works
Cherry
Tree
Farm
THE LANE
Ashby
St Ledgers
Home
Farm
Jurassic Way
5
MAIN ST
Inn
The
Cottage
68
4
3
Welton
Fields
67
Hobberhill
Farm
NN11
2
Bragborough
Hall
Cemy
Welton
ASHBY RD
THE RIDGEWAY
Oaklands
Farm
ROUND CL
WELL LA
STATION RD
BURROWS CL
1
Home
Farm
Welton CE
Prim Sch
Road
Spinney
The
Rookery
Welton
Place
WELTON PK
HIGH ST
PH
CROCKWELL HILL
66
56
57
58
135
120

119
101

119
136

102
122

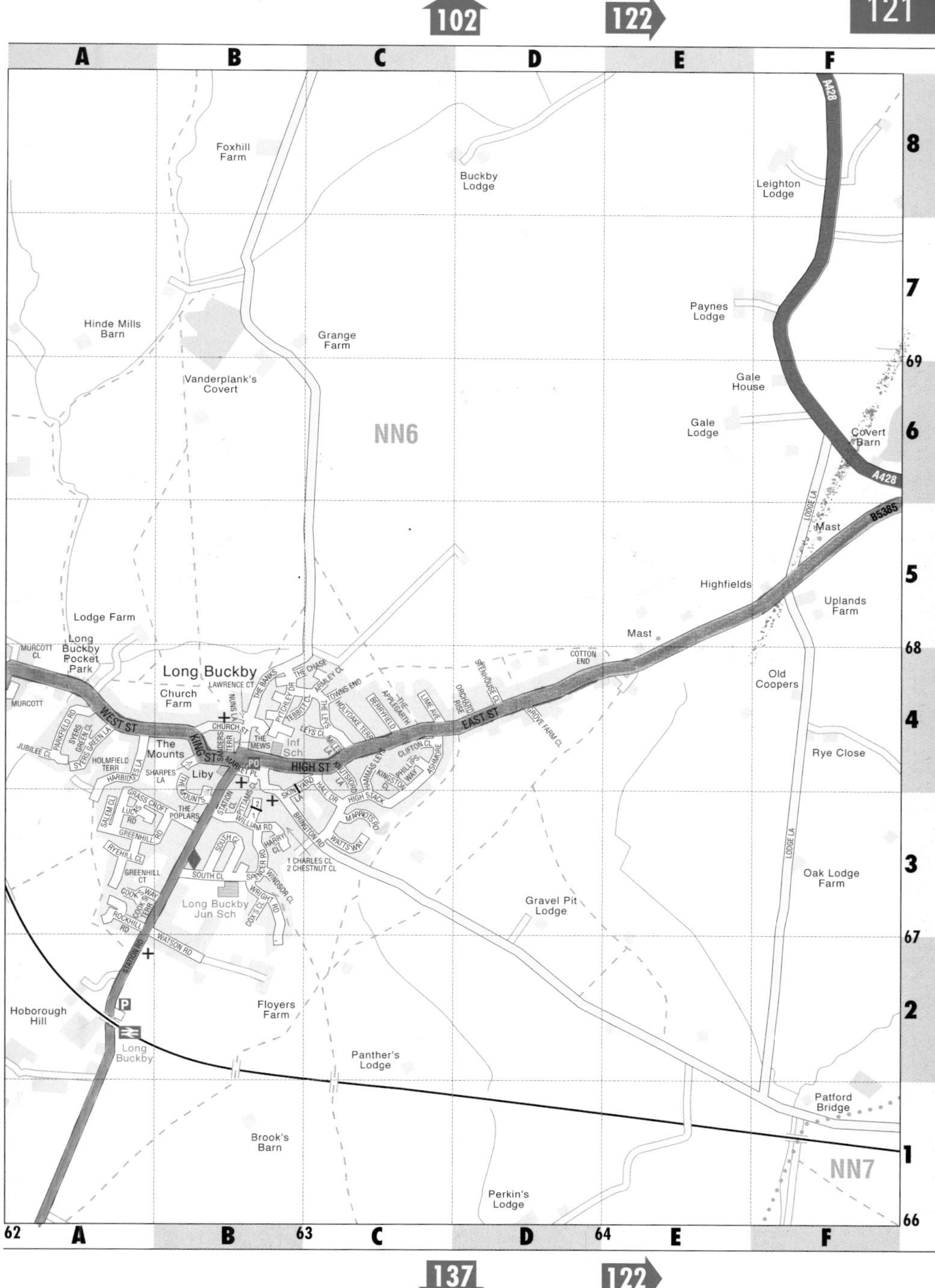

137
122

121
103

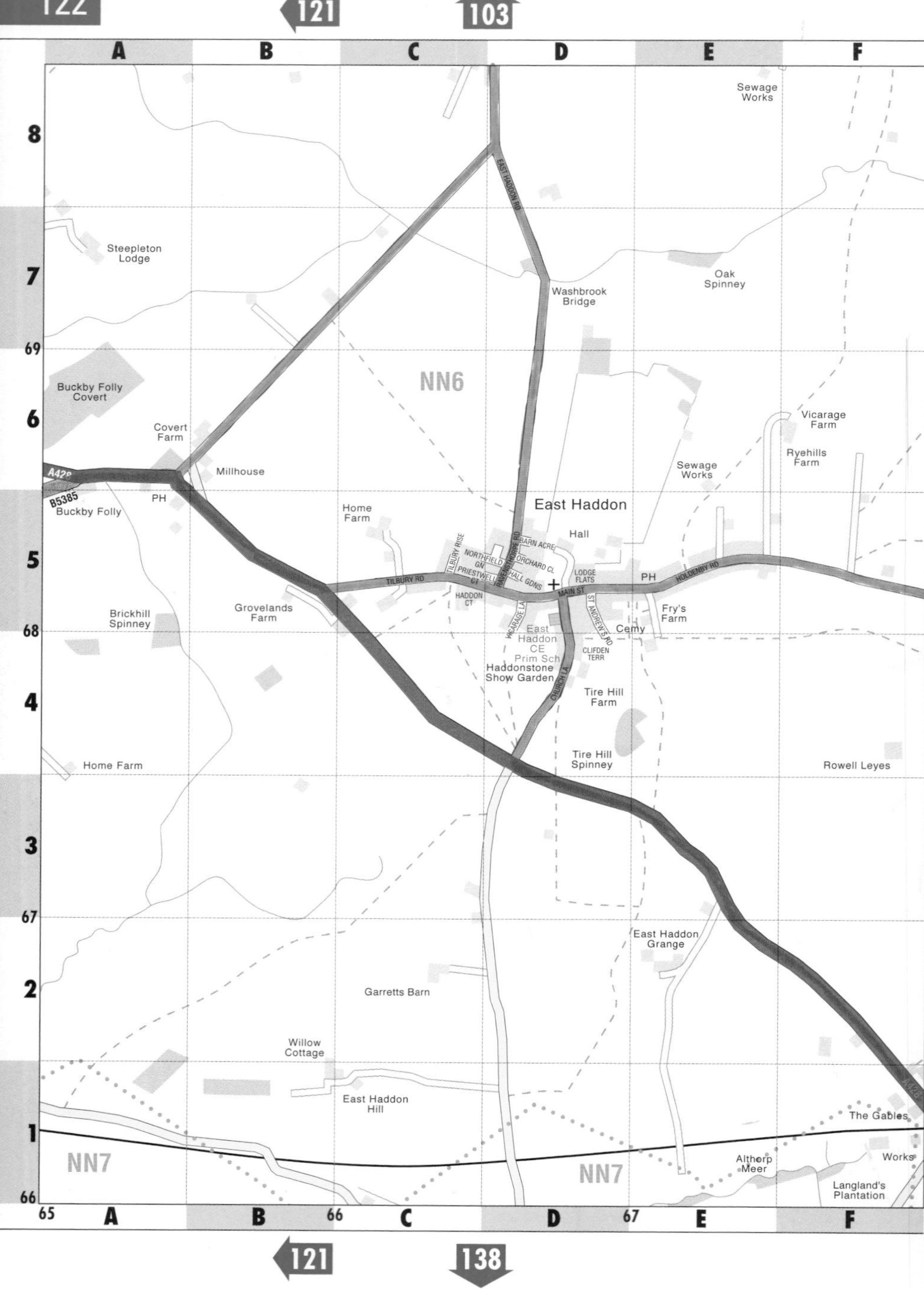

121
138

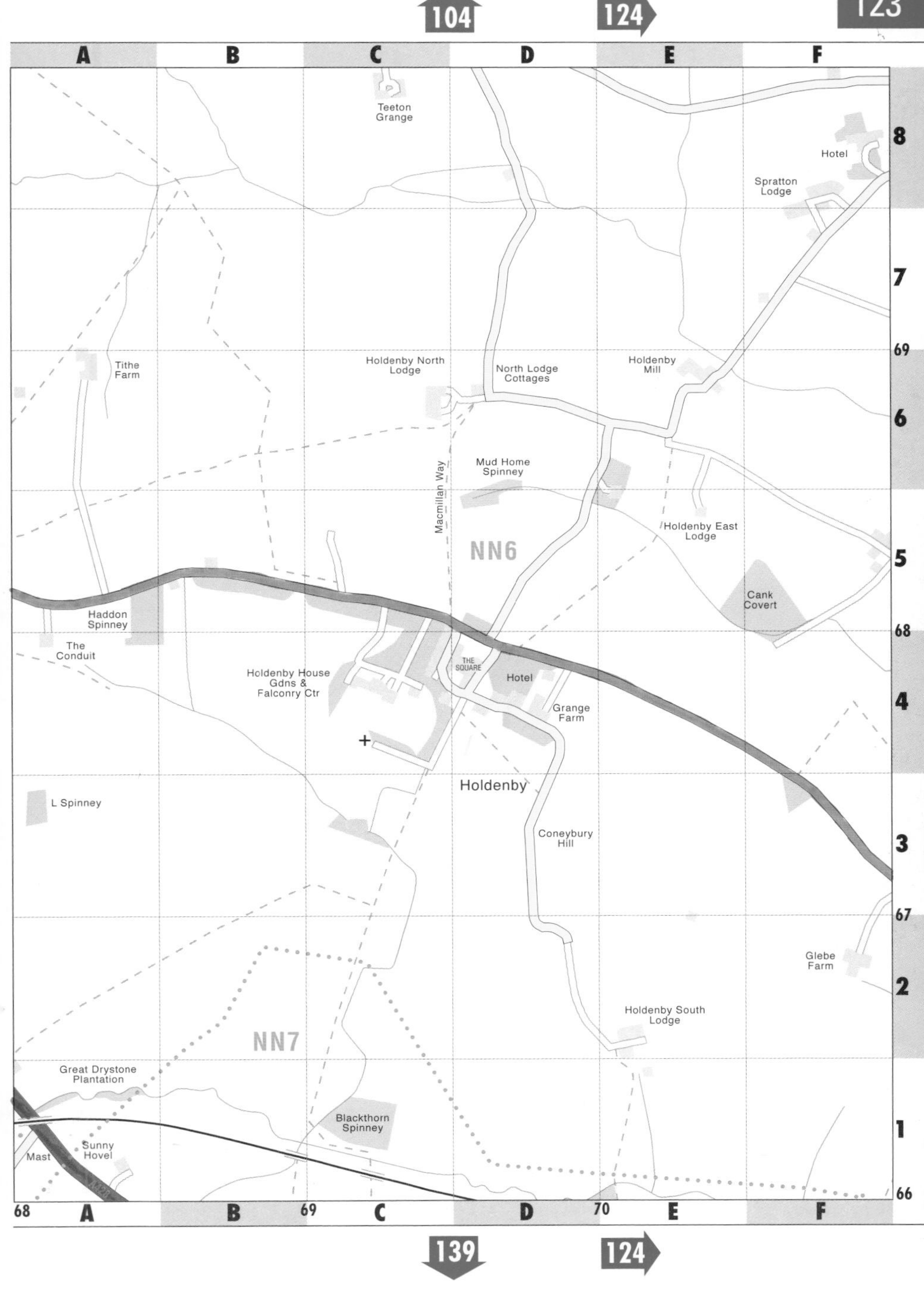
104
124
A
B
C
D
E
F
Teeton Grange
Hotel
Spratton Lodge
Tithe Farm
Holdenby North Lodge
North Lodge Cottages
Holdenby Mill
Macmillan Way
Mud Home Spinney
Holdenby East Lodge
NN6
Cank Covert
Haddon Spinney
The Conduit
Holdenby House Gdns & Falconry Ctr
THE SQUARE
Hotel
Grange Farm
Holdenby
L Spinney
Coneybury Hill
Glebe Farm
Holdenby South Lodge
NN7
Great Drystone Plantation
Blackthorn Spinney
Sunny Hovel
Mast
8
7
69
6
5
68
4
3
67
2
1
66
68
69
70
139
124

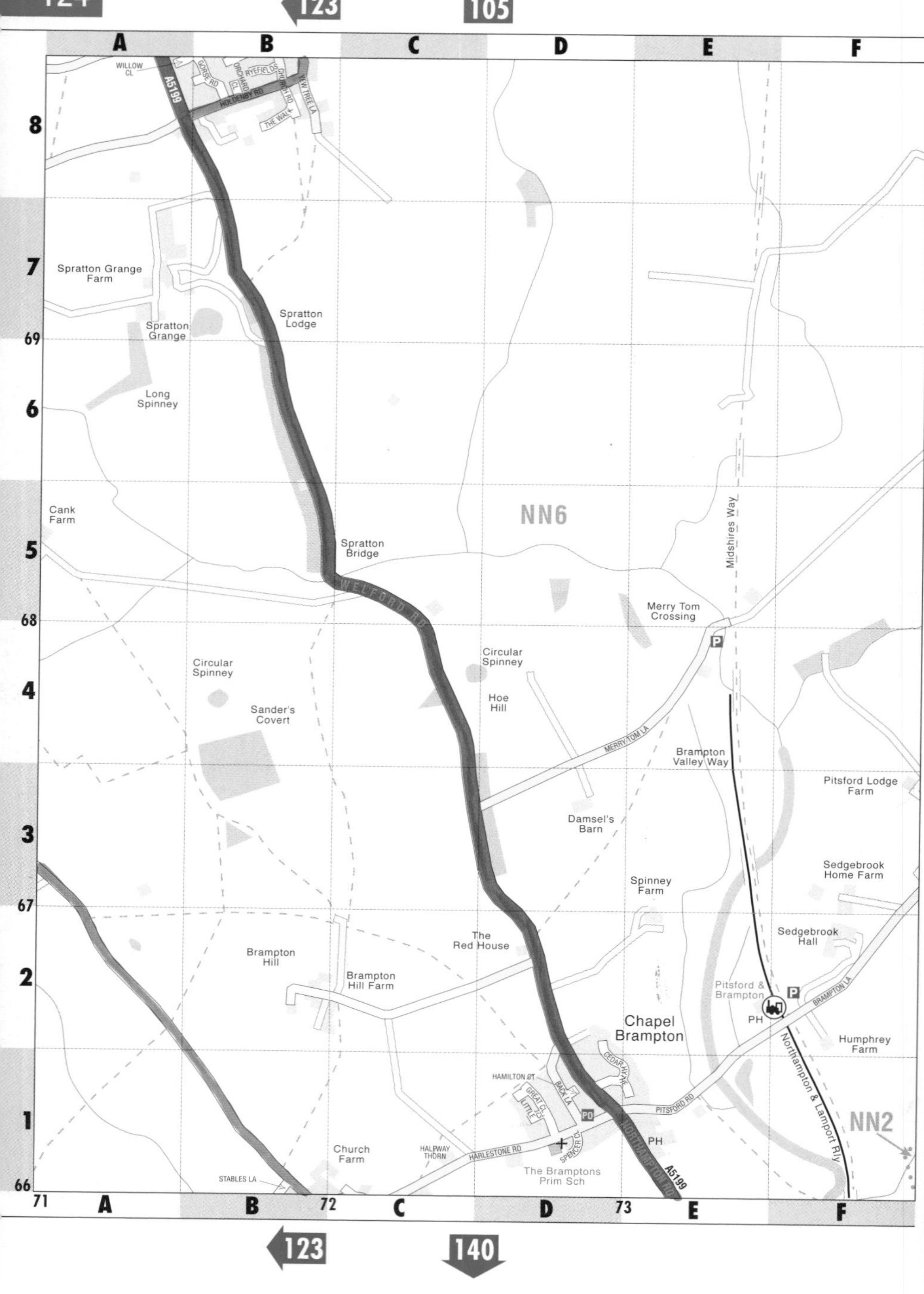
123
105
A
B
C
D
E
F
8
7
69
6
5
68
4
3
67
2
1
66
71
72
73
WILLOW CL
GORSE RD
ORCHARD CL
RYEFIELDS
CHURCH RD
YEW TREE LA
HOLDENBY RD
THE WALK
A5199
Spratton Grange Farm
Spratton Grange
Spratton Lodge
Long Spinney
Cank Farm
Spratton Bridge
NN6
Midshires Way
WELFORD RD
Merry Tom Crossing
Circular Spinney
Circular Spinney
Hoe Hill
Sander's Covert
MERRY TOM LA
Brampton Valley Way
Pitsford Lodge Farm
Damsel's Barn
Sedgebrook Home Farm
Spinney Farm
The Red House
Sedgebrook Hall
Brampton Hill
Brampton Hill Farm
Pitsford & Brampton
BRAMPTON LA
PH
Chapel Brampton
Humphrey Farm
CEDAR HYTHE
HAMILTON CT
BACK LA
GREAT CL
LITTLE CL
PO
PITSFORD RD
Northampton & Lamport Rly
NN2
Church Farm
HALFWAY THORN
HARLESTONE RD
SPENCER CL
PH
NORTHAMPTON RD
A5199
The Bramptons Prim Sch
STABLES LA
123
140

106
126

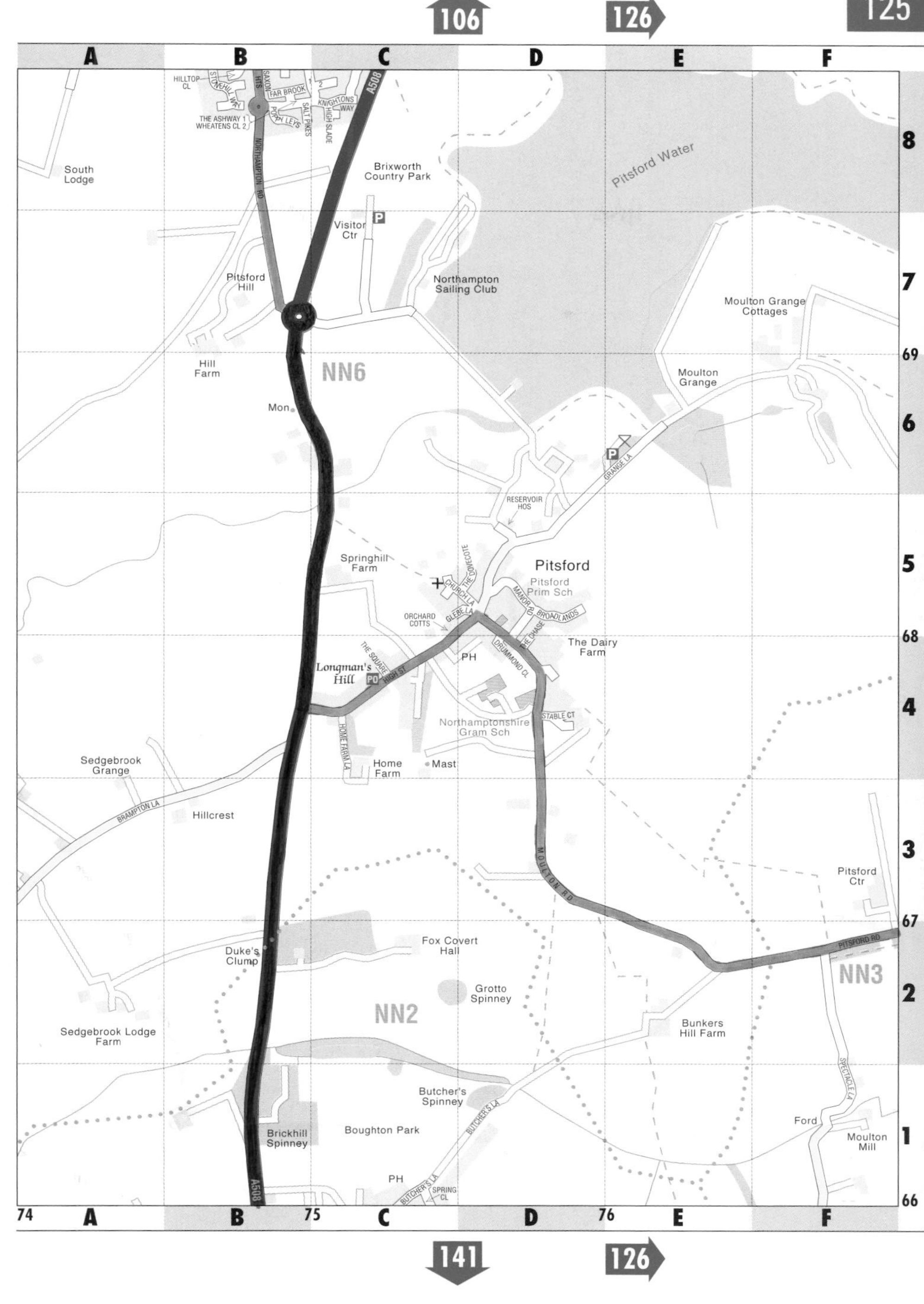

141
126

125
107

C1
1 LEONARD LA
2 BLUEBELL PK CVN PK
3 THE NURSERIES
4 ASHBY GDNS
5 CHAPPELL HO
6 WELLS CT
7 LUNCHFIELD WLK
8 STOCKS HILL

125
142

108 128

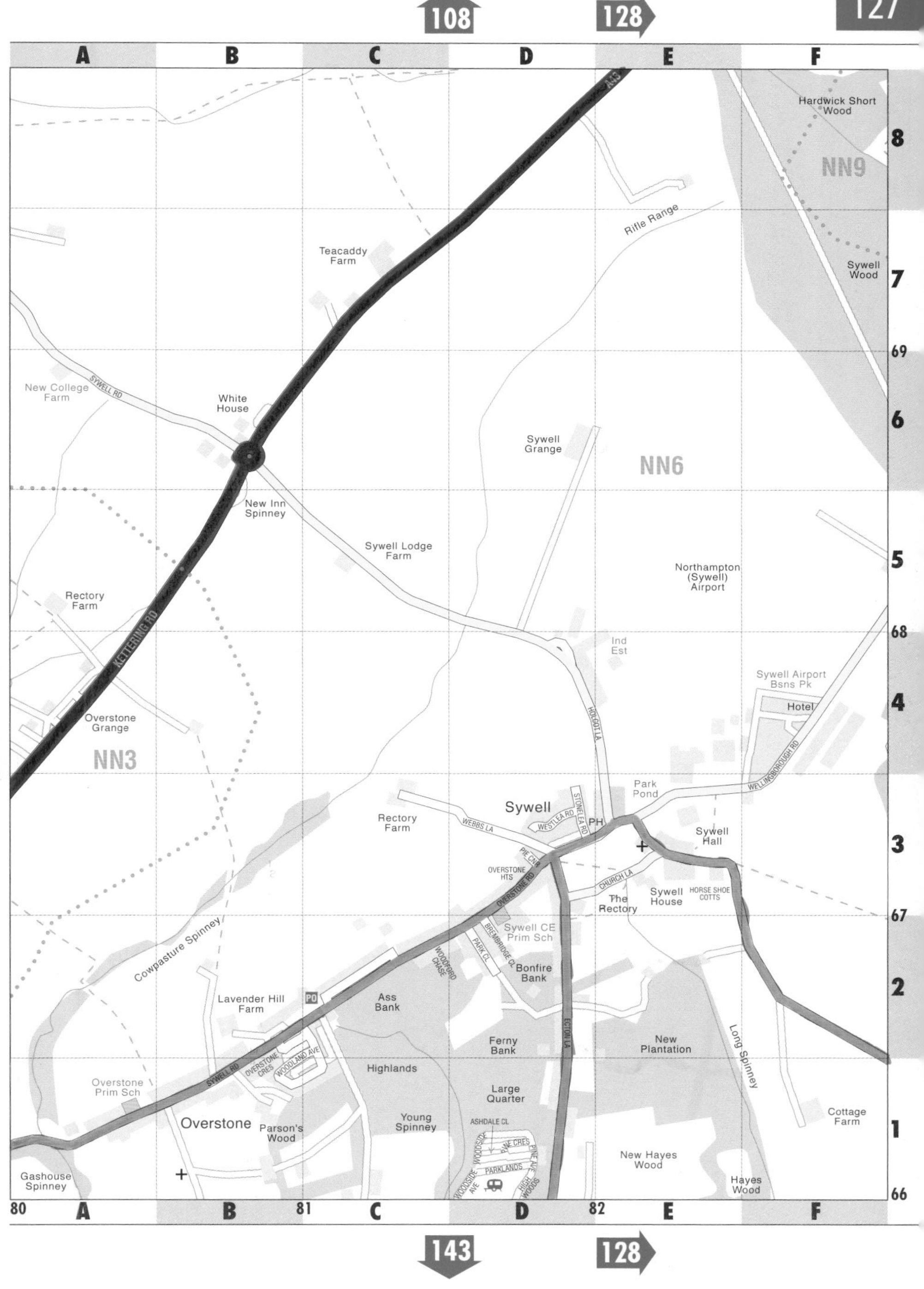

143 128

127
109

127
144

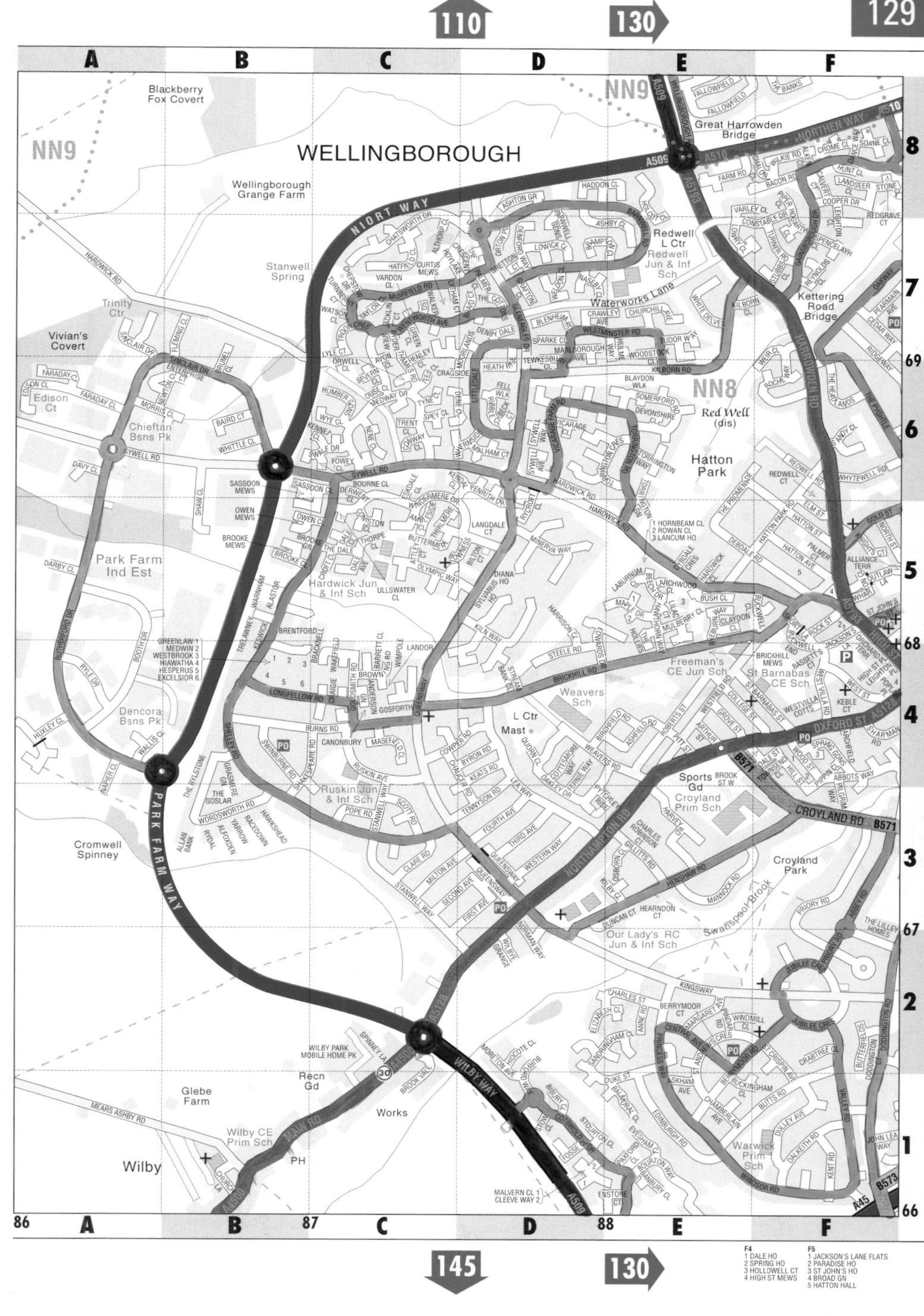

110
130
A
B
C
D
E
F
NN9
NN8
WELLINGBOROUGH
Blackberry Fox Covert
Wellingborough Grange Farm
Stanwell Spring
Trinity Ctr
Vivian's Covert
Edison Ct
Chieftain Bsns Pk
Park Farm Ind Est
Dencora Bsns Pk
Cromwell Spinney
Glebe Farm
Wilby
Wilby CE Prim Sch
PH
Recn Gd
Works
WILBY PARK MOBILE HOME PK
Great Harrowden Bridge
Redwell L Ctr
Redwell Jun & Inf Sch
Waterworks Lane
Kettering Road Bridge
Red Well (dis)
Hatton Park
Hardwick Jun & Inf Sch
Freeman's CE Jun Sch
St Barnabas CE Sch
Weavers Sch
L Ctr
Mast
Sports Gd
Croyland Prim Sch
Croyland Park
Ruskin Jun & Inf Sch
Our Lady's RC Jun & Inf Sch
Swanspool Brook
Warwick Prim Sch
NIORT WAY
PARK FARM WAY
WILBY WAY
NORTHAMPTON RD
HARROWDEN RD
SYWELL RD
HARDWICK RD
BRICKHILL RD
KINGSWAY
CROYLAND RD
OXFORD ST
HIGH ST
NORTHEN WAY
MAIN RD
RUTHERFORD DR
SINCLAIR DR
MEARS ASHBY RD
A509
A510
A5193
A5128
A4500
B571
B573
A45
8
7
69
6
5
68
4
3
67
2
1
66
86
87
88
GREENLAW 1
MEDWIN 2
WESTBROOK 3
HIAWATHA 4
HESPERUS 5
EXCELSIOR 6
1 HORNBEAM CL
2 ROWAN CL
3 LANCUM HO
MALVERN CL 1
CLEEVE WAY 2
145
130
F4
1 DALE HO
2 SPRING HO
3 HOLLOWELL CT
4 HIGH ST MEWS
F5
1 JACKSON'S LANE FLATS
2 PARADISE HO
3 ST JOHN'S HO
4 BROAD GN
5 HATTON HALL

129
111

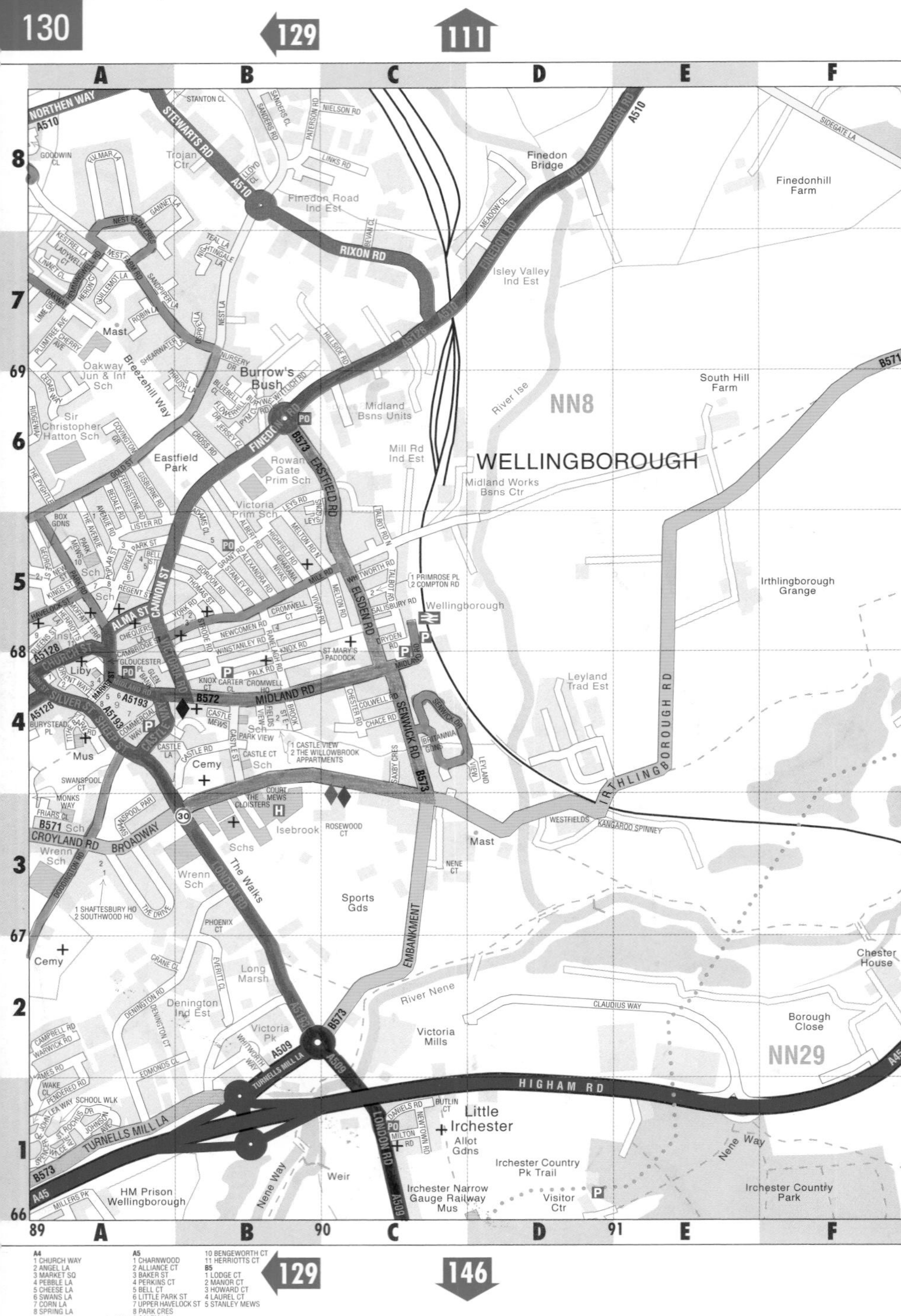

A4
1 CHURCH WAY
2 ANGEL LA
3 MARKET SQ
4 PEBBLE LA
5 CHEESE LA
6 SWANS LA
7 CORN LA
8 SPRING LA
9 The Swansgate Ctr

A5
1 CHARNWOOD
2 ALLIANCE CT
3 BAKER ST
4 PERKINS CT
5 BELL CT
6 LITTLE PARK ST
7 UPPER HAVELOCK ST
8 PARK CRES
9 SALEM LA
10 BENGEWORTH CT
11 HERRIOTTS CT

B5
1 LODGE CT
2 MANOR CT
3 HOWARD CT
4 LAUREL CT
5 STANLEY MEWS

129
146

112
132

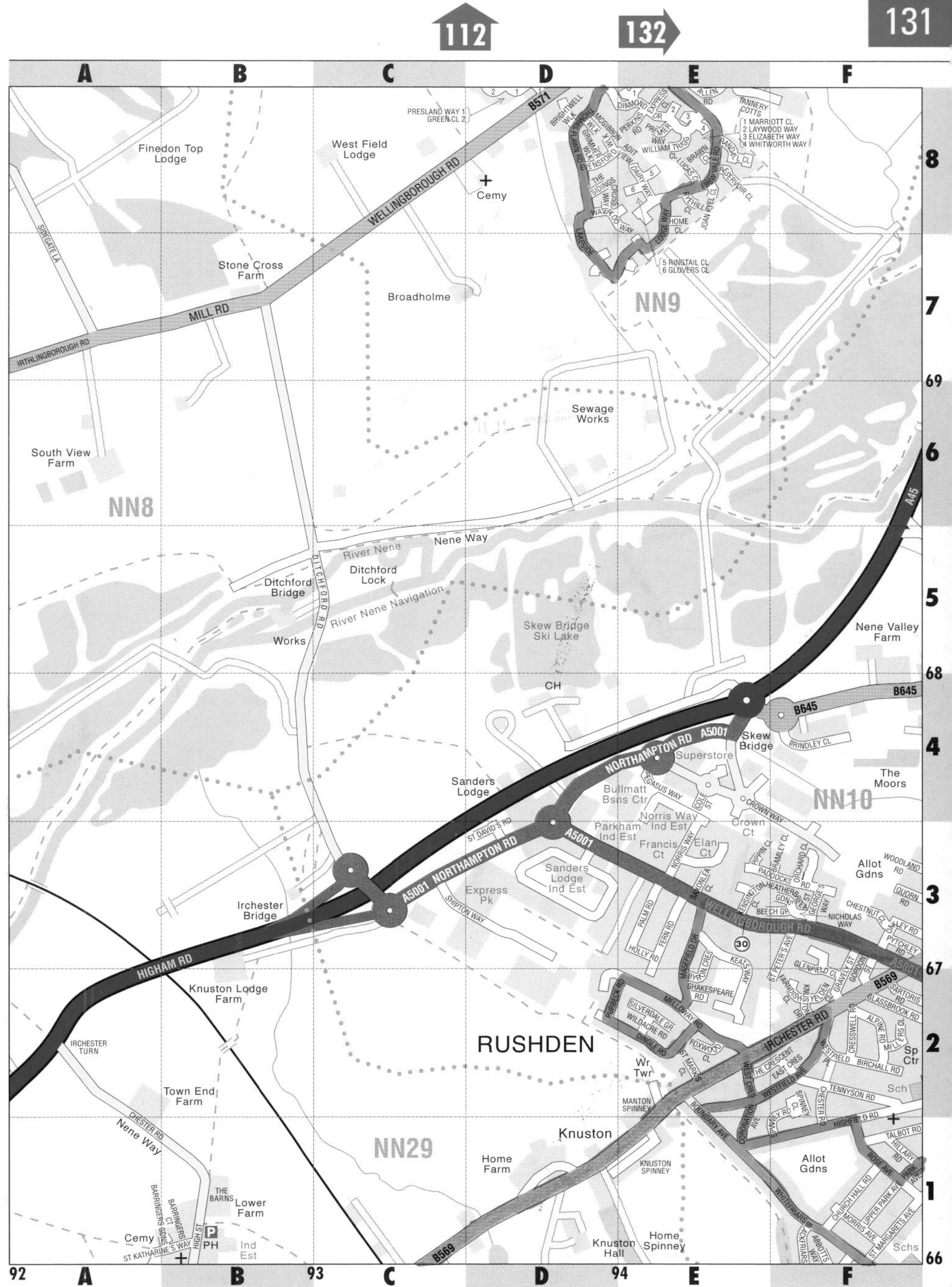

147
132

131 113

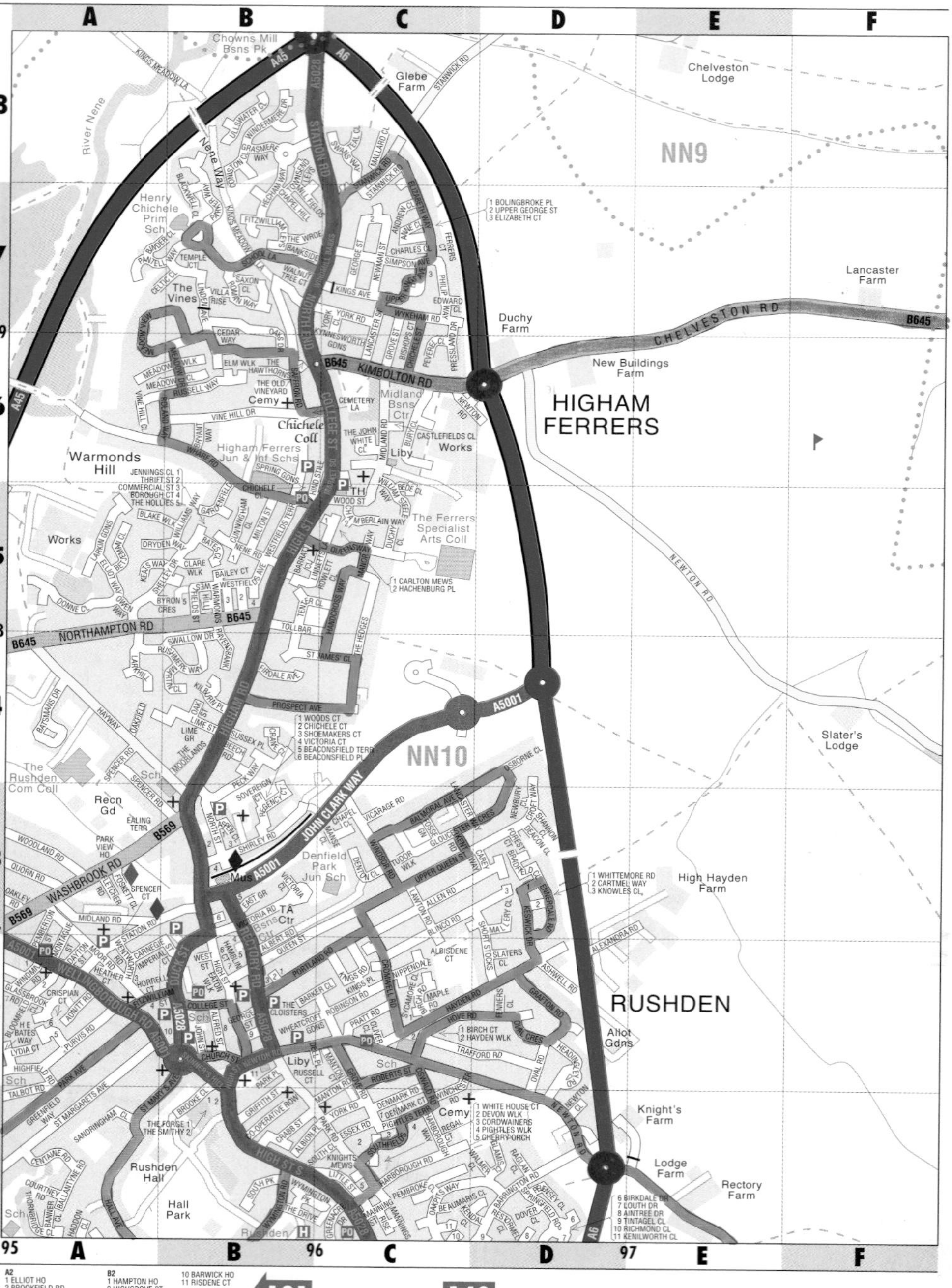

A B C D E F

8 7 69 6 5 68 4 3 67 2 1 66

Chowns Mill Bsns Pk
Glebe Farm
Chelveston Lodge
NN9
River Nene
Nene Way
Henry Chichele Prim Sch
The Vines
Lancaster Farm
Duchy Farm
CHELVESTON RD
B645
New Buildings Farm
KIMBOLTON RD
HIGHAM FERRERS
Cemy
Chichele Coll
Midland Bsns Ctr
Works
Liby
TH
Warmonds Hill
Higham Ferrers Jun & Inf Schs
The Ferrers Specialist Arts Coll
Works
NEWTON RD
NORTHAMPTON RD
A5001
Slater's Lodge
NN10
The Rushden Com Coll
Recn Gd
Sch
JOHN CLARK WAY
WASHBROOK RD
B569
Mus
Denfield Park Jun Sch
High Hayden Farm
TA Ctr
RUSHDEN
WELLINGBOROUGH RD
HIGHAM RD
HIGH ST
STATION RD
COLLEGE ST
RECTORY RD
Allot Gdns
Liby
Sch
Cemy
Knight's Farm
Lodge Farm
Rectory Farm
Rushden Hall
Hall Park
Rushden
A45
A6
A5028

1 BOLINGBROKE PL
2 UPPER GEORGE ST
3 ELIZABETH CT

JENNINGS CL 1
THRIFT ST 2
COMMERCIAL ST 3
BOROUGH CT 4
THE HOLLIES 5

1 CARLTON MEWS
2 HACHENBURG PL

1 WOODS CT
2 CHICHELE CT
3 SHOEMAKERS CT
4 VICTORIA CT
5 BEACONSFIELD TERR
6 BEACONSFIELD PL

1 WHITTEMORE RD
2 CARTMEL WAY
3 KNOWLES CL

1 BIRCH CT
2 HAYDEN WLK

1 WHITE HOUSE CT
2 DEVON WLK
3 CORDWAINERS
4 PIGHTLES WLK
5 CHERRY ORCH

THE FORGE 1
THE SMITHY 2

6 BIRKDALE DR
7 LOUTH DR
8 AINTREE DR
9 TINTAGEL CL
10 RICHMOND CL
11 KENILWORTH CL

95 A B 96 C D 97 E F

A2
1 ELLIOT HO
2 BROOKFIELD RD
3 CHILTERN CT
4 FITZWILLIAM CT
5 WILSON RD
6 CHARLOTTES ROW
7 Windmill Bsns Ctr

B2
1 HAMPTON HO
2 HIGHGROVE CT
3 GATCOMBE HO
4 HADLEIGH HO
5 DENBEIGH HO
6 ASHLEIGH HO
7 BURLEIGH HO
8 PALACE CT
9 COFFEE TAVERN LA
10 BARWICK HO
11 RISDENE CT

131 148

114

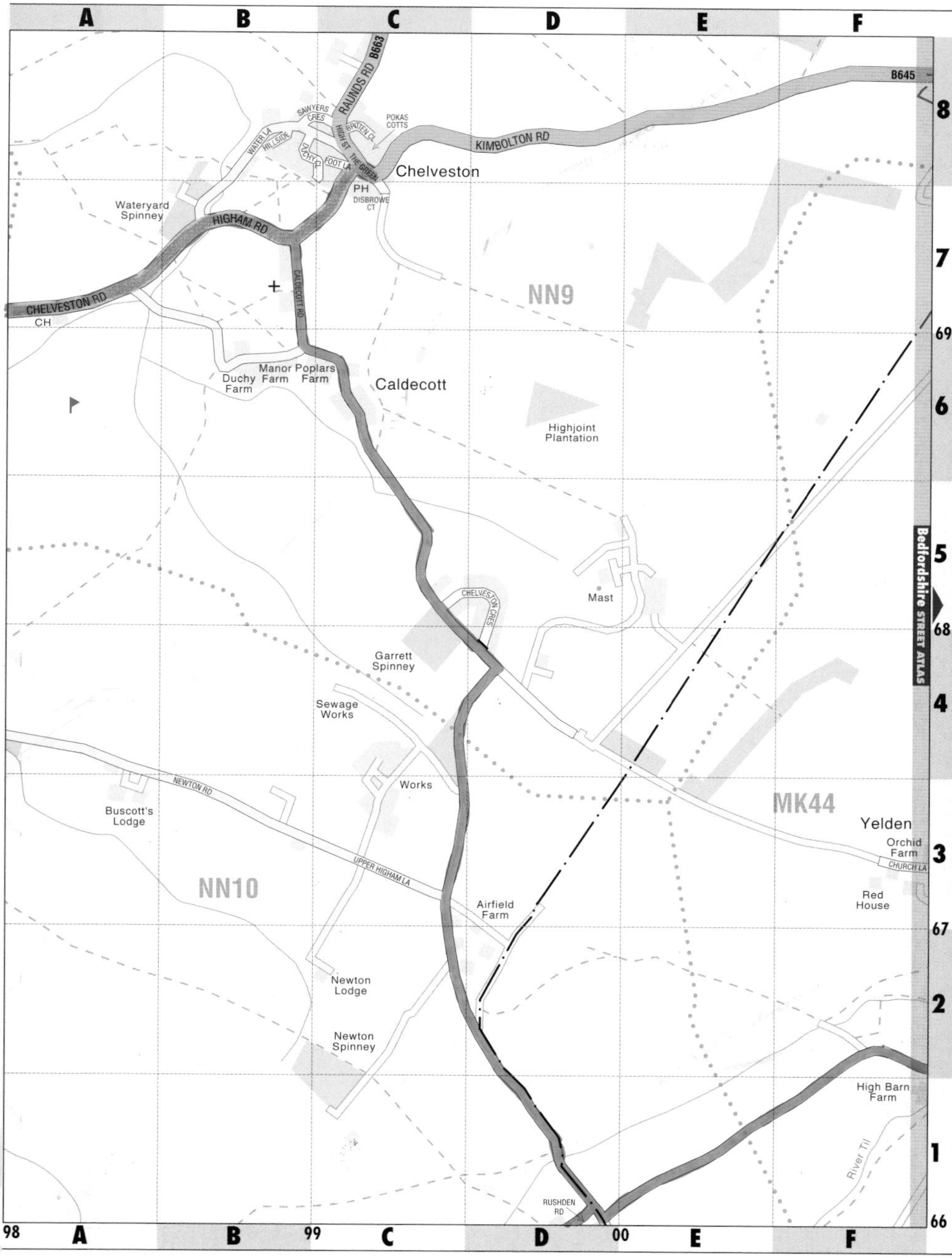

A
B
C
D
E
F
8
7
69
6
5
68
4
3
67
2
1
66
98
99
00
B663
RAUNDS RD
SAWYERS CRES
POKAS COTTS
BRITEN CL
HIGH ST
WATER LA
HILLSIDE
DUCHY CL
FOOT LA
THE GREEN
KIMBOLTON RD
B645
Chelveston
PH
DISBROWE CT
Wateryard Spinney
HIGHAM RD
CALDECOTT RD
NN9
CHELVESTON RD
CH
Duchy Farm
Manor Farm
Poplars Farm
Caldecott
Highjoint Plantation
Mast
CHELVESTON CRES
Garrett Spinney
Sewage Works
Works
NEWTON RD
Buscott's Lodge
MK44
Yelden
Orchid Farm
CHURCH LA
UPPER HIGHAM LA
NN10
Airfield Farm
Red House
Newton Lodge
Newton Spinney
High Barn Farm
River Til
RUSHDEN RD
Bedfordshire STREET ATLAS

118

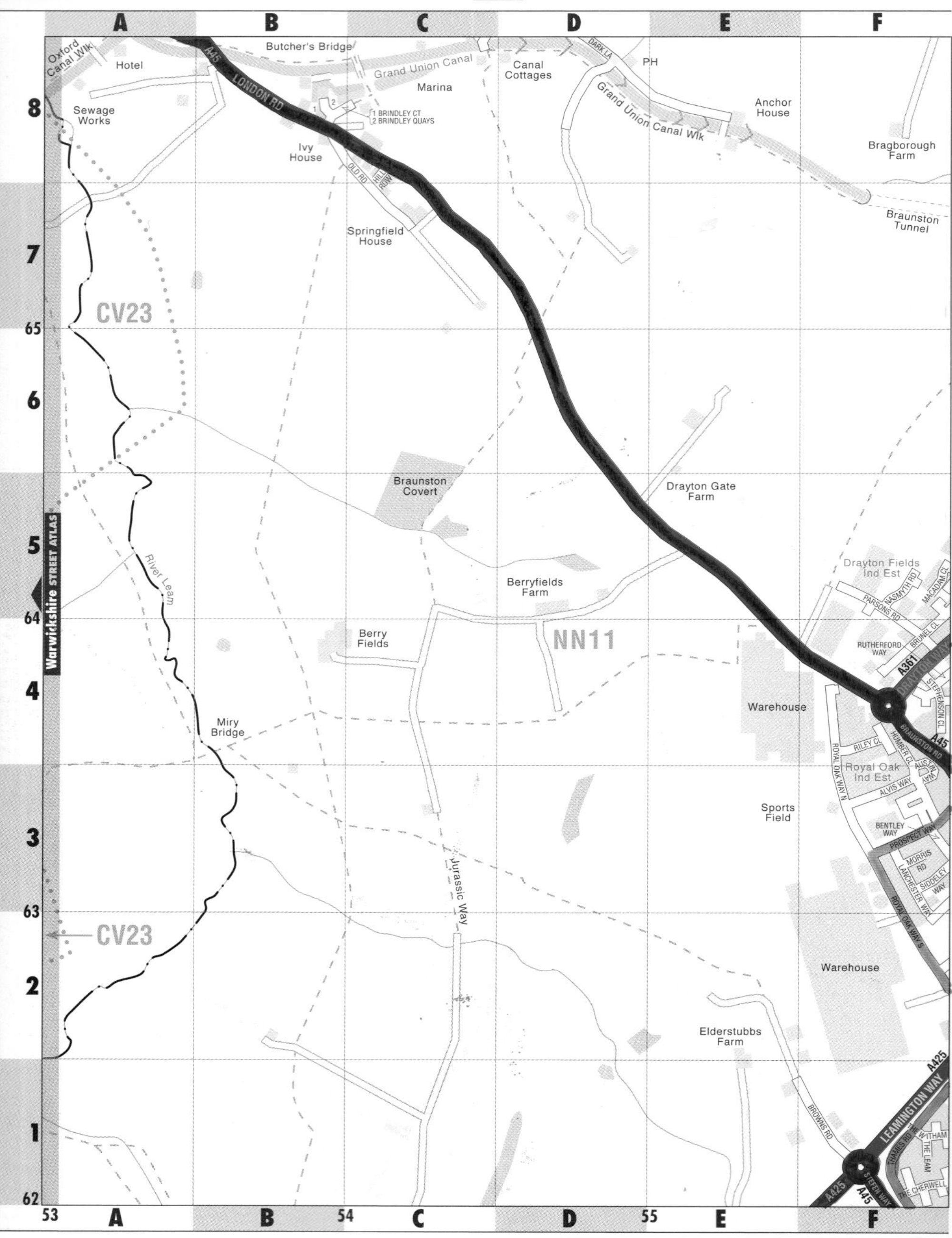
A B C D E F
8 7 65 6 5 64 4 3 63 2 1 62
53 54 55
Oxford Canal Wlk
Hotel
Butcher's Bridge
Grand Union Canal
Marina
Canal Cottages
DARK LA
PH
A45
LONDON RD
1 BRINDLEY CT
2 BRINDLEY QUAYS
Sewage Works
Grand Union Canal Wlk
Anchor House
Bragborough Farm
Ivy House
OLD RD
HILL ROW
Braunston Tunnel
Springfield House
CV23
Braunston Covert
Drayton Gate Farm
River Leam
Drayton Fields Ind Est
NASMYTH RD
MACADAM CL
PARSONS RD
Berryfields Farm
Berry Fields
NN11
RUTHERFORD WAY
BRUNEL CL
A361
DRAYTON WAY
STEPHENSON CL
Warehouse
Miry Bridge
RILEY CL
HUMBER CL
BRAUNSTON RD
Royal Oak Ind Est
ROYAL OAK WAY N
AUSTIN WAY
ALVIS WAY
Sports Field
BENTLEY WAY
PROSPECT WAY
MORRIS RD
LANCHESTER WAY
SIDDELEY WAY
ROYAL OAK WAY S
Jurassic Way
CV23
Warehouse
Elderstubbs Farm
A425
LEAMINGTON WAY
BROWNS RD
THAMES RD
THE WITHAM
THE LEAM
THE CHERWELL
STEFEN WAY
Warwickshire STREET ATLAS

152

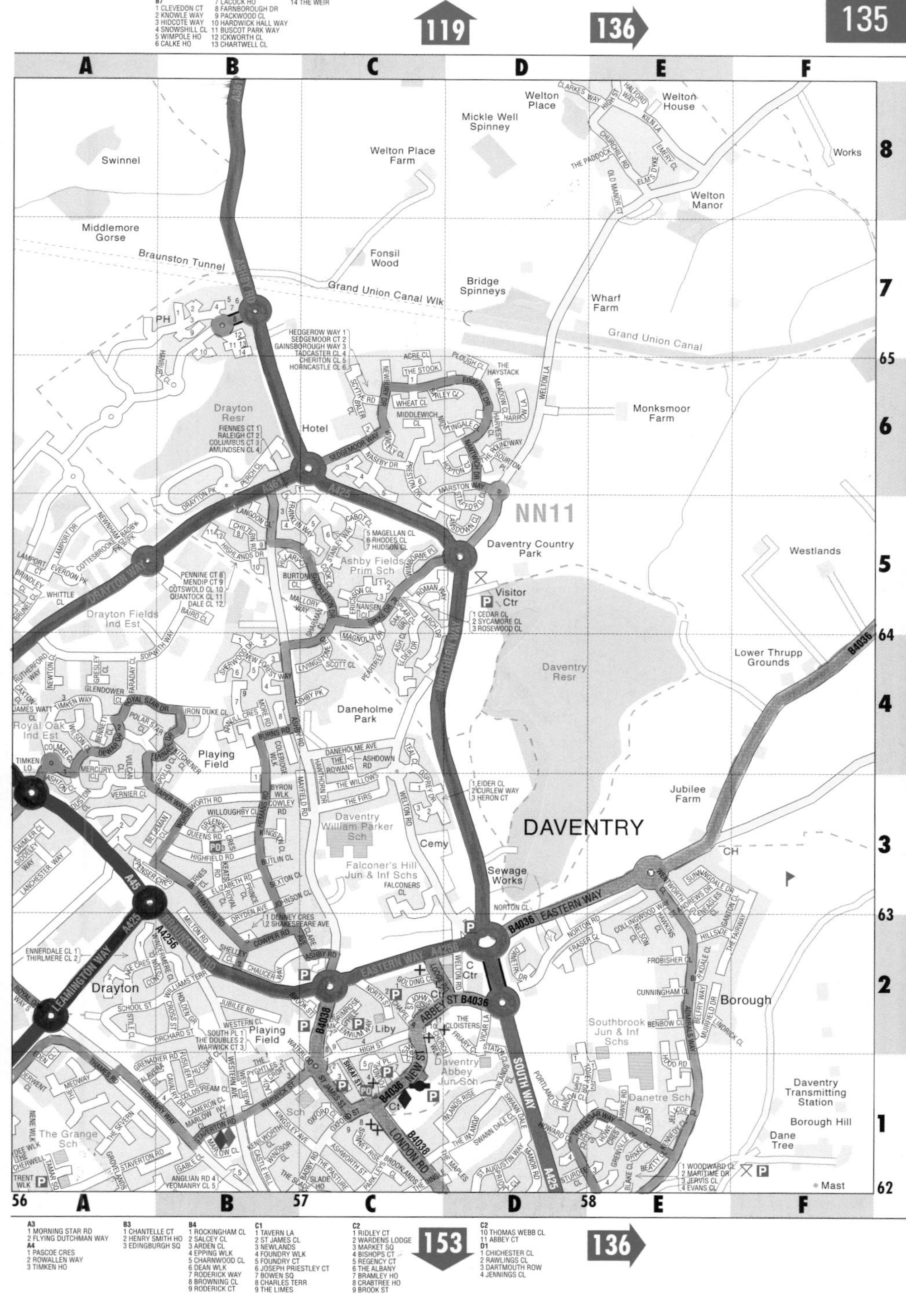
135
119
136
153
136
B7
1 CLEVEDON CT
2 KNOWLE WAY
3 HIDCOTE WAY
4 SNOWSHILL CL
5 WIMPOLE HO
6 CALKE HO
7 LACOCK HO
8 FARNBOROUGH DR
9 PACKWOOD CL
10 HARDWICK HALL WAY
11 BUSCOT PARK WAY
12 ICKWORTH CL
13 CHARTWELL CL
14 THE WEIR
A
B
C
D
E
F
8
7
65
6
5
64
4
3
63
2
1
62
56
57
58
Swinnel
Middlemore Gorse
Braunston Tunnel
Welton Place Farm
Fonsil Wood
Mickle Well Spinney
Welton Place
Welton House
Works
Welton Manor
Bridge Spinneys
Grand Union Canal Wlk
Wharf Farm
Grand Union Canal
ASHBY RD
HEDGEROW WAY 1
SEDGEMOOR CT 2
GAINSBOROUGH WAY 3
TADCASTER CL 4
CHERITON CL 5
HORNCASTLE CL 6
Drayton Resr
FIENNES CT 1
RALEIGH CT 2
COLUMBUS CT 3
AMUNDSEN CL 4
Hotel
Monksmoor Farm
NN11
Daventry Country Park
Westlands
5 MAGELLAN CL
6 RHODES CL
7 HUDSON CL
Ashby Fields Prim Sch
PENNINE CT 8
MENDIP CT 9
COTSWOLD CL 10
QUANTOCK CL 11
DALE CL 12
Drayton Fields Ind Est
Visitor Ctr
1 CEDAR CL
2 SYCAMORE CL
3 ROSEWOOD CL
Daventry Resr
Lower Thrupp Grounds
B4036
Royal Oak Ind Est
Daneholme Park
Playing Field
1 EIDER CL
2 CURLEW WAY
3 HERON CT
Jubilee Farm
DAVENTRY
Daventry William Parker Sch
Cemy
Falconer's Hill Jun & Inf Schs
Sewage Works
CH
EASTERN WAY
1 DENNEY CRES
2 SHAKESPEARE AVE
ENNERDALE CL 1
THIRLMERE CL 2
LEAMINGTON WAY
Drayton
C Ctr
Borough
Playing Field
SOUTH PL 1
THE DOUBLES 2
WARWICK CT 3
Liby
Southbrook Jun & Inf Schs
Daventry Abbey Jun Sch
Danetre Sch
Daventry Transmitting Station
Borough Hill
Dane Tree
The Grange Sch
Sch
LONDON RD
SOUTH WAY
ANGLIAN RD 4
YEOMANRY CL 5
1 WOODWARD CL
2 MARITIME DR
3 JERVIS CL
4 EVANS CL
Mast
A3
1 MORNING STAR RD
2 FLYING DUTCHMAN WAY
A4
1 PASCOE CRES
2 ROWALLEN WAY
3 TIMKEN HO
B3
1 CHANTELLE CT
2 HENRY SMITH HO
3 EDINGBURGH SQ
B4
1 ROCKINGHAM CL
2 SALCEY CL
3 ARDEN CL
4 EPPING WLK
5 CHARNWOOD CL
6 DEAN WLK
7 RODERICK WAY
8 BROWNING CL
9 RODERICK CT
C1
1 TAVERN LA
2 ST JAMES CL
3 NEWLANDS
4 FOUNDRY WLK
5 FOUNDRY CT
6 JOSEPH PRIESTLEY CT
7 BOWEN SQ
8 CHARLES TERR
9 THE LIMES
C2
1 RIDLEY CT
2 WARDENS LODGE
3 MARKET SQ
4 BISHOPS CT
5 REGENCY CT
6 THE ALBANY
7 BRAMLEY HO
8 CRABTREE HO
9 BROOK ST
C2
10 THOMAS WEBB CL
11 ABBEY CT
D1
1 CHICHESTER CL
2 RAWLINGS CL
3 DARTMOUTH ROW
4 JENNINGS CL

135
120

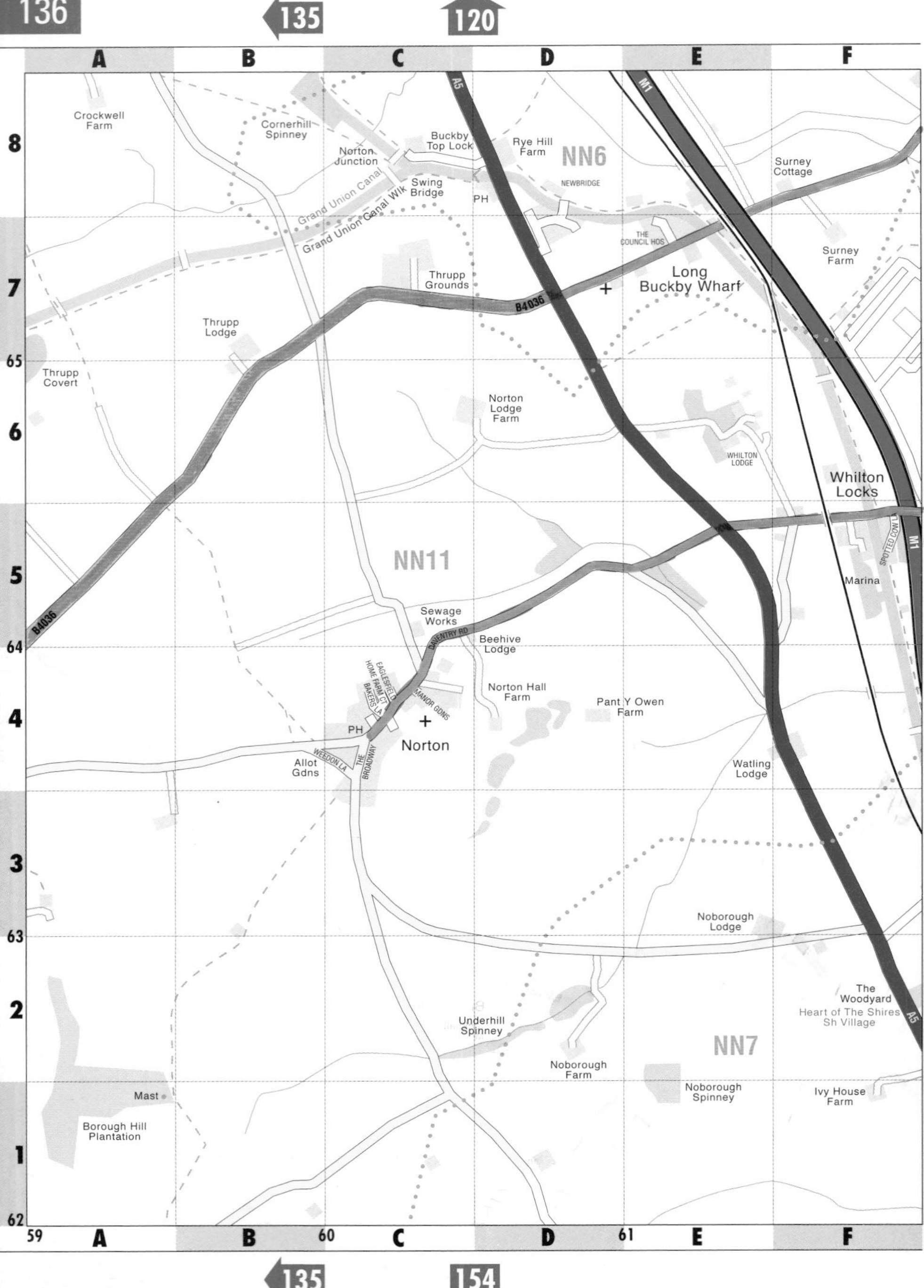

135
154

121
138

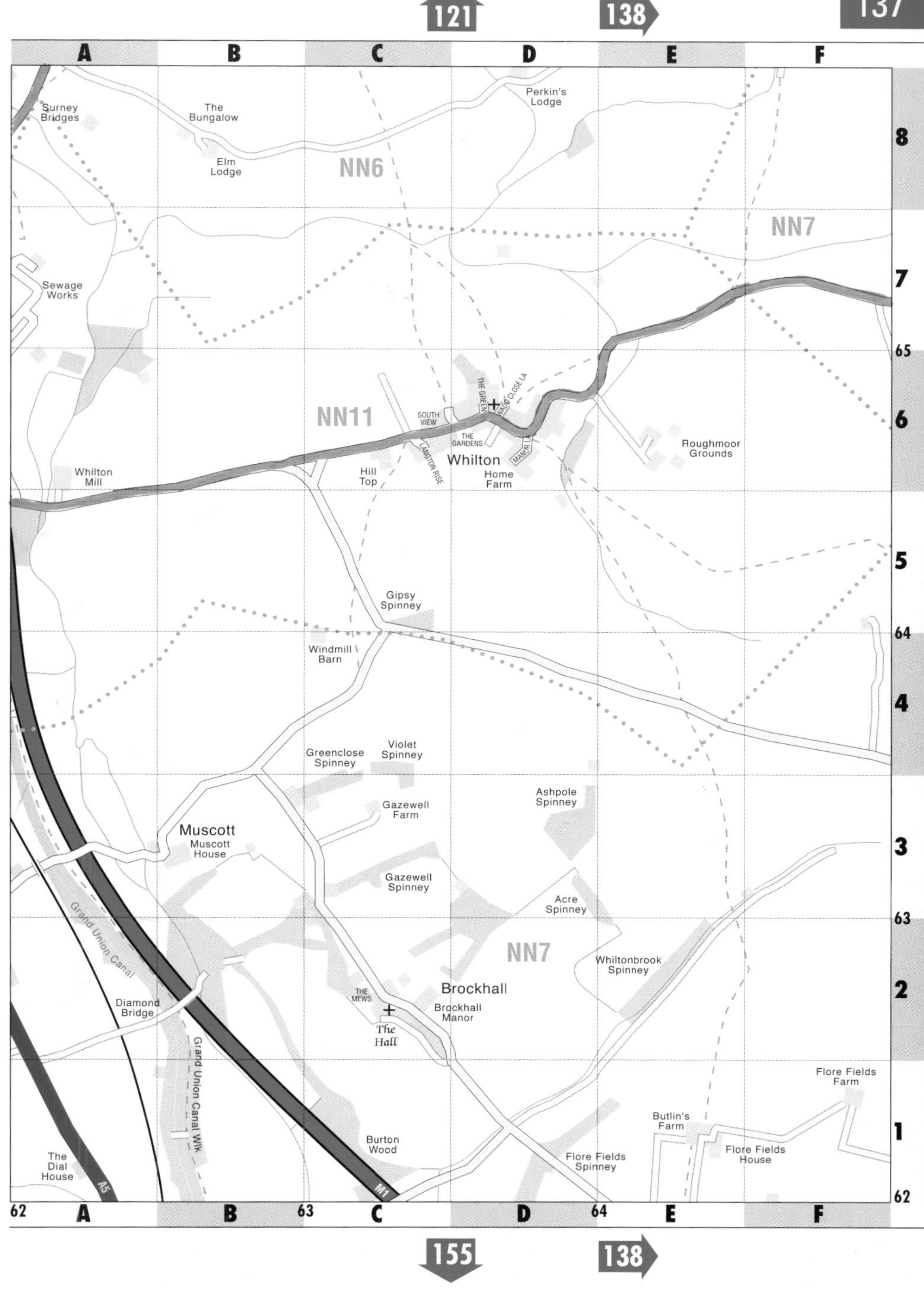

155
138

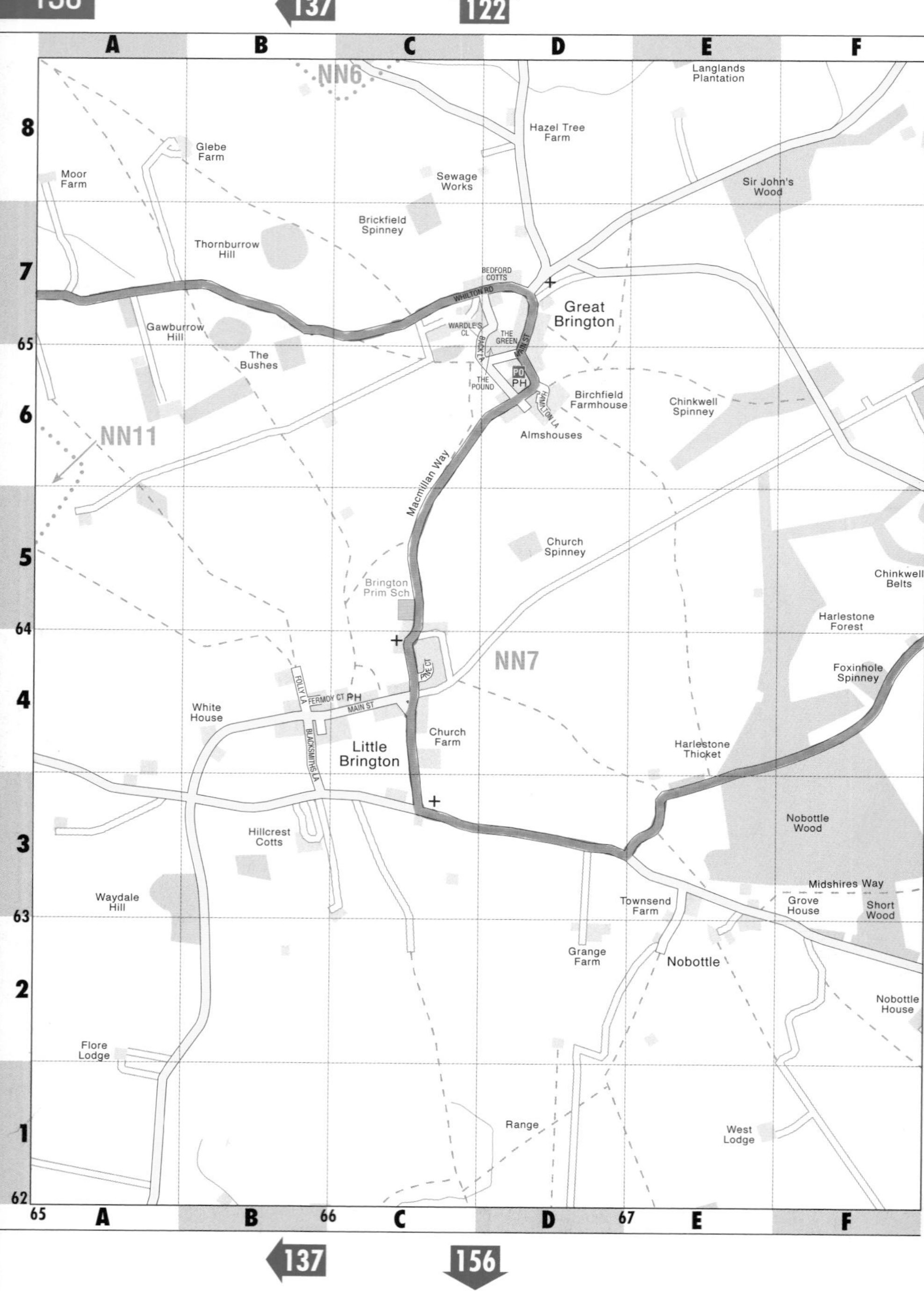
137
122
A
B
C
D
E
F
NN6
Langlands Plantation
8
Hazel Tree Farm
Glebe Farm
Moor Farm
Sewage Works
Sir John's Wood
Brickfield Spinney
Thornburrow Hill
7
BEDFORD COTTS
WHILTON RD
Great Brington
Gawburrow Hill
WARDLE'S CL
BACK LA
THE GREEN
MAIN ST
65
The Bushes
PO
PH
THE POUND
Birchfield Farmhouse
HAMILTON LA
Chinkwell Spinney
6
NN11
Almshouses
Macmillan Way
Church Spinney
5
Chinkwell Belts
Brington Prim Sch
Harlestone Forest
64
NN7
Foxinhole Spinney
FOLLY LA
FERMOY CT
PH
MAIN ST
4
White House
Church Farm
Little Brington
Harlestone Thicket
BLACKSMITHS LA
Hillcrest Cotts
Nobottle Wood
3
Waydale Hill
Midshires Way
Townsend Farm
Grove House
Short Wood
63
Grange Farm
Nobottle
2
Nobottle House
Flore Lodge
1
Range
West Lodge
62
65
66
67
137
156

123
140
A
B
C
D
E
F
8
7
65
6
5
64
4
3
63
2
1
62
68
69
70
Pedigree Buildings Farm
Delf Spinney
NN6
Millholme Plantation
Lucas's Field Plantation
East Lodge
Glebe Farm
Althorp
Glebe Cotts
GLEBE LA
Old Lodge Plantation
Dog Pond
Althorp Park
Three Corner Plantation
New Park Plantation
Oaktree Stew
Obelisk
PARK FARM BARNS
Great Stew
CHURCH LA
HARLESTONE RD
Mill
CH
PH
The Paddocks
Harlestone Prim Sch
Lower Harlestone
Chinkwell Clumps
PO
Harlestone
A428
Midshires Way
Yew Tree Farm
THE GREEN
Upper Harlestone
SWEDISH HOS
Sand Pit
Yewtree Spinney
Standingwell Spinney
Round Oak Plantation
NN5
Broadgow Spinney
NN7
PORT RD
Fleetland Farm
Sowditch Thicket
BERGERAC CL
ANJOU CT
Nobottle Belt
Oldfield Thicket
Heath Farm
TOURAINE CL
ROCHELLE WAY
SANDY LA
ALSACE CL
MACON CL
BEAUVAIS CT
PROVENCE CT
VELOCETTE WAY
MARSEILLES CL
HIRONDELLE CL
BEAUNE CL
Wr Twr
Lodge Barn
NORTHAMPTON
ST EMILION CL
BORDEAUX CT
The Lodge
BLOSSAC CT
AQUITAINE CL
GREEVES CL
BROUGH CL
POITIERS CT
TRIUMPH GDNS
A
B
C
D
E
F
157
140

139
124

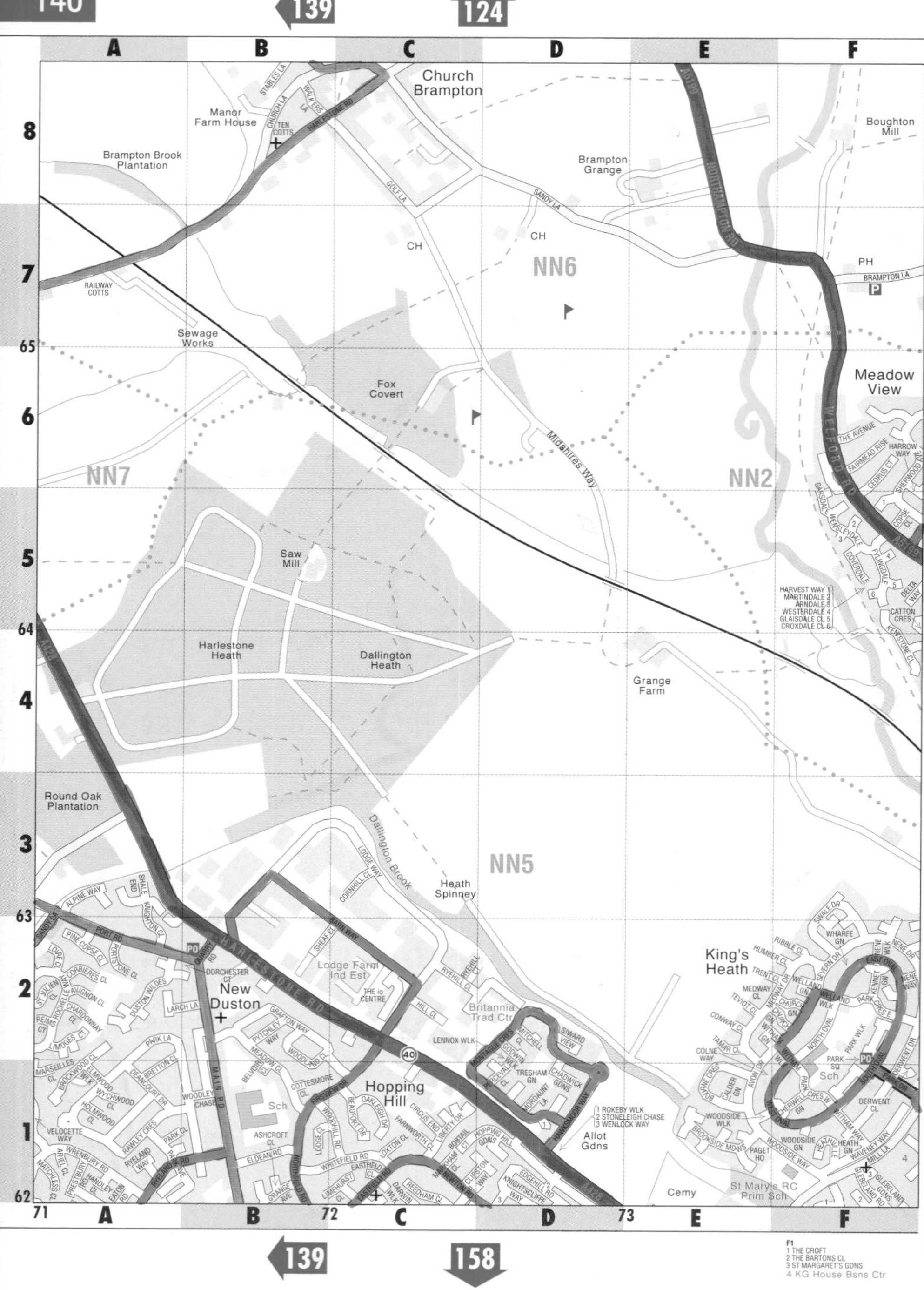

F1
1 THE CROFT
2 THE BARTONS CL
3 ST MARGARET'S GDNS
4 KG House Bsns Ctr

139
158

125
142

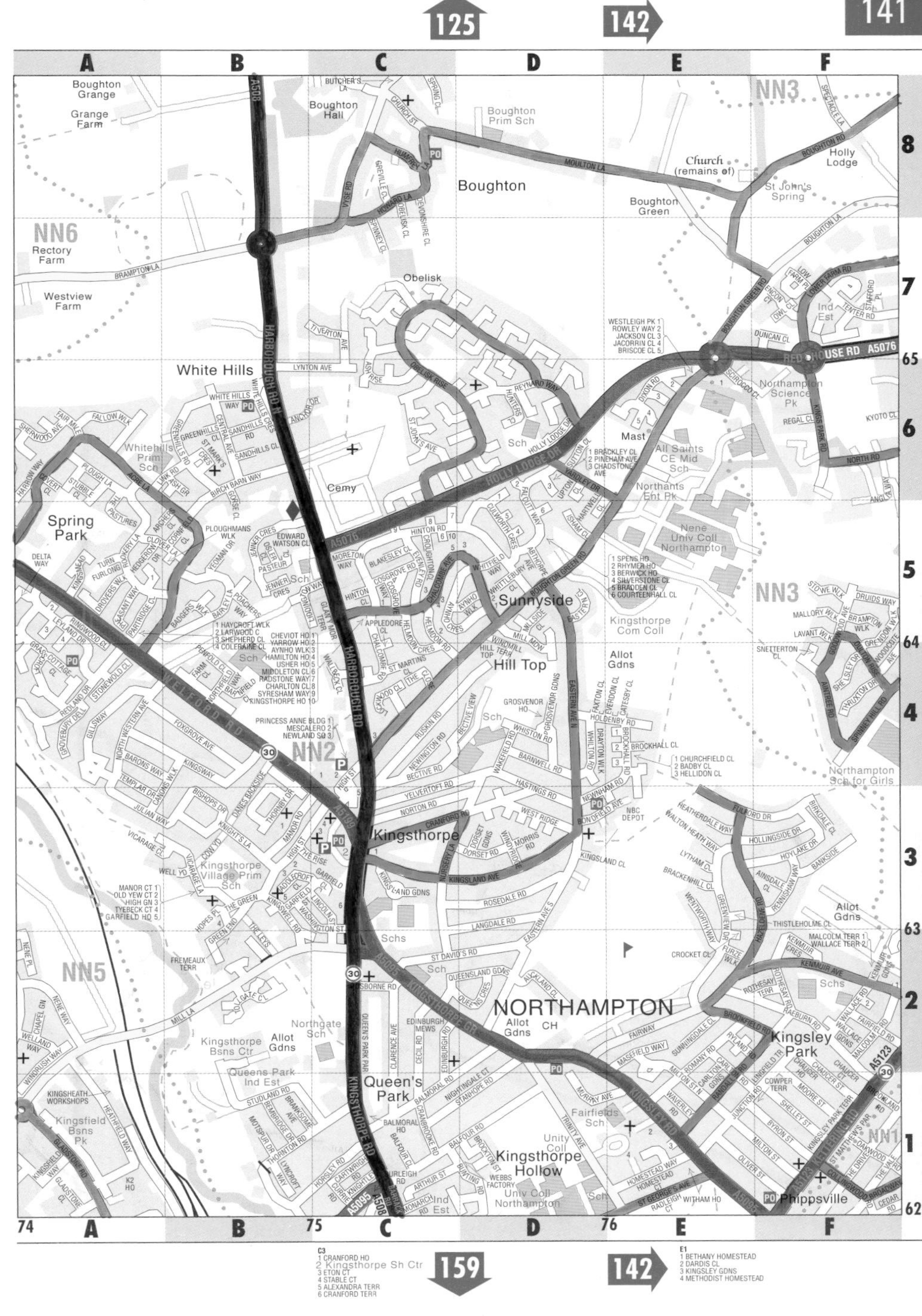

C3
1 CRANFORD HO
2 Kingsthorpe Sh Ctr
3 ETON CT
4 STABLE CT
5 ALEXANDRA TERR
6 CRANFORD TERR

E1
1 BETHANY HOMESTEAD
2 DARDIS CL
3 KINGSLEY GDNS
4 METHODIST HOMESTEAD

159
142

141 126

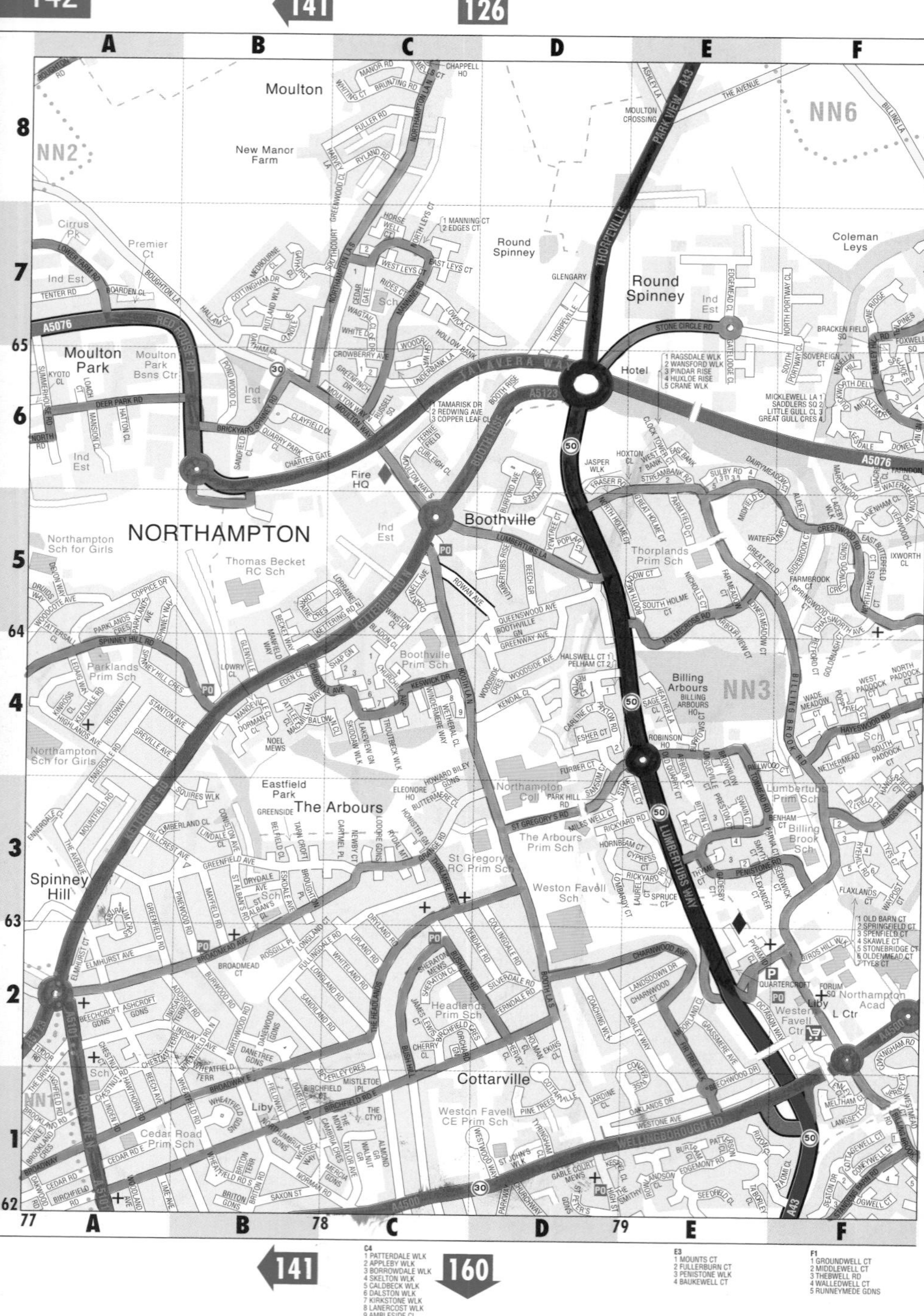

141 160

C4
1 PATTERDALE WLK
2 APPLEBY WLK
3 BORROWDALE WLK
4 SKELTON WLK
5 CALDBECK WLK
6 DALSTON WLK
7 KIRKSTONE WLK
8 LANERCOST WLK
9 AMBLESIDE CL

E3
1 MOUNTS CT
2 FULLERBURN CT
3 PENISTONE WLK
4 BAUKEWELL CT

F1
1 GROUNDWELL CT
2 MIDDLEWELL CT
3 THEBWELL RD
4 WALLEDWELL CT
5 RUNNEYMEDE GDNS

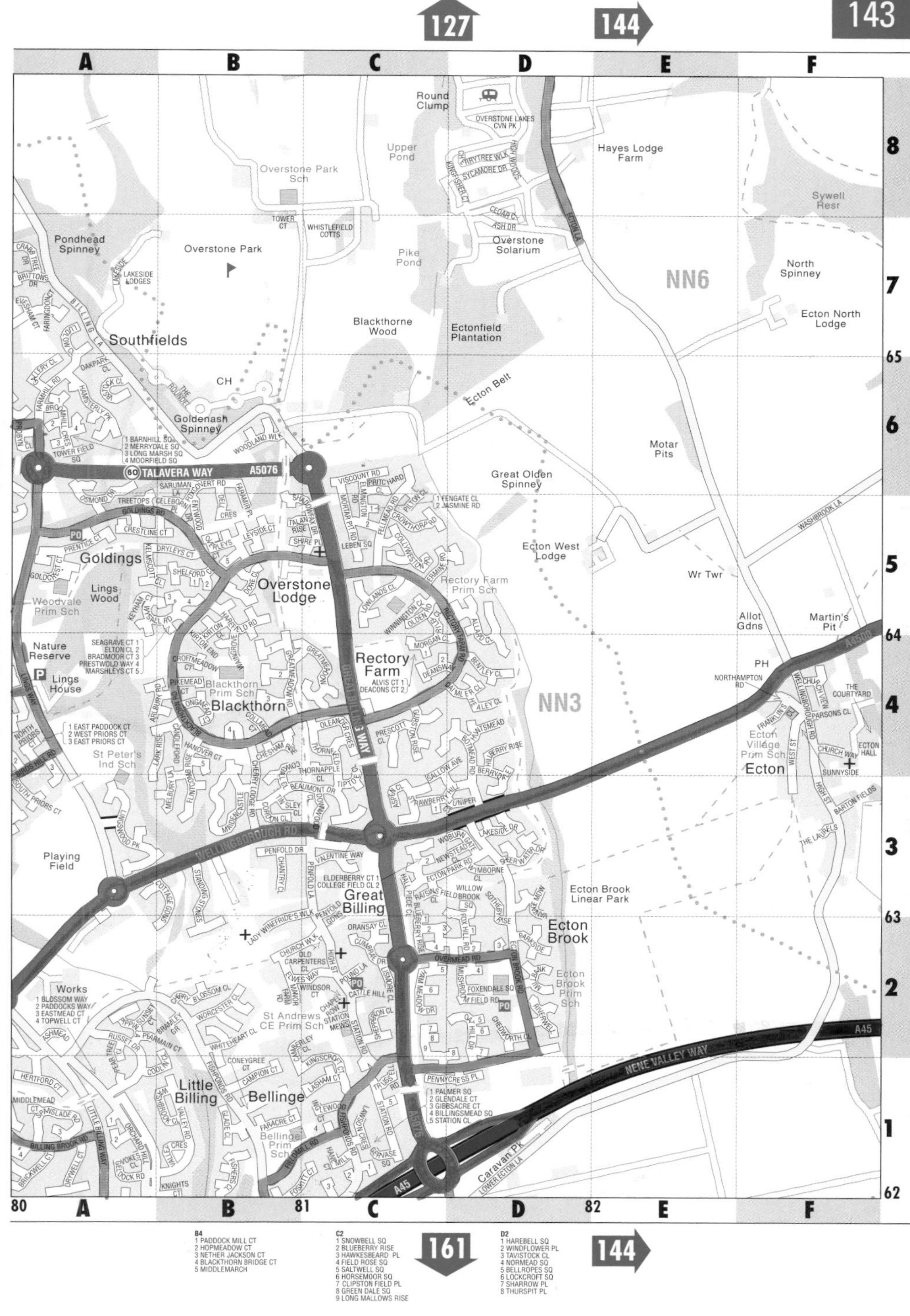
127
144
A
B
C
D
E
F
8
7
65
6
5
64
4
3
63
2
1
62
80
81
82
Round Clump
OVERSTONE LAKES CVN PK
Upper Pond
Hayes Lodge Farm
Overstone Park Sch
CHERRYTREE WLK
SYCAMORE DR
HIGH WOODS
KINGFISHER CT
CEDAR CL
ASH DR
Sywell Resr
ECTON LA
TOWER CT
WHISTLEFIELD COTTS
Overstone Solarium
Pondhead Spinney
Overstone Park
Pike Pond
NN6
North Spinney
CRABTREE DR
BRITTONS DR
LAKESIDE LODGES
EVESHAM CT
FARINGDON CT
BILLING LA
Blackthorne Wood
Ectonfield Plantation
Ecton North Lodge
Southfields
LUDLOW CL
OAKPARK CL
CH
Ecton Belt
THE ROUNDEL
FARMHILL RD
HAMSTERLY PK
BROOMHILL CRES
Goldenash Spinney
1 BARNHILL SQ
2 MERRYDALE SQ
3 LONG MARSH SQ
4 MOORFIELD SQ
TOWER FIELD SQ
WOODLAND WLK
TALAVERA WAY
A5076
Motar Pits
VISCOUNT RD
PRITCHARD CL
ELMINGTON
MORTAR PIT RD
FELLMEAD RD
PILTON CL
1 FENGATE CL
2 JASMINE RD
Great Olden Spinney
SARUMAN LA
FOXCOVERT RD
OSMOND DR
TREETOPS
CELEBORN
FARAMIR PL
GOLDINGS RD
ENTWOOD
DELL CRES
SHADOWFAX DR
TALAN RISE
CROWTHORP RD
WASHBROOK LA
CRESTLINE CT
LEYSIDE CT
SHIRE PL
LEBEN SQ
COLLYWESTON RD
PRENTICE CT
DRYLEYS CT
Ecton West Lodge
Goldings
KELMSCOTT
SHELFORD CT
ERMINE RD
Wr Twr
Overstone Lodge
Lings Wood
Woodvale Prim Sch
Rectory Farm Prim Sch
LOWLANDS CL
WINNINGTON CL
OLDEN RD
RECTORY FARM RD
KEYHAM CT
WALSALL RD
HAREFIELD RD
KIRTON END
WOOLGROVE
GREATMEADOW
Allot Gdns
Martin's Pit
Nature Reserve
SEAGRAVE CT 1
ELTON CL 2
BRADMOOR CT 3
PRESTWOLD WAY 4
MARSHLEYS CT 5
MORGAN CL
ALLARD CL
A4500
CROFTMEADOW CT
Rectory Farm
DEANSWAY
BENTLEY CL
PH
Lings House
PIKEMEAD CT
Blackthorn Prim Sch
ALVIS CT 1
DEACONS CT 2
NORTHAMPTON RD
WELLINGBOROUGH RD
CHURCH VIEW
THE COURTYARD
LONGMEAD CT
DAIMLER CL
HEALEY CL
Blackthorn
NN3
FRANKLIN'S CL
PARSONS CL
ARLBURY RD
COLLMEAD CT
GREAT BILLING WAY
1 EAST PADDOCK CT
2 WEST PRIORS CT
3 EAST PRIORS CT
OLEANDER CRES
PRESCOTT CL
GIBSTON RISE
HUNTSMEAD
Ecton Village Prim Sch
NORTH PRIORS CT
CANDLEFORD
CHESHAM RISE
THORNFIELD
BOTMEAD RD
HILLBERRY RISE
WEST ST
CHURCH WAY
ECTON HALL
Ecton
St Peter's Ind Sch
LARK RISE
HANOVER CT
THORNAPPLE CL
SALLOW AVE
BERRYDALE
SUNNYSIDE
BIRDS HILL RD
MELBURY LA
FLINTON RISE
CHERRY LODGE RD
BEAUMONT DR
TIPTO
SOUTH PRIORS CT
MAIDENCASTLE
CORDON CL
TINSLEY CL
STRAWBERRY HILL
JUNIPER
HIGH ST
BARTON FIELDS
LINGSWOOD PK
WELLINGBOROUGH RD
DOWNWOOD
LAKESIDE DR
THE LAURELS
Playing Field
PENFOLD DR
VALENTINE WAY
WOBURN GATE
NEWSTEAD CT
SEDGEWATER DR
CHANTRY CL
COTTAGE GDNS
STANDING STONES
ELDERBERRY CT 1
COLLEGE FIELD CL 2
PENFOLD LA
HALL PIECE CL
ECTON PARK RD
WIMBORNE CL
Ecton Brook Linear Park
Great Billing
RAISINS FIELD CL
WILLOW BROOK
SOTHEBY RISE
BLUEBERRY RISE
FOX HILL RD
PENFOLD GDNS
ORANSAY CL
LADY WINEFRIDE'S WLK
Ecton Brook
PARKSIDE
CHURCH WLK
CUMBRAE DR
LISMORE CL
OVERMEAD RD
ECTON BROOK RD
OLD CARPENTERS CL
ELWES WAY
POUND LA
HAM MEADOW DR
MUSHROOM FIELD RD
FOXENDALE SQ
Ecton Brook Prim Sch
Works
1 BLOSSOM WAY
2 PADDOCKS WAY
3 EASTMEAD CT
4 TOPWELL CT
BLOSSOM CL
MANOR FARM
WINDSOR CT
CATTLE HILL CL
WORCESTER CL
CHAPEL ROW
STATION MEWS
RIVERWELL
St Andrews CE Prim Sch
CHEDWORTH CL
ASHMEAD
PIPPIN
SUNSET
PEARMAIN CT
WHITEHEART CL
BRAMLEY
FOX HILL DR
A45
RUSSET DR
PEAR TREE CL
CAMBERLEY CL
KINGSCROFT CT
STATION RD
NENE VALLEY WAY
HERTFORD CT
CONEYGREE CT
CAMPION CT
COOLING
FISHPONDS RD
LASHAM CT
PENNYCRESS PL
Little Billing
Bellinge
TRUSS RD
1 PALMER SQ
2 GLENDALE CT
3 GIBBSACRE CT
4 BILLINGSMEAD SQ
5 STATION CL
MIDDLEMEAD CT
SPANSLADE RD
LITTLE BILLING WAY
VALLEY RD
FARACRE CT
BILLING BROOK RD
Bellinge Prim Sch
BRICKWELL CT
DRYWELL CT
ORCHARD HILL
GLADE CL
Caravan Pk
LOWER ECTON LA
REDMILL RD
LAWSON CRES
GERVASE
FOSKITT CT
KNIGHTS CT
FISHERS CL
SEDLOCK RD
B4
1 PADDOCK MILL CT
2 HOPMEADOW CT
3 NETHER JACKSON CT
4 BLACKTHORN BRIDGE CT
5 MIDDLEMARCH
C2
1 SNOWBELL SQ
2 BLUEBERRY RISE
3 HAWKESBEARD PL
4 FIELD ROSE SQ
5 SALTWELL SQ
6 HORSEMOOR SQ
7 CLIPSTON FIELD PL
8 GREEN DALE SQ
9 LONG MALLOWS RISE
161
D2
1 HAREBELL SQ
2 WINDFLOWER PL
3 TAVISTOCK CL
4 NORMEAD SQ
5 BELLROPES SQ
6 LOCKCROFT SQ
7 SHARROW PL
8 THURSPIT PL
144

143
128

143
162

129
146

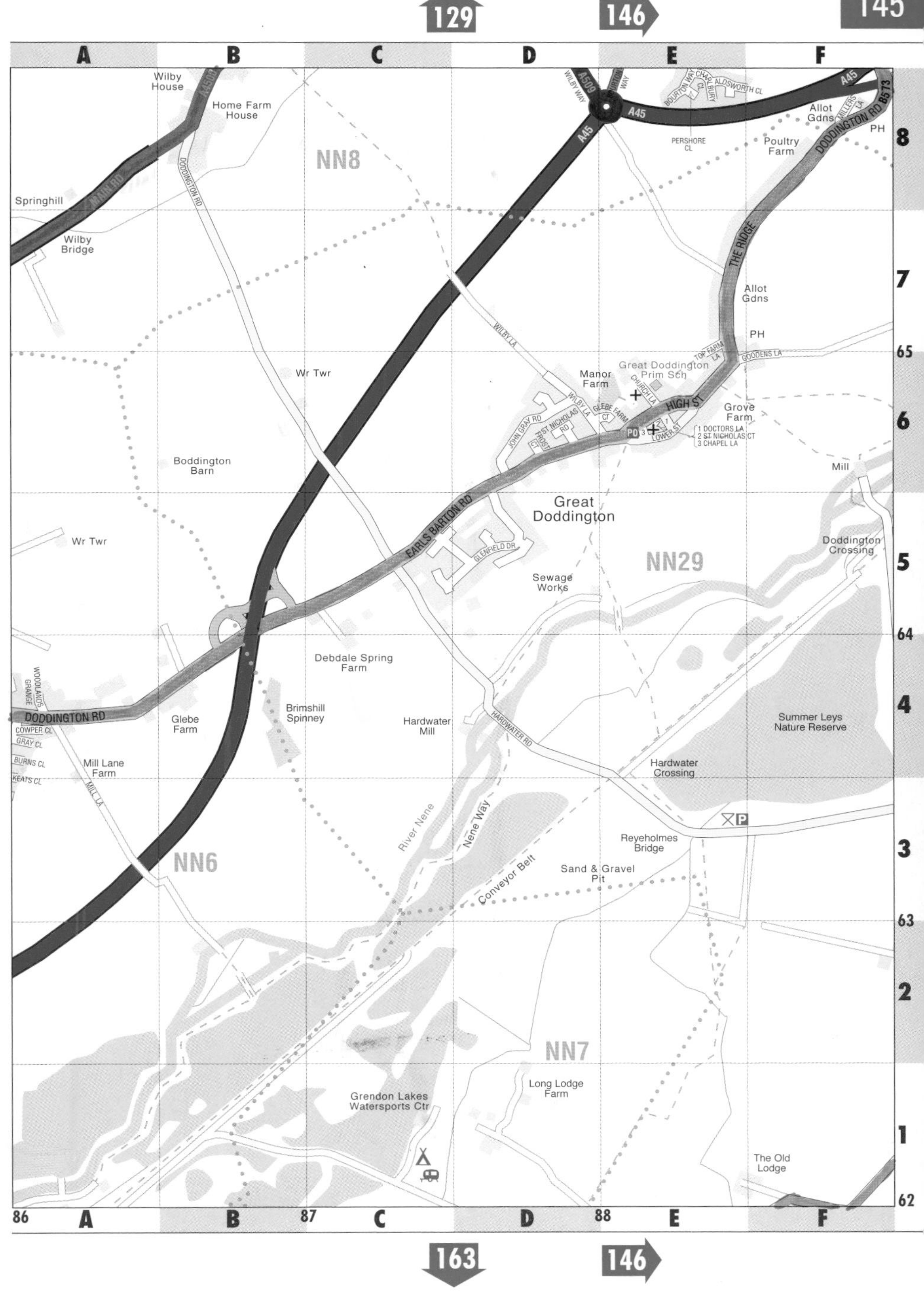

163
146

145
130

145
164

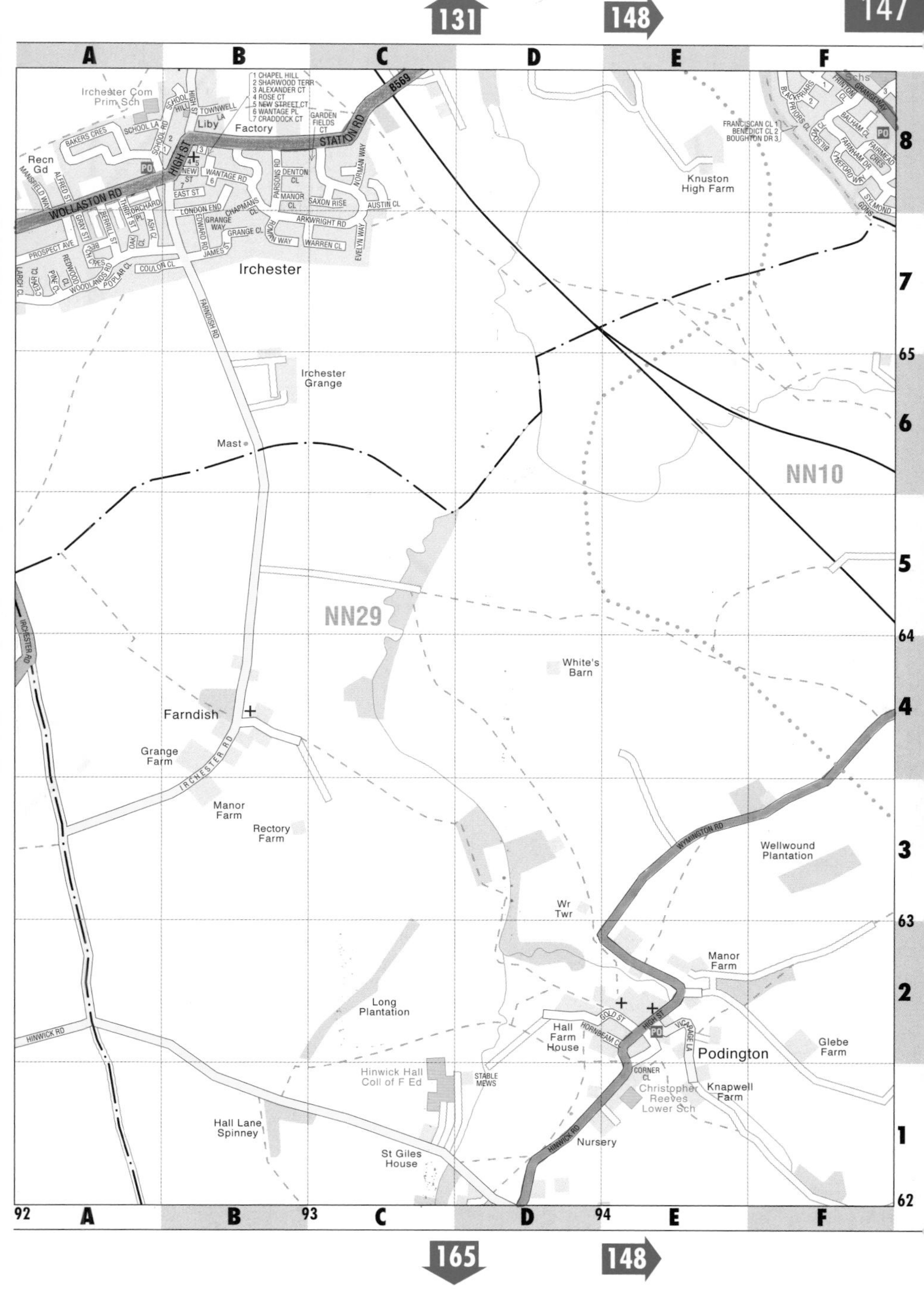
131
148
A
B
C
D
E
F
Irchester Com Prim Sch
1 CHAPEL HILL
2 SHARWOOD TERR
3 ALEXANDER CT
4 ROSE CT
5 NEW STREET CT
6 WANTAGE PL
7 CRADDOCK CT
Liby
Factory
GARDEN FIELDS CT
B569
STATION RD
WOLLASTON RD
HIGH ST
Recn Gd
Irchester
FARNDISH RD
Knuston High Farm
FRANCISCAN CL 1
BENEDICT CL 2
BOUGHTON DR 3
Irchester Grange
Mast
NN10
NN29
White's Barn
Farndish
Grange Farm
IRCHESTER RD
Manor Farm
Rectory Farm
WYMINGTON RD
Wellwound Plantation
Wr Twr
Manor Farm
Long Plantation
Hall Farm House
Podington
Glebe Farm
HINWICK RD
Hinwick Hall Coll of F Ed
STABLE MEWS
Christopher Reeves Lower Sch
Knapwell Farm
Hall Lane Spinney
St Giles House
Nursery
8
7
65
6
5
64
4
3
63
2
1
62
92
93
94
165
148

147
132

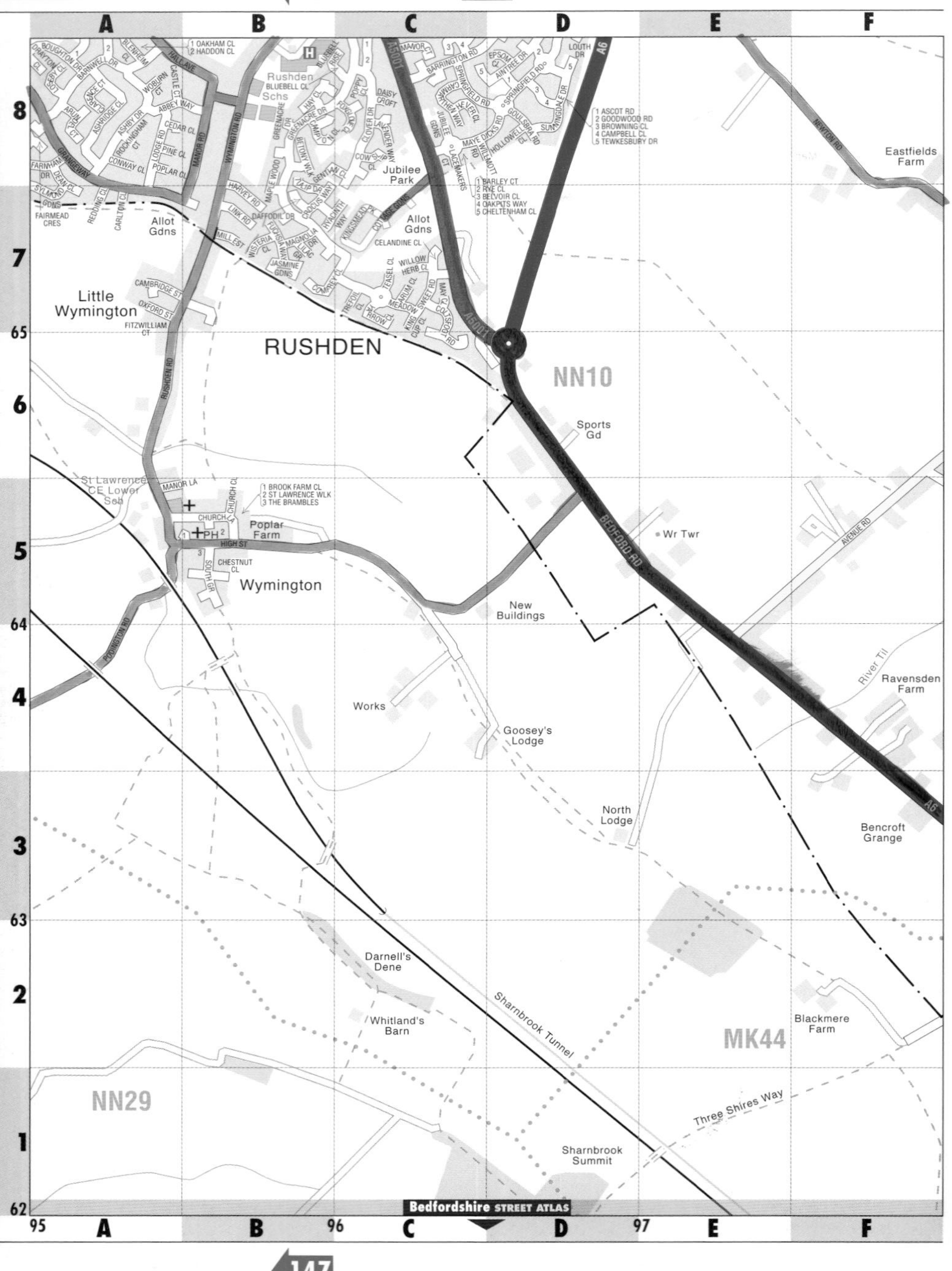
A
B
C
D
E
F
8
7
65
6
5
64
4
3
63
2
1
62
95
96
97
RUSHDEN
Rushden Schs
Jubilee Park
Allot Gdns
Little Wymington
NN10
Eastfields Farm
Sports Gd
Wr Twr
St Lawrence CE Lower Sch
Poplar Farm
Wymington
New Buildings
Works
Goosey's Lodge
Ravensden Farm
River Til
North Lodge
Bencroft Grange
Darnell's Dene
Whitland's Barn
Sharnbrook Tunnel
MK44
Blackmere Farm
NN29
Three Shires Way
Sharnbrook Summit
A6
A5001
BEDFORD RD
AVENUE RD
NEWTON RD
RUSHDEN RD
WYMINGTON RD
PODINGTON RD
HIGH ST
MANOR LA
CHURCH LA
CHESTNUT CL
SOUTH GR
1 BROOK FARM CL
2 ST LAWRENCE WLK
3 THE BRAMBLES
1 OAKHAM CL
2 HADDON CL
1 ASCOT RD
2 GOODWOOD RD
3 BROWNING CL
4 CAMPBELL CL
5 TEWKESBURY DR
1 BARLEY CT
2 RYE CL
3 BELVOIR CL
4 OAKPITS WAY
5 CHELTENHAM CL
FAIRMEAD CRES
CAMBRIDGE ST
OXFORD ST
FITZWILLIAM CT
CELANDINE CL

147

133

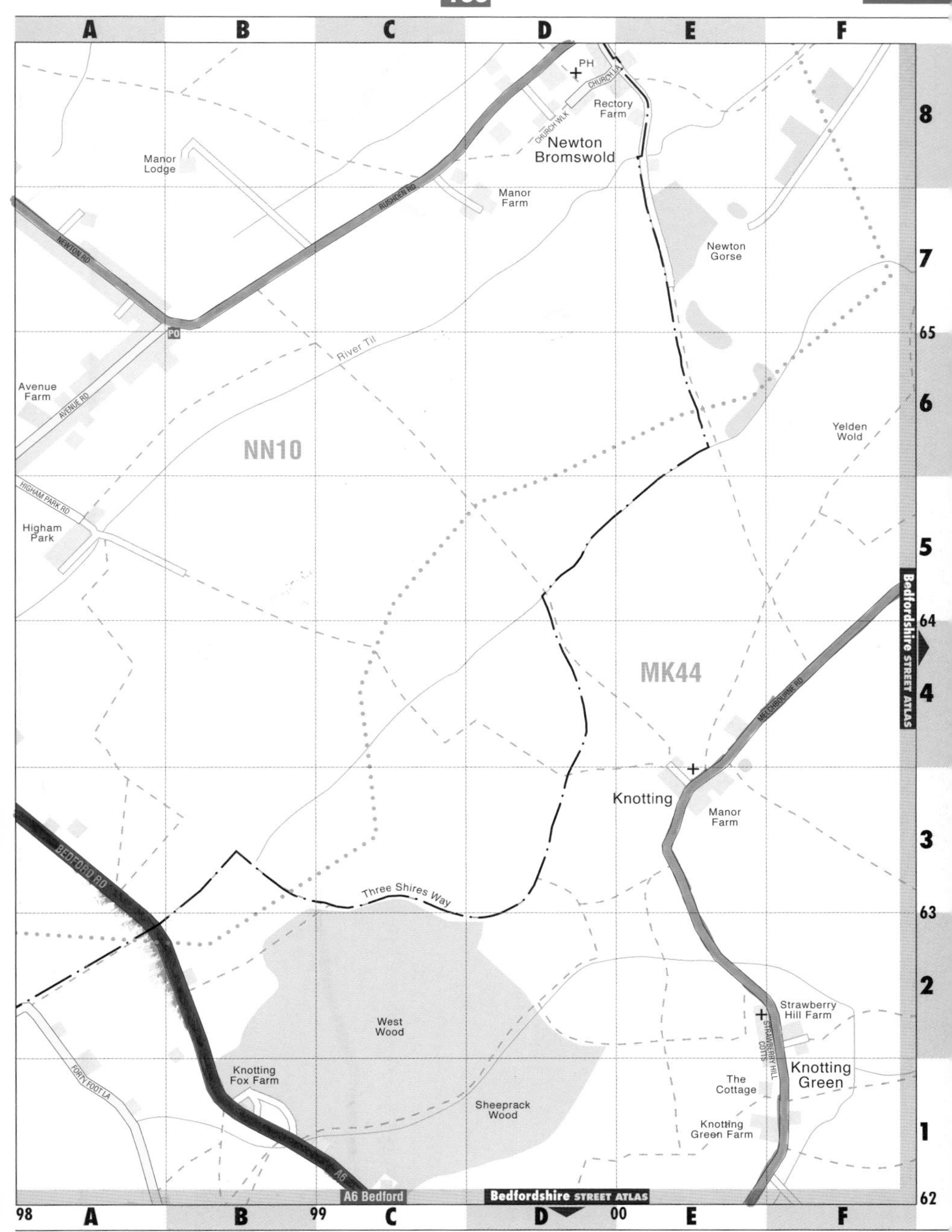
A
B
C
D
E
F
8
7
65
6
5
64
4
3
63
2
1
62
98
99
00
PH
CHURCH LA
CHURCH WLK
Rectory Farm
Newton Bromswold
Manor Lodge
Manor Farm
RUSHDEN RD
NEWTON RD
Newton Gorse
PO
River Til
Avenue Farm
AVENUE RD
Yelden Wold
NN10
HIGHAM PARK RD
Higham Park
MK44
MELCHBOURNE RD
Bedfordshire STREET ATLAS
Knotting
Manor Farm
BEDFORD RD
Three Shires Way
West Wood
Strawberry Hill Farm
STRAWBERRY HILL COTTS
Knotting Green
The Cottage
Knotting Fox Farm
FORTY FOOT LA
Sheeprack Wood
Knotting Green Farm
A6
A6 Bedford
Bedfordshire STREET ATLAS

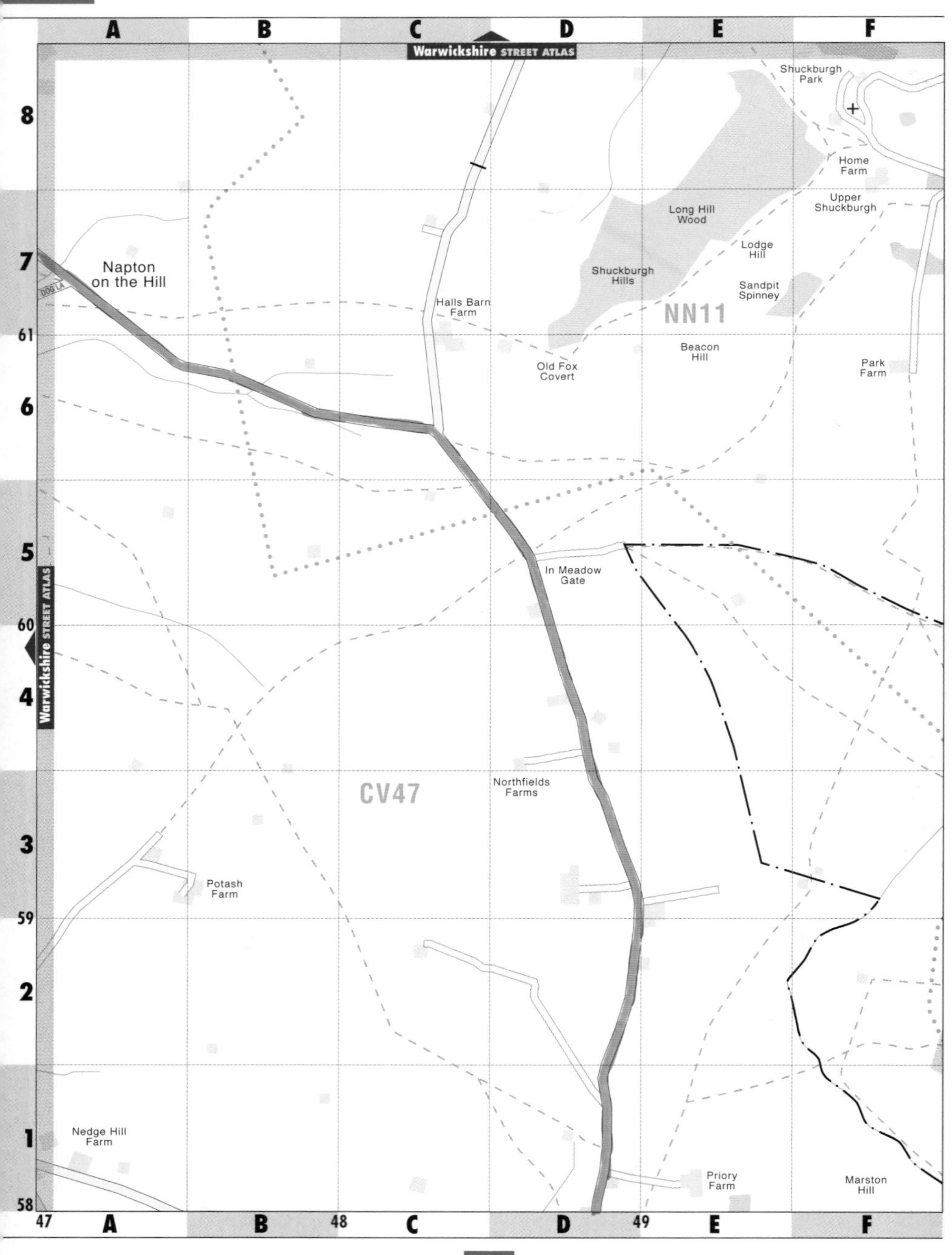
A
B
C
D
E
F
Warwickshire STREET ATLAS
8
7
61
6
5
60
4
3
59
2
1
58
47
48
49
Shuckburgh Park
Home Farm
Upper Shuckburgh
Long Hill Wood
Lodge Hill
Shuckburgh Hills
Sandpit Spinney
NN11
Napton on the Hill
DOG LA
Halls Barn Farm
Beacon Hill
Old Fox Covert
Park Farm
In Meadow Gate
CV47
Northfields Farms
Potash Farm
Nedge Hill Farm
Priory Farm
Marston Hill

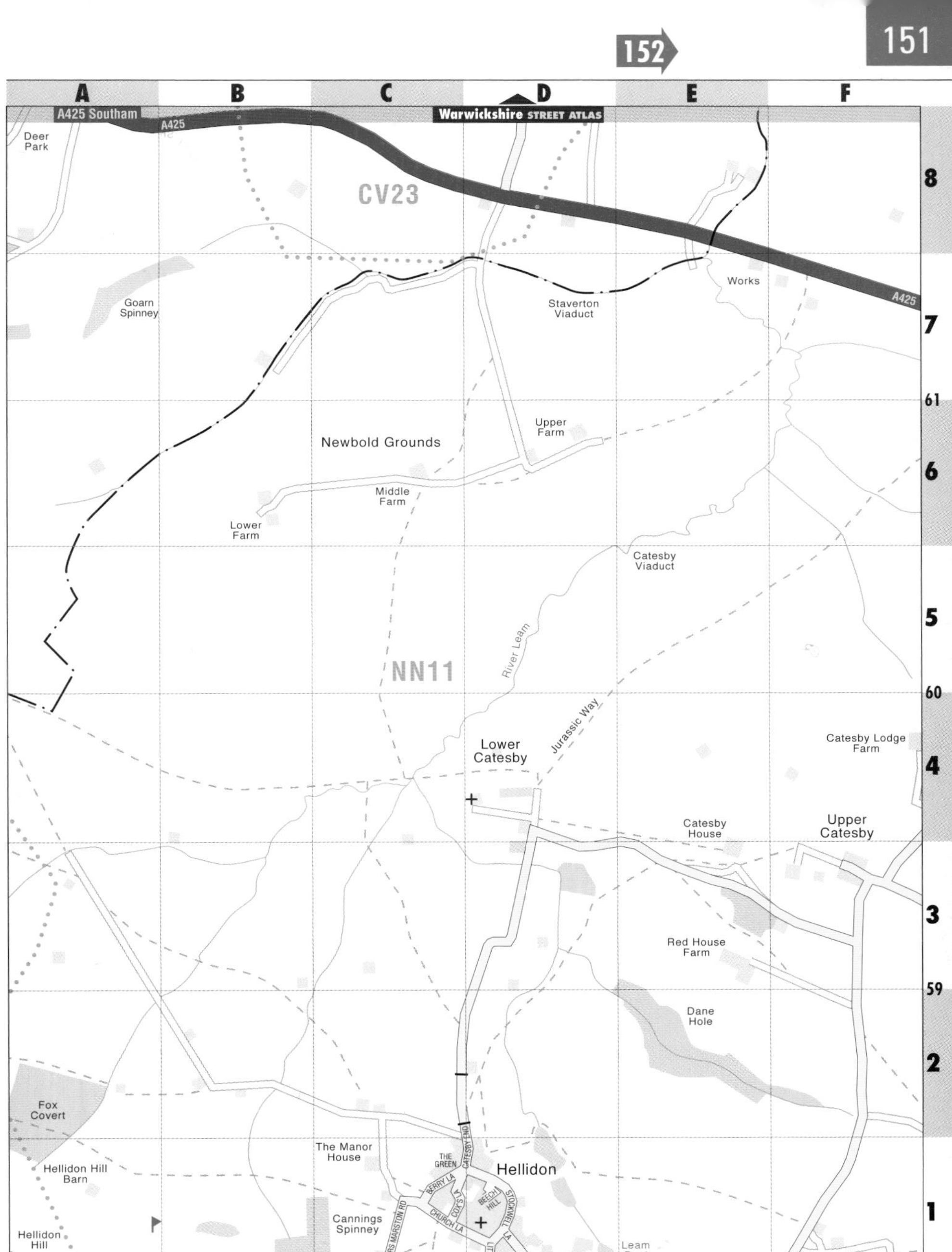
A B C D E F
A425 Southam
A425
Warwickshire STREET ATLAS
Deer Park
CV23
8
Goarn Spinney
Works
Staverton Viaduct
A425
7
61
Upper Farm
Newbold Grounds
6
Middle Farm
Lower Farm
Catesby Viaduct
5
River Leam
NN11
60
Jurassic Way
Lower Catesby
Catesby Lodge Farm
4
Catesby House
Upper Catesby
3
Red House Farm
59
Dane Hole
2
Fox Covert
The Manor House
THE GREEN
CATESBY END
Hellidon
Hellidon Hill Barn
BERRY LA
COX'S LA
BEECH HILL
STOCKWELL LA
CHURCH LA
PRIORS MARSTON RD
Cannings Spinney
1
Hellidon Hill
Leam Pool
PH
LITTLE BACK LA
MAIN ST
Hotel
CH
CV47
58
50 A B 51 C D 52 E F

151
134

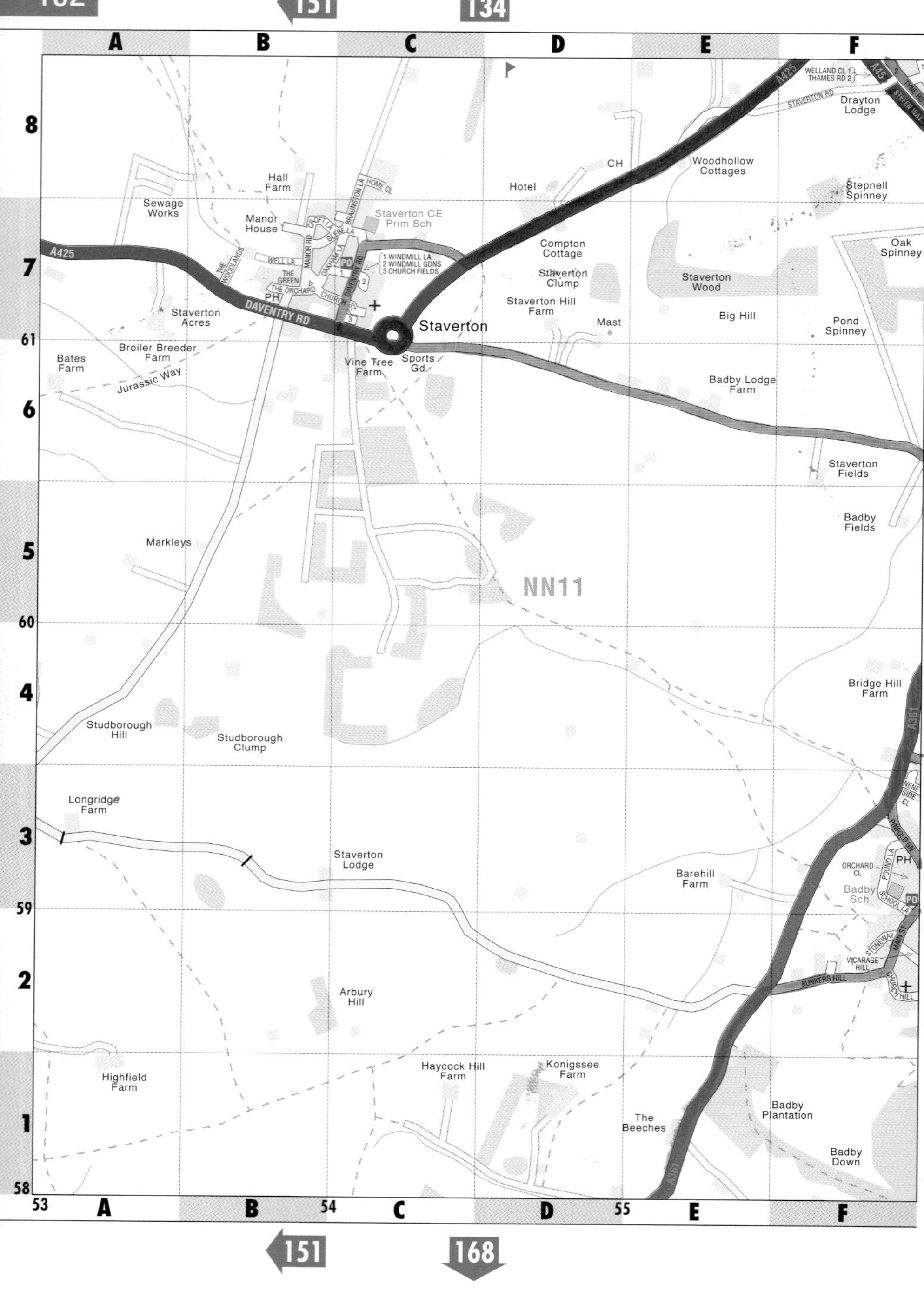

151
168

135
154

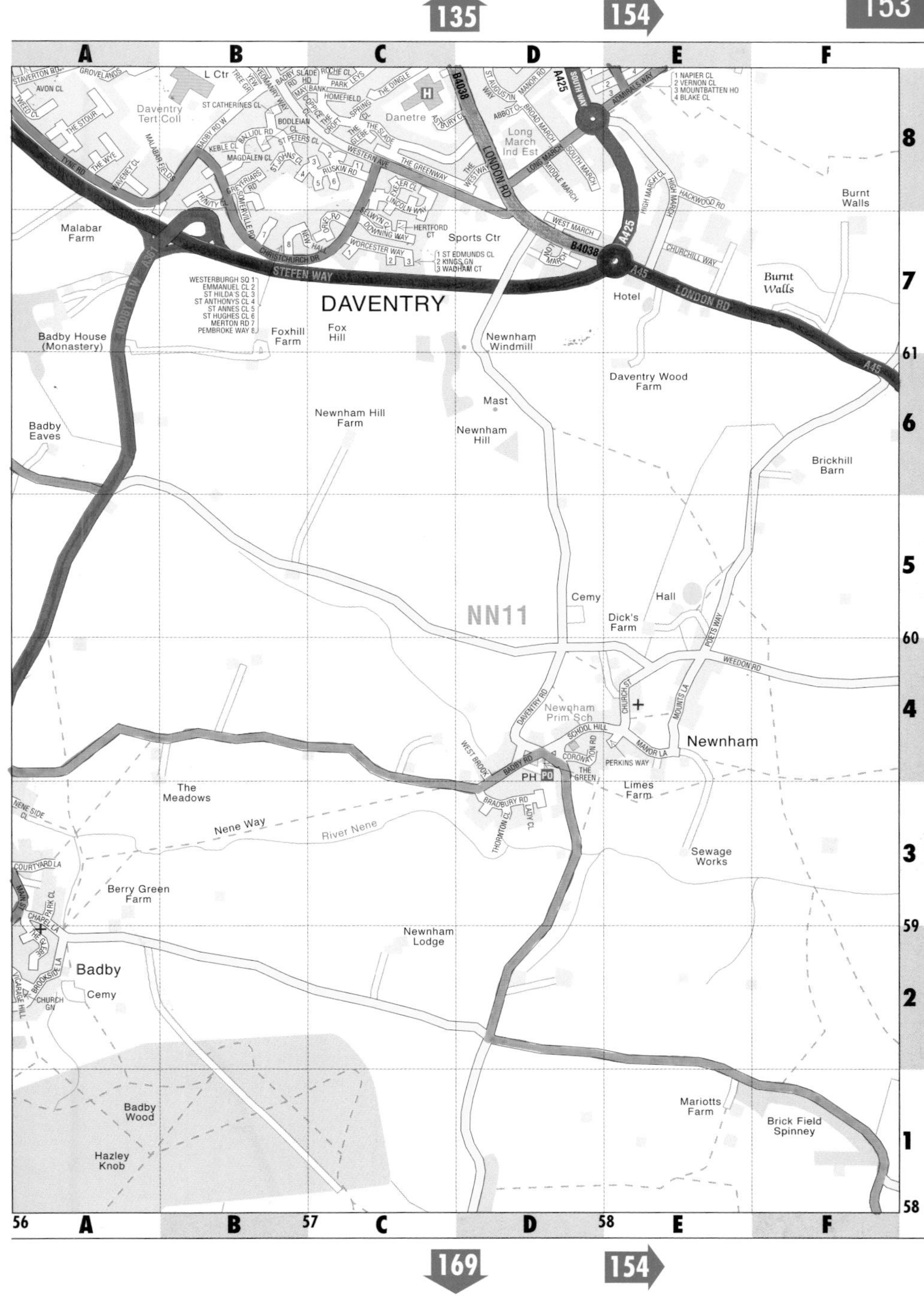

169
154

153

136

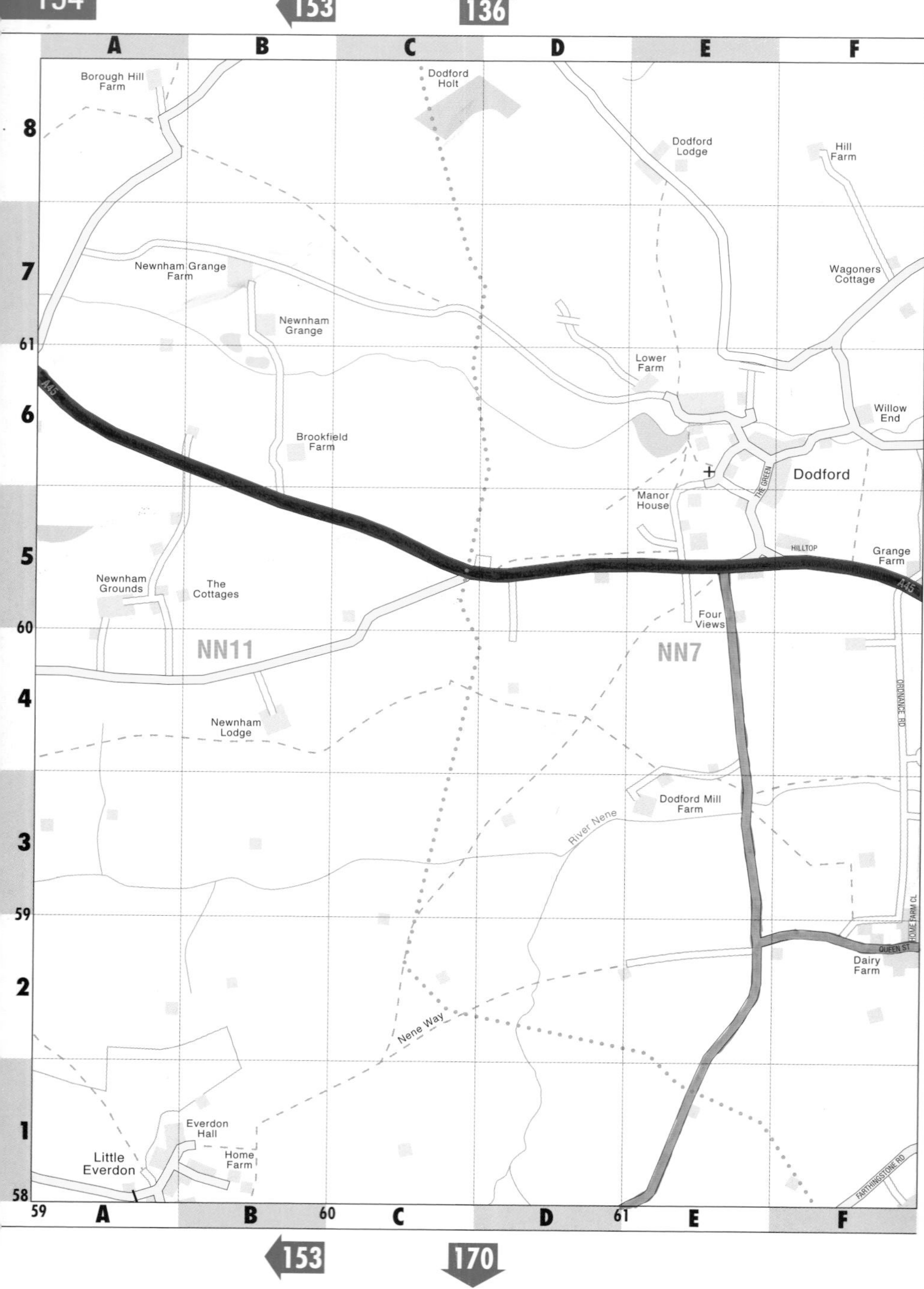

153

170

137
156

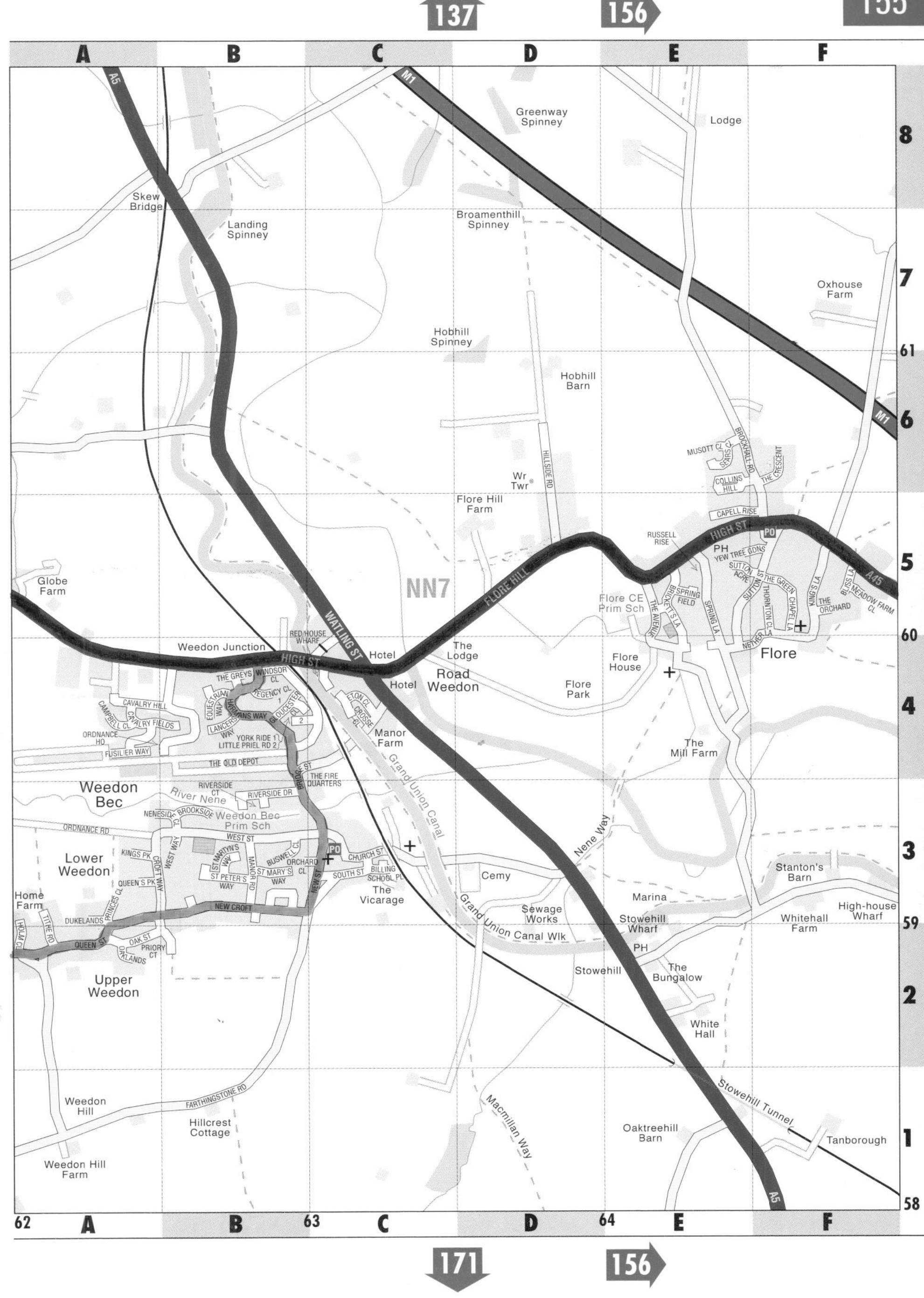

171
156

155
138

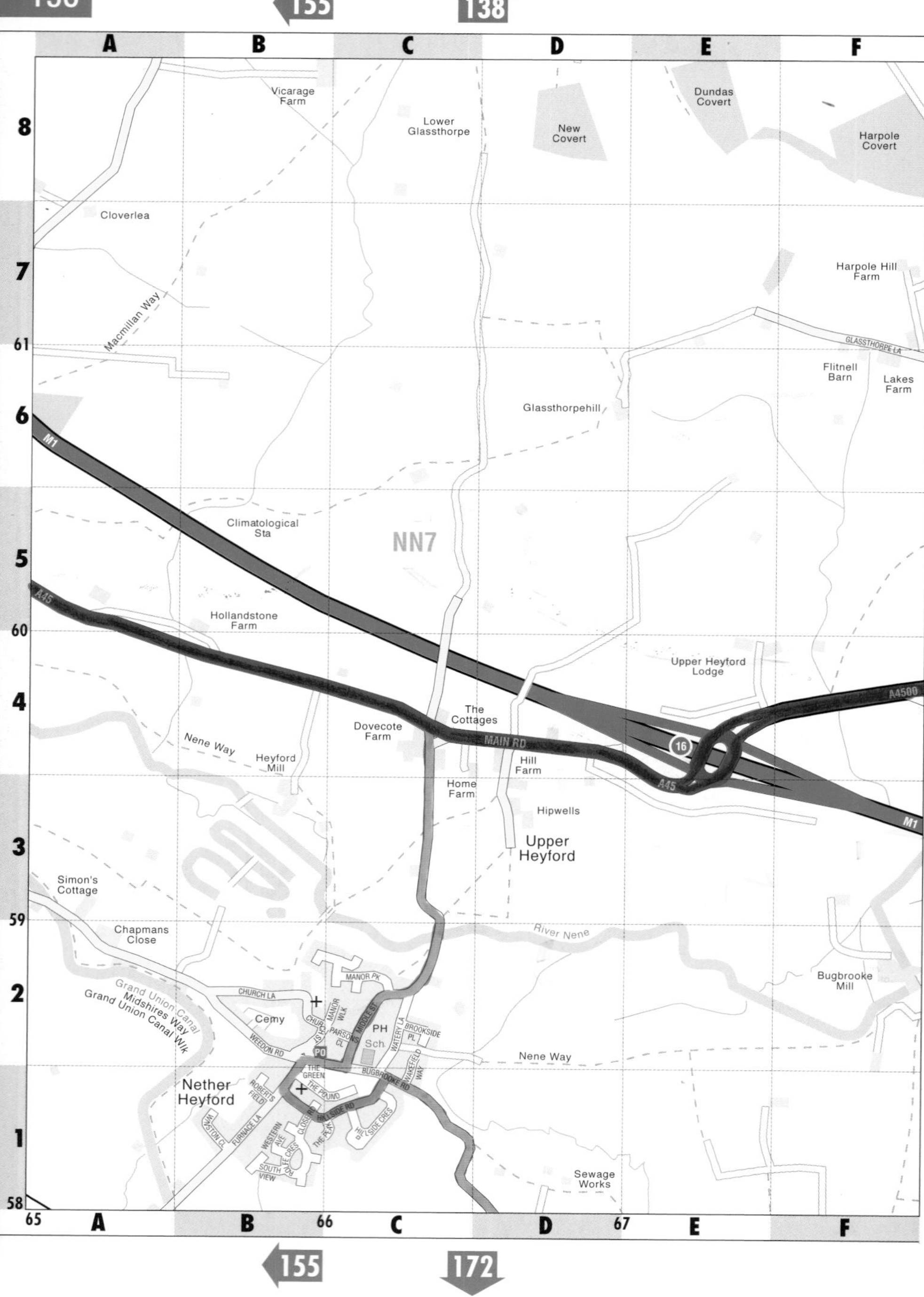

155
172

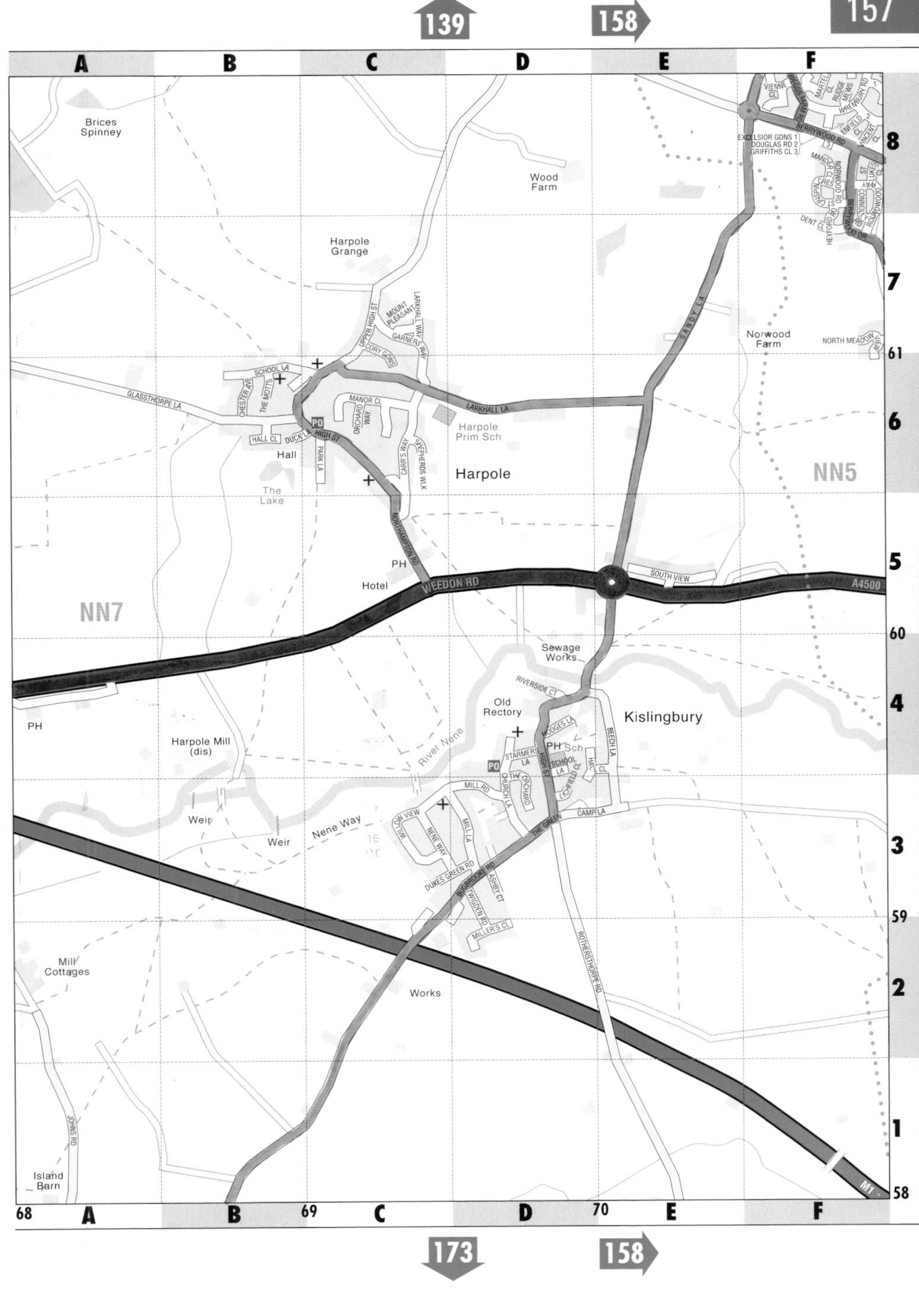

139
158
Brices Spinney
Wood Farm
Harpole Grange
Norwood Farm
NORTH MEADOW VIEW
BERRYWOOD RD
EXCELSIOR GDNS 1
DOUGLAS RD 2
GRIFFITHS CL 3
SANDY LA
UPPER HIGH ST
MOUNT PLEASANT
LARKHALL WAY
GARNERS WAY
CORY GDNS
SCHOOL LA
CHESTER AVE
THE MOTTS
GLASSTHORPE LA
MANOR CL
ORCHARD WAY
LARKHALL LA
Harpole Prim Sch
HALL CL
DUCK'S LA
HIGH ST
PARK LA
CARR'S WAY
SHEPHERDS WLK
Hall
Harpole
NN5
The Lake
NORTHAMPTON RD
PH
Hotel
WEEDON RD
SOUTH VIEW
A4500
NN7
Sewage Works
RIVERSIDE CT
Old Rectory
Kislingbury
HODGES LA
BEECH LA
PH
Sch
Harpole Mill (dis)
River Nene
STARMERS LA
SCHOOL LA
HIGH ST
LICHFIELD CL
MILL RD
CHURCH LA
THE ORCHARD
CAMP LA
Weir
Weir
Nene Way
WILLOW VIEW
NENE WAY
MILL LA
THE GREEN
DUKES GREEN RD
BUGBROOKE RD
ASHBY CT
TWIGDEN RD
MILLER'S CL
ROTHERSTHORPE RD
Mill Cottages
Works
JOHNS RD
Island Barn
M1
173
158

157
140

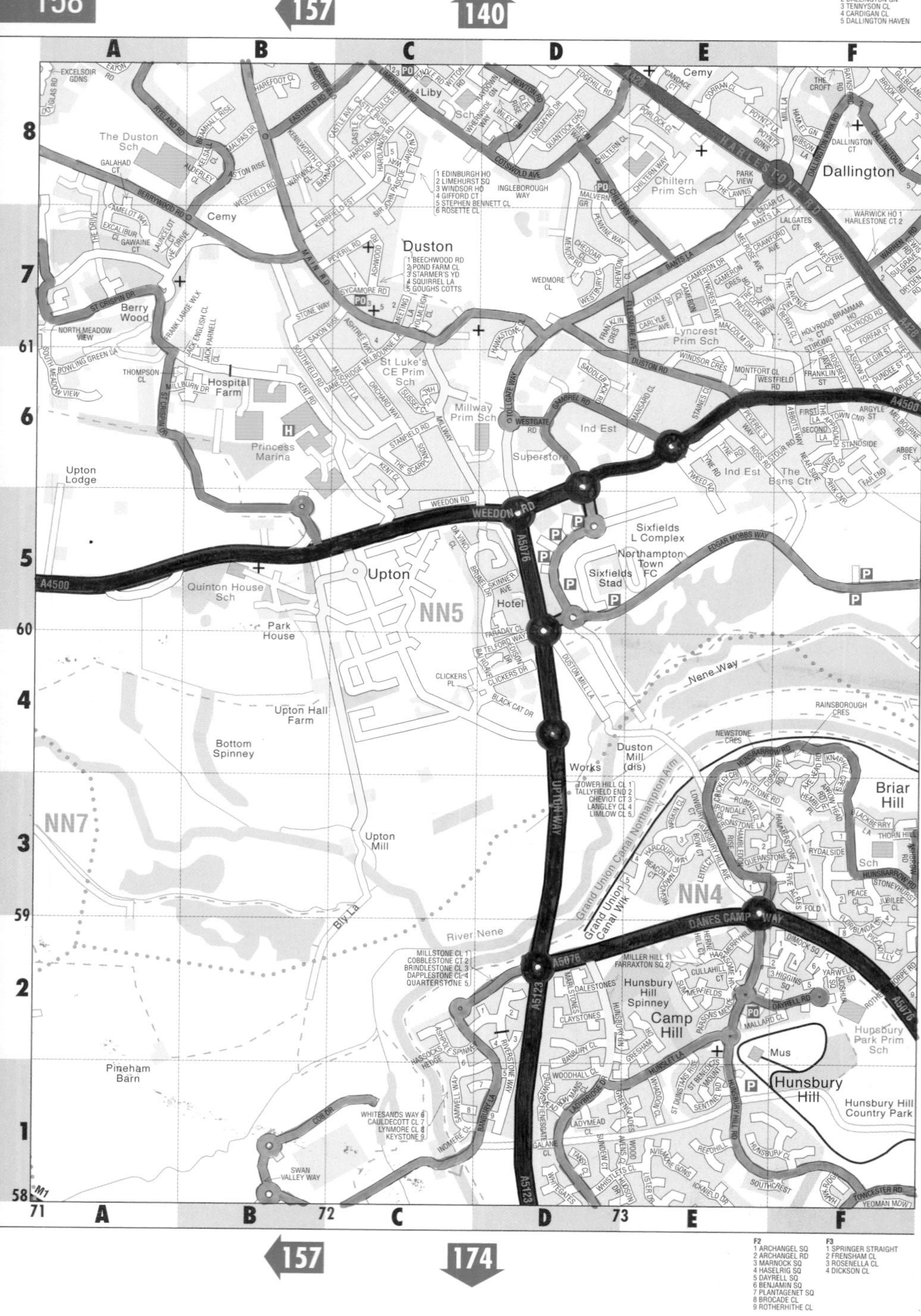

157
174

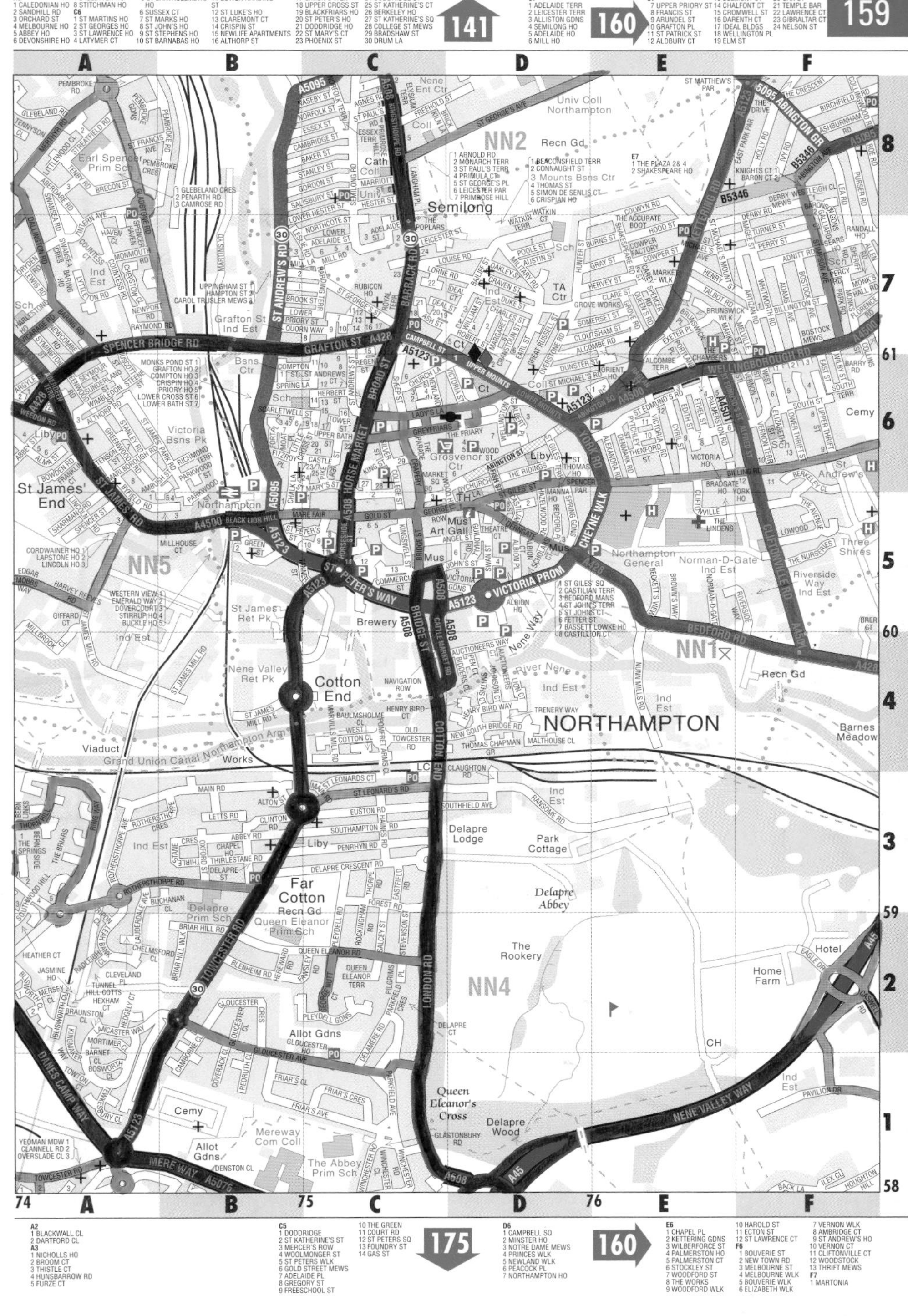
A6
1 CALEDONIAN HO
2 SANDHILL RD
3 ORCHARD ST
4 MELBOURNE HO
5 ABBEY HO
6 DEVONSHIRE HO
7 EYELETTER HO
8 STITCHMAN HO
C6
1 ST MARTINS HO
2 ST GEORGES HO
3 ST LAWRENCE HO
4 LATYMER CT
5 ST BARTHOLEMEWS HO
6 SUSSEX CT
7 ST MARKS HO
8 ST JOHN'S HO
9 ST STEPHENS HO
10 ST BARNABAS HO
11 LOWER HARDING ST
12 ST LUKE'S HO
13 CLAREMONT CT
14 CRISPIN ST
15 NEWLIFE APARTMENTS
16 ALTHORP ST
17 SIMON'S WLK
18 UPPER CROSS ST
19 BLACKFRIARS HO
20 ST PETER'S HO
21 DODDRIDGE HO
22 ST MARY'S CT
23 PHOENIX ST
24 DODDRIDGE ST
25 ST KATHERINE'S CT
26 BERKELEY HO
27 ST KATHERINE'S SQ
28 COLLEGE ST MEWS
29 BRADSHAW ST
30 DRUM LA
141
C7
1 ADELAIDE TERR
2 LEICESTER TERR
3 ALLISTON GDNS
4 SEMILONG HO
5 ADELAIDE HO
6 MILL HO
160
C7
7 UPPER PRIORY ST
8 FRANCIS ST
9 ARUNDEL ST
10 GRAFTON PL
11 ST PATRICK ST
12 ALDBURY CT
13 BELMONT CT
14 CHALFONT CT
15 CROMWELL ST
16 DARENTH CT
17 IDEAL BLDGS
18 WELLINGTON PL
19 ELM ST
20 OAK ST
21 TEMPLE BAR
22 LAWRENCE CT
23 GIBRALTAR CT
24 NELSON ST
A B C D E F
8 7 61 6 5 60 4 3 59 2 1 58
NN2
NN5
NN1
NN4
Semilong
Univ Coll Northampton
Recn Gd
Earl Spencer Prim Sch
St James' End
Northampton
Victoria Bsns Pk
Grafton St Ind Est
St James Ret Pk
Nene Valley Ret Pk
Cotton End
Brewery
Grosvenor St Ctr
Northampton General
Norman-D-Gate Ind Est
Riverside Way Ind Est
Three Shires
Barnes Meadow
NORTHAMPTON
Grand Union Canal Northampton Arm
River Nene
Viaduct
Works
Delapre Lodge
Park Cottage
Delapre Abbey
Far Cotton
Queen Eleanor Prim Sch
Delapre Prim Sch
The Rookery
Home Farm
Hotel
Allot Gdns
Cemy
Mereway Com Coll
The Abbey Prim Sch
Queen Eleanor's Cross
Delapre Wood
SPENCER BRIDGE RD
GRAFTON ST A428
ST ANDREW'S RD
A508 KINGSTHORPE RD
BARRACK RD
A508 HORSE MARKET
BROAD ST
WELLINGBOROUGH RD
A4500
BILLING RD
BEDFORD RD
CLIFTONVILLE RD
KETTERING RD
ABINGTON GR
ST JAMES' RD
WEEDON RD
A4500 BLACK LION HILL
ST PETER'S WAY
A5123
VICTORIA PROM
CHEYNE WLK
YORK RD
BRIDGE ST
COTTON END
LONDON RD
TOWCESTER RD
MERE WAY A5076
DANES CAMP WAY
NENE VALLEY WAY
A45
ROTHERSTHORPE RD
GLOUCESTER AVE
ST LEONARD'S RD
74 75 76
A2
1 BLACKWALL CL
2 DARTFORD CL
A3
1 NICHOLLS HO
2 BROOM CT
3 THISTLE CT
4 HUNSBARROW RD
5 FURZE CT
C5
1 DODDRIDGE
2 ST KATHERINE'S ST
3 MERCER'S ROW
4 WOOLMONGER ST
5 ST PETERS WLK
6 GOLD STREET MEWS
7 ADELAIDE PL
8 GREGORY ST
9 FREESCHOOL ST
10 THE GREEN
11 COURT RD
12 ST PETERS SQ
13 FOUNDRY ST
14 GAS ST
175
D6
1 CAMPBELL SQ
2 MINSTER HO
3 NOTRE DAME MEWS
4 PRINCES WLK
5 NEWLAND WLK
6 PEACOCK PL
7 NORTHAMPTON HO
160
E6
1 CHAPEL PL
2 KETTERING GDNS
3 WILBERFORCE ST
4 PALMERSTON HO
5 PALMERSTON CT
6 STOCKLEY ST
7 WOODFORD ST
8 THE WORKS
9 WOODFORD WLK
10 HAROLD ST
11 ECTON ST
12 ST LAWRENCE CT
F6
1 BOUVERIE ST
2 NEW TOWN RD
3 MELBOURNE ST
4 MELBOURNE WLK
5 BOUVERIE WLK
6 ELIZABETH WLK
7 VERNON WLK
8 AMBRIDGE CT
9 ST ANDREW'S HO
10 VERNON CT
11 CLIFTONVILLE CT
12 WOODSTOCK
13 THRIFT MEWS
F7
1 MARTONIA

159 142

F8
1 CARRINGTON GDNS
2 WOLLATON GDNS
3 CHILWELL CT
4 PORTCHESTER GDNS
5 WOODBOROUGH GDNS

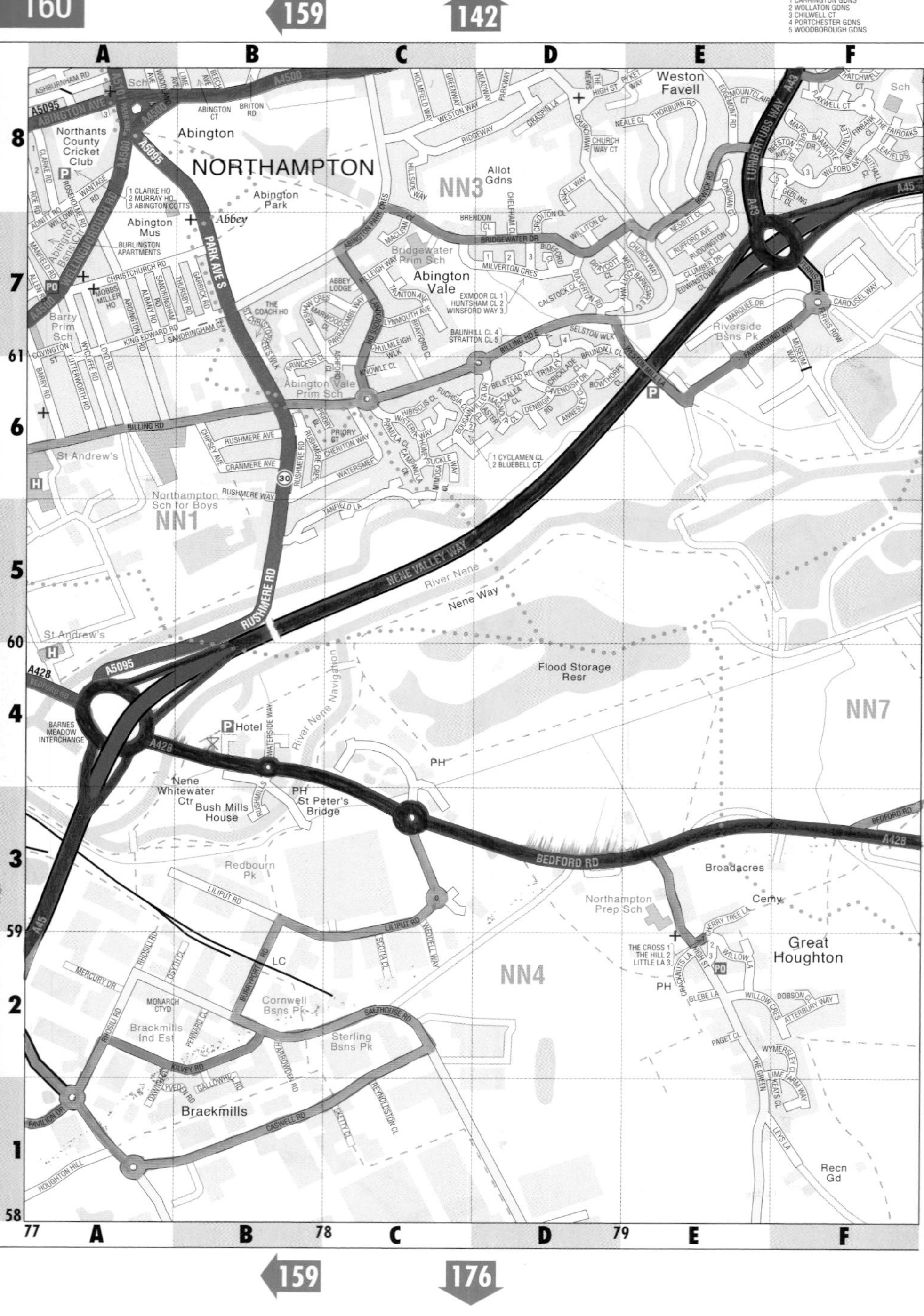

A8
1 SLADESWELL CT
2 PADWELL CT
3 BESTWELL CT
4 LEYSWELL CT
5 MARSHWELL CT
6 WALLINGFORD END
7 TWYFORD CL
8 BROMFORD CL

143
162

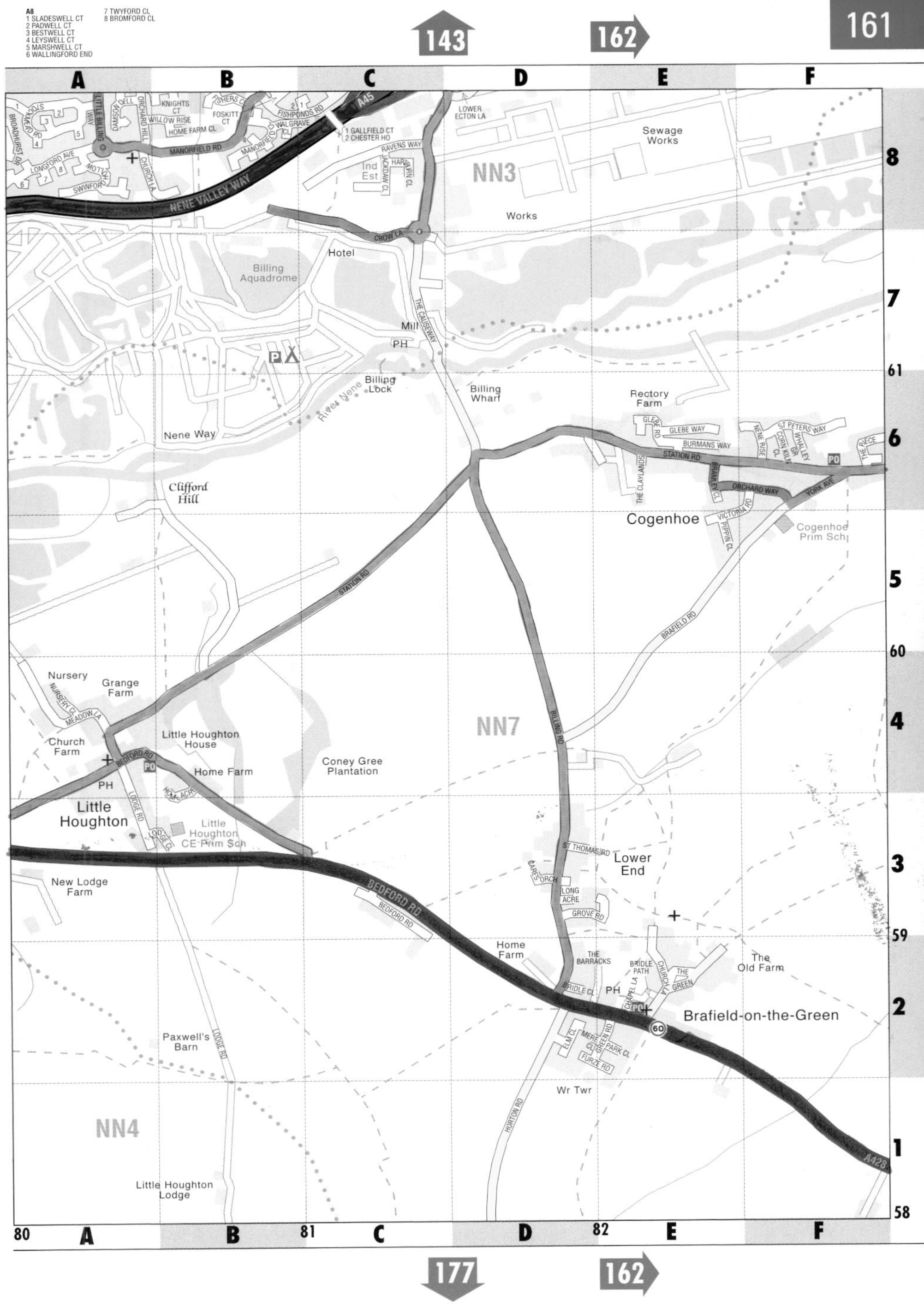

177
162

161
144

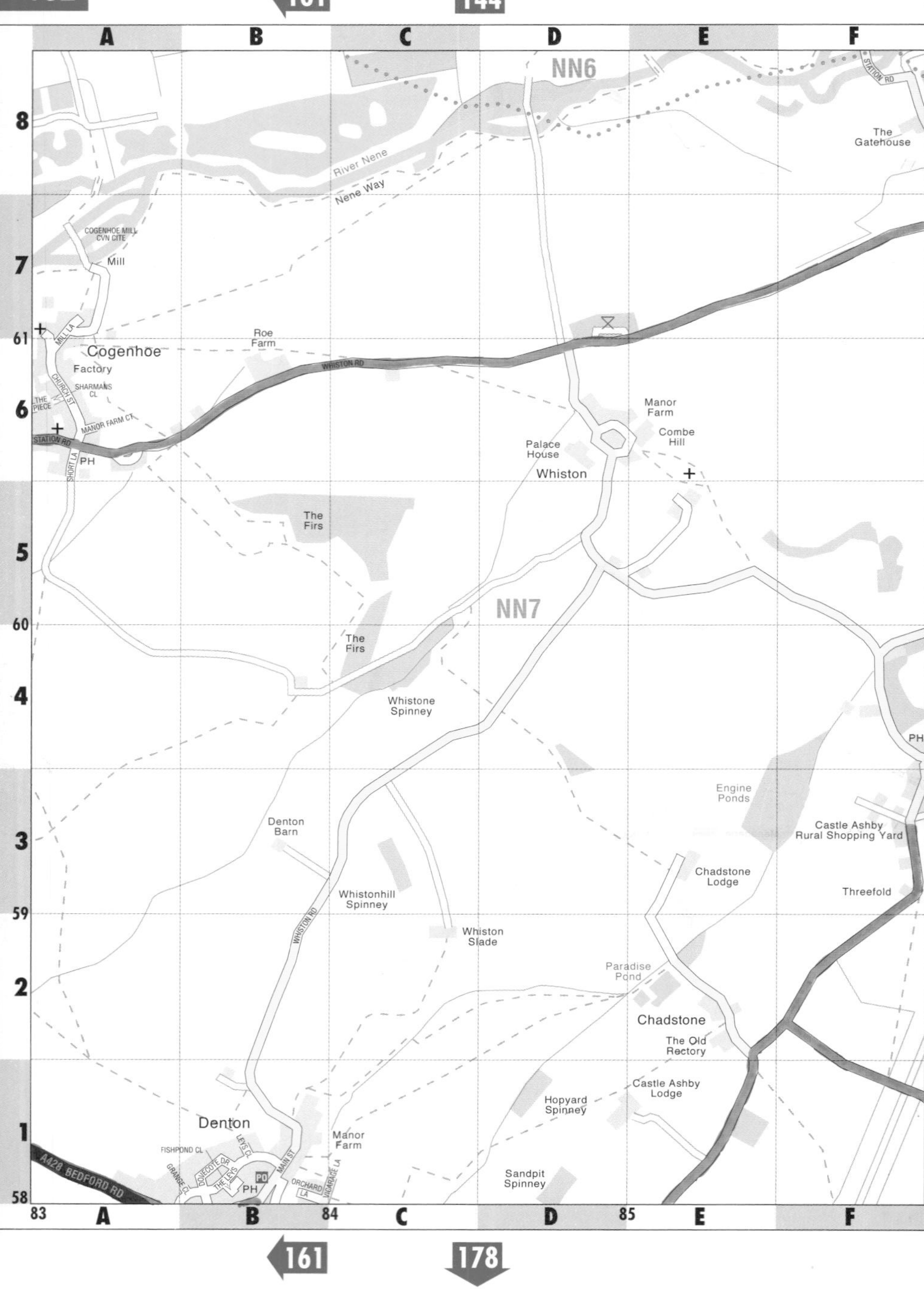

161
178

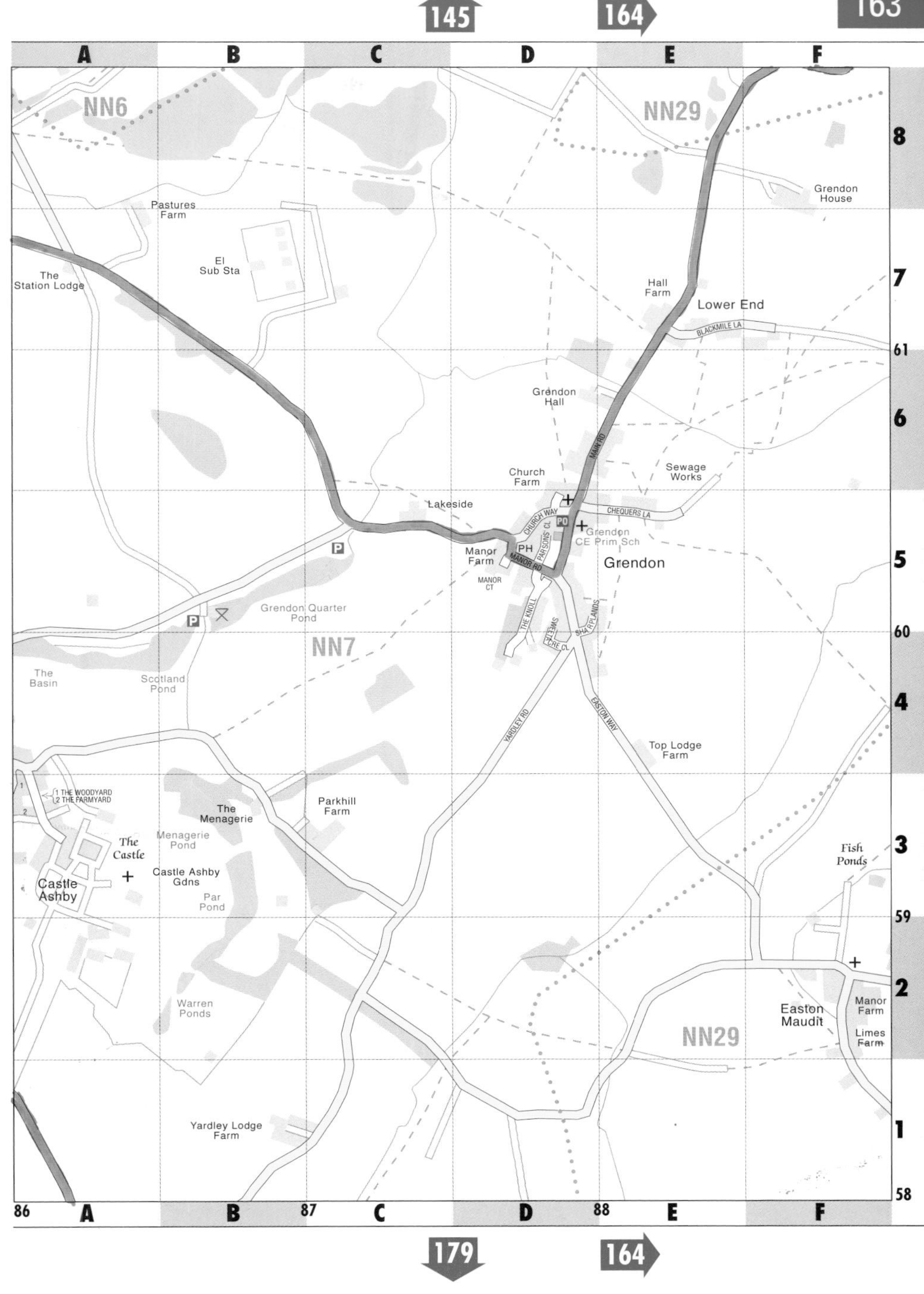
145
164
A
B
C
D
E
F
NN6
NN29
Pastures
Farm
El
Sub Sta
The
Station Lodge
Grendon
House
Hall
Farm
Lower End
BLACKMILE LA
Grendon
Hall
MAIN RD
Church
Farm
Sewage
Works
Lakeside
CHURCH WAY
CHEQUERS LA
PO
Grendon
CE Prim Sch
PH
Manor
Farm
MANOR RD
PARSONS' CL
Grendon
MANOR
CT
Grendon Quarter
Pond
NN7
THE KNOLL
SWEETBRIAR CL
SHARPLANDS
The
Basin
Scotland
Pond
YARDLEY RD
EASTON WAY
Top Lodge
Farm
1 THE WOODYARD
2 THE FARMYARD
The
Menagerie
Parkhill
Farm
The
Castle
Menagerie
Pond
Castle Ashby
Gdns
Castle
Ashby
Par
Pond
Fish
Ponds
Easton
Maudit
Manor
Farm
Limes
Farm
NN29
Warren
Ponds
Yardley Lodge
Farm
8
7
61
6
5
60
4
3
59
2
1
58
86
87
88
179
164

163
146

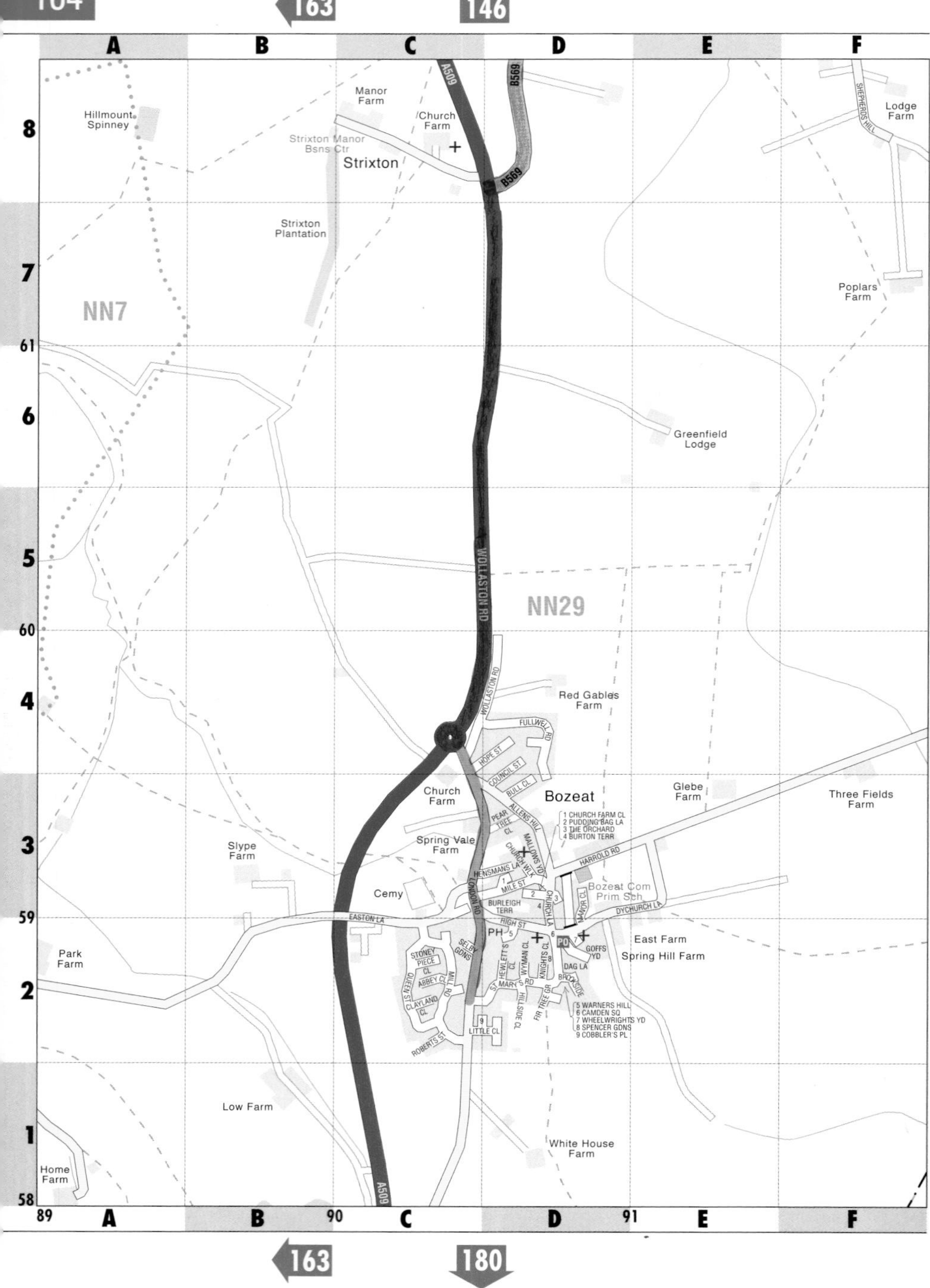

163
180

147

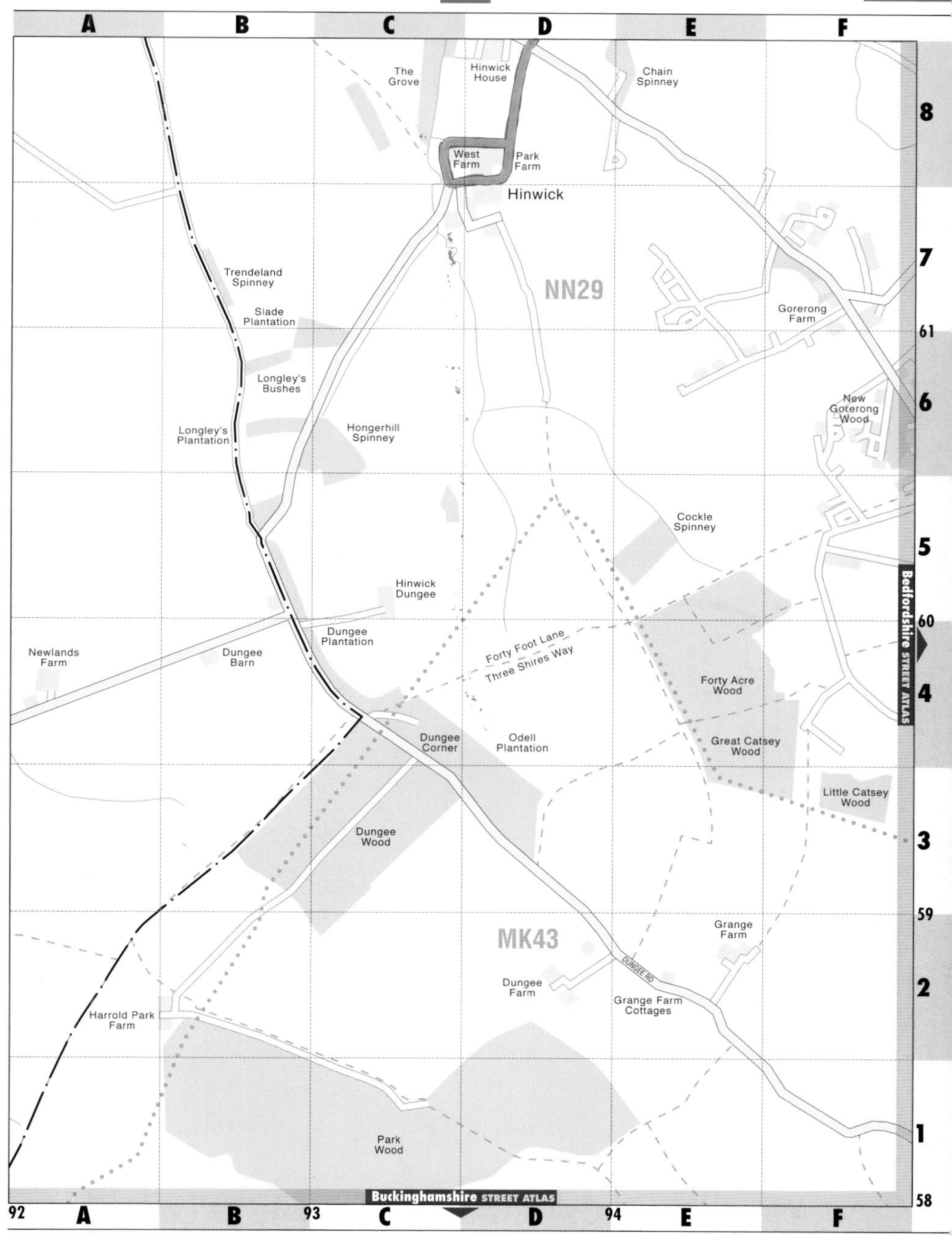

A
B
C
D
E
F
The Grove
Hinwick House
Chain Spinney
West Farm
Park Farm
Hinwick
Trendeland Spinney
NN29
Gorerong Farm
Slade Plantation
Longley's Bushes
New Gorerong Wood
Longley's Plantation
Hongerhill Spinney
Cockle Spinney
Hinwick Dungee
Bedfordshire STREET ATLAS
Newlands Farm
Dungee Barn
Dungee Plantation
Forty Foot Lane
Three Shires Way
Forty Acre Wood
Dungee Corner
Odell Plantation
Great Catsey Wood
Little Catsey Wood
Dungee Wood
MK43
Grange Farm
DUNGEE RD
Dungee Farm
Grange Farm Cottages
Harrold Park Farm
Park Wood
Buckinghamshire STREET ATLAS
8
7
61
6
5
60
4
3
59
2
1
58
92
93
94

150

A
B
C
D
E
F
The Meadows
TURVINS MDW
PO
SHUCKBURGH RD
KEYS LA
VICARAGE LA
Priors Marston
Hill Farm
Marston Hill
The Priors Sch
ST LEONARDS CL 1
WESTFIELD BARNS 2
SCHOOL LA
PH
HOLLY BUSH LA
MARSTON HILL
SOUTHAM RD
THE HOLLOWAY
THE GREEN
HELLIDON RD
PRIORS CT
Westover Farm
Chestnuts Farm
Manor Farm
HARDWICK RD
BYFIELD RD
Sewage Works
CV47
ST MARY'S CL
Church End
THE CLOISTERS
Priors Hardwick
PH
AGRICULTURAL HOS
Grange Farm
London End
WELSH RD
The Old Vicarage
Warwickshire STREET ATLAS
Rump Hall
Fields Farm
NN11
8
7
57
6
5
56
4
3
55
2
1
54
47
48
49

182

151
168

183
168

167
152

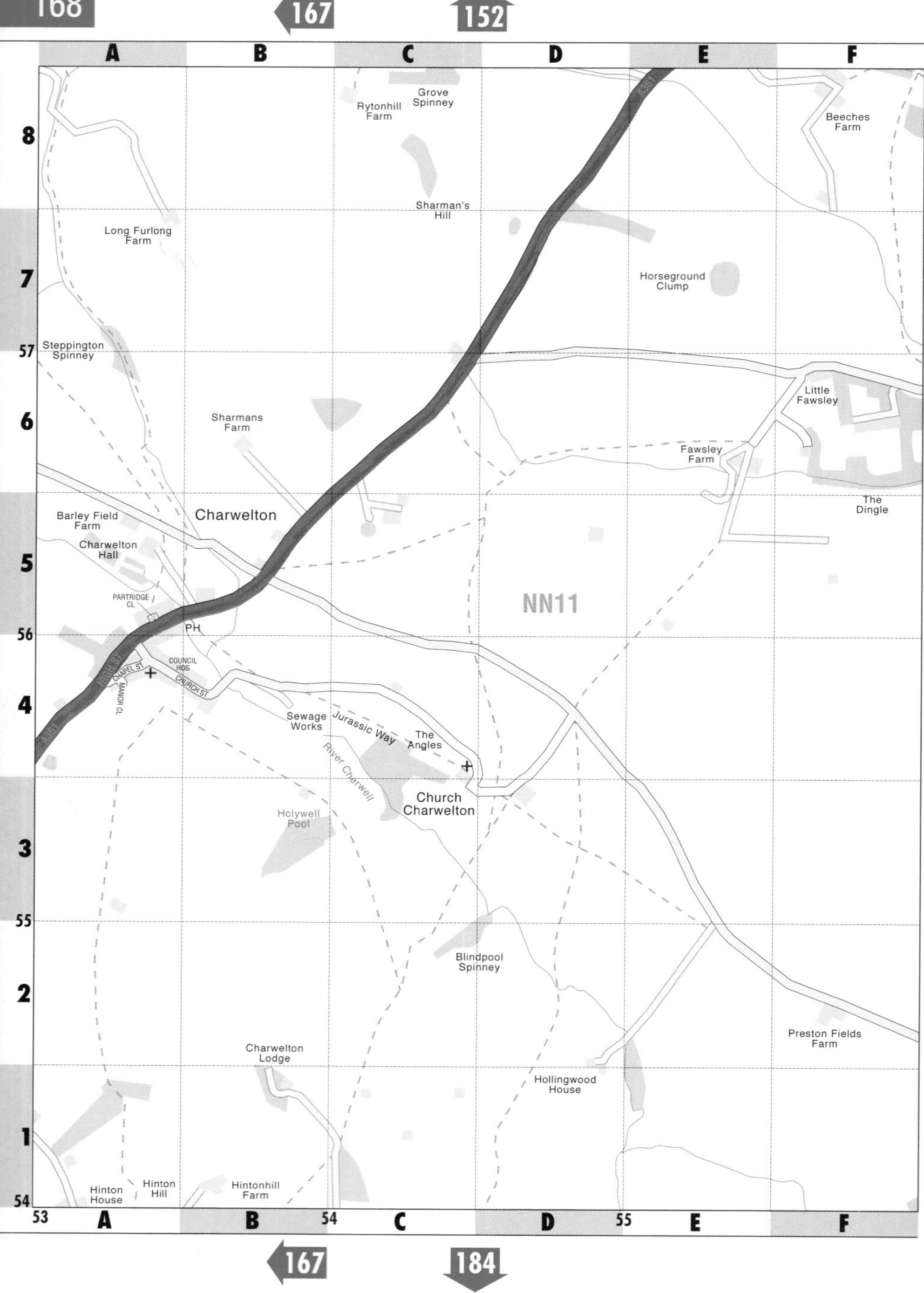

167
184

153
170

185
170

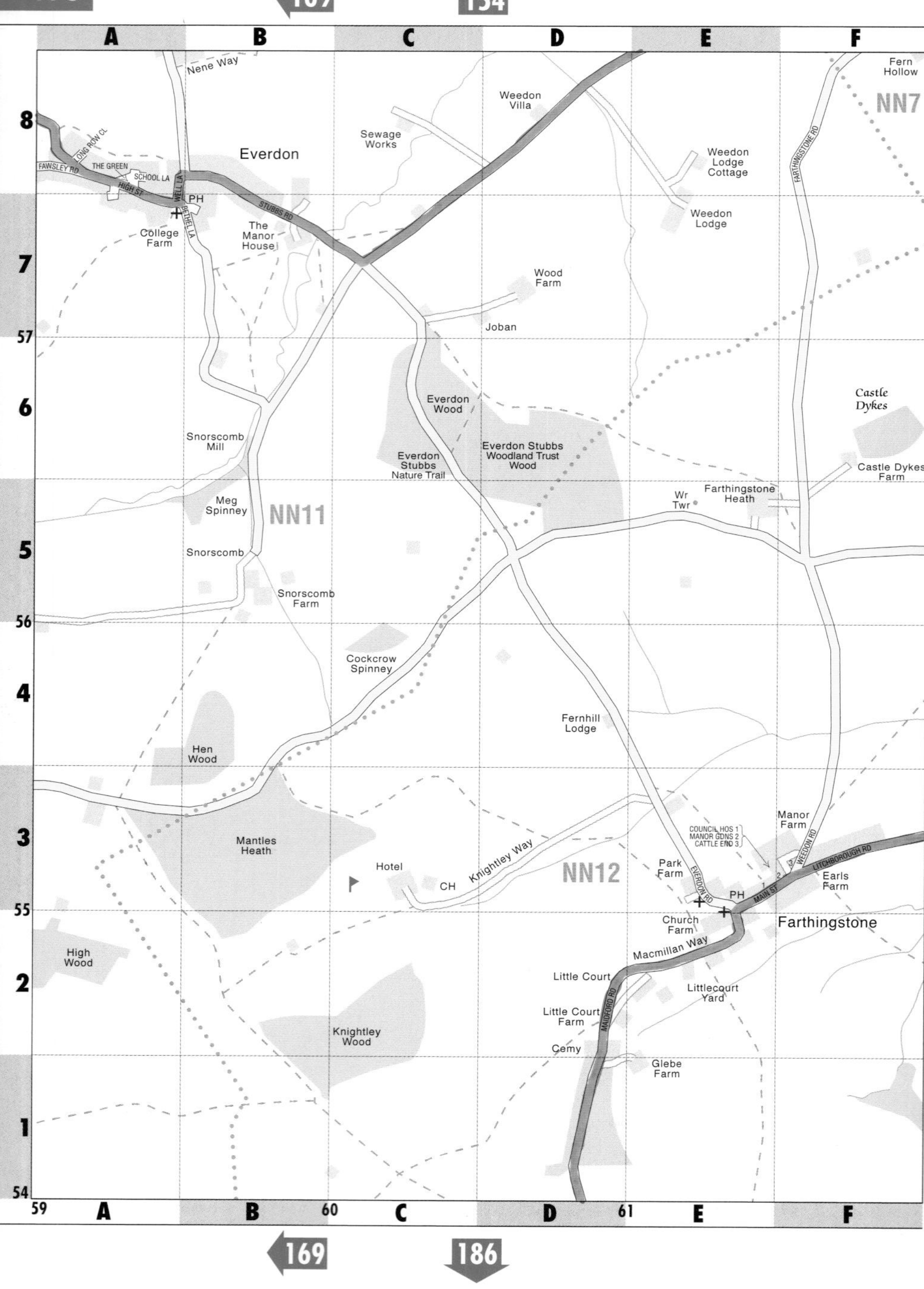
A
B
C
D
E
F
8
7
57
6
5
56
4
3
55
2
1
54
59
60
61
Nene Way
Everdon
FAWSLEY RD
LONG ROW CL
THE GREEN
SCHOOL LA
HIGH ST
WELL LA
PH
BETHEL LA
STUBBS RD
College Farm
The Manor House
Sewage Works
Weedon Villa
Weedon Lodge Cottage
Weedon Lodge
Fern Hollow
NN7
FARTHINGSTONE RD
Wood Farm
Joban
Everdon Wood
Everdon Stubbs Nature Trail
Everdon Stubbs Woodland Trust Wood
Snorscomb Mill
Meg Spinney
NN11
Snorscomb
Snorscomb Farm
Castle Dykes
Castle Dykes Farm
Wr Twr
Farthingstone Heath
Cockcrow Spinney
Hen Wood
Fernhill Lodge
Mantles Heath
Hotel
CH
Knightley Way
NN12
COUNCIL HOS 1
MANOR GDNS 2
CATTLE END 3
Manor Farm
WEEDON RD
LITCHBOROUGH RD
Park Farm
EVERDON RD
PH
MAIN ST
Earls Farm
Church Farm
Farthingstone
Macmillan Way
High Wood
Little Court
Littlecourt Yard
MAIDFORD RD
Little Court Farm
Knightley Wood
Cemy
Glebe Farm

155
172

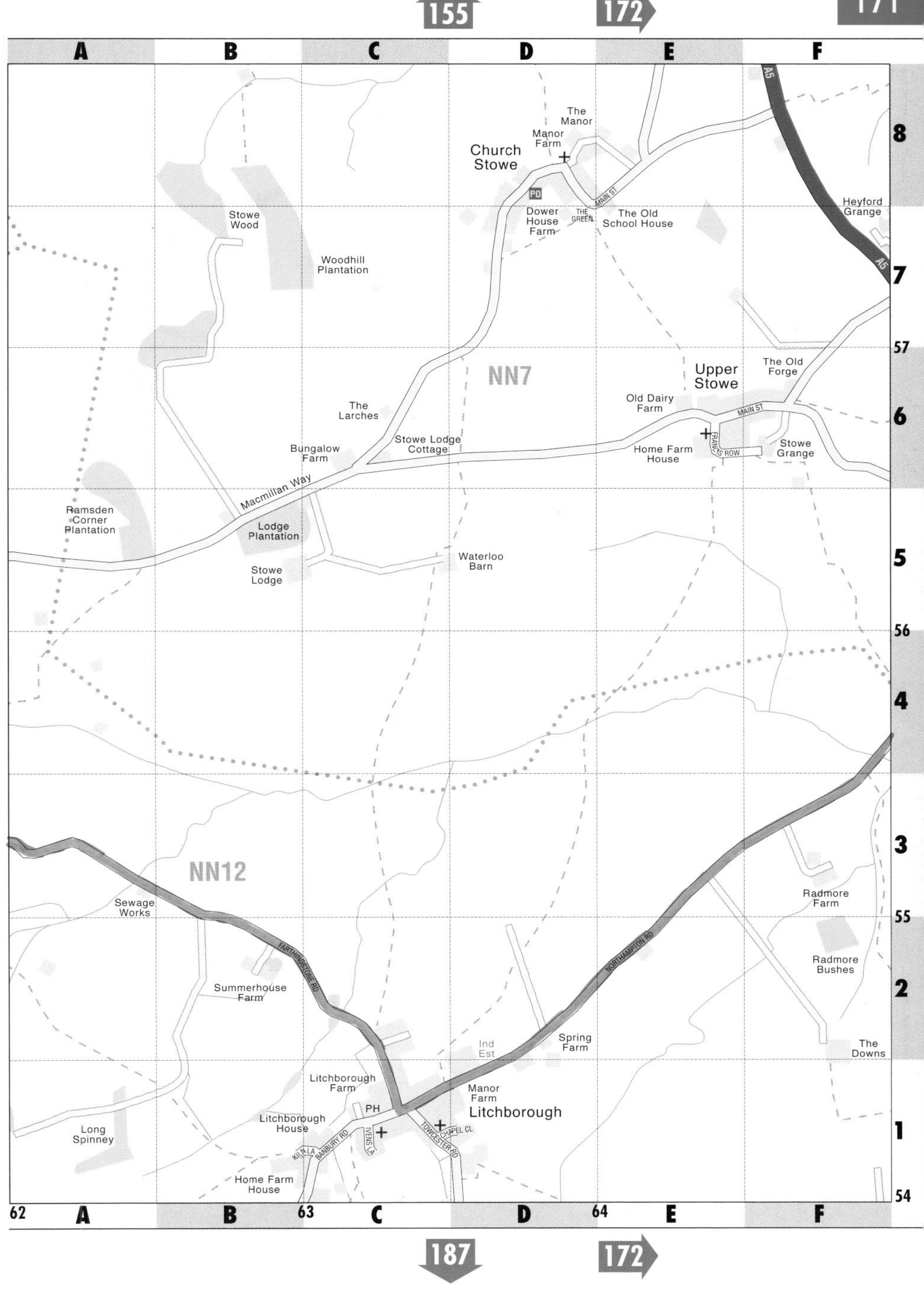

187
172

171
156

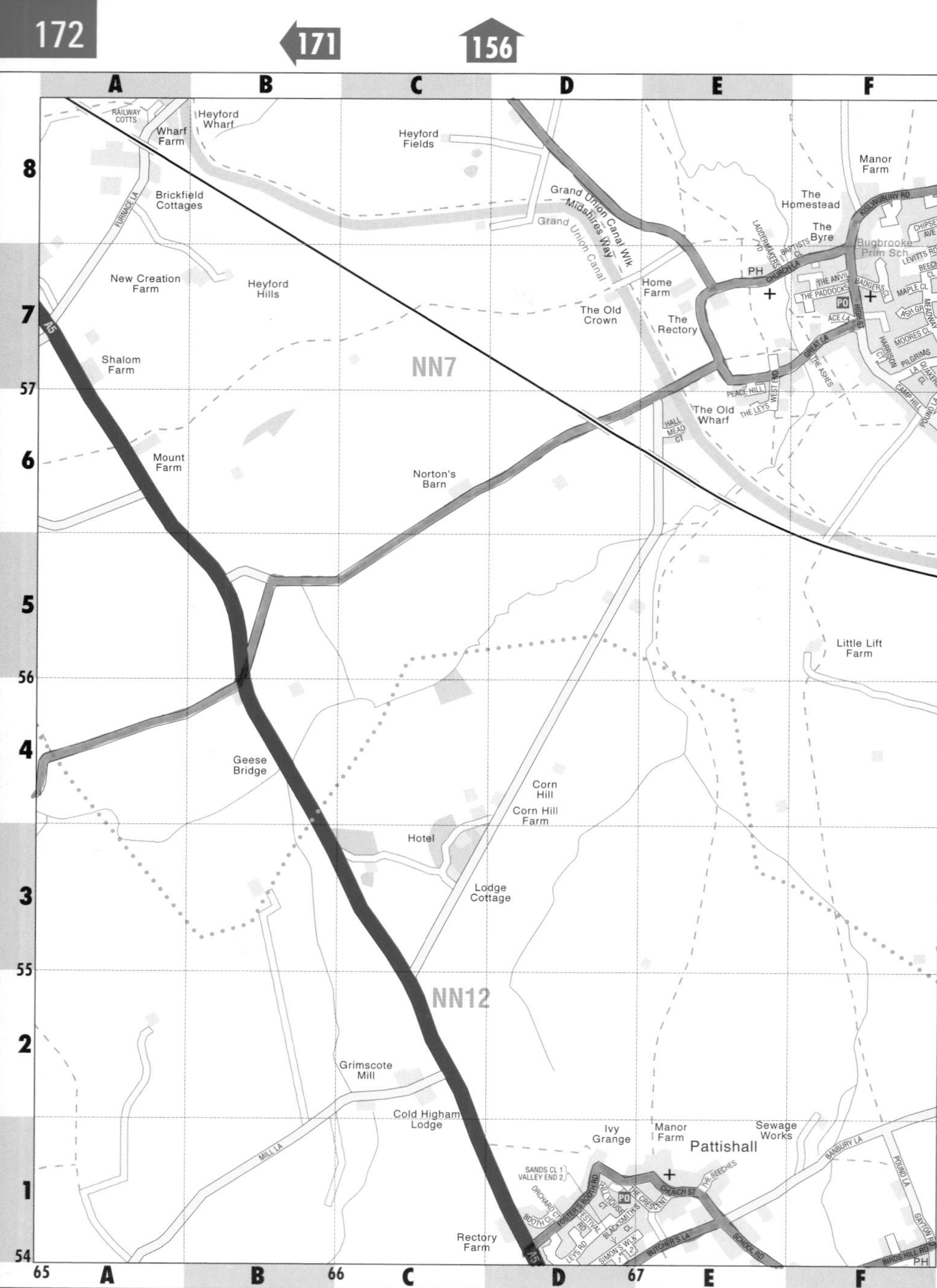

171
188

157
174

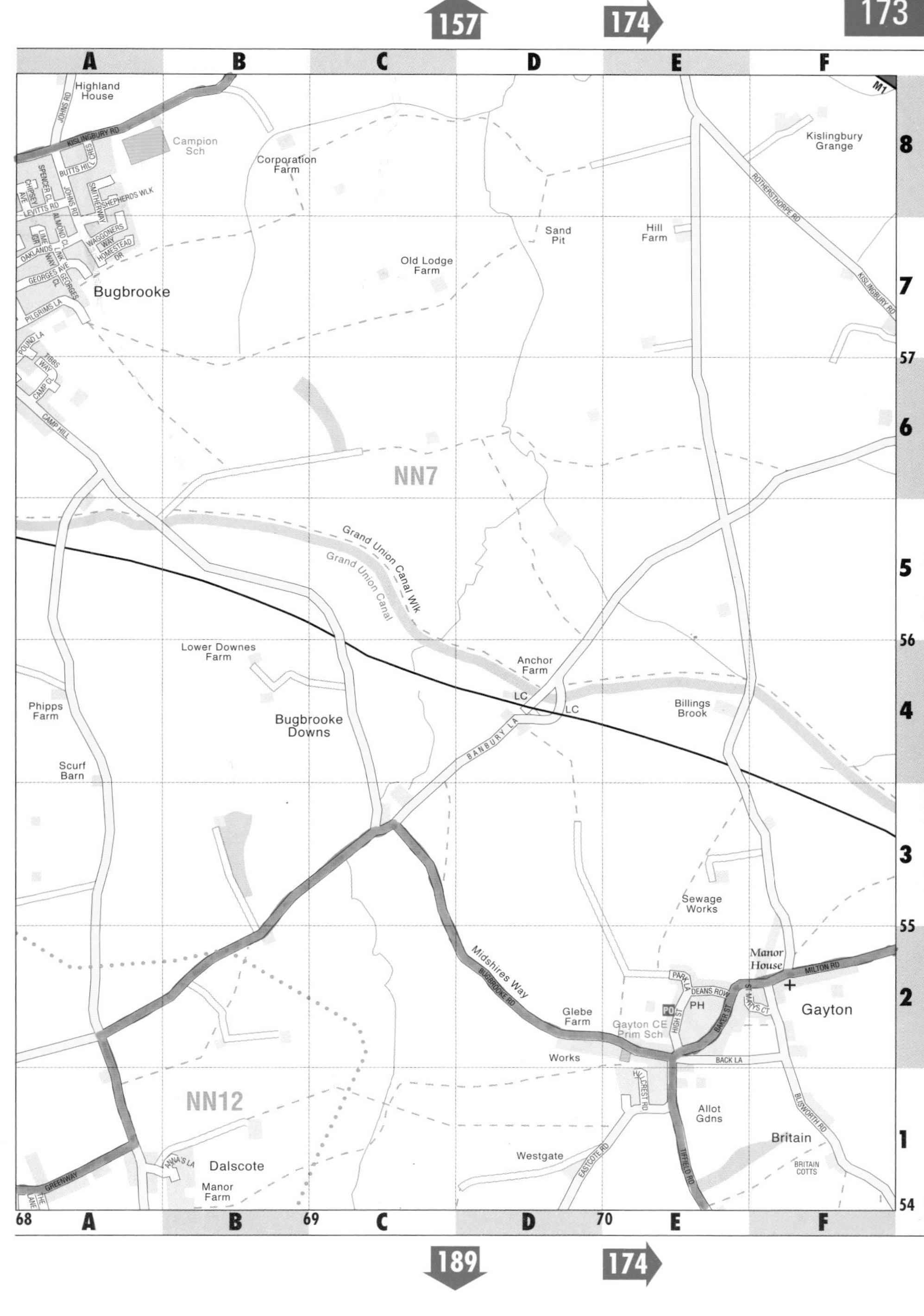

189
174

173
158

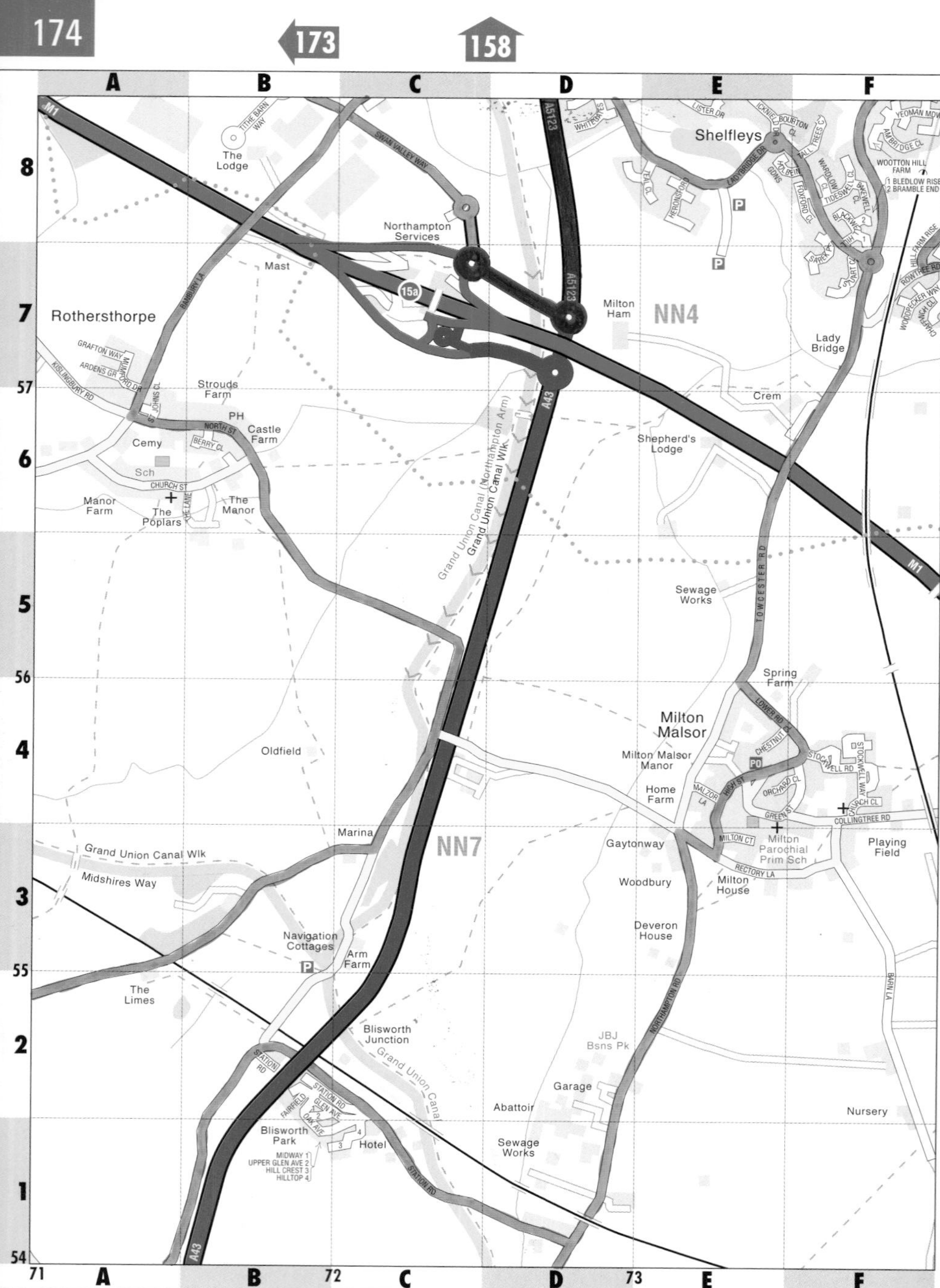

173
190

B8
1 MERE CL
2 SPRINGBANKS WAY
3 WAYSIDE ACRES
4 LONG ACRES
5 MERLIN GR
6 OSPREY VIEW

C8
1 SCOTNEY CL
2 STAGSHAW CL
3 KEDLESTON CL
4 BELTON CL
5 LONGLEAT CT
6 HATFIELD CL
7 OXBURGH CT

D6
1 VERDANT VALE
2 SHATTERSTONE
3 ROCKCROFT
4 RAKESTONE CL
5 CINNAMON CL
6 MARJORAM CL

E7
1 TANCRED CL
2 CRIMEA CL
3 BLANCHARD CL
4 LOUISBURG CL
5 QUEBEC CL
6 SENTRY CL
7 INSIGNIA CL
8 SCULLY CL
9 CAMPAIGN CL
10 PIONEER CL
11 TOULOUSE CL
12 PENINSULAR CL

159 176

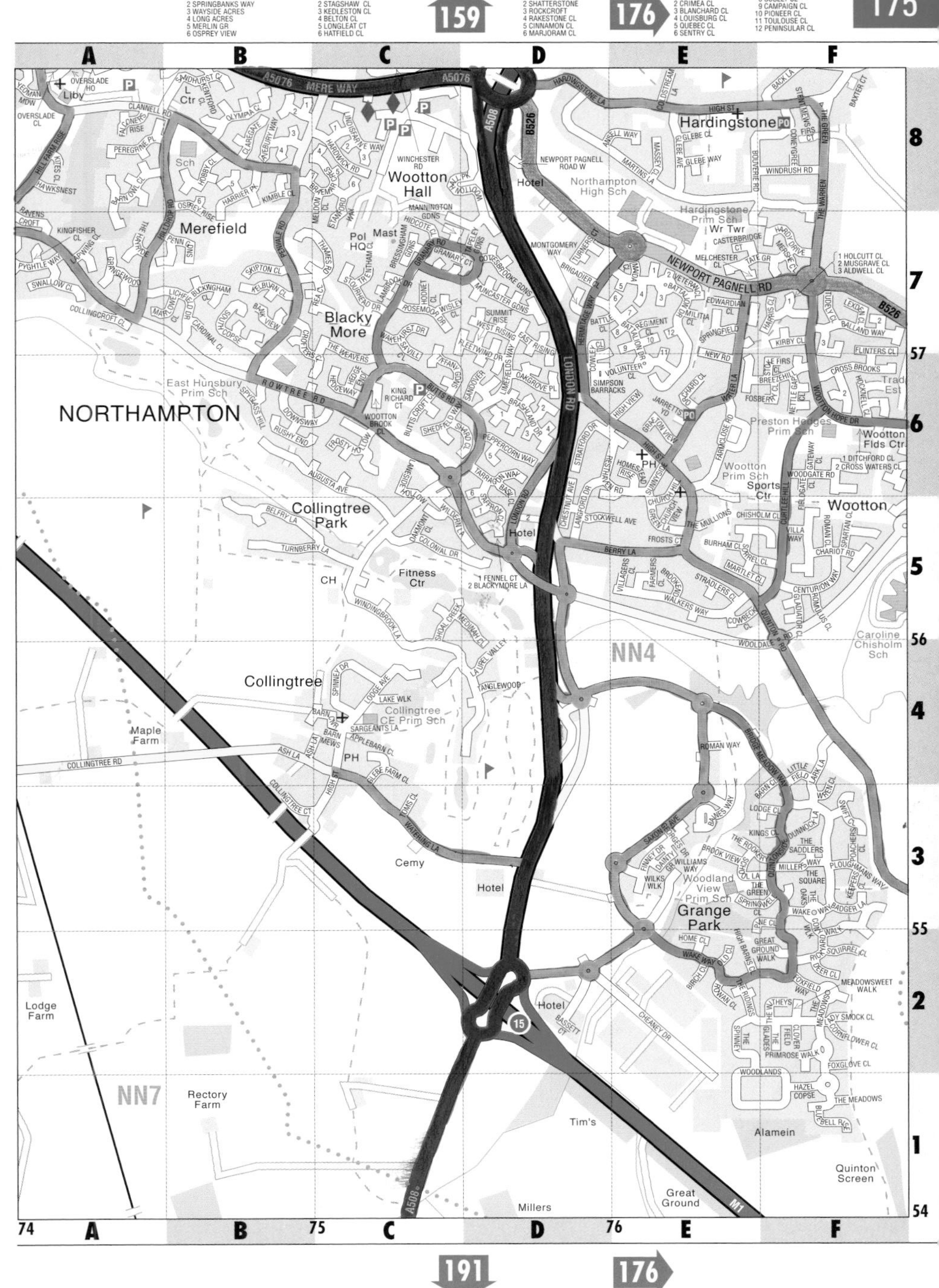

191 176

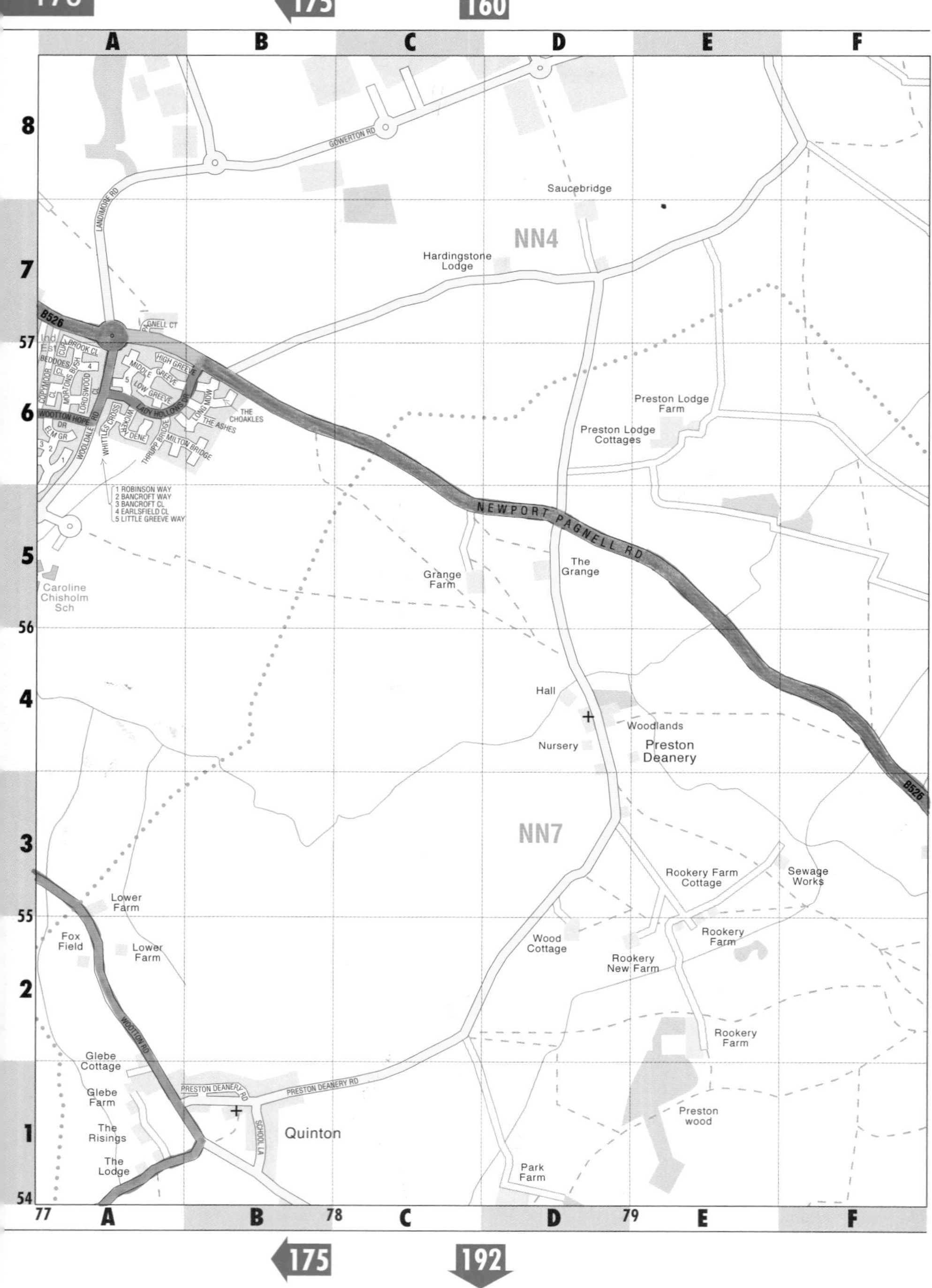
A
B
C
D
E
F
8
7
57
6
5
56
4
3
55
2
1
54
77
78
79
GOWERTON RD
LANDIMORE RD
Saucebridge
NN4
Hardingstone
Lodge
B526
GNELL CT
Ind
Est
BROOK CL
BEDDOES
MORTONS BUSH
LORDSWOOD
HIGH GREEVE
MIDDLE GREEVE
LOW GREEVE
LADY HOLLOWS DR
LONG MDW
THE CHOAKLES
THE ASHES
WOOTTON HOPE DR
WOOLDALE RD
WHITTLES CROSS
WICKEN DENE
THRUPP BRIDGE
MILTON BRIDGE
ELM GR
1 ROBINSON WAY
2 BANCROFT WAY
3 BANCROFT CL
4 EARLSFIELD CL
5 LITTLE GREEVE WAY
Preston Lodge
Farm
Preston Lodge
Cottages
NEWPORT PAGNELL RD
The
Grange
Grange
Farm
Caroline
Chisholm
Sch
Hall
Woodlands
Nursery
Preston
Deanery
B526
NN7
Rookery Farm
Cottage
Sewage
Works
Lower
Farm
Fox
Field
Lower
Farm
Wood
Cottage
Rookery
Farm
Rookery
New Farm
Rookery
Farm
WOOTTON RD
Glebe
Cottage
Glebe
Farm
PRESTON DEANERY RD
PRESTON DEANERY RD
SCHOOL LA
Quinton
The
Risings
The
Lodge
Preston
wood
Park
Farm

161
178

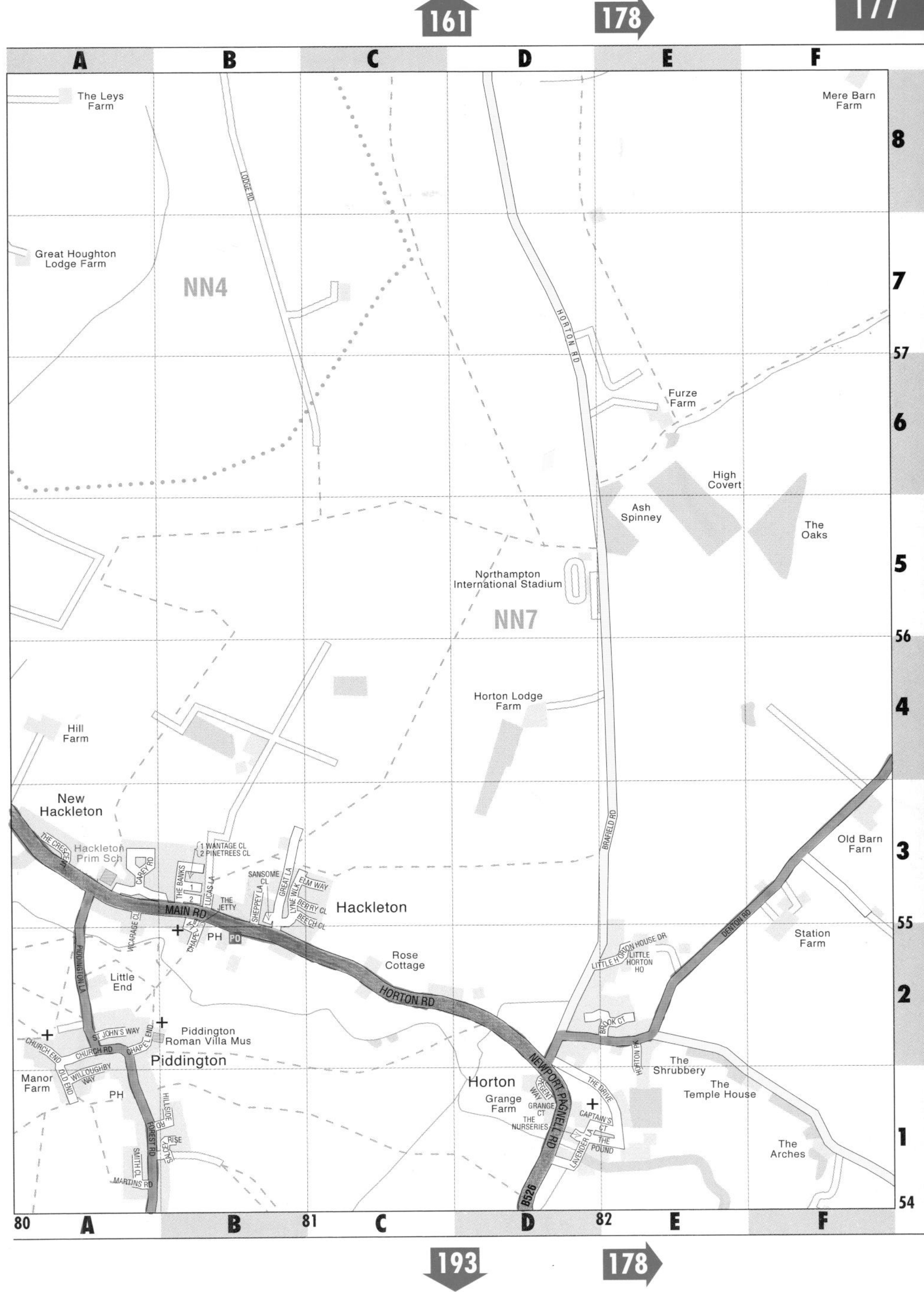

193
178

177
162

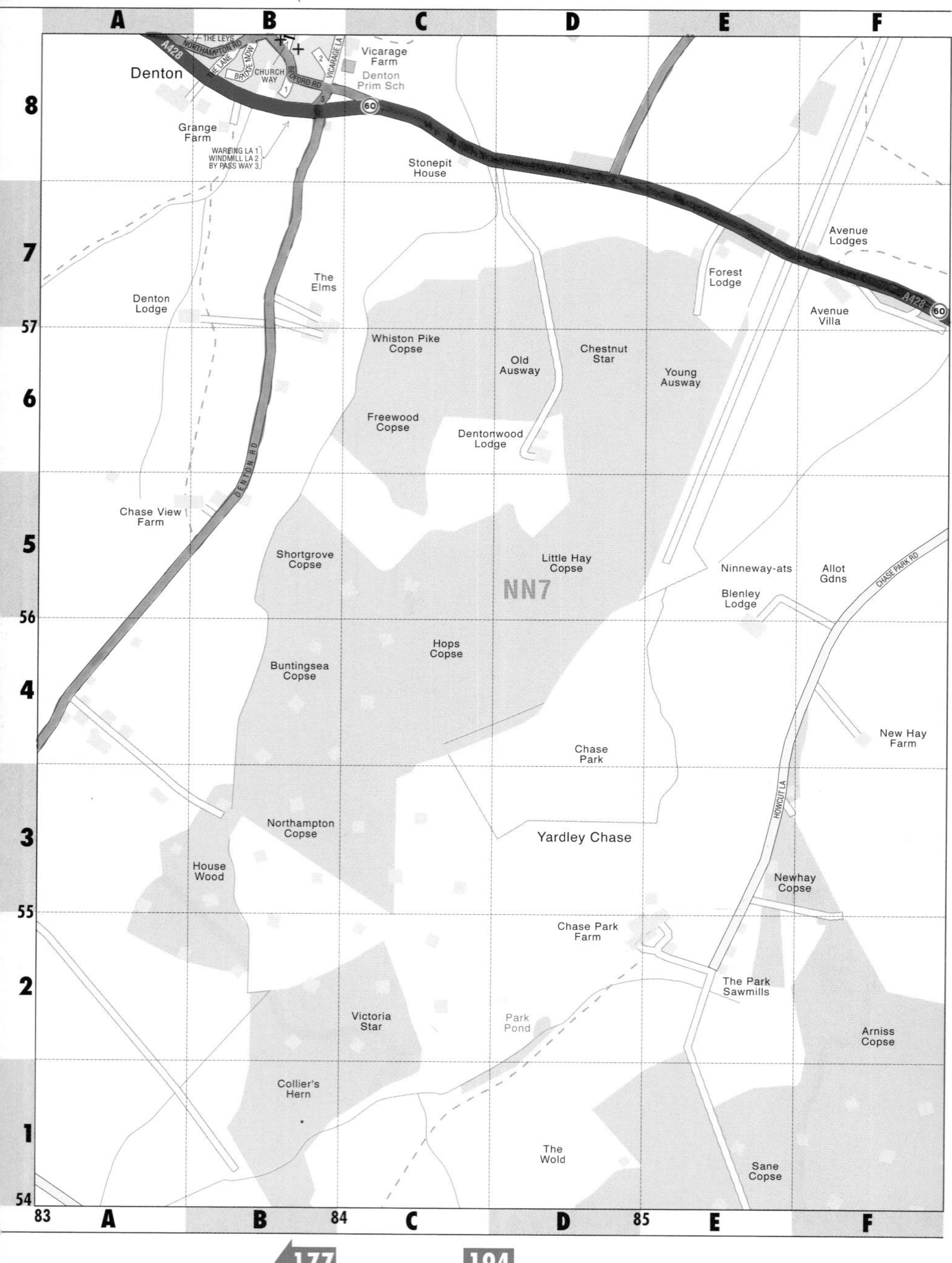

177
194

163
180

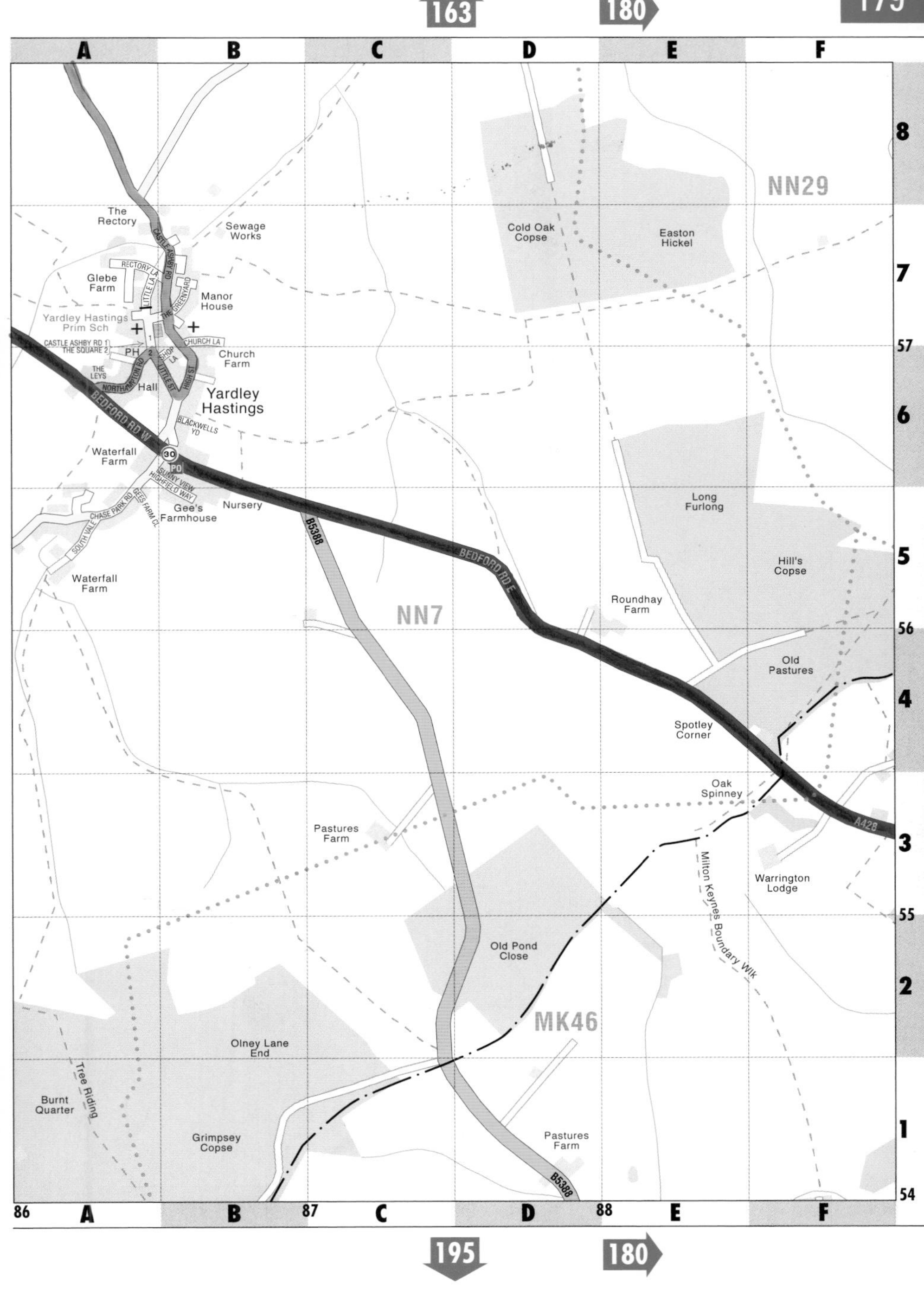

195
180

179
164

A
B
C
D
E
F
8
7
57
6
5
56
4
3
55
2
1
54
89
90
91
Horn Wood
A509
Stocking Hollow
The Belts
NN29
Wold Barn
Santon Barn
The Lodge
Bozeat Grange
Bozeat Wood
The Slipe
MK43
Nunwood Barn
Mast
The Oaks Wood
Northey Farm
Milton Keynes Boundary Wk
Three Shires Way
Nun Wood
Threeshire Wood
New Pastures Farm
Lavendon Lodge Farm
Barslay Spinney
A428
Broadlane Spinney
Warrington House
Nursery
Nunirons
Nuniron Spinney
MK46
Park Farm
Castle Farm
The Nest Farm
Lower Farm
Castle Rd
Brickfield Plantation
Warrington
Warrington House Farm
Home Farm
Lavendon
A509 Milton Keynes
Buckinghamshire STREET ATLAS
A428 Bedford
Bedfordshire STREET ATLAS

179

182

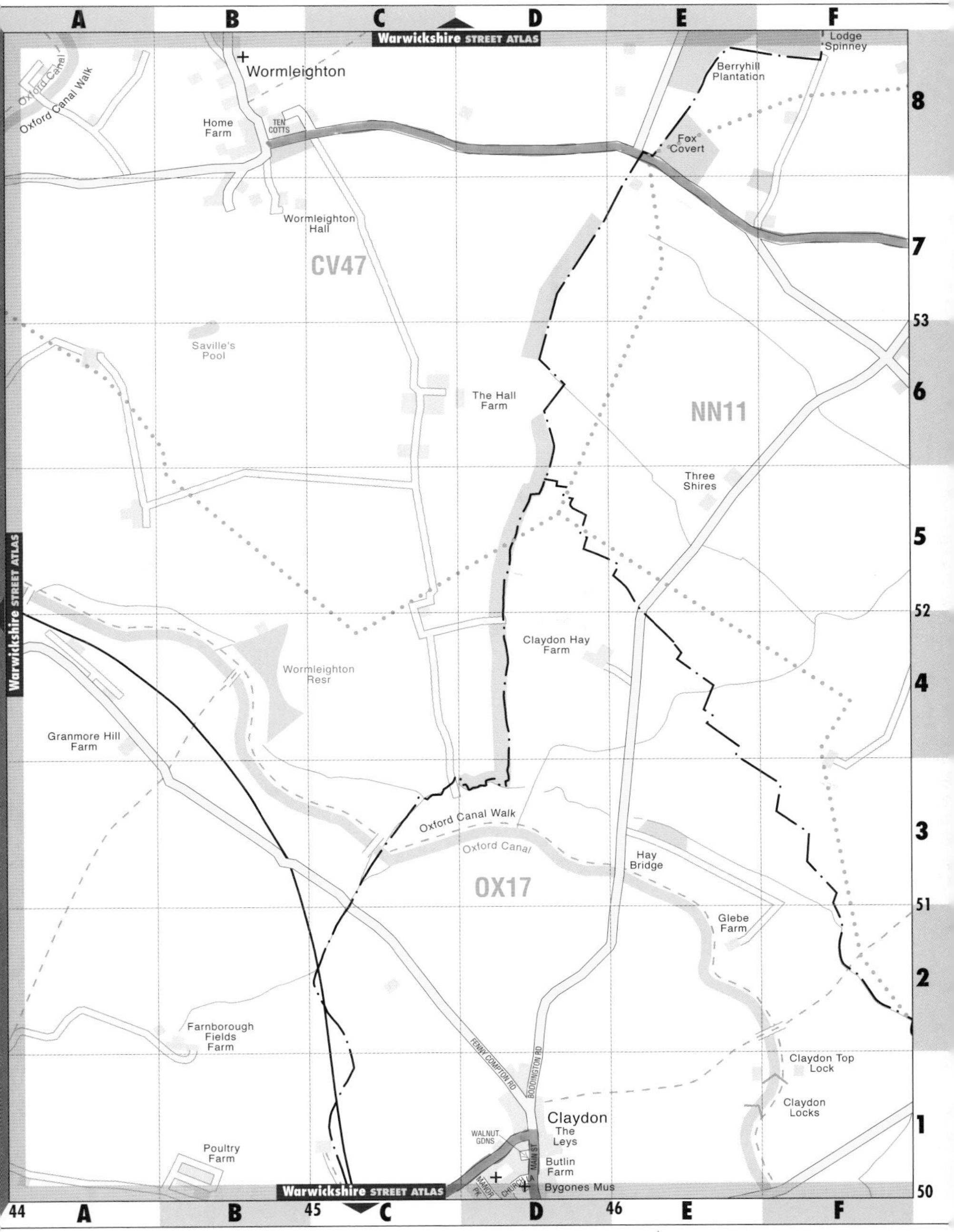

A
B
C
D
E
F
Warwickshire STREET ATLAS
Lodge Spinney
Wormleighton
Berryhill Plantation
Oxford Canal
Oxford Canal Walk
8
Home Farm
TEN COTTS
Fox Covert
Wormleighton Hall
7
CV47
53
Saville's Pool
The Hall Farm
6
NN11
Three Shires
5
Warwickshire STREET ATLAS
52
Claydon Hay Farm
Wormleighton Resr
4
Granmore Hill Farm
Oxford Canal Walk
3
Oxford Canal
Hay Bridge
OX17
51
Glebe Farm
2
Farnborough Fields Farm
FENNY COMPTON RD
BODDINGTON RD
Claydon Top Lock
Claydon Locks
Claydon
1
The Leys
WALNUT GDNS
Poultry Farm
Butlin Farm
MAIN ST
MANOR PK
CHURCH LA
Bygones Mus
Warwickshire STREET ATLAS
50
44
A
B
45
C
D
46
E
F

182

181
166

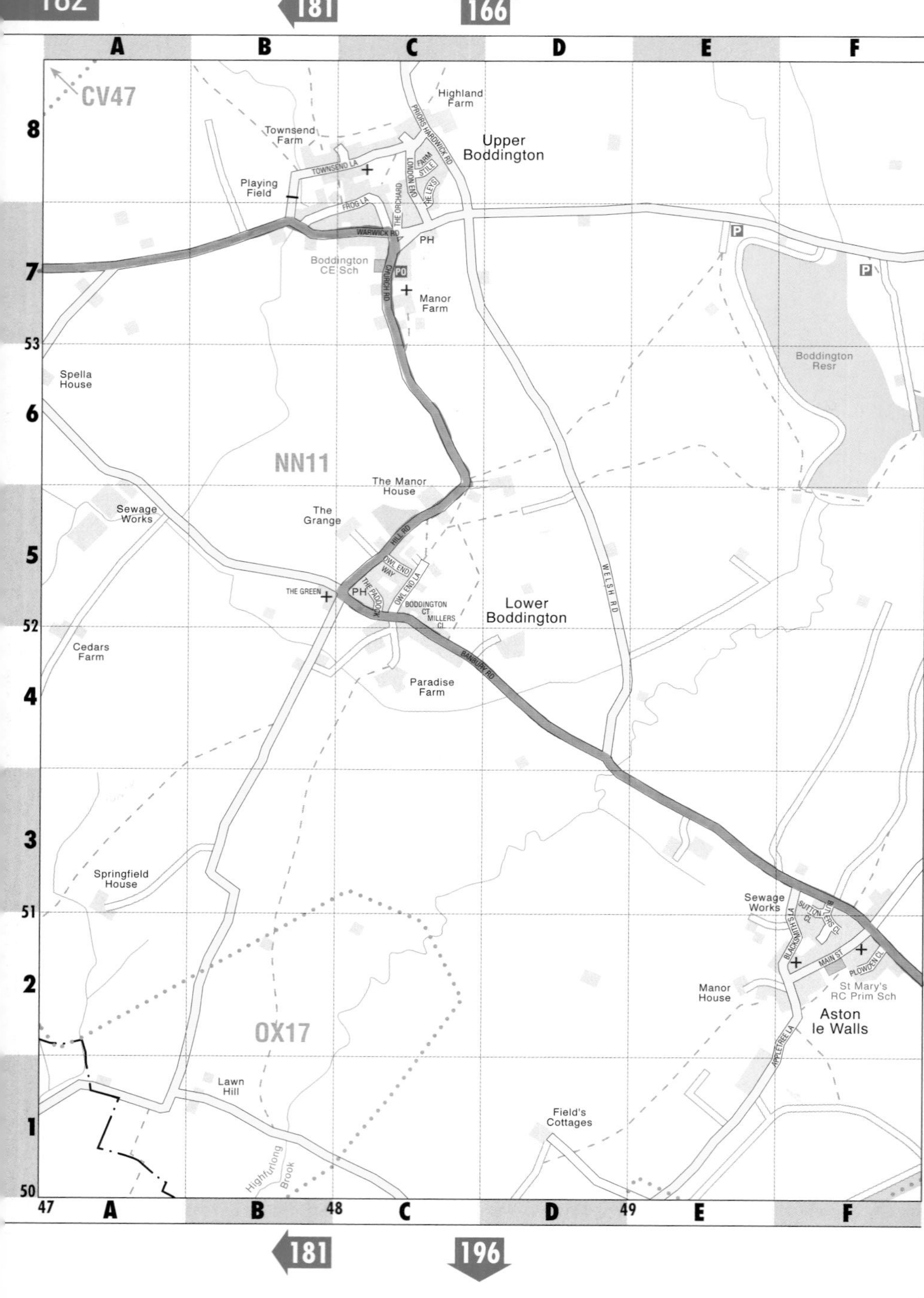

181
196

167
184

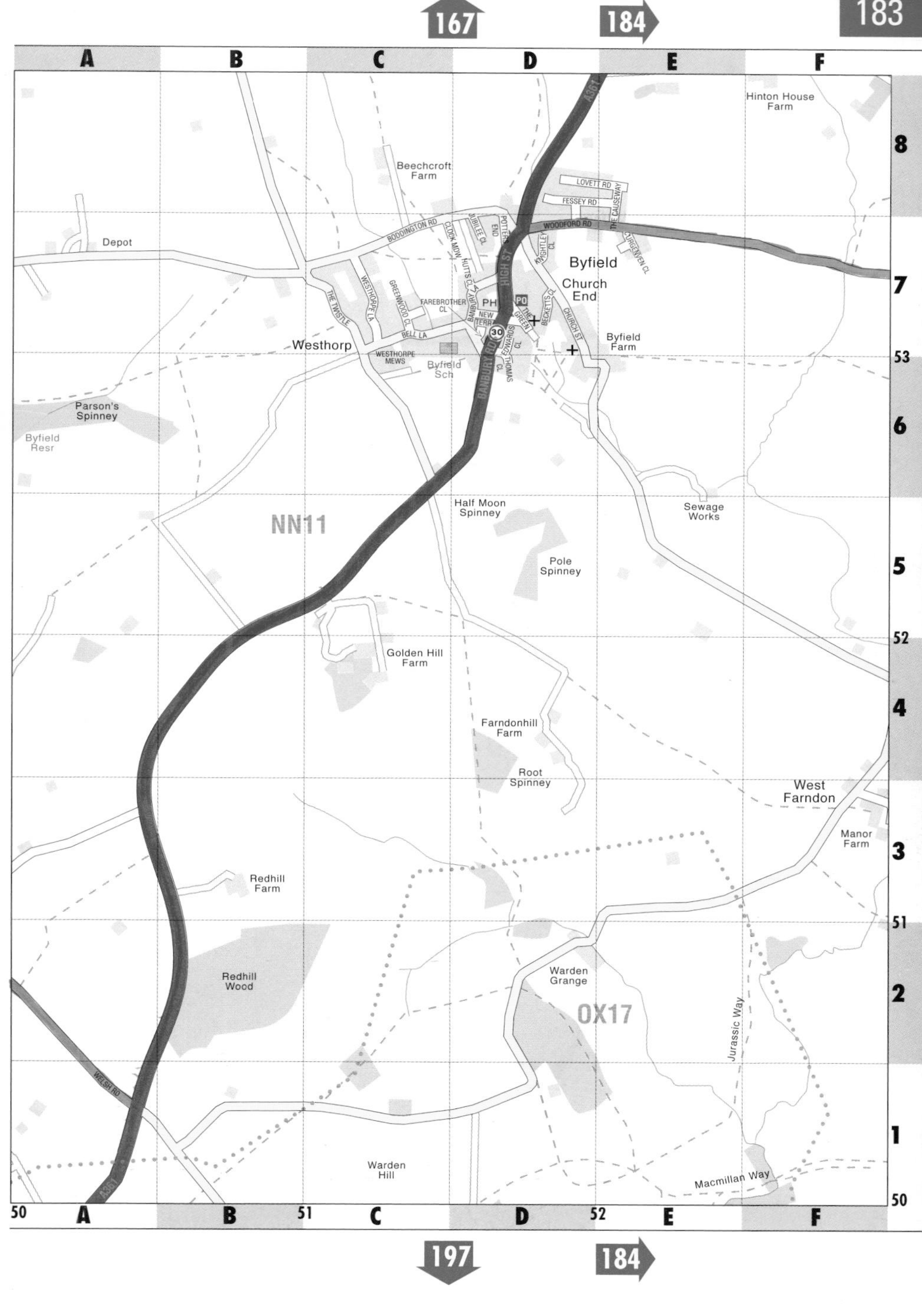

197
184

183
168

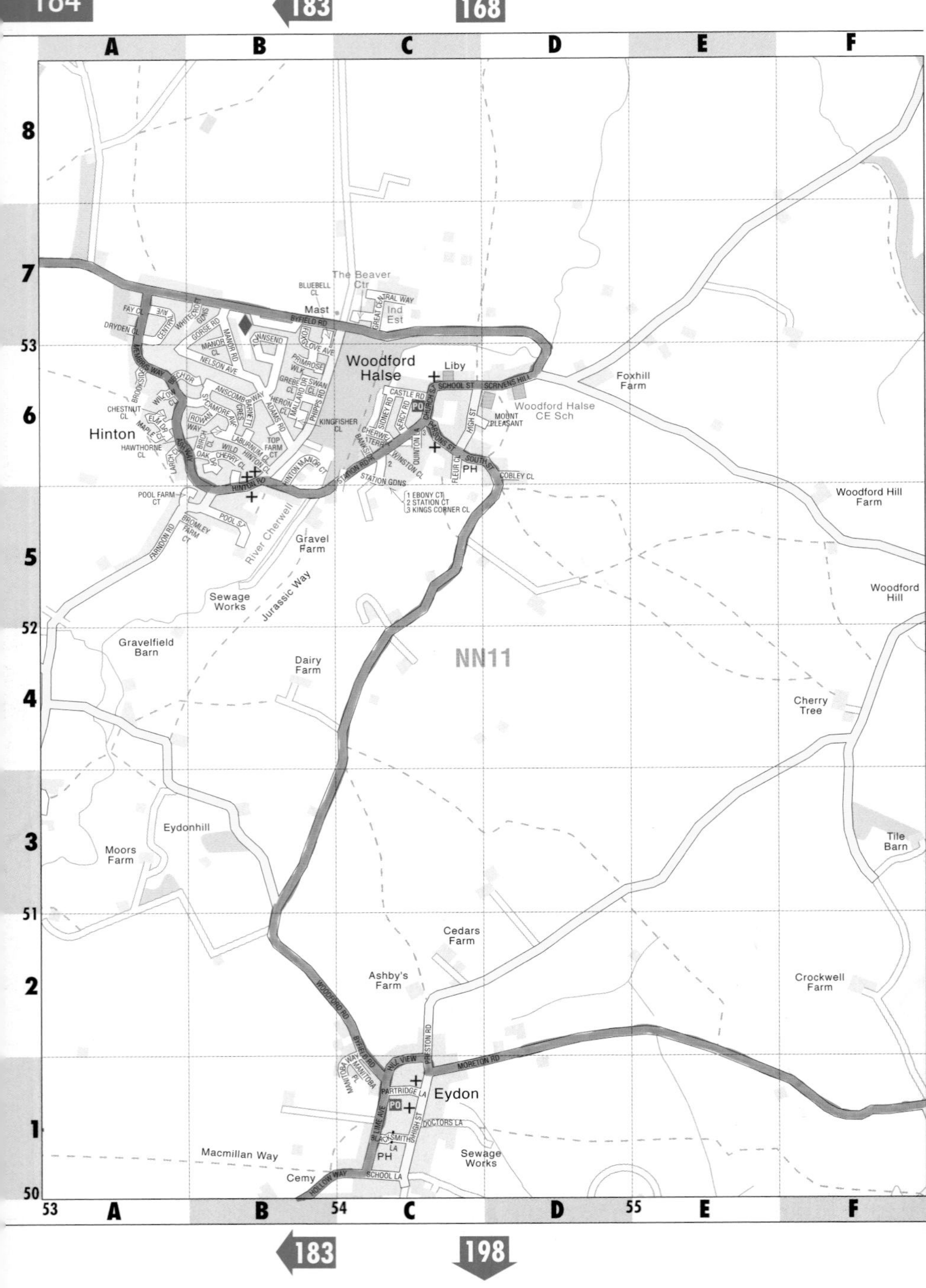
A B C D E F
8
7
53
6
5
52
4
3
51
2
1
50
53 54 55
The Beaver Ctr
Bluebell Cl
Mast
Central Way
Ind Est
Byfield Rd
Fay Cl
Dryden Cl
Woodford Halse
Liby
School St
Castle Rd
PO
Woodford Halse CE Sch
Mount Pleasant
Foxhill Farm
Hinton
Chestnut Cl
Hawthorne Cl
Kingfisher Cl
Hinton Rd
Station Gdns
1 Ebony Ct
2 Station Ct
3 Kings Corner Cl
Cobley Cl
South St
PH
Pool Farm Ct
Pool St
Farndon Rd
Bromley Farm Ct
River Cherwell
Gravel Farm
Sewage Works
Jurassic Way
Woodford Hill Farm
Woodford Hill
Gravelfield Barn
Dairy Farm
NN11
Cherry Tree
Eydonhill
Moors Farm
Tile Barn
Cedars Farm
Ashby's Farm
Crockwell Farm
Woodford Rd
Preston Rd
Hill View
Moreton Rd
Partridge La
Eydon
Doctors La
Lime Ave
High St
Macmillan Way
Sewage Works
Cemy
Hollow Way
School La

169
186

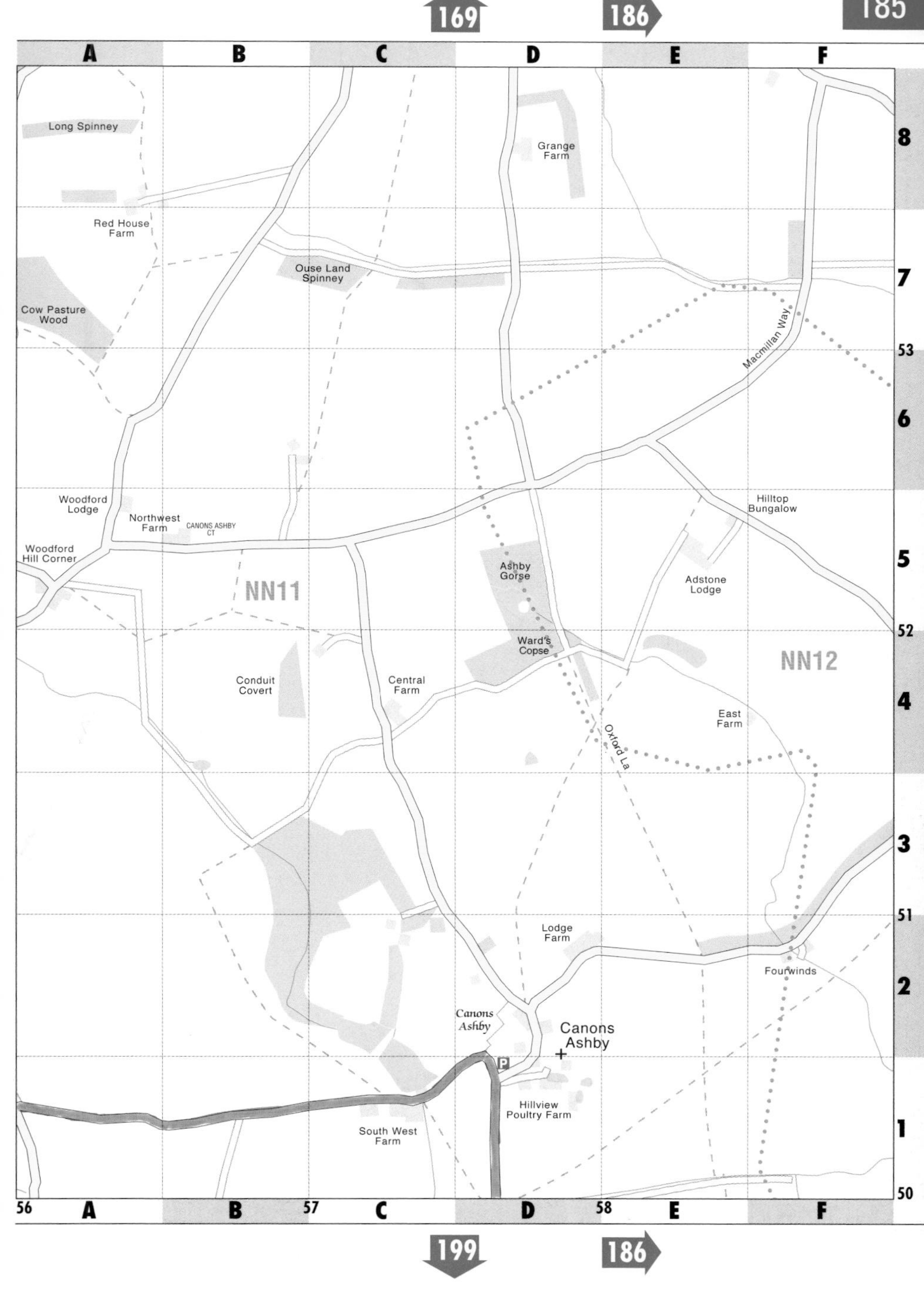

199
186

185
170

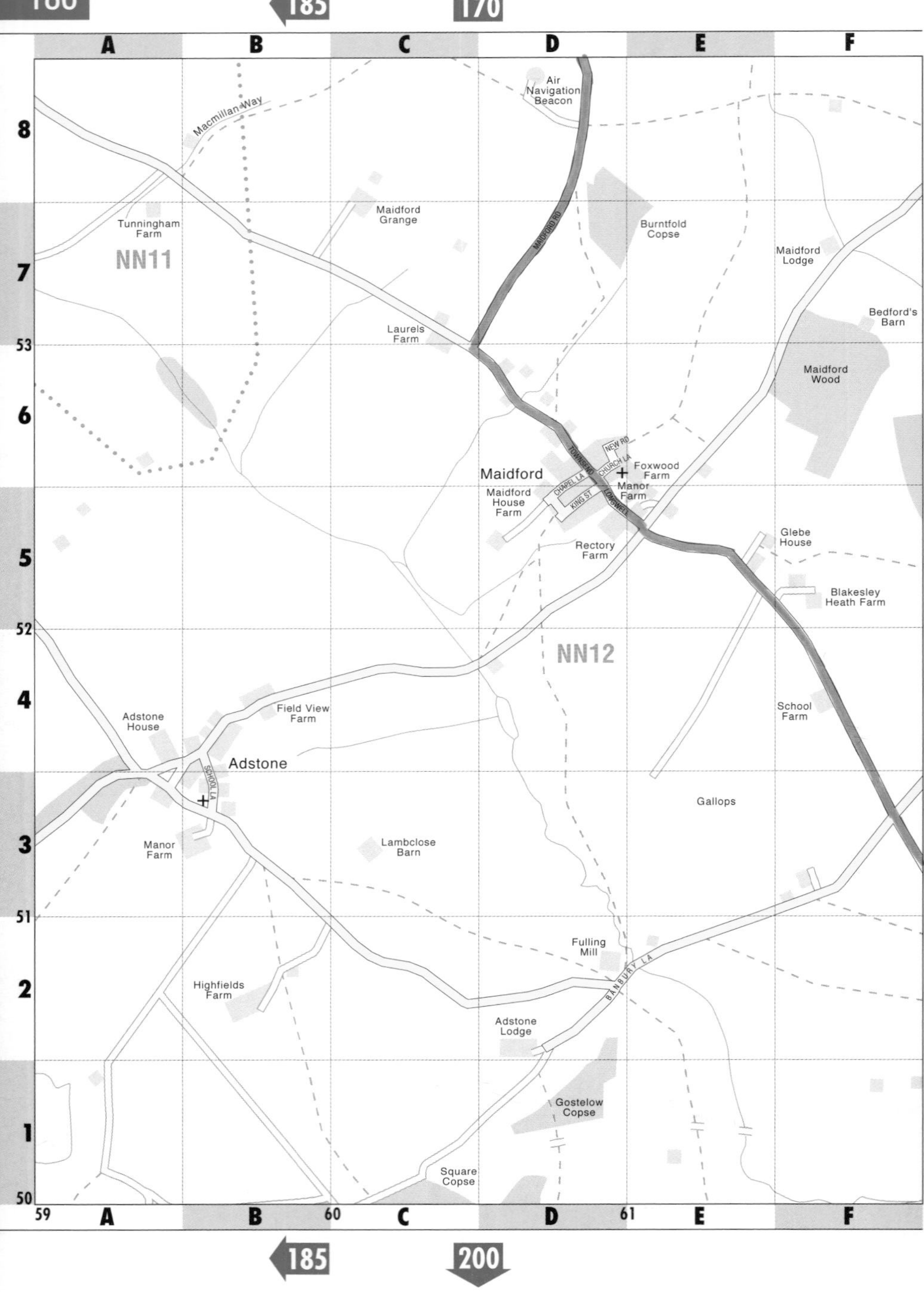

185
200

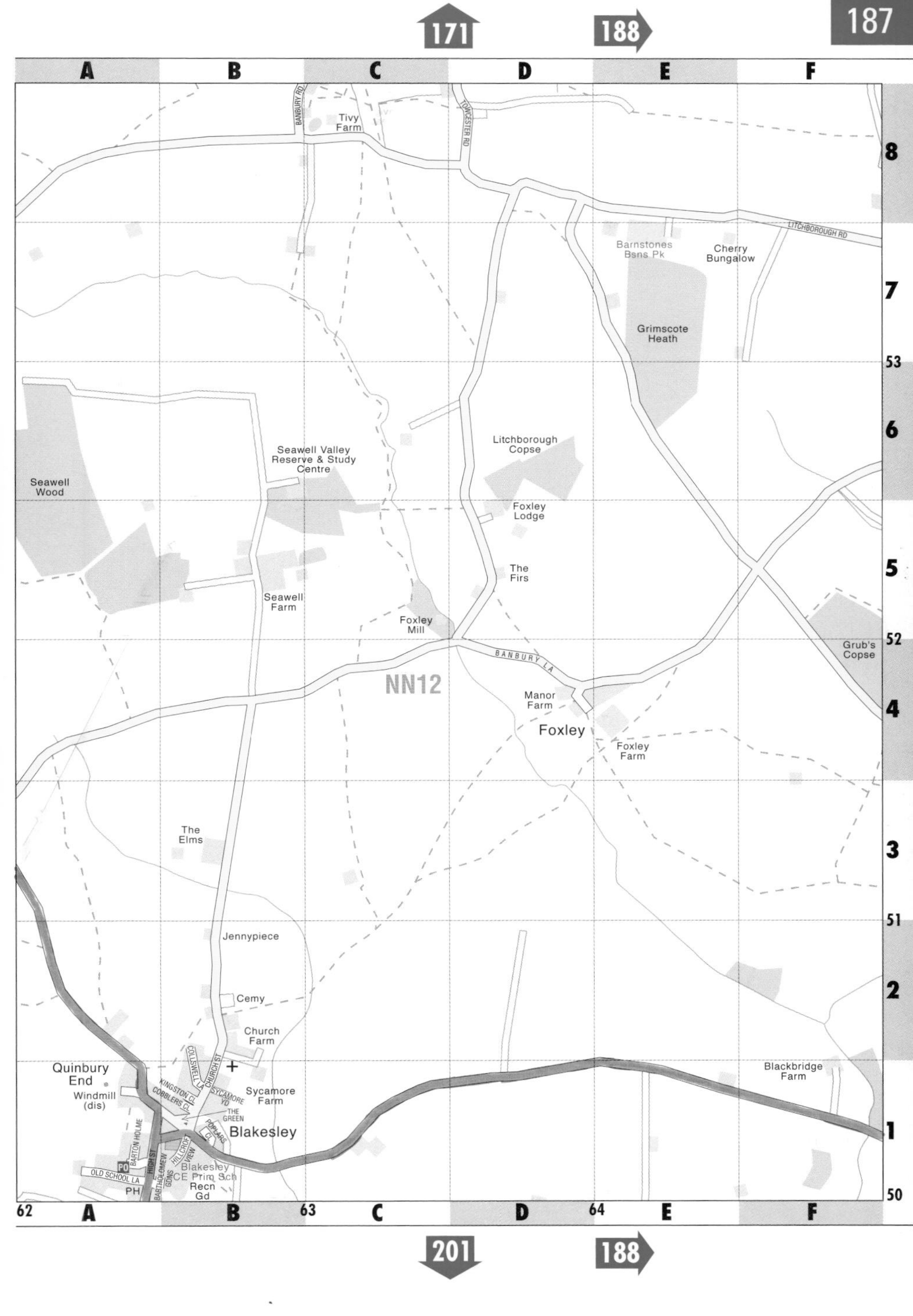
171
188
A
B
C
D
E
F
8
7
53
6
5
52
4
3
51
2
1
50
62
63
64
201
188
BANBURY RD
Tivy Farm
TOWCESTER RD
LITCHBOROUGH RD
Barnstones Bsns Pk
Cherry Bungalow
Grimscote Heath
Litchborough Copse
Seawell Valley Reserve & Study Centre
Seawell Wood
Foxley Lodge
The Firs
Seawell Farm
Foxley Mill
Grub's Copse
BANBURY LA
NN12
Manor Farm
Foxley
Foxley Farm
The Elms
Jennypiece
Cemy
Church Farm
Blackbridge Farm
Quinbury End
Windmill (dis)
COLLSWELL LA
CHURCH ST
KINGSTON CL
COBBLERS CL
SYCAMORE YD
Sycamore Farm
THE GREEN
POPLARS CL
Blakesley
BARTON HOLME
HILLCROFT
VIEW
HIGH ST
BARTHOLOMEW GDNS
PO
OLD SCHOOL LA
PH
Blakesley CE Prim Sch
Recn Gd

187
172

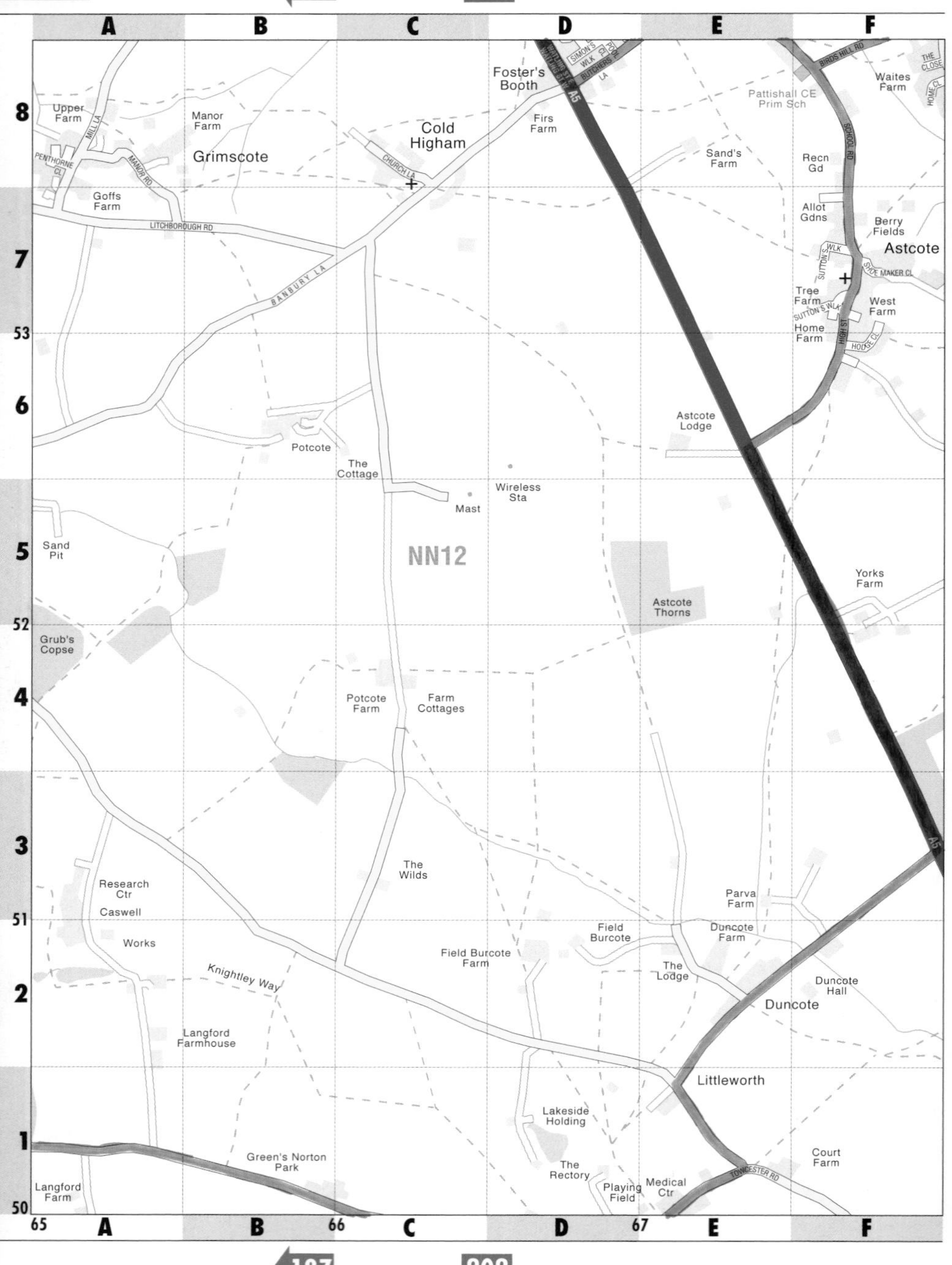

187
202

173
190

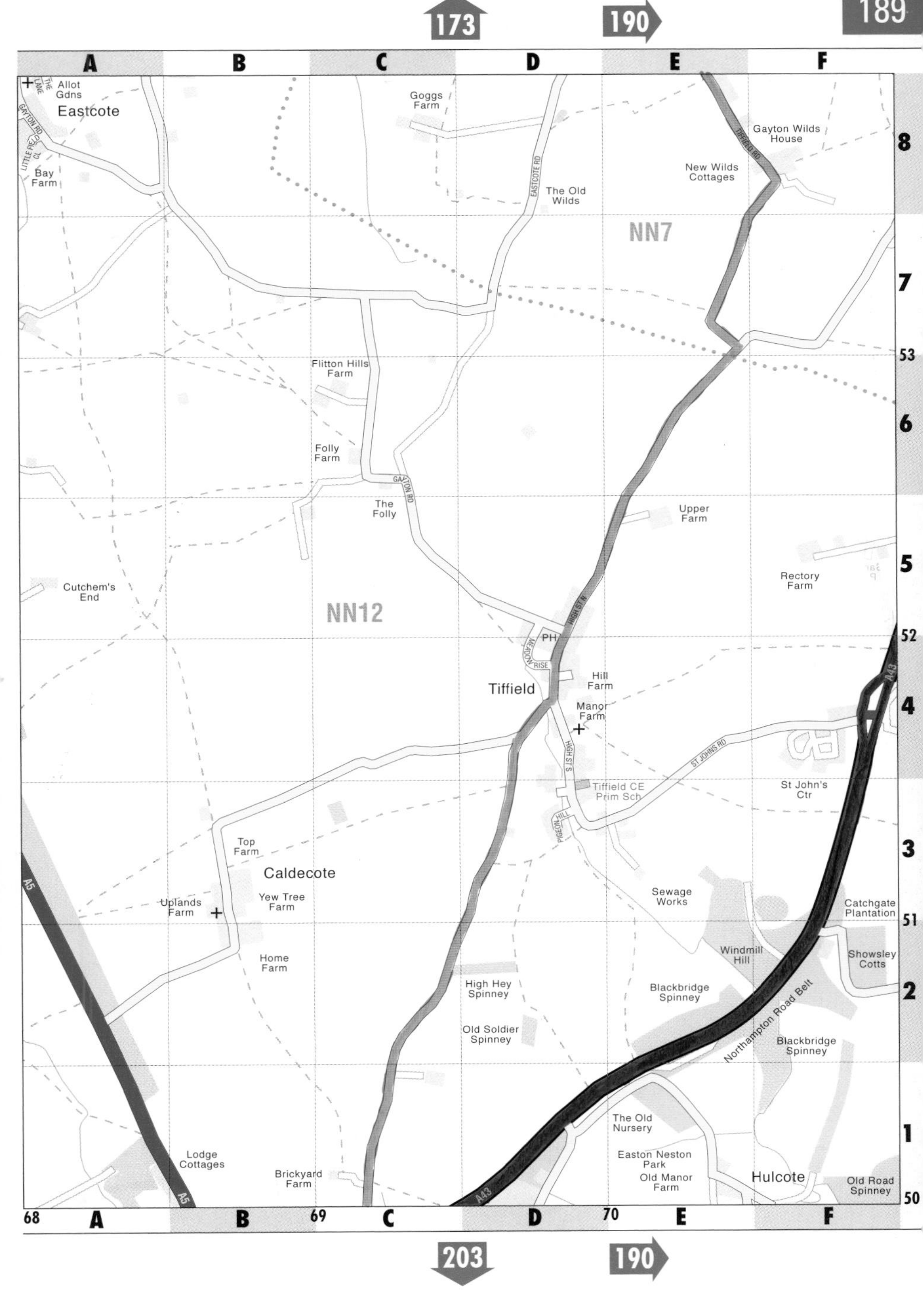

203
190

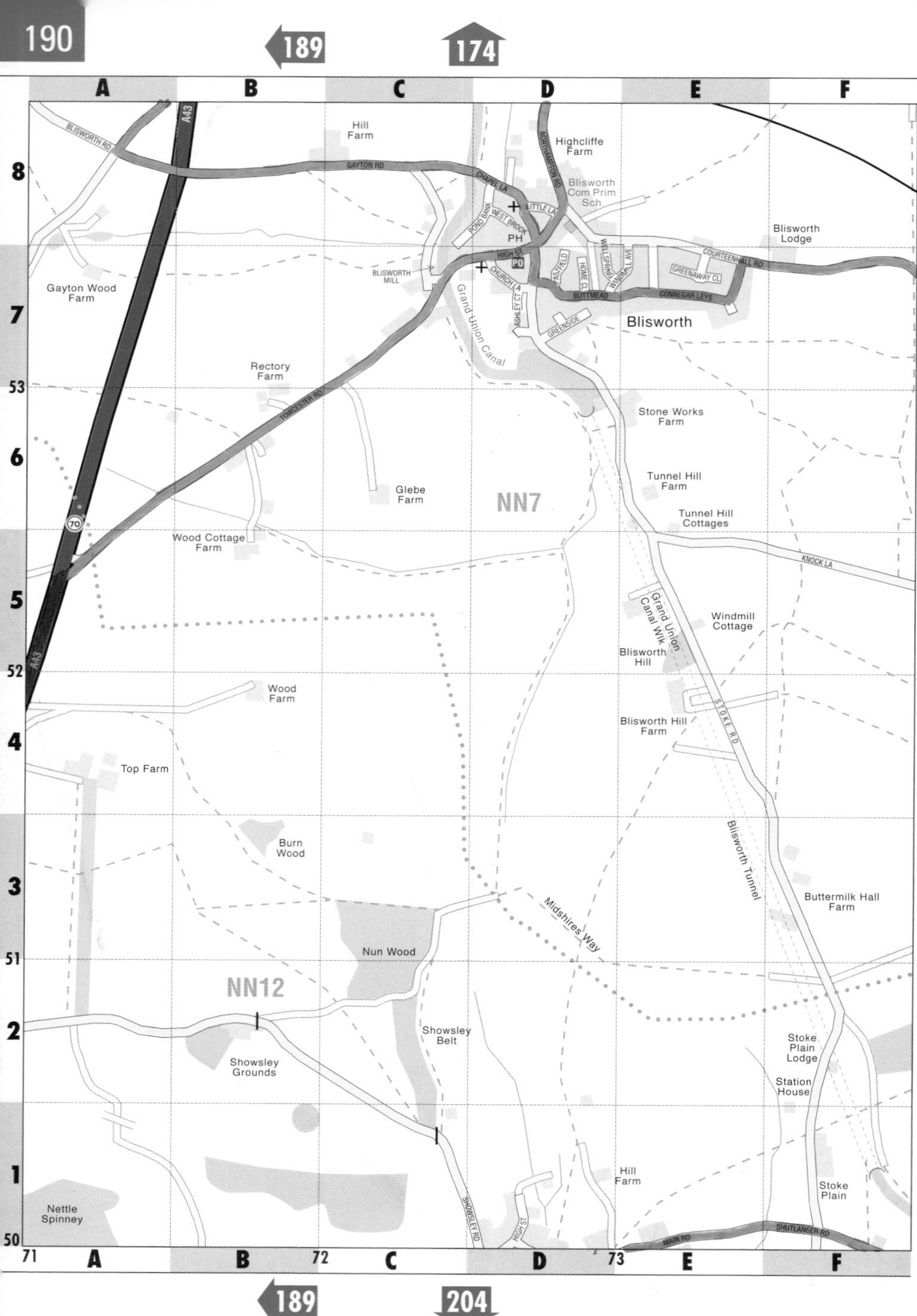
A
B
C
D
E
F
8
7
53
6
5
52
4
3
51
2
1
50
71
72
73
Hill Farm
Highcliffe Farm
Blisworth Com Prim Sch
BLISWORTH RD
A43
GAYTON RD
CHAPEL LA
NORTHAMPTON RD
LITTLE LA
POND BANK
WEST BROOK
PH
HIGH ST
PO
CHURCH LA
BLISWORTH MILL
Gayton Wood Farm
ASHLEY CT
FASTFIELD
HOME CL
WELLSPRING
WINDMILL AVE
COURTEENHALL RD
GREENAWAY CL
BUTTMEAD
CONNEGAR LEYS
GREENSIDE
Blisworth
Blisworth Lodge
Grand Union Canal
Rectory Farm
TOWCESTER RD
Stone Works Farm
Tunnel Hill Farm
Tunnel Hill Cottages
Glebe Farm
NN7
Wood Cottage Farm
70
KNOCK LA
Grand Union Canal Wlk
Windmill Cottage
Blisworth Hill
Wood Farm
STOKE RD
Blisworth Hill Farm
Top Farm
Burn Wood
Blisworth Tunnel
Buttermilk Hall Farm
Midshires Way
Nun Wood
NN12
Showsley Belt
Showsley Grounds
Stoke Plain Lodge
Station House
Hill Farm
Stoke Plain
Nettle Spinney
SHOWSLEY RD
HIGH ST
MAIN RD
SHUTLANGER RD

175
192

205
192

191
176

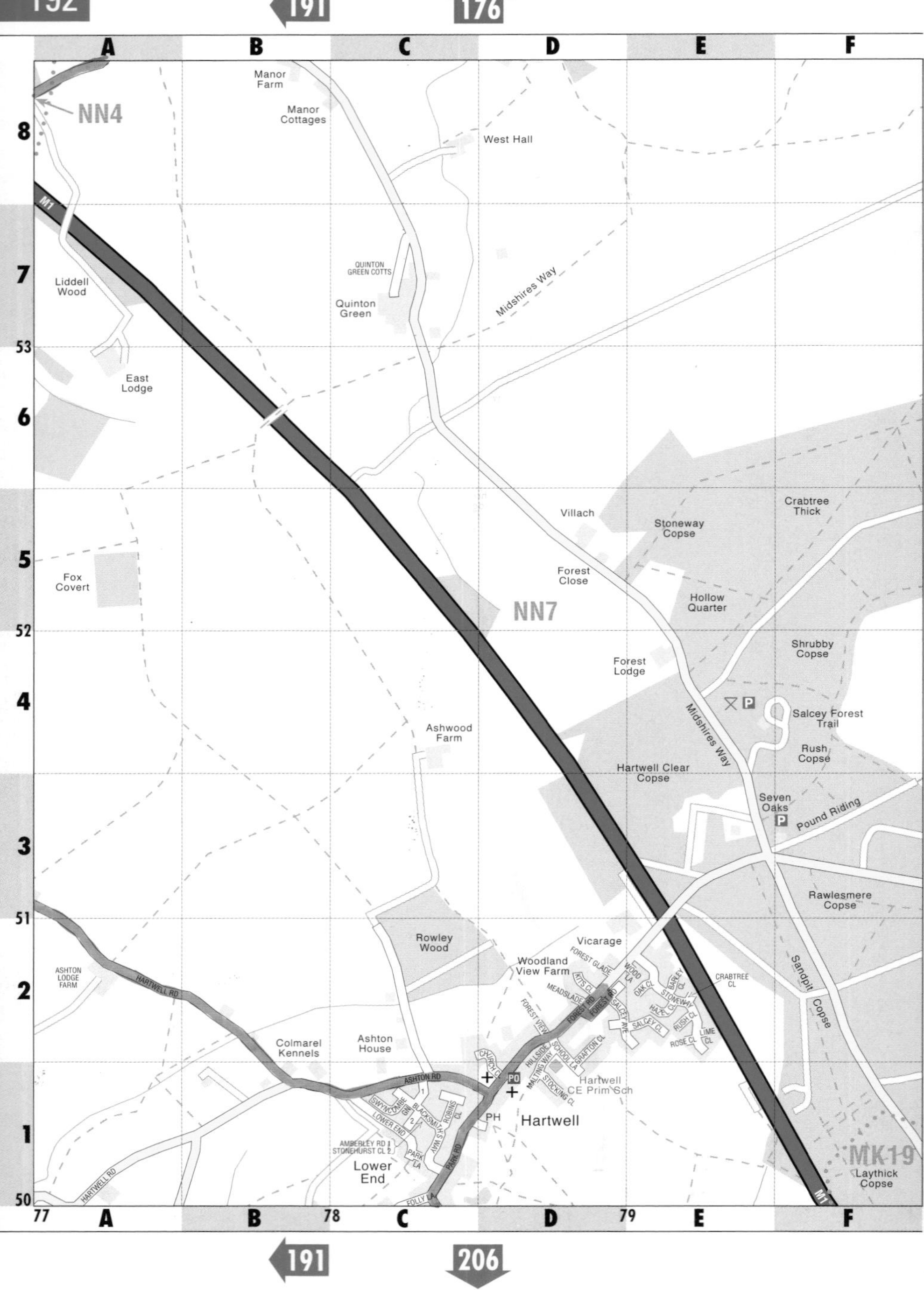

191
206

177
194

207
194

193
178

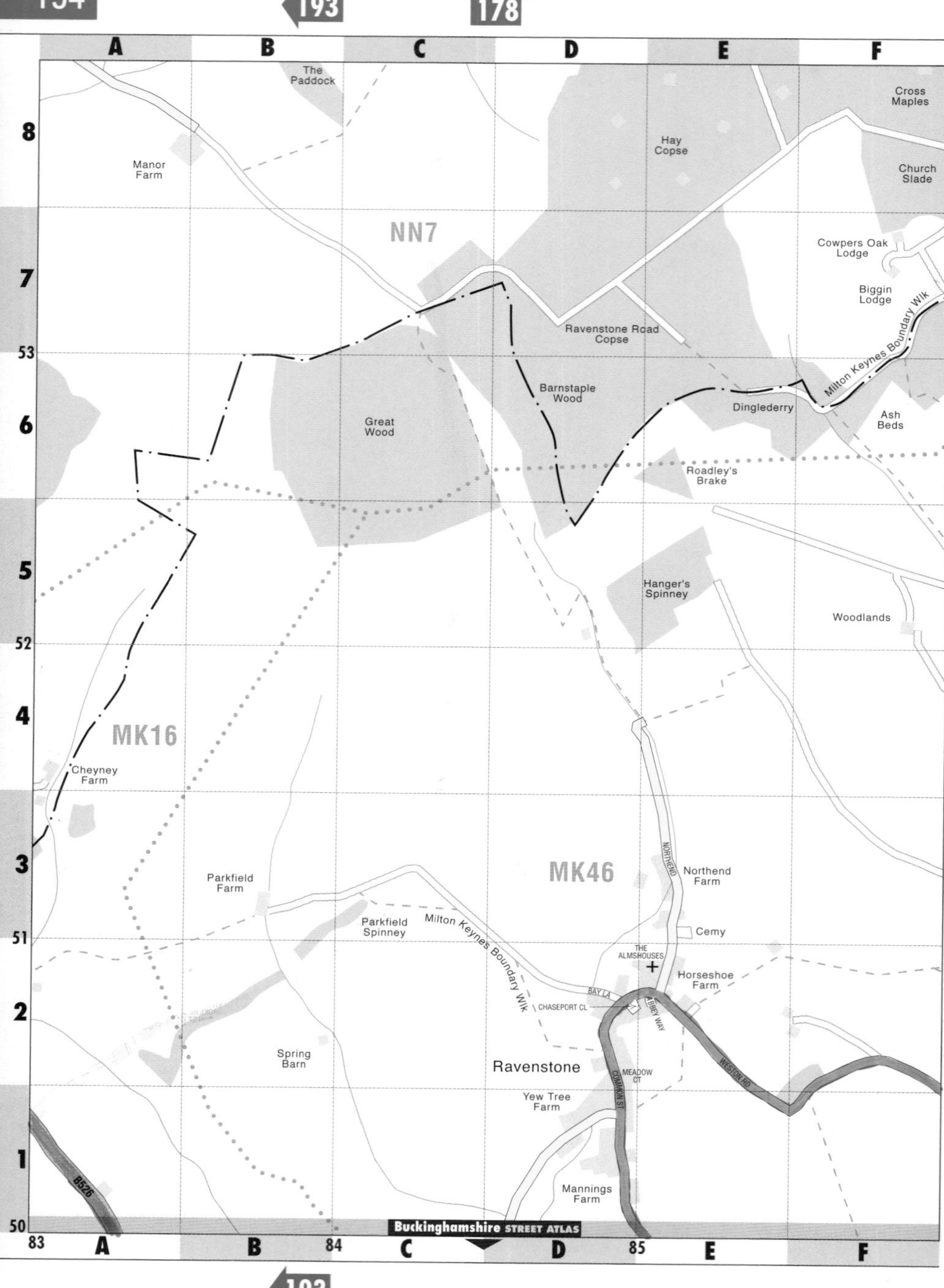
A
B
C
D
E
F
8
7
6
5
4
3
2
1
53
52
51
50
83
84
85
The Paddock
Manor Farm
Hay Copse
Cross Maples
Church Slade
NN7
Cowpers Oak Lodge
Biggin Lodge
Ravenstone Road Copse
Milton Keynes Boundary Wlk
Barnstaple Wood
Great Wood
Dinglederry
Ash Beds
Roadley's Brake
Hanger's Spinney
Woodlands
MK16
Cheyney Farm
MK46
NORTHEND
Northend Farm
Parkfield Farm
Parkfield Spinney
Cemy
THE ALMSHOUSES
Horseshoe Farm
BAY LA
CHASEPORT CL
ABBEY WAY
WESTON RD
Spring Barn
Ravenstone
MEADOW CT
COMMON ST
Yew Tree Farm
B526
Mannings Farm

193

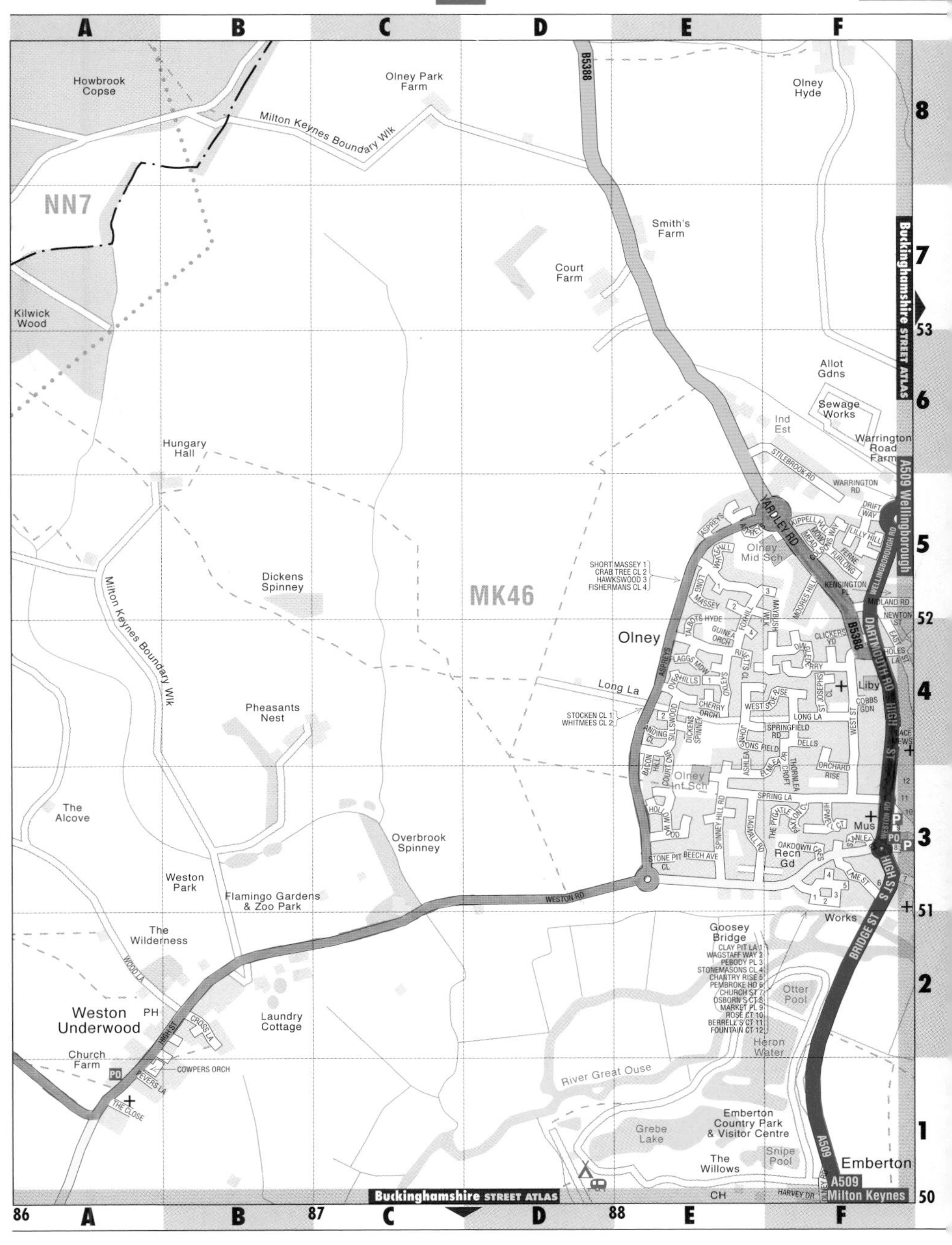
A
B
C
D
E
F
Howbrook Copse
Olney Park Farm
Olney Hyde
B5388
Milton Keynes Boundary Wlk
NN7
Smith's Farm
Court Farm
Kilwick Wood
Buckinghamshire STREET ATLAS
53
Allot Gdns
Sewage Works
Ind Est
Warrington Road Farm
Hungary Hall
STILEBROOK RD
WARRINGTON RD
A509 Wellingborough
YARDLEY RD
ASPREYS
Olney Mid Sch
SHORT MASSEY 1
CRAB TREE CL 2
HAWKSWOOD 3
FISHERMANS CL 4
Dickens Spinney
MK46
KENSINGTON PL
MIDLAND RD
NEWTON ST
52
Olney
B5388
DARTMOUTH RD
CLICKERS YD
Long La
Liby
COBBS GDN
Pheasants Nest
STOCKEN CL 1
WHITMEES CL 2
WEST ST
LONG LA
SPRINGFIELD RD
DELLS
HIGH ST
ORCHARD RISE
Olney Inf Sch
SPRING LA
The Alcove
Mus
Overbrook Spinney
Recn Gd
OAKDOWN CRES
STONE PIT CL
BEECH AVE
Weston Park
Flamingo Gardens & Zoo Park
WESTON RD
HIGH ST S
51
Works
The Wilderness
Goosey Bridge
CLAY PIT LA 1
WAGSTAFF WAY 2
PEBODY PL 3
STONEMASONS CL 4
CHANTRY RISE 5
PEMBROKE HO 6
CHURCH ST 7
OSBORN'S CT 8
MARKET PL 9
ROSE CT 10
BERRELL'S CT 11
FOUNTAIN CT 12
BRIDGE ST
WOOD LA
Otter Pool
Weston Underwood
PH
HIGH ST
CROSS LA
Laundry Cottage
Heron Water
Church Farm
PO
COWPERS ORCH
EVERS LA
River Great Ouse
THE CLOSE
Emberton Country Park & Visitor Centre
Grebe Lake
A509
The Willows
Snipe Pool
Emberton
A509 Milton Keynes
CH
HARVEY DR
Buckinghamshire STREET ATLAS
86
87
88
50
8
7
6
5
4
3
2
1

182

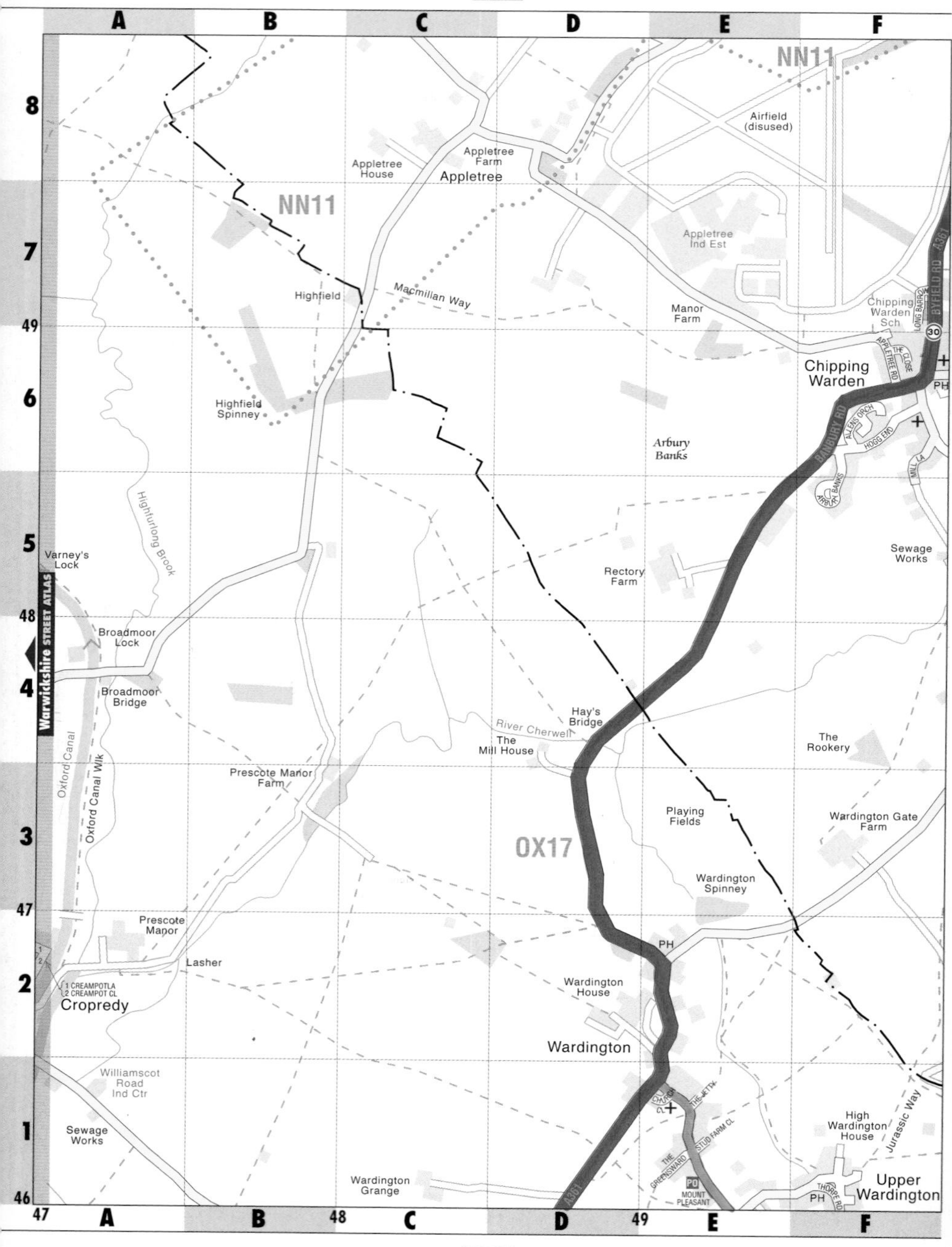
A
B
C
D
E
F
8
7
49
6
5
48
4
3
47
2
1
46
47
48
49
NN11
Airfield (disused)
Appletree House
Appletree Farm
Appletree
Appletree Ind Est
Highfield
Macmillan Way
Manor Farm
Chipping Warden Sch
Chipping Warden
BYFIELD RD
A361
LONG BARROW
APPLETREE RD
THE CLOSE
PH
Highfield Spinney
ALLENS ORCH
HOGG END
BANBURY RD
Arbury Banks
MILL LA
ARBURY BANKS
Highfurlong Brook
Varney's Lock
Sewage Works
Rectory Farm
Broadmoor Lock
Warwickshire STREET ATLAS
Broadmoor Bridge
Hay's Bridge
River Cherwell
The Mill House
The Rookery
Oxford Canal
Oxford Canal Wlk
Prescote Manor Farm
Playing Fields
Wardington Gate Farm
OX17
Wardington Spinney
Prescote Manor
Lasher
PH
1 CREAMPOTLA
2 CREAMPOT CL
Cropredy
Wardington House
Wardington
Williamscot Road Ind Ctr
CHURCH LA
THE JETTY
Jurassic Way
Sewage Works
STUD FARM CL
High Wardington House
THE GREENSWARD
Wardington Grange
PO
MOUNT PLEASANT
Upper Wardington
THORPE RD
PH

208

183
198

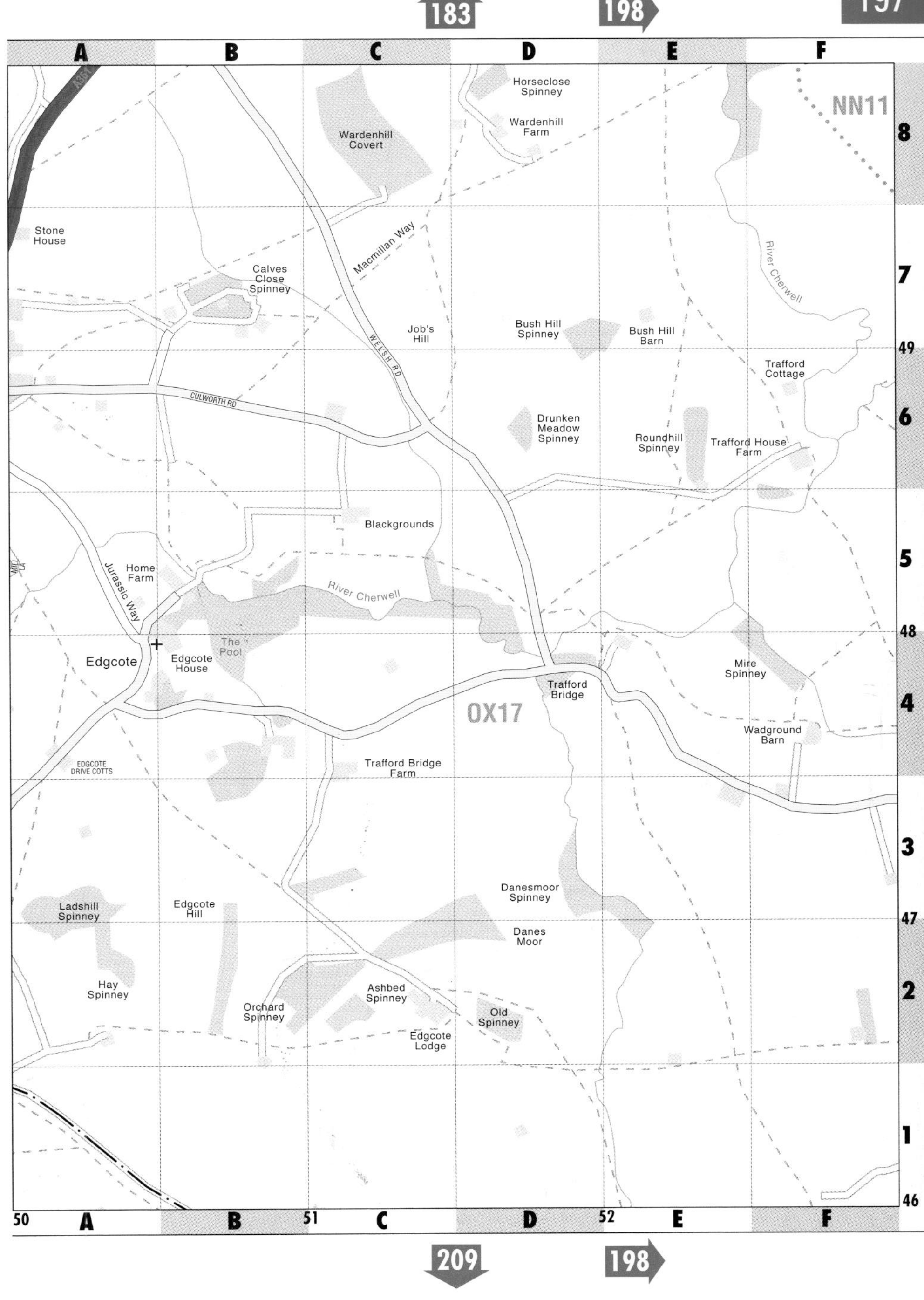

209
198

197
184

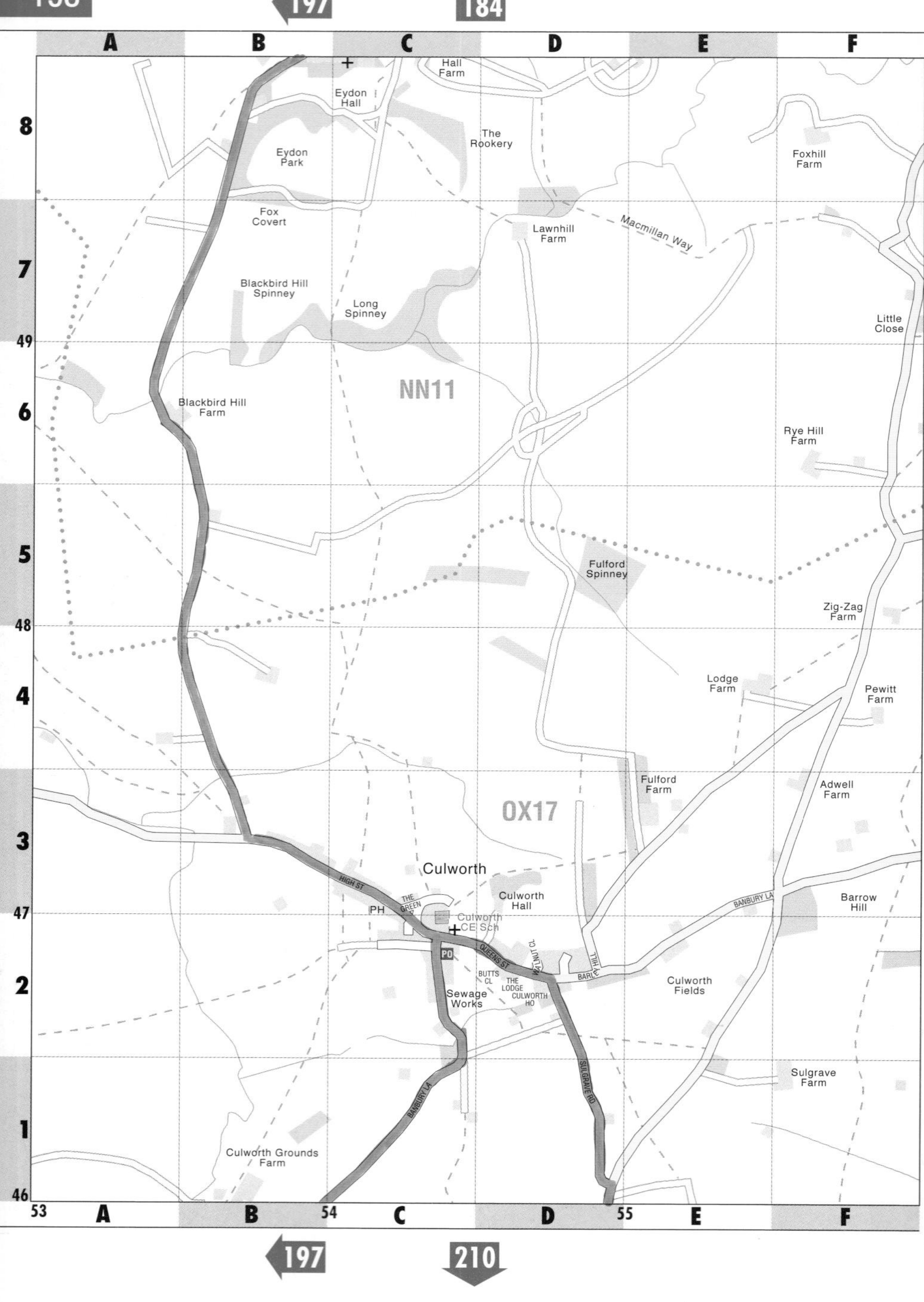

197
210

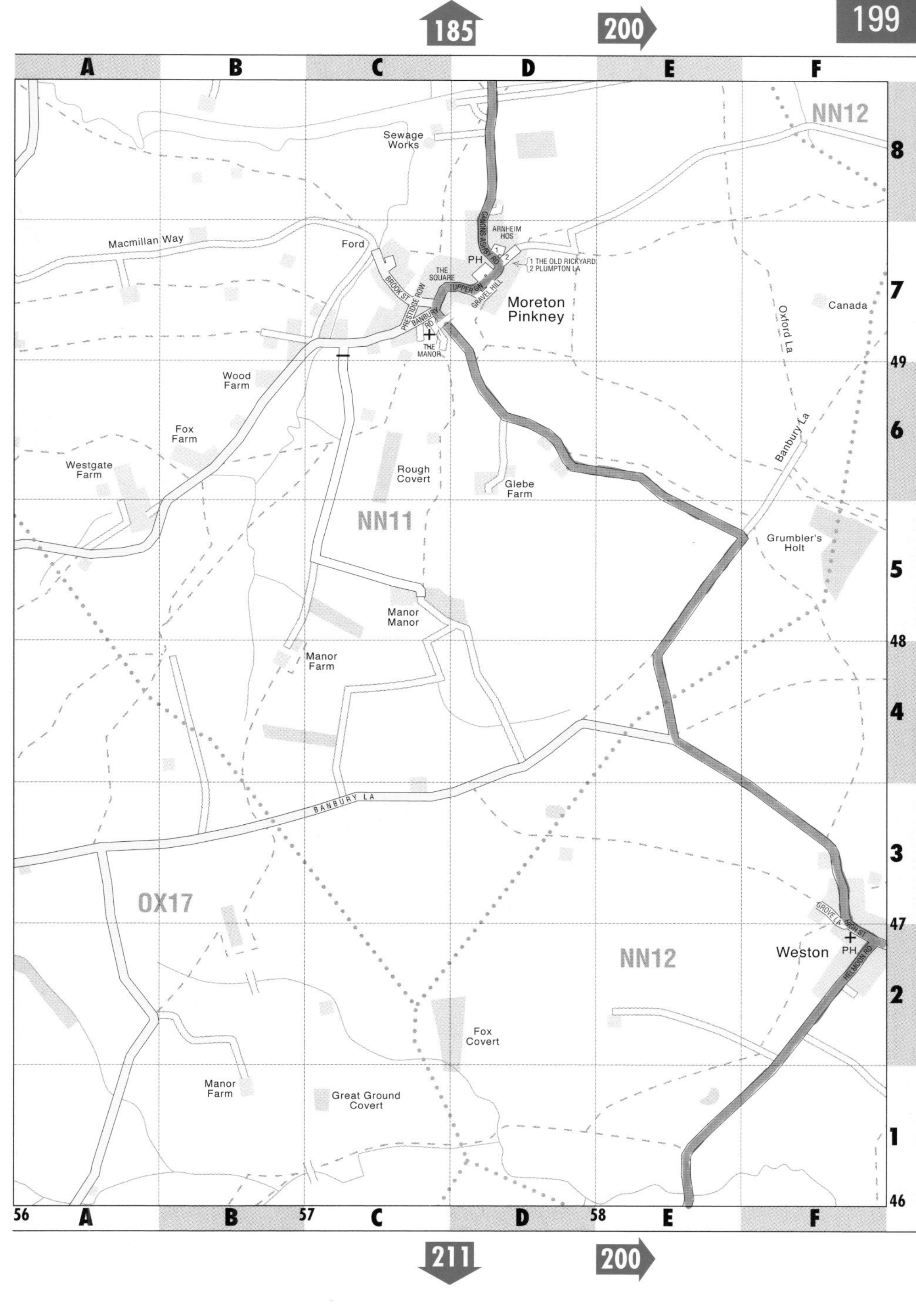
185
200
A
B
C
D
E
F
NN12
8
Sewage Works
Macmillan Way
Ford
ARNHEIM HOS
CANONS ASHBY RD
PH
1 THE OLD RICKYARD
2 PLUMPTON LA
THE SQUARE
BROOK ST
PRESTIDGE ROW
UPPER GN
GRAVEL HILL
BANBURY RD
Moreton Pinkney
THE MANOR
7
Oxford La
Canada
49
Wood Farm
Fox Farm
Westgate Farm
Rough Covert
Glebe Farm
Banbury La
6
NN11
Grumbler's Holt
5
Manor Manor
Manor Farm
48
4
BANBURY LA
3
OX17
GROVE LA
HIGH ST
47
NN12
Weston
PH
HELMDON RD
2
Fox Covert
Manor Farm
Great Ground Covert
1
46
56
57
58
211
200

199
186

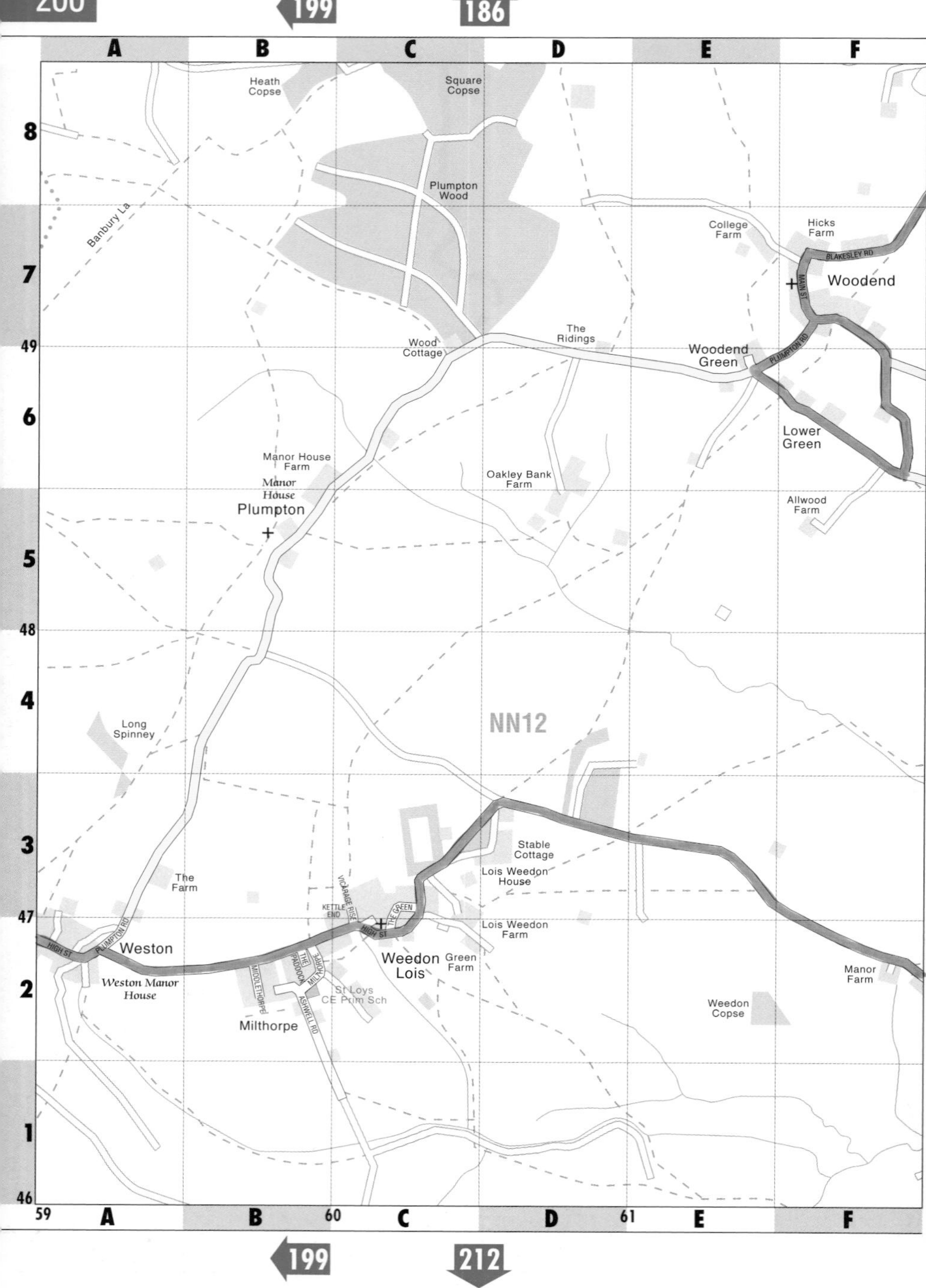

199
212

187 202

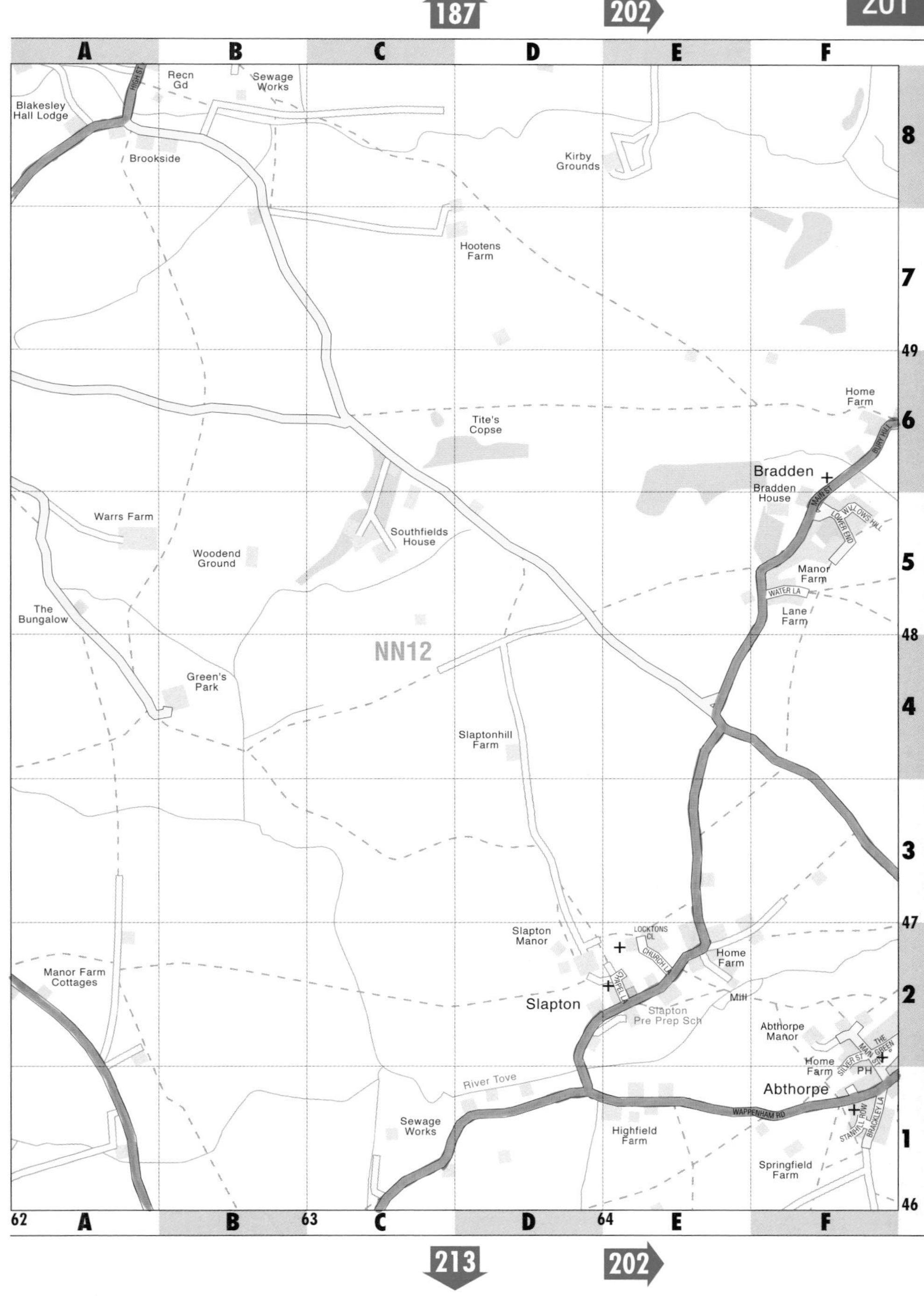

213 202

201
188

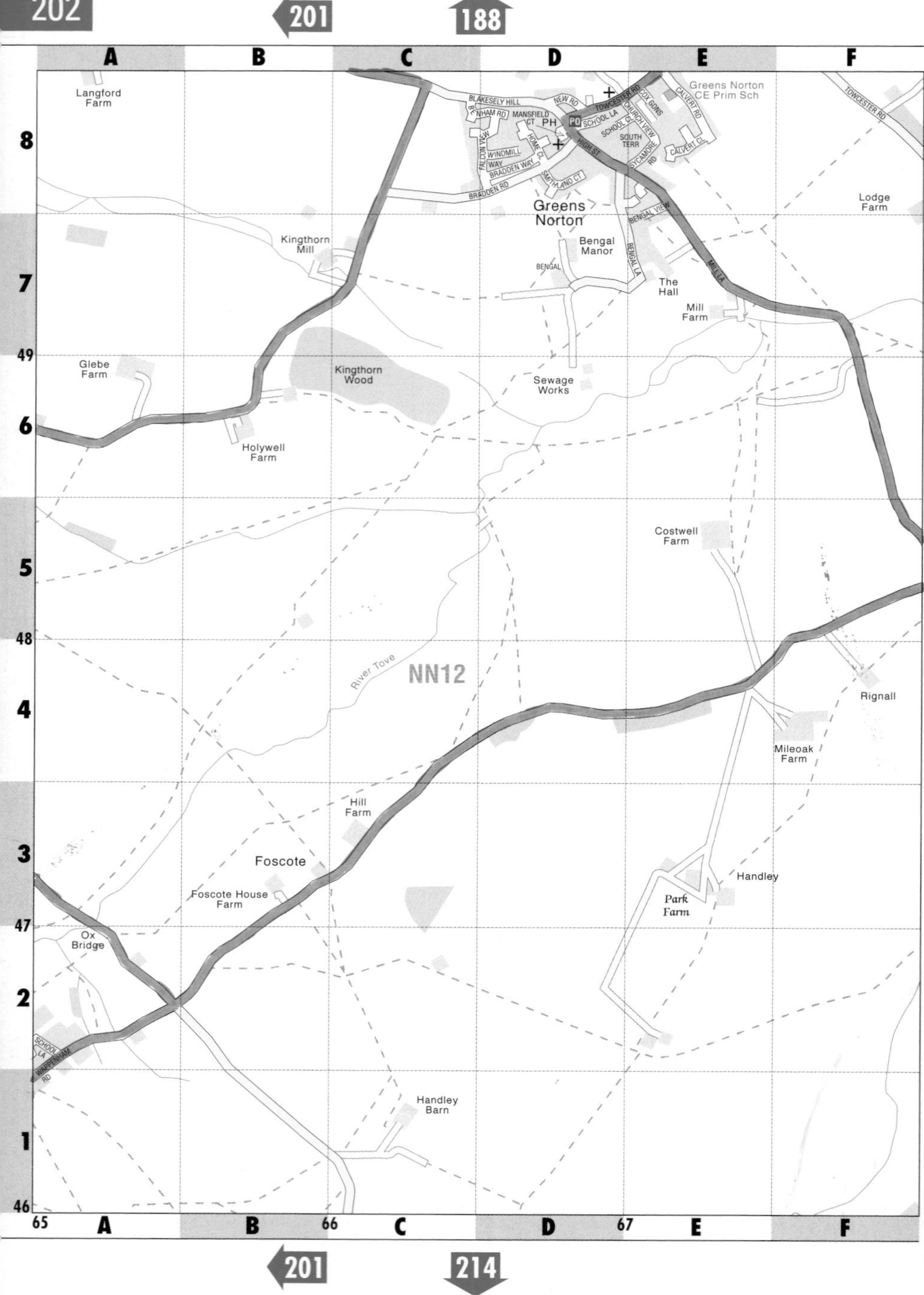

201
214

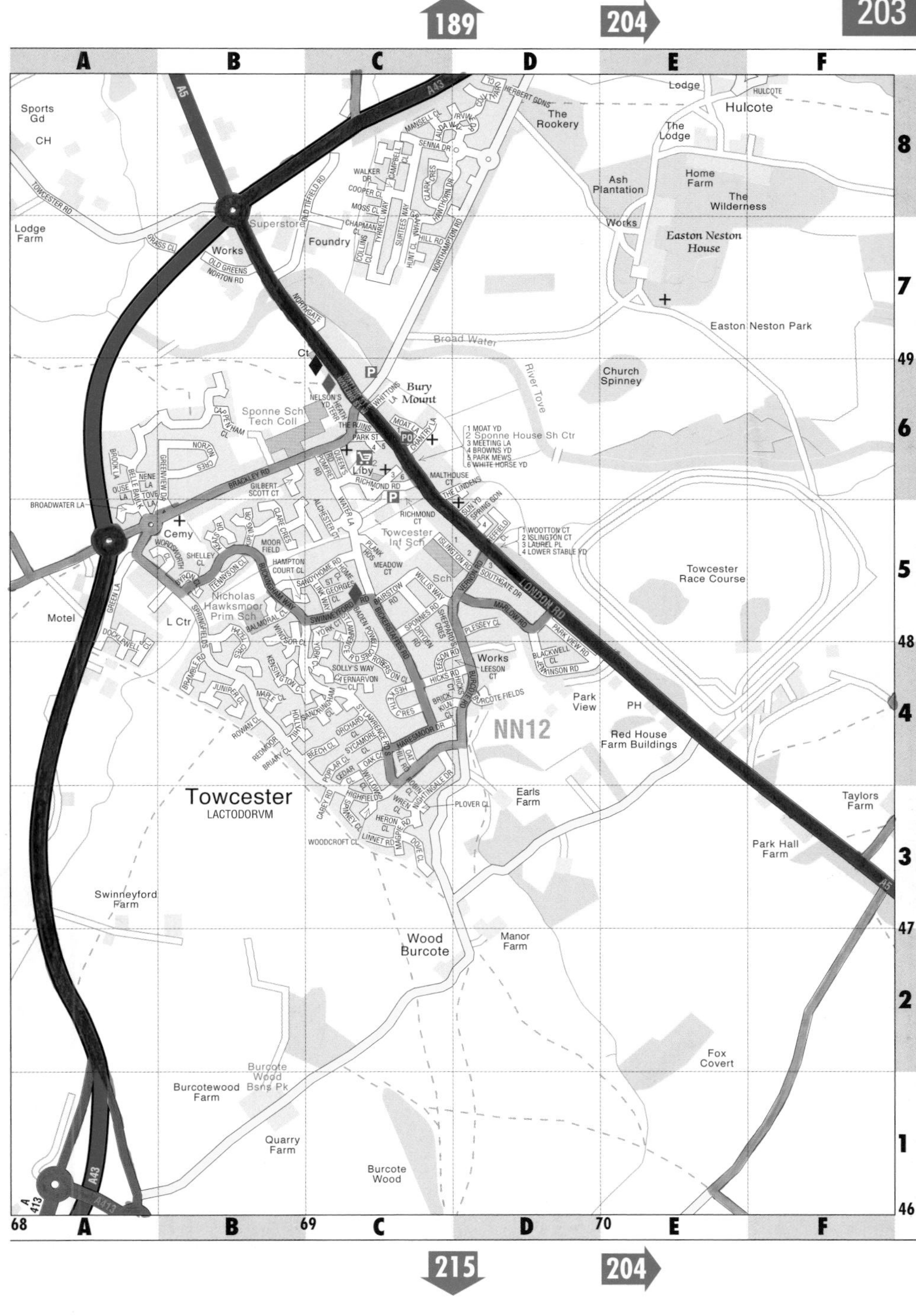
189
204
Hulcote
The Rookery
Ash Plantation
Home Farm
The Wilderness
Easton Neston House
Easton Neston Park
Broad Water
River Tove
Church Spinney
Bury Mount
Towcester Race Course
Sponne Sch Tech Coll
Nicholas Hawksmoor Prim Sch
Towcester Inf Sch
NN12
Towcester
LACTODORVM
Earls Farm
Red House Farm Buildings
Park View
Taylors Farm
Park Hall Farm
Swinneyford Farm
Wood Burcote
Manor Farm
Burcotewood Farm
Burcote Wood Bsns Pk
Quarry Farm
Burcote Wood
Fox Covert
Lodge Farm
Sports Gd
215
204

203
190

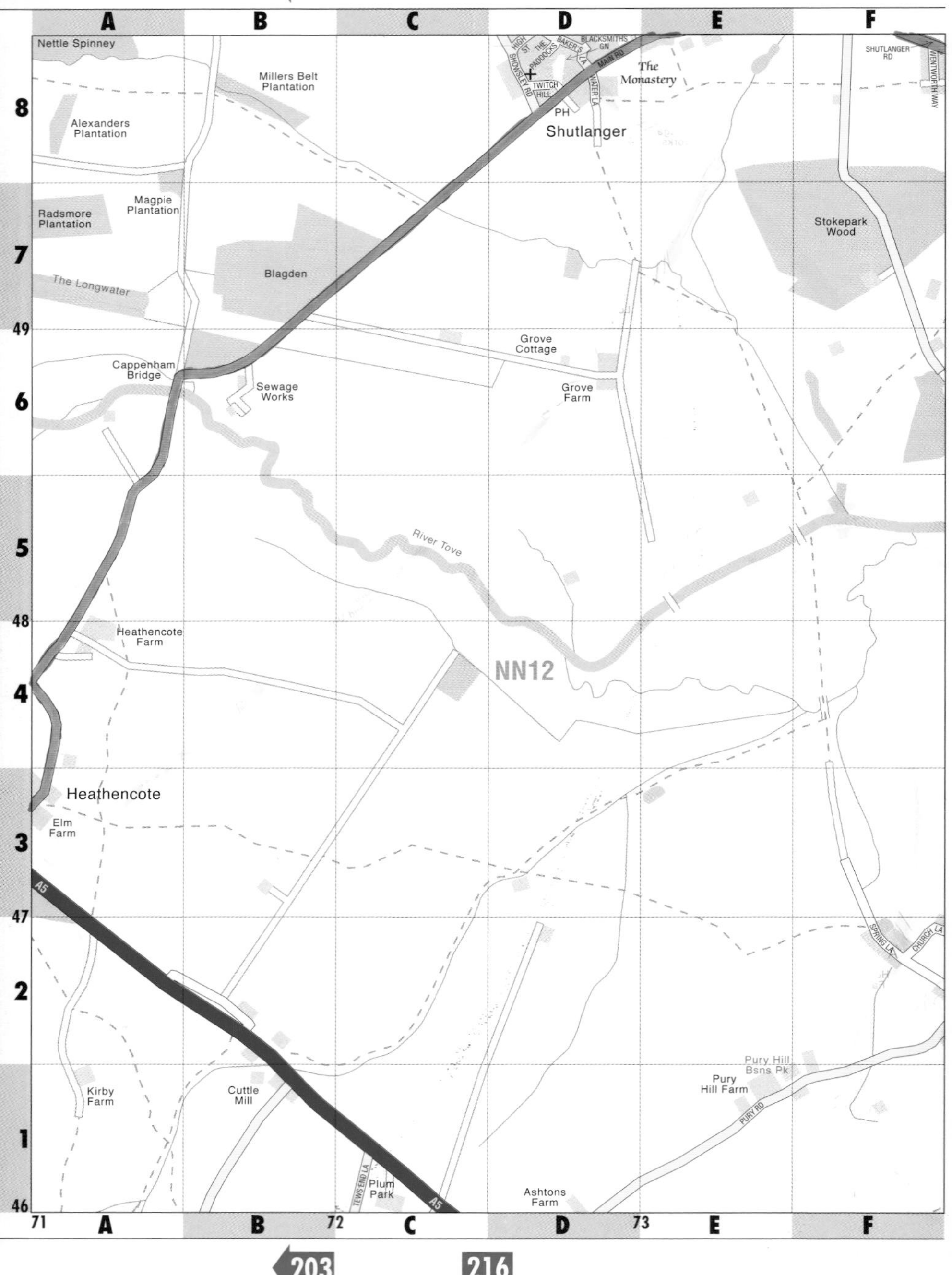

203
216

191
206

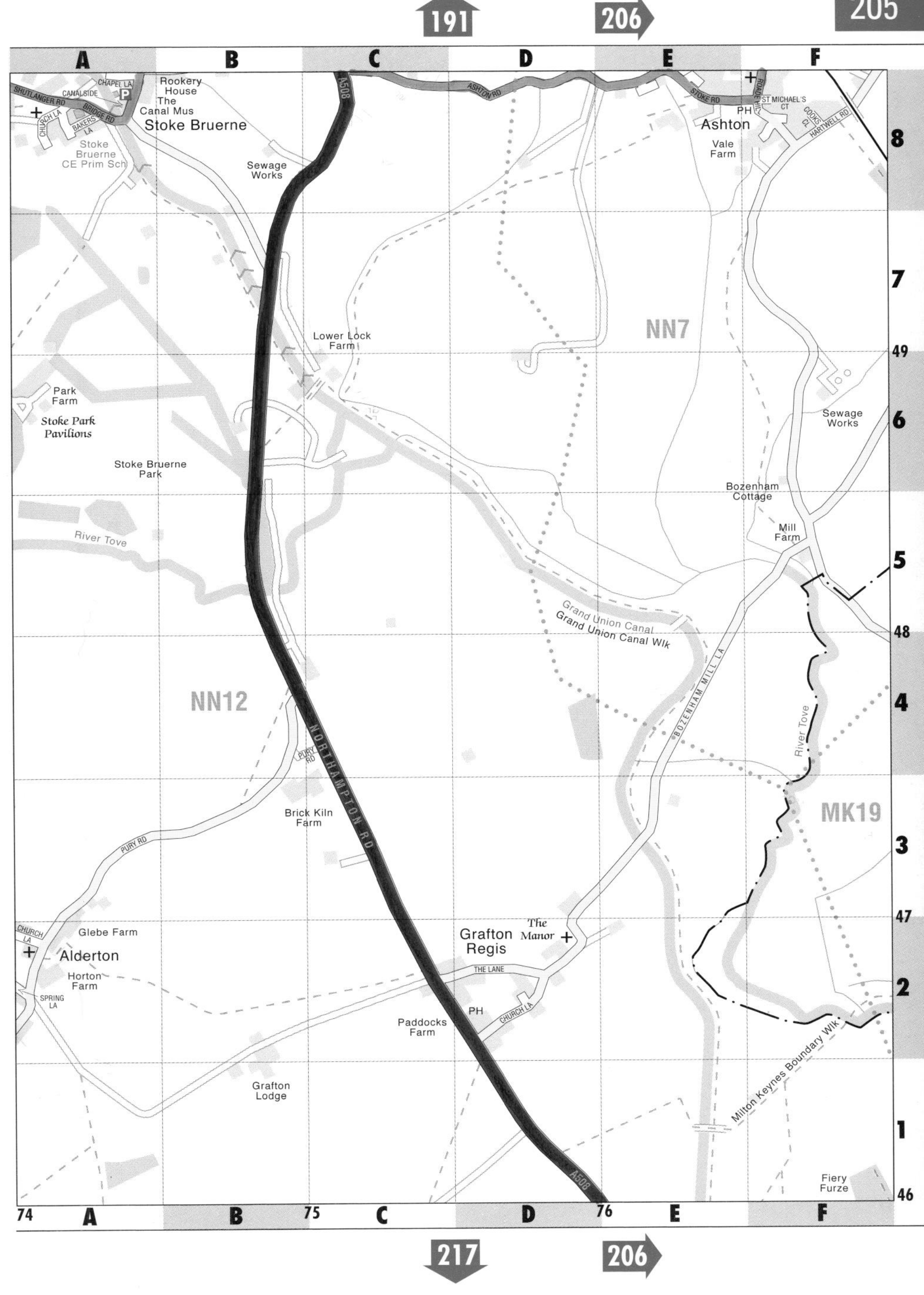

217
206

205
192

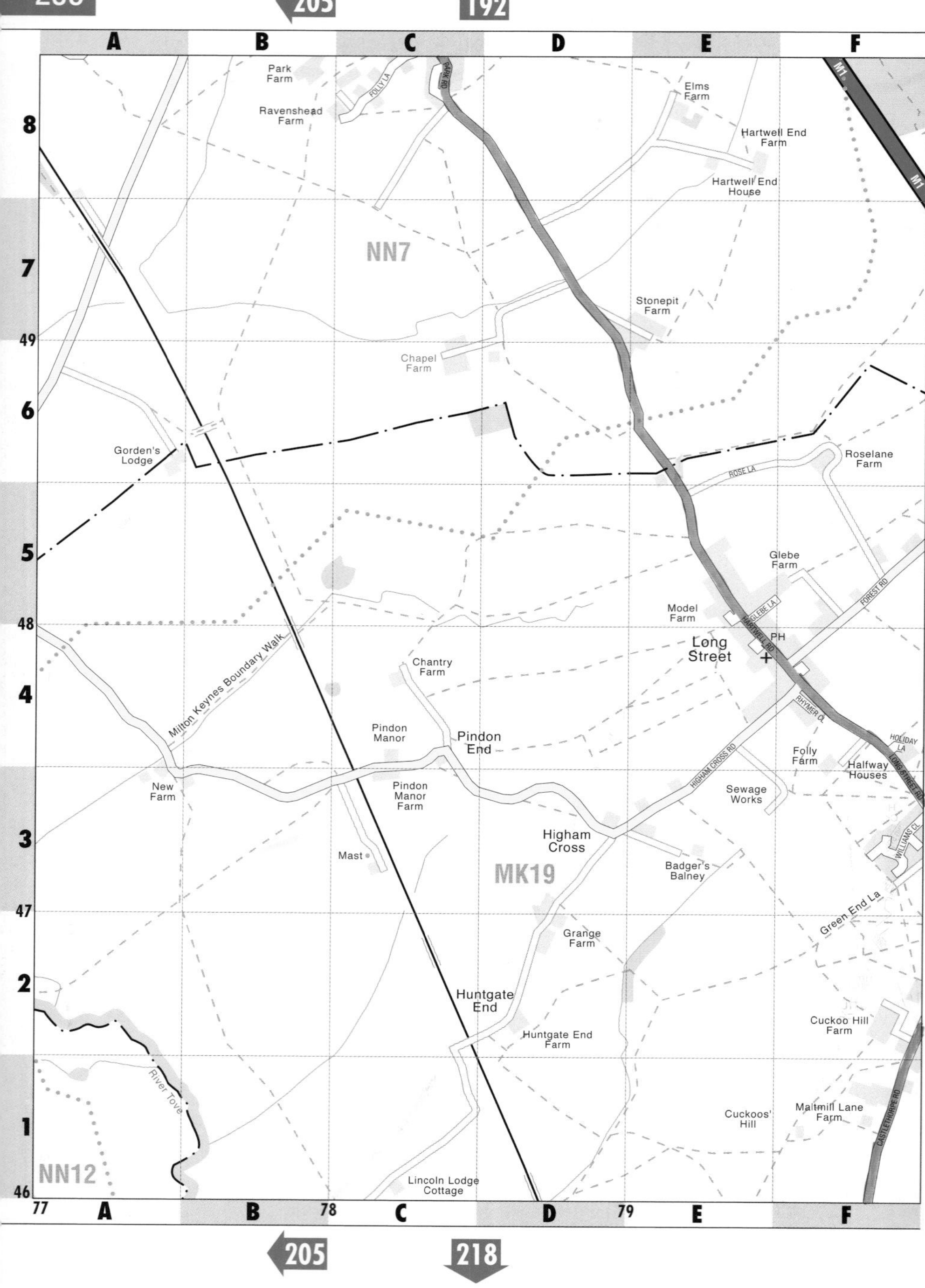

205
218

193

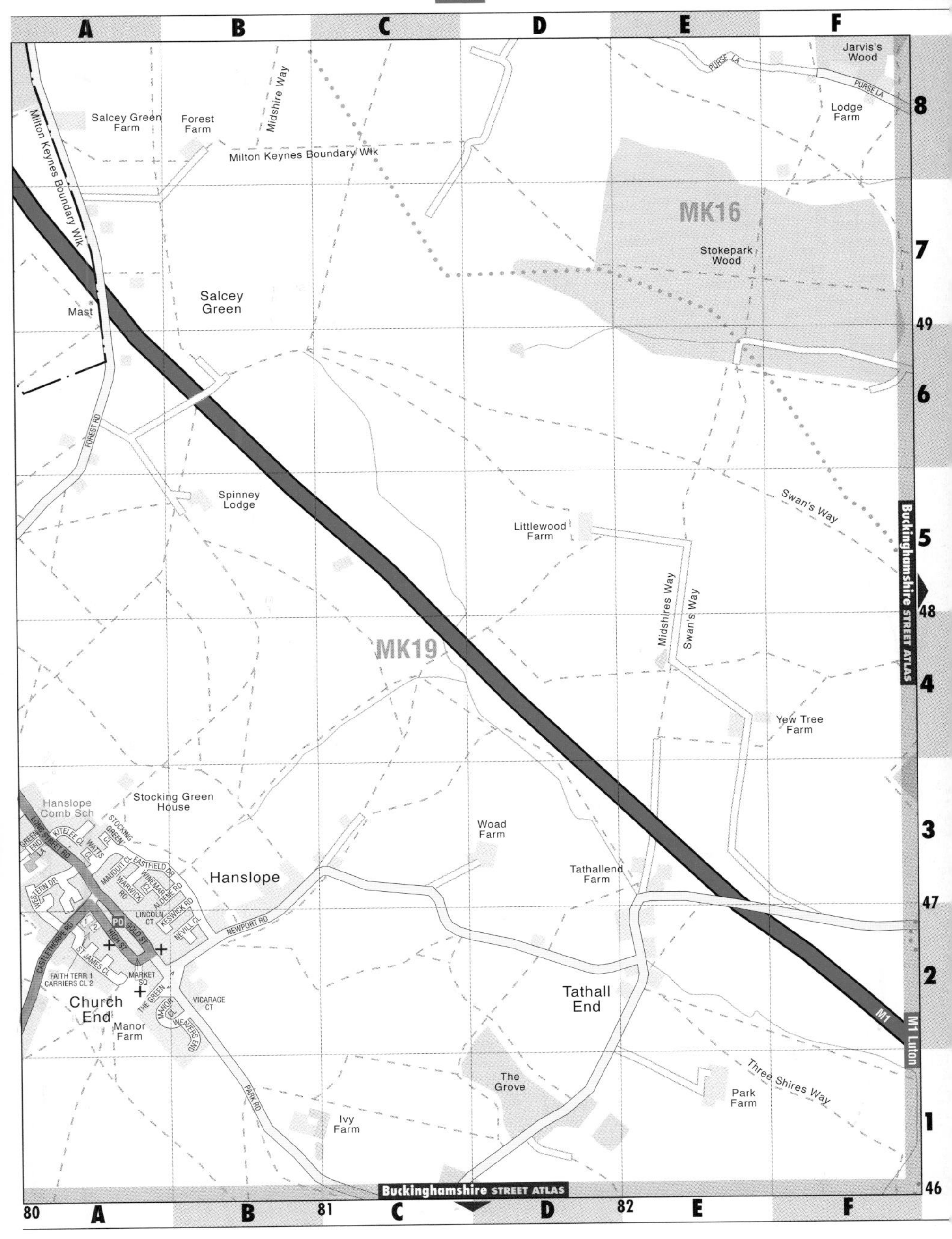

Buckinghamshire STREET ATLAS

Buckinghamshire STREET ATLAS

196

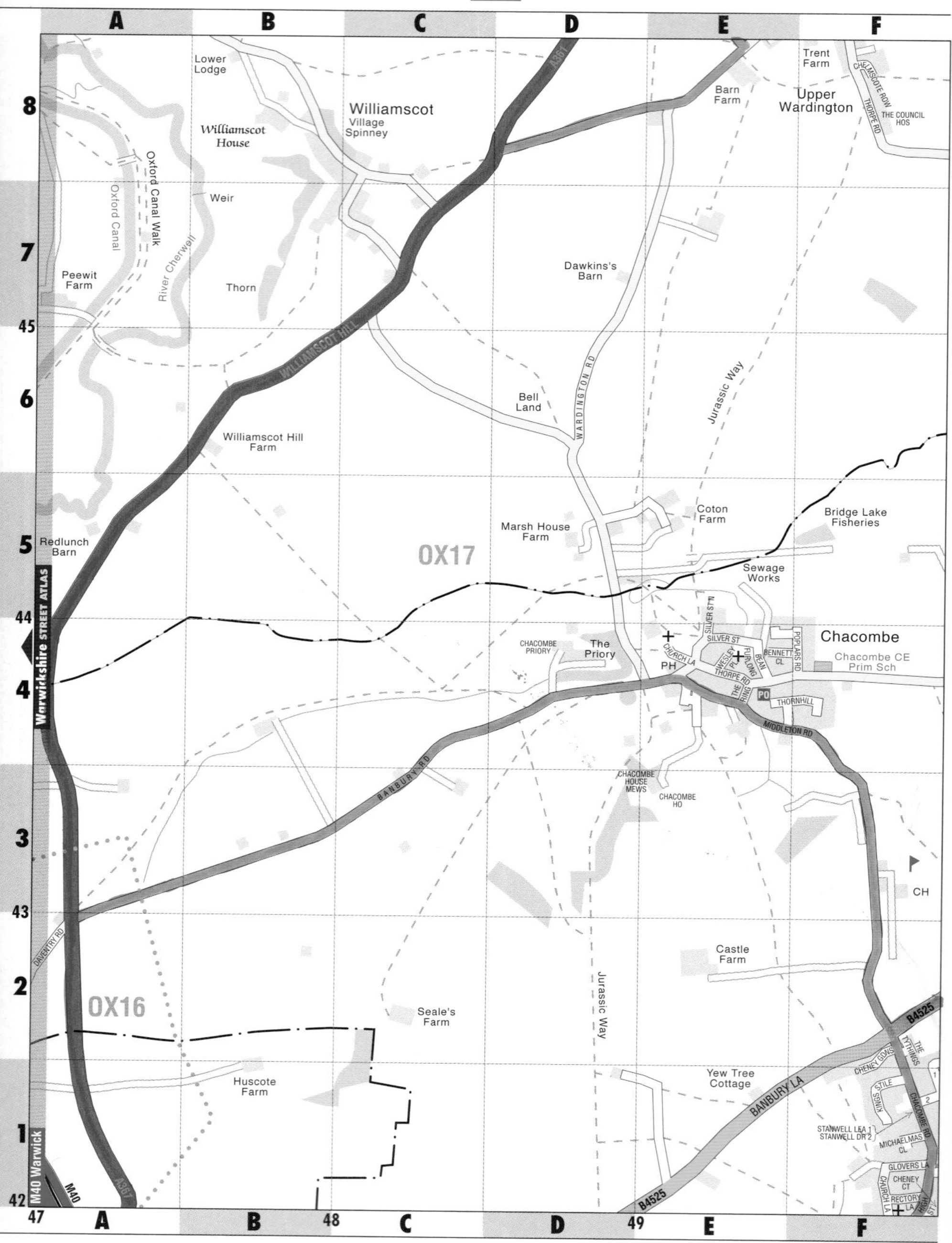
A
B
C
D
E
F
Lower Lodge
Williamscot
Village Spinney
Williamscot House
Oxford Canal Walk
Oxford Canal
Weir
River Cherwell
Peewit Farm
Thorn
A361
Barn Farm
Trent Farm
Upper Wardington
CHELMSCOTE ROW
THORPE RD
THE COUNCIL HOS
Dawkins's Barn
WILLIAMSCOT HILL
Bell Land
WARDINGTON RD
Jurassic Way
Williamscot Hill Farm
Coton Farm
Bridge Lake Fisheries
Marsh House Farm
Redlunch Barn
OX17
Sewage Works
Warwickshire STREET ATLAS
SILVER ST
Chacombe
CHACOMBE PRIORY
The Priory
CHURCH LA
WESLEY PL
FURLONG
BEAN
BENNETT CL
POPLARS RD
Chacombe CE Prim Sch
PH
THORPE RD
THE RING
PO
THORNHILL
MIDDLETON RD
BANBURY RD
CHACOMBE HOUSE MEWS
CHACOMBE HO
CH
DAVENTRY RD
Castle Farm
OX16
Seale's Farm
Jurassic Way
B4525
Huscote Farm
Yew Tree Cottage
BANBURY LA
CHENEY GDNS
THE TYTHINGS
STILE
KINGS
CHACOMBE RD
STANWELL LEA 1
STANWELL DR 2
MICHAELMAS CL
GLOVERS LA
CHENEY CT
CHURCH LA
RECTORY LA
HIGH ST
M40 Warwick
M40
A361
B4525
8
7
45
6
5
44
4
3
43
2
1
42
47
48
49

219

197
210

220
210

209 198

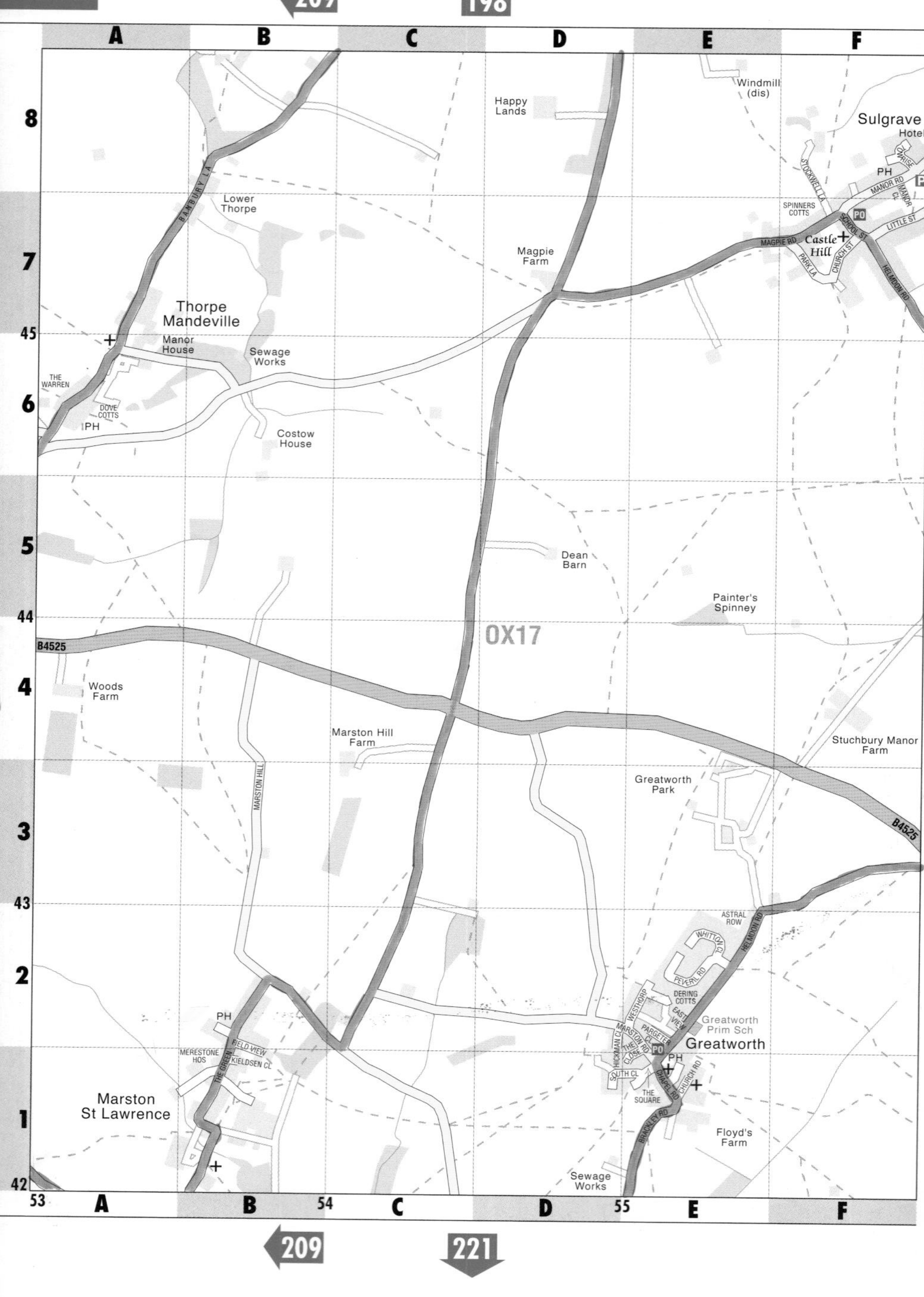

209 221

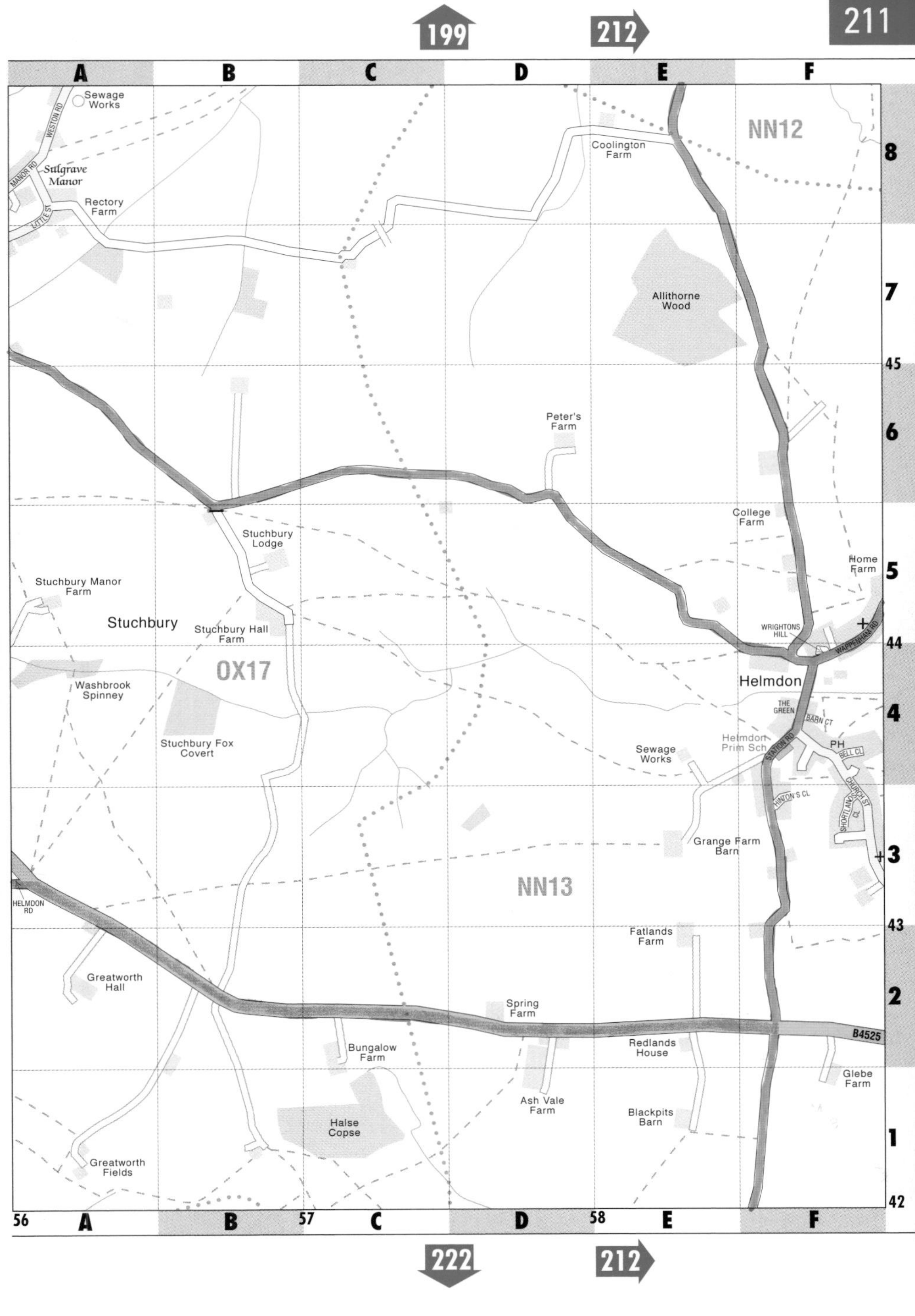
199
212
A
B
C
D
E
F
Sewage Works
WESTON RD
MANOR RD
Sulgrave Manor
LITTLE ST
Rectory Farm
Coolington Farm
NN12
8
7
Allithorne Wood
45
Peter's Farm
6
College Farm
Stuchbury Lodge
Home Farm
5
Stuchbury Manor Farm
Stuchbury
Stuchbury Hall Farm
WRIGHTONS HILL
WAPPENHAM RD
44
OX17
Washbrook Spinney
Helmdon
THE GREEN
BARN CT
4
Stuchbury Fox Covert
Sewage Works
Helmdon Prim Sch
STATION RD
PH
BELL CL
CHURCH ST
HINTON'S CL
SHORTLANDS CL
Grange Farm Barn
3
NN13
HELMDON RD
43
Fatlands Farm
Greatworth Hall
2
Spring Farm
B4525
Bungalow Farm
Redlands House
Glebe Farm
Ash Vale Farm
Halse Copse
Blackpits Barn
1
Greatworth Fields
42
56
57
58
222
212

211

200

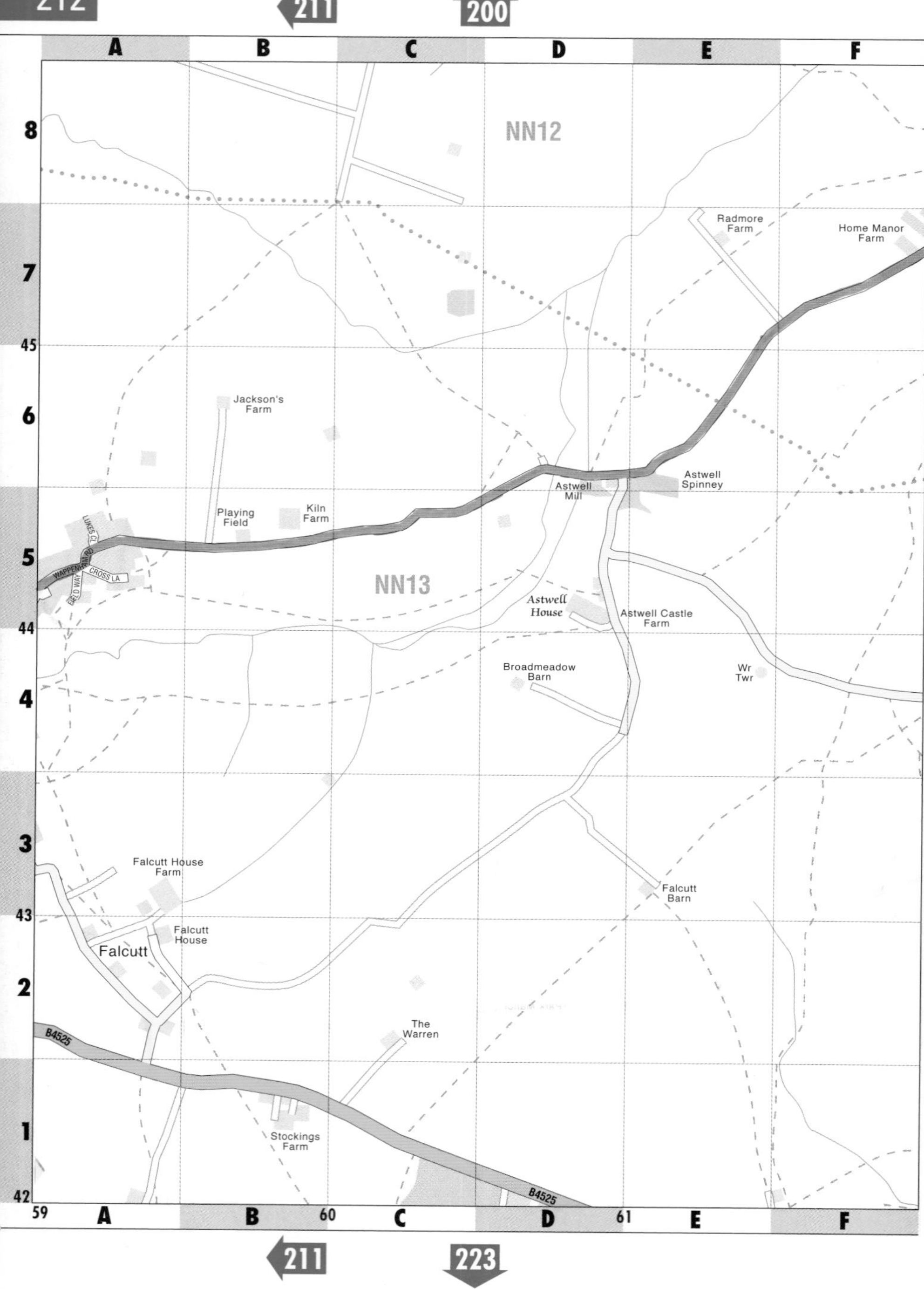

211

223

201
214

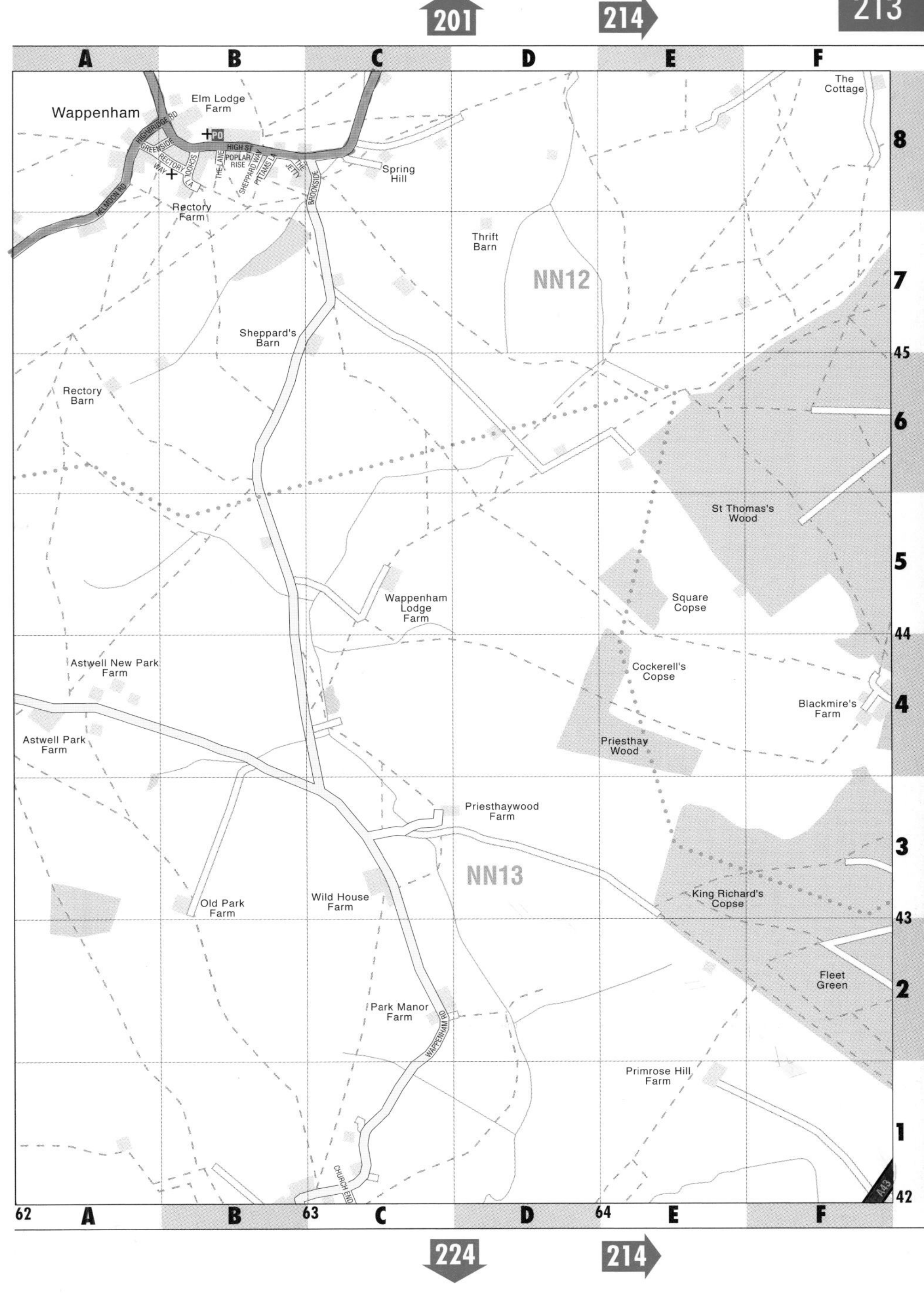
A
B
C
D
E
F
Wappenham
Elm Lodge Farm
PO
HIGHBRIDGE RD
GREENSIDE
HIGH ST
RECTORY WAY
SCHOOL LA
THE LANE
POPLAR RISE
SHEPPARD WAY
PITTAMS LA
THE JETTY
BROOKSIDE
HELMDON RD
Spring Hill
Rectory Farm
Thrift Barn
NN12
Sheppard's Barn
Rectory Barn
St Thomas's Wood
Square Copse
Wappenham Lodge Farm
Astwell New Park Farm
Cockerell's Copse
Blackmire's Farm
Astwell Park Farm
Priesthay Wood
Priesthaywood Farm
NN13
Old Park Farm
Wild House Farm
King Richard's Copse
Fleet Green
Park Manor Farm
WAPPENHAM RD
Primrose Hill Farm
CHURCH END
A43
The Cottage
8
7
45
6
5
44
4
3
43
2
1
42
62
63
64

224
214

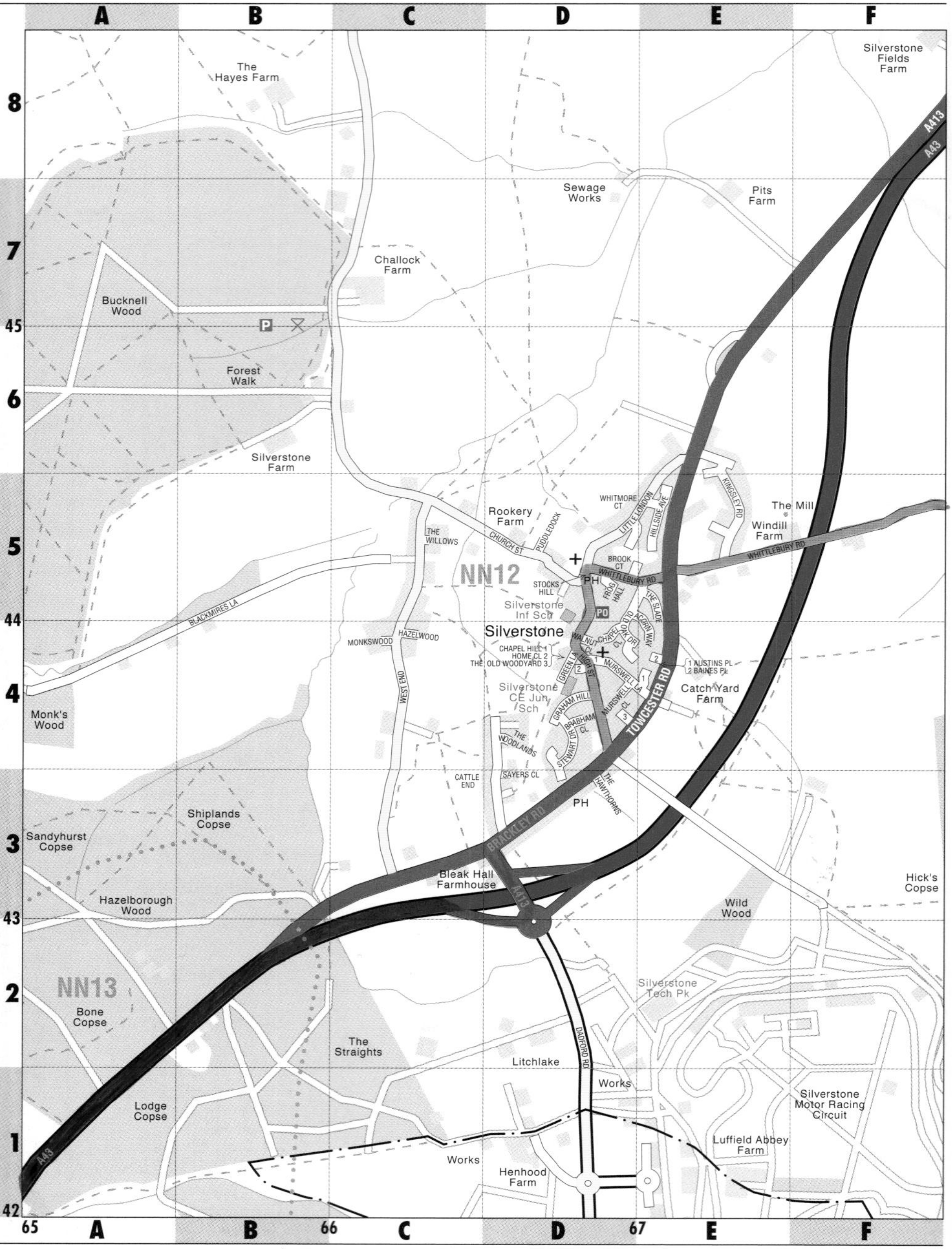
A
B
C
D
E
F
8
7
45
6
5
44
4
3
43
2
1
42
65
66
67
The Hayes Farm
Silverstone Fields Farm
A413
A43
Sewage Works
Pits Farm
Challock Farm
Bucknell Wood
P
Forest Walk
Silverstone Farm
The Mill
Windill Farm
WHITTLEBURY RD
WHITMORE CT
LITTLE LONDON
HILLSIDE AVE
KINGSLEY RD
Rookery Farm
PUDDLEDOCK
CHURCH ST
THE WILLOWS
BROOK CT
PH
NN12
STOCKS HILL
FROG HALL
THE SLADE
Silverstone Inf Sch
PO
OLD OAK DR
ACORN WAY
Silverstone
CHAPEL CL
WALNUT CL
HIGH ST
MONKSWOOD
HAZELWOOD
CHAPEL HILL 1
HOME CL 2
THE OLD WOODYARD 3
GREEN LA
MURSWELL LA
1 AUSTINS PL
2 BAINES PL
BLACKMIRES LA
WEST END
Silverstone CE Jun Sch
GRAHAM HILL
MURSWELL CL
TOWCESTER RD
Catch Yard Farm
Monk's Wood
BRABHAM CL
THE WOODLANDS
STEWART DR
CATTLE END
SAYERS CL
THE HAWTHORNS
Shiplands Copse
Sandyhurst Copse
BRACKLEY RD
Bleak Hall Farmhouse
Hazelborough Wood
Hick's Copse
Wild Wood
NN13
Bone Copse
Silverstone Tech Pk
DADFORD RD
The Straights
Litchlake
Works
Silverstone Motor Racing Circuit
Lodge Copse
Luffield Abbey Farm
Henhood Farm

203
216

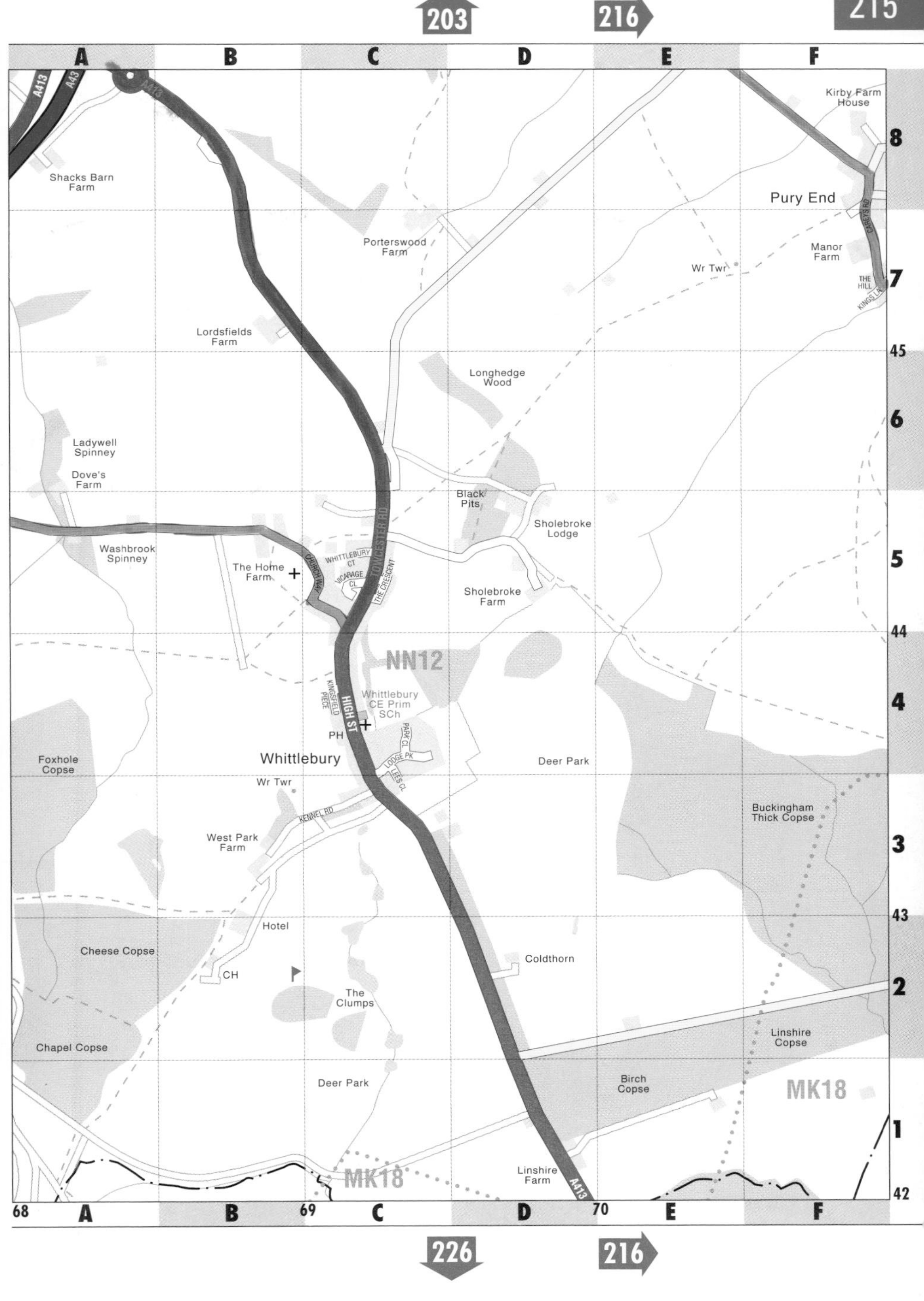

226
216

215
204

215
227

205
218

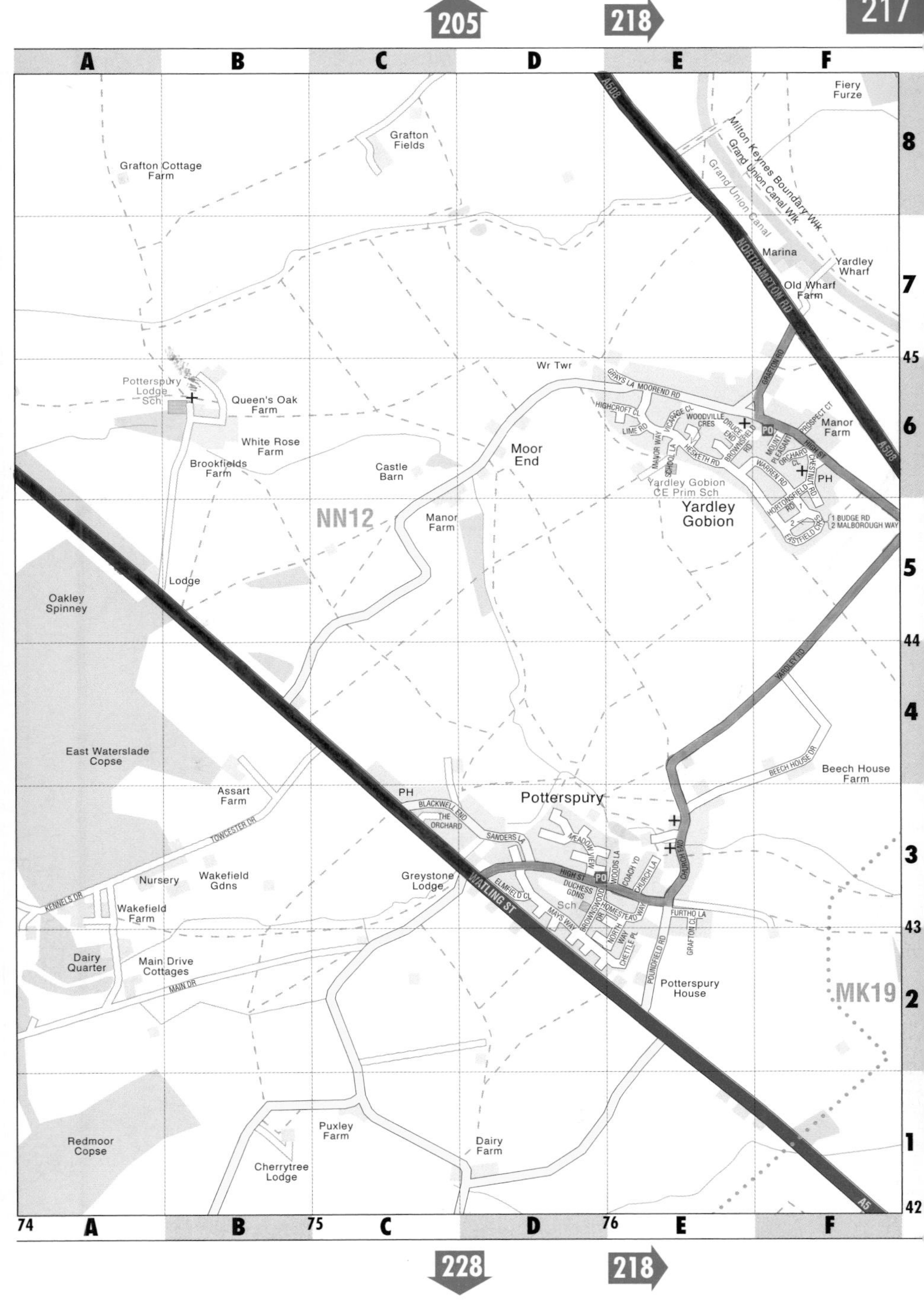

228
218

217
206

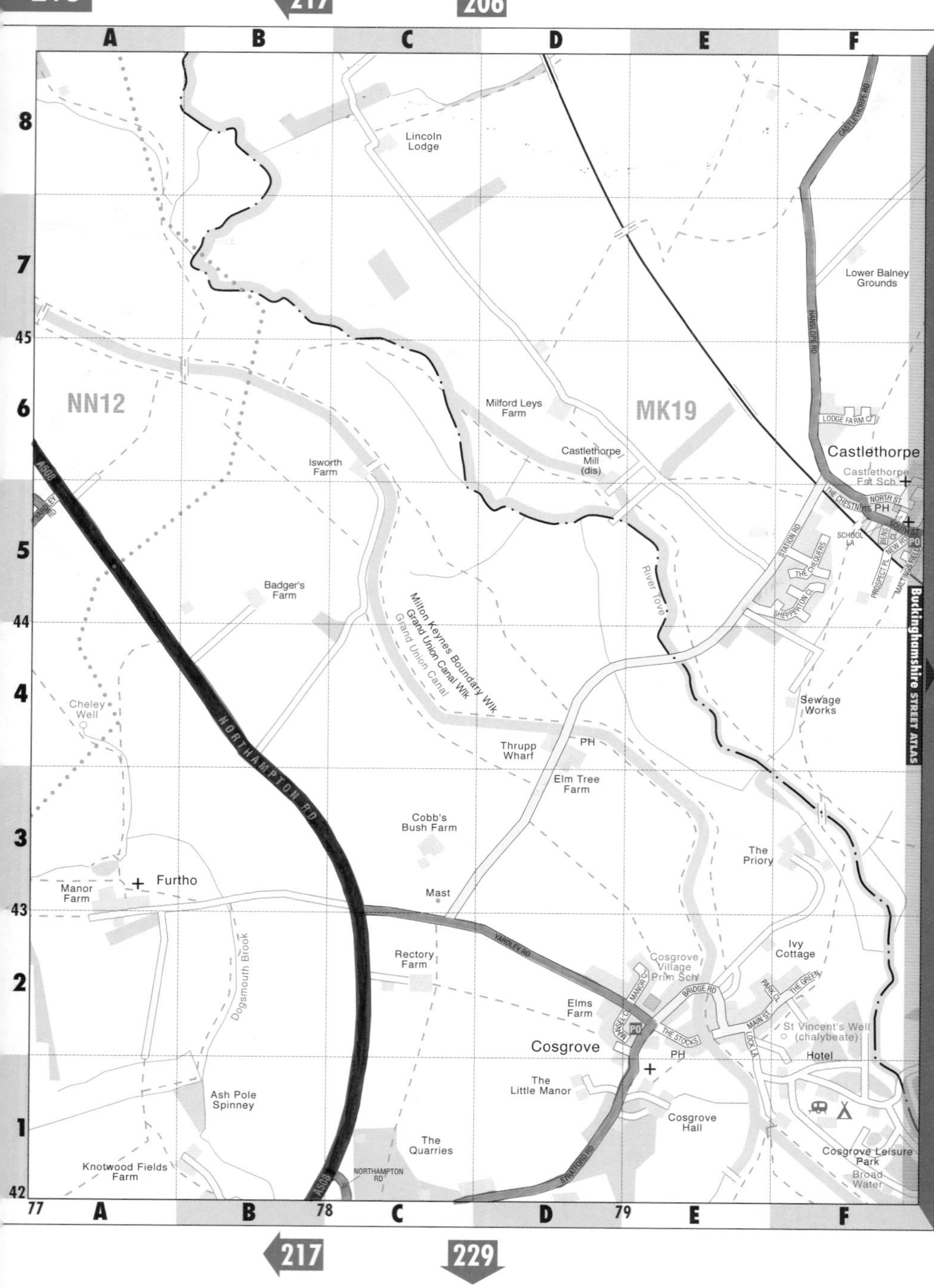

217
229

208
220

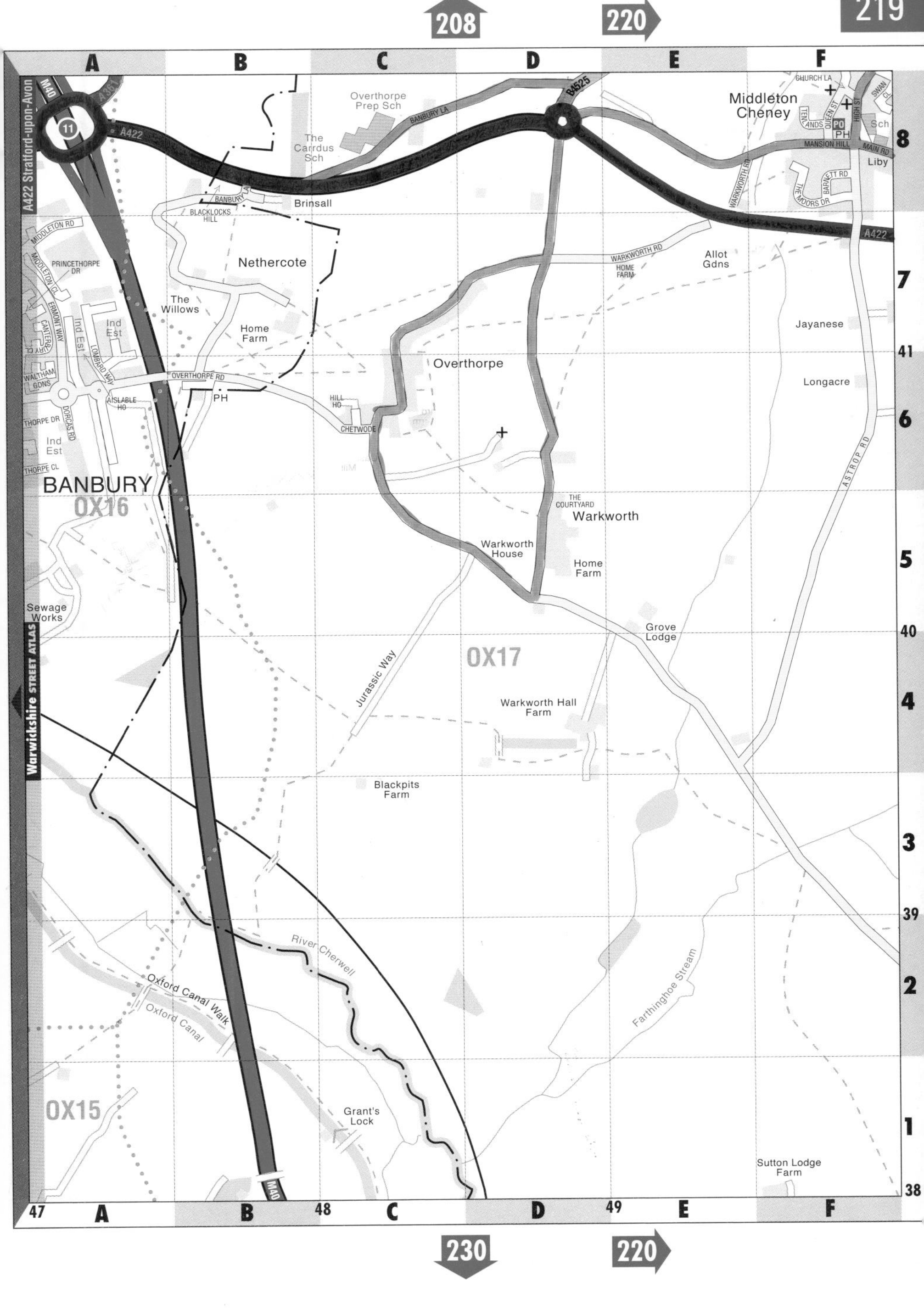

230
220

219 209

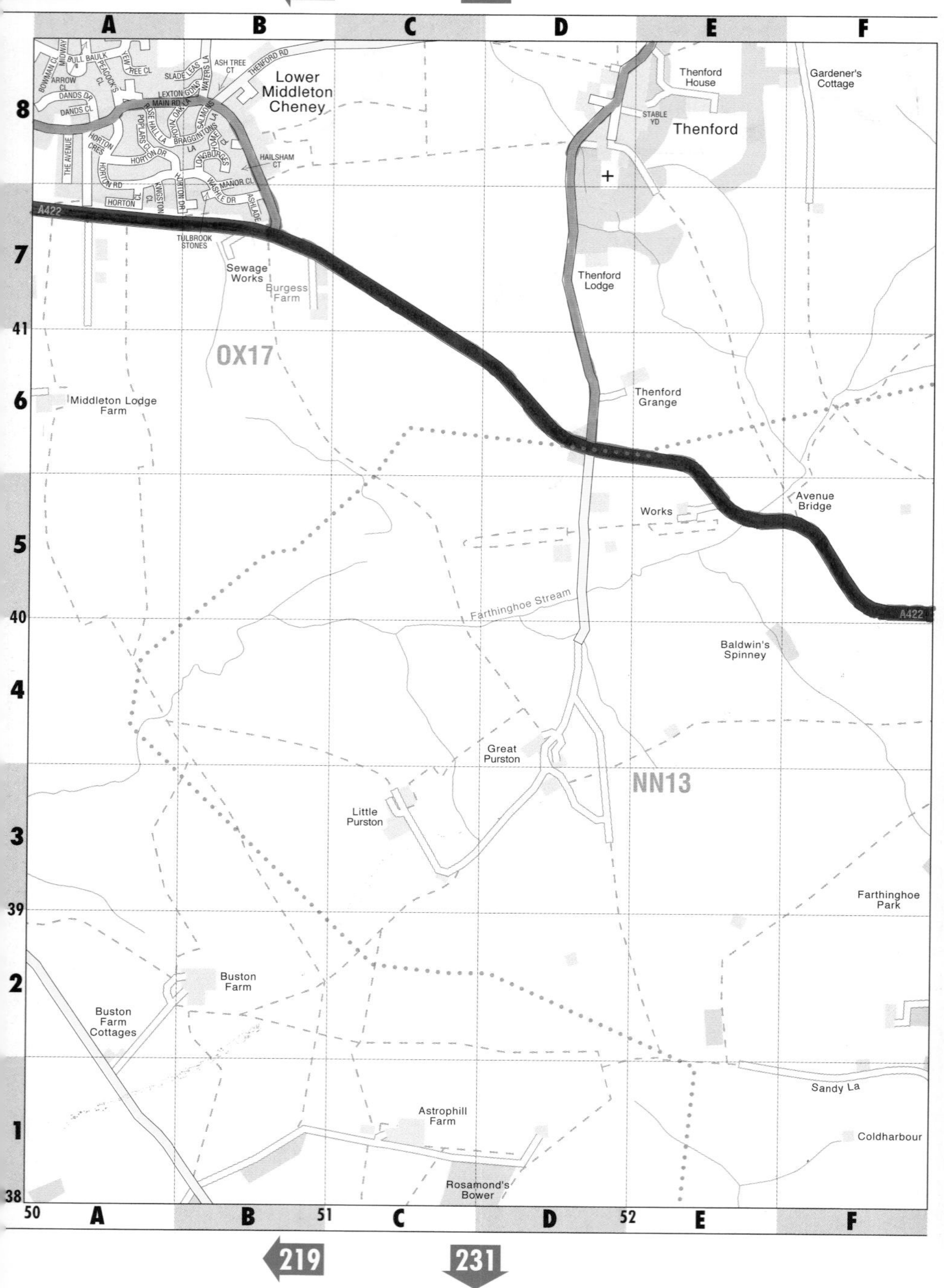

219 231

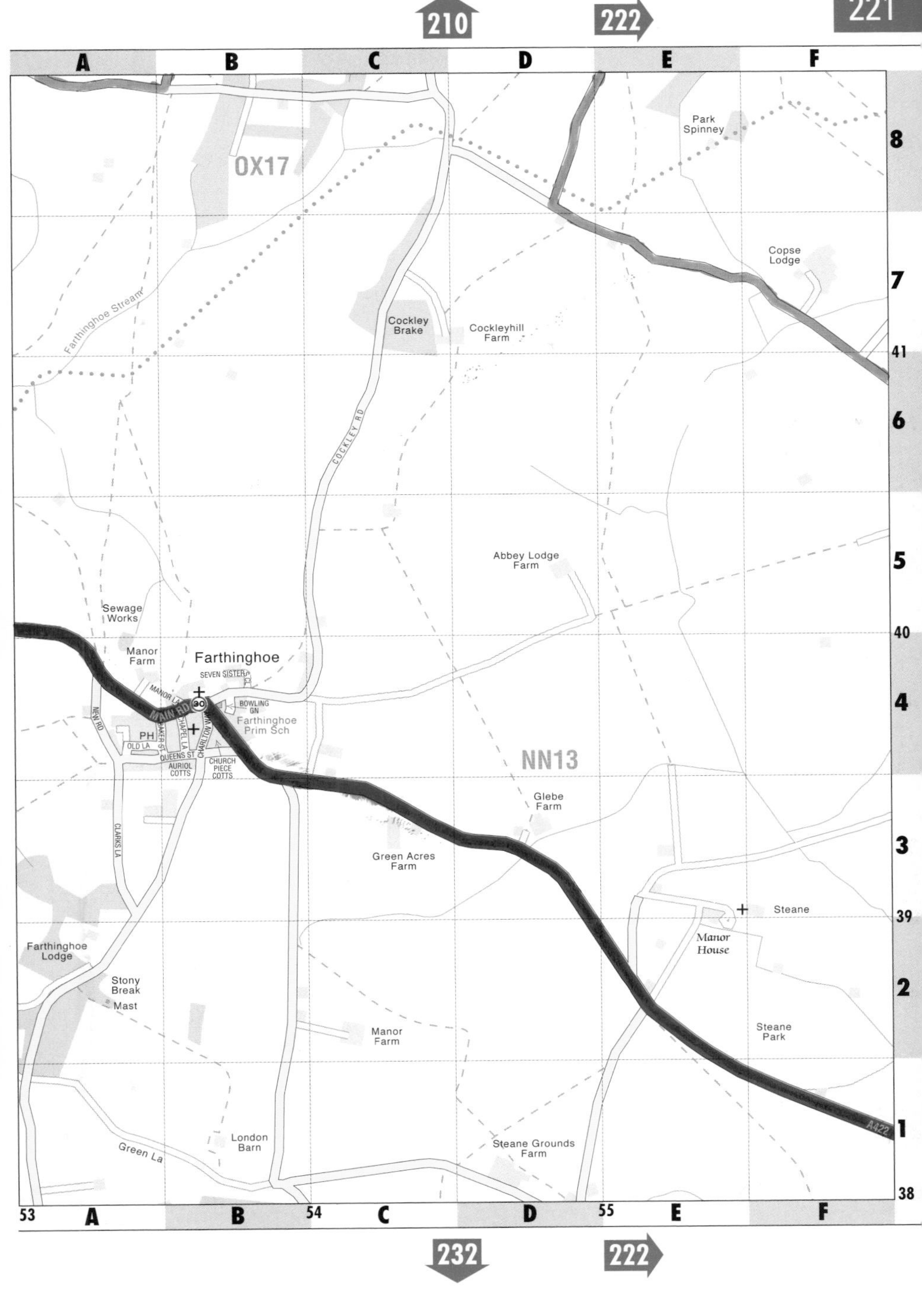
210
222
A
B
C
D
E
F
8
7
41
6
5
40
4
3
39
2
1
38
53
54
55
232
222
OX17
Park Spinney
Copse Lodge
Farthinghoe Stream
Cockley Brake
Cockleyhill Farm
COCKLEY RD
Abbey Lodge Farm
Sewage Works
Manor Farm
Farthinghoe
SEVEN SISTERS CL
MANOR LA
MAIN RD
BOWLING GN
Farthinghoe Prim Sch
NEW RD
PH
BAKER ST
CHAPEL LA
CHARLTON WAY
OLD LA
QUEENS ST
AURIOL COTTS
CHURCH PIECE COTTS
NN13
Glebe Farm
CLARKS LA
Green Acres Farm
Steane
Manor House
Farthinghoe Lodge
Stony Break
Mast
Steane Park
Manor Farm
A422
London Barn
Green La
Steane Grounds Farm

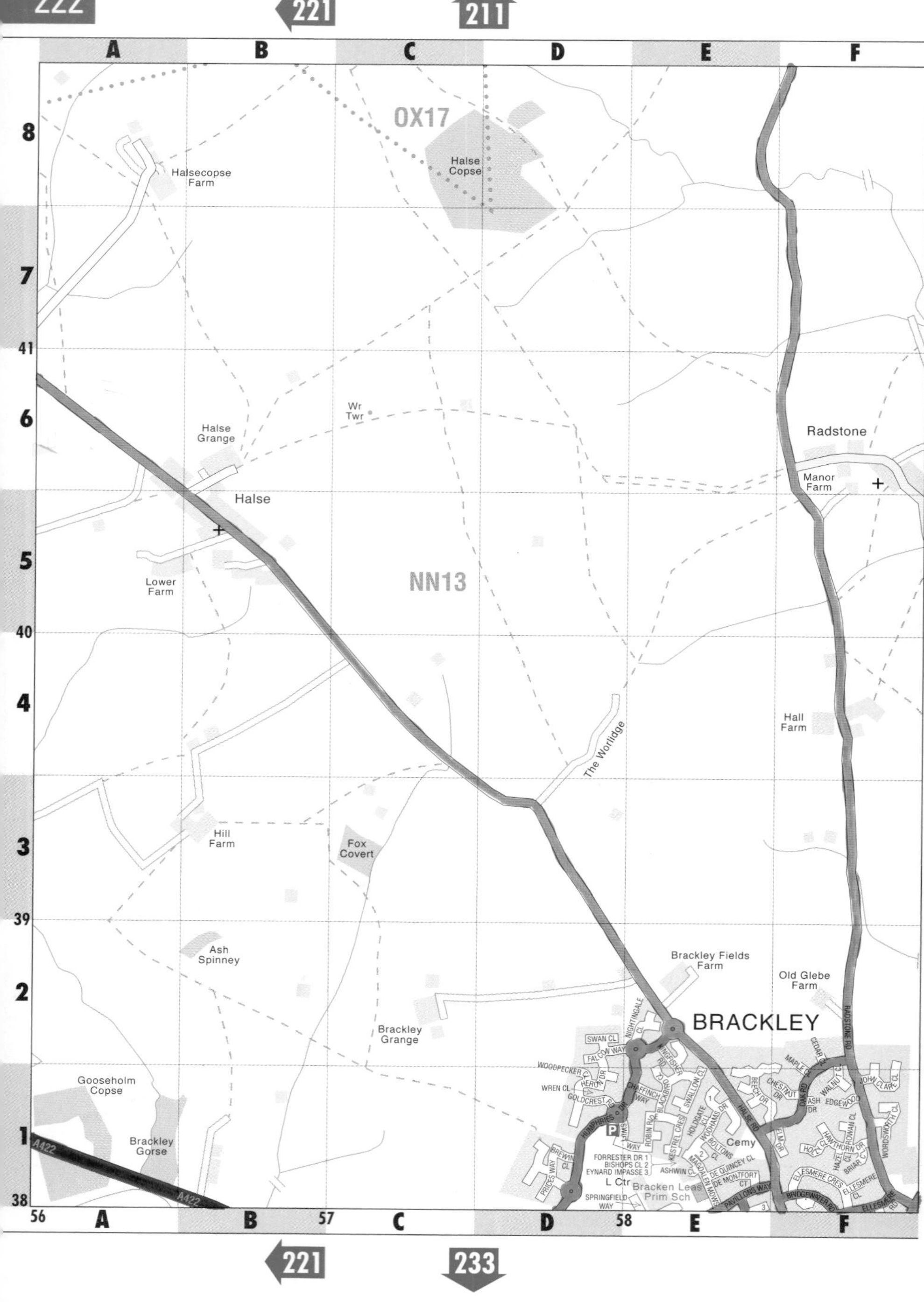

221
211
OX17
Halsecopse Farm
Halse Copse
Wr Twr
Halse Grange
Halse
Radstone
Manor Farm
Lower Farm
NN13
Hall Farm
The Worlidge
Hill Farm
Fox Covert
Ash Spinney
Brackley Fields Farm
Old Glebe Farm
BRACKLEY
Brackley Grange
Gooseholm Copse
Brackley Gorse
A422
Cemy
L Ctr
Bracken Leas Prim Sch
RADSTONE RD
HALSE RD
PAVILLONS WAY
BRIDGEWATER RD
ELLESMERE CRES
FORRESTER DR 1
BISHOPS CL 2
EYNARD IMPASSE 3
SPRINGFIELD WAY
56
57
58
38
39
40
41
221
233

212
224

234
224

223
213

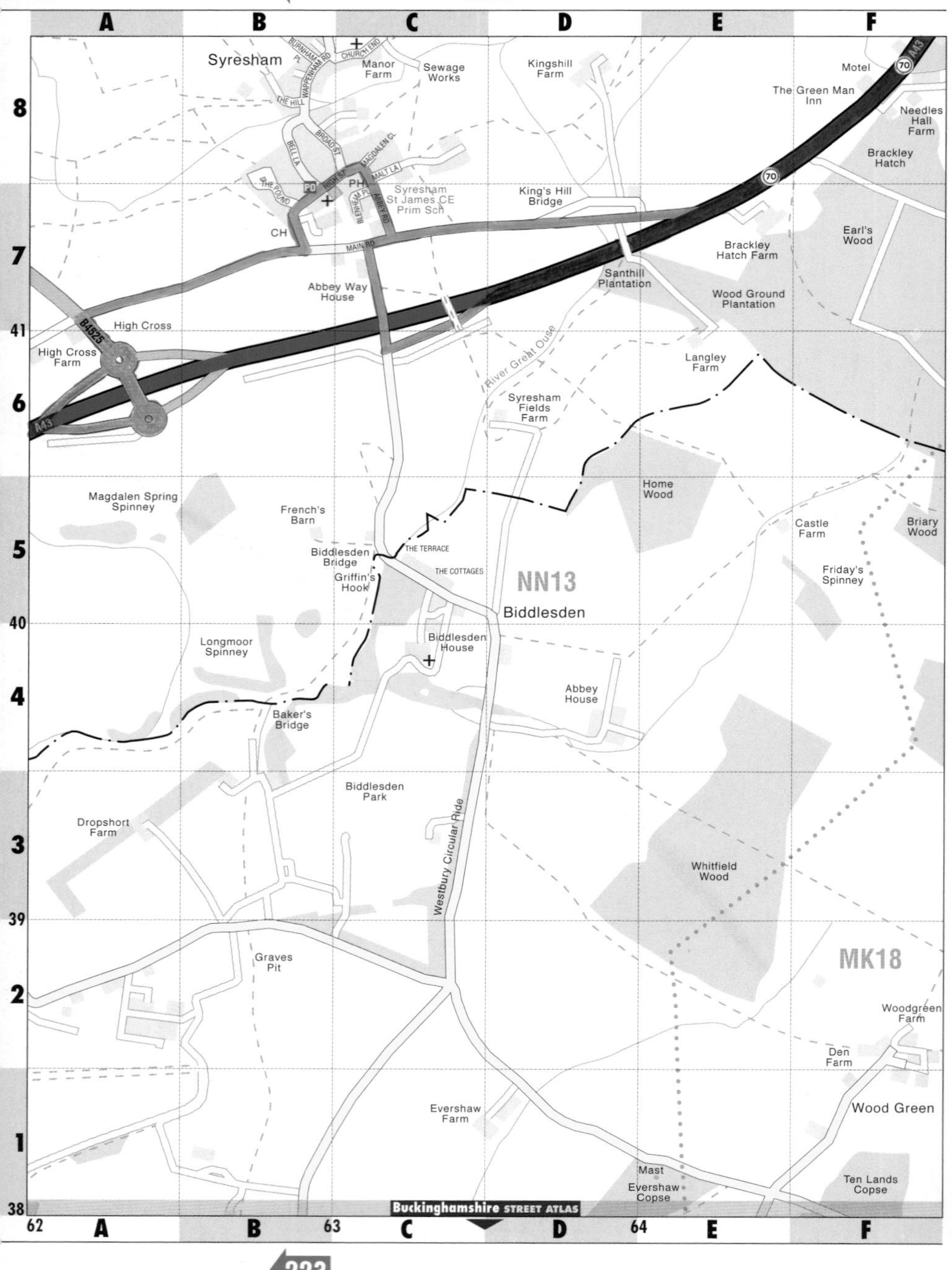
A
B
C
D
E
F
Syresham
Manor Farm
Sewage Works
Kingshill Farm
Motel
The Green Man Inn
Needles Hall Farm
Brackley Hatch
Syresham St James CE Prim Sch
King's Hill Bridge
Earl's Wood
Brackley Hatch Farm
Santhill Plantation
Wood Ground Plantation
Abbey Way House
High Cross
High Cross Farm
B4525
A43
Langley Farm
River Great Ouse
Syresham Fields Farm
Magdalen Spring Spinney
French's Barn
Home Wood
Castle Farm
Briary Wood
Biddlesden Bridge
THE TERRACE
THE COTTAGES
Griffin's Hook
NN13
Friday's Spinney
Biddlesden
Longmoor Spinney
Biddlesden House
Abbey House
Baker's Bridge
Biddlesden Park
Dropshort Farm
Westbury Circular Ride
Whitfield Wood
MK18
Graves Pit
Woodgreen Farm
Den Farm
Evershaw Farm
Wood Green
Mast
Evershaw Copse
Ten Lands Copse
8
7
41
6
5
40
4
3
39
2
1
38
62
63
64

223

214
226

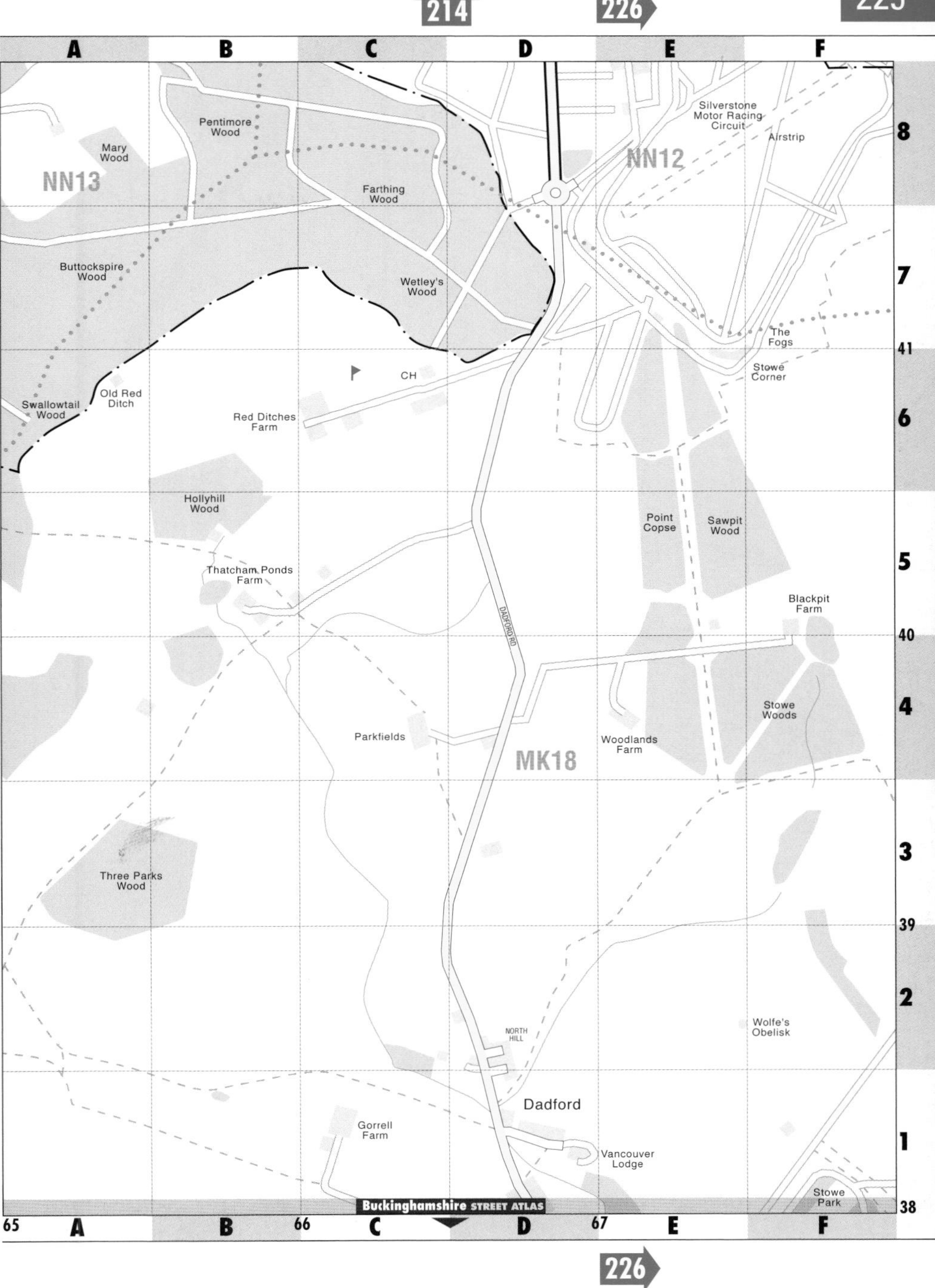
A
B
C
D
E
F
Pentimore Wood
Mary Wood
NN13
Farthing Wood
Silverstone Motor Racing Circuit
Airstrip
NN12
Buttockspire Wood
Wetley's Wood
The Fogs
Stowe Corner
Swallowtail Wood
Old Red Ditch
CH
Red Ditches Farm
Hollyhill Wood
Point Copse
Sawpit Wood
Thatcham Ponds Farm
Blackpit Farm
DADFORD RD
Stowe Woods
Parkfields
Woodlands Farm
MK18
Three Parks Wood
Wolfe's Obelisk
NORTH HILL
Dadford
Gorrell Farm
Vancouver Lodge
Stowe Park
8
7
41
6
5
40
4
3
39
2
1
38
65
66
67

226

225
215

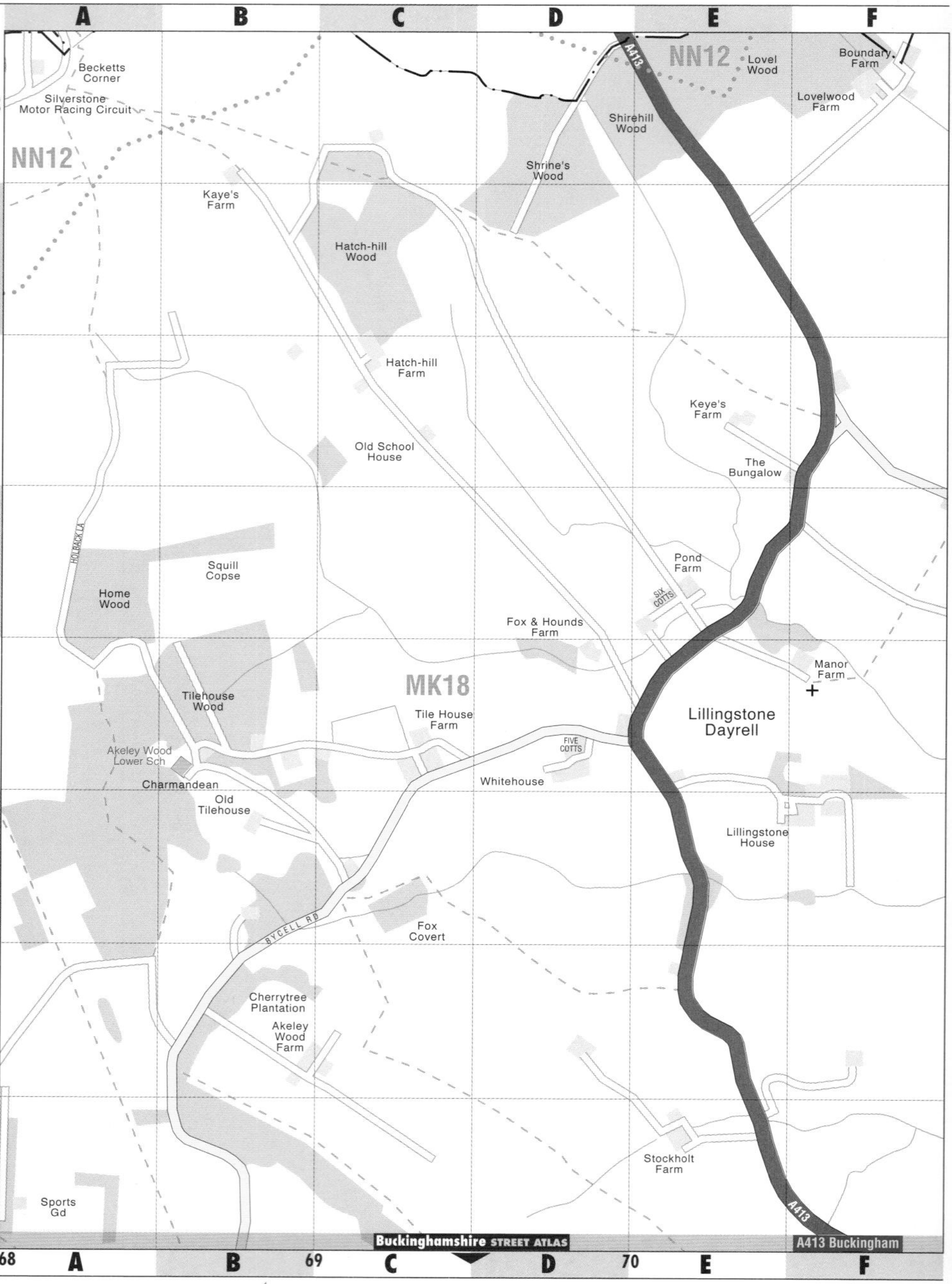
A
B
C
D
E
F
8
7
41
6
5
40
4
3
39
2
1
38
68
69
70
Beckets Corner
Silverstone Motor Racing Circuit
NN12
Kaye's Farm
Hatch-hill Wood
Hatch-hill Farm
Shrine's Wood
Shirehill Wood
NN12
Lovel Wood
Boundary Farm
Lovelwood Farm
A413
Keye's Farm
The Bungalow
Old School House
HOLBACK LA
Home Wood
Squill Copse
Pond Farm
SIX COTTS
Fox & Hounds Farm
Manor Farm
MK18
Tilehouse Wood
Tile House Farm
Lillingstone Dayrell
FIVE COTTS
Akeley Wood Lower Sch
Charmandean
Whitehouse
Old Tilehouse
Lillingstone House
BYCELL RD
Fox Covert
Cherrytree Plantation
Akeley Wood Farm
Stockholt Farm
Sports Gd
A413
A413 Buckingham

225

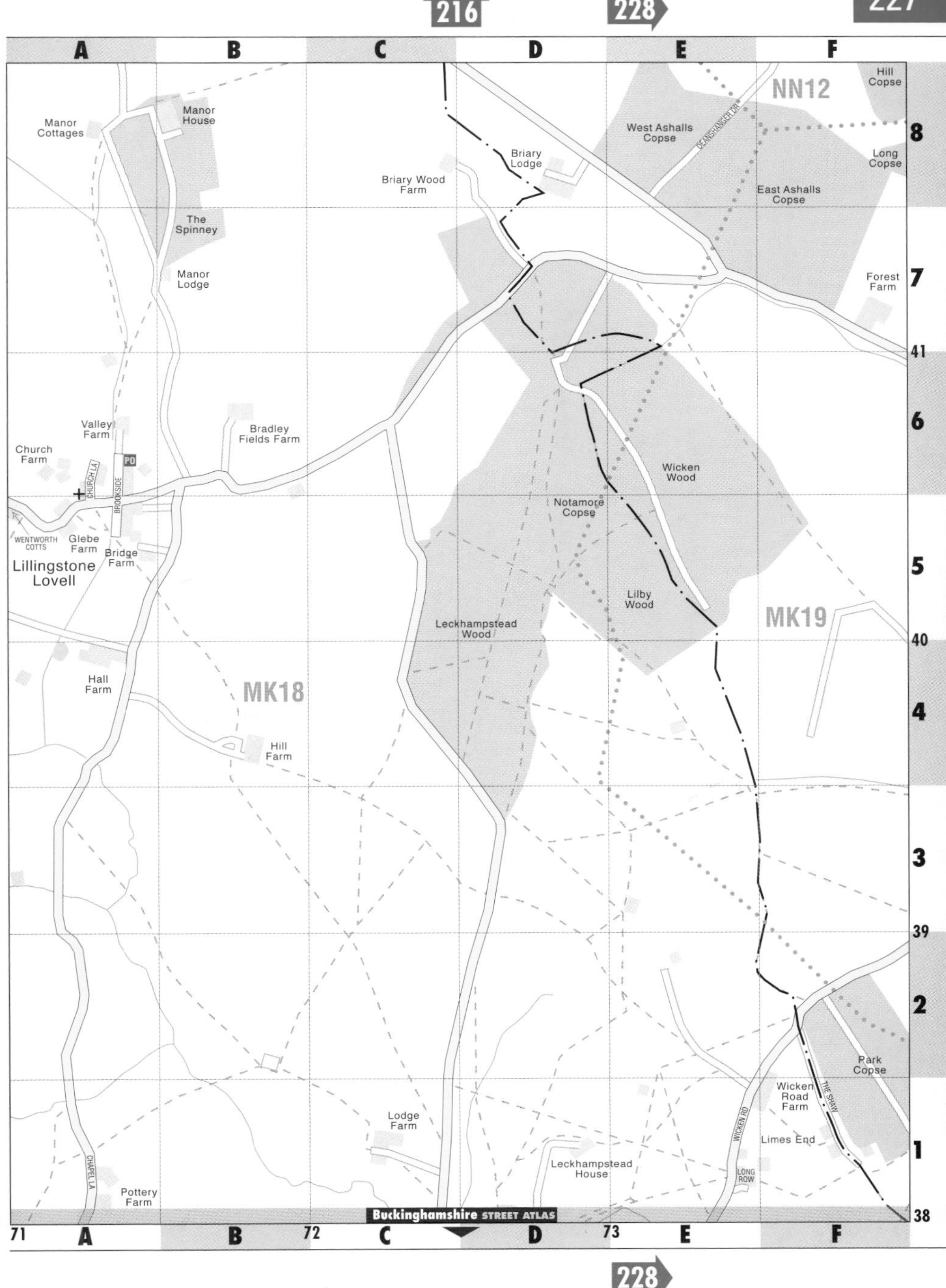
216
228
A
B
C
D
E
F
Manor Cottages
Manor House
The Spinney
Manor Lodge
Briary Wood Farm
Briary Lodge
West Ashalls Copse
DEANSHANGER DR
NN12
Hill Copse
Long Copse
East Ashalls Copse
Forest Farm
Valley Farm
Church Farm
CHURCH LA
BROOKSIDE
PO
Bradley Fields Farm
WENTWORTH COTTS
Glebe Farm
Bridge Farm
Lillingstone Lovell
Notamore Copse
Wicken Wood
Lilby Wood
Leckhampstead Wood
MK19
Hall Farm
MK18
Hill Farm
Church
Lodge Farm
Leckhampstead House
Wicken Road Farm
Park Copse
THE SHAW
WICKEN RD
Limes End
LONG ROW
CHAPEL LA
Pottery Farm
8
7
41
6
5
40
4
3
39
2
1
38
71
72
73
228

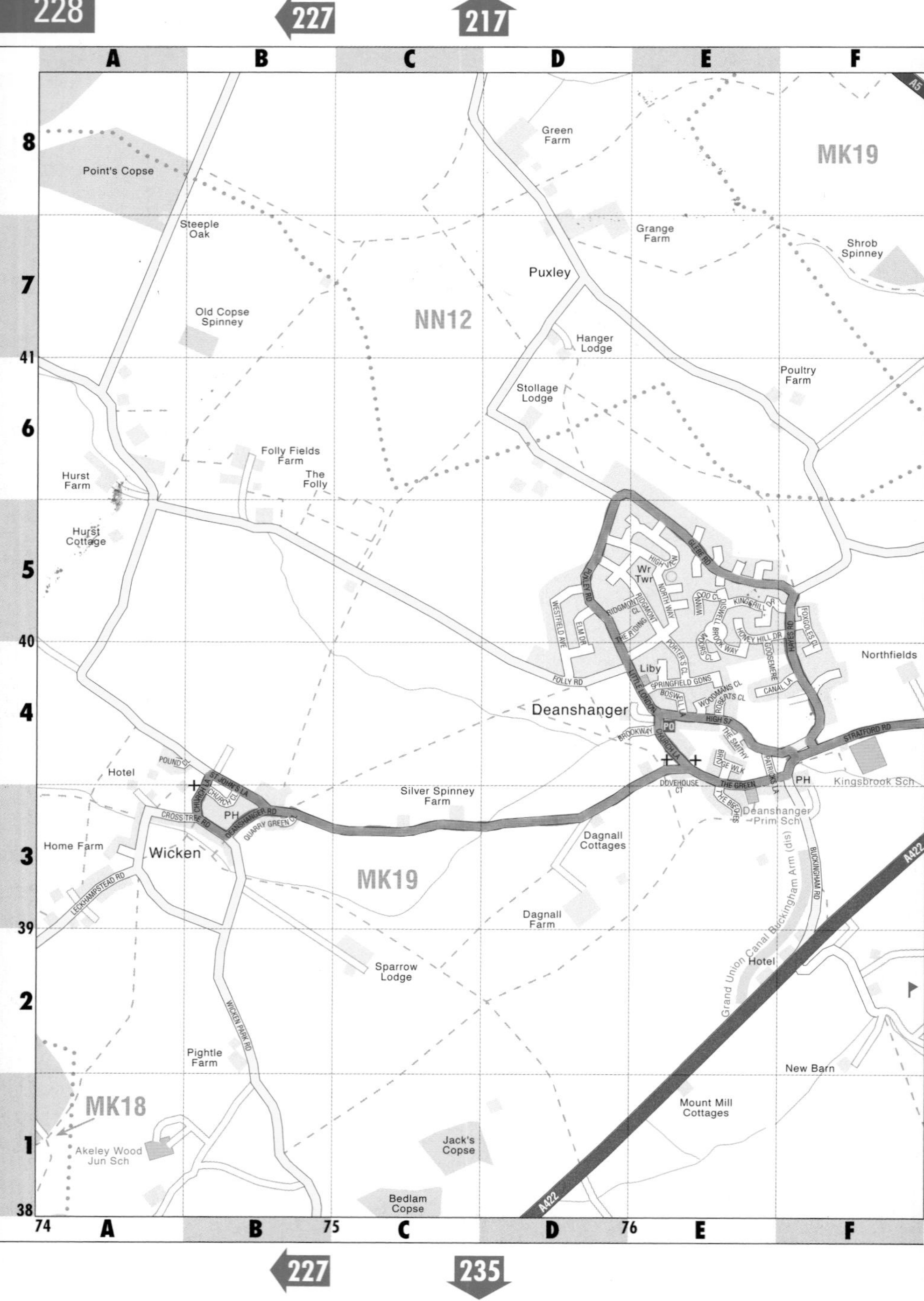
A
B
C
D
E
F
8
7
41
6
5
40
4
3
39
2
1
38
74
75
76
Point's Copse
Steeple Oak
Old Copse Spinney
Green Farm
MK19
Grange Farm
Shrob Spinney
Puxley
NN12
Hanger Lodge
Stollage Lodge
Poultry Farm
Folly Fields Farm
The Folly
Hurst Farm
Hurst Cottage
Wr Twr
GLEBE RD
PUXLEY RD
WESTFIELD AVE
ELM DR
RIDGMONT
NORTH WAY
THE RIDING
PORTER'S CL
KINGSHILL
HONEY HILL DR
GOOSEMERE
CANAL LA
FOXGOLES CL
Northfields
Liby
SPRINGFIELD GDNS
WOODMANS CL
ROBERTS CL
LITTLE LONDON
FOLLY RD
Deanshanger
HIGH ST
PO
BROOKWAY
CHURCH LA
THE SMITHY
STRATFORD RD
BRIDGE WLK
PATRICKS LA
DOVEHOUSE CT
THE GREEN
PH
Kingsbrook Sch
Deanshanger Prim Sch
POUND
Hotel
ST JOHN'S LA
CHURCH CL
CROSS TREE RD
DEANSHANGER RD
QUARRY GREEN CL
Silver Spinney Farm
Dagnall Cottages
Home Farm
Wicken
MK19
LECKHAMPSTEAD RD
BUCKINGHAM RD
A422
Grand Union Canal Buckingham Arm (dis)
Dagnall Farm
Sparrow Lodge
Hotel
WICKEN PARK RD
Pightle Farm
New Barn
MK18
Mount Mill Cottages
Akeley Wood Jun Sch
Jack's Copse
Bedlam Copse
A422
A5

218

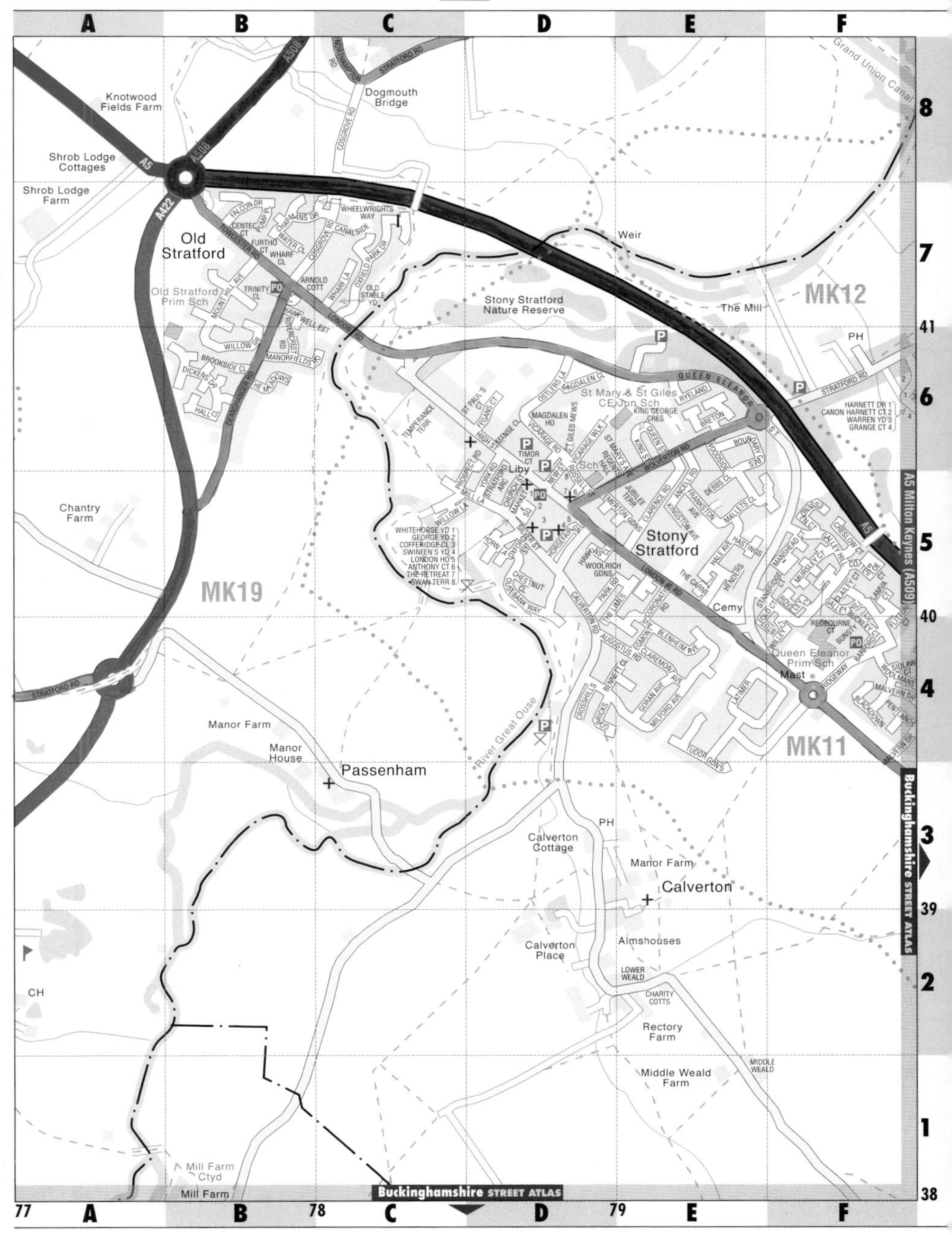
A
B
C
D
E
F
8
7
41
6
5
40
4
3
39
2
1
38
77
78
79
Knotwood Fields Farm
Shrob Lodge Cottages
Shrob Lodge Farm
Dogmouth Bridge
Grand Union Canal
Old Stratford
Old Stratford Prim Sch
Weir
Stony Stratford Nature Reserve
The Mill
MK12
PH
St Mary & St Giles CE Jun Sch
Stony Stratford
Chantry Farm
MK19
Cemy
Queen Eleanor Prim Sch
Mast
MK11
Manor Farm
Manor House
Passenham
River Great Ouse
Calverton Cottage
Manor Farm
Calverton
Calverton Place
Almshouses
Rectory Farm
Middle Weald Farm
Mill Farm Ctyd
Mill Farm
CH
A5
A508
A422
QUEEN ELEANOR ST
LONDON RD
WOLVERTON RD
STRATFORD RD
CALVERTON RD
HARNETT DR 1
CANON HARNETT CT 2
WARREN YD 3
GRANGE CT 4
WHITEHORSE YD 1
GEORGE YD 2
COFFERIDGE CL 3
SWINEEN'S YD 4
LONDON HO 5
ANTHONY CT 6
THE RETREAT 7
SWAN TERR 8
LOWER WEALD
CHARITY COTTS
MIDDLE WEALD
A5 Milton Keynes (A509)
Buckinghamshire STREET ATLAS

219

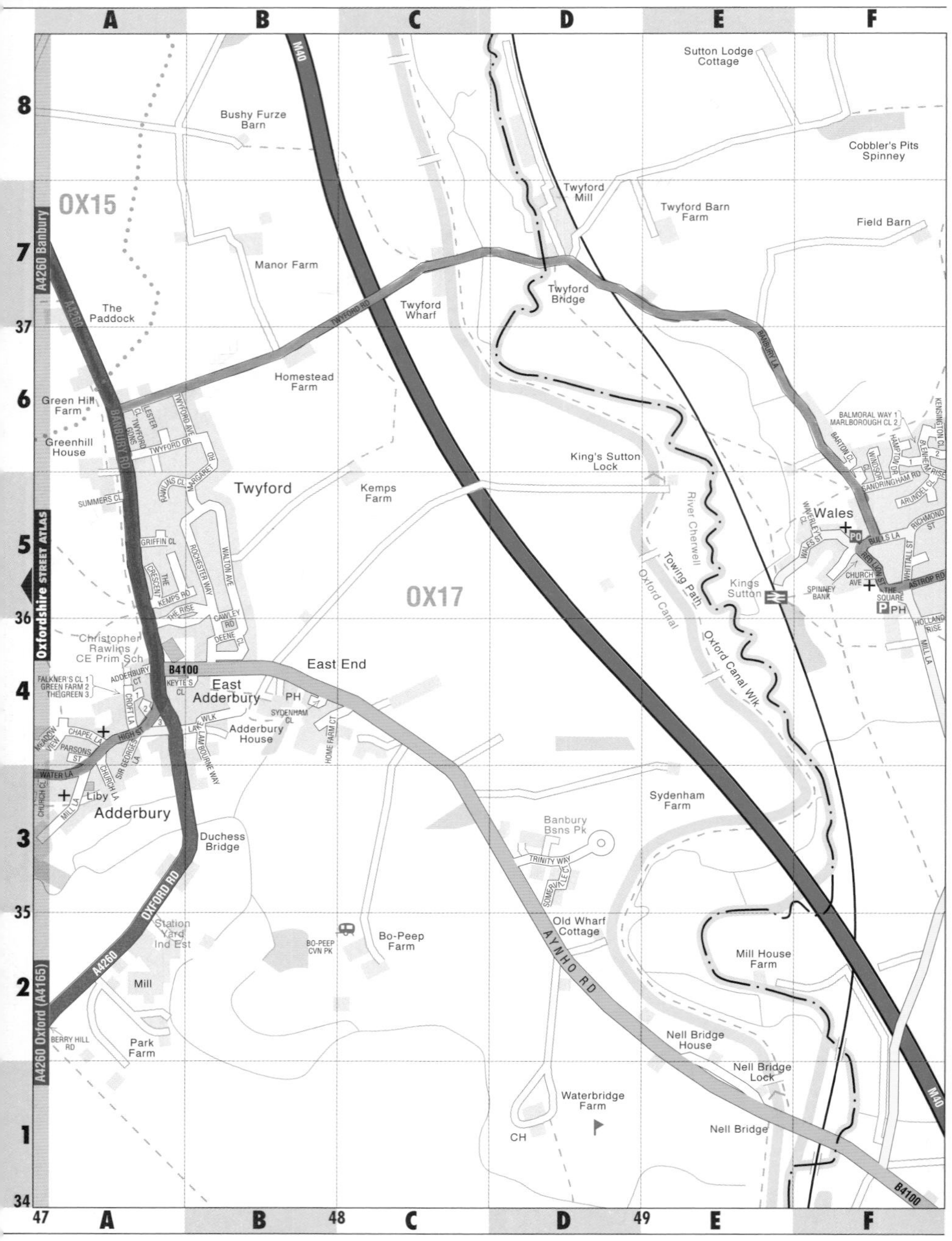

A B C D E F
8 7 6 5 4 3 2 1
37 36 35 34
47 48 49
OX15
OX17
A4260 Banbury
A4260 Oxford (A4165)
Oxfordshire STREET ATLAS
M40
Sutton Lodge Cottage
Bushy Furze Barn
Cobbler's Pits Spinney
Twyford Mill
Twyford Barn Farm
Field Barn
Manor Farm
The Paddock
Twyford Wharf
Twyford Bridge
TWYFORD RD
BANBURY LA
Homestead Farm
Green Hill Farm
Greenhill House
BANBURY RD
King's Sutton Lock
Twyford
Kemps Farm
SUMMERS CL
Wales
River Cherwell
Towing Path
Oxford Canal
Kings Sutton
Christopher Rawlins CE Prim Sch
East End
B4100
East Adderbury
PH
Oxford Canal Wlk
Adderbury House
Liby
Adderbury
Sydenham Farm
Banbury Bsns Pk
TRINITY WAY
Duchess Bridge
OXFORD RD
Station Yard Ind Est
BO-PEEP CVN PK
Bo-Peep Farm
Old Wharf Cottage
AYNHO RD
Mill House Farm
Mill
Park Farm
BERRY HILL RD
Nell Bridge House
Nell Bridge Lock
Waterbridge Farm
CH
Nell Bridge
B4100

236

220
232

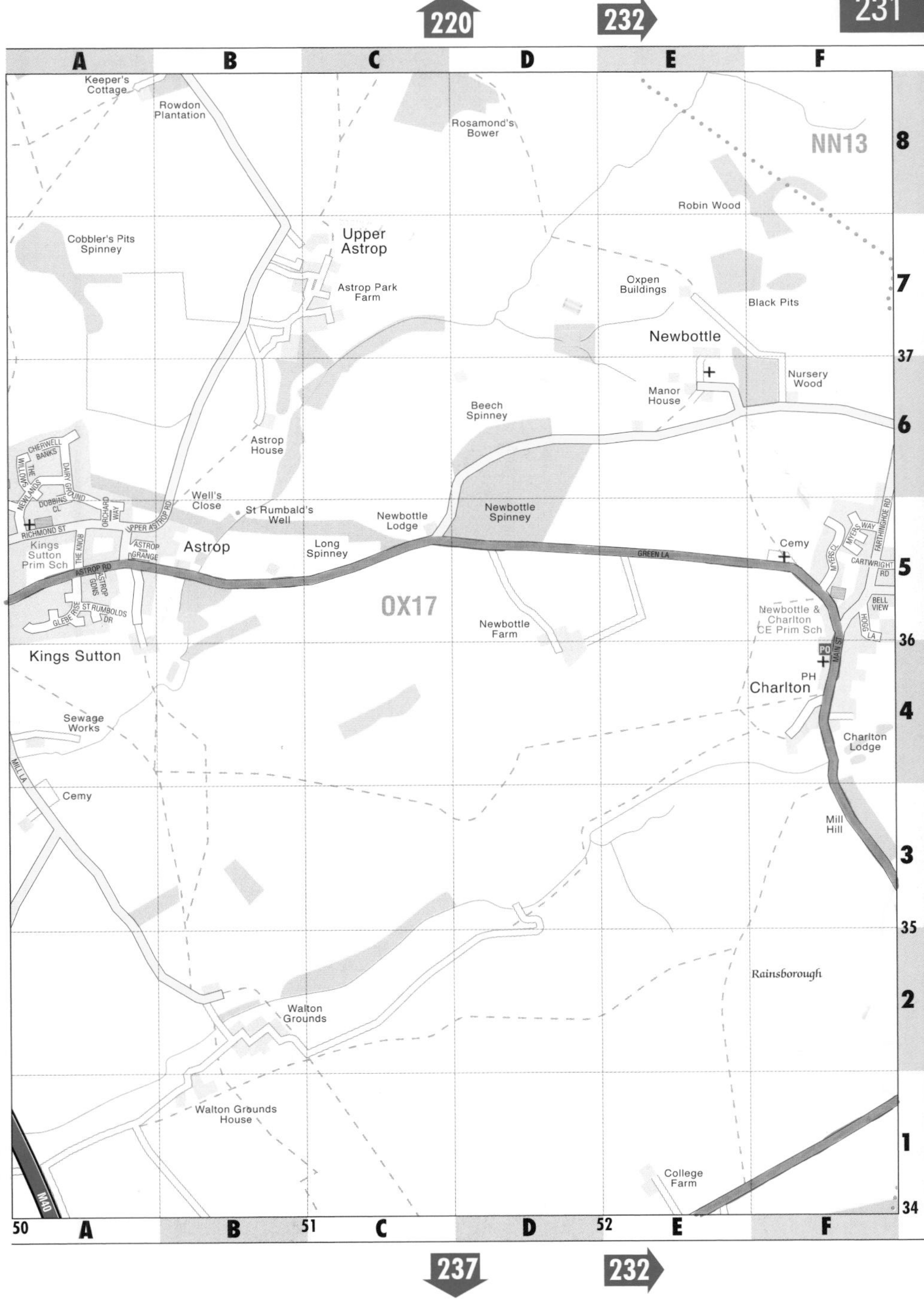

237
232

231
221

231
238

222
234

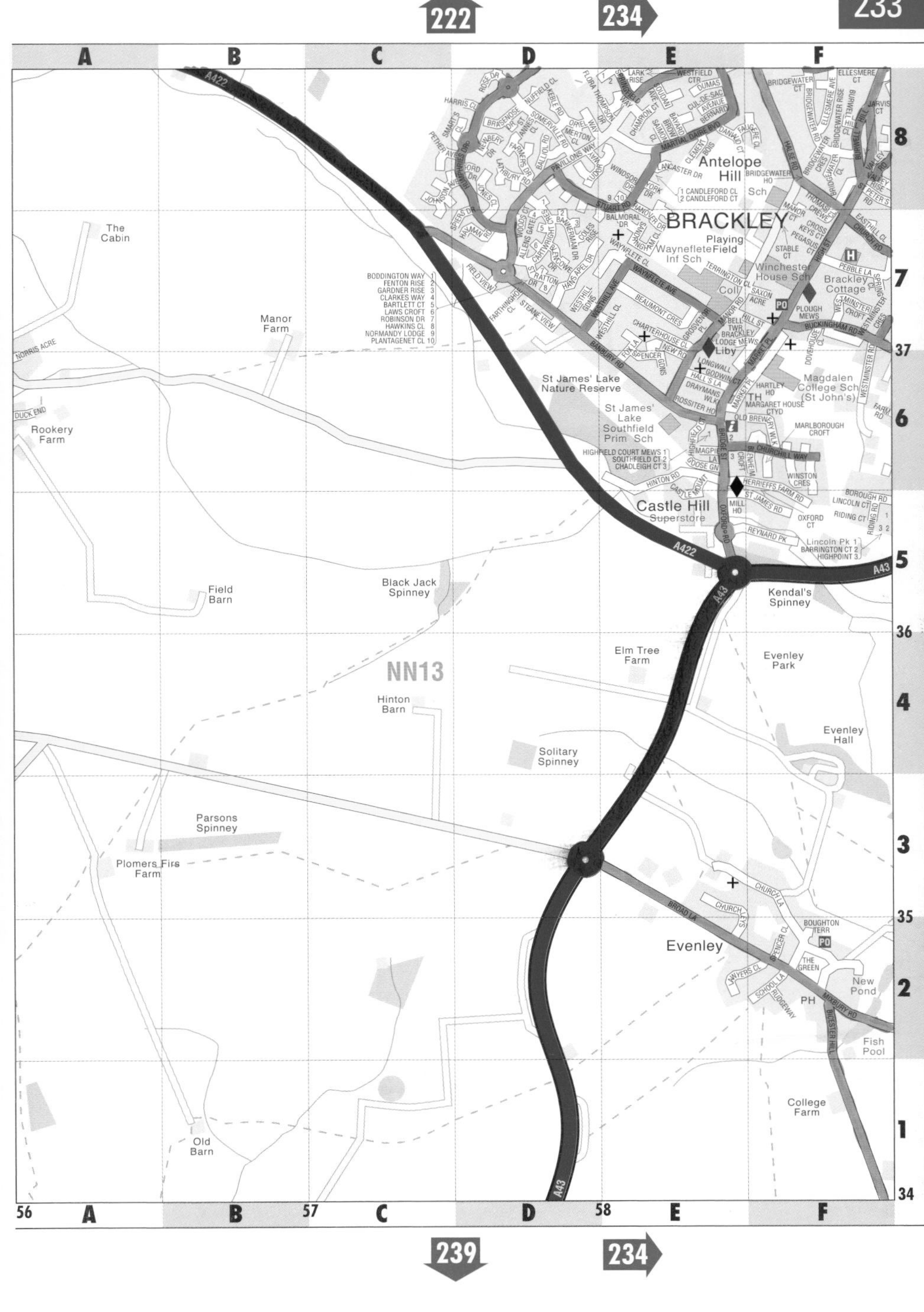

239
234

233
223

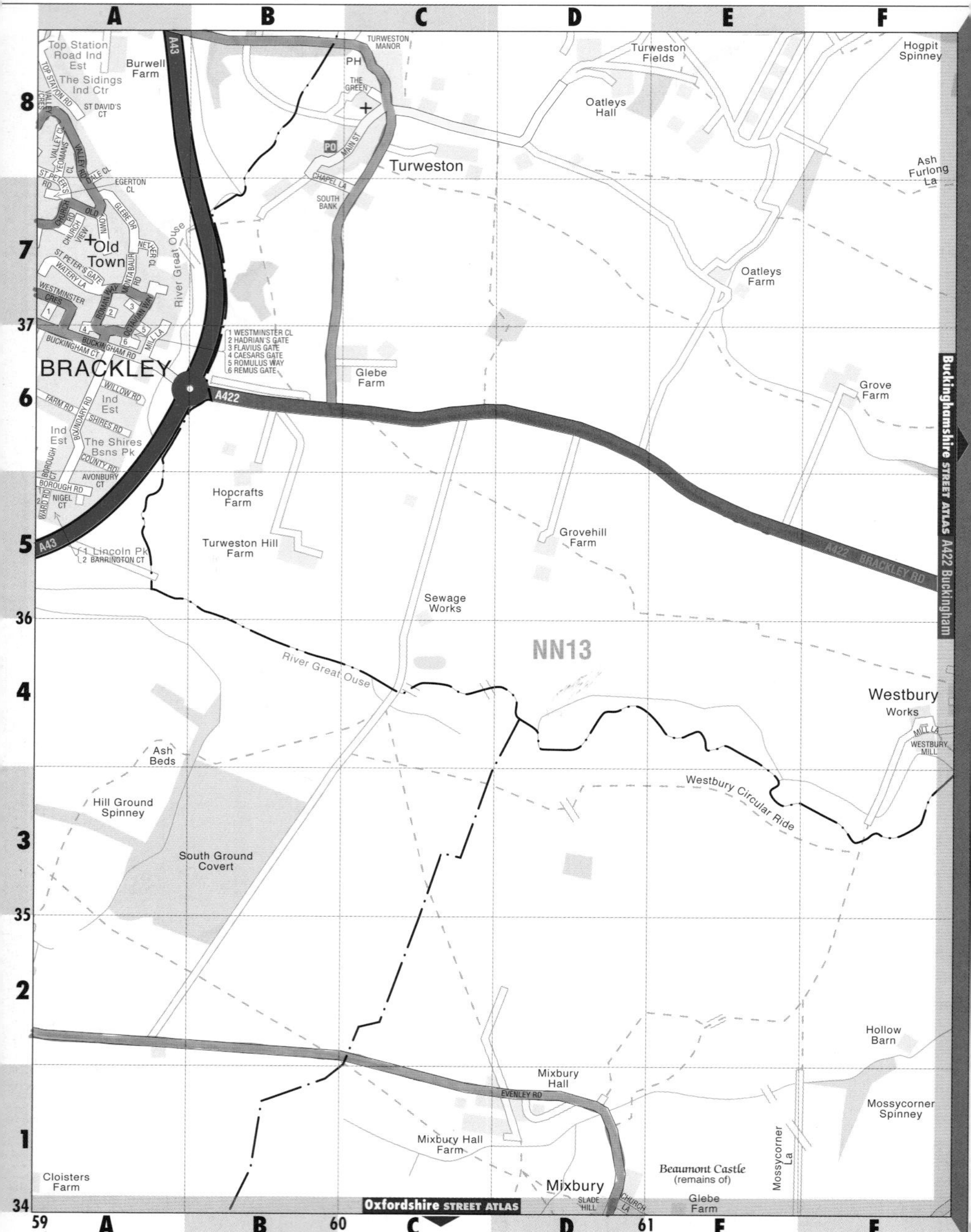

A B C D E F
8 7 37 6 5 36 4 3 35 2 1 34
59 60 61
Top Station Road Ind Est
Burwell Farm
The Sidings Ind Ctr
TOP STATION RD
ST DAVID'S CT
TURWESTON MANOR
PH
THE GREEN
Turweston Fields
Oatleys Hall
Hogpit Spinney
PO
MAIN ST
Turweston
CHAPEL LA
SOUTH BANK
EGERTON CL
GLEBE DR
OLD TOWN
Old Town
Ash Furlong La
Oatleys Farm
WESTMINSTER CRES
ROMAN WAY
MONTABAUR RD
OCTAVIAN WAY
River Great Ouse
1 WESTMINSTER CL
2 HADRIAN'S GATE
3 FLAVIUS GATE
4 CAESARS GATE
5 ROMULUS WAY
6 REMUS GATE
BUCKINGHAM CT
BUCKINGHAM RD
MILL LA
BRACKLEY
A43
A422
Glebe Farm
Grove Farm
WILLOW RD
FARM RD
BOUNDARY RD
Ind Est
SHIRES RD
The Shires Bsns Pk
COUNTY RD
AVONBURY CT
BOROUGH RD
NIGEL CT
WARD RD
Hopcrafts Farm
Grovehill Farm
Turweston Hill Farm
1 Lincoln Pk
2 BARRINGTON CT
A422 BRACKLEY RD
Sewage Works
NN13
River Great Ouse
Westbury
Works
MILL LA
WESTBURY MILL
Ash Beds
Westbury Circular Ride
Hill Ground Spinney
South Ground Covert
Hollow Barn
Mixbury Hall
EVENLEY RD
Mossycorner Spinney
Mixbury Hall Farm
Mossycorner La
Beaumont Castle (remains of)
Cloisters Farm
Mixbury
SLADE HILL
CHURCH LA
Glebe Farm
Oxfordshire STREET ATLAS
Buckinghamshire STREET ATLAS
A422 Buckingham

233

228

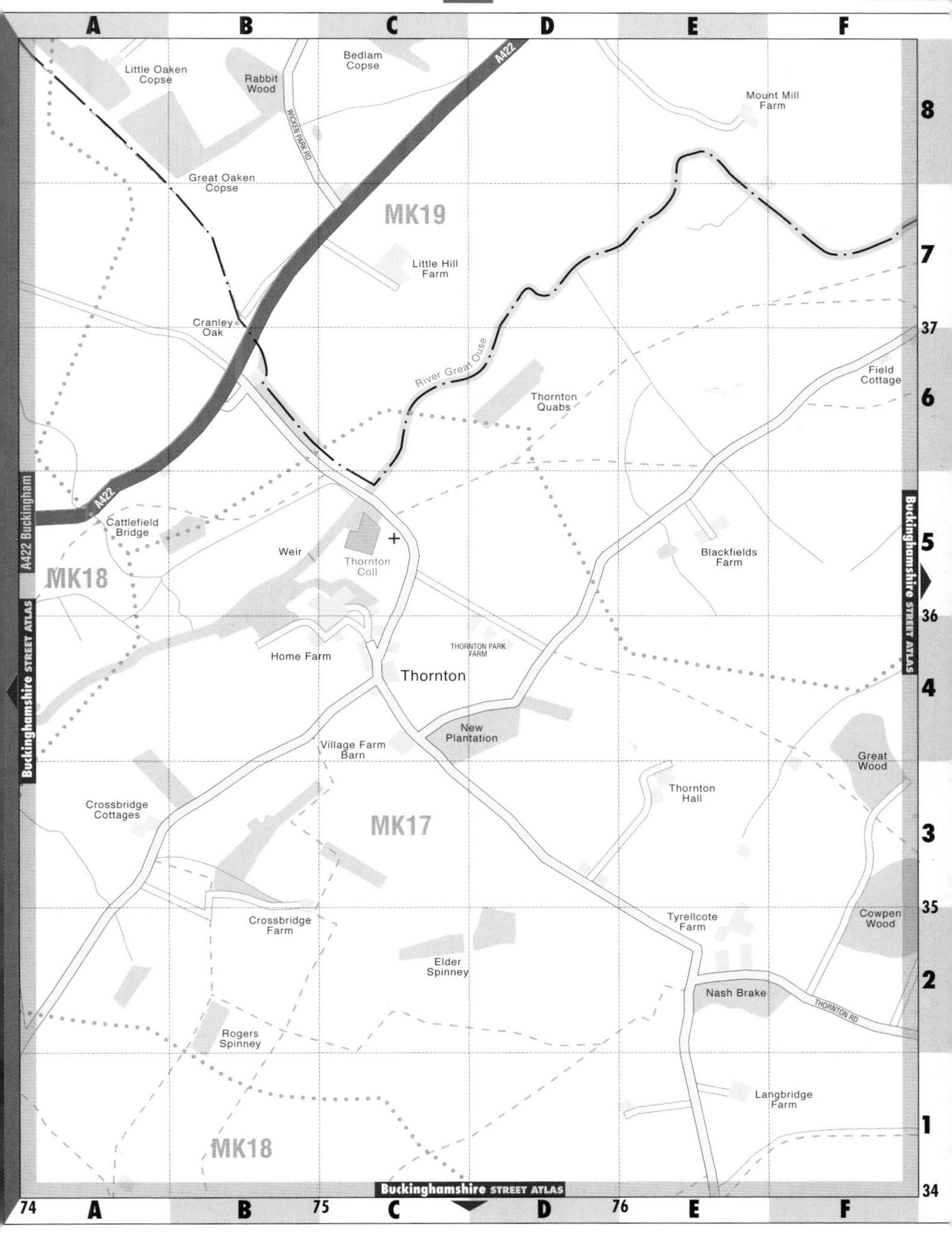

A
B
C
D
E
F
Little Oaken Copse
Rabbit Wood
Bedlam Copse
A422
WICKEN PARK RD
Mount Mill Farm
8
Great Oaken Copse
MK19
Little Hill Farm
7
37
Cranley Oak
River Great Ouse
Field Cottage
Thornton Quabs
6
A422
Cattlefield Bridge
A422 Buckingham
Weir
Thornton Coll
Blackfields Farm
5
MK18
36
Buckinghamshire STREET ATLAS
Home Farm
THORNTON PARK FARM
Thornton
4
New Plantation
Village Farm Barn
Great Wood
Crossbridge Cottages
Thornton Hall
MK17
3
Crossbridge Farm
Tyrellcote Farm
Cowpen Wood
35
Elder Spinney
Nash Brake
THORNTON RD
2
Rogers Spinney
Langbridge Farm
1
MK18
Buckinghamshire STREET ATLAS
34
74
75
76

230

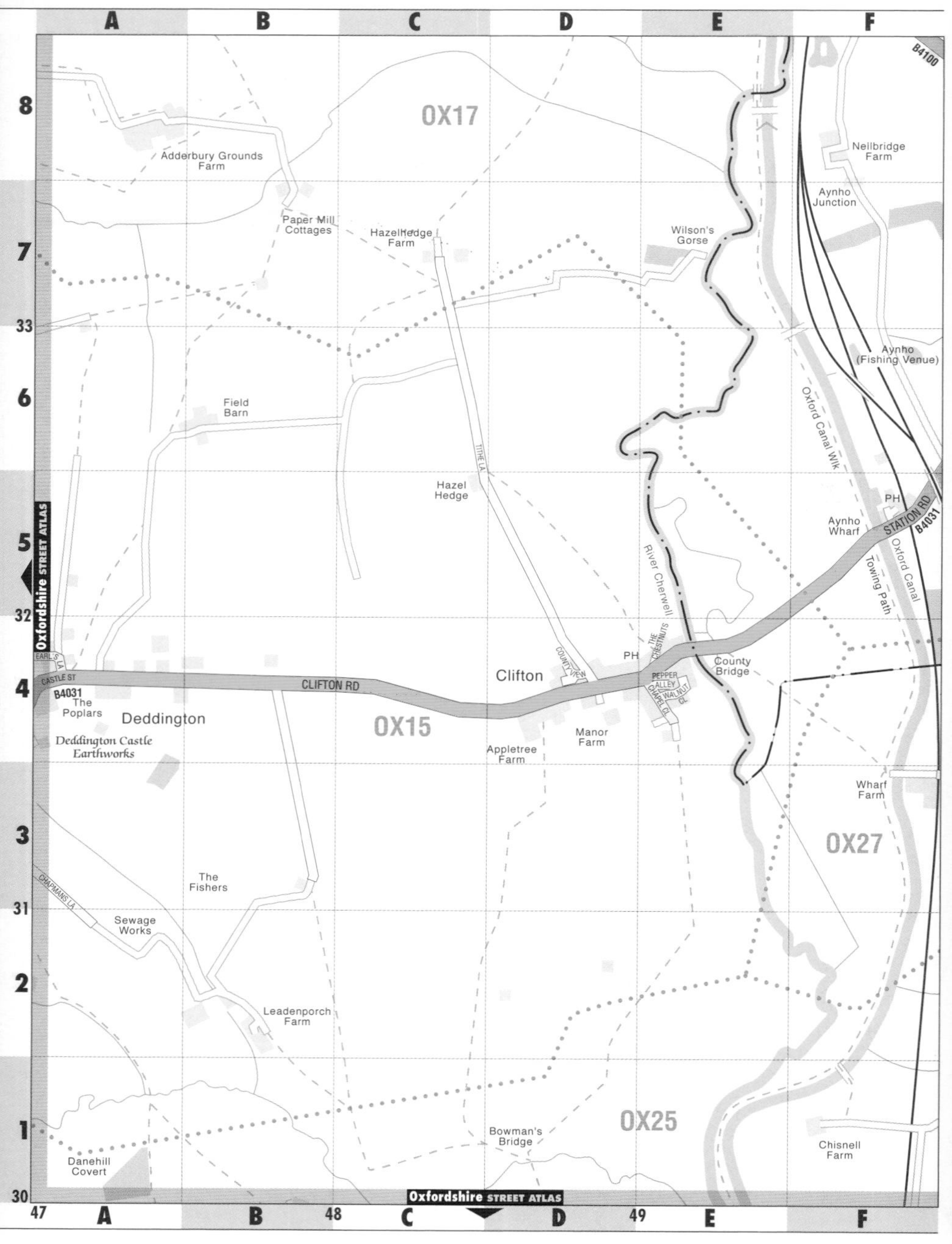

Oxfordshire STREET ATLAS

Oxfordshire STREET ATLAS

231
238
A
B
C
D
E
F
M40
Ox House
Allot Gdns
Bricklands Farm
Pesthouse Wood
NN13
8
Recn Gd
BLACKSMITHS HILL 1
SKITTLE ALLEY 2
THE HILL 3
THE SQUARE 4
B4100 BANBURY RD
CHARLTON RD
AINCLIFFE CL
THE BUTTS
PORTWAY
PORTWAY GDNS
BUTTS CL
BOWMENS LEA
THE GLEBE
COLLEGE FIELDS
College Farm
SCHOOL END
HOLLOW WAY
LITTLE LA
PH
B4031
ROUNDTOWN
CROUGHTON RD
CARTWRIGHT GDNS
AYNHO CT
B4100
B4031
7
Friar's Well
AYNHOE PK
Aynho
Aynho Fields
33
STATION RD
Ryeland Hill
OX17
Northcotehill Covert
6
Ash Grove
Puckwell
Keeper's Hill
Aynho Park
The Firs
The Mill House
Lower Aynho Grounds
5
Park Flat
Holloway's Flat
The Oaks
Ockley Brook
32
Sewage Works
Risley's Corner
Upper Aynho Grounds
4
Souldern Mill
Old Shaws
WHARF LA
Souldern Manor
PH
FOX LA
BATES LA
HIGH ST
BOVEWELL
1 CHAPEL ROW
2 THE PADDOCKS
3 COTSWOLD CT
3
OX27
FOXHILL LA
Souldern
Mast
31
Ploughley Hill
B4100
2
Foxhill La
Souldern Grounds
Holtage La
Fox Hill
Foxhill Barn
Inkerman Farm
OX25
Upper Souldern Grounds Farm
1
M40
Oxfordshire STREET ATLAS
M40 Oxford (A34)
30
50
51
52
238

237
232

A
B
C
D
E
F
8
7
33
6
5
32
4
3
31
2
1
30
53
54
55
OX17
Cemy
Croughton
Croughton
All Saints
CE Prim Sch
Recn
Gd
Warren
Farm
PH
HIGH ST
WHEELER'S RISE
BRACKLEY RD
YEW TREE
RISE
CHURCH
END
MANOR
FARM
COTTS
CHURCH
LA
CHAPEL END
PARK END
PO
The
Moors
B4031
BLENHEIM
MILL LA
The
Green
Park End
Works
PORTWAY
PORTWAY DR
PORTWAY
B4031
Old Down
Pond
Old Down
Covert
Sewage
Works
Park
Farm
SIXTH ST
FIFTH AVE
FIFTH ST E
FIFTH ST
BARKSDALE AVE
FOURTH AVE
FOURTH ST
ANDREWS AVE
THIRD ST
SECOND ST
FIRST ST
Padbury's
Bottom
NN13
New
Buildings
Smanhill
Covert
Masts
Middle
Covert
OX17
Pimlico
Farm
Crook's
Firs
Ockley Brook
Thriftwood
House
OX27
A43
Tower
Fields
Roundhill
Farm
B4100
Horwell
Corner
Round Hill
Lower
Rookery
Park Farm
Horwell
Farm
B4100
A43
Oxford
Lodge
Hermitage
Belt
A43 Junc. 10 M40

237

233

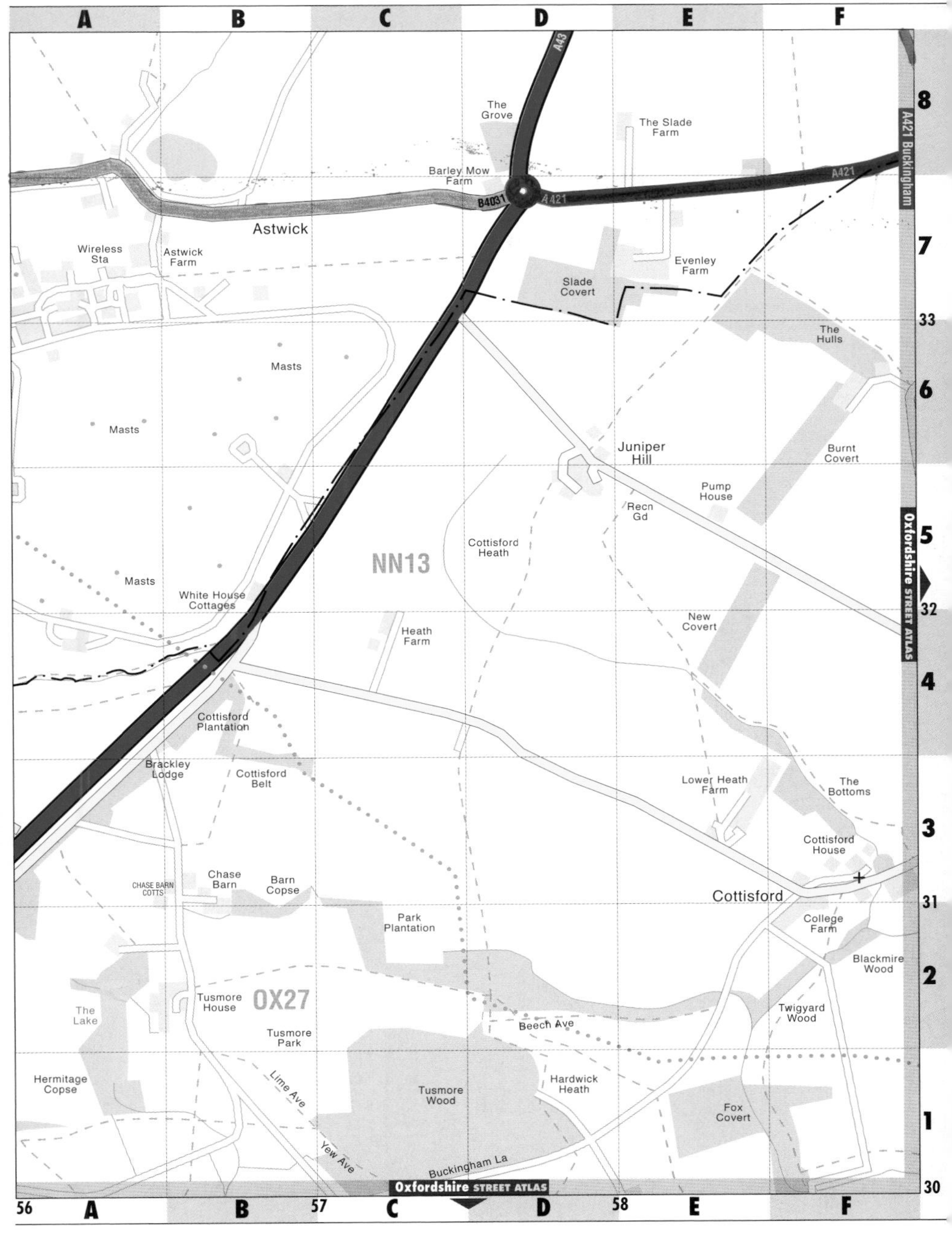

Oxfordshire STREET ATLAS

Oxfordshire STREET ATLAS

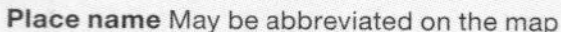

Index

Place name May be abbreviated on the map

Location number Present when a number indicates the place's position in a crowded area of mapping

Locality, town or village Shown when more than one place has the same name

Postcode district District for the indexed place

Page and grid square Page number and grid reference for the standard mapping

Church Rd 6 Beckenham BR2..........**53** C6

Cities, towns and villages are listed in CAPITAL LETTERS

Public and commercial buildings are highlighted in magenta

Places of interest are highlighted in **blue** with a star★

Abbreviations used in the index

Acad	**Academy**	Comm	**Common**	Gd	**Ground**	L	**Leisure**	Prom	**Promenade**
App	**Approach**	Cott	**Cottage**	Gdn	**Garden**	La	**Lane**	Rd	**Road**
Arc	**Arcade**	Cres	**Crescent**	Gn	**Green**	Liby	**Library**	Recn	**Recreation**
Ave	**Avenue**	Cswy	**Causeway**	Gr	**Grove**	Mdw	**Meadow**	Ret	**Retail**
Bglw	**Bungalow**	Ct	**Court**	H	**Hall**	Meml	**Memorial**	Sh	**Shopping**
Bldg	**Building**	Ctr	**Centre**	Ho	**House**	Mkt	**Market**	Sq	**Square**
Bsns, Bus	**Business**	Ctry	**Country**	Hospl	**Hospital**	Mus	**Museum**	St	**Street**
Bvd	**Boulevard**	Cty	**County**	HQ	**Headquarters**	Orch	**Orchard**	Sta	**Station**
Cath	**Cathedral**	Dr	**Drive**	Hts	**Heights**	Pal	**Palace**	Terr	**Terrace**
Cir	**Circus**	Dro	**Drove**	Ind	**Industrial**	Par	**Parade**	TH	**Town Hall**
Cl	**Close**	Ed	**Education**	Inst	**Institute**	Pas	**Passage**	Univ	**University**
Cnr	**Corner**	Emb	**Embankment**	Int	**International**	Pk	**Park**	Wk, Wlk	**Walk**
Coll	**College**	Est	**Estate**	Intc	**Interchange**	Pl	**Place**	Wr	**Water**
Com	**Community**	Ex	**Exhibition**	Junc	**Junction**	Prec	**Precinct**	Yd	**Yard**

Index of towns, villages, streets, hospitals, industrial estates, railway stations, schools, shopping centres, universities and places of interest

1st Drift PE9..............**2** D8
78 Derngate★ NN1 ..... **159** D5

A

A6 Bsns Ctr NN16.........**71** E4
Abbey Cl NN29 .... **164** C2
Abbey Ct
11 Daventry NN11....... **135** C2
Wollaston NN29......... **146** D3
Abbey Ho 5 NN5....... **159** A6
Abbey Lo NN3.......... **160** C7
Abbey Prim Sch The
NN4.................. **159** C1
Abbey Rd
Northampton NN4........**159** B3
Roade NN7 .... **191** C4
Syresham NN13......... **224** C7
Wellingborough NN8......**129** F3
Abbey Rise NN29 .... **146** D3
Abbey St
Daventry NN11 .... **135** C2
Market Harborough LE16 ...**31** E3
Northampton NN5 .... **159** A6
Abbey Way
Ravenstone MK46........**194** E2
Rushden NN10.......... **148** A8
Abbot Cl NN11.......... **153** D8
Abbots Cl NN15...........**91** B7
Abbots Way
Kettering NN15...........**91** A6
Northampton NN5........**158** F6
Roade NN7 .... **191** C4
Wellingborough NN8......**129** F4
Abbotts Cl NN14..........**77** D3
Abbotts Way NN10.......**131** F1
Aberdare Rd NN5....... **159** A8
Aberdeen Terr NN5 ..... **159** A6
ABINGTON **160** B8
Abington Ave NN3 ...... **160** A8
Abington Bsns Ctr
NN1.................. **160** A7
Abington Cotts NN1 .... **160** A8
Abington Ct NN3 ....**160** B8
Abington Gr NN1 ....**159** F8
Abington Mus★ NN1.... **160** A7
Abington Park Cres
NN3.................. **160** C7
Abington Rd NN17........**36** B7
Abington Sq NN1........**159** E6
Abington St NN1 .... **159** D6
ABINGTON VALE **160** C7
Abington Vale Prim Sch
NN3.................. **160** C6
Ablett Cl NN14 ....**76** D2
ABTHORPE **201** F1
Abthorpe Ave NN2...... **141** D5
Accurate Boot The
NN1...................**159** E7
Ace La NN7 ....**172** F7
ACHURCH **58** C2
Acorn Cl
Islip NN14...............**76** B3
Kettering NN15...........**92** B5
Lubenham LE16...........**30** E3
Acorn Ind Est NN14........**76** B3
Acorn Pk NN15...........**92** D4
Acorn Way NN12.........**214** E4
Acre Cl NN11........... **135** C6
Acre Ct NN16.............**72** D3
Acre La NN2............ **141** A6
Acremead PE8............**28** B3
Acre St NN16.............**72** D3
Adam Bsns Ctr NN16......**71** F5
Adam & Eve St 8 LE16 ...**31** E3
Adams Ave NN1 ....**159** F7
Adams Cl
Stanwick NN9 .... **114** A5
Wellingborough NN8......**130** B5
Adams Dr NN14 ....**70** B7
Adams Rd NN11 ....**184** B6
Adamswood Cl LE16 ......**31** C3
ADDERBURY **230** A3
Adderbury Ct OX17 ..... **230** A4
Addington Park Ind Est
NN14................. **113** C7
Addington Rd
Irthlingborough NN9..... **113** A5
Woodford NN14...........**94** D6
Addis Cl NN15............**92** C1
Addison Rd
Desborough NN14.........**50** F3
Northampton NN3 ....**142** B2
Addlecroft Cl NN2 ....**141** B3
Adelaide Ho
Corby NN17 ....**22** F1
5 Northampton NN2 .... **159** C7
Adelaide Pl 7 NN1 ..... **159** C5
Adelaide St NN2........ **159** C7
Adelaide Terr 1 NN2 ... **159** C7
Adit View NN9.......... **131** D8
Admiral Ct
Kettering NN16 ....**72** C3
Market Harborough
LE16 ....**31** D3
Admirals Way NN11......**135** E2
Adnitt Ho LE17 ....**45** E5
Adnitt Rd
Northampton NN1........**159** F7
Rushden NN10.......... **132** A2
ADSTONE **186** B4
Afan Cl NN16.............**72** A5
Affleck Bridge NN9......**111** F4
Aggate Way NN6 .... **144** D4
Agnes Rd NN2.......... **159** C8
Agricultural Hos
CV47 .... **166** A5
Ainsdale Cl NN2.........**141** F3
Aintree Dr NN10........ **148** D8
Aintree Rd
Corby NN18..............**36** E1
Northampton NN3 ....**141** F4
Aislable Ho OX16....... **219** A7
Akela Cl NN15 ....**91** C8
Akeley Wood Jun Sch
MK19 .... **228** A1
Akeley Wood Lower Sch
MK18..................**226** B4
Alanbrooke Cl NN15 ......**72** E1
Alastor NN8.............**129** B5
Albany Ct LE16 ....**31** F4
Albany Gdns NN18........**36** B2
Albany Rd
Market Harborough
LE16 ....**31** F4
Northampton NN1....... **160** A7
Albany The 6 NN11..... **135** C2
Alberta Cl NN18 ....**36** C3
Albert Pl NN1 .... **159** D6
Albert Rd
Finedon NN9 ....**111** F5
Market Harborough LE16 ...**31** F3
Rushden NN10...........**132** B2
Wellingborough NN8......**130** B5
Albert St 3 NN16.........**72** C2
Albion Ct
Little Harrowden NN9.... **110** C4
Northampton NN1 ...... **159** D5
Albion Ho NN1 .... **159** D5
Albion Pl
Northampton NN1....... **159** D5
Rushden NN10...........**132** B1
Albion Rd NN16 ....**72** B3
Albisdene Ct NN10...... **132** C2
Alchester Ct NN12...... **203** C5
Alcombe Rd NN1 ....**159** E7
Alcombe Terr NN1 ....**159** E7
Aldbury Ct 12 NN1...... **159** C7
Aldene Rd MK19.........**207** B3
Alder Cl NN14 ....**51** C3
Alder Ct NN3............**142** F5
Alderley Cl NN5 ....**158** B8
ALDERTON **205** A2
ALDGATE **1** B5
Aldgate Ct PE9 ....**1** A5
Aldsworth Cl NN8 ....**145** E8
Aldwell Cl NN4 ....**175** F7
ALDWINCLE **76** F8
Aldwincle Rd NN14 ....**76** A6
Aldwinkles Yd 4 LE16 ....**31** E3
Alexander Ct
Corby NN17...............**22** A2
Irchester NN29..........**147** B8
Northampton NN3........**142** E3
Alexander Pl NN9....... **113** A4
Alexander Rd NN9 ...... **113** A4
Alexandra Rd
Corby NN17 ....**36** E6
Desborough NN14.........**50** F3
Northampton NN1........**159** E6
Rushden NN10.......... **132** D2
Wellingborough NN8......**130** B5
Alexandra St
Burton Latimer NN15 ......**92** B2
Kettering NN16 ....**72** C2
Alexandra Terr 5
NN2.................. **141** C3
Alfoxden NN8 ....**129** B3
Alfred St
Irchester NN29......... **147** A8
Kettering NN16 ....**72** C2
Northampton NN1........**159** F6
Rushden NN10...........**132** B2
Stanwick NN9 ....**113** F4
Alfred Street Jun Sch
NN10..................**132** B2
Alibone Cl NN3......... **126** D1
Alice Ct NN6 ....**100** F6
Alice Dr NN15 ....**92** B1
Alice Gdns NN16..........**72** D3
Alington Cl NN9 .... **112** A5
Alken Cl NN8............**129** F8
Allan Bank NN8 ....**129** B3
Allans Cl CV23............**80** A5
Allans Dr CV23 ....**80** A5
Allard Cl NN3........... **143** D4
Allebone Rd NN6 ....**144** E3
Alledge Dr NN14..........**94** D7
Allen Ct NN9 .... **112** A5
Allen Rd
Finedon NN9 .... **112** A5
Irthlingborough NN9......**112** E1
Northampton NN1....... **160** A7
Rushden NN10.......... **132** C3
Allens Gate NN13....... **233** D7
Allens Hill NN29 .... **164** D3
Allens Orch OX17 ....**196** F6
Alliance Ct 2 NN8...... **130** A5
Alliance Terr NN8........**129** F5
Alliston Gdns 3 NN2 ... **159** C7
All Saints CE Mid Sch
NN2...................**141** E6
All Saints' CE Prim Sch
NN8 ....**130** B4
Alma St
Northampton NN5 .... **159** A6
Wellingborough NN8..... **130** A5
Almond Cl
Barby CV23 ....**99** C1
Bugbrooke NN7......... **173** A7
Almond Gr NN3 .... **142** C1
Almond Rd NN16 ....**72** D4
Almshouses NN6 ....**102** B5
Almshouses The
MK46..................**194** E2
Alness Cl NN15 ....**91** E8
Alpine Rd NN10..........**131** F2
Alpine Way NN5........ **140** A3
Alsace Cl NN5............**139** F2
Altendiez Way NN15 ......**92** B4
Althorp★ NN7 .... **139** A7
Althorp Cl
Market Harborough
LE16 ....**32** B3
Wellingborough NN8..... **129** C7
Althorpe Pl NN16.........**72** D3
Althorp Pl NN18...........**36** B3
Althorp Rd NN5 .... **159** A6
Althorp St 16 NN1 ...... **159** C6
Alton St NN4 ....**159** B3
Alvington Way LE16........**31** D5
Alvis Ct NN3.............. **143** C4
Alvis Way NN11...........**134** F3
Amber Dr NN6........... **108** A5
Amberley Rd NN7........ **192** C1
Ambleside Cl
9 Northampton NN3 .... **142** C4
Wellingborough NN8..... **129** C5
Ambridge Cl NN4........**174** F8
Ambridge Ct 8 NN1.....**159** F6

Ambush St NN5 159 B6
Amen Cnr NN14 113 C8
Amen Pl NN14 113 C8
Amundsen Cl NN11 135 B5
Ancell Rd MK11 229 E5
Anchor Dr NN2 141 B6
Anderson Ave CV22 98 A8
Anderson Dr NN15 72 F1
Anderson Gn NN8 129 C4
Anding Cl MK46 195 E4
Andrew Cl NN10 132 C7
Andrew Macdonald Cl
LE16 31 F3
Andrews Ave NN13 238 E6
Andrews Way NN9 114 B5
Angel Ct 2 LE16 31 E3
Angel La 2 NN8 130 A4
Angel St
1 Market Harborough
LE16 31 E3
Northampton NN1 159 D5
Angel Yd 10 NN16 72 B2
Anglian Rd NN11 135 B1
Anglia Way NN3 141 F6
Angus Ho NN17 36 F6
Anjou Ct NN5 139 F2
Annandale Rd NN17 36 E7
Anna's La NN12 173 B1
Anne Cl NN10 132 C7
Anne Rd NN8 129 E2
Annesley Cl NN3 160 D6
Anne St NN17 36 E5
Ann Sq NN16 72 E3
Anscomb Way NN11 184 B6
Ansell Way NN4 175 E8
Anson Cl
Corby NN17 36 B7
Daventry NN11 135 D1
ANTELOPE HILL 233 E8
Anthony Ct MK11 229 D5
Antona Cl NN9 114 B4
Antona Dr NN9 114 B4
Antona Gdns NN9 114 B4
Anvil The NN7 172 F7
APETHORPE 14 C3
Apethorpe Rd PE8 15 C6
Apollo Cl NN11 135 B3
Applebarn Cl NN4 175 C4
Appleby Cl NN9 110 F1
Appleby Wlk 2 NN3 142 C4
Appledore Cl NN2 141 C4
Applegarth Cl NN18 36 D3
Applegarth The NN6 121 C4
APPLETREE 196 C8
Appletree Ct NN9 111 F5
Appletree Ind Est
OX17 196 E7
Appletree La NN11 182 F2
Appletree Rd OX17 196 F6
Approach The NN5 158 F6
Aquitaine Cl NN5 139 F1
Arbour Ct NN3 142 E4
Arbours Prim Sch The
NN3 142 D3
Arbour View Ct NN3 142 E5
Arbury Banks OX17 196 F5
Archangel Rd 2 NN4 158 F2
Archangel Sq 1 NN4 158 F2
Archer Ave NN11 118 C1
Archers Cl NN2 141 B5
Archers Spinney CV21 99 B8
Archery Rd OX17 209 A1
Archfield NN8 129 F4
Archfield Terr 2 NN9 112 F2
Arden Cl
3 Daventry NN11 135 B4
Kettering NN15 91 F5
Market Harborough
LE16 32 A4
Ardens Gr NN7 174 A7
Arden Way LE16 31 F5
Ardington Rd NN1 160 A7
Argyle Pk LE16 48 E8
Argyle St NN5 159 A6
Argyll Ho NN17 36 E6
Argyll St
Corby NN17 36 F6
Kettering NN15 91 B8
Ariel Cl NN5 140 A1
Arkwright Rd
Corby NN17 22 C1
Irchester NN29 147 C7
Arlbury Rd NN3 143 B4
Armley Cl NN6 121 C4
ARMSTON 59 E8
Armston Rd PE8 59 B8
Arndale NN2 140 F5
Arnheim Hos NN11 199 D7
Arnhill Rd NN17 10 B1
Arnills Way CV23 100 A2
Arnold Cott MK19 229 B7
Arnold Rd NN2 159 C8
Arnsby Cres NN3 126 B1
Arnsley Rd NN17 23 A1
Arnull Cres NN11 135 B4
Arran Way NN17 36 C8
Arrow Cl OX17 220 A8
Arrow Head Rd NN4 158 F3
ARTHINGWORTH 68 C8
Arthingworth Rd NN14 50 E4
Arthur St
Northampton NN2 141 C1
Wellingborough NN8 129 E4
Arthur's Way 1 NN16 72 C2
Artizan Rd NN1 159 F7
Arum Cl NN10 148 C7
Arundel Cl
Kings Sutton OX17 230 F5

Arundel Cl *continued*
Thrapston NN14 76 F2
Arundel Ct
Kettering NN15 91 F8
Rushden NN10 148 A8
Arundel St 9 NN1 159 C7
Arundel Wlk NN18 36 B5
Ascot Cl NN18 36 E1
Ascot Rd NN10 148 D8
Ashbourne Dr NN14 50 E4
Ashbrook Cl NN14 90 A4
Ashbrow Rd NN4 158 F3
Ashburnham Rd NN1 159 F8
Ashby Cl NN8 129 E7
Ashby Ct
Guilsborough NN6 103 E7
Kislingbury NN7 157 D3
Moulton NN3 126 C1
Ashby Dr
Crick NN6 100 F5
Rushden NN10 148 A8
Ashby Fields Prim Sch
NN11 135 C5
Ashby Gdns 4 NN3 126 C1
Ashby Pk NN11 135 C4
Ashby Rd
Braunston NN11 118 C1
Daventry NN11 135 B4
Daventry NN11 135 B7
Daventry NN11 135 C2
Kilsby CV23 100 A2
Welton NN11 119 D1
ASHBY ST LEDGERS 119 D5
Ash Cl
Daventry NN11 135 C4
Irchester NN29 147 A7
Ashcroft Cl NN5 140 B1
Ashcroft Gdns NN3 142 A2
Ash Ct NN14 76 D1
Ashdale Cl NN6 127 D1
Ashdown Cl NN15 92 A5
Ashdown Pl NN17 36 E7
Ashdown Rd NN11 135 C4
Ash Dr
Brackley NN13 222 F1
Sywell NN6 143 D7
Ashes The
Bugbrooke NN7 172 F7
Northampton NN4 176 B6
Weldon NN17 38 C8
Ashfield Ave NN9 114 D6
Ashfield Rd
3 Market Harborough
LE16 31 E4
Wellingborough NN8 129 E4
Ashfield Rise NN9 114 C6
Ashford Cl NN3 160 C6
Ashford Lea NN14 50 E4
Ashgate Ct NN14 70 C7
Ash Gr
Bugbrooke NN7 172 F7
Desborough NN14 50 E4
Northampton NN2 141 B6
Ash La NN4 175 B4
Ashlade OX17 220 B7
Ashlawn Rd CV22 98 C7
Ashlawn Sch CV22 98 E7
Ashlea MK46 195 E3
Ashleigh Cl CV23 99 C2
Ashleigh Ho 6 NN10 132 B2
ASHLEY 18 E2
Ashley Ave NN17 36 B7
Ashley Ct
Blisworth NN7 190 D7
Kettering NN16 72 A3
Ashley La NN3 126 D1
Ashley Rd
Medbourne LE16 18 E6
Middleton LE16 20 B2
Stoke Albany LE16 34 A5
Weston by W LE16 18 C3
Ashley Way
Market Harborough
LE16 32 B3
Northampton NN3 142 E2
Ashmead NN3 143 A2
Ashmore NN6 121 C4
Ashpole Spinney NN4 158 C2
Ash Rd NN15 72 D1
Ashridge Cl NN10 148 A8
Ash Rise NN2 141 C6
Ash St NN1 159 C7
ASHTON
Oundle 42 D5
Roade 205 E8
Ashton CE Prim Sch
NN7 191 F1
Ashton Cl NN11 135 A3
Ashton Gr NN8 129 D8
Ashton Lodge Farm
NN7 192 A2
Ashton Rd
Hartwell NN7 192 C1
Oundle PE8 42 B5
Roade NN7 191 E2
Stoke Bruerne NN12 205 D8
Ash Tree Ct OX17 220 B8
Ashtree Gdns PE9 1 D2
Ashtree Way NN5 158 C7
Ashurst Cres NN18 36 B4
Ash Way
Braunston NN11 118 B1
Hinton NN11 184 A6
Ashway The
Brixworth NN6 106 C1
Brixworth NN6 125 B8
Ashwell Rd
Rushden NN10 132 D2

Ashwell Rd *continued*
Weedon Lois NN12 200 B2
Ashwells La NN6 82 B4
Ashwin Cl NN13 222 E1
Ashwood Rd NN5 158 C7
Ashworth Cl NN6 101 A6
Ashworth St NN11 135 C1
Askham Ave NN8 129 E1
Aspen Cl
Northampton NN3 143 C3
Rushden NN10 132 B3
Aspen Ho NN15 72 A1
Aspreys MK46 195 E4
Astbury Cl NN11 153 C8
ASTCOTE 188 F7
Aster Cl NN3 160 D6
Aster Rd NN16 72 D4
Astley Cl LE16 31 D1
Astley Pl CV21 99 B7
ASTON LE WALLS 182 F2
Aston Rise NN5 158 B8
Astral Row OX17 210 E2
ASTROP 231 B5
Astrop Gdns OX17 231 A5
Astrop Grange OX17 231 A5
Astrop Rd
Kings Sutton OX17 231 A5
Middleton Cheney
OX17 219 F6
ASTWICK 239 B7
Athelstan Rd NN16 72 D2
Atterbury Cl NN6 102 D4
Atterbury Way NN4 160 F2
Attlee Cl NN3 142 B4
Attley Ct NN8 129 C5
Attley Way NN9 113 A3
Auctioneers Ct NN1 159 D4
Auctioneers Way
NN1 159 D4
Auden Way NN17 36 C8
Audley Cl LE16 32 B2
Augusta Ave NN4 175 C6
Augustus Rd MK11 229 E4
Auriga St LE16 31 F2
Auriol Cotts NN13 221 B4
Austin Cl NN29 147 C8
Austin Ho NN14 70 D7
Austins Cl LE16 31 D3
Austins Pl NN12 214 E4
Austin St NN1 159 D7
Austins Yd NN6 144 E4
Austin Way NN11 134 F4
Avalon Ct NN14 70 E7
Avebury Way NN4 175 B8
Avenue Bernard
NN13 233 E8
Avenue Cl NN9 111 E5
Avenue Inf Sch The
NN8 130 A5
Avenue Rd
Finedon NN9 111 E5
Rushden NN10 148 F5
Wellingborough NN8 130 A5
Avenue Terr NN16 72 E3
Avenue The
Flore NN7 155 E5
Medbourne LE16 19 C8
Middleton Cheney
OX17 220 A8
Moulton NN3 142 E8
Northampton, Dallington
NN5 158 F7
Northampton, Meadow View
NN2 140 F6
Northampton NN1 159 F5
Northampton, Spinney Hill
NN3 142 A3
Rothwell NN14 70 D7
Stanwick NN9 114 A3
Wellingborough NN8 130 A5
Whitfield NN13 223 D4
Aviemore Gdns NN4 158 E1
Avignon Cl NN5 140 A2
Avonbury Ct NN13 234 A5
Avon Cl
Daventry NN11 153 A8
Kettering NN16 72 A5
Wellingborough NN8 129 C6
Avondale Jun & Inf Schs
NN16 72 D4
Avondale Mews NN16 72 D3
Avondale Rd NN16 72 D3
Avon Dr NN5 140 E1
Avon Fields NN6 64 E6
Avon Wks NN16 72 D3
Axe Head Rd NN4 158 F4
AYNHO 237 D7
Aynho Cres NN2 141 C5
Aynho Ct OX17 237 D7
Aynhoe Pk OX17 237 C7
Aynho (Fishing Venue)*
OX17 236 F6
Aynho Rd OX17 230 D2
Aynho Wlk NN2 141 D5
Aynsley Cl NN14 50 F3
Ayr Cl NN18 36 E1
Azalea Cl NN3 160 D6

B

Back La
Brigstock NN14 55 F8
Chapel Brampton NN6 124 D1
Collyweston PE8 1 D2
East Farndon LE16 48 B7
Elton PE8 28 D8
Gayton NN7 173 E2

Back La *continued*
Great Brington NN7 138 C6
Holcot NN6 126 E8
Little Addington NN14 113 B8
Morcott LE15 3 A6
Northampton NN4 175 F8
Ringstead NN14 95 B3
Scaldwell NN6 106 F5
South Luffenham LE15 3 D8
Backley Cl NN15 90 E8
Back Rd LE15 3 E5
Backway NN29 146 D2
Backway The LE16 31 F2
Bacon Hill MK46 195 E4
Bacon Rd NN8 129 F8
BADBY 153 A2
Badby Cl NN2 141 E4
Badby Leys CV22 98 A7
Badby Pk NN11 135 A5
Badby Rd
Daventry NN11 135 C1
Newnham NN11 153 D4
Badby Rd W
Daventry NN11 153 A7
Daventry NN11 153 B8
Badby Sch NN11 152 F3
Baden Powell Cres
NN12 203 C4
Badger La NN4 175 F3
Badgers Cl NN7 172 F7
Badgers Hyde NN13 232 F6
Badgers La NN14 89 C5
Badgers Wlk NN2 141 B5
Baffin Cl NN14 70 E7
Bailey Brooks Cl NN7 191 C5
Bailey Brooks La NN7 191 C5
Bailey Ct NN10 132 B5
Bailiff St NN1 159 D7
Baines Pl NN12 214 E4
Baines Way NN4 175 E3
Baird Ave NN5 158 D4
Baird Cl NN11 135 B5
Baird Ct NN8 129 B6
Baird Rd NN17 22 D1
Bairstow Rd NN12 203 C5
Bakehouse Hill
Geddington NN14 54 A3
Little Addington NN14 113 B8
Bakehouse La
Burton Latimer NN15 92 C3
Mears Ashby NN6 128 B2
Bakehouse Mews
NN14 90 B4
Bakehouse Rise NN6 85 B8
Baker Ave NN14 90 A3
Baker Ct NN14 76 D1
Bakers Cres NN29 147 A8
Bakers La
Norton NN11 136 C4
Spratton NN6 105 B1
Stoke Bruerne NN12 205 A8
Walgrave NN6 108 A4
Woodford NN14 94 D6
Baker's La NN12 204 D8
Baker St
Farthinghoe NN13 221 B4
Gayton NN7 173 E2
Irthlingborough NN9 112 E1
Northampton NN2 159 C8
3 Wellingborough
NN8 130 A5
Bakewell Cl NN4 174 F8
Balcombe Ct CV22 98 E8
Balcombe Pl NN18 36 A5
Balcombe Rd CV22 98 D8
Balding Cl CV23 99 C1
Baldwin Cl NN3 142 B4
Baler Cl NN11 135 C6
Balfour Cl NN2 141 C1
Balfour Dr NN14 70 E7
Balfour Gdns LE16 31 D1
Balfour Rd NN2 141 D1
Balfour St NN16 72 C4
Balham Cl NN10 147 F8
Balland Way NN4 175 F7
Ballantyne Rd NN10 132 A1
Balliol Rd
Brackley NN13 233 D8
Daventry NN11 153 B8
Balmoral NN18 36 C3
Balmoral Ave NN10 132 C3
Balmoral Cl
Earls Barton NN6 144 F3
Market Harborough LE16 32 B2
Towcester NN12 203 B5
Wellingborough NN8 129 E1
Balmoral Ct NN15 91 C5
Balmoral Dr NN13 233 E7
Balmoral Ho NN2 141 C1
Balmoral Rd NN2 141 C1
Balmoral Way OX17 230 F6
Baltic Cl NN18 36 A2
Bamburg Cl NN18 36 A1
Bamburgh Cl LE16 32 B3
Bampton Ct NN18 36 F4
BANBURY 219 A6
Banbury Bsns Pk
OX17 230 D3
Banbury Cl
Northampton NN4 158 D2
Wellingborough NN8 129 E1
Banbury La
Banbury OX17 219 B8
Banbury OX17 219 C8
Blakesley NN12 186 D2
Byfield NN11 183 D7
Cold Higham NN12 188 B7
Culworth OX17 198 E3

Banbury La *continued*
Foxley NN12 187 D4
Gayton NN7 173 D4
Great Easton LE16 20 D6
Kings Sutton OX17 230 E6
Middleton Cheney
OX17 209 C4
Northampton NN4 158 D1
Rothersthorpe NN7 174 B7
Thorpe Mandeville
OX17 210 B8
Weston NN12 199 C3
Banbury Rd
Aynho OX17 237 C7
Brackley NN13 233 E6
Byfield NN11 183 D7
Chacombe OX17 208 C3
Chipping Warden OX17 196 F6
Litchborough NN12 171 C1
Lower Boddington
NN11 182 C4
Moreton Pinkney NN11 199 C7
Twyford OX17 230 A6
Bancroft Cl NN4 176 A6
Bancroft Rd LE16 20 D1
Bancroft Way NN4 176 A6
Bangrave Rd NN17 37 F8
Bangrave Rd S NN17,
NN18 37 F6
Bank Cotts LE16 46 C8
Bankfield Dr LE16 32 A5
Bank Hill View NN9 110 C4
Bankside
Corby NN18 36 D3
Higham Ferrers NN10 132 B7
Northampton NN2 141 F3
Woodford Halse NN11 184 C6
Banks The
Broughton NN14 90 B5
Hackleton NN7 177 B3
Kilsby CV23 100 A2
Long Buckby NN6 121 B4
Wellingborough NN9 129 F8
Bank View NN4 175 B7
Banner Cl NN10 132 A1
Bannerman Dr NN13 233 D7
Bants La NN5 158 E7
Baptists Cl NN7 172 F7
BARBY 99 D1
Barby CE Prim Sch
CV23 118 C8
Barby La
Braunston NN11 118 C2
Rugby CV23 99 B5
BARBY NORTOFT 99 F6
Barby Rd
Kilsby CV23 99 F3
Rugby CV22 98 B7
Bardsley Rd NN17 21 E3
Barford MK11 229 F4
Baring Ho NN5 159 A7
Baring Rd NN5 159 A7
Barker Cl NN10 132 C2
Barker Rd NN6 144 E3
Barksdale Ave NN13 238 E6
Barley Cl
Daventry NN11 135 C6
Hartwell NN7 192 E2
Rugby CV21 99 A8
Barley Croft NN6 100 F6
Barley Ct NN10 148 C8
Barley Dr NN15 92 C2
Barley Hill OX17 198 D2
Barley Hill Rd NN3 142 F6
Barley La NN2 141 B5
Barlow Cl NN14 70 B7
Barlow Ct NN15 92 B1
Barlow La NN3 126 C1
Barlows La LE16 34 C5
Barn Acre NN6 122 D5
Barnard NN18 36 C3
Barnard Cl NN5 158 B8
Barnard Gdns LE16 48 D8
Barnard's Way NN14 56 A6
Barn Cl
Corby NN18 36 B1
Northampton NN4 175 F3
Barn Cnr NN4 175 C4
Barn Ct
Helmdon NN13 211 F4
Little Harrowden NN9 110 C4
Barnes Cl
Daventry NN11 135 B3
Kettering NN15 91 B7
Old NN6 107 D7
Barnes Mdw* NN4 159 F4
Barnes Meadow Intc
NN4 160 A4
Barneswell Cl NN6 106 B2
Barnet Cl NN4 159 A2
Barnett Cres NN11 184 B6
Barnett Rd OX17 219 F8
Barnfield Cl NN2 141 B4
Barnhill Sq NN3 143 A6
Barn La NN7 174 F2
Barn Mews NN4 175 C4
Barn Owl Cl NN4 175 A8
Barnsdale LE16 20 D6
Barnsdale Cl LE16 20 D6
Barnsley Sq NN18 36 C4
Barnstaple Cl NN3 160 E7
Barns The
Irchester NN29 131 B1
Mears Ashby NN6 128 C2

Barnstones Bsns Pk NN12 187 E7
Barn Way NN5 140 C2
BARNWELL 59 B6
Barnwell CE Prim Sch PE8 59 B6
Barnwell Cl NN14 76 E2
Barnwell Ctry Pk* PE8 41 E3
Barnwell Ctry Pk Visitor Ctr* PE8 41 F3
Barnwell Dr NN10 148 A8
Barnwell Gdns NN8 129 D7
Barnwell Rd
Northampton NN2 141 D4
Oundle PE8 41 F3
Wellingborough NN8 129 E7
Barnwell St NN16 72 D2
Barnwell Workshops PE8 59 B8
Baron Ave
Earls Barton NN6 144 F6
Kettering NN16 71 E3
Baron Ct
Corby NN17 22 E1
Northampton NN1 159 F8
Baronson Gdns NN1 159 F8
Barons Way NN2 141 A4
Barrack Rd NN1, NN2 159 C7
Barracks The NN7 161 D2
Barratt Cl NN10 132 B5
Barrett Cl NN8 129 C4
Barringers Ct NN29 131 B1
Barringers Gdns NN29 131 B1
Barrington Ct NN13 233 F5
Barrington Rd NN10 148 C8
Barron Cl NN15 91 C6
BARROWDEN 3 E5
Barrowden La LE15 3 E8
Barrowden Rd
Barrowden PE9 4 C8
Ketton PE9 1 A4
South Luffenham LE15 3 F7
Barry Prim Sch NN1 160 A7
Barry Rd NN1 160 A6
Barth Cl NN18 36 B2
Bartholomew Gdns NN12 187 A1
Bartlett Ct NN13 233 D7
Bartley Dr NN16 71 F4
Barton Cl OX17 230 F6
Barton Fields NN6 143 F3
Barton Holme NN12 187 A1
Barton Rd NN15 91 E7
Bartons Cl The 2 NN5 140 F1
BARTON SEAGRAVE 92 A7
Barton Seagrave Prim Sch NN15 92 A6
Barton Sq NN18 36 B6
Barwick Ho 10 NN10 132 B2
Basil Cl NN4 175 D6
Bassett Ct NN4 175 D2
Bassett Ford Rd PE8 42 A4
Bassett Lowke Ho NN1 159 D5
Bassett Pl PE8 42 A4
Bassett's Ct NN8 129 F4
Bassett Way LE16 67 A8
Bates Ave NN14 95 B3
Bates Cl
Higham Ferrers NN10 132 B5
Market Harborough LE16 31 E5
Bates La OX27 237 D3
Bath La NN16 72 C3
Bath Rd NN16 72 C4
Bath St LE16 31 E1
Batsmans Dr NN10 132 A4
Battalion Dr NN4 175 E7
Battle Cl
Cranford St John NN14 93 A6
Northampton NN4 175 D7
Baukewell Ct 4 NN3 142 E3
Baulmsholme Cl NN4 159 C4
Baunhill Cl NN3 160 D7
Baxter Ct NN4 175 F8
Bayard Brow NN13 233 E8
Bayes St NN16 72 A3
Bay La MK46 194 D2
Baysdale Ave NN17 36 E6
Beacon Ct NN4 158 E3
Beaconsfield Pl NN10 132 B3
Beaconsfield Terr
Northampton NN1 159 D7
Rushden NN10 132 B3
Beanfield Ave NN18 36 B5
Beanfield Prim Sch NN18 36 A5
Bean Furlong OX17 208 E4
Beardsley Ct NN18 36 D5
Beardsley Gdns NN15 92 A7
Beatrice Rd NN16 72 B5
Beatty Cl NN11 135 E1
Beatty Gdns NN17 36 B7
Beaufort Dr
Kettering NN15 92 A6
Northampton NN5 140 C1
Beauly Ct NN15 91 E8
Beaumaris Cl NN10 132 C1
Beaumont Cl NN16 72 B6
Beaumont Cres NN13 233 E7
Beaumont Dr NN3 143 C3
Beaune Cl NN5 139 F1
Beauvais Ct NN5 139 F1
Beaver Ctr The NN11 184 C7
Beck Ct NN8 129 D6
Becketts Cl NN11 183 D7
Beckett's View NN1 159 E5
Becket Way NN3 142 B4
Bective Rd NN2 141 C4
Bective View NN2 141 D4
Bedale Rd NN8 130 A6
Beddoes Cl NN4 176 A6
Bede Cl
Corby NN18 36 A1
Higham Ferrers NN10 132 C5
Bede Ho* LE15 9 D7
Bedford Cl NN15 91 F5
Bedford Cotts NN7 138 D7
Bedford Mans NN1 159 D5
Bedford Pl NN1 159 D5
Bedford Rd
Denton NN7 178 B8
Little Houghton NN7 160 F3
Northampton NN1 159 E4
Rushden NN10 148 D5
Bedford Rd E NN7 179 D5
Bedford Rd W NN7 179 A6
Beech Ave
Northampton NN3 142 A1
Olney MK46 195 E3
Beech Cl
Bugbrooke NN7 172 F7
Corby NN17 21 E1
Desborough NN14 51 A3
Hackleton NN7 177 B3
Towcester NN12 203 C4
Beech Cres
Irchester NN29 147 A7
Kettering NN15 72 D1
Beechcroft Gdns NN3 142 A2
Beech Ct
Rugby CV22 98 F8
Thrapston NN14 76 D2
Beech Dr
Brackley NN13 222 E1
Hinton NN11 184 B6
Wellingborough NN8 129 E5
Beeches Cl LE16 46 F2
Beeches The
Deanshanger MK19 228 E3
Pattishall NN12 172 E1
Beech Gr
Northampton NN3 142 D5
Rushden NN10 131 F3
Beech Hill NN11 151 D1
Beech House Dr NN12 217 F4
Beech La NN7 157 E4
Beech Rd NN10 132 B4
Beechwood Dr NN3 142 E1
Beechwood Rd NN5 158 C7
Beeston Ave NN3 160 F8
Beeston Pl NN18 36 C5
Belfield Cl NN3 142 B3
Belfry La NN4 175 B5
Belfry Way NN11 135 E2
Belgrave Cl NN15 92 A5
Bellamy Rd PE8 41 F7
Bell Cl NN13 211 F4
Bell Ct
Corby NN18 36 D4
5 Wellingborough NN8 130 A5
Belle Baulk NN12 203 A6
Bell End NN29 146 D2
Bellfield LE15 3 E8
Bellfields La LE16 32 A2
Bellfields St LE16 32 A2
Bellfoundry La 4 NN16 72 B2
Bell Hill
Finedon NN9 111 E4
Rothwell NN14 70 D7
BELLINGE 143 B1
Bellinge Prim Sch NN3 143 B1
Bell La
Byfield NN11 183 C7
Husbands Bosworth LE17 45 E5
Syresham NN13 224 B8
Bellropes Sq 5 NN3 143 D2
Bells Cl NN14 55 E8
Bell St NN8 130 A5
Bell Twr NN13 233 F7
Bell View OX17 231 F5
Bellway Cl NN16 72 A3
Bell Wlk CV21 99 A8
Belmont Ct 13 NN1 159 C7
Belmont Gdns NN9 114 C6
Belstead Rd NN3 160 D6
Belton Cl 4 NN4 175 C8
Belvedere Cl NN5 158 F7
Belvedere Rd NN15 72 D1
Belvoir Cl
Corby NN18 36 E2
Northampton NN5 140 B1
Rushden NN10 148 C8
Belvoir Dr NN15 92 A6
Bembridge Dr NN2 141 B1
Benbow Cl NN11 135 E2
Benedict Cl NN10 147 F8
Benefield Rd
Brigstock NN14 39 B2
Deenethorpe NN17 24 C4
Oundle PE8 41 C5
Bengal NN12 202 D7
Bengal La NN12 202 E7
Bengal View NN12 202 E8
Bengeworth Ct 10 NN8 130 A5
Benham Ct NN3 142 F3
Benham Rd NN12 202 D8
Benjamin Sq 6 NN4 158 F2
Bennett Cl
Chacombe OX17 208 E4
Daventry NN11 135 A4
Stony Stratford MK11 229 D4
Bennett Rd NN18 36 D1
Bens Cl MK19 218 F5
Bentley Cl NN3 143 D4
Bentley Ct NN9 111 B1
Bentley Way NN11 134 F3
Bentley Wlk NN18 36 C5
Bergen Wlk NN18 36 A2
Bergerac Cl NN5 139 F2
Berkeley Cl NN1 159 F6
Berkeley Ho 28 NN1 159 C6
Berkeley St LE16 46 F2
Berneshaw Cl NN18 36 D3
Bern Links NN4 159 A3
Bern Side NN4 159 A3
Berrell's Ct MK46 195 F3
Berridges La LE17 45 E5
Berrill St NN29 147 A7
Berrister Pl NN9 114 E7
Berry Cl
Earls Barton NN6 144 E5
Great Bowden LE16 32 A5
Hackleton NN7 177 B3
Rothersthorpe NN7 174 B6
Berrydale NN3 143 D4
Berryfield NN6 121 C4
Berry Field Rd LE16 20 C1
Berry Green Ct NN9 111 F5
Berry Green Pk NN14 78 E6
Berry Green Rd NN9 111 E5
Berry Hill Rd OX17 230 A2
Berry La
Hellidon NN11 151 C1
Northampton NN4 175 E5
Berrymoor Ct NN8 129 E2
Berrymoor Rd NN8 129 E2
Berry Rd LE16 20 C1
Berrywood Dr NN5 157 F7
Berrywood Rd NN5 158 A7
Bertha Way NN16 72 E4
Berwick Ho NN2 141 D5
Berwick Rd NN14 37 E3
Berwick Way NN15 92 A8
Bessemer Gr NN18 37 B6
Bestwell Ct 3 NN3 161 A8
Bestwood Cl NN14 50 F4
Beswood Gn NN18 36 C5
Beswick Cl NN14 52 C3
Bethany Homestead 1 NN2 141 E1
Bethel La NN11 170 B7
Betjeman Cl
Daventry NN11 135 A3
Higham Ferrers NN10 132 A5
Betony Wlk NN10 148 B8
Bettycroft Cl NN6 103 E1
Bevan Cl
Warmington PE8 28 B3
Wellingborough NN8 130 C7
Beverley Cl NN14 70 B7
Beverley Cres NN3 142 C1
Beverley Rd NN15 91 D8
Beverley Wlk NN18 36 C5
Bewick Ct NN18 36 E4
Bewick Rd NN3 160 E8
Bexhill Wlk NN18 36 B4
Bibury Cl NN8 129 D1
Bibury Cres NN3 142 D6
Bicester Hill NN13 233 F2
Bickerstaffes Rd NN12 203 C5
Bidders Cl NN1 159 D4
BIDDLESDEN 224 D5
Bideford Cl NN3 160 D7
Bideford Sq NN18 36 F5
Bies Cl NN18 36 C2
Big Gn PE8 28 C3
Bignal Ct NN15 90 E8
Billing Aquadrome* NN7 161 B7
Billing Arbours Ho NN3 142 E4
Billing Brook Rd NN3 142 F4
Billing Brook Specl Sch NN3 142 F3
Billing La
Moulton NN6 126 F1
Northampton NN3, NN6 143 A7
Billing Rd
Brafield-on-t-G NN7 161 D4
Northampton NN1 159 F6
Billing Rd E NN3 160 D7
Billing School Pl NN7 155 C3
Billington St NN1 159 F7
Bilsdon Cl NN10 147 F8
Bilton Ct NN8 129 D5
Binbrook Wlk NN18 36 C4
Binder Cl NN10 132 A7
Binders Ct NN14 37 F2
Bingham Wlk NN18 36 C5
Birchall Rd NN10 131 F2
Birch Ave NN18 36 D4
Birch Barn Way NN2 141 B6
Birch Cl
Hinton NN11 184 B6
Northampton NN4 175 E2
Birch Ct NN10 132 C2
Birchfield Cres NN3 142 C2
Birchfield Ct NN3 142 B1
Birchfield Rd
Northampton NN1, NN3 142 A1
Wellingborough NN8 129 E4
Birchfield Rd E NN3 142 C1
Birchington Rd NN17 22 F2
Birch Rd
Kettering NN16 72 D3
Rushden NN10 132 C2
Birch Spinney NN14 89 A4
Birch Tree Gdns LE16 31 F4
Birchvale Ct NN14 50 E4
Birds Hill Rd
Eastcote NN12 188 F8
Northampton NN3 142 F3
Birds Hill Wlk NN3 142 F2
Bird St NN15 92 D3
Birkdale Cl
Daventry NN11 135 E2
Northampton NN2 141 F3
Birkdale Dr NN10 132 D1
Birling Pl NN18 36 B5
Birtley Coppice LE16 31 D4
Bishop Cl LE16 48 E8
Bishops Cl NN13 222 E1
Bishops Ct
4 Daventry NN11 135 C2
Higham Ferrers NN10 132 C7
Bishops Dr NN2 141 B3
Bishop's Dr NN15 91 B6
Bishop Stopford Sch NN15 91 B7
Bishops Way NN18 36 A4
Bitten Ct NN3 142 E3
Blackberry Cl NN16 72 B6
Blackberry La NN4 158 F3
Blackbird Cl NN13 222 E1
Blackbridge Ct NN14 76 C2
Black Cat Dr NN5 158 D4
Blackdown MK11 229 F4
Blackfriars NN10 147 F8
Blackfriars Ho 19 NN1 159 C6
Black Lion Hill NN1 159 B5
Blacklocks Hill OX17 219 B8
Blackmile La NN7 163 E7
Blackmires La NN12 214 B5
Blackmoor Ave NN18 36 F4
Blackpot La PE8 42 A5
Blacksmith's Cl NN12 172 D1
Blacksmiths Gn NN12 204 D8
Blacksmiths Hill OX17 237 C7
Blacksmiths La
Eydon NN11 184 C1
Little Brington NN7 138 B4
Blacksmith's La
Aston le W NN11 182 F2
Pytchley NN14 90 F2
Blacksmith's Way NN7 192 C1
Black Swan Spinney PE8 8 A4
BLACKTHORN 143 B4
Blackthorn Bridge Ct 4 NN3 143 B4
Blackthorn Cl
Kettering NN16 72 C6
Spratton NN6 105 A1
Blackthorn Prim Sch NN3 143 B4
Blackthorn Rd NN3 143 B4
Blackwall Cl 1 NN4 159 A2
Blackwell Cl
Earls Barton NN6 144 E4
Higham Ferrers NN10 132 B7
Towcester NN12 203 D4
Blackwell End NN12 217 C3
Blackwell Hill NN4 174 F8
Blackwell Rd NN15 91 F4
Blackwells Yd NN7 179 B6
BLACKY MORE 175 C7
Blackymore La NN4 175 D5
Bladon Cl NN3 142 C4
Blake Cl NN11 153 E8
Blake Ct NN15 92 A8
Blake Rd NN18 36 D4
Blakesely Hill NN12 202 D8
BLAKESLEY 187 B1
Blakesley CE Prim Sch NN12 187 B1
Blakesley Cl NN2 141 C5
Blakesley Rd NN12 200 F7
Blake Wlk NN10 132 A5
Blanchard Cl 3 NN4 175 E7
Blandford Ave NN16 72 B5
Blandford Ct NN18 36 A6
BLATHERWYCKE 12 E4
Blatherwycke Rd PE8 13 E7
Blaydon Wlk NN8 129 E6
Bleaklow Cl NN14 50 E3
Bledlow Rise NN4 174 F8
Blencowe Dr NN13 233 D7
Blenheim NN13 238 B7
Blenheim Ave MK11 229 E4
Blenheim Cl NN10 148 A8
Blenheim Croft NN13 233 F6
Blenheim Pl NN13 224 C7
Blenheim Rd
Northampton NN4 159 B2
Wellingborough NN8 129 D7
Blenheim Rise OX17 230 F6
Blenheim Way
Kettering NN15 91 C5
Market Harborough LE16 31 E5
Blenheim Wlk NN18 36 C3
Blinco Rd NN10 132 C3
Blind La LE16 20 D1
Bliss Charity Sch The NN7 156 C2
Bliss La NN7 155 F5
BLISWORTH 190 E7
Blisworth Cl NN4 159 A2
Blisworth Com Prim Sch NN7 190 D8
Blisworth Mill NN7 190 C7
Blisworth Rd
Gayton NN7 173 F1
Roade NN7 191 B4
Bloomfield Cl NN10 132 A2
Blossac Ct NN5 139 F1
Blossom Ct 2 NN16 72 C4
Blossom Way NN3 143 A1
Blotts Barn Bsns Ctr NN9 114 F8
Bluebell Cl
Corby NN18 36 D2
Hinton NN11 184 B7
Kettering NN16 72 E4
Rushden NN10 148 C8
Wellingborough NN8 130 B6
Bluebell Ct NN3 160 C6
Bluebell Pk Cvn Pk 2 NN3 126 C1
Bluebell Rise
Northampton NN4 175 F1
Rushden NN10 148 B8
Blueberry Cl NN6 87 B6
Blueberry Rise 2 NN3 143 C2
Bluecoat La LE15 9 D7
Blythe Cl NN14 70 E6
Blyton Ct NN18 36 C4
Boarden Cl NN3 142 A7
Boardman Rd NN15 90 F8
Board St NN9 112 F2
Boat Horse La NN6 101 A5
Boathouse The LE16 31 D4
Bobtail Ct NN5 140 C1
Boddington CE Sch NN11 182 C7
Boddington Ct NN11 182 C5
Boddington Mews NN15 91 C8
Boddington Rd
Byfield NN11 183 C7
Claydon OX17 181 D1
Kettering NN15 91 C8
Boddington Way NN13 233 D8
Boden Cl NN18 36 A2
Bodiam CL NN14 76 E2
Bodiam Pl NN18 36 A5
Bodleian Cl NN11 153 B8
Bognor Rd NN18 36 B4
Bolingbroke Pl NN10 132 C7
Bollinger Cl NN5 139 F1
Boltons Cl NN13 222 E1
Bondfield Ave NN2 141 D3
Bonham Ct NN16 72 C3
Bonington Wlk NN18 36 D5
Bonnington Cl CV21 80 B1
Bonsor Gdns NN14 95 A3
Boon Wlk NN17 37 B7
Booth Cl NN12 172 D1
Booth Dr NN8 129 A4
Booth La N NN3 142 C4
Booth La S NN3 142 D2
Booth Meadow Ct NN3 142 E5
Booth Rise NN3 142 D6
BOOTHVILLE 142 D5
Boothville Gn NN3 142 D5
Boothville Prim Sch NN3 142 C4
Bo-Peep Cvn Pk OX17 230 C2
Bordeaux Cl NN5 139 F1
Bordeaux Ct NN5 139 F1
BOROUGH 135 E2
Borough Ct
Brackley NN13 234 A5
Higham Ferrers NN10 132 B5
Borough Rd NN13 234 A5
Borrowdale Rd NN17 36 D8
Borrowdale Wlk 3 NN3 142 C4
Bostock Ave NN1 159 F7
Bostock Mews NN1 159 F7
Boston Cl NN18 36 C4
Boswell La MK19 228 E4
Bosworth Cl
Northampton NN4 159 A1
Warmington PE8 28 B3
Bosworth Independent Coll NN2 159 C8
Bosworth Rd
Husbands Bosworth LE17 45 A8
Theddingworth LE17 46 C7
Bothy The OX17 237 D7
Botmead Rd NN3 143 D4
Bottom La LE16 34 B5
Bougainvillea Dr NN3 160 C6
BOUGHTON 141 D8
Boughton NN15 91 D4
Boughton Cl NN18 36 A4
Boughton Dr NN10 148 A8
Boughton Fair La NN3 126 B4
Boughton Green Rd NN2, NN3 141 D5
Boughton Ho* NN14 73 C8
Boughton La NN3 141 F7
Boughton Prim Sch NN2 141 D8

Boughton Rd
Boughton NN2, NN3 141 F8
Corby NN18 36 D2
Moulton NN3 126 A1
Boughton Terr NN13 233 F2
Boundary Ave NN10 131 E1
Boundary Cres MK11 229 E6
Boundary Rd NN13 234 A6
Bourne Cl
Corby NN18 36 D2
Wellingborough NN8 129 C6
Bourne Cres NN5 140 E1
Bourton Cl NN4 174 E8
Bourton Way NN8 129 E1
Bouverie Rd NN4 175 E8
Bouverie St 1 NN1 159 F6
Bouverie Wlk 5 NN1 159 F6
Bovewell OX27 237 E3
Bow Ct NN4 158 E3
Bowden La
Market Harborough LE16 31 E4
Welham LE16 17 E4
Bowden Rd
Northampton NN5 159 A6
Thorpe Langton LE16 17 A4
Bowden Ridge LE16 32 A5
Bowen Rd CV22 98 D8
Bowen Sq 7 NN11 135 C1
Bowhill NN16 72 A1
Bowland Dr NN15 92 A5
Bowling Gn NN13 221 B4
Bowling Green Ave NN15 72 B1
Bowling Green La NN5 158 A6
Bowling Green Rd NN15 72 B1
Bowman Cl OX17 220 A8
Bowmans Cl NN4 158 D1
Bowmens Lea OX17 237 C7
Bowness NN8 129 D5
Bowthorpe Cl NN3 160 D6
Box Gdns NN8 130 A5
Boxwood Dr CV23 100 A3
Boyle Rd NN17 22 C1
BOZEAT 164 D3
Bozeat Com Prim Sch NN29 164 D3
Bozenham Mill La NN7 205 E4
Brabham Cl NN12 214 D4
Bracadale Wlk NN17 21 C1
Bracken Borough NN6 106 C2
Bracken Cl NN16 72 B5
Brackendale Dr CV23 99 C1
Bracken Field Sq NN3 142 F7
Brackenhill Cl NN2 141 E3
Bracken Leas Prim Sch NN13 222 E1
BRACKLEY 233 E7
Brackley CE Jun Sch NN13 233 F8
Brackley Cl NN2 141 D6
Brackley Cottage Hospl NN13 233 F7
Brackley Jun Sch NN13 233 E6
Brackley La NN12 201 F1
Brackley Lodge Mews NN13 233 F7
Brackley Rd
Croughton NN13 238 D8
Greatworth OX17 210 E1
Silverstone NN12 214 D3
Towcester NN12 203 B6
Westbury NN13 234 F5
Brackley Waynflete Inf Sch NN13 233 E7
BRACKMILLS 160 B1
Brackmills Ind Est NN4 160 A2
Bracknell NN8 129 C4
Bradbury Rd NN11 153 D3
BRADDEN 201 F6
Bradden Cl NN2 141 D5
Bradden Rd NN12 202 D8
Bradden Way NN12 202 D8
Bradfield Cl
Rushden NN10 132 D3
Wellingborough NN8 111 A1
Bradfield Rd NN8 111 A1
Bradford Wlk NN18 36 C5
Bradgate Ho NN1 159 E6
Bradmoor Ct NN3 143 B5
Bradmore Gdns NN18 36 C6
Bradshaw St 29 NN1 159 C6
Bradshaw Way NN29 146 F8
Braemar Cl NN15 91 E8
Braemar Cres NN4 175 C8
Brafield Leys CV22 98 A6
BRAFIELD-ON-THE-GREEN 161 E2
Brafield Rd
Cogenhoe NN7 161 E5
Horton NN7 177 E3
Braggintons La OX17 220 B8
Braid Ct NN8 129 D7
Braithwaite Cl NN15 90 F8
Brakey Rd NN17 37 F8
Bramber Ct NN18 36 A5
Bramble Cl
Kettering NN16 72 B6
Ringstead NN14 95 A3
Bramble End NN4 174 F8
Bramble Rd NN12 203 B4
Brambleside
Kettering NN16 72 C6
Thrapston NN14 76 D1
Brambleside Com Prim Sch NN16 72 C6
Brambleside Ct NN16 72 B6
Brambles The NN10 148 B5
Bramblewood Rd NN17 38 A8
BraMCote Dr NN3 160 F8
Bramhall Rise NN5 158 B8
Bramley Cl
Cogenhoe NN7 161 E6
Market Harborough LE16 31 F5
Rushden NN10 131 F3
Bramley Ct NN29 146 D3
Bramley Gr NN3 143 B2
Bramley Ho 7 NN11 135 C2
Brammar Ho NN5 158 F7
BRAMPTON ASH 33 E3
Brampton Cl
Kettering NN15 92 A5
Wellingborough NN8 129 D7
Brampton Hill LE16 33 F4
Brampton La
Boughton NN2, NN6 141 A7
Chapel Brampton NN6 125 A3
Bramptons Prim Sch The NN6 124 D1
Brampton Valley Way* NN6 124 E4
Brampton Way NN6 106 B1
Brampton Wlk NN3 141 F5
Brampton Wood La NN14 50 F7
Bramshill Ave NN16 72 A6
Bramston Cl PE8 42 A4
Brandenburg Rd NN18 35 F2
Brangwyn Wlk NN18 36 E5
Branksome Ave NN2 141 B1
Branksome Ct NN18 36 A6
Branson Ct NN16 72 A3
Branson Mews NN17 38 A8
Brasenose Dr NN13 233 D8
Brashland Dr NN4 175 D6
BRAUNSTON 118 C2
Braunston CE Prim Sch NN11 118 C1
Braunston Cl NN4 159 A2
Braunston La NN11 152 C8
Braunston Pl CV22 98 D8
Braunston Rd NN11 135 B2
Braunton Pl NN18 36 F4
Brawn Cl NN9 131 E8
Brawn Way PE8 16 D1
BRAYBROOKE 49 F5
Braybrooke Cl NN14 95 C3
Braybrooke Prim Sch LE16 49 E6
Braybrooke Rd
Arthingworth LE16 68 D8
Desborough NN14 50 F4
Dingley LE16 33 A3
Great Oxendon LE16 49 A3
Market Harborough LE16 32 B1
Brayford Ave NN18 36 F5
Brayford Cl NN3 160 C7
Breach Cl NN6 106 C2
Breakleys Rd NN14 51 B2
Breck Cl NN18 53 B8
Brecon Cl NN16 72 B6
Brecon St NN5 159 A8
Breedon Cl NN18 36 A1
Breezehill NN4 175 F6
Brembridge Cl NN6 127 D2
Brendon Cl NN3 160 D7
Brent Cl NN15 92 A2
Brentford NN8 129 B5
Brer Ct NN4 159 F5
Bressingham Gdns NN4 175 C7
Breton MK11 229 E6
Bretton Cl NN5 140 A1
Bretts La NN7 191 E4
Brewery Ct PE8 41 F4
Brewery Yd NN14 56 E1
Brewin Cl NN13 222 D1
Briar Cl NN13 222 F1
Briar Ct NN9 112 F2
BRIAR HILL 158 F3
Briar Hill Prim Sch NN4 158 F3
Briar Hill Rd NN4 159 B2
Briar Hill Wlk NN4 159 B2
Briar Rd NN16 72 E5
Briars The NN4 159 A3
Briarwood Way NN29 146 D1
Briary Cl NN12 203 B4
Brickett's La NN7 155 E5
Brickhill Mews NN8 129 E4
Brickhill Rd NN8 129 D4
Brick Kiln Cl NN12 203 D4
Brick Kiln La NN2 159 D8
Brick Kiln Rd NN9 114 D8
Brickwell Ct NN3 143 A1
Brickyard Spinney Rd NN3 142 B6
Bridewell Ho 21 NN16 72 B2
Bridewell La 11 NN16 72 B2
Bridge Ct
Corby NN17 37 A7
Thrapston NN14 76 C2
Bridge End PE8 8 A3
Bridge Ho NN14 70 D7
Bridge Mdw NN7 178 B8
Bridge Meadow Way NN4 175 F4
Bridgend NN6 82 B4
Bridge Rd
Cosgrove MK19 218 E2
Desborough NN14 50 F4
Stoke Bruerne NN12 205 A8
Bridge St
Apethorpe PE8 14 D4
Brackley NN13 233 E6
Brigstock NN14 55 E7
Geddington NN14 54 A2
Kettering NN16 72 C3
King's Cliffe PE8 14 A7
Northampton NN1 159 C5
Olney MK46 195 F2
Raunds NN9 114 D7
Rothwell NN14 70 D7
Thrapston NN14 76 C2
Weedon Bec NN7 155 B4
Weldon NN17 38 B8
Bridge View PE8 42 A6
Bridgewater Cl NN13 233 F8
Bridgewater Cres NN13 233 F8
Bridgewater Ct NN13 233 F8
Bridgewater Dr NN3 160 D7
Bridgewater Ho NN13 233 F8
Bridgewater Prim Sch NN3 160 C7
Bridgewater Rd NN13 233 F8
Bridgewater Rise NN13 233 F8
Bridge Wlk MK19 228 E4
Bridgford Pl NN18 36 C6
Bridgwater Ct NN18 36 A6
Bridle Cl
Brafield-on-t-G NN7 161 D2
Wellingborough NN8 111 A1
Bridle La NN6 84 B6
Bridle Path NN7 161 E2
Bridle Rd
Burton Latimer NN15 92 A2
Hannington NN6 108 C3
Old NN6 107 D7
Bridle Way NN14 90 A6
Briery Cl NN18 36 B1
Brigadier Cl NN4 175 D7
Brigg Ct NN18 36 C4
Brighouse Cl NN18 36 C4
Brighton Rd NN18 36 B4
Bright Trees Rd NN14 54 B3
Brightwell Wlk NN9 131 D8
BRIGSTOCK 55 E7
Brigstock Latham's CE Prim Sch NN14 55 F7
Brigstock Rd NN14 38 A2
Brindlestone Cl NN4 158 D2
Brindley Cl
Daventry NN11 135 A5
Rushden NN10 131 F4
Brindley Ct NN11 134 B8
Brindley Quay NN11 134 B8
Brindley Rd CV21 80 B1
BRINGHURST 20 C5
Bringhurst Prim Sch LE16 20 C6
Brington Dr NN15 91 F5
Brington Prim Sch NN7 138 C5
Brington Rd NN6 121 C3
Brinkhill Wlk NN18 36 C4
Brinsley Gn NN18 36 C6
Brisbane Gdns NN18 36 B2
Briscoe Cl NN2 141 E6
BRITAIN 173 F1
Britain Cotts NN7 173 F1
Britannia Gdns NN8 130 C4
Britannia Rd NN16 72 B5
Britannia Trad Ctr NN5 140 D2
Britannia Wlk LE16 31 F2
British La 17 NN16 72 B2
Briton Gdns NN3 142 B1
Briton Rd NN3 142 B1
Briton Terr NN3 142 B1
Britten Cl NN9 133 C8
Brittens View NN6 126 E8
Brittons Dr NN3 143 A7
Brixham Wlk NN18 36 F5
BRIXWORTH 106 A2
Brixworth CE Prim Sch NN6 106 B1
Brixworth Ctry Pk* NN6 125 C8
Brixworth Ctry Pk Visitor Ctr* NN6 125 C7
Brixworth Hall Pk NN6 106 B2
Brixworth Rd
Creaton NN6 104 F4
Holcot NN6 126 D8
Spratton NN6 105 D1
Broadgate LE16 20 D7
Broadgate Way PE8 28 C2
Broad Gn 4 NN8 129 F5
Broadhurst Dr NN3 161 A8
Broad La NN13 233 E3
Broadlands
Brixworth NN6 106 A1
Desborough NN14 51 C2
Pitsford NN6 125 D5
Raunds NN9 114 E6
Broad March NN11 153 D8
Broadmead Ave NN3 142 B2
Broadmead Ct NN3 142 B2
Broad St
Brixworth NN6 106 B1
Earls Barton NN6 144 E4
Northampton NN1 159 C6
Syresham NN13 224 B8
Broadstone Ct NN18 36 A6
Broadwater La NN12 203 A5
Broadway
Kettering NN15 91 B8
Northampton NN1, NN3 142 A1
Wellingborough NN8 130 A3
Broadway E NN3 142 B1
Broadway Terr LE16 31 F4
Broadway The
Market Harborough LE16 31 F4
Norton NN11 136 C4
Brocade Cl 8 NN4 158 F2
BROCKHALL 137 D2
Brockhall Cl NN2 141 E4
Brockhall Rd
Flore NN7 155 E6
Northampton NN2 141 E4
Brockhill Cl NN15 72 E1
Brockton St NN2 141 D1
Brockwood Cl NN5 140 A1
Bromford Cl 8 NN3 161 A8
Bromley Farm Ct NN11 184 B5
Bromwich Rd 1 CV21 80 A1
Bronte Cl NN16 72 C6
Brontes The NN17 36 D8
Brook Ct
Horton NN7 177 E2
Silverstone NN12 214 D5
Brooke Cl
Rushden NN10 132 B1
Wellingborough NN8 129 B5
Brooke Gn NN8 129 B5
Brooke Ho NN17 36 E6
Brooke House Coll LE16 31 E4
Brooke Mews NN8 129 B5
Brookend NN4 175 E5
Brooke Rd NN18 53 B8
Brookes Gr NN17 21 E1
Brookes Mews NN6 144 E5
Brooke Weston City Tech Coll NN18 36 D1
Brook Farm Cl NN10 148 B5
Brookfield Rd
Market Harborough LE16 31 C3
Northampton NN2 141 E2
2 Rushden NN10 132 A2
Brookhaven NN14 90 B4
Brook La
Great Easton LE16 20 D6
Northampton NN5 158 F8
Towcester NN12 203 A6
Brookland Cres NN1 142 A1
Brookland Rd NN1, NN3 142 A1
Brooklands Cl NN11 135 C1
Brooklands Gdns LE16 31 E2
Brook St E NN8 130 B4
Brook St W NN8 129 F4
Brooks Cl
Burton Latimer NN15 92 C1
Willoughby CV23 117 D4
Brooksdale Cl NN16 72 B6
Brookside
Bozeat NN29 164 D2
Desborough NN14 51 B2
Glapthorn PE8 26 C1
Hinton NN11 184 A6
Lillingstone Lovell MK18 227 A6
Southwick PE8 26 B5
Stanwick NN9 114 A3
Wappenham NN12 213 C8
Weedon Bec NN7 155 B3
Brookside Cl
Old Stratford MK19 229 B6
Yelvertoft NN6 82 B4
Brookside La NN11 153 A2
Brookside Mdws NN5 140 E1
Brookside Mews NN6 82 B4
Brookside Pl NN7 156 C2
Brooks Rd NN9 114 F8
Brook St
9 Daventry NN11 135 C2
Hargrave NN9 115 E3
Moreton Pinkney NN11 199 C7
Northampton NN1 159 B7
Raunds NN9 114 D6
Brook Terr
1 Irthlingborough NN9 112 F2
Medbourne LE16 18 F6
Brook Vale NN8 129 C2
Brook View NN4 175 E3
Brookway MK19 228 E4
Brook Wlk NN14 95 A3
Broom Ct 2 NN4 159 A3
Broomhill Cres NN3 143 A6
Broom Way NN15 90 F8
Brough Cl NN5 139 F1
BROUGHTON 90 B4
Broughton Hill NN14 90 A6
Broughton Pl NN3 142 B3
Broughton Prim Sch NN14 90 A4
Broughton Rd
Mawsley Village NN14 89 B3
Old NN6 107 E8
Pytchley NN14 90 E2
Browning Ave NN16 72 C5
Browning Cl
8 Daventry NN11 135 B4
Rushden NN10 148 D8
Browning Rd
Rugby CV21 99 B8
Wellingborough NN8 129 C4
Browning Wlk NN17 36 D8
Brownlow Ct NN3 142 E4
Browns Cl
Mawsley Village NN14 89 B4
Moulton NN3 126 D2
Brownsfield Rd NN12 217 E6
Brown's La NN14 95 C6
Browns Rd NN11 134 F1
Brown's Way NN1 159 E5
Brownswood Dr NN12 217 D3
Browns Yd NN12 203 C6
Bruce St NN5 158 F6
Brundall Cl NN3 160 D7
Brunel Cl
Daventry NN11 134 F4
Kettering NN16 72 A3
Wellingborough NN8 129 B6
Brunel Ct NN17 22 A2
Brunel Dr NN5 158 D5
Brunel Rd NN17 22 A2
Brunswick Gdns NN18 35 F2
Brunswick Pl NN1 159 E7
Brunswick Wlk NN1 159 E7
Brunting Rd NN3 142 C8
Bryant Rd NN15 91 C7
Bryant Way NN10 132 B6
Bsns Ctr The NN5 158 F6
Bsns Exchange The NN16 72 B3
Buccleuch St NN16 72 B3
Buchanan Cl NN4 159 A3
Buckfast Sq NN18 36 F4
Buckingham Cl
Northampton NN4 175 B7
Wellingborough NN8 129 E1
Buckingham Ct
Brackley NN13 234 A6
Kettering NN15 91 F7
Buckingham Rd
Brackley NN13 234 A6
Deanshanger MK19 228 F3
Buckingham Way NN12 203 B5
Buckle Ho NN5 159 B5
Buckley Ct MK11 229 F4
Bucknell Wood Forest Wlk* NN12 214 B6
Bucknill Cres CV21 99 B7
Bucknills La NN6 100 F5
Buckwell Cl
Desborough NN14 51 A3
Wellingborough NN8 129 E5
Buckwell End NN8 129 F4
Buckwell La CV23 80 B6
Budge Rd NN12 217 F5
BUGBROOKE 173 A7
Bugbrooke Com Prim Sch NN12 172 F7
BUGBROOKE DOWNS 173 C4
Bugbrooke Rd
Gayton NN7 173 D2
Kislingbury NN7 157 D3
Nether Heyford NN7 156 C1
Bugby Dr NN9 113 B5
Bugby Way NN9 114 D7
Bull Baulk OX17 220 A8
Bull Cl NN29 164 D3
Bull La PE9 1 A6
Bullmatt Bsns Ctr NN10 131 E4
Bullock Rd PE7 29 D5
Bulls La OX17 230 F5
Bulwell Gn NN18 36 C6
BULWICK 12 C1
Bungalows The
Theddingworth LE17 46 D8
Walgrave NN6 108 A5
Bunkers Hill
Badby NN11 152 F2
Foxton LE17 30 A5
Bunsty Ct MK11 229 F5
Bunting Cl NN15 92 A2
Bunting Rd NN2 141 D1
Bunting's La PE8 28 B3
Burcote Fields NN12 203 D4
Burcote Rd NN12 203 D4
Burcote Wood Bsns Pk NN12 203 B1
Burditt Cl NN14 70 F6
Burdock Way NN14 51 A4
Burford Ave NN3 142 D5
Burford Cl LE16 31 D1
Burford Way NN8 129 D1
Burgess Ct NN18 36 A4
Burgess Farm OX17 220 B7
Burgess Row LE16 21 B8
Burghley Cl
Corby NN18 36 F4
Desborough NN14 51 A4
Market Harborough LE16 32 A3
Burghley Dr NN18 36 F5
Burghley St NN16 72 C4
Burham Cl NN4 175 E5
Burkitt Rd NN17 21 F3
Burleigh Ho 7 NN10 132 B2
Burleigh Rd NN2 141 C1
Burleigh Terr NN29 164 D3
Burlington Apartments NN1 160 A7

Burmans Way NN7 161 E6
Burnell Cl NN14 95 B3
Burnham Pl NN13 224 B8
Burnmill Rd LE16 31 E5
Burns Cl NN6 144 F4
Burns Dr NN17 36 D8
Burns Rd
Daventry NN11 135 B4
Kettering NN16 72 C5
Wellingborough NN8 129 C4
Burns St NN1 159 E7
BURROW'S BUSH 130 B6
Burrows Cl NN11 119 E1
Burrows Ct NN3 142 E4
Burrows Farm La NN14 113 B8
Burrows Vale NN6 106 C2
Burryport Rd NN4 160 B2
Burton Cl NN11 135 C5
Burtone Cl NN14 90 A4
Burton Ho NN15 92 C2
BURTON LATIMER 92 A1
Burton Rd NN9 111 F6
Burton Terr NN29 164 D3
Burtram Cl NN3 142 E1
Burwell Hill NN13 233 F8
Burwell Hill Cl NN13 233 F8
Burwell Wlk NN18 36 C4
Burwood Rd NN3 142 B2
Bury Cl
Cottingham LE16 20 C1
Higham Ferrers NN10 132 C6
Bury Dyke NN6 101 A6
Bury Hill NN12 201 F6
Burystead Pl NN8 130 A4
Burystead Rise NN9 114 E7
Burywell Rd NN8 130 B6
Buscot Park Way 11 NN11 135 B7
Bushacre Ct NN16 71 F3
Bush Cl NN8 129 E5
Bushey Balk Cl NN18 36 B1
Bush Hill NN3 142 C2
Bushland Rd NN3 142 C2
Buswell Cl NN7 155 B3
Buswell Rise NN14 70 E7
Butcher's La
Boughton NN2 125 C1
Pattishall NN12 172 E1
Pytchley NN14 90 F2
Butchers Paddock NN14 93 A7
Bute Cl NN17 36 B8
Butland Rd NN18 36 D2
Butler Gdns LE16 31 C1
Butlers Cl NN11 182 F2
Butlin Cl
Daventry NN11 135 B3
Rothwell NN14 70 B7
Butlin Ct NN8 130 C1
Butlins La NN7 191 D4
Buttercup Cl NN18 36 C2
Buttercup Rd NN14 51 A5
Butterfields NN8 129 F2
Buttermere NN8 129 C5
Buttermere Cl
Kettering NN16 71 E3
Northampton NN3 142 C3
Butterwick Wlk NN18 36 C4
Butt La LE17 45 E5
Buttmead NN7 190 D7
Butts Cl
Aynho OX17 237 C7
Culworth OX17 198 D2
Butts Croft Cl NN4 175 C6
Butts Hill Cres NN7 173 A8
Butts Rd
Northampton NN4 175 C6
Raunds NN9 114 E6
Wellingborough NN8 129 F1
Butts The OX17 237 D8
Buxton Dr NN14 50 E4
Bycell Rd MK18 226 B3
BYFIELD 183 D7
Byfield Rd
Chipping Warden OX17 196 F7
Eydon NN11 184 C2
Hinton NN11 184 B7
Northampton NN5 159 A5
Priors Marston CV47 166 E7
Byfield Sch NN11 183 C7
Bygones Mus* OX17 181 D1
By Pass Way NN7 178 B8
Byron Cl NN12 203 B5
Byron Cres
Higham Ferrers NN10 132 A5
Rushden NN10 131 E2
Byron Rd
Corby NN17 36 D8
Kettering NN16 72 C5
Wellingborough NN8 129 D4
Byron St NN2 141 F1
Byron Wlk NN11 135 B3
BYTHORN 97 D4

C

Cabot Cl
Daventry NN11 135 C5
Rothwell NN14 70 E6
Caernarvon Cl NN12 203 C4
Caesars Gate NN13 234 A6
Caistor Rd NN17 10 C1
Caldbeck Wlk 5 NN3 142 C4
CALDECOTE 189 B3
Caldecote Rd LE16 20 E6
CALDECOTT
Corby 21 C8
Higham Ferrers 133 C6
Caldecott Rd
Chelveston NN9 133 B7
Rockingham LE16 21 B5
Calder Cl NN17 21 D1
Calder Gn NN5 140 E1
Caledonian Ho 1 NN5 159 A6
Calke Ho 6 NN11 135 B7
Callcott Dr NN15 92 A8
Calstock Cl NN3 160 D7
Calvert Cl NN12 202 E8
Calvert Ct NN8 129 F8
CALVERTON 229 E3
Calverton Rd MK11 229 D4
Calvert Rd NN12 202 E8
Camberley Cl NN3 143 B2
Cambium Cl NN16 72 C6
Camborne Cl NN4 159 B2
Cambria Cres NN3 142 C1
Cambridge Ave NN17 36 B6
Cambridge St
Kettering NN16 72 C3
Northampton NN2 159 C8
Rothwell NN14 70 D8
Wellingborough NN8 130 A5
Wymington NN10 148 A7
Cam Cl NN17 21 C1
Camden Sq NN29 164 D2
Camelot Way NN5 158 A7
Cameron Cl
Daventry NN11 135 B1
Northampton NN5 158 E7
Cameron Cres NN5 158 E7
Cameron Ct NN17 36 F5
Cameron Dr NN5 158 E7
Campaign Cl 9 NN4 175 E7
Campanula Cl NN3 160 C6
Campbell Cl
Rushden NN10 148 D8
Towcester NN12 203 C8
Weedon Bec NN7 155 A4
Campbell Rd
Corby NN17 36 F5
Wellingborough NN8 130 A2
Campbell Sq 1 NN1 159 D6
Campbell St NN1 159 C7
Camp Cl NN7 173 A6
CAMP HILL 158 E2
Camp Hill NN7 173 A6
Campion Cl NN10 148 B8
Campion Ct NN3 143 B1
Campion Sch NN7 173 A8
Camp La NN7 157 D3
Camrose Rd NN5 159 A8
Camsdale Wlk LE16 35 C8
Canada Sq NN18 36 C3
Canal La MK19 228 E4
Canal Mus The* NN12 205 A8
Canalside
Market Harborough LE16 31 D4
Old Stratford MK19 229 C7
Stoke Bruerne NN12 205 A8
Canberra Ho NN17 22 F1
Candace Ct NN5 158 E8
Candleford NN3 143 B4
Candleford Cl NN13 233 E8
Candleford Ct NN13 233 E8
Canford Gn NN18 36 A6
Cannam Cl LE16 20 B1
Cannock Rd NN17 36 F8
Cannon St NN8 130 A5
Canonbury NN8 129 C4
Canon Harnett Ct MK12 229 F6
CANONS ASHBY 185 D2
Canons Ashby* NN11 185 D2
Canons Ashby Ct NN11 185 B5
Canons Ashby Rd NN11 199 D7
Canon St NN16 72 B3
Canons Wlk NN2 141 B4
Canterbury Cl OX16 219 A7
Cantle Cl NN18 36 D3
Capell Gdns NN18 36 E4
Capell Rise NN7 155 E5
Cappenham Cl NN12 203 B6
Captain's Ct NN7 177 E1
Cardigan Cl 4 NN5 158 F8
Cardigan Ho NN17 36 E6
Cardigan Pl
Corby NN17 36 E5
Kettering NN16 72 D2
Cardigan Rd NN14 37 E2
Cardinal Cl NN4 175 B7
Cares Orch NN7 161 D3
Carey Cl NN3 126 B1
Carey Ct NN3 126 B1
Carey Dr NN17 36 C8
Carey Ho 2 NN16 72 B2
Carey Rd
Hackleton NN7 177 A3
Towcester NN12 203 C3
Careys Rd NN12 215 F7
Carey St
Kettering NN16 72 C2
Northampton NN1 159 E7
Carey Way NN10 132 D3
Carina Rd NN15 91 C5
Carisbrooke Cl NN15 91 F8
Carline Ct NN3 142 D4
Carlisle Cl NN18 36 D1
Carlow Rd NN14 95 A3
Carlow St NN14 95 A3
Carlton Cl NN10 148 A7
Carlton Gdns NN2 141 E2
Carlton Mews NN10 132 C5
Carlton Pl NN18 36 B6
Carlton Rd
Northampton NN2 141 E2
Wilbarston LE16 34 D5
Carlton St NN16 72 A3
Carlyle Ave NN5 158 E7
Carmarthen Way NN10 148 C8
Carnegie St NN10 132 A2
Carne The MK11 229 E5
Caroline Chisholm Sch NN4 175 F5
Carol Trusler Mews NN2 159 B7
Carousel Way NN3 160 F7
Carpetbeggar & Northants Aviation Mus* NN6 68 F3
Carradale Cl NN16 72 A6
Carrdus Sch The OX17 219 C8
Carriage Dr NN16 72 C6
Carriers Cl MK19 207 A2
Carrington Gdns 1 NN3 160 F8
Carrington St NN16 72 B2
Carron Cl NN17 21 C1
Carr's Way NN7 157 C6
Carsington Cl NN16 71 E3
Carter Ave NN14 90 A3
Carter Cl NN8 130 B4
Cartmel Pl NN3 142 C3
Cartmel Way NN10 132 D3
Cartrill St NN9 114 C6
Cartwright Cres NN13 233 D7
Cartwright Gdns OX17 237 D7
Cartwright Rd
Charlton OX17 231 F5
Northampton NN2 141 C1
Casterbridge Ct NN4 175 E7
Casterton Cl NN9 114 A5
Castilian St NN1 159 D5
Castilian Terr NN1 159 D5
Castillion Ct NN1 159 D5
CASTLE ASHBY 163 A3
Castle Ashby Craft Ctr* NN7 162 F3
Castle Ashby Gdns* NN7 163 B3
Castle Ashby Rd NN7 179 B7
Castle Ashby Rural Shopping Yd* NN7 162 F3
Castle Ave NN5 158 C8
Castle Bush NN5 158 C8
Castle Cl
Corby NN18 36 A4
Northampton NN5 158 C8
Castle Ct
Rushden NN10 148 A8
Wellingborough NN8 130 B4
Castlefields Cl NN10 132 C6
Castle Gdns NN14 54 B3
CASTLE HILL 233 E5
Castle Hill
Daventry NN11 135 B1
Rothwell NN14 70 D7
Castle La NN8 130 B4
Castle Mews NN8 130 B4
Castle Mound CV23 99 C2
Castle Mount NN13 233 E5
Castle Prim Sch NN1 159 D7
Castle Rd
Lavendon MK46 180 F1
Wellingborough NN8 130 B4
Woodford Halse NN11 184 C6
Castle St
Deddington OX15 236 A4
Northampton NN1 159 C6
Wellingborough NN8 130 B4
CASTLETHORPE 218 F6
Castlethorpe Fst Sch MK19 218 F5
Castlethorpe Rd MK19 206 F1
Castleton Rd NN14 50 E4
Castle View
Barnwell PE8 59 B7
Wellingborough NN8 130 B4
Castle Way
Kettering NN15 91 F6
Wellingborough NN8 130 A4
Caswell Rd NN4 160 B1
Catchland Cl NN18 36 C2
Catchpole Cl NN18 36 D3
Catesby Cl NN2 141 E4
Catesby End NN11 151 D1
Catesby Rd NN14 70 E7
Catesby St NN16 72 C3
Catlow Cl NN9 114 C8
Catterick Cl NN18 36 E1
Cattle End
Farthingstone NN12 170 F3
Silverstone NN12 214 C3
Cattle Hill NN3 143 C2
Cattle Market Rd NN1 159 C4
Catton Cl NN6 85 B8
Catton Cres NN2 140 F5
Cauldecott Cl NN4 158 D1
Causeway Rd NN17 21 E2
Causeway The
Byfield NN11 183 E8
Northampton NN3 161 C7
Causin Cl NN14 55 F8
Causin Way PE8 40 C6
Cavalry Dr NN11 135 B1
Cavalry Fields NN7 155 A4
Cavalry Hill NN7 155 A4
Cavendish Cl NN15 91 F5
Cavendish Ctyd NN17 22 E1
Cavendish Dr NN3 160 D6
Cawley Rd OX17 230 B5
Caxton Cl NN11 135 A4
Caxton St LE16 31 F1
Caythorpe Sq NN18 36 B6
Cecil Cl NN18 36 E4
Cecil Dr NN18 36 F4
Cecil Rd NN2 141 C2
Cecil St
Kettering NN16 72 C4
Rothwell NN14 70 D7
Cedar Cl
Brackley NN13 222 F2
Daventry NN11 135 C5
Desborough NN14 51 C2
Irchester NN29 147 A7
Rushden NN10 148 A8
Sywell NN6 143 D8
Towcester NN12 203 C4
Cedar Ct
Corby NN17 21 E1
Northampton NN5 158 E8
Cedar Dr NN14 76 D1
Cedar Gate NN3 142 C7
Cedar Hythe NN6 124 D1
Cedar Rd
Kettering NN16 72 C4
Northampton NN1, NN3 142 A1
Cedar Rd E NN3 142 A1
Cedar Road Prim Sch NN3 142 A1
Cedar Way
Higham Ferrers NN10 132 B6
Wellingborough NN8 130 A7
Cedrus Ct NN2 140 F6
Celandine Cl NN10 148 C7
Celeborn Pl NN3 143 B5
Celtic Cl NN10 132 B7
Celtic Way NN6 100 C6
Cemetery La NN10 132 B6
Centaine Rd NN10 132 A1
Centec Ct MK19 229 B7
Central Ave
Hinton NN11 184 A7
Kettering NN16 72 D3
Northampton NN2 141 B6
Wellingborough NN8 129 E2
Central Mus & Art Gall* NN1 159 D5
Centre 2000 NN16 71 F4
Centre Par NN16 72 D4
Centurion Way NN4 175 F5
Chace Rd NN8 130 C4
CHACOMBE 208 F4
Chacombe CE Prim Sch OX17 208 F4
Chacombe Ho OX17 208 E3
Chacombe House Mews OX17 208 E3
Chacombe Priory OX17 208 D4
Chacombe Rd OX17 208 F1
Chadleigh Ct NN13 233 E6
CHADSTONE 162 E2
Chadstone Ave NN2 141 D6
Chadwick Gdns NN5 140 D1
Chaffinch Cl NN4 174 F7
Chaffinch Way NN13 222 E1
Chainbridge Ct NN14 76 C2
Chainbridge La PE28 97 F1
Chalcombe Ave NN2 141 C5
Chalcombe Rd NN2 141 C4
Chalfont Ct 14 NN1 159 C7
Chalk La NN1 159 B6
Chalon Cl NN8 129 F8
Chamberlain Ave NN8 129 E1
Chamberlain Rd CV21 99 B8
Chamberlain Way
Higham Ferrers NN10 132 C5
Raunds NN9 114 C5
Chambers Hill NN14 89 B4
Chambers Row NN6 64 E6
Chambers The NN1 159 E6
Champion Ct NN13 233 E8
Chancel Terr PE8 59 B5
Chancery La NN14 76 D2
Chandler Gdns NN14 76 E1
Chandlers Way NN17 36 E5
Channing St 8 NN16 72 C2
Chantelle Ct 1 NN11 135 B3
Chantry Cl NN3 143 B3
Chantry La NN12 203 C6
Chantry Rise MK46 195 F3
CHAPEL BRAMPTON 124 E2
Chapel Cl
Clifton OX15 236 E4
Great Addington NN14 94 B2
Litchborough NN12 171 C1
Rushden NN10 132 C3
Silverstone NN12 214 D4
Chapel Ct PE8 8 B2
CHAPEL END 44 D4
Chapel End
Croughton NN13 238 C8
Great Gidding PE28 61 D2
Piddington NN7 177 A2
Chapel Farm NN7 206 C6
Chapel Fields LE17 62 B3
Chapel Gn NN5 141 A2
Chapel Hill
Higham Ferrers NN10 132 B7
Irchester NN29 147 B8
Islip NN14 76 B2
Little Addington NN14 113 B7
Silverstone NN12 214 D4
Chapel Ho NN4 159 B3
Chapel La
Adderbury OX17 230 A4
Badby NN11 153 A3
Barrowden LE15 3 F5
Blisworth NN7 190 D8
Brafield-on-t-G NN7 161 E2
Clipston LE16 66 F8
Corby NN17 37 B6
Crick NN6 101 A5
Daventry NN11 135 C2
Denford NN14 95 C6
Elton PE8 28 C8
Farthinghoe NN13 221 B4
Flore NN7 155 F5
Geddington NN14 54 A2
Great Doddington NN29 145 E6
Hackleton NN7 177 B2
Ketton PE9 1 A5
Lilbourne CV23 81 A6
Lillingstone Lovell MK18 227 A1
Little Harrowden NN9 110 C4
Maidford NN12 186 D6
Old NN6 107 C7
Rushton NN14 52 C2
Slapton NN12 201 E2
Stanion NN14 37 E2
Stanwick NN9 114 A3
Stoke Albany LE16 34 B4
Stoke Bruerne NN12 205 A8
Turweston NN13 234 B7
Whitfield NN13 223 D3
Wilbarston LE16 34 C5
Chapel Pl 1 NN1 159 E6
Chapel Rd
Greatworth OX17 210 E1
Weldon NN17 38 A8
Chapel Row
Northampton NN3 143 C2
Souldern OX27 237 E3
Chapel St
Charwelton NN11 168 A4
Kilsby CV23 100 A2
Ringstead NN14 95 A3
Swinford LE17 62 B3
Titchmarsh NN14 77 C4
Warmington PE8 28 B3
Chapel View NN14 90 B5
Chaplins La NN14 51 A3
Chapman Cl NN12 203 C7
Chapman Gr NN17 36 E8
Chapmans Cl
Irchester NN29 147 B8
Stoke Albany LE16 34 B4
Chapmans Ct 11 NN16 72 C2
Chapmans Dr MK19 229 B7
Chapmans La OX15 236 A3
Chappell Ho 5 NN3 126 C1
Chardonnay Cl NN5 140 A2
Chariot Rd NN4 175 F5
Charity Cotts MK19 229 E2
Charlbury Cl NN8 145 E8
Charles Cl
Higham Ferrers NN10 132 C7
Long Buckby NN6 121 B3
Old NN6 107 D7
Charlesfield Rd CV22 98 A8
Charles Robinson Ct NN8 129 E3
Charles St
Corby NN17 36 F5
Kettering NN16 72 B4
Market Harborough LE16 31 D3
Northampton NN1 159 D7
Rothwell NN14 70 C6
Thrapston NN14 76 E2
Wellingborough NN8 129 E2
Charles Terr 8 NN11 135 C1
Charlotte Pl NN16 72 E4
Charlottes Row 6 NN10 132 A2
CHARLTON 231 F4
Charlton Cl NN2 141 C5
Charlton Rd OX17 237 C7
Charlton Way NN13 221 B4
Charnwood 1 NN8 130 A5
Charnwood Ave NN3 142 E2
Charnwood Cl 5 NN11 135 B4
Charnwood Ct NN3 142 E2
Charnwood Dr NN15 92 A5
Charnwood Rd NN17 36 F7
Charter Ct NN18 36 D2
Charter Gate NN3 142 B6
Charterhouse Cl NN13 233 E7
Charter Rd CV22 98 E8
Chartwell Ave NN3 142 C5
Chartwell Cl 13 NN11 135 B7
CHARWELTON 168 B5
Charwelton La NN11 167 D8

Charwelton Rd NN11 .... 169 C2
Chase Barn Cotts
OX27 .... 239 B3
Chase Cl NN14 .... 37 E3
Chase Farm NN14 .... 54 B2
Chase Hill NN14 .... 54 A3
Chase Park Rd NN7 .... 179 A5
Chaseport Cl MK46 .... 194 D2
Chase The
Long Buckby NN6 .... 121 B4
Pitsford NN6 .... 125 D4
Chase View Rd NN14 .... 54 B3
Chaston Pl NN16 .... 72 E5
Chatellerault Ct NN17 .... 36 D8
Chater Cl LE16 .... 32 A6
Chater La PE9 .... 1 A7
Chater Mews PE9 .... 1 A7
Chater St NN3 .... 126 D1
Chatsworth Ave
Kettering NN15 .... 91 C5
Northampton NN3 .... 142 F5
Chatsworth Dr
Market Harborough
LE16 .... 32 B3
Wellingborough NN8 .... 129 C7
Chatsworth Rd NN18 .... 36 D1
Chaucer Ct NN2 .... 141 F1
Chaucer Ho NN2 .... 141 F2
Chaucer Rd
Rugby CV22 .... 98 A7
Wellingborough NN8 .... 129 D4
Chaucer St NN2 .... 141 F1
Chaucer Way NN11 .... 135 B2
Cheaney Dr NN4 .... 175 E2
Cheddar Cl NN5 .... 158 D7
Cheddar Wlk NN18 .... 36 A6
Chedington Cl NN15 .... 92 A5
Chedworth Cl NN3 .... 143 D2
Cheese La [5] NN8 .... 130 A4
Chelfham Cl NN3 .... 160 D7
Chelmorton Vale NN14 .... 50 E4
Chelmscote Row
OX17 .... 208 F8
Chelmsford Cl NN4 .... 159 A2
Cheltenham Cl NN10 .... 148 C8
Cheltenham Rd NN18 .... 36 E1
CHELVESTON 133 C8
Chelveston Cres NN9 .... 133 D5
Chelveston Dr NN17 .... 36 B7
Chelveston Rd
Higham Ferrers NN10 .... 132 E7
Raunds NN9 .... 114 C4
Stanwick NN9 .... 114 B3
Chenderit Sch OX17 .... 209 A1
Cheney Ct OX17 .... 208 F1
Cheney Gdns OX17 .... 208 F2
Chepstow Cl
Kettering NN15 .... 91 F8
Northampton NN5 .... 159 A7
Chepstow Dr NN8 .... 129 C7
Chepstow Rd
Corby NN18 .... 36 D1
Corby NN18 .... 36 E1
Chequers Cl NN18 .... 36 E2
Chequers La
Grendon NN7 .... 163 E5
Ravensthorpe NN6 .... 103 D1
Wellingborough NN8 .... 130 A5
Chequers The MK19 .... 218 F5
Cheriton Cl NN11 .... 135 C6
Cheriton Rd NN18 .... 36 F4
Cheriton Way NN1 .... 160 C6
Cherradene Ct NN9 .... 114 D6
Cherry Ave NN8 .... 130 A7
Cherry Blossom Cl
NN3 .... 143 B2
Cherry Cl NN3 .... 142 C2
Cherry Ct NN9 .... 112 E1
Cherry Hill NN6 .... 107 E6
Cherry Lodge Rd NN3 .... 143 B3
Cherry Orch
Olney MK46 .... 195 E4
Rushden NN10 .... 132 C1
Cherry Rd NN16 .... 72 D4
Cherry St
Irthlingborough NN9 .... 112 E1
Ringstead NN14 .... 95 B3
Cherry Tree Cl
Desborough NN14 .... 51 B2
Husbands Bosworth
LE17 .... 45 E5
Cherry Tree La NN4 .... 160 E3
Cherrytree Wlk NN6 .... 143 D8
Cherry Wlk NN9 .... 114 B5
Cherwell Banks OX17 .... 231 A6
Cherwell Gn NN5 .... 140 F1
Cherwell Terr NN11 .... 184 C6
Cherwell The NN11 .... 134 F1
Cherwell Wlk NN17 .... 21 C1
Chesham Rise NN3 .... 143 B4
Chesil Wlk NN18 .... 36 A6
Chester Ave NN7 .... 157 B6
Chester Ct NN15 .... 91 B6
Chester Ho NN3 .... 161 B8
Chester Rd
Irchester NN29 .... 131 A1
Rushden NN10 .... 131 F2
Wellingborough NN8 .... 130 C4
Chestnut Ave
Corby NN17 .... 21 D1
Kettering NN15 .... 72 C1
Northampton NN4 .... 175 D5
Chestnut Cl
Hinton NN11 .... 184 A6
Long Buckby NN6 .... 121 B3
Milton Malsor NN7 .... 174 E4
Rushden NN10 .... 131 F3
Stony Stratford MK11 .... 229 D5

Chestnut Cl *continued*
Wymington NN10 .... 148 B5
Chestnut Ct
Northampton NN3 .... 142 A2
Raunds NN9 .... 114 D7
Chestnut Dr
Brackley NN13 .... 222 F1
Desborough NN14 .... 51 C2
Thrapston NN14 .... 76 D1
Chestnut Gn NN13 .... 223 E4
Chestnut Gr LE16 .... 67 A8
Chestnut Rd
Northampton NN3 .... 142 A1
Yardley Gobion NN12 .... 217 F6
Chestnuts The
Castlethorpe MK19 .... 218 F5
Clifton OX15 .... 236 E4
Hinton-in-t-H NN13 .... 232 F6
Chestnut Terr NN3 .... 142 A2
Chettle Pl NN12 .... 217 E2
Chetwode OX17 .... 219 C6
Cheviot Cl NN16 .... 72 B7
Cheviot Ct NN4 .... 158 E3
Cheviot Ho NN2 .... 141 C5
Chewton Cl NN5 .... 158 D7
Cheyne Wlk
Kettering NN15 .... 91 E8
Northampton NN1 .... 159 E5
Chichele Cl NN10 .... 132 B5
Chichele Coll* NN10 .... 132 B6
Chichele Ct NN10 .... 132 B3
Chichele St NN10 .... 132 C6
Chicheley Cotts NN14 .... 76 D2
Chichester Cl
[1] Daventry NN11 .... 135 D1
Rothwell NN14 .... 70 E6
Chieftan Bsns Pk
NN8 .... 129 A6
Child's St NN14 .... 95 C6
Chiltern Ave NN5 .... 158 D8
Chiltern Cl
Market Harborough
LE16 .... 31 F5
Northampton NN5 .... 158 D8
Chiltern Ct [3] NN10 .... 132 A2
Chiltern Prim Sch
NN5 .... 158 E8
Chiltern Rd
Daventry NN11 .... 135 B5
Kettering NN16 .... 72 B6
Chiltern Way NN5 .... 158 E8
Chilwell Ct [3] NN3 .... 160 F8
CHIPPING WARDEN 196 F6
Chipping Warden Sch
OX17 .... 196 F7
Chipsey Ave
Bugbrooke NN7 .... 172 F8
Northampton NN1 .... 160 B6
Chisholm Cl NN4 .... 175 F5
Choakles The NN4 .... 176 B6
Chowns Mill Bsns Pk
NN9 .... 113 B1
Christchurch Dr
NN11 .... 153 B7
Christchurch Rd NN1 .... 160 A7
Christie Way NN15 .... 90 F8
Christine Ct NN9 .... 114 D6
Christopher Ct NN6 .... 64 D5
Christopher Rawlins CE
Prim Sch OX17 .... 230 A4
Christopher Reeves Lower
Sch NN29 .... 147 E1
Chulmleigh Wlk NN3 .... 160 C7
Church Ave OX17 .... 230 F5
Church Bank LE16 .... 20 D7
CHURCH BRAMPTON
.... 140 C8
CHURCH CHARWELTON
.... 168 C3
Church Cl
Adderbury OX17 .... 230 A3
Braybrooke LE16 .... 49 E6
Caldecott LE16 .... 21 B8
Clipston LE16 .... 67 A8
Hartwell NN7 .... 192 D2
Milton Malsor NN7 .... 174 F4
Wardington OX17 .... 196 E1
West Haddon NN6 .... 102 C5
Wicken MK19 .... 228 B3
Wymington NN10 .... 148 B5
Churchcroft NN7 .... 191 D4
Church Dr NN18 .... 53 C8
CHURCH END 183 D7
Church End NN13 .... 238 D8
CHURCH END 207 A2
Church End
Piddington NN7 .... 177 A2
Potterspury NN12 .... 217 E3
Roade NN7 .... 191 D4
Syresham NN13 .... 224 C8
Church Farm Cl
NN29 .... 164 D3
Church Farm Way
LE16 .... 68 C7
Churchfield Cl NN2 .... 141 E4
Church Fields NN11 .... 152 C7
Church Gdns NN6 .... 103 E1
Church Gn
Badby NN11 .... 153 A2
Barnwell PE8 .... 59 B6
Northampton NN5 .... 140 F2
Woodford NN14 .... 94 D6
Church Hall Rd NN10 .... 131 F1
Church Hill
Badby NN11 .... 152 F2
Barnwell PE8 .... 59 B6
Finedon NN9 .... 111 E4
Geddington NN14 .... 54 A3

Church Hill *continued*
Hollowell NN6 .... 104 B4
Moulton NN3 .... 126 C1
Northampton NN4 .... 175 E6
Ravensthorpe NN6 .... 103 D1
Churchill Ave
Irthlingborough NN9 .... 113 B5
Northampton NN3 .... 142 B4
Wellingborough NN8 .... 129 E7
Churchill Cl NN14 .... 70 E7
Churchill Rd
Earls Barton NN6 .... 144 F4
Welton NN11 .... 135 E8
Churchill Way
Brackley NN13 .... 233 F6
Burton Latimer NN15 .... 92 B2
Daventry NN11 .... 153 E7
Kettering NN15 .... 72 F1
Church La
Adderbury OX17 .... 230 A3
Alderton NN12 .... 204 F2
Barnwell PE8 .... 59 B6
Barrowden LE15 .... 3 F4
Blisworth NN7 .... 190 D7
Bozeat NN29 .... 164 D3
Brafield-on-t-G NN7 .... 161 E2
Broughton NN14 .... 89 F6
Bugbrooke NN7 .... 172 E7
Burton Latimer NN15 .... 92 C2
Bythorn PE28 .... 97 D4
Caldecott LE16 .... 21 B8
Chacombe OX17 .... 208 E4
Church Brampton NN6 .... 140 B8
Claydon OX17 .... 181 D1
Clipston LE16 .... 67 A8
Cold Ashby NN6 .... 84 A5
Cold Higham NN12 .... 188 C8
Covington PE18 .... 116 C2
Cranford St John NN14 .... 93 B7
Croughton NN13 .... 238 D8
Deanshanger MK19 .... 228 E4
Denford NN14 .... 95 C6
Dingley LE16 .... 33 A4
Duddington PE9 .... 5 B6
East Carlton LE16 .... 34 F7
East Carlton LE16 .... 35 A7
East Haddon NN6 .... 122 D4
Evenley NN13 .... 233 F3
Grafton Regis NN12 .... 205 D2
Great Doddington
NN29 .... 145 E6
Harlestone NN7 .... 139 E6
Harrington NN6 .... 69 B6
Hellidon NN11 .... 151 C1
Husbands Bosworth
LE17 .... 45 E5
Kislingbury NN7 .... 157 D3
Lillingstone Lovell
MK18 .... 227 A6
Lyddington LE15 .... 9 D6
Maidford NN12 .... 186 D6
Middleton Cheney
OX17 .... 208 F1
Morcott LE15 .... 3 A6
Nether Heyford NN7 .... 156 B2
Newton Bromswold
NN10 .... 149 D8
Northampton, Bellinge
NN3 .... 161 A8
Northampton NN1 .... 159 C6
Pitsford NN6 .... 125 D5
Potterspury NN12 .... 217 E3
Slapton NN12 .... 201 E2
Slipton NN14 .... 75 A3
South Kilworth LE17 .... 63 C8
South Luffenham LE15 .... 3 E8
Spratton NN6 .... 105 B1
Stanford on A NN6 .... 62 F2
Stibbington PE8 .... 8 D2
Stoke Bruerne NN12 .... 205 A8
Stoke Doyle PE8 .... 41 D1
Sywell NN6 .... 127 E3
Thornby NN6 .... 84 D4
Thorpe Langton LE16 .... 17 A5
Walgrave NN6 .... 108 A4
Warmington PE8 .... 28 B3
Welford NN6 .... 64 E5
Wicken MK19 .... 228 B3
Wilby NN8 .... 129 B1
Wollaston NN29 .... 146 D3
Wymington NN10 .... 148 B5
Yardley Hastings NN7 .... 179 B7
Yelden MK44 .... 133 F3
Church Leys NN13 .... 233 E3
Church Mount NN6 .... 103 F6
Church Piece Cotts
NN13 .... 221 B4
Church Pk PE8 .... 7 D8
Church Rd
Brackley NN13 .... 233 F7
Braunston NN11 .... 118 B1
Greatworth OX17 .... 210 E1
Hargrave NN9 .... 115 F1
Ketton PE9 .... 1 A5
Piddington NN7 .... 177 A2
Pytchley NN14 .... 91 A1
Spratton NN6 .... 124 B8
Upper Boddington
NN11 .... 182 C7
Church Row PE8 .... 42 F3
Church Sq [6] LE16 .... 31 E3
Church St
Blakesley NN12 .... 187 B1
Boughton NN2 .... 141 C8
Brigstock NN14 .... 55 F7
Brixworth NN6 .... 106 B3
Broughton NN14 .... 90 B4
Burton Latimer NN15 .... 92 C3

Church St *continued*
Byfield NN11 .... 183 D7
Charwelton NN11 .... 168 B4
Clifton u D CV23 .... 80 A5
Cogenhoe NN7 .... 162 A6
Cottingham LE16 .... 20 D1
Crick NN6 .... 100 F6
Easton o t H PE9 .... 2 A6
Finedon NN9 .... 111 E4
Hargrave NN9 .... 115 E2
Helmdon NN13 .... 211 F3
Husbands Bosworth
LE17 .... 45 E5
Irthlingborough NN9 .... 112 F2
Isham NN14 .... 91 F1
Long Buckby NN6 .... 121 B4
Market Harborough LE16 .... 31 E3
Mears Ashby NN6 .... 128 B2
Moulton NN3 .... 126 C1
Naseby NN6 .... 85 B8
Nassington PE8 .... 15 F5
Nether Heyford NN7 .... 156 B2
Newnham NN11 .... 153 E4
Olney MK46 .... 195 F3
Oundle PE8 .... 42 A5
Pattishall NN12 .... 172 E1
Polebrook PE8 .... 42 F3
Raunds NN9 .... 114 E7
Ringstead NN14 .... 95 B3
Rothersthorpe NN7 .... 174 A6
Rushden NN10 .... 132 B2
Sibbertoft LE16 .... 47 A2
Silverstone NN12 .... 214 D5
Stanwick NN9 .... 114 A3
Staverton NN11 .... 152 C7
Stony Stratford MK11 .... 229 D5
Sulgrave OX17 .... 210 F7
Titchmarsh NN14 .... 77 C4
Wadenhoe PE8 .... 58 A3
Warmington PE8 .... 28 B2
Watford NN6 .... 120 C6
Weedon Bec NN7 .... 155 C3
Weldon NN17 .... 38 B7
Wellingborough NN8 .... 130 A4
Wilbarston LE16 .... 34 C5
Woodford Halse NN11 .... 184 C6
Woodford NN14 .... 94 D6
CHURCH STOWE 171 D8
Church View
Brackley NN13 .... 234 A7
Broughton NN14 .... 90 A4
Burton Latimer NN15 .... 92 C3
Ecton NN6 .... 143 F4
Greens Norton NN12 .... 202 E8
Keyston PE28 .... 97 A3
Moulton NN3 .... 126 C2
Northampton NN4 .... 175 E5
Raunds NN9 .... 114 D7
Walgrave NN6 .... 108 A5
Weldon NN17 .... 38 B7
Church View Rd NN14 .... 51 B2
Churchway NN3 .... 160 D8
Church Way
Denton NN7 .... 178 B8
Ecton NN6 .... 143 F4
Grendon NN7 .... 163 D5
Northampton NN3 .... 160 E7
Preston Capes NN11 .... 169 D2
Thorpe Malsor NN14 .... 71 A3
[1] Wellingborough
NN8 .... 130 A4
Whittlebury NN12 .... 215 C5
Church Way Ct NN3 .... 160 D8
Church Wlk
Barby CV23 .... 99 C1
Bozeat NN29 .... 164 D3
Corby NN17 .... 37 B6
Daventry NN11 .... 135 C2
Denford NN14 .... 95 C6
[5] Irthlingborough
NN9 .... 112 F2
Kettering NN16 .... 72 B2
Kilsby CV23 .... 100 A3
King's Cliffe PE8 .... 13 E7
Little Addington NN14 .... 113 B8
Lubenham LE16 .... 30 F3
Market Harborough
LE16 .... 32 A2
Newton Bromswold
NN10 .... 149 D8
Northampton NN3 .... 143 B2
Ringstead NN14 .... 95 B3
Weldon NN17 .... 38 B7
Cider Cl LE15 .... 3 F5
Cinnamon Cl [5] NN4 .... 175 D6
Circus End NN5 .... 140 C1
Circus Gr PE8 .... 42 F2
Cirrus Pk NN3 .... 142 A7
Cissbury Rd NN4 .... 158 F4
Clailey Ct MK11 .... 229 F5
Clannell Rd NN4 .... 175 A8
Clare Ave NN11 .... 135 C2
Clare Cl NN6 .... 144 F3
Clare Cres NN12 .... 203 B5
Clare Dr NN14 .... 76 E3
Claregate NN4 .... 175 B8
Claremont Ave MK11 .... 229 E4
Claremont Ct [13] NN1 .... 159 C6
Claremont Dr LE16 .... 32 A3
Clarence Ave NN2 .... 141 C2
Clarence Ct NN10 .... 148 A8
Clarence Rd
Kettering NN16 .... 72 C3
Stony Stratford MK11 .... 229 E5
Clarence St LE16 .... 31 F3
Clare Rd NN8 .... 129 C3
Clare St
Northampton NN1 .... 159 E7

Clare St *continued*
Raunds NN9 .... 114 D6
Clare Wlk NN10 .... 132 B5
Clark Cres NN12 .... 203 C8
Clarke Cl
Kettering NN16 .... 72 A4
Little Addington NN9 .... 113 B4
Clarke Ct NN6 .... 144 F4
Clarke Ho NN1 .... 160 A8
Clarke Rd
Corby NN17 .... 36 D8
Northampton NN1 .... 160 A8
Clarkes Dale LE16 .... 20 D6
Clarke St LE16 .... 31 D3
Clarkes Way
Brackley NN13 .... 233 D7
Welton NN11 .... 135 D8
Clarks La NN13 .... 221 A3
Claudius Way NN6 .... 130 E2
Claughton Rd NN4 .... 159 D3
CLAY COTON 82 A6
CLAYDON 181 D1
Claydon Cl NN8 .... 129 E5
Clayfield Cl NN3 .... 142 B6
Clay La NN17 .... 10 B1
Clayland Cl NN29 .... 164 C2
Claylands The NN7 .... 161 E6
Clay Pit La MK46 .... 195 F3
Claystones NN4 .... 158 D2
Clearway House Ind Est
OX16 .... 219 A7
Cleaver Ct NN15 .... 72 A1
Cleavers La NN6 .... 107 D7
Cleburne Cl NN9 .... 114 A4
Clee Rise NN5 .... 158 D8
Cleeve Way NN8 .... 129 D1
Clement Bois NN13 .... 233 E8
Clevedon Ct [1] NN11 .... 135 B7
Cleveland Ave NN16 .... 72 C6
Cleveland Pl NN4 .... 159 A2
Clickers Dr NN5 .... 158 D4
Clickers Pl NN5 .... 158 C4
Clickers Yd MK46 .... 195 F4
Clifden Terr NN6 .... 122 D4
Cliffe Rd PE9 .... 2 A3
CLIFTON 236 D4
Clifton Cl
Kettering NN15 .... 72 C1
Long Buckby NN6 .... 121 C4
Clifton Dr PE8 .... 41 E5
Clifton Gr NN15 .... 72 C1
Clifton Rd OX15 .... 236 B4
Clifton Sq NN17 .... 36 E8
CLIFTON UPON
DUNSMORE 80 A6
Cliftonville NN1 .... 159 E5
Cliftonville Ct [11] NN1 .... 159 F6
Cliftonville Rd NN1 .... 159 F5
Clinton Rd NN4 .... 159 B3
CLIPSTON 66 F8
Clipstone Ct NN14 .... 70 C6
Clipston Endowed Prim
Sch LE16 .... 67 A8
Clipston Field Pl [7]
NN3 .... 143 C2
Clipston La LE16 .... 48 E3
Clipston Rd
East Farndon LE16 .... 48 B4
Great Oxendon LE16 .... 48 D2
Clipston St LE16 .... 31 F1
Clipston Way NN5 .... 140 D1
Clive Cl NN15 .... 72 E1
Clock Mdw NN11 .... 183 C7
Clock Tower Ct NN3 .... 142 E6
Cloisters The
Daventry NN11 .... 135 D2
Priors Hardwick CV47 .... 166 A5
Rushden NN10 .... 132 B2
Wellingborough NN8 .... 130 B3
CLOPTON 78 E5
Close Rd NN7 .... 156 B1
Close The
Chipping Warden
OX17 .... 196 F6
Eastcote NN12 .... 188 F8
Easton o t H PE9 .... 1 F4
Greatworth OX17 .... 210 E1
Irthlingborough NN9 .... 112 F1
Kettering NN15 .... 91 B8
Northampton NN2 .... 141 C4
Roade NN7 .... 191 D4
Swinford LE17 .... 62 B4
Weston Underwood
MK46 .... 195 A1
Cloutsham St NN1 .... 159 E7
Clovelly Ct NN18 .... 36 F4
Clover Dr
Rushden NN10 .... 148 C8
Thrapston NN14 .... 76 D2
Clover Field NN4 .... 175 F2
Clover Gdns NN16 .... 72 B4
Clover La NN2 .... 141 B5
Club La NN14 .... 94 D6
Club St NN16 .... 72 C3
Clumber Ct NN18 .... 36 B6
Clumber Dr NN3 .... 160 E7
Clun Wlk NN17 .... 21 C1
Clwyd Wlk NN17 .... 21 C1
Clydesdale Rd NN17 .... 36 D7
Coach Ho The NN3 .... 160 B7
Coaching Wlk NN3 .... 142 D2
Coach Yd NN12 .... 217 E3
Coales Gdns LE16 .... 31 D5
Coalport Cl NN14 .... 50 F3
Cobblers Cl NN12 .... 187 B1

Cobbler's Pl NN29 164 D2
Cobblestone Ct NN4 158 D2
Cobbs Gdn MK46 195 F4
Cobb's La NN29 146 D3
Cobden St NN16 72 A3
Cob Dr NN4 158 B1
Cobley Cl NN11 184 D6
Cockbrook La PE28 79 C2
Cockerell Rd NN17 37 B8
Cockerill's Mdw CV21 99 A8
Cockley Rd NN13 221 C6
Codlin Cl NN3 143 B1
Coffee Tavern La 9
NN10 132 B2
Cofferidge Cl MK11 229 D5
Cogan Cres NN14 70 B6
COGENHOE 161 E5
Cogenhoe Mill Cvn Cite
NN7 162 A7
Cogenhoe Prim Sch
NN7 161 F5
Coggins Cl NN9 114 C6
COLD ASHBY 84 B5
Cold Ashby Rd
Guilsborough NN6 103 E7
Thornby NN6 84 D4
Coldermeadow Ave
NN18 36 A3
COLD HIGHAM 188 C8
Coldstream Cl NN11 135 B1
Coldstream La NN4 175 E8
Cole Ct
Kettering NN16 72 B4
Raunds NN9 114 C5
Coleman Cl NN6 101 A6
Coleman St NN9 114 D6
Coleraine Cl NN2 141 A5
Coleridge Way NN17 36 C8
Coleridge Wlk NN11 135 B4
Coles Cl NN15 92 B2
Coles Rise NN13 233 D7
Cole St NN10 131 E4
College Field Cl NN3 143 C3
College Fields OX17 237 C7
College Grounds The
NN3 126 B1
College Rd CV23 117 E3
College St Mews 28
NN1 159 C6
College St
Higham Ferrers
NN10 132 C6
Irthlingborough NN9 112 F2
Northampton NN1 159 C6
Rushden NN10 132 B2
Wellingborough NN8 129 E4
Wollaston NN29 146 D2
Colley Rise LE15 9 C7
Collingcroft Cl NN4 175 A7
Collingdale Rd NN3 142 D2
Collingham Cl NN9 114 A5
COLLINGTREE 175 B4
Collingtree CE Prim Sch
NN4 175 C4
Collingtree Ct NN4 175 B3
COLLINGTREE PARK 175 C5
Collingtree Rd NN4,
NN7 175 A4
Collingwood Ave NN17 36 A7
Collingwood Bsns Ctr
NN1 159 C6
Collingwood Rd NN1 141 F1
Collingwood Way
NN11 135 E3
Collins Cl NN12 203 C7
Collins Hill NN7 155 E6
Collins St NN1 159 F7
Collmead Ct NN3 143 B4
Collswell La NN12 187 B1
Collyns Way PE9 1 D2
COLLYWESTON 1 D2
Collyweston Cross Rds
PE8 6 A6
Collyweston Rd NN3 143 C5
Colmar Cl NN11 135 A4
Colne Cl NN17 21 C1
Colne Way NN5 140 E1
Colonial Dr NN4 175 C5
Colseed Rd NN14 89 B4
Colsons Way MK46 195 F5
Coltsfoot Rd NN10 148 C7
Columbus Cres NN14 70 E6
Columbus Ct NN11 135 B5
Colwell Rd NN8 130 C4
Colwyn Rd NN1 159 E8
Colyers Ave NN18 36 B3
Comfrey Cl NN10 148 B7
Commercial Rd
Corby NN17 37 B6
Kettering NN16 72 B2
Commercial St
Higham Ferrers NN10 132 B5
Northampton NN1 159 C5
Commercial Way
NN8 130 A4
Common St MK46 194 D1
Compton Gn NN18 36 A6
Compton Ho NN1 159 B6
Compton Pl NN16 72 E2
Compton Rd NN8 130 C5
Compton St
Desborough NN14 51 A3
Northampton NN1 159 B6
Compton Way NN6 144 E3
Coneygree NN4 175 F8
Coneygree Ct NN3 143 B1
Coneywell Ct NN3 142 F1
Conifer Rise NN3 142 E1
Coniston Ave NN3 142 B3
Coniston Cl
Daventry NN11 135 B2
Higham Ferrers NN10 132 B8
Wellingborough NN8 129 C5
Coniston Rd NN16 71 F2
Connaught Rd LE16 31 F4
Connaught St
Kettering NN16 72 D3
Northampton NN1 159 D7
Connegar Leys NN7 190 E7
Connell Cl LE16 30 F3
Connell Ct NN17 36 F5
Connolly Cl NN14 70 F7
Connolly Dr NN14 70 F7
Connolly Rd NN5 157 F8
Constable Dr
Kettering NN15 92 A7
Wellingborough NN8 129 F7
Constable Rd
Corby NN18 36 E5
Rugby CV21 80 B1
Constable Wlk NN14 94 D7
Conway Cl
Northampton NN5 140 E2
Rushden NN10 148 A8
Wellingborough NN8 129 C6
Conway Dr
Burton Latimer NN15 92 B2
Thrapston NN14 76 F2
Conway Wlk NN17 21 D1
Conyngham Rd NN3 142 F2
Cony Wlk NN4 175 F3
Cook Cl
Daventry NN11 135 C5
Rothwell NN14 70 E6
Cooks Cl NN7 205 F8
Cooks Rd NN17 37 F8
Cook's Terr NN6 121 A3
Cook's Way NN6 121 A3
Coomb Rd NN18 36 D1
Co-operative Row
NN10 132 B1
Cooper Cl NN12 203 C8
Cooper Ct NN14 76 D1
Cooper Dr NN8 129 F8
Copelands Rd NN14 51 C3
Copenhagen Rd NN18 36 A1
Copperfield Cl NN16 72 C6
Copper Leaf Cl NN3 142 C6
Coppertree Wlk NN14 76 D1
Coppice Cl
Burton Latimer NN15 92 C4
Daventry NN11 153 C8
Coppice Dr NN3 142 A5
Coppice The NN14 76 D1
Copse Cl
Burton Latimer NN15 92 C3
Northampton NN2 140 F5
Copymoor Cl NN4 176 A6
Cora Rd NN16 72 E4
Corbieres Cl NN5 140 A2
CORBY 36 E3
Corby Com Coll NN17 36 F6
Corby Com Hospl
NN17 36 D6
Corby Gate NN17 22 F1
Corby Gate Bsns Pk
NN17 22 F1
Corby Rd
Cottingham LE16 35 E8
Gretton NN17 22 B6
Stanion NN14 37 E3
Weldon NN17 38 A7
Cordon Cl NN3 143 B3
Cordon Cres NN6 144 F4
Cordwainer Gr NN14 76 D1
Cordwainer Ho NN5 159 A5
Cordwainers NN10 132 C1
Corfe Cl NN18 36 E2
Corner Cl NN29 147 E1
Cornfield Cl NN2 141 B5
Cornfield Way NN15 92 C1
Cornflower Cl NN4 175 F2
Cornhill Cl NN5 140 C3
Corn Kiln Cl NN7 161 F6
Corn La 7 NN8 130 A4
Cornwall Cl NN17 36 C6
Cornwall Rd NN16 72 D3
Cornwell Bsns Pk
NN4 160 B2
Coronation Ave
Rothwell NN14 70 D7
Rushden NN10 131 E1
Coronation Cres PE8 39 E7
Coronation Rd
Newnham NN11 153 D4
Stony Stratford MK11 229 E5
Corporation St NN17 36 E6
Corran Cl NN5 158 E8
Cory Gdns NN7 157 C7
COSGROVE 218 D2
Cosgrove L Pk*
MK19 218 F1
Cosgrove Rd
Northampton NN2 141 C5
Old Stratford MK19 229 C7
Cosgrove Village Prim Sch
MK19 218 E2
Cosgrove Way NN2 141 C5
Cosy Nook NN14 76 C2
COTON 103 E4
Coton Manor Gdns*
NN6 103 E4
Coton Rd
Guilsborough NN6 103 F5
Ravensthorpe NN6 103 E1
Rugby CV21 80 A1
Cotswold Ave
Kettering NN16 72 B5
Northampton NN5 158 D8
Cotswold Cl NN11 135 B5
Cotswold Ct OX27 237 E3
Cotswold Dr NN8 129 D1
Cottage Cl NN2 141 A4
Cottage Gdns
Northampton NN3 143 B3
Rushden NN10 148 C7
Cottages The NN13 224 C5
Cottagewell Ct NN3 142 F1
COTTARVILLE 142 D1
Cottarville NN3 142 D1
COTTERSTOCK 27 A2
Cotterstock Rd PE8 41 F7
COTTESBROOKE 104 F8
Cottesbrooke Gdns
NN4 175 D7
Cottesbrooke Grange
NN6 105 A8
Cottesbrooke Hall*
NN6 105 A8
Cottesbrooke Hall Gdns*
NN6 105 A8
Cottesbrooke Pk
NN11 135 A5
Cottesbrooke Rd NN17 36 B7
Cottesloe Ct MK11 229 F5
Cottesmore Ave NN15 92 A5
Cottesmore Cl NN5 140 B1
Cottesmore Way NN8 129 D4
COTTINGHAM 20 D1
Cottingham CE Prim Sch
LE16 20 C1
Cottingham Dr NN3 142 B7
Cottingham Rd
Corby NN17 36 E6
Corby NN18 36 B7
Rockingham LE16 21 A4
Cottingham Way NN14 76 C2
COTTISFORD 239 E3
COTTON END 159 C4
Cotton End
Long Buckby NN6 121 D4
Northampton NN4 159 C4
Cotton Mdw NN5 158 E7
Cottons The
Rockingham LE16 21 B4
Wellingborough NN8 129 D7
Coulon Cl NN29 147 A7
Coulthard Cl NN12 203 D8
Council Hos
Farthingstone NN12 170 E3
Guilsborough NN6 103 F7
Hannington NN6 108 C3
Podington NN29 147 E1
Council Ho's LE16 48 B8
Council Hos The
Long Buckby Wharf
NN6 136 E7
Upper Wardington
OX17 208 F8
Council Houses NN6 106 F6
Council St
Bozeat NN29 164 D4
Wollaston NN29 146 D2
Countess Ct NN5 159 A7
Countess Rd NN5 159 A7
Countryman Mews
LE16 32 A5
Countryside NN11 118 B1
Counts Farm Rd NN18 36 F4
County Rd NN13 234 A6
County View OX15 236 D4
Courier Rd NN17 37 B8
Court Cnr MK46 195 E4
Court Dr NN16 72 B6
COURTEENHALL 191 E7
Courteenhall Cl NN2 141 D5
Courteenhall Rd NN7 191 A7
Court House Cl NN6 104 F4
Court La NN6 64 D3
Courtman Rd NN9 114 A4
Court Mews NN8 130 B4
Courtney Rd NN10 132 A1
Court Rd 11 NN1 159 C5
Courtwood NN9 114 A3
Courtyard La NN11 153 A3
Courtyard The
Ecton NN6 143 F4
Islip NN14 76 B3
4 Kettering NN16 72 C3
Middleton Cheney
OX17 219 D5
Northampton NN3 142 C1
Courtyard Workshops
LE16 31 E1
Coventry Rd LE16 31 D3
Coverack Cl NN4 159 B1
Coverdale NN2 140 F5
Covert Cl NN2 141 A6
COVINGTON 116 D2
Covington Gr NN8 130 A6
Covington St NN1 160 A7
Cowbeck Cl NN4 175 E5
Cowgill Cl NN3 143 B3
Cowley Cl NN4 175 D6
Cowley Rd NN11 135 B3
Cowley Way CV23 99 F2
Cowper Cl
Earls Barton NN6 145 A4
Irthlingborough NN9 112 D1
Cowper Factory NN1 159 E7
Cowper & Newton Mus
The*MK46 195 F3
Cowper Rd
Daventry NN11 135 B2
Wellingborough NN8 129 C4
Cowpers Orch MK46 195 A1
Cowper St
Kettering NN16 72 B4
Northampton NN1 159 E7
Cowper Terr NN2 141 F1
Cowslip Cl
Corby NN18 36 D2
Rushden NN10 148 C8
Cowslip Hill NN14 89 B5
Cow Yd NN2 141 B3
Cox Gdns NN12 202 E8
Cox's Cl NN6 121 B3
Cox's La NN14 90 A5
Cox's La NN11 151 C1
Crab Apple Way NN14 76 E1
Crabb St NN10 132 B1
Crabb Tree Dr NN3 143 A7
Crabtree Cl
Hartwell NN7 192 E2
Wellingborough NN8 129 F2
Crab Tree Cl MK46 195 E5
Crabtree Ho 8 NN11 135 C2
Crabtree La NN6 84 B5
Cracknuts La NN4 160 E2
Craddock Ct NN29 147 B8
Cragside NN8 129 C6
Craigie NN8 129 C4
Cranbrooke Rd NN2 141 C1
Crane Cl
Broughton NN14 90 A5
Rushden NN10 132 B4
Wellingborough NN8 130 A2
Cranesbill Cl NN14 51 A4
Crane Wlk NN3 142 E6
Cranford CE Prim Sch
NN14 93 B7
Cranford Ho 1 NN2 141 C3
Cranford Rd
Burton Latimer NN15 92 D4
Great Addington NN14 94 A4
Kettering NN15 92 C6
Northampton NN2 141 C3
CRANFORD ST ANDREW
93 A8
CRANFORD ST JOHN 93 A7
Cranford Terr 6 NN2 141 C3
Cranleigh Rd NN15 91 B7
Cranmere Ave NN1 160 B6
Cransley Ct NN14 89 B3
Cransley Gdns NN17 36 B7
Cransley Hill NN14 90 A4
Cransley Rd NN14 70 E1
Cransley Rise NN14 89 B4
Cranstoun St NN1 159 D7
Craven St NN1 159 D7
Crawford Ave NN5 158 E7
Crawford Gr NN17 36 E8
Crawley Ave NN8 129 D7
Craxford Rd NN17 10 B1
Creampot Cl OX17 196 A2
Creampot La OX17 196 A2
CREATON 104 E4
Creaton Rd NN6 104 D5
Crediton Cl NN3 160 D7
Creed Rd PE8 41 E7
Creighton Cres NN15 91 F6
Crescent Cl LE16 31 F4
Crescent The
Burton Latimer NN15 92 C4
Easton o t H PE9 1 F5
Flore NN7 155 F6
Hackleton NN7 177 A3
Kettering NN15 91 B8
Ketton PE9 1 A7
Market Harborough LE16 31 F4
Moulton NN3 126 D1
Northampton NN1 159 F8
Pattishall NN12 172 E1
Rothwell NN14 70 C6
Rushden NN10 131 E2
Twyford OX17 230 A5
Wellingborough NN8 129 D7
Whittlebury NN12 215 C5
Creslow Ct MK11 229 F5
Cresswell Rd NN10 131 F2
Crestline Ct NN3 143 A5
Crestwood Gdns NN3 142 F5
Crestwood Rd NN3 142 F5
Creswell Wlk NN17 21 C1
CRICK 101 A5
Crick Cl NN17 22 A1
Cricketers Gn NN17 38 C8
Cricklade Cl NN3 160 D6
Crickley Cres NN4 158 E3
Crick Prim Sch NN6 100 F6
Crick Rd
Rugby CV21, CV23 99 D7
West Haddon NN6 102 A5
Yelvertoft NN6 82 A2
Crimea Cl 2 NN4 175 E7
Crispian Ct NN10 132 A2
Crispian Ho NN1 159 D7
Crispin Cotts NN6 108 A4
Crispin Ho NN1 159 B6
Crispin Pl 14 NN16 72 B2
Crispin St
14 Northampton NN1 159 C6
Rothwell NN14 70 E7
Crispin Way St NN9 114 C8
Crocket Cl NN2 141 E2
Crockwell Hill NN11 119 F1
Crocus Way NN10 148 B7
Croft Cl NN8 129 C5
Crofters Cl NN4 175 B7
Croft La
Adderbury OX17 230 A4
Roade NN7 191 D4
Staverton NN11 152 B7
Croftmeadow Ct NN3 143 B4
Croft The
Daventry NN11 153 C8
Hanging Houghton NN6 106 C8
1 Northampton NN5 140 F1
Rugby CV21 99 A8
Croft Way
Rushden NN10 132 D3
Weedon Bec NN7 155 A3
Cromarty Ct NN17 36 F5
Cromarty Ho NN17 36 F5
Crome Cl NN8 129 F8
Cromer Rd NN9 111 F4
Cromwell Cl NN14 51 A3
Cromwell Cres LE16 31 D1
Cromwell Ct NN8 130 B5
Cromwell Ho NN8 130 B4
Cromwell Rd
Kettering NN16 72 A2
Rushden NN10 132 C2
Cromwell St 15 NN1 159 C7
Cronin Ctyd NN18 37 E7
Cronin Rd NN18 37 E7
CROPREDY 196 A2
Crosby Rd LE16 31 F1
Cross Bank LE16 20 D6
Cross Brooks NN4 175 F6
Cross Ct NN16 72 A3
Crosse Cl NN7 155 C4
Cross Hill NN6 106 B3
Crosshills MK11 229 D4
Cross Keys Ct NN13 233 F7
Cross Keys Dr NN14 76 C2
Cross La
Aldwincle NN14 57 E1
Braunston NN11 118 C1
Helmdon NN13 212 A5
Weston Underwood
MK46 195 B2
Cross Rd NN8 130 B6
Cross St
Covington PE18 116 D2
Daventry NN11 135 B2
Kettering NN16 72 A3
Market Harborough LE16 31 F2
Moulton NN3 126 C1
Rothwell NN14 70 E7
Cross The
Great Houghton NN4 160 E2
Gretton NN17 10 B1
Cross Tree Rd MK19 228 B3
Cross Waters Cl NN4 175 F6
Cross Way NN9 131 D8
Crouch Rd NN9 112 F1
CROUGHTON 238 D8
Croughton All Saints CE
Prim Sch NN13 238 C8
Croughton Cl NN2 141 C5
Croughton Rd OX17 237 D7
Crowberry Ave NN3 142 C6
CROWFIELD 223 F8
Crow La NN3 161 C7
Crown Apartments 13
NN16 72 B2
Crown Ct
Corby NN18 36 E5
Oundle PE8 42 A5
Crown Ct NN10 131 E3
Crown La
Barrowden LE15 3 F5
Rothwell NN14 70 C7
West Haddon NN6 102 C4
Crownsmead NN4 158 D1
Crown St NN16 72 B3
Crown Way NN10 131 E4
Crowthorp Rd NN3 143 C5
Croxdale Cl NN2 140 F5
Croxen Cl NN15 92 C2
Croyde Ave NN18 36 F4
Croyland Hall Her Ctr
Mus*NN8 130 A4
Croyland Prim Sch
NN8 129 E3
Croyland Rd NN8 129 F3
Crucible Rd NN17 37 B7
Crystal Ct NN16 72 D3
Cubleigh Cl NN3 142 C6
Cuckoo Cl LE15 3 E5
Cukow Cl NN14 89 B4
Cullahill Ct NN4 158 E2
Culloden Ct NN17 36 F5
Culloden Dr NN15 91 F8
Culme Cl PE8 41 E7
Culross Wlk NN18 36 C3
CULWORTH 198 C3
Culworth CE Sch
OX17 198 C2
Culworth Cres NN2 141 D5
Culworth Ho OX17 198 D2
Culworth Rd OX17 197 B6
Cumberland Ave NN9 114 A4
Cumberland Cl NN3 142 A3
Cumbrae Dr NN3 143 C2
Cunliffe Dr NN16 72 A4
Cunliffe Rd Ind Est
NN16 72 A4
Cunningham Cl
Daventry NN11 135 E2
Higham Ferrers NN10 132 B5
Cupar Cres NN17 36 F5
Curgenven Cl NN11 183 E7
Curlbrook Cl NN4 176 A6
Curlew Way NN11 135 C3

Currie Rd NN2 141 C1
Curtis Mews NN8 129 C7
Curtlee Hill NN4 175 F5
Curver Way NN17 22 D1
Cyclamen Cl NN3 160 C6
Cypress Cl NN14 50 F3
Cypress Ct NN3 142 E3
Cyril St NN1 159 E6
Cytringen Cl NN15 91 A7

D

DADFORD 225 D1
Dadford Rd NN12, MK18 225 D5
Daffodil Dr NN10 148 B7
Dag La NN29 164 D2
Dagnall Rd MK46 195 E3
Dahlia Rd NN16 72 D4
Daimler Cl
Daventry NN11 135 A3
Northampton NN3 143 D4
Dainty Gr NN4 175 E3
Dairy Cl
Brixworth NN6 106 A1
West Haddon NN6 102 D4
Dairy Cotts LE17 45 A4
Dairy Field NN6 103 D1
Dairy Ground OX17 231 A6
Dairymeadow Ct NN3 142 F6
Dairy Way NN9 131 E8
Daisy Bank Ave NN14 70 C7
Daisy Cl NN18 36 C2
Daisy Croft NN10 148 C8
Dakin Cl PE8 13 F8
D'albini Cl LE16 34 B4
Dalby Cl NN16 72 A6
Dale Ave NN8 129 C5
Dale Cl
Brackley NN13 234 A7
Daventry NN11 135 B5
Mears Ashby NN6 128 C5
Wellingborough NN8 129 C5
Dale Farm Cotts NN6 128 C2
Dale Ho 1 NN8 129 F4
Dale St
Corby NN17 36 D7
Wellingborough NN8 129 F4
Dalestones NN4 158 D2
Daleswood Rise PE8 13 E7
Dale The NN8 129 C5
Dalkeith Ave 20 NN16 72 B2
Dalkeith Pl NN16 72 B2
Dalkeith Rd NN8 129 F1
Dallacre Dr LE16 34 C4
Dallacre Farm LE16 34 D4
DALLINGTON 158 F8
Dallington Cl NN14 54 A2
Dallington Ct NN5 158 F8
Dallington Gn 2 NN5 158 F8
Dallington Haven 5 NN5 158 F8
Dallington Park Rd NN5 158 F8
Dallington Rd NN5 159 A7
Dallison Cl LE16 48 E8
DALSCOTE 173 B1
Dalston Wlk 6 NN3 142 C4
Dalton Rd NN17 21 E2
Damherst Piece NN6 106 C2
Damson Cl NN14 76 E1
Damson Dell NN3 161 A8
Dance Way NN8 129 F8
Dando Cl NN29 146 D1
Dands Cl OX17 220 A8
Dands Dr OX17 220 A8
Dane Ct NN11 118 C1
Danefield Rd NN3 142 B1
Daneholme Ave NN11 135 C4
Dane Ridge NN5 158 C6
Danes Backside NN2 141 B3
Danes Camp Way NN4 158 E3
Danesholme Jun & Inf Sch NN18 36 A2
Danesholme Rd NN18 36 A2
Danes Way NN6 100 C7
Danetre Dr NN11 135 D2
Danetree Gdns NN3 142 B2
Danetre Hospl NN11 153 C8
Danetre Sch NN11 135 E1
Danewood Gdns NN3 142 B2
Danford Cl PE8 41 F4
Danfords PE8 41 F5
Daniaud Ct NN13 233 E8
Daniell Wlk NN18 36 D5
Daniels Rd NN8 130 C1
Dapplestone Cl NN4 158 D2
Darby Cl NN8 129 A5
Dardis Cl 2 NN2 141 E1
Darenth Ct 18 NN1 159 C7
Darescroft LE16 20 B1
Dark La
Braunston NN11 118 D1
Great Harrowden NN9 110 D2
Darley Cl NN16 72 C6
Darley Dale Rd NN17 36 D8
Dart Cl NN17 21 D2
Dartford Cl 2 NN4 159 A2
Dartmouth Rd MK46 195 F4
Dartmouth Row 3 NN11 135 D1
Darwin Ct NN17 37 C8
Darwin Ho NN17 22 F1
Darwin Rd NN17 37 C8
Darwin Wlk NN5 140 C1
Dash Farm Cl NN17 38 A8
DAVENTRY 135 D3
Daventry Abbey Jun Sch The NN11 135 D1
Daventry Cty Pk* NN11 135 D5
Daventry Cty Pk Visitor Ctr NN11 135 D5
Daventry Rd
Banbury OX16 208 A2
Barby CV23 118 C8
Kilsby CV23 100 A1
Newnham NN11 153 D4
Norton NN11 136 C5
Staverton NN11 152 B7
Staverton NN11 152 C7
Willoughby CV23 117 C7
Daventry Tert Coll NN11 153 B8
Daventry William Parker Sch NN11 135 C3
Davey Rd NN17 37 C8
Davies Cl
Kettering NN15 90 F8
Market Harborough LE16 31 D5
Da Vinci Cl NN5 158 C5
Davis Cl NN14 70 E6
Davis Ct NN17 37 A6
Davy Cl NN8 129 A6
Dawkins Ct NN14 90 A4
Dayrell Rd NN4 158 F2
Dayrell Sq 5 NN4 158 F2
Dayton St NN10 132 A2
Deacon Cl
Market Harborough LE16 31 D5
Rushden NN10 132 D3
Deacons Ct NN3 143 C4
Deal Ct NN1 159 D7
Deal St NN1 159 C7
Dean Cl
Raunds NN9 114 D7
Rushden NN10 148 A8
Deancourt Dr NN5 140 A1
Deane Par CV21 99 A8
Deane Rd CV21 99 B8
DEANSHANGER 228 D4
Deanshanger Dr NN12 216 F1
Deanshanger Prim Sch MK19 228 E3
Deanshanger Rd
Old Stratford MK19 229 B6
Wicken MK19 228 B3
Deans Row NN7 173 E2
Deansway NN3 143 C4
Dean Wlk 6 NN11 135 B4
Debbs Cl MK11 229 E5
Debdale Rd
Northampton NN3 142 D2
Wellingborough NN8 129 F5
Deben Rd NN17 21 D1
De Capel Cl NN14 94 D6
DEDDINGTON 236 A4
Deddington Castle Earthworks* OX15 236 A4
Deeble Rd NN15 72 F1
DEENE 23 F6
Deene Cl
Adderbury OX17 230 B4
Corby NN17 36 E7
Market Harborough LE16 32 A3
Deene End NN17 38 C8
Deene Pk* NN17 23 E5
Deene Rd
Deene NN17 11 D3
Harringworth NN17 10 F7
Deeneside NN17 38 B8
DEENETHORPE 24 B4
Deenethorpe La NN17 24 B5
Deepdale LE16 20 D7
Deep Side PE9 1 F4
Deer Cl NN4 175 F2
Deerings Rd CV21 99 A8
Deer Park Rd NN3 142 A6
Dee Wlk NN11 135 A1
De Ferneus Dr NN9 114 D7
Delamere Dr NN15 92 A5
Delamere Rd NN4 159 C2
Delapre Abbey* NN4 159 D3
Delapre Cres NN4 159 C3
Delapre Crescent Rd NN4 159 C3
Delapre Ct NN4 159 C2
Delapre Pl NN18 36 A3
Delapre Prim Sch NN4 159 B3
Delapre St NN4 159 B3
De Lisle Cl LE16 31 D2
Dell Cres NN3 143 B5
Dell Pl NN10 132 C2
Dells MK46 195 F4
Dells Cl PE28 61 D2
Dell The NN6 144 E4
Delta Way NN2 141 A5
Delves The NN9 114 C6
De Montfort Ct NN13 222 E1
Dempsey Dr NN14 70 F6
Demswell NN6 106 C2
Denbeigh Ho 5 NN10 132 B2
Denbigh Rd NN3 160 D6
Denby Dale NN8 129 D7
Dencora Bsns Pk NN8 129 A4
Dene Cl
Kettering NN16 72 A5
Dene Cl *continued*
Wellingborough NN8 129 C6
Denfield Park Jun Sch NN10 132 C3
DENFORD 95 C5
Denford Dr NN15 91 F5
Denford Rd
Corby NN17 36 B8
Ringstead NN14 95 C4
Thrapston NN14 95 D8
Denford Way NN8 129 D7
Denington Ct NN8 130 A2
Denington Ind Est NN8 130 B2
Denington Rd NN8 130 A2
Denman Cl LE16 34 A4
Denmark Cl NN18 35 F3
Denmark Ct NN10 132 C1
Denmark Rd
Northampton NN1 159 E6
Rushden NN10 132 C1
Denne Cl NN18 36 C1
Denney Cres NN11 135 B2
Denston Cl NN4 159 B1
Dent Cl NN5 157 F7
DENTON 178 A8
Denton Cl
Irchester NN29 147 B8
Rushden NN10 132 C3
Denton Ct NN15 92 B2
Denton Prim Sch NN7 178 C8
Denton Rd NN7 178 B6
De Quincey Cl NN13 222 E1
Derby Mews NN1 159 F8
Derby Rd NN1 159 F8
Dering Cotts OX17 210 E2
Derling Dr NN9 114 E6
Derngate NN1 159 D5
De Roos Way LE16 34 B4
Derry The NN6 100 F5
Derwent Cl
Daventry NN11 135 A1
Northampton NN5 140 F1
Wellingborough NN8 129 C6
Derwent Cres NN16 71 F2
Derwent Dr NN5 140 F2
Derwent Ho PE8 42 A6
Derwent Wlk NN17 21 D2
DESBOROUGH 51 C2
Desborough Rd
Arthingworth LE16 49 F1
Braybrooke LE16 49 F5
Rothwell NN14 70 C7
Rushton NN14 52 B2
Stoke Albany LE16 34 B3
De Vere Rd NN14 76 D2
Deveron Wlk NN17 21 D1
Devon Dr NN15 91 D6
Devon Ox Rd CV23 99 F2
Devonshire Cl
Boughton NN2 141 C8
Wellingborough NN8 129 E6
Devonshire Ho 6 NN5 159 A6
Devon Way NN3 142 A5
Devon Wlk NN10 132 C1
Dewar Dr NN11 135 A4
Dexter Way PE8 28 B3
Diamond Dr NN9 131 E8
Diamonds Bsns Ctr NN9 113 A3
Diamond Way NN9 113 A2
Diana Ho NN8 129 D5
Diana Way NN15 92 B1
Dibbin Cl NN17 38 B8
Dickens Dr
Kettering NN16 72 B6
Old Stratford MK19 229 B6
Dickens Spinney MK46 195 E4
Dick's Hill LE16 47 C5
Dickson Cl 4 NN4 158 F3
Digby St NN16 72 C3
Dimock Sq NN4 158 F2
Dinglederry MK46 195 F4
Dingle Rd NN10 131 E2
Dingle The
Daventry NN11 153 C8
Rugby CV21 99 B8
DINGLEY 33 A4
Dingley La LE16 32 F6
Dingley Rd LE16 32 B6
Dingley Terr LE16 31 F3
Disbrowe Ct NN9 133 C7
Diswell Brook Way MK19 228 E5
Ditchford Cl NN4 175 F6
Ditchford Rd NN8 131 C5
Dixon Rd NN2 141 E6
Dixon Wlk NN17 37 A6
Dobbins Cl OX17 231 A6
Dobson Cl NN4 160 F2
Dobson Wlk NN18 36 D5
Dockham Way NN6 100 E6
Docklewell Cl NN12 203 A4
Doctors La
Eydon NN11 184 C1
Great Doddington NN29 145 E6
Doddington Ct NN8 129 F2
Doddington Rd
Earls Barton NN6 145 A4
Great Doddington NN8 145 F8
Wellingborough NN8 129 F2
Wilby NN8 145 B8
Doddridge 1 NN1 159 C5
Doddridge Ho 21 NN1 159 C6
Doddridge Rd 1 LE16 31 E4
Doddridge St 24 NN1 159 C6
DODFORD 154 F6
Dog La
Napton on t H CV47 150 A7
South Kilworth LE17 63 C8
Dolben Ave NN9 113 F4
Dolben Cl NN9 111 E4
Dolben Sq NN9 111 F4
Dolver Cl NN18 36 C2
Donald Greaves Ho NN17 21 D1
Donaldson Ave NN14 90 A3
Don Cl NN17 21 D1
Donellan Gn NN3 142 F6
Donne Cl
Higham Ferrers NN10 132 A5
Kettering NN16 72 C6
Donovan Ct NN3 160 E8
Dorcas Rd OX16 219 A6
Dorchester Ct NN5 140 B2
Dore Cl NN3 143 B5
Doris Rd NN16 72 E4
Dorking Wlk NN18 36 C3
Dorman Cl NN3 142 B4
Dorothy Rd NN16 72 E3
Dorset Gdns NN2 141 D3
Dorset Rd
Corby NN17 36 C6
Northampton NN2 141 D3
Doubles The NN11 135 B1
Douglas Ct NN15 91 E8
Douglas Rd NN5 157 F8
Douglass Dr LE16 31 F4
Doulton Cl NN14 50 F3
Dove Cl NN12 203 C3
Dovecote Cl
Barrowden LE15 3 F5
Kettering NN15 91 F7
Raunds NN9 114 E7
Weston by W LE16 18 B3
Yarwell PE8 16 A8
Dovecote Dr
Denton NN7 162 B1
Little Addington NN14 113 B7
Dovecote Rd NN7 191 C4
Dovecote The
King's Cliffe PE8 13 F7
Pitsford NN6 125 D5
Dovecote Yd NN14 110 A5
Dove Cotts OX17 210 A6
Dovedale Gr NN14 50 E4
Dovedale Rd NN17 36 E7
Dovehouse Cl
Brackley NN13 233 F7
Stanwick NN9 113 F3
Welford NN6 64 E6
Dovehouse Ct MK19 228 E4
Dover Cl NN10 132 D1
Dovercourt NN5 159 B5
Dove's La NN3 126 D1
Downing Way NN11 153 C7
Downs The NN9 110 E1
Downsway NN4 175 B6
Downwood Cl NN3 143 C3
Dowthorpe End NN6 144 F4
Dowthorpe Hill NN6 144 F3
Drake Cl
Corby NN17 36 B8
Daventry NN11 135 E1
Rothwell NN14 70 E7
Drake Lee Mews NN16 72 B1
Draper's Cl PE8 28 C3
Drapery NN1 159 C6
DRAUGHTON 87 E6
Draughton Rd NN6 87 B7
Draycott Cl NN3 160 D7
Draymans Wlk NN13 233 E6
Drayson La NN6 100 F6
DRAYTON
Corby 20 A5
Daventry 135 A2
Drayton Cl
Corby NN18 36 B4
Islip NN14 76 B3
Rushden NN10 148 A8
Drayton Fields Ind Est NN11 135 A5
Drayton Leys CV22 98 A7
Drayton Pk NN11 135 B5
Drayton Pl NN9 112 F3
Drayton Rd
Bringhurst LE16 20 B5
Drayton LE16 19 D7
Irthlingborough NN9 112 F3
Lowick NN14 75 E6
Medbourne LE16 19 A5
Drayton Way NN11 135 A5
Drayton Wlk NN2 141 D4
Dresden Cl NN18 35 F2
Driffield Gr NN17 36 F7
Drift The
Collyweston PE9 1 D2
Sutton PE5 8 F3
Drift Way MK46 195 F5
Drill Hall Ct NN15 72 A1
Drive The
Horton NN7 177 E1
Kettering NN15 72 B1
Northampton, Duston NN5 158 A7
Northampton, Phippsville NN1 141 F1
Rushden NN10 132 C1
Wellingborough NN8 130 A3
Droue Ct NN14 70 C7
Drovers Wlk NN2 141 A5
Drove The
Collyweston PE9 1 D1
Nassington PE8 15 E5
Druce End NN12 217 E6
Druids Way NN3 141 F5
Drum La 30 NN1 159 C6
Drumming Well La PE8 42 A5
Drummond Cl NN6 125 D4
Drydale Ave NN3 142 B3
Dryden Ave NN11 135 B2
Dryden Cl NN11 184 A7
Dryden Rd
Northampton NN5 158 F7
Towcester NN12 203 C5
Wellingborough NN8 130 C5
Dryden's Cl NN14 77 C4
Dryden St
Kettering NN16 72 B3
Raunds NN9 114 C6
Dryden Way
Corby NN17 36 C8
Higham Ferrers NN10 132 B5
Dryland Rd NN3 142 C2
Dryland St NN16 72 B2
Dryleys Ct NN3 143 B5
Drywell Ct NN3 143 A1
Duchess Cl NN16 72 B4
Duchess End NN6 128 C2
Duchess Gdns NN12 217 D3
Duchy Cl
Chelveston NN9 133 B8
Higham Ferrers NN10 132 C5
Duck End
Cranford St John NN14 93 B7
Denford NN14 95 D6
Hinton-in-t-H NN13 232 F6
Wollaston NN29 146 D3
Duck La
Harpole NN7 157 C6
Oundle PE8 42 A5
Duck St
Elton PE8 16 D1
Rushden NN10 132 B2
Duckworth Dell NN3 142 F6
Duckworth Rd NN17 36 B7
DUDDINGTON 5 B6
Duffy Pl CV21 99 A8
Dugdale Cl NN14 76 D2
Dukelands NN7 155 A3
Dukes Ct NN15 92 C2
Dukes Green Rd NN7 157 D3
Duke St
Burton Latimer NN15 92 B2
Kettering NN16 72 B3
Northampton NN1 159 D7
Polebrook PE8 42 F3
Wellingborough NN8 129 E1
Dulce Rd NN5 158 C8
Dulley Ave NN8 129 F1
Dulverton Rd NN3 160 D7
Dumas Cul-De-Sac NN13 233 E8
Dumble Cl NN18 36 D2
Dunbar Ct NN15 91 F8
Duncan Cl NN3 141 F7
Duncan Ct NN8 129 D3
Duncan Rd NN17 36 B7
DUNCOTE 188 E2
Dundee St NN5 158 F6
Dunedin Rd NN18 36 C2
Dungee Rd MK43 165 E2
Dunkirk Ave NN14 51 B3
Dunmore Rd LE16 32 A1
Dunn Cl NN6 101 A6
Dunnock La NN4 175 F3
Dunnock Rd NN18 36 E3
Dunslade Cl LE16 32 B2
Dunslade Gr LE16 32 B2
Dunslade Rd LE16 32 A2
DUNSMORE 80 C6
Dunsmore Ave CV22 98 E8
Dunster St NN1 159 D6
Durban Rd NN16 72 D2
Durham Cl NN17 36 B6
Durness Cl NN15 91 E8
Dusthill Rd NN14 55 D8
DUSTON 158 C7
Duston Cl NN11 135 A3
Duston Eldean Prim Sch NN5 140 B1
Duston Mill La NN5 158 D4
Duston Rd NN5 158 E6
Duston Sch The NN5 158 A8
Duston Wildes NN5 140 A2
Dybdale Cres NN8 129 E5
Dychurch La
Bozeat NN29 164 E3
Northampton NN1 159 D6
Dyson Cl CV21 80 A1
Dyson Dr NN16 72 A4

E

Eady Cl NN3 126 E1
Eady Rd NN15 92 B1
Eady's Row NN14 94 D7
Eagle Dr NN4 159 F2
Eaglehurst NN6 106 C2
Eagle La NN14 71 B1
Eaglesfield NN11 136 C4
Eaglethorpe PE8 28 B4

EAKLEY LANES 193 D2
Ealing Terr NN10 132 A3
EARLS BARTON 144 F3
Earls Barton Inf Sch NN6 144 E4
Earls Barton Jun Sch NN6 144 E4
Earls Barton Mus* NN6 144 E4
Earls Barton Rd
Great Doddington NN29 145 C5
Mears Ashby NN6 128 B2
Earlsfield Cl NN4 176 A6
Earl's La OX15 236 A4
Earl Spencer Prim Sch NN5 159 A8
Earl St NN1 159 D7
Earlstrees Ct NN17 21 F2
Earlstrees Ind Est NN17 21 E2
Earlstrees Rd NN17 21 F2
EAST ADDERBURY 230 B4
East Ave
Burton Latimer NN15 92 B3
Corby NN17 36 F5
Kettering NN15 72 D2
East Bank NN3 142 E6
Eastbourne Ave NN18 36 B5
Eastbrook NN18 36 B4
Eastbrook Hill NN14 51 C3
East Butterfield Ct NN3 142 F5
EAST CARLTON 35 A7
East Carlton Countryside Pk* LE16 35 B8
East Carlton Pk LE16 35 B7
East Cl NN15 72 D2
EASTCOTE 189 A8
Eastcote Rd NN7 189 D8
East Cres
Rushden NN10 131 F2
Weldon NN17 38 C8
East Dr NN15 72 E2
EAST END 230 B4
East End NN6 106 F5
Eastern Ave N NN2 141 D4
Eastern Ave S NN2 141 D3
Eastern Cl NN2 141 D5
Eastern Way NN11 135 C2
EAST FARNDON 48 B7
Eastfield NN7 190 D7
Eastfield Cl NN5 140 C1
Eastfield Cres
Finedon NN9 112 A5
Yardley Gobion NN12 217 F5
Eastfield Dr MK19 207 A3
Eastfield Prim Sch NN3 142 B3
Eastfield Rd
Brixworth NN6 106 B1
3 Irthlingborough NN9 112 F2
Northampton, Duston NN5 158 B8
Northampton, Far Cotton NN4 159 C3
Wellingborough NN8 130 C6
Wollaston NN29 146 E2
Eastfields NN11 118 C1
Eastfields Cres PE8 15 E6
East Gr NN10 132 B3
EAST HADDON 122 D5
East Haddon CE Prim Sch NN6 122 D5
East Haddon Rd NN6 122 D8
Easthill Cl NN13 233 F7
East Hunsbury Prim Sch NN4 175 B6
Eastlands Rd NN9 112 A5
East Langham Rd NN9 114 D7
Eastleigh Rd NN15 91 D7
East Leys Ct NN3 142 C7
Eastmead Ct NN3 143 A1
Easton Garford CE Sch PE9 2 A5
Easton La NN29 164 C3
EASTON MAUDIT 163 F2
EASTON ON THE HILL 2 A4
Easton Way NN7 163 E4
Easton Wlk NN17 37 B6
East Oval NN5 140 F2
East Paddock Ct NN3 143 A4
East Park Par NN1 159 F8
East Priors Ct NN3 143 A4
East Rd PE8 42 A5
East Rising NN4 175 D7
East St
Irchester NN29 147 B8
Long Buckby NN6 121 D4
Market Harborough LE16 31 D3
Northampton NN1 159 F6
Olney MK46 195 F4
Stanwick NN9 114 A3
East View OX17 210 E2
East Wlk NN15 72 E2
Eastwood Gr CV21 99 C8
Eastwood Rd PE8 42 A5
Eaton Rd NN5 158 A8
Eaton Wlk NN10 132 B2
Ebbw Vale Rd NN9 131 E8
Ebenezer Pl 16 NN16 72 B2
Ebony Ct NN11 184 D5
Eccles Rd PE8 7 D8
Eckland Lodge Bsns Pk NN14 50 D6
ECTON 143 F4
ECTON BROOK 143 D2
Ecton Brook Prim Sch NN3 143 D2
Ecton Brook Rd NN3 143 D2
Ecton Hall NN6 143 F4
Ecton La NN6 127 D2
Ecton Leys CV22 98 A7
Ecton Park Rd NN3 143 C3
Ecton St 11 NN1 159 E6
Ecton Village Prim Sch NN6 143 F4
Edale Gn NN14 50 E4
Eden Cl
Daventry NN11 135 A1
Northampton NN3 142 B4
Eden Ct NN6 120 C6
Eden St NN16 72 B2
Edgar Mobbs Way NN5 158 E5
Edgar Rd NN16 72 D3
EDGCOTE 197 A4
Edgcote Drive Cotts OX17 197 A4
Edgehill Dr NN11 135 D6
Edgehill Rd NN5 140 D1
Edgell St NN16 72 C2
Edgemead Cl NN3 142 E7
Edgemont Rd NN3 142 E1
Edges Ct NN3 142 C7
Edgewood NN13 222 F1
Edinburgh Cl
Market Harborough LE16 31 F4
Rothwell NN14 70 C6
Edinburgh Ho NN5 158 C8
Edinburgh Mews NN2 141 C2
Edinburgh Rd
Kettering NN16 72 D3
Northampton NN2 141 C2
Wellingborough NN8 129 E1
Edinburgh Sq 3 NN11 135 B3
Edison Cl NN8 129 A6
Edison Ct NN8 129 A6
Edison Ctyd NN17 21 F3
Edison Dr NN5 158 D4
Edith Rd NN16 72 E4
Edith St NN1 159 E6
Edmonds Cl NN8 130 A2
Edmonds Dr PE9 1 A5
Edmund St NN16 72 D2
Edward Cl
Higham Ferrers NN10 132 C7
Kettering NN15 91 C7
Edwardian Cl NN4 175 E7
Edward Rd
Irchester NN29 147 B7
Kettering NN15 91 C7
Market Harborough LE16 31 D5
Edwards Cl NN11 183 D7
Edwards Dr NN8 129 D5
Edward Watson Cl NN2 141 B5
Edwinstowe Cl NN3 160 E7
Egerton Cl NN13 234 A7
Egmont Ave MK11 229 E4
Eider Cl
Burton Latimer NN15 92 A2
Daventry NN11 135 C3
Eismann Way NN17 37 C7
Ekins Cl NN3 142 D2
Elan Ct NN10 131 E3
Eldean Rd NN5 140 B1
Elderberry Ct NN3 143 C3
Elder Dr NN11 135 C4
Eldon Cl NN6 100 E6
Eldon Way NN6 100 E6
Eleanor Ct NN6 102 C5
Eleonore Ho NN3 142 C3
Elgin St NN5 158 F6
Eliot Cl NN16 72 C6
Elizabeth Cl
Earls Barton NN6 144 E5
Wellingborough NN8 129 D2
Elizabeth Ct NN10 132 C7
Elizabeth Rd
Daventry NN11 135 B3
Kettering NN16 72 D3
Rothwell NN14 70 C6
West Haddon NN6 102 C5
Elizabeth St
Corby NN17 36 E6
Northampton NN1 159 F6
Elizabeth Way
Earls Barton NN6 144 E5
Higham Ferrers NN10 132 C7
Irthlingborough NN9 131 E8
Elizabeth Wlk 6 NN1 159 F6
ELKINGTON 83 A5
Elkington La CV23 99 B1
Elkington Rd NN6 82 B4
Elkins Cl NN6 82 B4
Ellen Cl NN6 100 F6
Ellesmere Ave
Brackley NN13 233 F8
Northampton NN5 158 E7
Ellesmere Cl NN13 222 F1
Ellesmere Cres NN13 222 F1
Ellesmere Ct NN13 233 F8
Ellesmere Rd NN13 222 F1
Ellfield Ct NN3 142 F3
Elliot Ho 1 NN10 132 A2
Elliot Way NN10 132 A5
Ellis La NN14 89 B4
Ellison Cl NN9 114 C7
Elm Cl
Brafield-on-t-G NN7 161 D2
Hargrave NN9 115 F2
Elm Ct NN14 76 D1
Elm Dr
Brackley NN13 222 F1
Deanshanger MK19 228 D5
Hinton NN11 184 A6
Market Harborough LE16 31 C2
Elmfield Cl NN12 217 D3
Elm Gr NN4 176 A6
Elmhurst Ave NN3 142 A2
Elmhurst Ct NN3 142 A2
Elmington Cotts PE8 42 C8
Elmington Rd NN3 143 C5
Elmlea Dr MK46 195 F4
Elm Rd
Burton Latimer NN15 92 C4
Kettering NN15 72 D1
Elms Dr CV22 98 F8
Elms Dyke NN11 135 E8
Elm St
19 Northampton NN1 159 C7
Wellingborough NN8 129 F5
Elm Way NN7 177 C3
Elm Wlk
Corby NN17 21 D1
Higham Ferrers NN10 132 B6
Elmwood Wlk NN5 140 A1
Elsden Rd NN8 130 C5
ELTON 28 E8
Elton CE Prim Sch PE8 28 D8
Elton Cl
Desborough NN14 50 E3
Northampton NN3 143 B5
Elton Hall* PE8 28 D6
Elton Rd PE8 16 C7
Elwes Way NN3 143 B2
Elysium Terr NN2 159 C8
Embankment NN8 130 C2
EMBERTON 195 F1
Emberton Ctry Pk & Visitor Ctr* MK46 195 E1
Emerald Way NN1 159 B5
Emerton Gdns MK11 229 D5
Emery Cl NN11 135 E8
Emley Cl NN3 142 F1
Emmanuel Cl NN11 153 C8
Encon Ct NN3 141 F7
Enfield Cl NN5 157 F8
English Martyrs RC Prim Sch CV21 99 A7
Ennerdale Cl
Daventry NN11 135 A2
Kettering NN16 72 A2
Northampton NN3 142 A3
Ennerdale Rd
Corby NN17 21 E1
Northampton NN3 142 A4
Rushden NN10 132 D3
Ensleigh Cl NN15 92 C1
Enstone Ct NN8 129 E1
Enterprise Cl NN16 71 F4
Enterprise Ct NN8 129 B6
Enterprise Ind Pk NN17 22 F1
Enterprise Rd NN9 114 D7
Entwood Dr NN3 143 B5
Epping Cl NN15 92 A5
Epping Wlk 4 NN11 135 B4
Epsom Cl NN10 148 D8
Epsom Wlk NN18 36 C3
Equestrian Way NN7 155 B4
Ericsson Cl NN11 135 C5
Ermine Rd NN3 143 C5
Ermont Way OX16 219 A7
Erskin Wood NN6 105 B1
Esher Ct NN3 142 D4
Eskdaill Pl NN16 72 B3
Eskdaill St NN16 72 B3
Eskdale Ave
Corby NN17 36 E7
Northampton NN3 142 B3
Eskdale Cl NN8 129 C6
Essenden Ct MK11 229 F5
Essen La CV23 100 A3
Essex Cl NN17 36 B6
Essex Gdns LE16 31 D1
Essex Pl NN15 91 D6
Essex Rd NN10 132 C1
Essex St NN2 159 C8
Essex Terr NN2 159 C8
Ethel St NN1 159 E6
Eton Cl NN7 155 C4
Eton Ct 3 NN2 141 C3
Ettrick Cl NN16 72 A6
Euro Bsns Pk LE16 32 B4
Euro Hub NN18 37 A4
Euston Rd NN4 159 C3
Evans Cl NN11 135 E1
Eva Rd NN16 72 E3
Evelyn Way NN29 147 C7
Evelyn Wlk NN9 114 D6
EVENLEY 233 E2
Evenley Rd
Mixbury NN13 234 D1
Northampton NN2 141 C5
Evensford Wlk NN9 131 D8
Everard Cl CV23 80 A5
EVERDON 170 B8
Everdon Cl
Northampton NN2 141 E4
Rugby CV22 98 E8
Everdon Pk NN11 135 A5
Everdon Rd NN12 170 E3
Everdon Stubbs Nature Trail* NN11 170 C6
Everdon Stubbs Woodland Trust Wood* NN11 170 D6
Everest Ho NN17 36 E6
Everest La NN17 36 E6
Evergreen Dr NN14 113 B7
Everitt Cl NN8 130 B2
Evesham Cl NN8 129 E1
Evesham Ct NN3 143 A7
Evison Ct NN14 70 C6
Evison Rd NN14 70 C6
Ewenfield Rd NN9 111 F4
Excalibur Cl NN5 158 A7
Excelsior NN8 129 B4
Excelsior Cl NN9 112 E2
Excelsior Gdns NN5 157 F8
Exeter Cl NN11 153 C8
Exeter Inf Sch NN18 36 F5
Exeter Pl NN1 159 E7
Exeter St NN16 72 C5
Exmoor Cl NN3 160 D7
Exmouth Ave NN18 36 F4
Express Cl NN9 131 E8
Express Pk
Kettering NN16 71 F3
Rushden NN10 131 D3
Eyam Cl NN14 50 E3
EYDON 184 C1
Eyeletter Ho 7 NN5 159 A6
Eynard Impasse NN13 222 E1
Eynon Cl NN3 126 B1

F

Factory La 9 LE16 31 E3
Fairfax Rd LE16 31 E1
Fairfax Rise NN6 85 B8
Fairfield NN7 174 B2
Fairfield Rd
Isham NN14 91 E1
Market Harborough LE16 31 D4
Northampton NN2 141 F2
Paulerspury NN12 216 B7
Fairfields Sch NN2 141 E1
Fairground Way NN3 160 E7
Fairhurst Way NN6 144 F4
Fair La NN14 76 E3
Fairlight Ct 8 NN18 36 B5
Fairmead Cres NN10 147 F8
Fairmead Rise NN2 140 F6
Fair Mile NN2 141 A6
Fairoaks Dr NN9 114 C7
Fairoaks The NN3 160 F8
Fairway
Market Harborough LE16 31 D4
Northampton NN2 141 E2
Fairway The
Daventry NN11 135 F2
Kettering NN15 91 A8
Wellingborough NN9 110 E1
Faith Terr MK19 207 A2
Falcon Dr MK19 229 B7
Falconers Cl NN11 135 C3
Falconer's Hill Com Jun & Inf Schs NN11 135 C3
Falconers Rise NN4 175 A8
Falcon View NN12 202 D8
Falcon Way NN13 222 D2
FALCUTT 212 A2
Falcutt Way NN2 141 D5
Falkner's Cl OX17 230 A4
Fallowfield NN9 129 E8
Fallowfields NN6 101 A6
Fallow Wlk NN2 141 A6
Falmer Wlk NN18 36 B4
Falster Cl NN18 36 A2
Faracre Ct NN3 143 B1
Faraday Cl
Daventry NN11 135 A4
Northampton NN5 158 D5
Wellingborough NN8 129 A6
Faraday Ct
Thrapston NN14 76 E2
Wellingborough NN8 129 A6
Faraday Gr NN17 37 A8
Faramir Pl NN3 143 B6
Far Brook NN6 125 B8
FAR COTTON 159 B3
Farebrother Cl NN11 183 D7
Fareham Ave CV22 98 E8
Far End NN5 158 F6
Faringdon Ct NN3 143 A7
Farmbrook Ct NN3 142 F5
Farm Cl
Brigstock NN14 55 F7
Holcot NN6 126 E8
Northampton NN2 141 B4
Farmclose Rd NN4 175 E6
Far Meadow Ct NN3 142 E5
Farmers Cl NN4 175 E5
Farmers Dr NN13 233 D8
Farmfield Ct NN15 91 F4
Farm Field Ct NN3 142 E5
Farmhill Rd NN3 143 A6
Farm Rd
Brackley NN13 234 A6
Wellingborough NN8 129 E8
Farmstead Rd NN18 36 A5
Farm Stile NN11 182 C8
Farmyard The NN7 163 A3
Farnborough Cl
Corby NN18 36 E1
Farnborough Cl *continued*
Kettering NN15 91 D5
Farnborough Dr 8 NN11 135 B7
Farndale Ave NN17 36 E7
Farndale View LE16 31 C2
FARNDISH 147 B4
Farndish Cl NN10 131 F2
Farndish Rd NN29 147 B7
Farndon Cl NN3 142 F6
Farndon Ct LE16 31 D2
Farndon Fields Prim Sch LE16 48 E8
Farndon Rd
Great Oxendon LE16 48 D4
Hinton NN11 184 A5
Lubenham LE16 30 F2
Market Harborough LE16 31 D1
Marston Trussell LE16 47 D7
Farnham Dr NN10 147 F8
Farnworth Cl NN5 140 C1
Farraxton Sq NN4 158 E2
Farrer Cl NN13 223 D4
Farthing Ct CV21 99 B8
FARTHINGHOE 221 B4
Farthinghoe Cl NN13 233 D7
Farthinghoe Prim Sch NN13 221 B4
Farthinghoe Rd OX17 231 F5
FARTHINGSTONE 170 F2
Farthingstone Rd
Litchborough NN12 171 B2
Weedon Bec NN7 155 B1
Faugere Cl NN13 233 F8
Favell Way NN3 160 D8
Fawsley Leys CV22 98 A7
Fawsley Rd
Everdon NN11 170 A8
Northampton NN4 159 C2
FAXTON 88 C3
Faxton Cl NN2 141 D4
Faxton End NN6 107 D7
Fay Cl NN11 184 A7
Feast Field Cl NN29 146 D1
Featherbed La
Geddington NN18 37 B1
Rugby CV21 80 A1
Federation Ave NN14 50 F2
Fegans Ct MK11 229 D6
Fellmead Rd NN3 143 C5
Fellows Cl NN29 146 C3
Fellows Way CV21 98 F8
Fell Wlk NN8 129 D6
Fengate Cl NN3 143 C5
Fenn Cl PE8 15 E5
Fennel Ct NN4 175 D5
Fenners Cl NN10 132 D2
Fenny Compton Rd OX17 181 D1
Fenton Rise NN13 233 D7
Fenwick Dr CV21 99 A8
Ferguson's Cl PE8 43 A3
Fermoy Ct NN7 138 B4
Fermyn Cl NN14 55 F8
Fermyn Pl NN18 36 A3
Fermyn Woods Ctry Pk* NN14 56 A7
Fern Dale Cl NN14 54 B3
Ferndale Rd NN3 142 D2
Ferne Furlong MK46 195 F5
Fernfield Cl LE16 32 B4
Fernie Chase LE16 17 A6
Fernie Cl NN15 92 A5
Fernie Ct LE17 45 E6
Fernie Field NN3 142 C6
Fernie Rd LE16 31 F3
Fernie Way NN8 129 D4
Fern Ley Cl LE16 32 B2
Fernmoor Dr NN9 112 F2
Fern Rd NN10 131 E3
Ferrers Ct NN10 132 C7
Ferrers Specialist Arts Coll The NN10 132 C5
Ferrestone Rd NN8 130 A6
Ferris Row NN3 160 F7
Ferro Fields NN6 106 C3
Fessey Rd NN11 183 D8
Festival Cl NN9 113 B5
Festival Rd NN12 172 D1
Fetter St NN1 159 D5
Fettledine Rd NN9 113 B5
Field Cl NN6 102 C4
Field Cotts NN18 53 B8
Fieldgate Cl NN4 175 F6
Fieldhead Cl LE16 31 C3
Fieldmill Rd NN3 143 B1
Field Rose Sq 4 NN3 143 C2
Field St NN16 72 B3
Field Street Ave NN16 72 B3
Fields View NN8 130 B4
Field View
Brackley NN13 233 D7
Braunston NN11 118 C1
Marston St Lawrence OX17 210 B2
Fieldway NN3 142 B1
Field Way NN13 212 A5
Fiennes Ct NN11 135 B6
Fiensgate NN4 158 D1
Fife St NN5 158 F7
Fifth Ave NN13 238 E7
Fifth St E NN13 238 E7
Fifth St NN13 238 E7
Filey Ct NN18 36 B4
Filleigh Way NN3 160 C7
Finch Dr NN15 92 A6
Finch-Hatton Dr NN17 10 C1

FINEDON 111 E4
Finedon Hall NN9 111 E4
Finedon Inf Sch NN9 111 F5
Finedon Mulso CE Jun Sch NN9 112 A5
Finedon Rd
Burton Latimer NN15 92 B1
Irthlingborough NN9 112 E3
Wellingborough NN8 130 B6
Finedon Road Ind Est NN8 130 B8
Finedon St NN15 92 B1
Finedon Station Rd NN9 111 A6
Fineshade Cl
Kettering NN15 92 A5
King's Cliffe PE8 13 E7
Fineshade Gr NN17 36 E7
Finland Way NN18 36 A2
Finney Dr NN4 175 E3
Firbank Cl NN3 160 F8
Firdale Ave NN10 132 B4
Fire Quarters The NN7 155 C4
Fir Rd NN16 72 D2
Firs Ct NN4 175 F8
First Ave NN8 129 D3
Firs The
Daventry NN11 135 C3
Market Harborough LE16 31 C3
First La NN5 158 F6
First St NN13 238 F6
Firsview Dr NN5 140 C1
Fir Tree Gr NN29 164 D2
Firtree La LE17 62 C3
Fir Tree Wlk
Market Harborough LE16 31 E4
Northampton NN3 142 E2
Fisher Ave CV22 98 E8
Fisher Cl NN14 76 E1
Fishermans Cl MK46 195 E4
Fishers Cl
Kilsby CV23 99 F2
Northampton NN3 143 B1
Fishpond Cl NN7 162 B1
Fishponds Rd NN3 143 B1
Fish St NN1 159 D6
Fishton Cl NN15 91 C7
Fitzroy Ct NN6 102 B4
Fitzroy Pl NN1 159 B6
Fitzwilliam Ct
4 Rushden NN10 132 A2
Wymington NN10 148 A7
Fitzwilliam Dr NN15 92 A5
Fitzwilliam Leys NN10 132 B7
Fitzwilliam Rd NN9 112 F3
Fitzwilliam St NN10 132 A2
Five Acres Fold NN4 158 F3
Five Cotts MK18 226 D4
Fiveways NN6 104 C1
Fjord Wlk NN18 36 A2
Flaggs Mdw MK46 195 E4
Flamingo Gardens & Zoo Pk* MK46 195 B3
Flatford Cl NN18 36 D1
Flatlets The NN9 112 F2
Flavius Gate NN13 234 A7
Flaxland Cl LE16 32 B3
Flaxlands Ct NN3 142 F3
Flaxwell Ct NN3 160 F8
Fleet St NN16 72 A2
Fleetwind Dr NN4 175 D7
Fleetwood Cl LE16 31 D1
Fleetwood Gdns LE16 31 D1
Fleming Cl NN8 129 B7
Fleming Rd NN17 22 A2
Flensburg Cl NN18 36 B2
Fletcher Gdns NN14 76 D1
Fletcher Rd NN10 132 A3
Fletton Way PE8 41 F6
Fleur Cl NN11 184 C6
Flintcomb Rise NN3 143 B3
Flinters Cl NN4 175 F7
Flitton Ct MK11 229 F5
Flora Thompson Dr NN13 233 E8
FLORE 155 F4
Flore CE Prim Sch NN7 155 E5
Flore Hill NN7 155 D5
Florence Rd NN1 159 F7
Floribunda Dr NN4 158 F2
Florin Pl CV21 99 A8
Flowerhill Dr NN8 130 B6
Flying Dutchman Way 2 NN11 135 A3
Fog Cotts NN6 120 B5
Folly La
Hartwell NN7 206 C8
Little Brington NN7 138 B4
Folly Rd MK19 228 D4
Fontwell Cres NN18 36 E1
Foot La NN9 133 C8
Ford Bank LE16 20 D6
Ford Dr NN13 233 D8
Ford St NN16 72 C2
Forest App PE8 13 F7
Forest Cl NN15 92 D3
Forest Ct NN10 132 D3
Foresters Pl CV21 99 B7
Forest Gate Rd NN17 36 E7
Forest Glade
Hartwell NN7 192 D2
Kettering NN16 72 C6
Forest Rd
Hanslope MK19 207 A6
Hartwell NN7 192 D2
Northampton NN4 159 C3
Piddington NN7 177 A1
Forest View NN7 192 D2
Forfar St NN5 158 F7
Forge Ho NN14 70 D7
Forge The NN10 132 B1
Forrester Dr NN13 222 E1
Forrester Gr NN14 76 E1
Forresters The NN9 114 D5
Forstal Cl NN18 36 D3
Fort Pl NN1 159 B6
Forty Foot La MK44 149 A1
Fosberry Cl NN4 175 F6
FOSCOTE 202 B3
Foskett Cl NN10 132 A3
Foskitt Ct NN3 143 B1
Fosse Cl NN8 129 D1
Fosse Gn NN10 132 C3
Foster Cl NN15 90 F8
Foster Ct NN18 36 E5
FOSTER'S BOOTH 188 D8
Foster's Booth Rd NN12 172 D1
Fothergill Cl LE16 32 B3
FOTHERINGHAY 27 D7
Fotheringhay Castle* PE8 27 E6
Fotheringhay Ct NN14 76 E2
Fotheringhay Mews PE8 42 A5
Fotheringhay Rd
Corby NN17 36 B8
Nassington PE8 15 F4
Foundry Ct 5 NN11 135 C1
Foundry Pl NN11 135 C1
Foundry St 13 NN1 159 C5
Foundry Wlk
4 Daventry NN11 135 C1
Thrapston NN14 76 C1
Fountain Ct MK46 195 F3
Four Crosses Ho CV23 117 E3
Fourth Ave
Croughton NN13 238 E6
Wellingborough NN8 129 D3
Fourth St NN13 238 E6
Fowey Cl NN8 129 C6
Fox Cl CV21 80 B1
Fox Covert Dr NN7 191 E3
Foxcovert Rd NN3 143 B6
Fox Coverts NN14 89 A4
Foxendale Sq NN3 143 D2
Foxfield Way NN4 175 F2
Foxford Cl NN4 174 F8
Foxglove Ave NN11 184 B6
Foxglove Cl
Corby NN18 36 E2
Northampton NN4 175 F2
Rushden NN10 148 C8
Foxglove Rd NN14 51 A5
Foxgoles Cl MK19 228 F5
Foxgrove Ave NN2 141 B4
Foxhill MK46 195 E5
Foxhill La OX27 237 E3
Foxhill Rd NN6 102 B3
Fox Hill Rd NN3 143 D2
Fox La
Brackley NN13 233 E7
Souldern OX27 237 E3
Foxlands NN14 51 B2
FOXLEY 187 D4
Fox St NN14 70 C7
FOXTON 30 E8
Foxton Canal Mus* LE16 30 C8
Foxton Ct NN15 72 A1
Foxton Locks Ctry Pk* LE16 30 C8
Foxton Prim Sch LE16 30 D8
Foxton Rd
Foxton LE16 30 B7
Lubenham LE16 30 D5
Foxwell Sq NN3 142 F7
Foxwood Cl NN10 131 E2
Fox Yd 7 LE16 31 E3
Franciscan Cl NN10 147 F8
Francis Ct NN10 131 E3
Francis Dickins Cl NN29 146 E3
Francis Row NN7 171 E6
Francis St
8 Northampton NN1 159 C7
Raunds NN9 114 B4
Francis Terr NN9 114 B4
Frank Large Wlk NN5 158 A7
Franklin Cres NN5 158 D7
Franklin Ct NN5 159 A6
Franklin Fields NN17 37 A8
Franklin's Cl NN6 143 F4
Franklin St NN5 158 F6
Franklin Way NN11 135 B5
Frankston Ave MK11 229 E5
Fraser Cl NN11 135 D2
Fraser Rd NN3 142 D6
Freehold St NN2 159 C8
Freeman's Endowed CE Jun Sch NN8 129 E4
Freeman's La NN14 95 C6
Freeman Way NN9 112 B5
Freeschool St 9 NN1 159 C5
Fremeaux Terr NN2 141 B2
French Dr NN15 72 F1
Frensham Cl 2 NN4 158 F3
Friar's Ave NN4 159 C1
Friars Cl NN8 130 A3
Friar's Cl NN4 159 B1
Friar's Cres NN4 159 C1
Friars Sch NN8 130 A3
Friary Cl NN11 135 D2
Friary The NN1 159 D6
Frinton Cl NN10 147 F8
Frisby La LE15 3 D8
Friston Cl NN15 92 A5
Frobisher Cl NN11 135 E2
Frog Hall
Brixworth NN6 106 A2
Silverstone NN12 214 D5
Frog La NN11 182 C7
Front St NN14 95 C6
Frost Cl NN14 51 B4
Frost Ct NN29 145 D6
Frosts Ct NN4 175 E5
Frosty Hollow NN4 175 C6
Froxhill Cres NN6 106 A1
Froxhill Wlk NN6 106 A1
Fuchsia Cl NN3 160 C6
Fuchsia Way NN10 148 B7
Fulford Dr NN2 141 E3
Fullen La NN17 22 D8
Fullerburn Ct 2 NN3 142 E3
Fuller Rd NN3 142 C8
Fullers Cl NN14 76 F8
Fuller St NN16 72 C2
Fullingdale Rd NN3 142 B2
Fullwell Rd NN29 164 D4
Fulmar La NN8 130 A8
Fulwell Ave NN17 10 C1
Furber Ct NN3 142 D4
Furlong Rd NN14 51 C3
Furlongs The LE16 32 B3
Furnace Cotts NN9 111 A5
Furnace Dr
Daventry NN11 135 A4
Thrapston NN14 76 D1
Furnace La
Finedon NN9 111 A5
Kettering NN16 72 A5
Nether Heyford NN7 172 A8
Furnace Lane Ind Est NN9 111 B5
Furnells Cl NN9 114 D7
FURTHO 218 A3
Furtho Ct MK19 229 B7
Furtho La NN12 217 E3
Furze Ct 5 NN4 159 A3
Furze Rd NN7 161 D2
Furze Wlk NN2 141 E2
Fusilier Rd NN11 135 B1
Fusilier Way NN7 155 A4
Fydell Row LE15 3 A6
Fyfe Rd NN17 36 B8
Fylingdale NN2 140 F5

G

Gable Cl NN11 135 B1
Gable Court Mews NN3 142 D1
Gables The NN15 72 B1
Gadesby Ct NN3 142 E3
Gainage Cl NN18 36 C1
Gainsborough Ave NN15 92 A7
Gainsborough Cres CV21 80 B1
Gainsborough Ct NN18 36 D5
Gainsborough Dr NN8 129 F7
Gainsborough Rd NN18 36 C4
Gainsborough Way NN11 135 C6
Gains La PE28 61 D2
Galahad Ct NN5 158 A8
Galane Cl NN4 158 D1
Gallery Cl NN3 143 A6
Gallery La PE8 42 A5
Gallery The* PE8 42 A5
Galley Hill MK11 229 F5
Gallfield Ct NN3 161 C8
Galliard Ct NN1 159 F7
Gallow Field Rd LE16 30 E7
Gallowhill Rd NN4 160 B1
Gambrel Rd NN5 158 D6
Gamston Wlk NN18 36 B6
Gander Cl NN17 38 A7
Gannet La NN8 130 A8
Ganton Cl NN11 135 F3
Gapstile Cl NN14 51 A4
Gap The NN29 146 E2
Gardenfield NN10 132 B5
Gardenfields Cl NN9 113 B5
Garden Fields Ct NN29 147 C8
Gardens The
East Carlton LE16 35 A7
Kettering NN16 72 A4
Whilton NN11 137 D6
Gardiner St LE16 31 C3
Gardner Cl NN9 114 C7
Gardner Rise NN13 233 D7
Garfield Cl NN2 141 C3
Garfield Ho NN2 141 B3
Garfield St
Kettering NN15 91 B8
Northampton NN2 141 B3
Garford La PE9 2 A5
Garners Way NN7 157 C7
Garrard Way NN16 71 F3
Garrick Rd NN1 160 B7
Garrow Cl NN9 112 E3
Garsdale NN2 140 F5
Garston Rd NN18 36 C1
Gas St 14 NN1 159 C5
Gatcombe Ho 3 NN10 132 B2
Gateford Ct NN18 36 B6
Gatehouse Cl CV21 99 A8
Gatehouse La LE16 20 F6
Gate La NN14 90 B5
Gatelodge Cl NN3 142 E6
Gates Cl NN9 112 E3
Gateway Cl NN4 175 F6
Gaultney The NN14 51 A3
Gawaine Ct NN5 158 A7
Gaydon Ho NN17 22 C1
Gayhurst Cl NN3 142 B7
GAYTON 173 F2
Gayton CE Prim Sch NN7 173 E2
Gayton Rd
Blisworth NN7 190 C8
Eastcote NN12 172 F1
Tiffield NN12 189 C6
GEDDINGTON 54 B3
Geddington CE Prim Sch NN14 54 B2
Geddington Rd NN18 37 D5
Gedling Cl NN3 160 F8
Gees Farm Cl NN7 179 A5
GEESTON 1 B4
Geeston Rd PE9 1 B5
Geldock Rd NN3 143 A1
Genner Rd NN17 22 B1
Gentian Cl NN10 148 C8
George Blackall Ct NN17 36 C8
George Nutt Ct NN4 159 C2
George Row NN1 159 C5
Georges Ave NN7 173 A7
Georges Cl NN7 173 A7
Georges Dr NN4 175 E3
George St
Burton Latimer NN15 92 D3
Corby NN17 36 E6
Higham Ferrers NN10 132 C7
Irthlingborough NN9 112 E1
Kettering NN16 72 B1
Rushden NN10 132 B2
Wellingborough NN8 130 A5
George Yd MK11 229 D5
Gerandria Ct CV22 98 E8
Gerrard Gdns LE16 48 D8
Gervase Sq NN3 143 C1
Gharana Nivas NN8 130 B5
Gibbons Dr NN14 70 E7
Gibbsacre Ct NN3 143 C1
Gibraltar Ct 23 NN1 159 C7
Gibson Dr
Rugby CV21 80 A1
Upper Benefield PE8 39 F7
Gibson La NN5 158 F8
Giffard Ct
Market Harborough LE16 31 D3
Northampton NN5 159 A5
Gifford Ct NN5 158 C8
Gilbert Cl LE16 32 B2
Gilbert Scott Ct NN12 203 B6
Gilbey Cl NN9 110 E1
Gilchrist Ave NN17 37 A8
Gillingham Rd NN15 90 F8
Gillitts Rd NN8 129 E3
Gillsway NN2 141 A4
Gilson's Cl LE15 3 A6
Gingles Ct CV21 99 A8
Gipsy La
Irchester NN29 146 E8
Kettering NN16 71 E2
Gipsy Lane Turn NN29 146 F7
Gisburne Rd NN8 130 A6
Glade Cl
Burton Latimer NN15 92 C3
Northampton NN3 143 B1
Glades The NN4 175 F2
Glade The NN9 110 E1
Gladiator Cl NN4 175 F5
Gladstone Cl NN5 141 A1
Gladstone Ct 7 NN16 72 C2
Gladstone Rd NN5 159 A8
Gladstone St
Desborough NN14 51 A4
Kettering NN16 72 C2
Market Harborough LE16 31 F2
Raunds NN9 114 D6
Ringstead NN14 95 C3
Rothwell NN14 70 D7
Glaisdale Cl NN2 140 F5
Glaister Pl NN16 72 D2
Glamis Cl NN10 132 D1
Glan y Mor Terr NN2 141 C5
GLAPTHORN 26 C2
Glapthorn CE Lower Sch PE8 26 B2
Glapthorn Rd PE8 41 F6
Glasgow St NN5 158 F6
Glassbrook Rd NN10 132 A2
Glassthorpe La NN7 157 A6
Glastonbury Cl NN15 91 F8
Glastonbury Rd
Corby NN18 36 A6
Northampton NN4 159 C1
Glaston Rd LE15 3 A5
Glebe Ave
Broughton NN14 90 B4
Kettering NN15 91 B8
Northampton NN4 175 E8
Glebe Cl
Holcot NN6 126 E8
Glebe Cl *continued*
Northampton NN4 175 E8
Glebe Ct PE8 58 A4
Glebe Dr NN13 234 A7
Glebe Farm Cl NN4 175 C4
Glebe Farm Ct NN29 145 E6
Glebe La
Great Houghton NN4 160 E2
Hanslope MK19 206 E5
Harlestone NN7 139 E7
Pitsford NN6 125 D5
Staverton NN11 152 C7
Glebeland Cres NN5 159 A8
Glebeland Gdns NN5 140 F1
Glebeland Rd NN5 158 F8
Glebelands NN6 105 B1
Glebeland Wlk 1 NN5 158 F8
Glebe Rd
Burton Latimer NN15 92 A2
Cogenhoe NN7 161 E6
Deanshanger MK19 228 E5
Market Harborough LE16 32 A2
Mears Ashby NN6 128 B2
Glebe Rise OX17 231 A5
Glebe The
Aynho OX17 237 D7
Badby NN11 153 A2
Daventry NN11 153 C8
Glebe Way
Cogenhoe NN7 161 E6
Northampton NN4 175 E8
Glen Ave NN7 174 B2
Glen Bank NN8 130 A4
Glen Baulk Rd NN14, NN16 71 C4
Glencoe Dr NN15 91 E8
Glendale Ct NN3 143 C1
Glendon Rd NN14 70 E7
Glendower Cl NN11 135 A4
Gleneagles Cl
Daventry NN11 135 E3
Kettering NN15 91 F8
Gleneagles Dr NN8 129 D7
Glenfield Cl NN10 131 F2
Glenfield Dr NN29 145 D5
Glengary NN3 142 D7
Glenshee Cl NN15 91 E8
Glenville NN3 142 B4
Gloucester Ave NN4 159 B1
Gloucester Cl
2 Kettering NN16 72 C2
Northampton NN4 159 B2
Weedon Bec NN7 155 B4
Gloucester Cres
Northampton NN4 159 B2
Rushden NN10 132 C3
Gloucester Ct NN14 70 C6
Gloucester Ho NN4 159 C2
Gloucester Pl NN8 130 A4
Glover Ct LE16 20 C1
Glovers Cl NN9 131 E8
Glovers La
Middleton Cheney OX17 208 F1
Raunds NN9 114 C5
Glyndebourne Gdns NN18 36 A4
Goadby's Yd 9 NN16 72 B2
Gocker Wood Cl NN18 36 B1
Goddard Ct 5 LE16 31 E4
Godwin Ct NN13 233 E6
Godwin Rd NN17 21 F3
Godwin Wlk NN5 140 D2
Goffs Yd NN29 164 D2
Goldcrest Ct NN3 143 A5
Goldcrest Rd NN13 222 D1
Goldenash Ct NN3 142 F5
Golding Cl NN11 135 C2
GOLDINGS 143 A5
Goldings Rd NN3 143 A5
Goldsmith Dr NN17 36 D8
Goldsmith Rd NN8 129 C4
Gold St
Clipston LE16 66 F8
Desborough NN14 51 A3
Hanslope MK19 207 A2
Kettering NN16 72 B2
Northampton NN1 159 C5
Podington NN29 147 E2
Walgrave NN6 108 A5
Wellingborough NN8 130 A6
Gold Street Mews 6 NN1 159 C5
Golf La NN6 140 C8
Goodacre Cl CV23 80 A5
Goodens La NN29 145 F6
Goodhew Cl NN15 90 F8
Good Shepherd RC Prim Sch The NN2 141 C3
Goodwin Cl NN8 130 A8
Goodwood Ave NN3 141 F5
Goodwood Cl
Corby NN18 36 E1
Market Harborough LE16 32 B3
Goodwood Rd NN10 148 D8
Goose Gn NN13 233 E6
Goosemere MK19 228 E4
Goran Ave MK11 229 E4
Gordon Rd
Oundle PE8 42 A6
Wellingborough NN8 130 B5
Gordon St
Kettering NN16 72 C2

Gordon St *continued*
Northampton NN2 . . . . 159 C8
Rothwell NN14 . . . . 70 D6
Rushden NN10 . . . . 131 F2
Gordon Terr NN14 . . . . 74 F2
Gores La LE16 . . . . 32 A3
Gorricks MK11 . . . . 229 D4
Gorse Cl NN2 . . . . 141 B6
Gorseholm Ct 10 NN9 . . . . 112 F2
Gorse Rd
Hinton NN11 . . . . 184 B7
Kettering NN16 . . . . 72 E4
Spratton NN6 . . . . 124 B8
Gosforth NN8 . . . . 129 C4
Goslar The NN8 . . . . 129 B3
Gotch Cl NN15 . . . . 91 F4
Gotch Rd NN15 . . . . 91 F5
Gough Cl NN15 . . . . 72 E1
Goughs Cotts NN5 . . . . . . 158 C7
Gould Cl NN11 . . . . 118 B1
Goulsbra Rd NN10 . . . . . . 148 D8
Goward St LE16 . . . . 31 E3
Gower Cl NN15 . . . . 91 C6
Gowerton Rd NN4 . . . . . . 176 C8
Grace Ct NN15 . . . . 92 B1
Gracelands LE16 . . . . 31 C2
Graeme Rd PE5 . . . . 8 F2
Grafton Cl
Hartwell NN7 . . . . 192 D2
Potterspury NN12 . . . . 217 E3
Wellingborough NN8 . . . . . 129 D7
Grafton Ct NN7 . . . . 193 A8
Grafton Dr NN17 . . . . 36 B8
Grafton Ho NN1 . . . . 159 B6
Grafton Pl 10 NN1 . . . . . . 159 C7
Grafton Rd
Brigstock NN14 . . . . 55 E4
Cranford St John NN14 . . . . . 93 A7
Geddington NN14 . . . . 54 B2
Roade NN7 . . . . 191 C4
Rushden NN10 . . . . 132 D2
Yardley Gobion NN12 . . . . . . 217 F6
GRAFTON REGIS 205 D2
Grafton St Ind Est
NN1 . . . . 159 B7
Grafton St
Kettering NN16 . . . . 72 A4
Northampton NN1 . . . . 159 C7
Grafton View NN4 . . . . 175 E6
Grafton Way
Northampton NN5 . . . . 140 B2
Rothersthorpe NN7 . . . . . . 174 A7
Graham Hill NN12 . . . . . . 214 D4
Graham Hill Rd NN12 . . . 203 C7
Granary Cl LE16 . . . . 31 F6
Granary Ct NN4 . . . . 175 C7
Granary Rd NN4 . . . . 175 C7
Granby Cl NN18 . . . . 36 B6
Grandborough Cl
NN6 . . . . 106 C1
Grange Ave NN5 . . . . 140 B1
Grange Cl
Denton NN7 . . . . 162 B1
Earls Barton NN6 . . . . 144 E5
Irchester NN29 . . . . 147 B7
Grange Com Sch NN16 . . . . 72 E3
Grange Ct
Brixworth NN6 . . . . 106 B2
Horton NN7 . . . . 177 D1
Stony Stratford MK12 . . . . . 229 F6
Grange La
Pitsford NN6 . . . . 125 E6
Thorpe Langton LE16 . . . . 17 A5
GRANGE PARK 175 E3
Grange Pl NN16 . . . . 72 E4
Grange Rd
Broughton NN14 . . . . 90 B5
Geddington NN14 . . . . 53 F2
Islip NN14 . . . . 76 B1
Kettering NN16 . . . . 72 A3
Northampton NN3 . . . . 142 C3
Stanion NN14 . . . . 37 E2
Stanwick NN9 . . . . 114 A3
Wellingborough NN9 . . . . . . 110 E1
Grange Road Workshops
NN14 . . . . 53 F2
Grange Sch The
NN11 . . . . 135 A1
Grangeway NN10 . . . . 148 A8
Grange Way NN29 . . . . 147 B7
Grangewood NN4 . . . . 175 A7
Grant Cl NN15 . . . . 90 F7
Grantham Wlk NN18 . . . . . . 36 B4
Grantown Cl NN15 . . . . 91 E8
Grant Rd NN8 . . . . 130 B5
Granville St
Kettering NN16 . . . . 72 C2
Market Harborough LE16 . . . 31 F2
Grasmere Gn NN8 . . . . 129 B4
Grasmere Rd NN16 . . . . 71 F2
Grasmere Way NN10 . . . . 132 B8
Graspin La NN3 . . . . 160 D8
Grass Cl NN12 . . . . 203 B7
Grasscroft NN2 . . . . 141 A4
Grass Croft NN6 . . . . 121 A3
Grassmere Ave NN3 . . . . . 142 E2
Grass Slade NN6 . . . . 106 C2
Gravel Hill NN11 . . . . 199 D7
Gravely St NN10 . . . . 131 F2
Gray Cl NN6 . . . . 145 A4
Grays Cl NN12 . . . . 216 D8
Gray's Cl NN17 . . . . 36 E8
Grays Dr NN14 . . . . 37 E3
Grays La
Paulerspury NN12 . . . . 216 D8
Grays La *continued*
Yardley Gobion NN12 . . . . . . 217 E6
Gray St
Irchester NN29 . . . . 147 A7
Northampton NN1 . . . . 159 E7
Greasley Wlk NN18 . . . . 36 B6
GREAT ADDINGTON 94 B2
Great Addington CE Prim Sch NN14 . . . . 94 B3
GREAT BILLING 143 C3
Great Billing Way
NN3 . . . . 143 C4
GREAT BOWDEN 32 A6
Great Bowden CE Prim Sch LE16 . . . . 32 A6
Great Bowden Hall
LE16 . . . . 31 E7
Great Bowden Rd LE16 . . . . 32 A4
GREAT BRINGTON 138 D7
Great Central Walk Nature Trail* CV22 . . . . 98 D6
Great Central Way
NN11 . . . . 184 C7
Great Cl NN6 . . . . 124 D1
GREAT CRANSLEY 89 F6
Great Creaton Prim Sch
NN6 . . . . 104 F4
GREAT DODDINGTON
. . . . 145 D5
Great Doddington Prim Sch NN29 . . . . 145 E6
GREAT EASTON 20 E7
Great Easton Rd
Bringhurst LE16 . . . . 20 C6
Caldecott LE16 . . . . 21 A7
Drayton LE16 . . . . 20 A5
Great Easton LE16 . . . . 20 F6
Great Field Ct NN3 . . . . . . 142 E5
Great Folds Rd NN18 . . . . . . 35 F1
GREAT GIDDING 61 D3
Great Gidding CE Prim Sch PE28 . . . . 61 D3
Great Ground Wlk
NN4 . . . . 175 F2
Great Gull Cres NN3 . . . . . 142 F6
GREAT HARROWDEN
. . . . 110 D2
Great Holme Ct NN3 . . . . . 142 E5
GREAT HOUGHTON 160 F2
Great La
Bugbrooke NN7 . . . . 172 F7
Hackleton NN7 . . . . 177 B3
Greatmeadow NN3 . . . . . 143 C4
Greatmeadow Rd
NN3 . . . . 143 B4
Great North Rd
Stibbington PE8 . . . . 8 C2
Wothorpe PE9 . . . . 2 B8
GREAT OAKLEY 53 B8
GREAT OXENDON 48 E3
Great Park St NN8 . . . . . . 130 A5
Great Russell St NN1 . . . 159 D7
GREATWORTH 210 E2
Greatworth Prim Sch
OX17 . . . . 210 E2
Grebe Cl
Hinton NN11 . . . . 184 B6
Thrapston NN14 . . . . 76 E3
Greenacre Dr
Rushden NN10 . . . . 148 B8
Stanion NN14 . . . . 37 E2
Green Acres Cvn Pk
LE16 . . . . 31 C6
Greenaway Cl NN7 . . . . . . 190 E7
Greenbank Ave NN15 . . . . . 72 D1
Greenbank Terr NN14 . . . . . 95 B3
Green Cl
Irthlingborough NN9 . . . . . 131 D8
Wellingborough NN8 . . . . . 129 C7
Green Dale Sq 8
NN3 . . . . 143 C2
Green End NN2 . . . . 141 B2
Green End La MK19 . . . . . . 207 A3
Green Farm OX17 . . . . 230 A4
Green Farm Cl CV23 . . . . . . 81 A6
Greenfield Ave
Kettering NN15 . . . . 71 F1
Northampton NN3 . . . . 142 B3
Greenfield Rd NN3 . . . . . . 142 A2
Greenfields Sch NN2 . . . . . 141 B5
Greenfield Way NN10 . . . . 132 A1
Greenfinch Dr NN3 . . . . . 142 C6
Greenglades NN4 . . . . 158 E1
Greenhill Cres NN11 . . . . . 135 B3
Greenhill Ct NN6 . . . . 121 A3
Greenhill Rd
Elton PE7 . . . . 29 B6
Elton PE8 . . . . 28 F8
Kettering NN15 . . . . 91 A8
Long Buckby NN6 . . . . 121 A3
Greenhill Rise NN18 . . . . . . 36 B5
Greenhills Cl NN2 . . . . 141 B6
Greenhills Rd NN2 . . . . 141 B6
Greening Rd NN14 . . . . 70 C7
Green La
Ashley LE16 . . . . 18 F2
Braybrooke LE16 . . . . 49 F5
Charlton OX17 . . . . 231 E5
Desborough NN14 . . . . 50 D3
Duddington PE9 . . . . 5 B6
Husbands Bosworth
LE17 . . . . 45 E5
Kettering NN16 . . . . 72 B2
Market Harborough LE16 . . . 31 E1
Northampton NN4 . . . . 175 E5
Silverstone NN12 . . . . 214 D4
Stanwick NN9 . . . . 113 F3
Stoke Albany LE16 . . . . 34 B4
Green La *continued*
Thrapston NN14 . . . . 76 D2
Towcester NN12 . . . . 203 A5
Weston by W LE16 . . . . 18 C6
Greenland Wlk NN18 . . . . . . 36 A2
Greenlaw NN8 . . . . 129 B4
Green Oaks Prim Sch
NN2 . . . . 141 D4
Green Rd NN7 . . . . 161 E2
Greenside
Blisworth NN7 . . . . 190 D7
Northampton NN3 . . . . 142 B3
Wappenham NN12 . . . . 213 B8
Greenslade Cl NN15 . . . . . . 91 A8
GREENS NORTON 202 D8
Greens Norton CE Prim Sch NN12 . . . . 202 E8
Green St
Milton Malsor NN7 . . . . 174 E4
Northampton NN1 . . . . 159 B5
Wollaston NN29 . . . . 146 E2
Greensward The
OX17 . . . . 196 E1
Green The
Abthorpe NN12 . . . . 201 F2
Adderbury OX17 . . . . 230 A4
Barby CV23 . . . . 99 C1
Blakesley NN12 . . . . 187 B1
Brafield-on-t-G NN7 . . . . . . 161 E2
Braunston NN11 . . . . 118 C1
Byfield NN11 . . . . 183 D7
Caldecott LE16 . . . . 21 B8
Chelveston NN9 . . . . 133 C8
Church Stowe NN7 . . . . 171 D7
Clipston LE16 . . . . 67 A8
Cosgrove MK19 . . . . 218 F2
Cranford St John NN14 . . . . . 93 A6
Culworth OX17 . . . . 198 C3
Deanshanger MK19 . . . . 228 E4
Dodford NN7 . . . . 154 E6
Evenley NN13 . . . . 233 F2
Everdon NN11 . . . . 170 A8
Flore NN7 . . . . 155 F5
Great Bowden LE16 . . . . 32 B6
Great Brington NN7 . . . . . . 138 D7
Great Houghton NN4 . . . . . . 160 E2
Guilsborough NN6 . . . . 103 E7
Hanslope MK19 . . . . 207 A2
Harlestone NN7 . . . . 139 D4
Hellidon NN11 . . . . 151 C1
Helmdon NN13 . . . . 211 F4
Hollowell NN6 . . . . 104 B4
Husbands Bosworth
LE17 . . . . 45 E5
Kislingbury NN7 . . . . 157 D3
Lilbourne CV23 . . . . 81 A6
Little Addington NN14 . . . . . 113 B8
Lower Boddington
NN11 . . . . 182 B5
Lubenham LE16 . . . . 30 E3
Lyddington LE15 . . . . 9 D7
Marston St Lawrence
OX17 . . . . 210 B1
Mawsley Village NN14 . . . . . . 89 B4
Nether Heyford NN7 . . . . . . 156 B1
Newnham NN11 . . . . 153 D4
Northampton, Grange Park
NN4 . . . . 175 F3
Northampton, Hardingstone
NN4 . . . . 175 F8
Northampton, Kingsthorpe
NN2 . . . . 141 B3
10 Northampton NN1 . . . . 159 C5
Orlingbury NN14 . . . . 110 A5
Paulerspury NN12 . . . . 216 B7
Priors Marston CV47 . . . . . . 166 D7
Roade NN7 . . . . 191 D4
Staverton NN11 . . . . 152 B7
Titchmarsh NN14 . . . . 77 C4
Turweston NN13 . . . . 234 C8
Twywell NN14 . . . . 75 A1
Wadenhoe PE8 . . . . 58 A4
Weedon Lois NN12 . . . . 200 C3
West Haddon NN6 . . . . 102 B4
Weston by W LE16 . . . . 18 B3
Whilton NN11 . . . . 137 D6
Woodford NN14 . . . . 94 D6
Greenview Dr
Northampton NN2 . . . . 141 E3
Towcester NN12 . . . . 203 B6
Greenway
Braunston NN11 . . . . 118 B1
Eastcote NN12 . . . . 173 A1
Northampton NN3 . . . . 160 C8
Greenway Ave NN3 . . . . . 142 D4
Greenway The NN11 . . . . 153 C8
Greenwood Cl
Byfield NN11 . . . . 183 C7
Moulton NN3 . . . . 142 C8
Greenwood Rd NN5 . . . . . 159 A6
Greenyard The NN7 . . . . . . 179 B7
Greeve Cl NN18 . . . . 36 C1
Greeves Cl NN5 . . . . 139 F1
Gregory St 8 NN1 . . . . . . 159 C5
Gregory Wlk NN18 . . . . 36 D4
Grenadier Rd NN11 . . . . . . 135 B1
GRENDON 163 E5
Grendon Ave NN17 . . . . 36 B7
Grendon CE Prim Sch
NN7 . . . . 163 D5
Grendon Lakes Watersports Ctr*
NN7 . . . . 145 C1
Grendon Rd NN6 . . . . 144 E1
Grendon Wlk NN3 . . . . 141 F5
Grenville Cl
Corby NN17 . . . . 36 A8
Daventry NN11 . . . . 135 E1
Grenville Cl *continued*
Rothwell NN14 . . . . 70 E6
Grenville Gdns LE16 . . . . . . 31 D1
Gresham Dr NN4 . . . . 158 E2
Gresley Cl NN11 . . . . 135 A4
GRETTON 10 C1
Gretton Brook Rd
Corby NN17 . . . . 21 E3
Corby NN17 . . . . 22 C4
Gretton Ct NN8 . . . . 129 D7
Gretton Prim Sch
NN17 . . . . 22 C8
Gretton Rd
Corby NN17 . . . . 22 F3
Harringworth NN17 . . . . 10 E7
Lyddington LE15 . . . . 9 D5
Rockingham LE16 . . . . 21 B5
Weldon NN17 . . . . 38 A8
Gretton Road Ind Est
NN17 . . . . 38 A8
Greville Ave NN3 . . . . 142 A4
Greville Cl NN2 . . . . 141 C8
Greyfriars NN1 . . . . 159 C6
Greyfriars Rd NN11 . . . . . 153 B8
Greys The NN7 . . . . 155 B4
Grieg Wlk NN18 . . . . 36 A2
Griffin Cl OX17 . . . . 230 A5
Griffin Rd LE16 . . . . 49 E4
Griffiths Cl NN5 . . . . 157 F8
Griffith St NN10 . . . . 132 B1
Grimmer Wlk NN9 . . . . . . 131 D8
Grimsby Cl NN18 . . . . 36 C4
GRIMSCOTE 188 B8
Grindleford Cl NN14 . . . . . . 50 E3
Grizedale Cl
Corby NN17 . . . . 36 D8
Kettering NN16 . . . . 72 A6
Grombold Ave NN9 . . . . . . 114 C6
Grooms La NN6 . . . . 105 A4
Grosvenor Cl NN15 . . . . 92 A5
Grosvenor Ctr NN1 . . . . 159 D6
Grosvenor Gdns NN2 . . . . 141 D4
Grosvenor Ho NN2 . . . . . . 141 D4
Grosvenor Pl NN13 . . . . . . 233 E7
Grosvenor Rd NN15 . . . . 92 A5
Grosvenor Way NN15 . . . . . 91 F5
Groundwell Ct 1
NN3 . . . . 142 F1
Grovebury Dell NN2 . . . . . 141 A4
Grove Farm Cl NN6 . . . . . . 121 D4
Grove Farm La NN3 . . . . . . 126 D2
Grove La NN12 . . . . 199 F3
Grovelands NN11 . . . . 153 A8
Grove Pl NN9 . . . . 114 D5
Grove Rd
Brafield-on-t-G NN7 . . . . . . 161 D3
Northampton NN1 . . . . 159 E7
Rushden NN10 . . . . 132 C2
Thrapston NN14 . . . . 76 D1
Grove St
Higham Ferrers
NN10 . . . . 132 C6
Raunds NN9 . . . . 114 D5
Wellingborough NN8 . . . . . . 129 E4
Grove The
Corby NN18 . . . . 37 C6
Kettering NN15 . . . . 72 B1
Moulton NN3 . . . . 126 C2
Ringstead NN14 . . . . 95 A3
Roade NN7 . . . . 191 E3
Wollaston NN29 . . . . 146 D1
Grove Way NN9 . . . . 111 E3
Grove Works NN1 . . . . 159 E7
Grundy Ct NN15 . . . . 91 B8
Guildhall Rd NN1 . . . . 159 D5
Guillemot La NN8 . . . . 130 A7
GUILSBOROUGH 103 E6
Guilsborough CE Prim Sch
NN6 . . . . 103 E7
Guilsborough Hill
NN6 . . . . 104 B5
Guilsborough Rd
Ravensthorpe NN6 . . . . 103 D1
West Haddon NN6 . . . . 102 C5
Guilsborough Sch
NN6 . . . . 103 D8
Guinea Orch MK46 . . . . 195 E4
Gullet La LE16 . . . . 18 F2
Gumley Rd LE16 . . . . 30 C7
Gunnell Cl NN15 . . . . 90 F8
Gunnsbrook Cl LE16 . . . . . . 32 A6
Gunthorpe Pl NN18 . . . . 36 B6
Gurston Rise NN3 . . . . 143 C4
Gynwell NN6 . . . . 85 B8

H

Hachenburg Pl NN10 . . . . 132 C5
HACKLETON 177 C3
Hackleton Prim Sch
NN7 . . . . 177 A3
Hackwood Rd NN11 . . . . . . 153 E8
Haddon Cl
Rushden NN10 . . . . 132 A1
Wellingborough NN8 . . . . . 129 D8
Haddon Ct NN6 . . . . 122 C5
Haddonian Rd LE16 . . . . 31 F1
Haddonstone Show Gdn*
NN6 . . . . 122 D4
Hadfield Cl CV23 . . . . 80 A5
Hadleigh Ho 4 NN10 . . . . 132 B2
Hadrian's Gate NN13 . . . . 234 A7
Hafod Cl NN18 . . . . 36 C2
Hagley Cl LE16 . . . . 32 B3
Haigh Dr NN15 . . . . 72 E1
Hailsham Ct OX17 . . . . 220 B8
Haines Rd NN4 . . . . 159 C3
Hale Ave MK11 . . . . 229 E5
Halfmoon Mews PE8 . . . . . . 42 A5
Halford St NN14 . . . . 76 C1
Halford Way NN11 . . . . 135 E8
Halfway Thorn NN6 . . . . . 124 C1
Halifax Sq NN18 . . . . 36 B5
Hallam Cl NN3 . . . . 142 B7
Hallaton Rd LE16 . . . . 18 F7
Hall Ave NN10 . . . . 132 A1
Hall Cl
Arthingworth LE16 . . . . 68 C7
Harpole NN7 . . . . 157 B6
Kettering NN15 . . . . 90 F8
Kilsby CV23 . . . . 100 A3
Kislingbury NN7 . . . . 157 D4
Naseby NN6 . . . . 66 B1
Northampton NN5 . . . . 158 C6
Old Stratford MK19 . . . . 229 B6
Weston by W LE16 . . . . 18 B4
Hall Dr
Finedon NN9 . . . . 111 E4
Long Buckby NN6 . . . . 121 C4
Hall Farm Cl NN6 . . . . 106 B3
Hall Gdns
East Haddon NN6 . . . . 122 D5
Loddington NN14 . . . . 70 C1
Polebrook PE8 . . . . 43 A3
Hall Hill NN14 . . . . 55 F7
Hall La
Ashley LE16 . . . . 18 E2
Drayton LE16 . . . . 20 A5
Kettering NN15 . . . . 90 F8
South Luffenham LE15 . . . . 3 E8
Welford NN6 . . . . 64 D6
Wittering PE8 . . . . 7 C8
Hall Mead Ct NN7 . . . . 172 E6
Hall Meadow Prim Sch
NN15 . . . . 90 F7
Hall Piece Cl NN3 . . . . . . 143 C3
Hall's Cl
Geddington NN14 . . . . 54 B3
Weldon NN17 . . . . 38 A8
Hall's La NN13 . . . . 233 E6
Hallwood Rd NN16 . . . . 72 C5
Hall Yd
Collyweston PE9 . . . . 1 C2
King's Cliffe PE8 . . . . 13 F7
HALSE 222 B5
Halse Rd NN13 . . . . 222 F1
Halswell Ct NN3 . . . . 142 D4
Hambledon Rise NN4 . . . . 158 E3
Hamblin Ct NN10 . . . . 132 B2
Hamilton Ct NN6 . . . . 124 D1
Hamilton Ho
Corby NN17 . . . . 36 E5
Northampton NN2 . . . . 141 C5
Hamilton La NN7 . . . . 138 D6
Ham La NN14 . . . . 95 A4
Hamlet Gn NN5 . . . . 158 F8
Hammas Leys NN6 . . . . . . 121 C4
Ham Meadow Dr NN3 . . . . 143 C2
Hammerstone La
NN4 . . . . 158 F3
Hammond Way LE16 . . . . . . 31 E4
Hampden Cres NN16 . . . . . . 72 D3
Hampton Court Cl
NN12 . . . . 203 B5
Hampton Ct LE16 . . . . 31 F3
Hampton Dr OX17 . . . . 230 F6
Hampton Ho 1 NN10 . . . . 132 B2
Hampton St NN1 . . . . 159 B7
Hamsterly Pk NN3 . . . . . . 143 A6
Hanbury Cl NN11 . . . . 135 B6
Handcross Ct NN18 . . . . 36 B4
Handcross Way NN10 . . . . 132 C5
Handley Cl NN5 . . . . 140 A1
Hanemill Ct NN3 . . . . 143 C1
Hangerfield Ct NN3 . . . . . . 142 F4
HANGING HOUGHTON
. . . . 106 C8
HANNINGTON 108 C2
Hanover Cl NN15 . . . . 92 A7
Hanover Ct NN3 . . . . 143 B4
Hanover Dr NN13 . . . . 233 E7
Hans Apel Dr NN13 . . . . . 233 D7
HANSLOPE 207 B3
Hanslope Comb Sch
MK19 . . . . 207 A3
Hanslope Rd MK19 . . . . 218 F7
Harbidges La NN6 . . . . . . 121 A4
Harborough Rd
Braybrooke LE16 . . . . 49 D7
Brixworth NN6 . . . . 106 C3
Clipston LE16 . . . . 48 A2
Desborough LE16, NN14 . . . . 50 D7
Dingley LE16 . . . . 32 D5
Dingley LE16 . . . . 32 E1
Dingley LE16 . . . . 33 A3
East Farndon LE16 . . . . 48 C8
Great Oxendon LE16 . . . . 48 F4
Kelmarsh NN6 . . . . 67 F5
Lubenham LE16 . . . . 31 A3
Maidwell NN6 . . . . 87 B4
Market Harborough
LE16 . . . . 31 C7
Marston Trussell LE17 . . . . . . 30 A1
Northampton NN2 . . . . 141 C4
Rushden NN10 . . . . 132 C1
Stoke Albany LE16 . . . . 34 B4
Theddingworth LE17 . . . . 46 D8
Harborough Rd N
NN2 . . . . 141 B6
Harborough Way
NN10 . . . . 132 C1
Harcourt Sq NN6 . . . . 144 E4
Harcourt St
9 Kettering NN16 . . . . 72 C2

Harcourt St *continued*
Market Harborough
LE16 .... 31 D3
Raunds NN9 .... 114 D6
Harcourt Way NN4 .... 158 E3
Hardays La NN6 .... 102 B4
Harden Cl NN18 .... 53 A8
Harding Cl NN15 .... 72 F1
HARDINGSTONE 175 E8
Hardingstone La NN4 ... 175 D8
Hardingstone Prim Sch
NN4 .... 175 E7
Harding Terr NN1 .... 159 C7
Hardlands Rd NN5 .... 158 C8
Hardwater Rd NN29 .... 145 D4
HARDWICK 128 D8
Hardwick Cl NN8 .... 129 E5
Hard wick Hall Way 10
NN11 .... 135 B7
Hardwick Jun & Inf Sch
NN8 .... 129 C5
Hardwick Rd
Gretton NN17 .... 10 B1
Little Harrowden NN9 .... 110 B3
Northampton NN4 .... 175 C8
Priors Marston CV47 .... 166 D7
Wellingborough, Hatton Park
NN8 .... 129 D6
Wellingborough, Hatton Park
NN8 .... 129 E5
Wellingborough NN8 .... 129 A7
Hardy Dr NN4 .... 175 F7
Harebell Sq 1 NN3 .... 143 D2
Harefield Rd NN3 .... 143 B5
Harefoot Cl NN5 .... 158 B8
Haresmoor Dr NN12 .... 203 C4
Hares Run NN14 .... 89 C5
HARGRAVE 115 E2
Hargrave Ct NN9 .... 112 E1
Harksome Hill NN4 .... 158 E2
Harlech NN18 .... 36 C3
Harlech Ct NN14 .... 76 F2
HARLESTONE 139 D5
Harlestone Ct NN5 .... 158 F7
Harlestone Ho NN5 .... 159 A7
Harlestone Prim Sch
NN7 .... 139 E5
Harlestone Rd
Church Brampton
NN6 .... 124 D1
Harlestone NN7 .... 139 F6
Northampton NN5 .... 140 B2
Harley Way
Brigstock NN14 .... 56 C8
Lower Benefield PE8 .... 40 D3
Harmans Way NN7 .... 155 B4
Harnett Dr MK12 .... 229 F6
Harold St 10 NN1 .... 159 E6
Harpers Cl NN18 .... 53 B8
Harper's Ct NN14 .... 55 F7
HARPOLE 157 D6
Harpole Prim Sch
NN7 .... 157 D6
Harrier Pk NN4 .... 175 B8
HARRINGTON 69 B4
Harrington Rd
Desborough NN14 .... 50 F3
Kelmarsh NN6 .... 67 F3
Loddington NN14 .... 70 D1
Old NN6 .... 107 D7
Rothwell NN14 .... 70 C6
HARRINGWORTH 10 F7
Harringworth Rd NN17 .... 10 C2
Harris Cl
Brackley NN13 .... 233 D8
Northampton NN4 .... 175 F7
Raunds NN9 .... 114 D7
Harrison Cl
Market Harborough
LE16 .... 48 D8
Rugby CV21 .... 99 B8
Wellingborough NN8 .... 129 D5
Harrison Ct NN7 .... 172 F7
Harris Rd NN17 .... 21 C1
Harrod Dr LE16 .... 32 A4
Harrogate Ct NN18 .... 36 B4
Harrold Rd NN29 .... 164 D3
Harrowden Rd
Finedon NN9 .... 111 D3
Northampton NN4 .... 160 B2
Orlingbury NN14 .... 110 A5
Wellingborough NN8 .... 129 F6
Harrowick La NN6 .... 144 E4
Harrow La NN11 .... 135 D6
Harrow Way NN2 .... 140 F6
Harry Cl NN6 .... 121 B3
Harry Potter Ho NN15 .... 72 B1
Hartburn Cl NN3 .... 161 C8
Hartland Dr LE16 .... 32 B3
Hartley Dr NN15 .... 92 A7
Hartley Ho NN13 .... 233 F6
HARTWELL 192 D1
Hartwell CE Prim Sch
NN7 .... 192 D1
Hartwell Cl NN2 .... 141 D5
Hartwell Rd
Ashton NN7 .... 205 F8
Hanslope MK19 .... 206 E4
Roade NN7 .... 192 A2
Hartwood Croft NN16 .... 72 C6
Harvest Cl
Burton Latimer NN15 .... 92 C2
Daventry NN11 .... 135 D6
Harvest Way NN2 .... 140 F5
Harvey Cl NN9 .... 114 B5
Harvey Dr MK46 .... 195 F1
Harvey La NN3 .... 142 B8
Harvey Rd
Rushden NN10 .... 148 B7
Wellingborough NN8 .... 129 E3
Harvey Reeves Rd
NN5 .... 159 A5
Harwood Dr NN16 .... 72 A6
HASELBECH 86 A8
Haselrig Sq 4 NN4 .... 158 F2
Hassocks Hedge NN4 .... 158 C2
Hastings MK11 .... 229 E5
Hastings Rd NN2 .... 141 D3
Hastings Wlk 4 NN18 .... 36 B5
Hatchdoyle La PE8 .... 41 D1
Hatfield Cl
Corby NN18 .... 36 E3
6 Northampton NN4 .... 175 C8
Wellingborough NN8 .... 129 C7
Hatherley Cl NN6 .... 101 A6
Hathersage Cl NN14 .... 50 E4
Hatton Ave NN8 .... 129 F5
Hatton Cl NN3 .... 142 A6
Hatton Hall 5 NN8 .... 129 F5
Hatton La NN17 .... 10 B1
HATTON PARK 129 E6
Hatton Park Rd NN8 .... 129 F5
Hatton St NN8 .... 129 F5
Hautboy La PE8 .... 28 B3
Havelock Cotts PE8 .... 42 A5
Havelock Ho 4 NN16 .... 72 C4
Havelock Jun & Inf Schs
NN14 .... 51 A3
Havelock Mews NN16 .... 72 B3
Havelock St
Desborough NN14 .... 51 A3
Kettering NN16 .... 72 C3
Wellingborough NN8 .... 130 A5
Haven Cl NN5 .... 159 A7
Haweswater Rd NN16 .... 71 E3
Hawfinch Gn NN14 .... 51 B4
Hawke Rd NN11 .... 135 E1
Hawkesbeard Pl 3
NN3 .... 143 C2
Hawkins Cl
Brackley NN13 .... 233 D7
Corby NN17 .... 21 B1
Daventry NN11 .... 135 E2
Rothwell NN14 .... 70 E7
Stony Stratford MK11 .... 229 D5
Hawk Ridge NN4 .... 158 F1
Hawkshead NN8 .... 129 B3
Hawksmoor Way
NN5 .... 140 D1
Hawksnest NN4 .... 175 A8
Hawkstone Cl NN5 .... 158 D7
Hawkswood MK46 .... 195 F5
Hawkwell Est MK19 .... 229 B7
Hawson Cl NN15 .... 91 C7
Hawthorn Ave NN14 .... 89 C5
Hawthorn Cl NN15 .... 92 B1
Hawthorn Com Prim Sch
NN15 .... 91 B8
Hawthorn Dr
Brackley NN13 .... 222 F1
Daventry NN11 .... 135 C3
Thrapston NN14 .... 76 D1
Towcester NN12 .... 203 C8
Hawthorne Cl NN11 .... 184 B6
Hawthorne Rd NN9 .... 112 A4
Hawthorne Wlk NN17 .... 21 E1
Hawthorn Rd
Burton Latimer NN15 .... 92 B1
Kettering NN15 .... 91 B8
Northampton NN3 .... 142 A1
Hawthorns The
Desborough NN14 .... 51 C2
Higham Ferrers NN10 .... 132 B6
Silverstone NN12 .... 214 D3
Hawthorn Way NN8 .... 129 E5
Hay Cl
Corby NN18 .... 53 B8
Rushden NN10 .... 148 B8
Haycroft Wlk NN2 .... 141 A5
Hayden Ave NN9 .... 112 A5
Hayden Rd NN10 .... 132 C2
Hayden Wlk NN10 .... 132 C2
Haydock Cl NN18 .... 53 E8
Haydown Gn NN5 .... 158 D8
Hayes Rd MK19 .... 228 F5
Hayes Wlk PE8 .... 16 D1
Hayeswood Rd NN3 .... 142 F4
Hay La NN9 .... 112 E1
Hayman Rd NN13 .... 233 D7
Haynes La NN6 .... 105 B1
Haynes Rd NN16 .... 72 D2
Hayride The NN4 .... 175 A7
Haystack The NN11 .... 135 D6
Hayway
Irthlingborough NN9 .... 112 E1
Rushden NN10 .... 132 A4
Hayway Inf Sch NN10 .... 132 B3
Hazeland Ho NN14 .... 51 A3
Hazel Cl
Brackley NN13 .... 222 F1
Hartwell NN7 .... 192 E2
Hazel Copse NN4 .... 175 F1
Hazel Cres NN12 .... 203 B5
Hazel Croft NN11 .... 118 C1
Hazelden Cl NN29 .... 146 D1
Hazeldene Rd NN2 .... 141 F3
Hazel Leys Prim Sch
NN18 .... 36 D4
Hazel Rd NN15 .... 72 C1
Hazelwood NN12 .... 214 C4
Hazelwood Ct 1 NN16 .... 72 B1
Hazelwood La NN16 .... 72 B1
Hazelwood Rd
Corby NN17 .... 36 E7
Northampton NN1 .... 159 D5
Headingley Rd NN10 .... 132 D2
Headlands
Desborough NN14 .... 51 C3
Kettering NN15 .... 91 B8
Headlands Prim Sch
NN3 .... 142 C2
Headlands The
Market Harborough
LE16 .... 31 F4
Northampton NN3 .... 142 C2
Wellingborough NN8 .... 129 F6
Headway NN18 .... 53 A8
Healey Cl NN3 .... 143 D4
Hearndon Ct NN8 .... 129 E3
Hearth St LE16 .... 31 D3
Heart Of The Shires Sh
Village NN7 .... 136 F2
Heathcote Gr NN14 .... 50 E4
HEATHENCOTE 204 A3
Heatherbreea Gdns
NN10 .... 131 F3
Heather Ct
Northampton NN4 .... 159 A2
Rushden NN10 .... 132 A2
Heatherdale Way
NN2 .... 141 E3
Heather La NN3 .... 142 E4
Heather Rd NN16 .... 72 D4
Heathers The NN29 .... 146 E2
Heathfield Way NN5 .... 141 A1
Heathfield Wlk NN18 .... 36 B4
Heath Gn NN5 .... 140 F1
Heath Rise NN8 .... 129 D6
Heath Terr NN12 .... 203 C6
Heathville NN5 .... 140 F1
Heath Way
Burton Latimer NN15 .... 92 C3
Rugby CV22 .... 98 D8
H E Bates Way NN10 .... 132 A2
Hecham Way NN10 .... 132 B7
Hedge End NN4 .... 175 C6
Hedgely Ct NN4 .... 159 A2
Hedgerow Dr NN2 .... 141 A5
Hedgerow La NN14 .... 89 C5
Hedgerow Way NN11 .... 135 C6
Hedges The NN10 .... 132 C4
Hedgeway NN4 .... 175 C6
HELLIDON 151 D1
Hellidon Cl NN2 .... 141 E4
Hellidon Rd CV47 .... 166 D7
HELMDON 211 F4
Helmdon Cres NN2 .... 141 C4
Helmdon Prim Sch
NN13 .... 211 F4
Helmdon Rd
Greatworth OX17 .... 210 E2
Northampton NN2 .... 141 C5
Sulgrave OX17 .... 210 F7
Wappenham NN12 .... 213 A8
Weston NN12 .... 199 F2
Helmsley Way NN18 .... 36 B5
Hemans Rd NN11 .... 135 B3
Hembury Pl NN4 .... 158 F3
Hemery Way NN15 .... 90 F8
HEMINGTON 60 E7
Hemington Rd PE8 .... 42 F2
Hemmingwell Rd
NN8 .... 130 A7
Hempland Cl NN18 .... 53 B8
Hemplow Dr NN6 .... 64 B2
Henders MK11 .... 229 E5
Henley Cl
Kettering NN15 .... 91 F5
Wellingborough NN8 .... 129 C6
Henley Ct NN6 .... 120 C6
Henley Ho NN17 .... 36 E6
Henry Bird Ct NN4 .... 159 D4
Henry Bird Way NN4 .... 159 D4
Henry Chichele Prim Sch
NN10 .... 132 B7
Henry Gotch Prim Sch
NN15 .... 72 D1
Henry Smith Ho 2
NN11 .... 135 B3
Henry St NN1 .... 159 E7
Henshaw Rd NN8 .... 129 E3
Hensmans La NN29 .... 164 D3
Henson Cl NN16 .... 71 F5
Henson Pk NN16 .... 71 F5
Henson Way NN16 .... 71 E4
Herbert Gdns NN12 .... 203 D8
Herbert St NN1 .... 159 C6
Hereford Cl NN14 .... 51 C4
Hereward Rd NN4 .... 159 B2
Herford Cl NN18 .... 36 A2
Heritage Ct NN16 .... 72 B1
Heritage Way
Corby NN17 .... 22 B2
Raunds NN9 .... 114 E7
Hermitage Rd LE16 .... 33 E3
Hermitage Way NN4 .... 175 D7
Herne Hill Ct NN4 .... 158 E2
Herne Rd PE8 .... 42 B4
Heron Ave NN14 .... 76 E3
Heron Cl
Burton Latimer NN15 .... 92 A2
Hinton NN11 .... 184 B6
Towcester NN12 .... 203 C3
Wellingborough NN8 .... 130 A7
Heron Ct NN11 .... 135 C3
Heron Dr NN13 .... 222 D1
Heronsford NN4 .... 174 E8
Herons Wood Cl PE8 .... 41 E5
Herrieffs Farm Rd
NN13 .... 233 F6
Herriotts Ct 11 NN8 .... 130 A5
Herriotts La NN8 .... 130 A5
Hertford Ct
Daventry NN11 .... 153 C7
Northampton NN3 .... 143 A1
Hertford Rd NN15 .... 91 C6
Hervey Cl NN3 .... 142 D2
Hervey St NN1 .... 159 E7
Hesketh Cres NN12 .... 203 C4
Hesketh Rd NN12 .... 217 E6
Hesperus NN8 .... 129 B4
Hester St NN2 .... 159 C8
Hever Cl
Rushden NN10 .... 148 C8
Thrapston NN14 .... 76 E2
Hewlett's Cl NN29 .... 164 D2
Hexham Ct NN4 .... 159 A2
Heyford Rd NN5 .... 157 F7
Heygate St LE16 .... 31 E4
Hiawatha NN8 .... 129 B4
Hibiscus Cl NN3 .... 160 C6
Hickman Cl OX17 .... 210 D2
Hickmire NN29 .... 146 D3
Hicks Ct NN12 .... 203 D4
Hicks Rd NN12 .... 203 C4
Hidcote Cl
Corby NN18 .... 36 E2
Northampton NN4 .... 175 C7
Wellingborough NN8 .... 129 D2
Hidcote Way 3 NN11 .... 135 B7
Hield Cl NN18 .... 36 C1
Higgins Sq NN4 .... 158 F2
HIGHAM CROSS 206 D3
Higham Cross Rd
MK19 .... 206 E4
HIGHAM FERRERS 132 D6
Higham Ferrers Jun & Inf
Schs NN10 .... 132 B6
Higham Park Rd
NN10 .... 149 A5
Higham Rd
Burton Latimer NN15 .... 92 C1
Chelveston NN9 .... 133 B7
Little Irchester NN8,
NN29 .... 130 D1
Rushden NN10 .... 132 B4
Stanwick NN9 .... 113 F3
High Barns Cl NN4 .... 175 E2
Highbridge Rd NN12 .... 213 A8
Highbrook NN18 .... 36 B4
Highcroft LE17 .... 45 E6
Highcroft Cl NN12 .... 217 E6
Highcross St LE16 .... 31 C3
Highdown Cl NN4 .... 158 E3
Highfield
Duddington PE9 .... 5 B7
Woodford NN14 .... 94 C7
Highfield Cotts LE15 .... 3 E8
Highfield Court Mews
NN13 .... 233 E6
Highfield Cres NN15 .... 91 C6
Highfield Ct NN13 .... 233 E6
Highfield Gr NN17 .... 36 F7
Highfield Pk NN6 .... 104 D4
Highfield Rd
Daventry NN11 .... 135 B3
Irthlingborough NN9 .... 112 F2
Kettering NN15 .... 91 B7
Mears Ashby NN6 .... 128 C4
Northampton NN1 .... 142 A1
Rushden NN10 .... 131 F1
Thrapston NN14 .... 76 E2
Wellingborough NN8 .... 130 B5
Highfields
Polebrook PE8 .... 42 F3
Towcester NN12 .... 203 C3
Highfields Com Prim Sch
NN15 .... 91 B7
Highfield St
Finedon NN9 .... 112 B5
Market Harborough
LE16 .... 31 D3
Highfield Way NN7 .... 179 B6
HIGHGATE 28 D8
Highgate Gn PE8 .... 28 D8
High Gn NN2 .... 141 B3
High Greeve NN4 .... 176 A6
Highgrove Ct 2
NN10 .... 132 B2
High Hill Ave NN14 .... 70 C7
Highlands Ave NN3 .... 142 A4
Highlands Dr NN11 .... 135 B5
High Leys The NN6 .... 100 F4
High March NN11 .... 153 E8
High March Cl NN11 .... 153 E8
Highpoint NN13 .... 233 F5
High St Mews 4 NN8 .... 129 F4
High St N NN12 .... 189 D5
High St Pl NN8 .... 129 F4
High St S
Olney MK46 .... 195 F3
Rushden NN10 .... 132 B1
Tiffield NN12 .... 189 D4
High St The NN6 .... 103 D1
High Slade NN6 .... 125 C8
High St
Adderbury OX17 .... 230 A4
Astcote NN12 .... 188 F7
Blakesley NN12 .... 187 A1
Blisworth NN7 .... 190 D7
Bozeat NN29 .... 164 D2
Brackley NN13 .... 233 F7
Braunston NN11 .... 118 B1
Brigstock NN14 .... 55 F8
Brixworth NN6 .... 106 B3
Broughton NN14 .... 90 A4
Bugbrooke NN7 .... 172 F7
Burton Latimer NN15 .... 92 C2
Byfield NN11 .... 183 D7
Charwelton NN11 .... 168 A4
High St *continued*
Chelveston NN9 .... 133 C8
Clipston LE16 .... 67 A8
Collyweston PE9 .... 1 D2
Corby NN17 .... 37 A6
Cottingham LE16 .... 20 C1
Cranford St John NN14 .... 93 A6
Creaton NN6 .... 104 F4
Crick NN6 .... 100 F5
Croughton NN13 .... 238 C8
Culworth OX17 .... 198 C3
Daventry NN11 .... 135 C2
Deanshanger MK19 .... 228 E4
Denford NN14 .... 95 C6
Desborough NN14 .... 51 A3
Duddington PE9 .... 5 B6
Earls Barton NN6 .... 144 E4
Easton o t H PE9 .... 2 A5
Ecton NN6 .... 143 F3
Everdon NN11 .... 170 A8
Eydon NN11 .... 184 C1
Finedon NN9 .... 111 F5
Flore NN7 .... 155 E5
Gayton NN7 .... 173 E2
Great Doddington NN7 .... 145 E6
Great Easton LE16 .... 20 D7
Great Houghton NN4 .... 160 E2
Greens Norton NN12 .... 202 D8
Gretton NN17 .... 10 C1
Guilsborough NN6 .... 103 F6
Hanslope MK19 .... 207 A2
Harpole NN7 .... 157 C6
Harrington NN6 .... 69 A5
Higham Ferrers NN10 .... 132 B5
Husbands Bosworth
LE17 .... 45 E5
Irchester NN29 .... 147 B8
Irthlingborough NN9 .... 112 E2
Islip NN14 .... 76 B2
Kettering NN16 .... 72 B2
Ketton PE9 .... 1 A6
Kislingbury NN7 .... 157 D4
Lamport NN6 .... 87 D2
Little Addington NN14 .... 113 B8
Long Buckby NN6 .... 121 C4
Market Harborough LE16 .... 31 E3
Middleton Cheney
OX17 .... 219 F8
Milton Malsor NN7 .... 174 E4
Morcott LE15 .... 3 A6
Moulton NN3 .... 126 C1
Naseby NN6 .... 85 B8
Northampton, Collingtree
NN4 .... 175 C4
Northampton, Great Billing
NN3 .... 143 C2
Northampton, Hardingstone
NN4 .... 175 F8
Northampton, Kingsthorpe
NN2 .... 141 B3
Northampton, Weston Favell
NN3 .... 142 D1
Northampton, Wootton
NN4 .... 175 E6
Olney MK46 .... 195 F4
Paulerspury NN12 .... 216 C8
Pitsford NN6 .... 125 C4
Podington NN29 .... 147 E2
Potterspury NN12 .... 217 D3
Preston Capes NN11 .... 169 D2
Pytchley NN14 .... 90 F2
Raunds NN9 .... 114 D7
Ringstead NN14 .... 95 B3
Roade NN7 .... 191 D4
Rothwell NN14 .... 70 C7
Rugby CV21 .... 99 A8
Rushden NN10 .... 132 B2
Rushton NN14 .... 52 C2
Scaldwell NN6 .... 106 F5
Shutlanger NN12 .... 190 D1
Silverstone NN12 .... 214 D4
Souldern OX27 .... 237 E3
Spratton NN6 .... 105 B1
Stanion NN14 .... 37 E2
Stanwick NN9 .... 113 F3
Stony Stratford MK11 .... 229 D6
Swinford LE17 .... 62 B3
Syresham NN13 .... 224 B8
Thrapston NN14 .... 76 D2
Titchmarsh NN14 .... 77 D4
Twywell NN14 .... 74 F1
Walgrave NN6 .... 108 A5
Wappenham NN12 .... 213 B8
Weedon Bec NN7 .... 155 B4
Weedon Lois NN12 .... 200 C2
Weldon NN17 .... 38 B8
Welford NN6 .... 64 E6
Wellingborough NN8 .... 129 F5
Welton NN11 .... 119 E1
West Haddon NN6 .... 102 C4
Weston NN12 .... 199 F2
Weston Underwood
MK46 .... 195 B2
Whittlebury NN12 .... 215 C4
Wollaston NN29 .... 146 D2
Woodford Halse NN11 .... 184 C6
Woodford NN14 .... 94 D7
Wymington NN10 .... 148 B5
Yardley Gobion NN12 .... 217 F6
Yardley Hastings NN7 .... 179 B6
Yelvertoft NN6 .... 82 B3
High Stack NN6 .... 121 C3
High View
Deanshanger MK19 .... 228 E5
Northampton NN4 .... 175 E6

High Woods NN6 143 D8
Hilda Pl NN16 72 E4
Hillary Cl NN11 135 B5
Hillary Rd NN10 131 F1
Hillberry Rise NN3 143 D4
Hill Cl
Northampton NN5 140 C2
Walgrave NN6 107 F5
Hill Crest NN7 174 C1
Hillcrest Ave
Burton Latimer NN15 92 B1
Kettering NN15 72 D1
Market Harborough LE16 31 D4
Northampton NN3 142 A3
Hillcrest Cl NN14 76 E3
Hillcrest La LE17 45 E5
Hillcrest Rd NN7 173 E1
Hillcroft View NN12 187 B1
Hilldrop Rd NN4 175 B7
Hill Farm Est NN14 113 C7
Hill Farm Rise NN4 175 A8
Hillfield Rd PE8 41 E6
Hill Gdns LE16 31 C3
Hill Ho OX17 219 C6
Hill House Ct NN12 172 D1
Hill House Gdns NN9 113 F3
Hillmorton La
Clifton u D CV23 80 A4
Lilbourne CV23 80 F5
Yelvertoft NN6 82 A4
Hillmorton Prim Sch CV21 99 B8
Hill Rd NN11 182 C5
Hill Row NN11 134 C8
Hillside
Chelveston NN9 133 B8
Daventry NN11 135 E2
Great Harrowden NN9 110 E4
Hartwell NN7 192 D2
West Haddon NN6 102 B4
Hillside Ave
Kettering NN15 91 C8
Silverstone NN12 214 E5
Hillside Cl NN29 164 D2
Hillside Cotts PE28 97 A4
Hillside Cres
Nether Heyford NN7 156 C1
Weldon NN17 38 A7
Hillside Rd
Flore NN7 155 D6
Market Harborough LE16 31 F4
Nether Heyford NN7 156 C1
Piddington NN7 177 B1
Wellingborough NN8 130 C7
Hillside Terr NN16 72 A2
Hillside Way NN3 160 C8
Hill St
Brackley NN13 233 F7
Kettering NN16 72 A3
Raunds NN9 114 D6
Wellingborough NN8 129 F4
Hillstone Ct NN9 113 F3
Hill The
Aynho OX17 237 C7
Great Houghton NN4 160 E2
Middleton LE16 35 B8
Pury End NN12 215 F7
Syresham NN13 224 B8
Hilltop
Blisworth NN7 174 C1
Dodford NN7 154 F5
Great Harrowden NN9 110 E5
HILL TOP 141 D4
Hill Top NN2 141 D4
Hilltop Ave
Desborough NN14 50 F4
Kettering NN15 91 F5
Hilltop Cl
Brixworth NN6 106 B1
Desborough NN14 50 F4
Hill Top Rd NN9 110 D4
Hill View NN11 184 C1
Hilmorton Rd CV22 98 F8
Hind Stile NN10 132 B5
HINTON 184 A6
Hinton Ave NN18 36 A4
Hinton Cl
Hinton NN11 184 B6
Northampton NN2 141 C5
HINTON-IN-THE-HEDGES 232 F6
Hinton Manor Ct NN11 184 B6
Hinton Rd
Brackley NN13 233 E6
Hinton NN11 184 B5
Northampton NN2 141 C5
Hinton's Cl NN13 211 F3
HINWICK 165 D7
Hinwick Cl NN15 91 D5
Hinwick Hall Coll of F Ed NN29 147 C1
Hinwick Rd
Podington NN29 147 D1
Wollaston NN29 146 E1
Hipwell Ct MK46 195 F3
Hirondelle Cl NN5 139 F1
Hobbs Hill NN14 70 C6
Hobby Cl NN4 175 B8
Hocknell Cl NN4 175 F6
Hockney Ave NN15 92 A7
Hodge Cl NN12 188 F6
Hodges La NN7 157 D4
Hodge Way NN16 72 D2
Hodnet Cl NN4 175 C7
Hoe Way NN7 191 C4
Hogarth Cl NN8 129 F7
Hogarth Dr NN15 92 A7
Hogarth Wlk NN18 36 E5
Hogg End OX17 196 F6
Hogg La OX17 231 F5
Holback La MK18 226 A5
Holbein Gdns NN4 174 E8
Holbein Wlk NN18 36 D5
Holbush Way NN9 112 E3
HOLCOT 126 E8
Holcot Cl NN8 129 E8
Holcot La
Scaldwell NN6 107 A5
Sywell NN6 127 E4
Holcot Leys CV22 98 A7
Holcot Rd
Brixworth NN6 106 D2
Moulton NN3 126 C5
Walgrave NN6 107 F4
Holcutt Cl NN4 175 F7
HOLDENBY 123 D3
Holdenby
Holdenby NN6 123 D4
Kettering NN15 91 D5
Holdenby Cl LE16 32 B3
Holdenby House Gdns & Falconry Ctr* NN6 123 C4
Holdenby Rd
East Haddon NN6 122 E5
Northampton NN2 141 E4
Spratton NN6 124 B8
Holden Gr NN11 135 B2
Holdgate Cl NN13 222 E1
Holes La MK46 195 F4
Holiday La MK19 206 F4
Holkham Cl NN18 36 D2
Holland Rise OX17 230 F4
Hollands Dr NN15 92 C2
Hollies The
Higham Ferrers NN10 132 B5
Moulton NN3 126 B2
Wellingborough NN8 129 E5
Hollingside Dr NN2 141 F3
Hollington Rd NN9 114 D6
Holloway The CV47 166 D7
Hollow Bank NN3 142 C6
HOLLOWELL 104 B5
Hollowell Cl NN10 148 D8
Hollowell Ct 3 NN8 129 F4
Hollowell Rd NN6 104 E4
Hollow The
Ravensthorpe NN6 103 E1
Stanwick NN9 114 A3
Hollow Way
Aynho OX17 237 C7
Eydon NN11 184 B1
Hollow Wood MK46 195 E3
Holly Bush La CV47 166 D7
Holly Cl
Brackley NN13 222 F1
Market Harborough LE16 31 E4
Hollyhill NN12 203 B4
Holly La NN14 90 A6
Holly Lodge Dr NN2 141 D6
Holly Rd
Kettering NN16 72 C4
Northampton NN1 159 F8
Rushden NN10 131 E3
Holly Wlk NN9 111 D4
Holman Cl NN3 142 D2
Holm Cl NN7 155 A2
Holme Cl
Wellingborough NN9 110 E1
Wilbarston LE16 34 D5
Holmecross Rd NN3 142 E5
Holmes Ave NN9 114 E5
Holmes Dr PE9 1 B5
Holme Way CV23 99 D1
Holmfield Dr NN9 114 E6
Holmfield Terr NN6 121 A4
Holmfield Way NN3 160 C8
Holmfirth Wlk NN18 36 C4
Holmleigh Cl NN5 158 C7
Holmwood Cl NN5 140 A1
Holt Rd LE16 19 C8
Holt View LE16 20 D7
Holyoake Rd NN29 146 D2
Holyoake Terr NN6 121 C4
Holyrood Ct NN5 158 F7
Holyrood Rd NN5 158 F7
Holyrood Wlk NN18 36 C3
Home Acre NN7 161 B4
Home Cl
Blisworth NN7 190 D7
Corby NN18 36 B1
Dingley LE16 33 A3
Eastcote NN12 188 F8
Greens Norton NN12 202 D8
Irthlingborough NN9 131 E8
Middleton Cheney OX17 220 B8
Northampton NN4 175 E2
Silverstone NN12 214 D4
Staverton NN11 152 C8
Towcester NN12 203 C5
Home Ct NN14 76 D2
Home Farm OX17 219 E7
Home Farm Cl
Corby NN18 53 B8
Creaton NN6 104 F5
East Farndon LE16 48 B7
Northampton NN3 161 B8
Weedon Bec NN7 154 F2
Home Farm Ct
Adderbury OX17 230 B4
Norton NN11 136 C4
Home Farm Gr LE16 68 C7
Home Farm La NN6 125 C4
Home Farm Rd NN14 37 E2
Home Farm Yd NN6 104 B5
Homefield NN11 153 C8
Homestead Cl NN3 126 D1
Homestead Ct NN2 141 E1
Homestead Dr NN7 173 A7
Homestead Rise NN4 175 E6
Homestead The NN14 74 F1
Homestead Way
Northampton NN2 141 E1
Potterspury NN12 217 E3
Homewelland Ho LE16 31 D4
Honey Hill Dr MK19 228 E5
Honey Holme NN6 106 A1
Honeypot La LE17 45 E5
Honeystones NN3 126 C1
Honeysuckle Rd NN14 51 A5
Honeysuckle Way NN3 160 C6
Honiton Gdns NN18 36 E4
Hood Ct NN17 36 B8
Hood Rd NN11 135 E1
Hood St NN1 159 E7
Hood Wlk NN15 91 D8
Hookhams Path NN29 146 E2
Hopes Pl NN2 141 B3
Hope St NN29 164 D4
Hopmeadow Ct 2 NN3 143 B4
Hoppet Cl NN18 53 A8
HOPPING HILL 140 C1
Hopping Hill Gdns NN5 140 D1
Hopping Hill Prim Sch NN5 158 C8
Hopton Cl NN11 135 D6
Hopton Fields LE16 48 D8
Hornbeam Cl
Podington NN29 147 E2
Wellingborough NN8 129 E5
Hornbeam Ct
Desborough NN14 51 D3
Northampton NN3 142 D3
Hornby Rd NN6 144 E5
Horncastle Cl NN11 135 C6
Horne Cl CV21 99 B8
Horn La MK11 229 D5
Horrell Ct NN10 132 A2
Horrock's Way NN15 72 F1
Horsefair Cl LE16 31 D4
Horsefair Gn MK11 229 D5
Horse La NN17 11 F5
Horselease Cl NN18 53 A8
Horse Market
Kettering NN16 72 B2
Northampton NN1 159 C6
Horsemoor Sq 6 NN3 143 C2
Horsepool The CV23 81 A7
Horseshoe Cl
Brixworth NN6 106 C2
Creaton NN6 104 F4
Horse Shoe La LE16 32 B6
Horseshoe St NN1 159 C5
Horse Well Ct NN3 142 C7
Horsham Wlk NN18 36 B5
Horsley Rd NN2 141 C1
HORTON 177 D1
Horton Cl OX17 220 A7
Horton Cres OX17 220 A8
Horton Dr OX17 220 A8
Horton Pk NN7 177 E2
Horton Rd
Brafield-on-t-G NN7 177 D7
Hackleton NN7 177 C2
Middleton Cheney OX17 220 A7
Hortonsfield Rd NN12 217 F5
Hortons' La NN14 76 D2
Hoskyn Cl CV21 98 F8
Hospital Bungalow NN6 126 D7
Hospital Hill NN14 70 D7
Hothorpe Rd LE17 46 D8
Houghton Hill NN4 160 A1
Hove Rd NN10 132 C2
Hove St NN18 36 B4
Howard Ave NN17 36 B7
Howard Biley Gdns NN3 142 C3
Howard Cl NN11 135 D1
Howard Ct 3 NN8 130 B5
Howard La NN2 141 C8
Howard Rd NN29 146 D2
Howard's Ct NN29 146 D2
Howards Mdw PE8 13 F7
Howard St NN16 72 A2
Howard Way LE16 31 D1
Howcut La NN7 178 E3
Howden Gn NN14 50 E4
Howe Cres
Corby NN17 36 A7
Daventry NN11 135 E1
Hoxton Cl NN3 142 E6
Hoylake NN8 129 C7
Hoylake Dr NN2 141 F3
Hoy Wlk NN17 21 C1
Hubble Rd NN17 21 F1
Hudson Cl
Corby NN18 36 C3
Daventry NN11 135 C5
Hudson Dr NN4 158 E1
HULCOTE 189 F1
Hulcote NN12 203 F8
Hulme Way NN8 129 E7
Humber Cl
Daventry NN11 134 F4
Northampton NN5 140 F2
Humber Gdns NN8 129 C6
Humber Wlk NN17 21 D2
Humfrey La NN2 141 C8
Humphries Dr NN13 233 D8
Hunsbarrow Rd NN4 158 E4
Hunsbury Cl NN4 158 F1
Hunsbury Gn NN4 158 D2
HUNSBURY HILL 158 F1
Hunsbury Hill Ave NN4 158 E3
Hunsbury Hill Ctry Pk* NN4 158 F1
Hunsbury Hill Rd NN4 158 E1
Hunsbury Ironstone Railway Mus* NN4 158 E2
Hunsbury Park Prim Sch NN4 158 F2
Hunslet La NN4 158 E2
Hunt Cl
Brixworth NN6 106 B2
Towcester NN12 203 C7
Wellingborough NN8 129 F8
Hunters Cl
Husbands Bosworth LE17 45 E6
Northampton NN2 141 D6
Hunters Rd NN17 22 F1
Hunter St NN1 159 D7
Hunters' Way NN6 106 B2
HUNTGATE END 206 D2
Huntingdon Cl NN18 36 E1
Huntingdon Gdns LE16 31 E1
Huntingdon Rd NN14 76 E2
Hunting Way PE8 14 C4
Huntsham Cl NN3 160 D7
Huntsmead NN3 143 D4
Hunt St NN18 36 D5
Hurst Cl NN15 92 C4
HUSBANDS BOSWORTH 45 D5
Husbands Bosworth CE Prim Sch LE17 45 E5
Hussar Cl NN11 135 B1
Hutchinson Ave NN14 90 B3
Hutts Cl NN11 183 D7
Huxley Cl NN8 129 A4
Huxloe Rise NN3 142 E6
Huxlow Science Coll NN9 112 E3
Hyacinth Way NN10 148 B7
Hyde Cl NN7 191 C4
Hyde Dr NN9 112 A5
Hyde Rd NN7 191 C4

I

Ibsen Wlk NN18 36 A2
Ibstock Cl NN3 143 A6
Icknield Dr NN4 158 E1
Ickworth Cl 12 NN11 135 B7
Ideal Bldgs 17 NN1 159 C7
Ilex Cl NN4 159 F1
Ilmor Ave NN6 106 C3
Imperial Ct NN10 132 A2
Independent St CV23 100 A3
Indmere Cl NN4 158 C1
Ingleborough Way NN5 158 D8
Inglewood Ct NN3 143 C1
Inham Cl NN18 36 C2
Inkerman Way PE8 41 F5
Inlands Cl NN11 135 D1
Inlands Rise NN11 135 D1
Inlands The NN11 135 D1
Inn Yard Ct LE16 68 C7
Insignia Cl 7 NN4 175 E7
Inwood Cl NN18 36 C2
io Centre The NN5 140 C2
Iona Rd NN17 36 C8
IRCHESTER 147 B7
Irchester Com Prim Sch NN29 147 A8
Irchester Country Pk Trail* NN8 130 D1
Irchester Country Pk Visitor Ctr* NN29 130 D1
Irchester Ctry Pk* NN29 130 F1
Irchester Narrow Gauge Rly Mus* NN8 130 D1
Irchester Rd
Podington NN10 147 B4
Rushden NN10 131 F2
Wollaston NN29 146 F3
Irchester Turn NN29 131 A2
Ireton Rd LE16 31 D2
Iron Cross NN11 167 B2
Irondale Cl NN4 158 E3
Iron Duke Cl NN11 135 B4
Iron Pikes NN6 106 C1
Ironstone Ct NN9 111 F4
Ironstone La NN4 158 E3
Ironstone Way NN6 106 C3
Ironwood Ave NN14 51 A4
IRTHLINGBOROUGH 112 D2
Irthlingborough Inf Sch NN9 112 E2
Irthlingborough Jun Sch NN9 112 E2
Irthlingborough Rd
Finedon NN9 112 B4
Little Addington NN14 113 B7
Wellingborough NN8 130 E4
Irvine Dr NN12 203 D8
Irving Gr NN17 36 E8
Isebrook Ct NN15 92 A2
Isebrook Hospl NN8 130 B3
Isebrook Sch NN15 91 E7
Ise Com Coll NN15 72 D1
Ise Rd NN15 72 D1
Ise Vale Ave NN14 51 B3
Ise View Rd NN14 51 B3
ISHAM 91 E1
Isham CE Prim Sch NN14 91 F1
Isham Cl NN2 141 D5
Isham Rd
Orlingbury NN14 110 A5
Pytchley NN14 91 B3
Islay Wlk NN17 36 C8
Isley Valley Ind Est NN8 130 D7
Islington NN14 77 B4
Islington Ct NN12 203 D5
Islington Rd NN12 203 D5
ISLIP 76 B3
Ivens La NN12 171 C1
Ivy Ct NN11 135 B1
Ivydene Terr NN14 90 A4
Ivy La NN9 111 F4
Ivy Rd
Kettering NN16 72 D4
Northampton NN1 159 F8
Ixworth Cl NN3 142 F5

J

Jackdaw Cl NN3 161 C8
Jacklin Ct NN8 129 C7
Jack Parnell Cl NN5 158 B6
Jackson Cl
Market Harborough LE16 48 E8
Northampton NN2 141 E6
Jackson Rd CV21 80 A1
Jackson's La NN8 129 F5
Jackson's Lane Flats 1 NN8 129 F5
Jackson Way NN15 90 F8
Jacorrin Cl NN2 141 E6
Jacques Rd NN15 92 C1
Jamb The NN17 37 A6
James Lewis Ct NN3 142 C2
James Rd NN8 130 A2
James St NN29 147 B7
James Watt Ave NN17 37 A8
James Watt Cl NN11 135 A4
Jardine Cl NN3 142 D1
Jarretts Yd NN4 175 E6
Jarvis Ct NN13 233 F8
Jasmine Ct NN16 72 D5
Jasmine Gdns NN10 148 B7
Jasmine Ho NN4 159 A2
Jasmine Rd
Kettering NN16 72 D4
Northampton NN3 143 C5
Jasper Wlk NN3 142 D6
Javelin Cl NN5 158 C8
Jay Rd NN18 36 E3
JBJ Bsns Pk NN7 174 D2
Jean Rd NN16 72 E3
Jellicoe Cl NN11 135 E1
Jenkinson Rd NN12 203 D4
Jenkins Rd CV21 80 A1
Jenner Cres NN2 141 B5
Jennings Cl
4 Daventry NN11 135 D1
Higham Ferrers NN10 132 B5
Jersey Cl NN8 130 B6
Jersey Ct NN3 142 F1
Jervis Cl NN11 135 E1
Jerwood Way LE16 31 F2
Jesus Hospl NN14 70 D7
Jetty The
Creaton NN6 104 F4
Hackleton NN7 177 B3
Wappenham NN12 213 B8
Wardington OX17 196 E1
Jeyes Cl NN3 126 B1
Jibwood NN14 89 B5
Jitty The NN14 89 B4
Joan Pyel Cl NN9 131 E8
Job's Yd NN16 72 B2
John Beverly Mews NN14 70 C6
John Clare Cl NN13 222 F1
John Clare Ct NN16 72 C6
John Clare Way NN17 36 D8
John Clark Way NN10 132 C3
John Eagle Cl NN9 113 F4
John Gray Rd NN29 145 D6
John Hellins Prim Sch NN12 217 D3
John Lea Way NN8 130 A1
John Pyel Rd NN9 112 E1
John Smith Ave NN14 70 E7
Johnson Ave
Brackley NN13 233 C8
Wellingborough NN8 130 A1
Johnson Cl NN11 135 B3
Johnson Ct NN4 159 D4
Johnsons Field MK46 195 E4
Johns Rd NN7 157 A1
John St
Rushden NN10 132 B2
Thrapston NN14 76 E2
John White Cl The NN10 132 C6
Jones Cl NN13 233 D8
Jordan Cl LE16 32 A3

Joseph Priestley Ct 6 NN11 135 C1
Joshua Sq NN4 158 F2
Jowett Cl NN15 92 A8
Jubilee Ave NN18 36 D5
Jubilee Cl
Byfield NN11 183 D7
Islip NN14 76 B3
Long Buckby NN6 121 A4
Northampton NN4 158 F3
Jubilee Cres NN8 129 F2
Jubilee Ct PE8 39 E7
Jubilee Dr NN6 108 B5
Jubilee Gdns
Market Harborough LE16 31 F4
Rushden NN10 148 C8
Jubilee Rd NN11 135 B2
Jubilee St
Irthlingborough NN9 112 E1
Rothwell NN14 70 D6
Jubilee Terr
Isham NN14 110 F8
Stony Stratford MK11 229 E5
Judes Ct NN15 72 A1
Judges Ct NN6 104 F4
Judith Rd NN16 72 E4
Julian Way NN2 141 A3
Junction Rd NN2 141 E1
Juniper Cl NN12 203 B4
Juniper Ct NN3 143 D3
JUNIPER HILL 239 E6
Juniper Thorn NN6 106 C1
Jura Cl NN17 36 B8
Justin Park Cvn Site LE16 48 F7
Jutland Way NN16 72 A2

K

K2 Ho NN5 141 A1
Kane Wlk NN17 36 E8
Kangaroo Spinney NN8 130 E3
Karlstad Cl NN18 36 A2
Kathleen Dr NN16 72 E4
Katrine Cl NN17 21 B1
Kealdale Rd NN3 142 A4
Keating Cl NN15 92 A8
Keats Cl
Earls Barton NN6 144 F4
Great Houghton NN4 160 F1
Keats Dr
Kettering NN16 72 C6
Towcester NN12 203 B5
Keats Rd
Daventry NN11 135 B3
Wellingborough NN8 129 D4
Keats Way
Corby NN17 36 C8
Higham Ferrers NN10 132 A5
Rushden NN10 131 E3
Keble Cl NN11 153 B8
Keble Ct NN8 129 F4
Keble Rd NN13 233 D8
Kedleston Cl 3 NN4 175 C8
Keebles Cl NN14 37 E2
Keepers Cl NN4 175 F3
Kelburn Cl NN4 175 B7
Keld Cl NN18 36 D2
KELMARSH 67 F3
Kelmarsh Hall* NN6 67 F4
Kelmarsh Rd
Arthingworth LE16 68 C7
Clipston LE16 67 A7
Corby NN17 36 C7
Kelmscott Cl NN3 143 A5
Kelsall Cl NN5 158 B8
Kelthorpe Cl PE9 1 A4
Kelvin Gr NN17 37 A7
Kemp Ho NN17 21 F3
Kemps Cl NN14 89 B4
Kemps Rd OX17 230 A5
Kempton Cl NN18 53 E8
Kendal Cl
Northampton NN3 142 D4
Rushden NN10 132 D1
Wellingborough NN8 129 D6
Kendalls Cl LE16 34 D5
Kenilworth NN18 36 C3
Kenilworth Cl
Daventry NN11 135 B1
Northampton NN5 158 B8
Rushden NN10 132 C1
Kenilworth Dr NN15 91 F8
Kenilworth Gdns NN14 76 F2
Kenmore Dr NN14 51 B2
Kenmuir Ave NN2 141 F2
Kenmuir Cres NN2 141 F2
Kenmuir Gdns NN2 141 F2
Kenmuir Rd NN9 111 F4
Kennedy Cl NN11 135 E1
Kennel Hill NN14 55 F7
Kennel Rd NN12 215 C3
Kennels Dr NN12 216 E3
Kennel Terr NN6 106 B2
Kennet Cl NN8 129 C6
Kennet Gn NN5 140 F2
Kensington Cl
Kings Sutton OX17 230 F6
Rushden NN10 131 E3
Towcester NN12 203 B4
Kensington Gdns NN15 91 B8
Kensington Pl MK46 195 F5
Kensington Wlk NN18 36 C3
Kent Cl
Corby NN17 36 C7
Kent Cl *continued*
Northampton NN5 158 C6
Kentford Cl NN4 175 B8
Kenton Ct NN15 92 A8
Kent Pl NN15 91 D6
Kent Rd
Northampton, Duston NN5 158 B6
Rushden NN10 132 C3
Wellingborough NN8 129 F1
Kentstone Cl NN2 140 F4
Kent The CV21 80 A2
Kerley Cl NN14 90 A3
Kerrfield Est NN5 158 C7
Kestian Cl LE16 31 D5
Keston Way NN9 114 B5
Kestrel Cl NN3 142 D1
Kestrel Cres NN13 222 E1
Kestrel La NN8 130 A7
Keswick NN8 129 B5
Keswick Dr
Northampton NN3 142 C4
Rushden NN10 132 D3
Keswick Rd MK19 207 B2
Ketco Ave PE9 1 B7
KETTERING 72 E3
Kettering Gdns 2 NN1 159 E6
Kettering General Hospl NN16 71 F2
Kettering Parkway NN15 91 D5
Kettering Rd
Broughton NN14 90 B5
Burton Latimer NN15 92 B3
Geddington NN14 54 A1
Great Harrowden NN9 110 E4
Isham NN14 91 E1
Islip NN14 75 E1
Market Harborough LE16 32 B2
Moulton NN3 126 F2
Northampton NN1 159 E8
Northampton, Spinney Hill NN3 142 A3
Pytchley NN14 90 F2
Rothwell NN14, NN16 70 E5
Stanion NN14 37 E2
Walgrave NN6 108 C6
Weldon NN17 38 B7
Woodford NN14 94 B8
Wothorpe PE9 2 C8
Kettering Rd N NN3 142 C5
Kettering Sta NN15 72 A1
Kettering Town FC NN16 72 B5
Kettle End NN12 200 C3
KETTON 1 A6
Kettonby Gdns NN15 91 B8
Ketton CE Prim Sch PE9 1 A5
Ketton Rd PE9 1 C3
Keyham Ct NN3 143 A5
Keys Cl NN11 135 D1
Keys La CV47 166 E8
KEYSTON 97 A4
Keystone NN4 158 C1
Keyston Rd PE18 116 D2
Keyte's Cl OX17 230 A4
KG House Bsns Ctr 4 NN5 140 F1
Kielder Ct NN15 92 A4
Kieldsen Ct OX17 210 B1
Kiel Wlk NN18 36 A2
Kilborn Cl NN8 129 E7
Kilborn Rd NN8 129 E6
Kilburn Pl NN10 132 B4
Kilby Cl NN8 129 E3
Kiln La
Litchborough NN12 171 C1
Welton NN11 135 E8
Kiln Way NN8 129 D4
KILSBY 100 A3
Kilsby CE Prim Sch CV23 100 A3
Kilsby La CV21 99 C7
Kilsby Rd
Barby CV23 99 C1
Crick NN6 100 F2
Watford NN6 120 B7
Kilvey Rd NN4 160 B2
Kilworth Rd
Husbands Bosworth LE17 45 D4
Rugby CV21 99 B7
Swinford LE17 62 C4
Kimble Cl NN4 175 B8
Kimbolton Ct NN14 76 E2
Kimbolton Rd
Chelveston NN9 133 D8
Higham Ferrers NN10 132 C6
Kinewell Cl NN14 95 A3
Kinewell Lake Nature Trail* NN14 95 A3
King Cup Cl NN10 148 C7
King Edward Rd NN1 160 A7
Kingfisher Cl
Hinton NN11 184 B6
Northampton NN4 175 A7
Ringstead NN14 95 A3
Kingfisher Ct NN6 143 D8
Kingfisher Rd NN13 222 E2
Kingfisher Way NN15 92 A2
King George Cres MK11 229 E6
King John Sch The NN14 76 D1
Kingmaker Way NN4 159 A2
King Richard Ct NN4 175 C6
Kings Arms La PE8 42 F3
Kings Ave NN10 132 C7
Kingsbrook NN18 36 B3
Kingsbrook Sch MK19 228 F4
Kings Cl NN4 175 F3
KING'S CLIFFE 13 E8
King's Cliffe Endowed Prim Sch PE8 13 F7
Kings Cliffe Rd PE8 14 C4
Kings Corner Cl NN11 184 C6
Kingscroft Ct NN3 143 C1
Kings Ct NN14 51 B3
King's Ct 2 LE16 31 E4
Kingsfield Bsns Pk NN5 141 A1
Kingsfield Cl NN5 141 A1
Kingsfield Piece NN12 215 C4
Kingsfield Way NN5 141 A1
King's Forest PE8 13 F7
Kings Gn NN11 153 C7
King's Head Pl LE16 31 E3
KING'S HEATH 140 E2
King's Heath Prim Sch NN5 140 F2
Kingshill Dr MK19 228 E5
Kings La
Barrowden LE15 3 F5
Pury End NN12 215 F7
Yelvertoft NN6 82 B4
King's La
Flore NN7 155 F5
Little Harrowden NN9 110 B3
Kingsland Ave NN2 141 D3
Kingsland Cl NN2 141 D3
Kingsland Gdns NN2 141 C3
Kingsley Ave
Daventry NN11 135 B1
Kettering NN16 72 B5
Rugby CV21 98 F8
Kingsley Dr NN17 36 D8
Kingsley Gdns 3 NN2 141 E1
KINGSLEY PARK 141 F2
Kingsley Park Mid Sch NN2 141 D1
Kingsley Park Terr NN2 141 F1
Kingsley Prim Sch NN2 141 F2
Kingsley Rd
Northampton NN2 141 E1
Rothwell NN14 70 C7
Silverstone NN12 214 E5
Kingsley Sch NN15 72 F1
Kingsmead
King's Cliffe PE8 13 F8
Northampton NN2 141 A5
Kings Meadow La NN10 132 B7
Kings Meadow Sch NN3 142 C7
Kingsmead Pk NN10 148 C7
Kingsmith Dr NN9 114 E6
Kings Park Rd NN3 141 F6
Kings Pk NN7 155 A3
Kings Pl NN10 132 C2
Kings Rd
Oundle PE8 42 A6
Rushden NN10 132 C2
Weldon NN17 38 B7
King's Rd LE16 31 E3
Kings St NN8 130 A5
Kings Stile OX17 208 F1
KINGS SUTTON 231 A4
Kings Sutton Prim Sch OX17 231 A5
Kings Sutton Sta OX17 230 E5
King St
Desborough NN14 51 B3
Earls Barton NN6 144 E5
Kettering NN16 72 C3
Long Buckby NN6 121 B4
Maidford NN12 186 D5
Northampton NN1 159 C6
Stony Stratford MK11 229 E6
Kingsthorne Distribution Pk NN16 71 E4
KINGSTHORPE 141 C3
Kingsthorpe Ave NN17 36 B7
Kingsthorpe Bsns Ctr NN2 141 B2
Kingsthorpe Com Coll NN2 141 E5
Kingsthorpe Gr NN2 141 C2
Kingsthorpe Grove Prim Sch NN2 141 C2
Kingsthorpe Ho NN2 141 C5
KINGSTHORPE HOLLOW 141 D1
Kingsthorpe Mid Com Sch NN2 141 B4
Kingsthorpe Rd NN2 141 C1
Kingsthorpe Sh Ctr 2 NN2 141 C3
Kingsthorpe Village Prim Sch NN2 141 B3
Kingston Ave MK11 229 E5
Kingston Cl
Blakesley NN12 187 B1
Daventry NN11 135 B3
Long Buckby NN6 121 C4
Middleton Cheney OX17 220 A7
Kingston Way LE16 31 E6
King Style Cl NN6 100 F6
Kingsway
Northampton NN2 141 B4
Wellingborough NN8 129 E2
Kingswell Rd NN2 141 B3
Kingswell St NN1 159 C5
Kingswood Pl NN18 36 A3
Kingswood Prim Sch NN18 36 C3
Kingswood Sch The NN18 36 A3
Kinross Cl NN3 142 A4
Kipling Dr NN12 203 B5
Kipling Rd
Corby NN17 36 D8
Kettering NN16 72 C5
Kippell Hill MK46 195 F5
Kipton Cl NN14 70 E7
Kipton Field NN14 70 E7
Kirby Cl
Corby NN18 36 A3
Northampton NN4 175 F7
Kirby Ct NN15 91 C5
Kirby Hall* NN17 23 B6
Kirby Ho LE16 31 F3
Kirby La NN17 23 C5
Kirby Rd NN17 10 C1
Kirkby Rd CV21 98 F8
Kirkhams Cl NN6 82 C3
Kirkstone Wlk 7 NN3 142 C4
Kirkwall NN17 21 C1
Kirton Cl NN3 143 B5
Kirton End NN3 143 B4
KISLINGBURY 157 E4
Kislingbury Prim Sch NN7 157 D4
Kislingbury Rd
Bugbrooke NN7 173 A8
Rothersthorpe NN7 174 A7
Kitchener Cl NN11 135 B4
Kitchen Gdns NN14 89 F6
Kitelee Cl MK19 207 A3
Kites Cl NN4 175 A8
Kits Cl NN7 192 D2
Knaphill Cres NN4 158 F4
Knibb Pl NN15 91 F6
Knibb St NN16 72 C2
Knightlands Rd NN9 112 F3
Knightley Cl NN11 183 D7
Knightley Rd NN2 141 C1
Knighton Cl NN5 140 A3
Knightons Way NN6 106 C1
Knights Cl
Bozeat NN29 164 D2
Corby NN18 36 A5
Earls Barton NN6 144 E4
Knightscliffe Way NN5 140 D1
Knights Ct
Northampton, Little Billing NN3 143 B1
Northampton NN1 159 F8
Wellingborough NN8 129 F5
Knight's End Rd LE16 32 B6
Knights Hill NN6 85 B8
Knight's La NN2 141 B3
Knights Mews NN10 132 C1
Knob The OX17 231 A5
Knock La NN7 190 F5
Knoll Ct NN16 72 B4
Knoll St LE16 31 C3
Knoll The
Brixworth NN6 106 C2
Grendon NN7 163 D5
KNOTTING 149 E3
KNOTTING GREEN 149 F1
Knowle Cl NN3 160 C6
Knowles Cl NN10 132 D3
Knowle Way 2 NN11 135 B7
Knox Ct NN8 130 B4
Knox Rd NN8 130 B5
KNUSTON 131 D1
Knuston Dr NN10 131 F2
Knuston Spinney NN10 131 E1
Knutsford La NN6 121 C4
Kylesku Cres NN15 91 E8
Kynnesworth Gdns NN10 132 C6
Kyoto Cl NN3 142 A6

L

Laburnum Cl
Hinton NN11 184 B6
Wellingborough NN8 129 E5
Laburnum Cres
Kettering NN16 72 D4
Northampton NN3 142 A3
Laceby Wlk NN3 142 F5
Lacemakers Ct NN10 148 C8
Lace Mews MK46 195 F4
Lacock Ho 7 NN11 135 B7
Laddermakers Yd NN7 172 E7
Ladybower Cl NN16 71 E3
Ladybridge Dr NN4 174 E8
Lady Cl NN11 153 D3
Lady Croft NN11 135 B1
Lady Hollows Dr NN4 176 A6
Ladymead Cl NN4 158 D1
Lady's La
Mears Ashby NN6 128 B2
Northampton NN1 159 C6
Lady Smock Cl NN4 175 F2
Ladywell Ct NN8 130 A7
Ladywell Mews NN14 70 D7
Lady Winefride's Wlk NN3 143 B2
Lahnstein Ct 12 NN16 72 B2
Lake Ave NN15 90 F8
Lake Cres NN11 135 A2
Lakeside
Irthlingborough NN9 131 D7
Northampton NN3 143 A7
Lakeside Bglws NN15 91 E6
Lakeside Cl NN14 76 D3
Lakeside Dr NN3 143 D3
Lakeside Lodges NN3 143 A7
Lakeview Gn NN3 142 C4
Lake Wlk
Adderbury OX17 230 B4
Northampton NN4 175 C4
Lalgates Ct NN5 158 F8
Lambert's Cl LE15 3 A6
Lambourne Way OX17 230 B4
Lambrook Dr NN4 175 C7
Lammas Cl
Husbands Bosworth LE17 45 E5
Orlingbury NN14 110 A5
Lammas Ctyd NN17 23 A1
Lammas Rd NN17 23 A1
LAMPORT 87 D2
Lamport Cl NN15 91 D5
Lamport Ct NN11 135 A5
Lamport Dr NN11 135 A5
Lamport Hall* NN6 87 D1
Lamport Rd
Draughton NN6 87 E6
Old NN6 107 C7
Lamva Ct MK11 229 F5
Lancaster Cl NN29 146 C3
Lancaster Dr
Brackley NN13 233 E8
Thrapston NN14 76 F2
Lancaster Rd
Kettering NN16 72 C3
Rothwell NN14 70 E7
Lancaster St NN10 132 C7
Lancaster Way
Northampton NN4 159 A1
Rushden NN10 132 C3
Lancers Way NN7 155 B4
Lanchester Way NN11 134 F3
Lancum Ho NN8 129 E5
Landcross Dr NN3 160 C7
Landimore Rd NN4 176 A7
Landor NN8 129 C4
Landor Cl NN17 21 D1
Landsdown Dr NN3 142 E2
Landseer Cl
Rugby CV21 80 B1
Wellingborough NN8 129 F8
Landseer Ct NN18 36 D5
Lanercost Wlk
Northampton NN3 142 C4
8 Northampton NN3 142 C4
Laneside Hollow NN4 175 C6
Lane The
Ashby St L CV23 119 B5
Denton NN7 178 B8
Eastcote NN12 173 A1
Easton o t H PE9 2 A5
Grafton Regis NN12 205 D2
Rothersthorpe NN7 174 B6
Wappenham NN12 213 B8
Weston by W LE16 18 B4
Langdale NN14 50 F3
Langdale Ct NN8 129 D5
Langdale Gr NN17 36 D8
Langdale Rd NN2 141 D3
Langdale Wlk LE16 31 E1
Langdon Cl NN11 135 B5
Langford Dr NN4 175 D5
Langham Cl NN6 104 F5
Langham Pl
Northampton NN2 159 C8
Walgrave NN6 108 A5
Langham Rd NN9 114 D7
Langley Cl NN4 158 E3
Langley Cres NN9 113 B5
Langley Ct NN15 92 B2
Langley Way NN15 91 C6
Langley Wlk NN18 36 D5
Langport Gn NN18 36 B6
Langsett Cl
Kettering NN16 71 E3
Northampton NN3 142 F1
Langton Ct
Corby NN18 36 B6
Market Harborough LE16 31 E3
Langton Pl NN14 91 E1
Langton Rd LE16 32 A7
Langton Rise NN11 137 C6
Lansdown Cl NN11 135 D5
Lansom Cl NN15 92 C3
Lapford Rd NN18 36 E4
Lapland Wlk NN18 36 B2
Lapstone Ho NN5 159 A5
Lapwing Cl NN4 175 A7
Larch Cl
Hinton NN11 184 A6
Irchester NN29 147 A7
Larch Dr NN11 135 C5
Larch La NN5 140 B2
Larch Rd
Corby NN17 21 D1
Kettering NN15 72 C1
Larchwood Cl NN8 129 E5
Larkhall La NN7 157 D6

Larkhall Way NN7 157 C7
Larkhill NN10 132 A4
Larkin Gdns NN10 132 A5
Lark La NN4 175 F4
Lark Rise
Brackley NN13 233 E8
Northampton NN3 143 B4
Larkwood Cl NN16 72 C6
Larratt Rd NN17 38 A8
Larwood Cl NN2 141 A5
Lasham Ct NN3 143 C1
Latham Rd PE8 41 F7
Latham's Hospl PE8 59 B6
Latham St NN14 55 F7
Lathbury Rd NN13 233 D8
Lathkill St LE16 31 F1
Latimer MK11 229 E4
Latimer Cl
Burton Latimer NN15 92 C2
Gretton NN17 10 C1
Latimer Com Arts Coll
NN15 92 A6
Latimer Cres LE16 31 F2
Latimer Rd NN17 36 E8
Lattimore Cl NN6 102 C5
Latymer Cl LE16 49 E5
Latymer Ct 4 NN1 159 C6
Lauda Way NN12 203 C8
Lauderdale Ave NN4 159 A2
Laud's Rd NN6 101 A5
Laughton Rd LE16 30 C4
Launcelot Ct NN5 158 A7
Launde Pk LE16 32 A2
Laundry Rd PE8 14 C4
Laurel Ct
Northampton NN3 142 E3
4 Wellingborough NN8 130 B5
Laurel Pl NN12 203 D5
Laurel Rd NN16 72 C4
Laurels The
Ecton NN6 143 F3
Moulton NN3 126 B2
Laurel Valley NN4 175 D4
Lavant Wlk NN3 141 F5
Lavender Cl
Corby NN18 36 D2
Thrapston NN14 76 D2
Lavender La NN7 177 D1
Lavender Way NN10 148 C8
Lavendon Ct NN15 92 A5
Lavenham Cl NN3 142 F5
Lavery Ct NN18 36 D5
Lawns The
Corby NN18 36 A4
Kettering NN16 72 A1
Kilsby CV23 100 A2
Northampton NN5 158 E8
Lawrence Cl
Kettering NN15 92 A8
Raunds NN9 114 B5
Lawrence Ct
Corby NN18 36 D5
Long Buckby NN6 121 B4
22 Northampton NN1 159 C7
Laws Croft NN13 233 D7
Laws La NN9 111 F4
Law's La PE8 13 F7
Lawson Cres NN3 143 C1
Lawson St
Kettering NN16 72 C3
Raunds NN9 114 D6
Lawton Rd NN10 132 C3
Lawyers Cl NN13 233 E2
LAXTON 11 F5
Laxton Cl NN17 36 B8
Laxton Ct NN15 92 A5
Laxton Dr PE8 42 B7
Laxton Jun Sch PE8 42 A5
Laywood Cl NN9 114 C7
Laywood Way NN9 131 E8
Leafields NN3 160 F8
Leah Bank NN4 159 A2
Leah Cl NN18 53 A8
Lealand The LE16 48 B8
Leamington Way
NN11 135 A2
Leam The NN11 134 F1
Lea Rd NN1 159 F8
Leatherland Ct 18
NN16 72 B2
Lea Way NN8 129 D3
Leben Sq NN3 143 C5
Leckhampstead Rd
MK19 228 A3
Ledaig Way NN3 142 A4
Ledbury Rd NN15 91 F5
Leeds Cl NN18 36 F2
Lees Cl NN12 215 C4
Leeson Cres NN15 91 F6
Leeson Ct NN12 203 D4
Leeson Rd NN12 203 C4
Lees St NN9 112 E1
Lee's Way NN14 54 A3
Lee Way NN9 114 D7
Legg Rd PE8 7 D8
Legion Cres NN16 71 F3
Leicester Cl NN16 72 A3
Leicester La LE16 31 D7
Leicester Par NN2 159 C8
Leicester Rd
Husbands Bosworth LE17 45 D7
Market Harborough LE16 31 D5
Leicester St
Kettering NN16 72 A3
Northampton NN1 159 C7
Leicester Terr 2
NN2 159 C7
Leighton Cl NN8 129 F8
Leighton Pl NN8 129 F4
Leighton Rd NN18 36 D5
Leith Ct NN4 158 E3
Lely Ct NN18 36 D5
Lennon Cl CV21 99 C8
Lennox Wlk NN5 140 D2
Lensway NN14 89 B5
Lenthall Sq LE16 31 E1
Lenton Cl NN14 90 A3
Leonard La 1 NN3 126 C1
Leonardo Ct NN18 36 D5
Lerwick Way NN17 36 C8
Leslie Rd NN2 159 B7
Lesson Rd NN6 106 B1
Lester Cl OX17 230 A6
Letts Rd NN4 159 B3
Leven Way NN17 21 B1
Lever Rd CV21 80 A1
Levitts Rd NN7 173 A8
Lewin Cl NN14 70 B7
Lewin Rd NN18 36 B1
Lewis Ho NN14 91 E1
Lewis Rd
Kettering NN15 91 C7
Northampton NN5 159 A7
Lexden Cl NN4 175 F7
Lexton Gdns OX17 220 B8
Leyland Dr NN2 141 A5
Leyland Trad Est NN8 130 D4
Leyland View NN8 130 D4
Leys Ave
Desborough NN14 51 C3
Rothwell NN14 70 C7
Leys Cl
Denton NN7 162 B1
Long Buckby NN6 121 C4
Leys Gdns NN8 130 B6
Leyside Ct NN3 143 B5
Leys La NN4 160 F1
Leys Rd
Earls Barton NN6 144 D4
Pattishall NN12 172 D1
Rugby CV21 99 C7
Wellingborough NN8 130 B6
Leys The
Bugbrooke NN7 172 E6
Denton NN7 162 B1
Long Buckby NN6 121 C4
Northampton NN2 141 B2
Orlingbury NN14 110 A5
Roade NN7 191 D4
Upper Boddington NN11 182 C8
Welford NN6 64 E5
Woodford NN14 94 D7
Yardley Hastings NN7 179 A6
Leyswell Ct 4 NN3 161 A8
Liberty Dr NN5 140 C1
Lichfield Cl NN7 157 D3
Lichfield Dr NN4 175 B7
Liddington Way NN2 141 B5
Lightfoot La LE16 20 B1
Lilac Cl NN14 76 D3
Lilac Ct NN8 129 E5
Lilac Gr NN10 148 B7
Lilac Pl NN15 72 D1
LILBOURNE 81 A6
Lilbourne Rd CV23 80 C5
LILFORD 58 E4
Lilford Pl NN16 72 D3
Lilford Rd NN14 77 C8
Liliput Rd NN4 160 C3
Lilley Homes The
NN8 129 F2
Lilley Terr NN9 112 F2
LILLINGSTONE DAYRELL 226 E4
LILLINGSTONE LOVELL 227 A5
Lillington Ct NN18 36 B6
Lillycourt Ho NN16 72 A2
Lilly Hill MK46 195 F5
Lime Ave
Eydon NN11 184 C1
Long Buckby NN6 121 C4
Northampton NN3 142 A1
Oundle PE8 41 F7
Lime Cl
Broughton NN14 90 B4
Hartwell NN7 192 E2
Lime Ct NN9 112 F2
Lime Farm Way NN4 160 F2
Limefields Way NN4 175 D6
Lime Gr
Bugbrooke NN7 173 A7
Rushden NN10 132 B4
Wellingborough NN8 130 A7
Limehurst Cl NN5 140 C1
Limehurst Rd NN5 158 C8
Limehurst Sq NN5 158 C8
Lime Rd
Kettering NN16 72 D4
Yardley Gobion NN12 217 E6
Lime St
Irthlingborough NN9 112 F2
Olney MK46 195 F3
Rushden NN10 132 B4
Limes The
9 Daventry NN11 135 C1
11 Irthlingborough NN9 112 F2
Stony Stratford MK11 229 E5
Limes The *continued*
Thorpe Langton LE16 17 A5
Thrapston NN14 76 E2
Lime Terr NN9 112 F2
Lime Tree Mews NN15 72 B1
Lime Trees Gr NN17 37 A6
Limlow Cl NN4 158 E3
Limoges Ct NN5 140 A2
Linacre Cl NN3 142 F6
Lincoln Ct
Brackley NN13 233 F5
Hanslope MK19 207 A2
Market Harborough LE16 31 F5
Lincoln Ho NN5 159 A5
Lincoln Pk NN13 233 F5
Lincoln Rd NN5 159 A5
Lincoln St NN2 141 C3
Lincoln Way
Corby NN18 36 C4
Daventry NN11 153 C8
Lindale Cl NN3 142 B3
Linden Ave
Higham Ferrers NN10 132 B7
Kettering NN15, NN16 72 D1
Linden Cl NN15 72 D1
Linden Gr PE28 97 A2
Linden Rd NN3 142 A1
Lindens The
Northampton NN1 159 E5
Towcester NN12 203 C6
Lindisfarne Dr NN15 91 F8
Lindisfarne Rd NN17 21 C1
Lindisfarne Way
Northampton NN4 175 C8
Thrapston NN14 76 F2
Lindrick Cl NN11 135 E2
Lindsay Ave NN3 142 B2
Lindsay St NN16 72 B3
Lindsay Terr NN3 142 A2
Lindsey Cl PE8 14 F1
Lindsey Gdns LE16 48 D8
Lingfield Terr NN2 141 F2
Lingfield Wlk NN18 36 C2
Lings Prim Sch NN3 142 F4
Lings Way NN3 143 A4
Lingswood Pk NN3 143 A3
Link La NN14 89 B4
Link Rd
Northampton NN2 141 B6
Rushden NN10 148 B7
Links Rd NN8 130 C8
Links The NN15 91 B8
Link Way
Bugbrooke NN7 173 A7
Towcester NN12 203 C5
Linley Dr NN14 50 F4
Linley Gn NN5 158 D8
Linnell Way NN16 71 F4
Linnet Cl NN8 130 A7
Linnet Dr NN15 92 A6
Linnet Rd NN12 203 C3
Linnetts La NN10 132 B5
Lion Ct NN4 159 D4
Lismore Cl NN3 143 C2
Lismore Wlk NN17 21 C1
Lister Cl NN17 22 A1
Lister Dr NN4 158 E1
Lister Rd NN8 130 A5
LITCHBOROUGH 171 D1
Litchborough Rd
Farthingstone NN12 170 F3
Grimscote NN12 188 A7
Litchfield Cl
Brixworth NN6 106 B2
Kettering NN16 72 C6
Litchfield La NN6 104 F4
LITTLE ADDINGTON 113 B7
Little Back La NN11 151 D1
LITTLE BILLING 143 B1
Little Billing Way
NN3 143 A1
LITTLE BOWDEN 32 A2
Little Bowden Manor
LE16 31 F3
Little Bowden Sch
LE16 31 F2
LITTLE BRAUNSTON 118 D1
LITTLE BRINGTON 138 C4
Little Cl
Bozeat NN29 164 C2
Chapel Brampton NN6 124 D1
LITTLE CRANSLEY 90 A5
LITTLE CREATON 105 A3
Little Cross St NN1 159 B6
Littledale NN8 129 D6
LITTLE EVERDON 154 A1
Little Field NN4 175 F4
Little Field Cl NN12 189 A8
Little Gn PE8 28 B3
Little Greeve Way
NN4 176 A6
Little Gull Cl NN3 142 F6
LITTLE HARROWDEN 110 B4
Little Harrowden Com Prim Sch NN9 110 C4
Little Horton Ho NN7 177 E2
Little Horton House Dr
NN7 177 E2
LITTLE HOUGHTON 161 A3
LITTLE IRCHESTER 130 C1
Little La
Aynho OX17 237 C7
Blisworth NN7 190 D8
Great Houghton NN4 160 E2
Ravensthorpe NN6 103 D1
Stanion NN14 37 E3
Wollaston NN29 146 D3
Little La *continued*
Yardley Hastings NN7 179 A7
Little London
Deanshanger MK19 228 E4
Silverstone NN12 214 D5
Little Mdw NN18 36 B1
LITTLE OAKLEY 54 A8
Little Park St 6 NN8 130 A5
Little Priel Rd NN7 155 B4
Little St
Rushden NN10 132 C1
Sulgrave OX17 211 A8
Yardley Hastings NN7 179 B6
Littlewood Cl NN5 159 A8
Littlewood St NN14 70 E7
LITTLEWORTH 188 E1
LITTLE WYMINGTON 148 A7
Livingstone Cl NN14 70 F7
Livingstone Rd NN11 135 C4
Llewellyn Wlk NN18 36 D5
Lloyd Cl NN8 130 B8
Lloyd's Rd NN17 37 B7
Loach Ct NN3 142 A6
Loatlands Prim Sch
NN14 50 F3
Loatland St NN14 50 F3
Lobelia Rd NN16 72 C4
Lockcroft Sq 6 NN3 143 D2
Lock La MK19 218 E2
Locks Gn PE8 16 A8
Locks The CV21 80 B1
Locktons Cl NN12 201 E2
Lockwood Cl NN2 141 C4
LODDINGTON 70 C2
Loddington CE Prim Sch
NN14 70 D1
Loddington Rd NN14 89 F7
Loddington Way NN14 89 B4
Lodge Ave NN4 175 C4
Lodge Cl
Little Houghton NN7 161 B3
Northampton, Hopping Hill NN5 140 B1
Northampton NN4 175 F3
Lodge Ct 1 NN8 130 B5
Lodge Farm Ct MK19 218 F6
Lodge Farm Ind Est
NN5 140 C2
Lodge Flats NN6 122 D5
Lodge Green Rd NN17 36 E8
Lodge La NN6 121 F3
Lodge Park Tech Coll
NN17 21 B1
Lodge Pk NN12 215 C4
Lodge Rd
Daventry NN11 135 C2
Little Houghton NN7 161 A3
Rushden NN10 148 A8
Lodge The OX17 198 D2
Lodge Way
Irthlingborough NN9 131 E8
Northampton NN5 140 C3
Lodore Gdns NN3 142 C3
Logan Cres LE16 31 C4
Logan Ct LE16 31 D4
Logan St LE16 31 D3
Logwell Ct NN3 142 F1
Loire Cl NN5 140 A2
Lombard Way OX16 219 A6
Lombardy Ct NN3 142 D3
Lomond Cl NN17 21 C1
Lomond Dr NN15 91 F8
London End
Earls Barton NN6 144 D4
Irchester NN29 147 B8
Titchmarsh NN14 77 D3
Upper Boddington NN11 182 C8
London Ho MK11 229 D5
London Rd
Bozeat NN29 164 C3
Braunston NN11 118 A1
Daventry NN11 153 D8
Kettering NN15 91 C8
Little Irchester NN8 130 C1
Northampton, Far Cotton NN4 159 C2
Northampton, Wootton NN4 175 D5
Old Stratford MK19 229 C6
Raunds NN9 114 C6
Roade NN7 191 C4
Stony Stratford MK11 229 E5
Towcester NN12 203 D5
Wansford PE8 8 B3
Wellingborough NN8 130 B3
Willoughby CV23 117 E3
Wollaston NN29 146 D1
Wothorpe PE9 2 F7
Lone Pine Ct NN6 106 B2
Long Acre NN7 161 D3
Long Acres 4 NN4 175 B8
Long Acres Dr NN9 112 E3
Long Barrow OX17 196 F7
Long Breech NN14 89 B5
Long Brimley Cl LE16 32 B3
LONG BUCKBY 121 B4
Long Buckby Inf Sch
NN6 121 B4
Long Buckby Jun Sch
NN6 121 B3
Long Buckby Pocket Pk*
NN6 121 A4
Long Buckby Rd NN6 120 E5
Long Buckby Sta NN6 121 A2
LONG BUCKBY WHARF 136 E7
Longburges OX17 220 B8
Long Cl NN18 36 B1
Longcroft La NN12 216 C8
Long Croft Rd NN14, NN18 37 C3
Longdown La CV23 118 B7
Longfellow Dr NN16 72 C6
Longfellow Rd NN8 129 B4
Longford Ave NN3 161 A8
Long Furlong CV22 98 A8
Long La
Olney MK46 195 F4
Warmington PE8 28 B2
Longland Ct NN3 142 B2
Longland Rd NN3 142 C2
Longlands The LE16 32 B3
Longleat Cl LE16 32 B3
Longleat Ct 5 NN4 175 C8
Longleat Gr NN15 91 C5
Long Mallows Rise 9
NN3 143 C2
Long March NN11 153 D8
Long March Ind Est
NN11 153 D8
Long Marsh NN8 130 B2
Long Marsh Sq NN3 143 A6
Long Massey MK46 195 E5
Long Mdw NN4 176 B6
Longmead Ct NN3 143 B4
Longmynd Dr NN5 158 D8
Long Row
Leckhampstead MK18 227 E1
Woodford NN14 94 D7
Long Row Cl NN11 170 A8
LONG STREET 206 E4
Long Street Rd MK19 207 A3
Longueville Ct NN3 142 E4
Long Wall NN13 233 E6
Longwell NN12 186 D5
Lonsborough Dr NN15 90 E8
Lonsdale Rd NN15 91 B7
Loop Rd PE28 97 A3
Lordswood Cl NN4 176 A6
Lorne Ct NN17 36 F6
Lorne Rd NN1 159 C7
Lorraine Cres NN3 142 B5
Lorraine Dr NN3 142 C5
Loseby Cl NN10 148 A8
Lotus Ct NN15 72 B1
Louisa Dr NN16 72 E4
Louisa Lilley Homes The
7 NN9 112 F2
Louisburg Cl 4 NN4 175 E7
Louise Rd NN1 159 D7
Lounts Cres LE16 20 D7
Lovap Way NN18 36 B1
Lovat Dr NN5 158 E7
Lovell Cl NN9 114 A4
Lovell Ct 12 NN9 112 F2
Lovers La PE5 8 F2
Lovett Rd NN11 183 D8
Lowbury Ct NN4 158 E3
Lower Adelaide St
NN2 159 C7
Lower Bath St NN1 159 B6
LOWER BENEFIELD 40 C6
LOWER BODDINGTON 182 D5
LOWER CATESBY 151 D4
Lower Cross St NN1 159 B6
Lower Ecton La NN3 143 D1
Lower End NN12 201 F5
LOWER END
Brafield-on-the-Green 161 E3
Grendon 163 E7
Hartwell 192 C1
Lower End
Hartwell NN7 192 C1
Pytchley NN14 91 A1
Lower Farm Rd NN3 141 F7
LOWER GREEN
Blakesley 200 F6
Willoughby 117 A5
Lower Harding St 11
NN1 159 C6
LOWER HARLESTONE 139 E5
Lower Hester St NN2 159 C8
Lower Hilmorton Rd 5
CV21 80 A1
Lower King St NN14 51 B3
Lower Lea Pl CV21 99 B8
Lower Meadow Ct
NN3 142 E5
LOWER MIDDLETON CHENEY 220 B8
Lower Mounts NN1 159 D6
Lower Pastures NN18 53 A8
Lower Priory St NN1 159 B7
Lower Rd
Milton Malsor NN7 174 E4
Stoke Albany LE16 34 B5
Lower St
Desborough NN14 51 A3
Great Addington NN14 94 B2
Great Doddington NN29 145 E6
Kettering NN16 72 A2
Pury End NN12 216 A7
Rugby CV21 99 C8
Twywell NN14 75 A1
Willoughby CV23 117 D4
Lower Stable Yd
NN12 203 D5
Lower Steeping NN14 51 B2
Lower Thrift St NN1 159 F6
Lower Weald MK19 229 E2

LOWER WEEDON 155 A3
Low Farm Pl NN3 141 F7
Low Greeve NN4 176 A6
LOWICK 75 F6
Lowick Cl NN8 129 D7
Lowick Ct NN3 142 C7
Lowick La NN14 76 F7
Lowick Rd
Aldwincle NN14 76 E7
Islip NN14 76 B3
Lowlands Cl NN3 143 C5
Low March NN11 153 D7
Lowood NN1 159 F5
Lowry Cl
Corby NN18 36 D4
Northampton NN3 142 B4
Wellingborough NN8 129 E7
Loxton Cl NN5 140 C1
Loyd Rd NN1 160 A6
LUBENHAM 30 E3
Lubenham All Saints CE Prim Sch LE16 30 F3
Lubenham Hill LE16 31 C2
Lubenham Rd
East Farndon LE16 31 B1
Marston Trussell LE16 30 D1
Lucas Cl NN9 131 E8
Lucas La NN7 177 B3
Lucas Rd NN6 121 A3
LUDDINGTON IN THE BROOK 61 B4
Luddington Rd PE8, PE28 61 C3
Ludlow Cl NN3 143 A7
Ludlow Wlk NN18 36 E1
Luffenham Rd LE15 3 F6
Lukes Cl NN13 212 A5
Lulworth Wlk NN18 36 A6
Lumber La NN12 216 B7
Lumbertubs La NN3 142 D5
Lumbertubs Prim Sch NN3 142 F3
Lumbertubs Rise NN3 142 D5
Lumbertubs Way NN3 142 E3
Lunchfield Ct NN3 126 C1
Lunchfield Gdns NN3 126 C1
Lunchfield La NN3 126 C1
Lunchfield Wlk [7] NN3 126 C1
Lundie Cl NN9 114 D7
Lundy Ave NN18 36 E4
Lupin Cl NN16 72 D4
Lutterworth Rd
Northampton NN1 160 A6
Swinford LE17 62 B6
LUTTON 44 C4
Lutton Rd PE8 43 C3
LYDDINGTON 9 C7
Lyddington Rd
Caldecott LE15, L16 9 D2
Gretton NN17 10 A1
Lydia Ct NN10 132 A2
Lyle Ct NN8 129 C7
Lyncrest Ave NN5 158 E7
Lyncrest Prim Sch NN5 158 E7
Lyncroft Way NN2 141 B1
Lyndhurst Rd CV21 98 F8
Lyneford Way NN10 147 F8
Lyne Wlk NN7 177 B3
Lynmore Cl NN4 158 C1
Lynmouth Ave NN3 160 C7
Lynmouth Pl NN18 36 E4
Lynton Ave NN2 141 C6
Lynton Gr NN18 36 F4
Lynwood Cl NN16 72 B5
Lytham Cl NN2 141 E3
Lytham Ct NN8 129 C7
Lyttleton Rd NN5 159 A7
Lyveden New Bield* PE8 57 A7
Lyveden Pl NN16 72 D3
Lyveden Rd
Brigstock NN14 55 F7
Northampton NN4 160 A1
Lyveden Way NN18 36 E2

M

Macadam Cl NN11 134 F5
Macadam Rd NN17 22 A1
McGibbon Wlk NN9 131 D8
McInnes Way NN9 114 D7
Mackenzie Rd NN9 114 C5
Mackintosh Ct NN15 92 B1
Mackworth Dr NN9 111 E4
Mackworth Gn NN9 111 F4
Maclean Cl NN3 160 C7
Macmillan Way NN3 142 B4
Macon Cl NN5 139 F2
Madams Gdns NN14 70 D7
Madams Hill NN14 70 D7
Madeline Cl LE16 32 A5
Madison Apartments NN16 72 A3
Magdalen Cl
Daventry NN11 153 B8
Stony Stratford MK11 229 D6
Syresham NN13 224 C8
Magdalen College Sch (St John's) NN13 233 F6
Magdalen College Sch (Waynflete) NN13 233 E7
Magdalene Cl NN14 54 B3
Magdalen Ho MK11 229 D6
Magdalen Mdws NN13 222 E1
Magdalen Rd CV23 117 E3
Magee St NN1 159 F7
Magellan Cl
Daventry NN11 135 C5
Rothwell NN14 70 E6
Magnolia Cl NN3 160 D6
Magnolia Dr
Daventry NN11 135 C4
Rushden NN10 148 B7
Magpie La NN13 233 E6
Magpie Rd
Sulgrave OX17 210 E7
Towcester NN12 203 C3
Maida Cl NN4 175 E7
Maidencastle NN3 143 B3
MAIDFORD 186 D6
Maidford Rd
Corby NN17 36 C7
Farthingstone NN12 170 D1
MAIDWELL 87 B7
Maidwell Hall (Prep Sch for Boys) NN6 87 B6
Maidwell Prim Sch NN6 87 B6
Maidwell Rd
Haselbech NN6 86 B8
Maidwell NN6 87 D7
Main Dr NN12 217 B2
Main Rd
Collyweston PE9 1 D2
Crick NN6 100 F5
Dingley LE16 32 F3
Earls Barton NN6 144 D6
Farthinghoe NN13 221 B4
Grendon NN7 163 D6
Hackleton NN7 177 B3
Kelmarsh NN6 67 F3
Kilsby CV23 99 F3
Middleton Cheney OX17 220 A8
Northampton, Duston NN5 158 B7
Northampton, Far Cotton NN4 159 B3
Shutlanger NN12 204 D8
Syresham NN13 224 C7
Upper Heyford NN7 156 D4
Wilby NN8 129 B1
Main St
Abthorpe NN12 201 F2
Aldwincle NN14 76 F8
Apethorpe PE8 14 C4
Ashby St L CV23 119 C5
Ashley LE16 18 F2
Aston le W NN11 182 F2
Badby NN11 152 F2
Barnwell PE8 59 B5
Barrowden LE15 3 F5
Bradden NN12 201 F5
Bythorn PE28 97 D4
Caldecott LE16 21 B8
Charlton OX17 231 F4
Church Stowe NN7 171 E8
Claydon OX17 181 D1
Clifton u D CV23 80 A5
Cold Ashby NN6 84 B5
Cosgrove MK19 218 E2
Cottesbrooke NN6 105 A8
Denton NN7 162 B1
Drayton LE16 20 A5
East Farndon LE16 48 B7
East Haddon NN6 122 D5
Farthingstone NN12 170 E3
Foxton LE16 30 A8
Great Addington NN14 94 B2
Great Bowden LE16 32 A6
Great Brington NN7 138 D7
Great Gidding PE28 61 D3
Great Oxendon LE16 48 E3
Hannington NN6 108 C3
Hellidon NN11 151 D1
Holcot NN6 126 E8
Little Brington NN7 138 C4
Little Harrowden NN9 110 C4
Loddington NN14 70 C1
Lowick NN14 75 F6
Lubenham LE16 30 F3
Lyddington LE15 9 C7
Mawsley Village NN14 89 B4
Medbourne LE16 19 A7
Middleton LE16 35 C8
Orton NN14 70 A3
Polebrook PE8 43 A3
Rockingham LE16 21 B4
Slipton NN14 75 A3
Southwick PE8 26 B5
Stoke Dry LE15 9 A7
Sudborough NN14 56 D1
Sutton Bassett LE16 18 A1
Tansor PE8 27 D2
Theddingworth LE17 46 D8
Thorpe by Water LE15 10 A5
Thurning PE8 60 D3
Turweston NN13 234 C8
Upper Stowe NN7 171 F6
Wadenhoe PE8 58 A4
Wakerley LE15 4 A4
Watford NN6 120 C6
Wilbarston LE16 34 C5
Willoughby CV23 117 E3
Woodend NN12 200 F7
Woodnewton PE8 14 E1
Yarwell PE8 15 F8
Makepeace Ho NN11 118 C1
Malabar Fields NN11 153 B8
Malaslea NN14 89 B4
Malborough Way NN12 217 F5
Malcolm Ct NN17 36 F6
Malcolm Dr NN5 158 E7
Malcolm Rd NN2 141 F2
Malcolm Terr NN2 141 F2
Malham Ct NN8 129 D6
Malham Dr NN16 72 A5
Mallard Cl
Earls Barton NN6 144 F5
Higham Ferrers NN10 132 C8
Northampton NN4 158 F2
Thrapston NN14 76 D3
Mallard Dr
Burton Latimer NN15 92 A2
Hinton NN11 184 B6
Mallery Cl NN10 132 D3
Mallets Cl MK11 229 E5
Mallory Way NN11 135 C5
Mallory Wlk NN3 141 F5
Mallows Dr NN9 114 C7
Mallows Yd NN29 164 D3
Mall The NN16 72 B2
Malmo Cl NN18 36 A2
Malpas Dr NN5 158 B8
Malthouse Cl
Irthlingborough NN9 112 F2
Northampton NN4 159 D4
Malthouse Ct NN12 203 C6
Malting La NN14 54 A3
Maltings Cl NN17 10 B1
Maltings Field MK19 218 F5
Maltings Rd NN17 10 B1
Maltings The
Ashley LE16 18 F3
[10] Market Harborough LE16 31 E3
Rothwell NN14 70 C7
Wollaston NN29 146 D3
Wothorpe PE9 2 E8
Malting Way NN7 192 D1
Malt La NN13 224 C8
Malt Mill Cl CV23 100 A2
Malt Mill Gn CV23 100 A2
Malton Wlk NN18 36 B5
Malvern Cl
Kettering NN16 72 B7
Wellingborough NN8 129 D1
Malvern Dr MK11 229 F4
Malvern Gr NN5 158 D8
Malzor La NN7 174 E4
Manchester Rd NN29 146 C3
Mander Cl NN5 157 F8
Mandeville Cl NN3 142 B4
Manfield Rd NN1 160 A7
Manfield Way NN3 142 B4
Manitoba Cl NN18 36 B3
Manitoba Pl NN11 184 C1
Manitoba Way NN11 184 C1
Manna Ho NN1 159 D6
Manning Ct NN3 142 C7
Manningham Rd NN9 114 A4
Manning Rd NN3 142 C7
Mannings Rise NN10 132 C1
Manning St NN10 132 C1
Mannington Gdns NN4 175 C7
Mannock Rd NN8 129 E3
Manor Cl
Bozeat NN29 164 D3
Charwelton NN11 168 A4
Cosgrove MK19 218 E2
Great Addington NN14 94 B2
Great Harrowden NN9 110 D2
Hanslope MK19 207 A2
Harpole NN7 157 C6
Hinton NN11 184 B7
Irchester NN29 147 B8
Isham NN14 110 F8
Middleton Cheney OX17 220 B7
Roade NN7 191 E4
Sulgrave OX17 210 F8
Thrapston NN14 76 D2
Manor Ct
Brackley NN13 233 F8
Cottingham LE16 20 C1
Grendon NN7 163 D5
Little Harrowden NN9 110 C4
Northampton NN2 141 B3
Rushden NN10 148 C8
[2] Wellingborough NN8 130 B5
Manor Dr
Corby NN18 36 A4
Irthlingborough NN9 113 A2
Manor Farm
Apethorpe PE8 14 C4
Hannington NN6 108 C3
Manor Farm Cl
Barby CV23 99 C2
Broughton NN14 90 B4
Walgrave NN6 108 A5
Manor Farm Cotts NN13 238 C8
Manor Farm Ct
Cogenhoe NN7 162 A6
Titchmarsh NN14 77 C4
Manor Farm Rd
Northampton NN3 143 B2
Raunds NN9 114 E6
Manorfield Cl NN3 161 B8
Manorfield Rd NN3 161 B8
Manorfields Rd MK19 229 B6
Manor Gdns
Farthingstone NN12 170 F3
Norton NN11 136 C4
Pytchley NN14 90 F2
Manor Gdns *continued*
Stanwick NN9 114 A3
Manor Ho The NN14 76 D2
Manor House Cl NN6 144 E5
Manor House Gdns NN9 114 D6
Manor House Mus* NN16 72 B1
Manor La
Clifton u D CV23 80 A5
Farthinghoe NN13 221 B4
Newnham NN11 153 E4
Whilton NN11 137 D6
Wymington NN10 148 A5
Manor Pk
Claydon OX17 181 D1
Nether Heyford NN7 156 C2
Manor Pl NN15 91 B8
Manor Rd
Brackley NN13 233 E7
Daventry NN11 135 D1
Earls Barton NN6 144 E5
Great Bowden LE16 32 A6
Grendon NN7 163 D5
Grimscote NN12 188 A8
Hanging Houghton NN6 106 C8
Hinton NN11 184 B6
Kilsby CV23 100 A3
Mears Ashby NN6 128 B2
Medbourne LE16 19 A7
Moulton NN3 142 C8
Northampton NN2 141 B3
Pitsford NN6 125 D5
Rothwell NN14 70 B7
Rushden NN10 148 B8
Rushton NN14 52 C2
Spratton NN6 105 B1
Stanion NN14 37 E2
Staverton NN11 152 B7
Sulgrave OX17 210 F8
Sutton PE5 8 F2
Weedon Bec NN7 155 B3
Manor Sch & Sports Coll NN9 114 E6
Manor St NN9 114 D6
Manor The NN11 199 C7
Manor View PE9 1 A6
Manor Way
Higham Ferrers NN10 132 C5
Yardley Gobion NN12 217 E6
Manor Wlk
Hanging Houghton NN6 106 C8
Market Harborough LE16 31 E3
Nether Heyford NN7 156 C2
Mansard Cl NN5 158 E6
Manse Cl
Rushden NN10 132 C3
Stony Stratford MK11 229 D6
Mansefield Cl NN14 51 A3
Mansel Cl MK19 218 D2
Mansell Cl NN12 203 C8
Mansfield Ct NN12 202 D8
Mansfield St NN9 113 F4
Mansfield Way NN29 147 A8
Manshead Ct MK11 229 F5
Mansion Cl NN3 142 A6
Mansion Hill OX17 219 F8
Mantlefield Rd NN18 36 B6
Manton Ct NN10 132 C2
Manton Rd
Corby NN17 22 A2
Irthlingborough NN9 112 E2
Rushden NN10 132 C1
Manton Spinney NN10 131 E2
Maple Cl
Brackley NN13 222 F1
Braunston NN11 118 D1
Bugbrooke NN7 172 F7
Hinton NN11 184 A6
Towcester NN12 203 B4
Maple Ct NN17 21 E1
Maple Dr NN8 129 E5
Maplefields Sch NN18 36 D5
Maple Rd
Kettering NN16 72 D4
Rushden NN10 132 C2
Maples The NN11 135 D1
Mapletoft St NN9 114 C5
Maple Wood NN10 148 B7
Mapperley Dr NN3 160 F8
Marchwood Cl NN3 142 F6
Marconi Ctyd NN17 22 B1
Marecroft LE16 66 F7
Mare Fair NN1 159 C5
Margaret Ave NN8 129 E2
Margaret House Ctyd NN13 233 F6
Margaret Rd
Kettering NN16 72 E3
Twyford OX17 230 B5
Margaret St NN1 159 D7
Marion Sq NN16 72 E3
Maritime Way NN11 135 E1
Marjoram Cl [6] NN4 175 D6
Market Cross NN9 112 F2
MARKET HARBOROUGH 31 C2
Market Harborough CE Prim Sch LE16 31 D3
Market Harborough District Hospl LE16 31 D3
Market Harborough Mus* LE16 31 E3
Market Harborough Sta LE16 32 A3
Market Hill NN14 70 D7
Market Pl
Brackley NN13 233 E6
Kettering NN16 72 B1
Long Buckby NN6 121 B4
Olney MK46 195 F3
Oundle PE8 42 A5
Market Rd NN14 76 D2
Market Sq
[3] Daventry NN11 135 C2
Hanslope MK19 207 A2
Higham Ferrers NN10 132 C6
Northampton NN1 159 C6
Stony Stratford MK11 229 D5
[3] Wellingborough NN8 130 A4
Market St
Kettering NN16 72 B2
Northampton NN1 159 E7
Wellingborough NN8 130 A4
Market Street Mews [10] NN16 72 B2
Market Wlk NN1 159 E7
Markham Cl NN5 140 C1
Markham Wlk NN18 36 B5
Marks Cl NN9 114 A3
Marlborough Ave NN8 129 D7
Marlborough Cl
Kettering NN15 72 F1
Kings Sutton OX17 230 F6
Marlborough Croft NN13 233 F6
Marlborough Rd NN5 159 A6
Marlborough Way LE16 31 E5
Marlow Cl
Daventry NN11 135 B1
Rothwell NN14 70 C6
Marlow Ct
Corby NN18 36 B5
Medbourne LE16 19 A8
Marlowe Cl NN4 175 B7
Marlow Rd NN12 203 D5
Marlstones NN4 158 D2
Marnock Sq [3] NN4 158 F2
Marquee Dr NN3 160 F7
Marriots Rd NN6 121 C3
Marriott Cl NN9 131 E8
Marriott St NN2 159 C8
Marseilles Cl NN5 139 F1
Marshall Ct [2] LE16 31 F2
Marshalls Ct NN9 114 D6
Marshall's Rd NN9 114 C6
Marsh Cl NN6 101 A5
Marsh La NN9 113 B3
Marshleys Ct NN3 143 B5
Marsh The NN6 101 A5
Marshwell Ct [5] NN3 161 A8
Marsons Dr NN6 100 F5
Marston Hill
Marston St Lawrence OX17 210 B3
Priors Marston CV47 166 E7
Marston La LE16 48 A7
Marston Rd
Greatworth OX17 210 E2
Lubenham LE16 30 D2
MARSTON ST LAWRENCE 210 A1
MARSTON TRUSSELL 47 C8
Marston Trussell Rd LE16 47 F7
Marston Way NN11 135 D6
Martel Cl NN5 157 F8
Martha Wallis Ct [1] NN16 72 B2
Martial Daire Bvd NN13 233 E8
Martin Cl NN10 132 B4
Martindale NN2 140 F5
Martin Rd NN15 91 C7
Martins La NN4 175 E8
Martins Rd NN7 177 A1
Martins Yd NN5 159 B7
Martlet Cl NN4 175 E5
Martonia [1] NN1 159 F7
Marvills Mill Rd NN4 159 C4
Marwood Cl NN3 160 C7
Masefield Cl NN8 129 C4
Masefield Dr NN10 131 E3
Masefield Rd NN16 72 C5
Masefield Way
Corby NN17 36 D8
Northampton NN2 141 E2
Mason Cl
Oundle PE8 42 A5
Thrapston NN14 76 D1
Massey Cl NN4 175 E8
Matchless Cl NN5 140 A1
Matlock Way NN14 50 E4
Matson Cl NN14 70 B6
Matson Ct NN9 114 E7
Matthew Clarke Ho [4] LE16 31 E4
Matthews Cl NN14 52 C3
Mauduit Cl MK19 207 A3
Maunsell Rise NN14 70 B6
Mauntley Ave NN14 55 F7
Maurice Rd LE16 48 D8
Mawsley Chase NN14 89 C5
Mawsley Cres NN16 71 F2
Mawsley La NN14 89 C8
Mawsley Lo NN14 89 B3

Mawsley Prim Sch
NN14 89 B5
MAWSLEY VILLAGE 89 A4
Maxwell Wlk NN18 36 E5
May Bank NN11 153 B8
Maybush Wlk MK46 195 E5
May Cl NN10 148 C7
Maye Dicks Rd NN10 148 C8
Mayfield Rd
Daventry NN11 135 C3
Desborough NN14 51 C3
Northampton NN3 142 B3
Maylan Rd NN17 21 F3
Mays Way NN12 217 D3
Mazewood Gate PE8 13 E7
Meacham Cl NN14 90 A3
Meadow Cl
Daventry NN11 135 D6
Higham Ferrers NN10 132 B6
Market Harborough LE16 31 F4
Northampton NN5 140 B2
Ringstead NN14 95 A3
Wellingborough NN8 130 D8
Meadow Ct
[6] Kettering NN16 72 B2
Ravenstone MK46 194 D2
Towcester NN12 203 C5
Meadowdale Prim Sch
LE16 32 B4
Meadow Dr NN10 132 B6
Meadow Farm Cl NN7 155 F5
Meadow Gate PE8 14 E2
Meadow La
Denford NN14 95 C6
Little Houghton NN7 161 A4
Raunds NN9 114 A6
Thornhaugh PE8 7 F5
Thrapston NN14 76 D2
Meadowlands NN9 110 B3
Meadow Rd
Kettering NN16 72 A2
Rothwell NN14 70 C6
Meadow Rise NN12 189 D4
Meadowside Inf Sch
NN15 92 B2
Meadowside Jun Sch
NN15 92 B2
Meadow St LE16 31 E4
Meadows The
Northampton NN4 175 F1
Northampton NN4 175 F2
Old Stratford MK19 229 B6
Wellingborough NN9 110 E1
Meadow Sweet Rd
NN10 148 C7
Meadowsweet Wlk
NN4 175 F2
Meadow The NN3 142 C1
Meadowvale NN9 112 F1
MEADOW VIEW 140 F6
Meadow View
Adderbury OX17 230 A4
Great Addington NN14 94 C3
Higham Ferrers NN10 132 A6
Potterspury NN12 217 D3
Meadow Way NN9 112 F1
Meadow Wlk
Higham Ferrers NN10 132 B6
[9] Irthlingborough
NN9 112 F2
Mead Rd NN15 90 F8
Meads Ct NN15 92 B1
Meadslade NN7 192 D2
Meadway
Bugbrooke NN7 172 F7
Northampton NN3 160 D8
Meadway Cl NN15 91 D8
MEARS ASHBY 128 C2
Mears Ashby Prim Sch
NN6 128 B2
Mears Ashby Rd
Earls Barton NN6 144 C6
Wilby NN8 129 A1
MEDBOURNE 18 F6
Medbourne Cl NN3 142 B7
Medbourne Rd
Ashley LE16 18 E4
Drayton LE16 19 E4
Medbourne LE16 18 C8
Medellin Hill NN3 142 F6
Medinah Cl NN4 175 D5
Medina Rd NN17 21 C1
Medlicott Cl NN18 53 A8
Medway Cl
Market Harborough
LE16 32 A3
Northampton NN5 140 E2
Medway Dr
Northampton NN5 140 F2
Wellingborough NN8 129 C6
Medway Ho PE8 42 A6
Medway The NN11 135 A1
Medwin NN8 129 B4
Meeting La
Burton Latimer NN15 92 C2
Corby NN17 37 B7
Irthlingborough NN9 112 F2
[15] Kettering NN16 72 B2
Northampton NN5 158 C7
Rothwell NN14 70 C6
Towcester NN12 203 C6
Meissen Ave NN14 50 F3
Melbourne Ho
Corby NN17 22 F1
[4] Northampton NN5 159 A6
Melbourne La NN5 158 C6
Melbourne Rd NN5 158 F6
Melbourne St [3] NN1 159 F6
Melbourne Wlk [4]
NN1 159 F6
Melbury La NN3 143 B3
Melbury Pl NN3 143 B3
Melchbourne Rd
MK44 149 F4
Melchester Cl NN4 175 E7
Meldon Cl NN4 175 C8
Melford Cl NN18 36 D2
Mellor Rd CV21 99 B8
Melloway Rd NN10 131 E2
Melrose Ave NN5 158 E7
Melrose Cl NN15 91 F8
Meltham Cl NN3 142 F1
Melton Rd NN8 130 C5
Melton Rd N NN8 130 B5
Melton St NN16 72 B3
Melville St NN1 159 F7
Membris Way NN11 184 A6
Memorial Gn NN7 191 E4
Mendip Cl NN16 72 B5
Mendip Ct NN11 135 B5
Mendip Rd NN5 158 D7
Meon Cl NN17 21 C1
Meon Way NN5 158 D8
Mercer Ct CV22 98 F8
Mercer's Row [3] NN1 159 C5
Mercia Gdns NN3 142 C1
Mercury Cl NN11 135 A4
Mercury Dr NN4 160 A2
Mere Cl
Brafield-on-t-G NN7 161 D2
[1] Northampton NN4 175 B8
Mere Farm Bsns Units
NN6 108 D4
MEREFIELD 175 B7
Merefields NN9 112 E3
Merestone Hos OX17 210 B1
Merestone Rd NN18 36 D3
Mere Way NN4 175 C8
Mereway Com Coll
NN4 159 B1
Merlin Gr [5] NN4 175 B8
Merrivale Cl NN15 90 F7
Merrycot La NN6 82 B4
Merrydale Sq NN3 143 A6
Merryhill NN4 158 E2
Merry Tom La NN6 124 D4
Mersey Cl NN4 159 A2
Mersey Gn NN17 21 C1
Mershe Cl NN4 175 F7
Merthyr Rd NN5 159 A8
Merton Cl NN13 233 D8
Merton Rd NN11 153 B7
Mescalero NN2 141 C4
Meshaw Cres NN3 160 B7
Methodist Homestead [4]
NN2 141 E1
Mews Cotts LE16 48 E3
Mews The
Brixworth NN6 106 B2
Brockhall NN11 137 C2
Great Bowden LE16 31 E7
Long Buckby NN6 121 B4
Northampton NN3 160 D8
[4] Rugby CV21 80 A1
Michaelmas Cl OX17 208 F1
Michael's Wlk LE16 21 B4
Mickleborough Cl
LE16 18 B3
Mickle Hill PE18 116 D7
Micklewell La NN3 142 F6
Middlebrook Gn LE16 32 A4
Middledale Rd LE16 32 A3
Middlefield Cl NN14 95 B3
Middle Grass NN9 112 E3
Middle Greeve NN4 176 A6
Middle La LE16 34 A3
Middlemarch [5] NN3 143 B4
Middle March NN11 153 D8
Middlemead Ct NN3 143 A1
Middlemore NN3 142 F6
Middle St
Elton PE8 28 D8
Foxton LE16 30 E8
Isham NN14 110 F8
Kilsby CV23 100 A3
Nether Heyford NN7 156 C2
Middlethorpe NN12 200 B2
MIDDLETON 35 B8
MIDDLETON CHENEY
209 A1
Middleton Cheney Com
Prim Sch OX17 219 F8
Middleton Cl
Banbury OX16 219 A7
Northampton NN2 141 C5
Middleton Rd
Ashley LE16 19 B3
Banbury OX16 219 A7
Bringhurst LE16 20 C4
Chacombe OX17 208 E4
Middle Weald MK19 229 E1
Middlewell Ct [2] NN3 142 F1
Middlewich Cl NN11 135 C6
Midfield Ct NN3 142 E5
Midland Bsns Ctr
NN10 132 C6
Midland Bsns Units
NN8 130 C6
Midland Cotts NN14 52 C3
Midland Rd
Higham Ferrers
NN10 132 C6
Olney MK46 195 F5
Midland Rd *continued*
Raunds NN9 114 E7
Rushden NN10 132 A3
Thrapston NN14 76 C1
Wellingborough NN8 130 B4
Midland Works Bsns Ctr
NN8 130 D6
Midway
Blisworth NN7 174 B2
Middleton Cheney
OX17 209 A1
Milbury NN6 144 F3
Milby La NN14 54 A2
Mildmay Cl PE8 41 E5
Miles Cl NN9 114 B5
Miles La NN6 121 C4
Mile St NN29 164 D3
Milestone Mews LE16 20 C1
Miles Well Ct NN3 142 D3
Milford Ave MK11 229 E4
Military Rd NN1 159 D7
Militia Cl NN4 175 E7
Milking Slade La PE28 61 F3
Millais Rd NN18 36 E5
Millbank NN3 143 D2
Millbrook Cl NN5 159 A4
Millbrook Inf Sch
NN15 91 F8
Millbrook Jun Sch
NN15 91 F8
Millburn Dr NN5 158 A6
Mill Cl
Braunston NN11 118 B1
Corby NN18 36 B1
Raunds NN9 114 C6
Milldale Gdns NN15 91 D8
Mill Dale Rd NN15 91 D8
Millenium Cl NN15 91 A7
Millennium Way
NN11 135 C2
Miller Cl
Kettering NN15 91 C6
Thrapston NN14 76 E1
Miller Hill NN4 158 E2
Miller Rd NN15 92 B1
Millers Cl
Lower Boddington
NN11 182 C5
Rushden NN10 131 F2
Miller's Cl
Finedon NN9 112 A5
Kislingbury NN7 157 D2
Millers Gdns LE16 31 B2
Millers La NN8 145 F8
Millers Pk NN8 130 A1
Miller St NN9 114 D7
Millers Way NN4 175 F3
Miller's Yd [5] LE16 31 E3
Mill Est NN10 148 B7
Mill Farm Ctyd MK19 229 B1
Millfield Ave LE16 20 D1
Millfields PE8 41 F6
Mill Fields NN10 132 B7
Millfields Ave CV21 98 F8
Millglade The NN14 91 F1
Mill Greene Ct [3]
NN16 72 C4
Mill Hill
Corby NN18 53 B7
Lubenham LE16 30 E3
Mill Hill Rd LE16 31 F3
Mill Ho
Brackley NN13 233 E5
[6] Northampton NN2 159 C7
Millholm Rd NN14 51 B2
Millhouse Ct NN5 159 B5
Millies La NN17 12 C1
Mill La
Adderbury OX17 230 A3
Barrowden LE15 4 A5
Brackley NN13 234 A6
Brigstock NN14 55 F7
Caldecott LE16 21 B8
Chipping Warden OX17 196 F6
Cogenhoe NN7 162 A7
Croughton NN13 238 C7
Earls Barton NN6 145 A3
Greens Norton NN12 202 E7
Grimscote NN12 172 B1
Isham NN14 91 F1
Islip NN14 76 C3
Ketton PE9 1 A5
Kings Sutton OX17 230 F4
Kislingbury NN7 157 D3
Lowick NN14 75 F6
Northampton, Kingsthorpe
NN2, NN5 141 B2
Northampton NN2 159 B7
Old NN6 88 E3
Oundle PE8 27 B1
Stoke Bruerne NN12 191 A1
Stony Stratford MK11 229 D5
Wadenhoe PE8 58 A3
Westbury NN13 234 F4
Mill Marina Cvn Pk
NN14 76 C1
Mill Mdw NN2 141 D5
Mill Rd
Bozeat NN29 164 C2
Cottingham LE16 20 C2
Great Gidding PE28 61 E3
Gretton LE15, NN17 9 F2
Irthlingborough NN8 131 B7
Islip NN14 76 B3
Kettering NN16 72 C2
Kislingbury NN7 157 D3
Northampton NN2 159 C7
Oundle PE8 41 F4
Mill Rd *continued*
Wellingborough NN8 130 B5
Whitfield NN13 223 E4
Woodford NN14 94 C7
Yarwell PE8 16 A7
Mill Rd Ind Est NN8 130 C6
Mill Road Pas [5] NN16 72 C2
Mills Cl NN6 144 F4
Millside Cl NN2 141 D5
Mill St PE9 5 B6
Millstone Cl NN4 158 D2
Millway NN5 158 C6
Millway Prim Sch
NN5 158 D6
Millwood Way PE8 13 E7
Milner Rd NN9 111 F4
MILTHORPE 200 B2
Milthorpe NN12 200 B2
Milton Ave NN8 129 C3
Milton Bridge NN4 176 A6
Milton Ct
Kettering NN16 72 C5
Milton Malsor NN7 174 E3
MILTON MALSOR 174 E4
Milton Parochial Prim Sch
NN7 174 E4
Milton Rd
Corby NN17 36 C8
Daventry NN11 135 B2
Gayton NN7 173 F2
Little Irchester NN8 130 C1
Oundle PE8 41 F5
Milton St N NN2 141 E1
Milton St
Higham Ferrers NN10 132 B5
Northampton NN2 141 F1
Milton Terr PE8 44 C4
Milverton Cres NN3 160 D7
Mimosa Cl NN3 160 C6
Minden Cl NN18 35 F2
Minehead Cl NN18 36 A6
Minerva Way NN8 129 D5
Minster Ho [2] NN1 159 D6
Minton Cl NN14 50 F3
Mirfield Cl NN18 36 C5
Mistletoe Pl NN3 142 C1
Mitchell Cl NN5 140 D2
Mitchell Rd NN17 22 B2
Mitchell St NN16 72 C5
Mitchison Cl CV23 118 C8
MIXBURY 234 D1
Mixbury Rd NN13 233 F2
Moat Farm Dr CV21 99 A7
Moat La NN12 203 C6
Moat Pl NN1 159 B6
Moat Yd NN12 203 C6
Mobbs Miller Ho NN1 160 A7
Moffatt Terr NN8 130 A5
Molesworth Bglws PE9 1 A6
Monarch Ctyd NN4 160 A2
Monarch Rd NN2 141 C1
Monarch Terr NN2 159 C8
Monkfield Coll NN14 50 E2
Monk's Hall Rd NN1 159 F7
Monks Park Rd NN1 159 F7
Monks Pond St NN1 159 B6
Monks Rd NN29 146 D3
Monks Way
Corby NN18 36 A4
Crick NN6 101 A6
Wellingborough NN8 130 A3
Monkswood NN12 214 C4
Monmouth Cl NN14 76 F2
Monmouth Rd NN5 159 A7
Monroe Cl LE16 31 D5
Monson Way PE8 41 E7
Montabaur Rd NN13 234 A7
Montagu Ct NN15 91 D5
Montague Cres NN5 140 D2
Montague Ct NN14 76 D2
Montague Dr CV23 100 A3
Montague St NN10 132 A2
Montagu Sch NN16 72 D5
Montagu St NN16 72 C2
Montagu Terr PE8 59 B6
Montcalm Cl NN15 72 F1
Monterly Gate NN14 55 F7
Montfort Cl NN5 158 E6
Montgomery Cl NN15 72 E1
Montgomery Way
NN4 175 D7
Montrose Cl LE16 31 D1
Montrose St NN17 36 F6
Montsaye Com Coll
NN14 70 B7
Moonshine Gap NN6 128 D6
Moore Cl
Corby NN17 36 D8
Kettering NN15 92 A7
Moor End PE8 60 D3
MOOR END 217 D6
Moorend Rd NN12 217 E6
Moores Cl NN7 172 F7
Moores Hill MK46 195 F5
Moore St NN2 141 F1
Moor Field NN12 203 B5
Moorfield Gn NN14 70 B6
Moorfield Rd NN14 70 B6
Moorfield Sq NN3 143 A6
Moorhouse Way NN15 90 E8
Moorings The NN14 94 E6
Moor La CV23 117 D3
Moorland Cl NN3 142 E2
Moorlands NN8 129 D7
Moorlands The NN10 132 B4
Moor Rd NN10 132 A2
Moors Cl MK19 228 E4
Moors Dr The OX17 219 F8
Moors La CV21, CV23 99 D8
Morby Ct NN15 92 B1
MORCOTT 3 A5
Morcott Rd LE15 3 D5
Mordaunt Cl NN14 75 E6
Mordaunt La NN5 140 D1
Morehay La
King's Cliffe PE8 13 E6
King's Cliffe PE8 13 F7
More Rd NN11 135 B4
Moreton Ave NN8 129 D2
MORETON PINKNEY 199 D7
Moreton Rd NN11 184 C1
Moreton Way NN2 141 C5
Morgan Cl NN3 143 C4
Morgan Dr NN6 106 C3
Morgans Cl PE8 43 A3
Moriston Cl NN17 21 C1
Morland Rd NN18 36 E5
Morley St
Kettering NN16 72 C4
Market Harborough
LE16 31 D3
Morley Wlk NN17 36 C8
Morning Star Rd [1]
NN11 135 A3
Morris Ave NN10 131 F1
Morris Cl NN8 129 A6
Morrison Park Rd
NN6 102 C5
Morris Rd
Daventry NN11 134 F3
Northampton NN2 141 D3
Morse Way NN14 51 B4
Mortar Pit Rd NN3 143 C5
Mortimer Cl NN4 159 A2
Morton Ct CV22 98 F8
Mortons Bush NN4 176 A6
Moss Cl NN12 203 C8
Moss Ct NN16 72 B3
Moss Wlk NN18 36 A2
Motala Cl NN18 36 A2
Motherwell Ho NN17 37 A8
Motspur Dr NN2 141 B1
Motts The NN7 157 B6
Moulds La LE16 20 D7
MOULTON 126 C2
Moulton Coll NN3 126 C1
Moulton Crossing
NN3 142 E8
Moulton La NN2, NN3 141 D8
MOULTON PARK 142 A6
Moulton Park Bsns Ctr
NN3 142 A6
Moulton Prim Sch
NN3 126 C1
Moulton Rd
Holcot NN6 126 D7
Pitsford NN6 125 D3
Moulton Sch & Science
Coll NN3 126 B1
Moulton Way NN3 142 C6
Moulton Way N NN3 142 C6
Moulton Way S NN3 142 C6
Mountbatten Dr NN14 95 C3
Mountbatten Ho
NN11 153 E8
Mountbatten Way
NN9 114 E6
Mountclair Ct NN3 160 E8
Mountfield Rd
Irthlingborough NN9 112 F3
Northampton NN3 142 A3
Mount Hill Ave MK19 229 B7
Mount Pleasant
Earls Barton NN6 144 F4
Harpole NN7 157 C7
Morcott LE15 3 A6
Wardington OX17 196 E1
Woodford Halse NN11 184 D6
Yardley Gobion NN12 217 F6
Mount Pleasant Rd
LE15 3 A6
Mounts Bsns Ctr NN1 159 D7
Mounts Ct [1] NN3 142 E3
Mounts La NN11 153 E4
Mounts The NN6 121 B3
Mow Mead MK46 195 F5
Mowsley Ct LE17 45 E6
Mowsley Rd
Husbands Bosworth
LE17 45 E6
Theddingworth LE16 46 C8
Moyeady Ave CV22 98 E8
Muirfield Dr NN11 135 E2
Muirfield Rd NN8 129 C7
Mulberry Cl
Desborough NN14 51 A5
Northampton NN5 158 F7
Wellingborough NN8 129 E5
Mulberry Ct LE16 20 A5
Mull Dr NN17 36 C8
Mullions The NN4 175 E5
Mulso Rd NN9 112 A4
Mumford Dr NN7 174 A7
Muncaster Gdns NN4 175 D7
Muncaster Way NN6 102 C5
Murcott NN6 121 A4
Murcott Cl NN6 121 A4
Murray Ave NN2 141 D1
Murray Ho NN1 160 A8
Murray Wlk NN18 36 E5
Mursley Ct MK11 229 F5
Murswell Cl NN12 214 D4
Murswell La NN12 214 D4
MUSCOTT 137 B3
Muscott La NN5 158 C6
Muscott St NN5 159 A6

Museum Way NN3 . . . . 160 F7
Musgrave Cl NN4 . . . . 175 F7
Mushroom Field Rd
NN3 . . . . 143 D2
Musk Cl LE16 . . . . 20 D7
Musott Cl NN7 . . . . 155 E6
Musson Cl NN9 . . . . 112 E2
Myers Cl OX17 . . . . 231 F5
Myers Rd CV21 . . . . 99 C8
Myers Way OX17 . . . . 231 F5
Myrtle Rd NN16 . . . . 72 D4

N

Nags Head La NN9 . . . . . . 115 F2
Nansen Cl
Daventry NN11 . . . . 135 C5
Rothwell NN14 . . . . 70 E6
Nansen Wlk NN18 . . . . 36 B2
Nantwich Dr NN11 . . . . . . 135 D6
Naomi Cl NN3 . . . . 142 F1
Napier Cl
Daventry NN11 . . . . 153 D8
Wellingborough NN8 . . . . . 129 A4
NAPTON ON THE HILL
. . . . 150 A7
Narvik Rd NN18 . . . . 36 A2
NASEBY 66 B1
Naseby Battle & Farm Mus* NN6 . . . . 85 B7
Naseby CE Prim Sch
NN6 . . . . 66 B1
Naseby Cl
Market Harborough
LE16 . . . . 31 E2
Wellingborough NN8 . . . . . 129 D7
Naseby Dr NN11 . . . . 135 C6
Naseby Ho NN16 . . . . 71 F3
Naseby Rd
Clipston LE16 . . . . 66 F8
Corby NN17 . . . . 36 C7
Haselbech NN6 . . . . 85 F8
Kettering NN16 . . . . 72 E3
Sibbertoft LE16 . . . . 46 F2
Thornby NN6 . . . . 84 E4
Welford NN6 . . . . 65 C5
Naseby Sq LE16 . . . . 31 E2
Naseby St NN2 . . . . 159 C8
Nash Ct NN15 . . . . 92 A8
Nasmith Ave NN17 . . . . 37 A8
Nasmyth Rd NN11 . . . . . . 134 F5
NASSINGTON 15 E5
Nassington Prim Sch
PE8 . . . . 15 F5
Nassington Rd
Woodnewton PE8 . . . . 14 F1
Yarwell PE8 . . . . 15 F7
Navigation Row NN1 . . . . 159 C4
Navisford Cl NN14 . . . . 76 E3
NBC Depot NN2 . . . . 141 E3
Neale Ave NN16 . . . . 72 B5
Neale Cl
Northampton NN3 . . . . 160 E8
Wollaston NN29 . . . . 146 C3
Near Side NN5 . . . . 158 F6
Near The Church LE16 . . . . 17 A5
Needham Rd NN9 . . . . 113 F4
Neene Ct [13] NN9 . . . . 112 F2
Nelson Ave NN11 . . . . 184 B6
Nelson Cl NN11 . . . . 135 E2
Nelson Dr NN14 . . . . 70 E7
Nelson Rd NN17 . . . . 36 B8
Nelson St
Kettering NN16 . . . . 72 C3
Market Harborough
LE16 . . . . 31 D3
[24] Northampton NN1 . . . . 159 C7
Nelson's Yd NN12 . . . . 203 C6
Nene Cl
Kettering NN15 . . . . 92 A5
Raunds NN9 . . . . 114 D7
Wansford PE8 . . . . 8 A3
Wellingborough NN8 . . . . . 129 C6
Nene Cres NN17 . . . . 21 C1
Nene Ct
Thrapston NN14 . . . . 76 D2
Wellingborough NN8 . . . . . 130 C3
Nene Dr NN5 . . . . 140 F2
Nene Ent Ctr NN2 . . . . . . 159 C8
Nene La NN12 . . . . 203 A6
Nene Park (Rushden & Diamonds FC) NN9 . . . . 113 A2
Nene Pl NN5 . . . . 141 A2
Nene Rd
Burton Latimer NN15 . . . . . . 92 A2
Higham Ferrers NN10 . . . . 132 B5
Nene Rise NN7 . . . . 161 F6
Neneside Cl NN7 . . . . 155 B3
Nene Side Cl NN11 . . . . . . 152 F3
Nene Univ Coll
Northampton NN2 . . . . . . 141 E5
Nene Valley Bsns Pk
PE8 . . . . 42 B5
Nene Valley Ret Pk
NN1 . . . . 159 B4
Nene Valley Way
NN3 . . . . 160 D5
Nene View
Irthlingborough NN14 . . . . 112 F2
Islip NN14 . . . . 76 B3
Oundle PE8 . . . . 41 F6
Nene Way
Kislingbury NN7 . . . . 157 C3
Northampton NN5 . . . . 141 A2
Oundle PE8 . . . . 41 F7
Sutton PE5 . . . . 8 F2
Nene Whitewater Ctr*
NN4 . . . . 160 B3
Nene Wlk
Daventry NN11 . . . . 135 A1
Northampton NN5 . . . . 140 F2
Nepcote Cl NN15 . . . . 91 D8
Nesbitt Cl NN3 . . . . 160 E8
Nest Farm Cres NN8 . . . . . 130 A8
Nest Farm Rd NN8 . . . . . . 130 A7
Nest La NN8 . . . . 130 B7
Nether Cl NN13 . . . . 234 A7
NETHERCOTE 219 B7
Netherfield Gr NN17 . . . . . . 36 F8
Netherfield Rd NN15 . . . . . . 91 C7
Nether Gn LE16 . . . . 67 A8
NETHER HEYFORD 156 B1
Nether Jackson Ct [3]
NN3 . . . . 143 B4
Nether La NN7 . . . . 155 F4
Nethermead Ct NN3 . . . . . 142 F4
Nethertown Way NN14 . . . . 89 B4
Nettle Gap Cl NN4 . . . . . . 175 F6
Neuville Way NN14 . . . . 50 F3
Nevill Cl MK19 . . . . 207 B2
Neville Day Cl PE9 . . . . 1 F5
Neville Ho NN17 . . . . 36 E6
NEVILL HOLT 19 D8
Nevill Holt Rd LE16 . . . . 19 F6
Nevis Cl NN17 . . . . 21 C1
Newark Dr NN18 . . . . 36 C6
NEW BARTON 144 F5
Newbery Dr NN13 . . . . 233 D8
New Bldgs [7] NN16 . . . . 72 B2
Newbold Cl PE8 . . . . 41 E6
Newbolt Cl NN12 . . . . 216 B8
NEWBOTTLE 231 E7
Newbottle & Charlton CE Prim Sch OX17 . . . . 231 F5
Newbridge NN6 . . . . 136 D8
Newbridge La NN9 . . . . . 114 A3
Newbury Cl
Corby NN18 . . . . 36 D1
Rushden NN10 . . . . 132 D3
Newbury Dr NN11 . . . . . . 135 C6
Newby Ct NN3 . . . . 142 C3
New College Farm
NN6 . . . . 127 A6
Newcombe Rd NN5 . . . . . . 159 A7
Newcombe St LE16 . . . . 31 E2
Newcomen Rd NN8 . . . . . . 130 B5
New Croft NN7 . . . . 155 B3
NEW DUSTON 140 B2
Newell Rd NN14 . . . . 95 B3
New Forest Way
NN11 . . . . 135 B4
NEW HACKLETON 177 A3
New Hall NN11 . . . . 153 B7
Newham Cl NN14 . . . . 70 C7
Newington Rd NN2 . . . . . . 141 C4
New La PE8 . . . . 8 C1
Newland NN1 . . . . 159 C6
Newland Rd NN6 . . . . 108 A5
Newlands
Brixworth NN6 . . . . 106 B2
[3] Daventry NN11 . . . . 135 C1
Kings Sutton OX17 . . . . . . 231 A6
Naseby NN6 . . . . 66 C1
Newlands Ctr NN16 . . . . 72 B2
Newland Sq NN2 . . . . 141 C4
Newlands Rd NN6 . . . . 64 E5
Newland St
Braybrooke LE16 . . . . 49 E5
Kettering NN16 . . . . 72 B2
Newland Wlk [5] NN1 . . . 159 D6
Newlife Apartments [15]
NN1 . . . . 159 C6
Newman St
Burton Latimer NN15 . . . . . . 92 B2
Higham Ferrers NN10 . . . . 132 C7
[6] Kettering NN16 . . . . 72 C2
Newmarket Cl NN18 . . . . . . 36 D1
NEWNHAM 153 E4
Newnham Dr NN11 . . . . . . 135 A5
Newnham Prim Sch
NN11 . . . . 153 D4
Newnham Rd NN2 . . . . . . 141 D3
Newnham Windmill*
NN11 . . . . 153 D7
Newport Pagnell Rd
Horton NN7 . . . . 177 D1
Northampton NN4,
NN7 . . . . 176 A7
Newport Pagnell Rd W
NN4 . . . . 175 D8
Newport Rd
Hanslope MK19 . . . . 207 B2
Northampton NN5 . . . . 159 A7
New Post Office Sq
NN17 . . . . 36 E6
New Rd
Brackley NN13 . . . . 233 E6
Castlethorpe MK19 . . . . . . 218 F5
Collyweston PE9 . . . . 1 C2
Easton o t H PE9 . . . . 2 A5
Farthinghoe NN13 . . . . 221 A4
Geddington NN14 . . . . 54 A2
Greens Norton NN12 . . . . . 202 D8
Maidford NN12 . . . . 186 D6
Northampton NN4 . . . . 175 E6
Oundle PE8 . . . . 42 A6
New South Bridge Rd
NN4 . . . . 159 C4
New St
Brixworth NN6 . . . . 106 A2
Daventry NN11 . . . . 135 C1
Desborough NN14 . . . . 51 A3
Earls Barton NN6 . . . . 144 F4
Irchester NN29 . . . . 147 B8
New St *continued*
Irthlingborough NN9 . . . . . 112 F2
Oundle PE8 . . . . 42 A5
Rothwell NN14 . . . . 70 D7
Stony Stratford MK11 . . . . 229 D5
Weedon Bec NN7 . . . . 155 C3
Wellingborough NN8 . . . . . 130 A5
Newstead Cl NN3 . . . . 143 D3
Newstead Ct NN15 . . . . 91 C5
Newstone Cres NN4 . . . . . 158 E4
New Street Ct NN29 . . . . . 147 B8
New Terr NN11 . . . . 183 D7
NEWTON 53 E3
NEWTON BROMSWOLD
. . . . 149 D8
Newton Cl
Daventry NN11 . . . . 135 A4
Rushden NN10 . . . . 132 D1
Wellingborough NN8 . . . . . 129 B6
Newton Ct CV23 . . . . 80 A8
Newton Gr NN17 . . . . 22 A1
Newton Manor La
CV23 . . . . 80 A8
Newton Rd
Clifton u D CV23 . . . . 80 A7
Geddington NN14 . . . . 54 A3
Higham Ferrers NN10 . . . . 132 E5
Kettering NN15 . . . . 91 F5
Northampton NN5 . . . . 158 D8
Rushden NN10 . . . . 132 E1
Wollaston NN29 . . . . 146 D2
Newton Road Com Prim Sch NN10 . . . . 132 C2
Newton St MK46 . . . . 195 F4
Newton Way LE16 . . . . 49 F6
Newtown
Brigstock NN14 . . . . 55 E8
Woodford NN14 . . . . 94 D7
New Town PE9 . . . . 2 A5
Newtown Rd
Little Irchester NN8 . . . . . 130 C1
Raunds NN9 . . . . 114 E5
New Town Rd [2] NN1 . . . . 159 F6
Newtown St NN14 . . . . 94 D7
Nibbits La NN11 . . . . 118 C1
Nicholas Hawksmoor Prim Sch NN12 . . . . 203 B5
Nicholas La NN9 . . . . 112 E1
Nicholas Rd NN9 . . . . 112 E1
Nicholas Way NN10 . . . . . . 131 F3
Nicholls Ct NN3 . . . . 142 E5
Nicholls Ho [1] NN4 . . . . . 159 A3
Nichols St NN14 . . . . 51 A4
Nichols Way NN9 . . . . 114 C7
Nielson Rd NN8 . . . . 130 C8
Nigel Ct NN13 . . . . 234 A5
Nightingale Cl
Brackley NN13 . . . . 222 E2
Daventry NN11 . . . . 135 D6
Nightingale Ct NN2 . . . . . . 141 D1
Nightingale Dr
Desborough NN14 . . . . 51 B4
Towcester NN12 . . . . 203 C3
Nightingale La NN8 . . . . . . 130 B7
Nine Arches Way
NN14 . . . . 76 C2
Niort Way NN8 . . . . 129 C8
Nippendale NN10 . . . . 132 C2
Nithsdale Ave LE16 . . . . 31 F2
Nithsdale Cres LE16 . . . . . . 31 F2
Nithsdale Rd NN17 . . . . 36 D7
Noble Ave NN9 . . . . 113 A5
Nobold Ct LE16 . . . . 66 F8
NOBOTTLE 138 E2
Noel Mews NN3 . . . . 142 B4
Nook The
Corby NN17 . . . . 37 B6
Cottingham LE16 . . . . 20 D1
Easton o t H PE9 . . . . 2 A5
Norbury Cl LE16 . . . . 31 D3
Norfolk Cl NN17 . . . . 36 C7
Norfolk St NN2 . . . . 159 C8
Norfolk Terr NN2 . . . . 159 C8
Norman-D-Gate NN1 . . . . 159 E5
Norman-D-Gate Ind Est
NN1 . . . . 159 E5
Normandy Lo NN13 . . . . . . 233 E8
Norman Rd NN3 . . . . 142 B1
Norman Way
Irchester NN29 . . . . 147 C8
Wellingborough NN8 . . . . . 129 D2
Normead Sq [4] NN3 . . . . . 143 D2
Norris Acre NN13 . . . . 232 F6
Norris Cl NN15 . . . . 92 A8
Norris Way NN10 . . . . 131 E3
Norris Way Ind Est
NN10 . . . . 131 E3
Norse Wlk NN18 . . . . 36 A2
Northall NN6 . . . . 108 A5
Northall Mews NN16 . . . . . . 72 A2
Northall St NN16 . . . . 72 B3
Northam Ct NN16 . . . . 72 B4
NORTHAMPTON 159 E4
Northampton Acad
NN3 . . . . 142 F2
Northampton Christian Sch NN1 . . . . 160 A8
Northampton Coll
Northampton NN1 . . . . 159 D6
Northampton, The Arbours
NN3 . . . . 142 D3
Northampton General Hospl NN1 . . . . 159 E5
Northampton High Sch
NN4 . . . . 175 E8
Northampton Ho [7]
NN1 . . . . 159 D6
Northampton La N
NN3 . . . . 142 C8
Northampton La S
NN3 . . . . 142 C7
Northampton Prep Sch
NN4 . . . . 160 E3
Northampton Rd
Blisworth NN7 . . . . 174 D1
Brackley NN13 . . . . 223 A1
Brixworth NN6 . . . . 106 B1
Broughton NN14 . . . . 90 A3
Chapel Brampton NN6 . . . . 124 E1
Cosgrove MK19 . . . . 217 F7
Denton NN7 . . . . 178 B8
Earls Barton NN6 . . . . 144 D5
Ecton NN6 . . . . 143 F4
Harpole NN7 . . . . 157 C5
Kettering NN15 . . . . 71 F1
Litchborough NN12 . . . . . . 171 E2
Market Harborough LE16 . . . 31 F3
Orlingbury NN14 . . . . 109 F5
Roade NN7 . . . . 191 D5
Rushden NN10 . . . . 131 E4
Towcester NN12 . . . . 203 C7
Welford NN6 . . . . 64 E4
Wellingborough NN8 . . . . . 129 D3
West Haddon NN6 . . . . 102 C4
Yardley Hastings NN7 . . . . 179 A6
Northampton Sch for Boys
NN1 . . . . 160 A6
Northampton Sch for Girls
Northampton NN3 . . . . 142 A4
Northampton NN3 . . . . 142 A5
Northampton Science Pk
NN3 . . . . 141 F6
Northamptonshire Fire & Rescue HQ NN3 . . . . 142 C6
Northamptonshire Gram Sch NN6 . . . . 125 D4
Northampton Sta
NN1 . . . . 159 B5
Northampton (Sywell) Airport NN6 . . . . 127 E5
Northampton Town FC
NN5 . . . . 158 E5
Northamton & Lamport Rly* NN6 . . . . 124 F1
Northants County Cricket Club* NN1 . . . . 160 A8
Northants Ent Pk
NN2 . . . . 141 E6
North Ave NN15 . . . . 92 B3
Northbank LE16 . . . . 31 E3
Northbrook NN18 . . . . 36 B4
North Cape Wlk NN18 . . . . . 36 A2
North Cl NN11 . . . . 118 D1
Northcote St NN2 . . . . 159 C7
Northend MK46 . . . . 194 E3
North End NN10 . . . . 132 B7
Northen Way NN8 . . . . 129 F8
Northern Cl NN17 . . . . 22 B8
Northern Way NN11 . . . . . 135 D4
Northfield Ave
Kettering NN16 . . . . 72 A3
Ringstead NN14 . . . . 95 B3
North Field Cl NN16 . . . . . . 72 A4
Northfield Gn NN6 . . . . 122 D5
Northfield La PE8 . . . . 15 E5
Northfield Point NN16 . . . . 72 A4
Northfield Rd
Broughton NN14 . . . . 71 C1
Northampton NN5 . . . . 140 B1
Northfield Way NN2 . . . . . 141 B4
North Folds Rd NN18 . . . . . 35 F1
Northgate NN12 . . . . 203 C7
Northgate Sch NN2 . . . . . 141 C2
North Hayes Ct NN3 . . . . . 142 F5
North Hill MK18 . . . . 225 D2
North Holme Ct NN3 . . . . . 142 D5
NORTH KILWORTH 45 A3
North La LE16 . . . . 30 D8
North Lea LE16 . . . . 18 B3
Northleigh Gr LE16 . . . . 31 D4
North Leys Ct NN3 . . . . . . 142 C7
North Luffenham Rd
LE15 . . . . 3 B8
North Meadow View
NN5 . . . . 157 F7
North Oval NN5 . . . . 140 F2
North Paddock Ct
NN3 . . . . 142 F4
North Park Dr NN16 . . . . . . 72 C5
North Portway Cl
NN3 . . . . 142 F7
North Priors Ct NN3 . . . . 143 A4
North Rd
Clifton u D CV23 . . . . 80 A6
Earls Barton NN6 . . . . 144 E5
Northampton NN3 . . . . 141 F6
South Kilworth LE17 . . . . 63 D8
North St
Castlethorpe MK19 . . . . . . 218 F5
Daventry NN11 . . . . 135 C2
Kilsby CV23 . . . . 99 F3
Mears Ashby NN6 . . . . 128 B2
Oundle PE8 . . . . 42 A5
Raunds NN9 . . . . 114 E7
Rothersthorpe NN7 . . . . . . 174 B6
Rushden NN10 . . . . 132 B3
Swinford LE17 . . . . 62 B4
Titchmarsh NN14 . . . . 77 C4
Wellingborough NN8 . . . . . 129 F5
Northumberland Cl
NN15 . . . . 91 D6
Northumberland Rd
NN15 . . . . 91 D6
Northumbria Gdns
NN3 . . . . 142 B1
North Way
Deanshanger MK19 . . . . . . 228 E5
Potterspury NN12 . . . . 217 E2
North Western Ave
NN2 . . . . 141 A4
Northwood Rd NN3 . . . . . . 142 B2
Norfoft NN6 . . . . 103 F7
NORTON 136 C4
Norton Cl NN11 . . . . 135 D2
Norton Cres NN12 . . . . . . 203 B6
Norton Leys CV22 . . . . 98 A6
Norton Rd
Corby NN17 . . . . 36 C7
Daventry NN11 . . . . 135 D2
Northampton NN2 . . . . 141 C3
Norton St NN14 . . . . 70 E7
Norway Cl NN18 . . . . 36 A3
Norwood Rd NN5 . . . . 157 F8
Notre Dame Mews [3]
NN1 . . . . 159 D6
Nuffield Cl NN13 . . . . 233 D8
Nunneley Way LE16 . . . . 31 F5
Nunnery Ave NN14 . . . . 70 C7
Nunn Mills Rd NN1 . . . . . . 159 E4
Nuns La NN6 . . . . 121 B4
Nurseries The
Horton NN7 . . . . 177 D1
[3] Moulton NN3 . . . . 126 C1
Northampton NN1 . . . . 159 F5
Nursery Cl
Little Houghton NN7 . . . . . 161 A4
Maidwell NN6 . . . . 87 B7
Nursery Ct NN6 . . . . 128 B2
Nursery Dr NN8 . . . . 130 B7
Nursery End LE16 . . . . 31 C2
Nursery Gdns NN9 . . . . . . 112 E2
Nursery La NN2 . . . . 141 C3
Nutcote NN6 . . . . 85 B8
Nuthall Cl NN3 . . . . 160 F8

O

Oak Ave NN7 . . . . 174 B1
Oak Cl
Broughton NN14 . . . . 90 B4
Hartwell NN7 . . . . 192 E2
Irchester NN29 . . . . 147 A7
Market Harborough LE16 . . . 31 F4
Towcester NN12 . . . . 203 C4
Oakdown Cres MK46 . . . . . 195 F3
Oak Dr NN11 . . . . 184 B6
Oakfield NN10 . . . . 132 A4
Oak Gr NN11 . . . . 135 C5
Oakgrove Pl NN4 . . . . 175 D6
Oakham Cl
Desborough NN14 . . . . 50 F4
Northampton NN3 . . . . 142 B7
Rushden NN10 . . . . 148 A8
Oakham La NN11 . . . . 152 B7
Oak La NN6 . . . . 100 F6
Oaklands
Bugbrooke NN7 . . . . 173 A7
Weedon Bec NN7 . . . . 155 A2
Oaklands Dr NN3 . . . . 142 E1
Oaklands Pk [4] LE16 . . . . . 31 F2
Oakleas Rise NN14 . . . . 76 D1
Oaklee Cl PE8 . . . . 58 A3
Oakleigh Cl NN9 . . . . 114 C7
Oakleigh Dr NN5 . . . . 140 C1
Oakley Ct NN18 . . . . 36 A1
Oakley Dr
Moulton NN3 . . . . 126 D1
Wellingborough NN8 . . . . . 129 D3
Oakley Hay Ind Est
NN18 . . . . 36 A1
Oakley Mews LE16 . . . . 31 D3
Oakley Pond NN18 . . . . 53 B8
Oakley Rd
Corby NN17 . . . . 37 A6
Corby NN18 . . . . 36 C3
Pipewell NN14 . . . . 52 D8
Rushden NN10 . . . . 131 F3
Rushton NN14 . . . . 52 E5
Oakley St
Kettering NN16 . . . . 72 B4
Northampton NN1 . . . . 159 D7
Oakmont Cl NN4 . . . . 175 C5
Oakpark Cl NN3 . . . . 143 A6
Oakpits Way NN10 . . . . . . 132 C1
Oak Rd
Brackley NN13 . . . . 222 F1
Kettering NN15 . . . . 72 D1
Oaks Dr NN10 . . . . 132 B6
Oak St
[20] Northampton NN1 . . . . 159 C7
Rushden NN10 . . . . 132 B4
Weedon Bec NN7 . . . . 155 A2
Oaks The NN4 . . . . 175 F3
Oak Terr [6] NN9 . . . . 112 F2
Oak Tree Cl NN14 . . . . 50 F3
Oaktree Ct [2] NN16 . . . . . . 72 B1
Oak Tree Ct NN14 . . . . 76 F8
Oak View NN9 . . . . 110 F1
Oakway NN8 . . . . 129 F7
Oak Way NN9 . . . . 112 F2
Oakway Jun & Inf Sch
NN8 . . . . 130 A7
Oakwood Cl PE8 . . . . 27 D2
Oakwood Rd NN1 . . . . 142 A1
Oathill Cl NN6 . . . . 106 B1
Oat Hill Dr NN3 . . . . 143 D2
Oat Hill Rd NN12 . . . . 203 C4
Oathill Rise NN15 . . . . 92 C2
Oban Cl NN15 . . . . 91 E8

Obelisk Cl NN2 141 C8
Obelisk Rd NN9 112 A5
Obelisk Rise NN2 141 C6
Occupation Rd
Corby NN17 36 F7
Middleton LE16 20 B2
Oundle PE8 42 A7
Octagon The NN17 37 A8
Octagon Way NN3 142 F2
Octavian Way NN13 234 A7
Odeon Bldgs NN17 37 A7
OLD 107 D7
Old Barn Ct NN3 142 F3
Old Brewery Wlk NN13 233 F6
Old Brickyard The NN6 102 C4
Old Carpenters Cl NN3 143 C2
Old Cl NN4 175 E2
Old Coach Ho The LE16 35 A7
Old Coffee Mills The 6 LE16 31 F2
Old Dairy Farm* NN7 171 E6
Old Depot The NN7 155 B4
Old Dry La NN14 55 F8
Olde Forde Cl NN6 106 B1
Olde Hall Cl NN6 105 B1
Oldenburg Rd NN18 35 F3
Old End NN7 177 A1
Oldenmead Ct NN3 142 F3
Olden Rd NN3 143 C5
Old Farm PE8 41 C1
Old Farm La NN14 76 B3
Old Forge Dr NN6 102 C4
Old Forge La NN11 169 C2
Old Gn LE16 18 F6
Old Gorse Way NN14 89 A4
Old Gram School The NN6 103 F6
Old Great North Rd PE8 8 C2
Old Greens Norton Rd NN12 203 B7
Old Hall La LE16 30 F3
Old Holt Rd LE16 19 A7
Old La NN13 221 A4
Oldland Rd NN18 36 D3
Old Leicester Rd PE8 8 A3
Old Manor Ct NN11 135 E8
Old North Rd PE8 8 A4
Old Oak Dr NN12 214 D4
Old Oundle Rd PE8 7 A6
Old Quarry Ct NN3 142 E4
Old Rd
Braunston NN11 134 C8
Scaldwell NN6 107 A7
Stanion NN14 37 E2
Walgrave NN6 107 F5
Old Rectory Dr PE8 8 A6
Old Rickyard The NN11 199 D7
Old School Cotts NN6 105 A8
Old School La NN12 187 A1
Old School Mews LE16 31 E3
Old Stable Yd MK19 229 C7
OLD STRATFORD 229 B7
Old Stratford Prim Sch MK19 229 B6
Old Sulehay Rd PE8 15 F8
Old Tiffield Rd NN12 203 C8
Old Towcester Rd NN4 159 C4
OLD TOWN 234 A7
Old Town NN13 234 A7
Old Vineyard The NN10 132 B6
Old Woodyard The NN12 214 D4
Old Yew Ct NN2 141 B3
Oleander Cres NN3 143 C4
Oliver Cl NN10 132 C2
Oliver St NN2 141 E1
Ollerton Wlk NN18 36 C5
Ollis Cl NN17 36 E8
OLNEY 195 E4
Olney Inf Sch MK46 195 E3
Olney Mid Sch MK46 195 F5
Olney Rd MK46 195 F1
Olympia Cl NN4 175 B8
Olympic Way
Kettering NN15 91 A7
Wellingborough NN8 129 C5
ONLEY 98 D2
Onley La CV22 98 D6
Onley Pk CV23 117 C8
Oransay Cl NN3 143 C2
Orchard Cl
Badby NN11 152 F3
Desborough NN14 50 E3
East Haddon NN6 122 D5
Finedon NN9 111 F5
Hannington NN6 108 C3
Hollowell NN6 104 B5
Milton Malsor NN7 174 E4
Northampton NN4 175 E6
Orlingbury NN14 110 A5
Oundle PE8 41 F6
Ringstead NN14 95 C3
Rushden NN10 131 F3
Spratton NN6 124 B8
Towcester NN12 203 C4
Walgrave NN6 107 F5
Orchard Cl *continued*
Warmington PE8 28 B3
Weedon Bec NN7 155 C3
Weldon NN17 38 B8
Wilbarston LE16 34 C5
Wollaston NN29 146 D3
Yardley Gobion NN12 217 F6
Yelvertoft NN6 82 B4
Orchard Cotts NN6 125 C5
Orchard Cres
Kettering NN16 72 C4
Woodnewton PE8 14 E2
Orchard Ct
Pattishall NN12 172 D1
Woodford NN14 94 C7
Orchard Est NN14 90 F2
Orchard Field NN14 93 A6
Orchard Gn NN3 142 C2
Orchard Hill NN3 143 A1
Orchard Ho NN17 38 B8
Orchard La
Denton NN7 162 B1
Gretton NN17 10 C1
King's Cliffe PE8 13 E7
Woodnewton PE8 14 E2
Orchard Pl NN29 147 A8
Orchard Rd
Finedon NN9 111 F5
Raunds NN9 114 B5
Orchard Rise
Long Buckby NN6 121 D4
Olney MK46 195 F3
Orchard Sch The NN16 72 B5
Orchard St
Daventry NN11 135 B2
Market Harborough LE16 31 E4
3 Northampton NN5 159 A6
Orchards The NN6 103 D1
Orchard Terr
Finedon NN9 111 F5
Welford NN6 64 E6
Wellingborough NN8 129 F5
Orchard The
Apethorpe PE8 14 C4
Bozeat NN29 164 D3
Flore NN7 155 F5
Kislingbury NN7 157 D3
Potterspury NN12 217 C3
Sibbertoft LE16 47 A2
Staverton NN11 152 B7
Upper Boddington NN11 182 C7
Orchard Way
Cogenhoe NN7 161 F6
Easton o t H PE9 1 F6
Harpole NN7 157 C6
Kings Sutton OX17 231 A5
Northampton NN5 158 C6
Roade NN7 191 D4
Thrapston NN14 76 E1
Orchid Cl NN14 51 A4
Ordnance Ho NN7 155 A4
Ordnance Rd NN7 154 F3
Oriel Rd NN11 153 C7
Oriel Way NN13 233 D8
Orient Ho NN1 159 E6
Orient Way NN8 130 A4
Orion Way NN15 91 C5
Orkney Wlk NN17 36 B8
ORLINGBURY 110 A5
Orlingbury Rd
Great Harrowden NN9 110 D2
Isham NN14 110 C7
Little Harrowden NN9 110 B4
Pytchley NN14 90 F1
Ormond Pl NN14 110 E8
Orson Leys CV22 98 A7
ORTON 70 A3
Orton Pl NN8 129 D7
Orton Rd
Kettering NN15 91 F5
Loddington NN14 70 D2
Orwell Cl
Clifton u D CV23 80 A5
Raunds NN9 114 D7
Wellingborough NN8 129 C6
Osborn Cl NN8 129 E3
Osborne Cl NN10 132 D4
Osborne Rd NN2 141 C2
Osborn's Ct MK46 195 F3
Osbourne Cl NN18 36 E2
Osier Bed La NN17 24 B5
Osiers The NN14 51 D2
Osier Way NN14 76 C1
Osler Cl NN2 141 B5
Oslo Gdns NN18 36 A3
Osmond Dr NN3 143 A5
Osprey Dr NN11 135 C3
Osprey La NN8 130 B7
Osprey Rise NN4 175 B8
Osprey View 6 NN4 175 B8
Ostlers La MK11 229 D6
Ostlers Way NN15 91 B7
Oswald Rd NN10 132 C2
Osyth Cl NN4 160 B2
Oulton Rise NN3 141 F4
OUNDLE 42 A6
Oundle CE Prim Sch PE8 41 F5
Oundle Dr NN3 142 B7
Oundle & Kings Cliffe Mid Sch PE8 41 E7
Oundle Mus* PE8 41 F5
Oundle Rd
Elton PE8 16 F1
Thrapston NN14 76 E2
Weldon NN17 38 E7
Oundle Rd *continued*
Woodnewton PE8 14 F1
Oundle Sch PE8 42 A5
Our Lady of Walsingham RC Prim Sch NN17 36 F7
Our Lady & Pope John RC Sch NN18 36 A4
Our Lady's Convent Prep Sch NN15 71 F1
Our Lady's RC Jun & Inf Sch NN8 129 D3
Ousebank Way MK11 229 D5
Ouse Cl NN8 129 C6
Ouse La NN12 203 A6
Outlaw La NN8 129 F5
Oval Cres NN10 132 D2
Oval Rd
Rugby CV22 98 D8
Rushden NN10 132 D2
Oval The
Kettering NN15 91 B8
Market Harborough LE16 31 E4
Overdale Cl LE16 32 A3
OVER END 28 E7
Overfield Ave LE16 31 F5
Overhills MK46 195 E4
Overleys Ct NN3 143 B5
Overmead Rd NN3 143 D2
Overslade Cl NN4 175 A8
Overslade Ho NN4 175 A8
OVERSTONE 127 B1
Overstone Cl NN3 126 E1
Overstone Cres NN6 127 B1
Overstone Hts NN6 127 D3
Overstone La NN6 126 F1
Overstone Lakes Cvn Pk NN6 143 D8
OVERSTONE LODGE 143 B5
Overstone Park Sch NN6 143 B8
Overstone Prim Sch NN6 127 A1
Overstone Rd
Moulton NN3 126 D1
Northampton NN1 159 D7
Sywell NN6 127 D3
OVERTHORPE 219 D6
Overthorpe Ind Est OX16 219 A7
Overthorpe Prep Sch OX17 219 C8
Overthorpe Rd OX16 219 B6
Ovett Cl NN15 90 F8
Owen Cl NN8 129 B5
Owen Mews NN8 129 B5
Owen Way NN10 132 A5
Owl Cl NN3 141 F7
Owl End La NN11 182 C5
Owl End Way NN11 182 C5
Oxburgh Ct 7 NN4 175 C8
Oxendon Hall LE16 48 E3
Oxendon Rd
Arthingworth LE16 49 A1
Braybrooke LE16 49 D5
Clipston LE16 48 B1
East Farndon LE16 48 B5
Oxfield Park Dr MK19 229 C7
Oxford Cl
Daventry NN11 135 C1
Earls Barton NN6 144 F3
Oxford Ct NN13 233 F5
Oxford Rd
Adderbury OX17 230 A3
Corby NN17 36 C6
Evenley NN13 233 E5
Oxford St
Daventry NN11 135 C1
Finedon NN9 112 B5
Kettering NN16 72 A3
Northampton NN4 159 B3
Rothwell NN14 70 D8
Stony Stratford MK11 229 D5
Wellingborough NN8 129 F4
Wymington NN10 148 A7
Oxleys MK46 195 E4
Oxwich Cl NN4 160 A1

P

Packer Rd NN15 90 E8
Packwood Ave CV21 99 C8
Packwood Cl 9 NN11 135 B7
Paddock Cl NN6 103 D1
Paddock Ct LE16 31 E3
Paddock End NN14 89 B4
Paddock La
Desborough NN14 51 A3
Mears Ashby NN6 128 B2
Medbourne LE16 19 D8
Paddock Mews NN14 51 A3
Paddock Mill Ct 1 NN3 143 B4
Paddocks Cl NN6 108 A5
Paddocks Rd NN10 131 F3
Paddocks The
Brixworth NN6 106 B3
Bugbrooke NN7 172 F7
Moulton NN3 126 C1
Orlingbury NN14 109 F5
Shutlanger NN12 204 D8
Souldern OX27 237 E3
Stanion NN14 37 F3
Yelvertoft NN6 82 A5
Paddocks Way NN3 143 A1
Paddock The
Crick NN6 100 F5
Paddock The *continued*
Lower Boddington NN11 182 C5
Raunds NN9 114 C4
Weedon Lois NN12 200 B2
Welton NN11 135 E8
Woodnewton PE8 14 E2
Paddox Cl CV22 98 F8
Paddox Ct CV23 100 A3
Paddox Prim Sch
Rugby CV22 98 D8
Rugby CV22 98 E8
Padmans Cl NN14 89 B4
Padwell Ct 2 NN3 161 A8
Pagent Ct NN15 91 A7
Pages Wlk NN17 37 B6
Paget Cl NN4 160 E2
Paget Ho NN5 140 E1
Paget Rd LE16 30 E3
Pagnell Ct NN4 176 A7
Palace Ct 8 NN10 132 B2
Palk Rd NN8 130 B4
Palmer Ave NN9 113 B4
Palmer Cl NN8 129 D7
Palmer Ct NN8 129 F5
Palmer's Cl CV21 99 B8
Palmer Sq NN3 143 C1
Palmerston Ct 5 NN1 159 E6
Palmerston Ho 4 NN1 159 E6
Palmerston Rd NN1 159 E6
Palm Rd NN10 131 E3
Pantell Way NN10 132 A7
Panters La NN14 75 A1
Parade Bank NN3 126 C1
Parade The NN1 159 C6
Paradise Ave NN15 91 D6
Paradise Ho 2 NN8 129 F5
Paradise La NN15 91 D6
Pargeter Cl OX17 210 E2
Park Ave
Kettering NN16 72 B4
Northampton, Abington NN1 160 A8
Northampton NN5 140 B1
Raunds NN9 114 E5
Rushden NN10 132 A2
Park Ave N NN3 142 A1
Park Ave S NN3 160 B7
Park Cl
Badby NN11 153 A3
Brafield-on-t-G NN7 161 E2
Cosgrove MK19 218 F2
Earls Barton NN6 144 D4
Isham NN14 110 F8
King's Cliffe PE8 14 A8
Northampton NN5 140 A1
Sywell NN6 127 D2
Watford NN6 120 C6
Whittlebury NN12 215 C4
Park Cnr NN5 158 F6
Park Cres 8 NN8 130 A5
Park Cres E NN5 140 F2
Park Cres W NN5 140 F1
Park Dr
Market Harborough LE16 31 E4
Northampton NN5 140 F1
Park End NN13 238 D8
Park End Works NN13 238 D7
Parker Rd PE8 7 D8
Parkers Terr NN9 111 F4
Parker Way NN10 132 B7
Park Farm Barns NN7 139 E6
Park Farm Ct NN14 77 C4
Park Farm Ind Est NN8 129 A5
Park Farm Way NN8 129 A3
Parkfield Ave NN4 159 C1
Parkfield Cres NN4 159 C2
Parkfield Rd
Brixworth NN6 106 A1
Long Buckby NN6 121 A4
Parkham Ind Est NN10 131 D3
Park Hill Rd NN3 142 D3
Park Ho LE16 31 E4
Park Jun Sch
Kettering NN16 72 C4
Wellingborough NN8 130 A5
Park La
Earls Barton NN6 144 D4
Gayton NN7 173 E2
Harpole NN7 157 C6
Hartwell NN7 192 C1
Northampton NN5 140 A2
Paulerspury NN12 216 B7
Sulgrave OX17 210 F7
Watford NN6 120 C6
Parklands
Crick NN6 100 C7
Stanwick NN9 113 F3
Sywell NN6 127 D1
Parklands Ave NN3 142 A5
Parklands Cl NN14 70 D1
Parklands Cres NN3 142 A5
Parklands Mid Sch NN3 142 A5
Parklands Prim Sch NN3 142 A4
Park Leys NN11 135 C1
Park Lo NN17 36 E6
Park Mews
Market Harborough LE16 31 E4
Towcester NN12 203 C6
Park Mews *continued*
Wellingborough NN8 130 A5
Park Pl NN10 132 B2
Park Rd
Burton Latimer NN15 92 B2
Hanslope MK19 207 B1
Hartwell NN7 192 C1
Irthlingborough NN9 112 F1
Kettering NN16 72 C4
Raunds NN9 114 E6
Rushden NN10 132 C1
Stony Stratford MK11 229 D5
Titchmarsh NN14 77 C4
Wellingborough NN8 130 A5
Parkside NN3 143 D2
Park Spinney Cl NN6 84 A5
Park Sq NN5 140 F2
Park St
Earls Barton NN6 144 D4
King's Cliffe PE8 13 F7
Raunds NN9 114 E6
Towcester NN12 203 C6
Wollaston NN29 146 E2
Park The PE28 97 A3
Park View
Kettering NN16 72 B4
Moulton NN3 142 E8
Northampton NN5 158 E8
Thrapston NN14 76 D2
Wellingborough NN8 130 B4
Park View Cl NN3 126 E1
Park View Ho NN10 132 A3
Park View Rd NN12 203 D5
Parkway
Nassington PE8 15 F5
Northampton NN3 142 D1
Parkway Cl PE8 15 F5
Park Wlk
Brigstock NN14 55 E7
Easton o t H PE9 2 A6
Northampton NN5 140 F2
Parkwood St NN5 159 B5
Parnell Cl NN6 102 C5
Parracombe Way NN3 160 C7
Parsons Cl
Ecton NN6 143 F4
Nether Heyford NN7 156 C2
Parsons' Cl NN7 163 D5
Parsons Gr NN17 22 A1
Parsons Meade NN4 158 E2
Parsons Rd
Daventry NN11 134 F5
Irchester NN29 147 B8
Parsons St
Adderbury OX17 230 A4
Woodford Halse NN11 184 C6
Partridge Cl
Charwelton NN11 168 A5
Northampton NN2 141 A5
Partridge La NN11 184 C1
Parva Ct NN3 142 E3
Pascoe Cres 1 NN11 135 A4
Pashler Gdns NN14 76 D2
PASSENHAM 229 C3
Pasteur Cl NN2 141 B5
Pasteur Ctyd NN17 37 B8
Pasture End NN14 89 C5
Pasture Mobile Home Pk NN14 51 C8
Pastures The
Market Harborough LE16 31 C3
Northampton NN2 141 A5
Wellingborough NN9 110 E1
Pasture The NN11 135 C1
Paterson Rd NN8 130 B8
Patrick Cl NN15 91 C6
Patrick Rd
Corby NN18 36 D4
Kettering NN15 91 C6
Patricks La MK19 228 E4
Patrick St LE16 31 F2
Patterdale Wlk 1 NN3 142 C4
Patterson Cl NN3 142 E1
PATTISHALL 172 E1
Pattishall CE Prim Sch NN12 188 F8
PAULERSPURY 216 C8
Paulerspury CE Prim Sch NN12 216 B8
Pavilion Dr
Northampton NN4 159 F1
Oundle PE8 41 E6
Pavillons Way NN13 233 E8
Paxford Cl NN8 129 E1
Paxton Cl MK46 195 F3
Paxton Rd NN3 142 D4
Payne's La LE16 18 F7
Peace Cl NN4 158 F3
Peace Hill NN7 172 E7
Peacock Dr NN14 95 B3
Peacock Pl 6 NN1 159 D6
Peacock's Cl OX17 220 A8
Peake Cl LE16 35 B8
Peak The NN7 156 C1
Pearmain Ave NN8 129 F7
Pearmain Ct NN3 143 A2
Pearson Mews NN29 146 D2
Peartree Cl NN11 135 C4
Pear Tree Cl
Bozeat NN29 164 D3
Northampton NN3 143 A2
Pear Tree Gdns LE16 31 D2
Peaselands NN14 50 F4
Pebble Cotts LE17 46 D8
Pebbleford Rd NN15 91 D8

Pebble La
Brackley NN13 233 F7
4 Wellingborough NN8 130 A4
Pebody Pl MK46 195 F3
Peck Way NN10 132 B4
Pegasus Ct NN13 233 F7
Pegasus Way NN10 131 E4
Peg's La
Clipston LE16 66 F8
Denford NN14 95 C6
Pelham Ct NN3 142 D4
Pell Ct NN3 142 E3
Pells Cl NN6 103 E7
Pemberton St NN10 132 A3
Pembroke Cl
Rushden NN10 132 C1
Thrapston NN14 76 E2
Pembroke Cres NN5 159 B8
Pembroke Gdns NN5 159 A8
Pembroke Ho MK46 195 F3
Pembroke Rd NN5 159 B8
Pembroke Way NN11 153 B7
Penarth Rd NN5 159 A8
Pen Ct NN1 159 D4
Pendered Rd NN8 130 A1
Pendle Ave NN16 72 A6
Pendle Rd NN5 158 C8
Penfold Cl NN2 141 B4
Penfold Dr NN3 143 B3
Penfold Gdns NN3 143 C3
Penfold La NN3 143 C3
Pen Gn La NN17 37 A8
Peninsular Cl 12 NN4 175 E7
Penistone Rd NN3 142 E3
Penistone Wlk 3 NN3 142 E3
Pennard Cl NN4 160 B2
Penn Gdns NN4 175 B7
Pennine Ct NN11 135 B5
Pennine Way
Kettering NN16 72 B6
Northampton NN5 158 D7
Pennycress Pl NN3 143 D1
Penny La NN9 114 D7
Penrhyn Cl NN18 36 F3
Penrhyn Ct NN14 76 E2
Penrhyn Rd NN4 159 C3
Penrith Dr NN8 129 D6
Pentelowes The PE18 116 D2
Penthorne Cl NN12 188 A8
Pentlands MK11 229 F4
Penvale Rd NN4 175 B7
Pepper Alley OX15 236 E4
Peppercorn Way NN4 175 D6
Perceval Cl NN5 140 D1
Perch Cl NN11 135 B6
Percival Rd CV22 98 D8
Percy Rd
Northampton NN1 159 F7
Woodford Halse NN11 184 C6
Peregrine Pl NN4 175 A8
Perkins Cl LE16 31 F4
Perkins Ct 4 NN8 130 A5
Perkins Rd NN9 131 E8
Perkins Way NN11 153 E4
Perry Cl NN15 91 A7
Perry St NN1 159 F7
Pershore Cl NN8 145 E8
Perth Ho NN17 22 F1
Peterborough Rd
Morcott LE15 3 D6
Wansford PE8 8 A3
Warmington PE8 28 C4
Peters La NN6 106 F5
Pether Ave NN13 233 C8
Petherton Ct NN16 72 B3
Pettiver Cres 2 CV21 80 A1
Petworth Dr LE16 32 B2
Petworth Gdns NN18 36 B5
Pevensey Cl NN10 132 D1
Pevensey Wlk 2 NN18 36 B5
Peverel Cl NN10 132 C6
Peverel's Way NN5 158 E6
Peveril Rd
Greatworth OX17 210 E2
Northampton NN5 158 C7
Pevers La MK46 195 A1
Pevrel Pl NN14 50 E4
Pexley Ct PE8 41 E5
Pheasant Way NN2 141 A5
Pheonix Parkway NN17 37 B8
Philip Way NN10 132 C7
Phillips Way NN6 121 C4
Phipps Rd NN11 184 B6
PHIPPSVILLE 141 F1
Phoenix Ct NN8 130 B3
Phoenix Parkway NN17 22 B2
Phoenix St 23 NN1 159 C6
Piccadilly Bldgs 3 NN16 72 B1
Piccadilly Cl NN4 158 F2
Pickering Ct NN18 36 B4
Pickerings The NN6 106 C1
Picks Cl LE16 32 B3
PIDDINGTON 177 B2
Piddington La NN7 177 A2
Piddington Roman Villa Mus* NN7 177 B2
Piece The
Cogenhoe NN7 161 F6
Spratton NN6 105 B1
Pie Cnr NN6 127 D3
Pied Bull Cl PE9 1 A6
Pierce Cres PE8 28 C3
Pigeon Hill NN12 189 D3
Pightles Terr NN10 132 C1
Pightles Wlk NN10 132 C1
Pigott's La NN15 92 C2
Pike La NN1 159 C6
Pikemead Ct NN3 143 B4
Pike Rd NN18 36 A1
Pilgrims La NN7 173 A7
Pilgrims Pl NN4 159 C2
Pilgrim Way NN8 129 F3
Pilot Rd NN17 37 C8
PILTON 58 C5
Pilton Cl NN3 143 C5
Pilton Rd PE8 58 A4
PIMLICO 223 F6
Pincet La LE17 45 A6
Pindar Rd NN8 129 E2
Pindar Rise NN3 142 E6
PINDON END 206 C4
Pine Ave NN6 127 D1
Pine Cl
Desborough NN14 51 C2
Irchester NN29 147 A7
Northampton NN4 175 F3
Rushden NN10 148 A8
Pine Copse Cl NN5 140 A2
Pine Cres NN6 127 D1
Pine Ct NN7 138 C4
Pine Gr CV21 80 A1
Pineham Ave NN2 141 D6
Pine Rd NN15 72 D1
Pine Ridge NN3 142 F7
Pines The LE16 32 A6
Pine Tree Ct NN14 76 B3
Pine Trees NN3 142 D1
Pinetrees Cl NN7 177 B3
Pine Wlk NN17 21 E1
Pinewood Cl NN16 72 B6
Pinewood Rd NN3 142 B3
Pinfold Cl LE15 3 E8
Pinfold Gn NN11 152 F3
Pinfold La LE15 3 E8
Pingle La LE15 3 B6
Pioneer Ave
Burton Latimer NN15 92 B2
Desborough NN14 50 F2
Pioneer Cl 10 NN4 175 E7
Piper Cl NN8 129 F8
Pipers Cl
Irthlingborough NN9 112 F2
Kettering NN15 72 C1
Piper's Hill Rd NN15 91 C8
PIPEWELL 52 C8
Pipewell Rd
Desborough NN14 51 C4
East Carlton LE16 35 B3
Pippin Cl
Cogenhoe NN7 161 E5
Rushden NN10 131 E3
Wellingborough NN8 129 F4
Pippin La NN3 143 A2
Pitchers La LE16 20 D7
Pit La PE9 1 A7
PITSFORD 125 D5
Pitsford & Brampton Sta* NN6 124 E2
Pitsford Prim Sch NN6 125 D5
Pitsford Rd
Chapel Brampton NN6 124 E1
Moulton NN3 126 B2
Pitstone Rd NN4 158 E3
Pittams Cl NN6 121 B3
Pittams La NN12 213 B8
Pittoms La CV23 99 C1
Pitt St NN8 129 E4
Plank Hos NN12 203 C5
Plantagenet Cl NN13 233 E8
Plantagenet Sq 7 NN4 158 F2
Playford Cl NN14 70 F7
Plaza 2& 4 The 1 NN1 159 E7
Pleasant Row NN14 94 D7
Plessey Cl NN12 203 D5
Pleydell Gdns NN4 159 C2
Pleydell Rd NN4 159 C2
Plough Cl
Daventry NN11 135 D6
Rothwell NN14 70 D7
Plough La NN2 141 A6
Ploughmans Way NN4 175 F3
Ploughmans Wlk NN2 141 B5
Ploughmans Yd 11 LE16 31 E3
Plough Mews NN13 233 F7
Plover Cl NN12 203 C3
Plowden Cl NN11 182 F2
Plum Park La NN12 216 D8
PLUMPTON 200 B5
Plumpton Ct NN18 36 B5
PLUMPTON END 216 D7
Plumpton La NN11 199 D7
Plumpton Rd
Weston NN12 200 A2
Woodend NN12 200 F6
Plumtree Ave NN8 130 A7
Poachers Cl NN4 175 F3
Poachers Way NN2 141 B5
Pochin Dr LE16 31 F5
PODINGTON 147 E2
Podington Rd NN10 148 A4
Podmore Way NN14 90 A3
Poets Way NN11 153 E5
Poitiers Ct NN5 139 F1
Pokas Cotts NN9 133 C8
Polar Star Cl NN11 135 A4
POLEBROOK 43 A3
Polebrook Airfield Nature Reserve* PE8 43 F3
Polebrook CE Prim Sch PE8 43 A3
Polebrook Ct PE8 42 F3
Polegate Ct NN18 36 B5
Police Flats NN17 36 E6
Pollards Cl LE15 3 F5
Pollard St NN16 72 B4
Polopit NN14 77 D3
Polwell La NN15 92 A4
Pomfret Arms Cl NN4 159 C4
Pomfret Rd NN12 203 C6
Pond Bank NN7 190 D8
Ponder St NN14 70 D7
Pond Farm Cl NN5 158 C7
Ponds Cl NN9 114 D6
Pond Wood Cl NN3 142 B6
Pool Cl NN12 188 D8
Poole St NN1 159 D7
Pool Farm Ct NN11 184 A5
Pool St NN11 184 B5
Pope Rd NN8 129 C3
Popham Cl NN9 114 C7
Poplar Cl
Daventry NN11 135 C5
Irchester NN29 147 A7
Rushden NN10 148 A8
Towcester NN12 203 C4
Poplar Ct NN3 142 D5
Poplar Pl
Wellingborough NN8 129 F4
Wollaston NN29 146 E2
Poplar Rd
Burton Latimer NN15 92 C4
Corby NN17 21 D1
Finedon NN9 112 A5
Kettering NN16 72 D2
Poplar Rise NN12 213 B8
Poplars Cl
Blakesley NN12 187 B1
Middleton Cheney OX17 220 A8
Raunds NN9 114 C6
Poplars Ct
Market Harborough LE16 31 D4
Scaldwell NN6 106 F6
Poplar's Farm Rd NN15 92 B8
Poplars La NN6 126 E8
Poplars Rd OX17 208 F4
Poplar St NN8 130 A5
Poplars The
Guilsborough NN6 103 E7
Long Buckby NN6 121 B3
Northampton NN1 159 C7
Poppy Cl NN10 148 C8
Poppyfield Ct
Northampton NN3 142 F4
Thrapston NN14 76 D3
Poppy Fields NN16 71 F3
Poppy Leys NN6 125 B8
Porlock Cl NN5 158 E8
Portchester Gdns 4 NN3 160 F8
Porter's Cl MK19 228 E4
Porter's La PE9 2 A5
Portland Cl NN11 135 D1
Portland Pl NN1 159 E6
Portland Rd
Irthlingborough NN9 112 F3
Rushden NN10 132 B2
Portlow La NN6 100 F6
Port Rd NN5 140 A2
Portree Wlk NN17 36 C8
Portstone Cl NN5 140 A2
Portway
Aynho OX17 237 D7
Croughton NN13 238 E7
Portway Cres NN13 238 E7
Portway Dr NN13 238 D7
Portway Gdns OX17 237 D7
Portwey Cl NN6 106 C1
Postle Cl CV23 99 F2
Post Office Cl NN17 37 B6
Potter Ct NN9 114 A4
Potters End NN11 183 D7
POTTERSPURY 217 D3
Potterspury Lodge Sch NN12 217 A6
Pound Cl
Corby NN18 36 B2
Ringstead NN14 95 B3
Wicken MK19 228 A4
Pound Ct NN3 126 B1
Poundfield Rd NN12 217 E2
Pound La
Badby NN11 152 F3
Bugbrooke NN7 173 A7
Eastcote NN12 172 F1
Moulton NN3 126 C1
Northampton NN3 143 C2
Pound Pl NN9 111 F4
Pound The
Great Brington NN7 138 D6
Horton NN7 177 E1
Nether Heyford NN7 156 B1
Syresham NN13 224 B7
Powys Cl NN18 36 E2
Poyntz Gdns NN5 158 E8
Poyntz La NN5 158 E8
Pratt Rd NN10 132 C2
Prebendal Gn PE8 15 F8
Premier Ct NN3 142 A7
Premier Way NN9 131 E8
Prentice Ct NN3 143 A5
Prentice Wlk NN17 37 A6
Prescott Cl NN3 143 C4
Presland Way NN9 112 D1
Pressland Dr NN10 132 C6
Prestbury Rd NN5 140 A1
Prestidge Row NN11 199 C7
PRESTON CAPES 169 D2
Preston Ct
Burton Latimer NN15 92 C3
Northampton NN3 142 E3
PRESTON DEANERY 176 E4
Preston Deanery Rd NN7 176 B1
Preston Dr NN11 135 C6
Preston Hedges Prim Sch NN4 175 F6
Preston Rd NN11 184 C2
Prestwold Way NN3 143 B5
Pretoria Cotts NN9 114 C1
Prices Way NN13 222 D1
Pride Pl LE16 31 D2
Pridmore Cl PE8 14 E2
Priestley Ct NN17 22 D1
Priestwell Ct NN6 122 D5
Primrose Cl
Corby NN18 36 C2
Kettering NN16 72 D4
Primrose Gdns NN9 114 D5
Primrose Hill
Daventry NN11 135 C2
Northampton NN2 159 C8
Raunds NN9 114 D6
Primrose Pl NN8 130 C5
Primrose Wlk
Hinton NN11 184 B6
Northampton NN4 175 F2
Primula Cl NN3 160 C6
Primula Ct NN2 159 C8
Prince Cl NN11 135 B3
Prince Of Wales Row NN3 126 D1
Prince Rupert Ave NN14 50 F3
Princes Ave NN14 51 B3
Princes Cl NN7 155 A3
Princes Ct NN16 72 B3
Princess Anne Bldg NN2 141 C4
Princess Cl NN3 160 B6
Princess Marina Hospl NN5 158 B6
Princes St NN16 72 C3
Princess Way NN8 129 E2
Prince St NN6 144 E5
Princes Wlk 4 NN1 159 D6
Princethorpe Dr OX16 219 A7
Prince William Rd PE8 41 E5
Prince William Sch PE8 42 B4
Princewood Rd NN17 21 E3
Printers Yd NN16 72 B2
Priors Cl NN10 147 F8
Priors Ct
Corby NN17 23 A1
Priors Marston CV47 166 D7
PRIORS HARDWICK 166 A5
Priors Hardwick Rd NN11 182 B8
Priors Haw Rd NN17 23 A1
PRIORS MARSTON 166 E8
Priors Marston Rd
Byfield NN11 167 B8
Hellidon NN11 151 C1
Priors Sch The CV47 166 D8
Priory Cl
Daventry NN11 135 D1
Northampton NN3 160 B6
Priory Cres NN7 191 C4
Priory Ct
Geddington NN14 54 A2
Weedon Bec NN7 155 A2
Priory Ho NN1 159 B6
Priory Rd
Wellingborough NN8 129 F3
Wollaston NN29 146 D3
Pritchard Cl NN3 143 C6
Probyn Cl NN3 143 A6
Promenade The NN8 129 E6
Prospect Ave
Irchester NN29 147 A7
Rushden NN10 132 B4
Prospect Cl NN29 146 D3
Prospect Ct NN12 217 F6
Prospect Pl MK19 218 F5
Prospect Rd MK11 229 C5
Prospect Way NN11 134 F3
Provence Ct NN5 139 F1
Pudding Bag La NN29 164 D3
Puddledock NN12 214 D5
Pumping Station Cott LE16 21 A7
Pump Pl MK19 229 B7
Purbeck Rd NN10 131 D2
Purse La MK16 207 F8
Purser Rd NN1 159 F8
Purvis Rd NN10 132 A2
PURY END 215 F8
Pury Hill Bsns Pk NN12 204 E1
Pury Rd NN12 205 A3
PUXLEY 228 D7
Puxley Rd MK19 228 D5
Pye Ct CV23 117 D4
Pyghtles The
Daventry NN11 135 B1
Pyghtles The *continued*
Wollaston NN29 146 D1
Pyghtle The
Earls Barton NN6 144 E5
Olney MK46 195 F3
Wellingborough NN8 129 F6
Pyghtle Way NN4 175 A7
Pyket Way NN3 160 E8
Pyke Way NN6 101 A6
Pym Cl NN8 130 B6
Pyramid Cl NN3 142 E2
PYTCHLEY 90 F2
Pytchley Cl NN6 106 B2
Pytchley Ct
Corby NN17 36 B8
West Haddon NN6 102 C4
Pytchley Dr NN6 121 B4
Pytchley Endowed CE Prim Sch NN14 90 F2
Pytchley La NN15 91 C5
Pytchley Lodge Ind Est NN15 91 C6
Pytchley Lodge Rd NN15 91 C5
Pytchley Rd
Kettering NN15 91 C6
Orlingbury NN14 109 F5
Rugby CV22 98 C8
Rushden NN10 131 F3
Pytchley Rise NN8 129 D3
Pytchley St NN1 159 E6
Pytchley View NN3 126 D1
Pytchley Way
Brixworth NN6 106 B2
Northampton NN5 140 B2
Pywell Ct NN17 22 E2
Pywell Rd NN17 22 E2

Q

Quakers Cl NN7 172 F7
Quantock Cl
Daventry NN11 135 B5
Kettering NN15 92 A5
Quantock Cres NN5 158 D8
Quarry Green Cl MK19 228 B3
Quarry Park Cl NN3 142 B6
Quarry Rd
Brixworth NN6 106 C3
Northampton NN5 140 B2
Quartercroft NN3 142 E2
Quarterstone NN4 158 D1
Quebec Cl
Corby NN18 36 C2
5 Northampton NN4 175 E7
Queen Eleanor Prim Sch
Northampton NN4 159 B2
Stony Stratford MK11 229 F4
Queen Eleanor Rd
Geddington NN14 54 A3
Northampton NN4 159 C2
Queen Eleanor St MK11 229 E6
Queen Eleanor Terr NN4 159 C2
Queensberry Rd NN15 72 B1
Queensbury Ct NN15 72 B1
Queens Cl LE16 34 C5
Queens Cres NN2 141 D2
Queensland Gdns NN2 141 D2
QUEEN'S PARK 141 C1
Queens Park Ind Est NN2 141 B1
Queen's Park Par NN2 141 C2
Queen's Pk NN7 155 A3
Queens Rd
Daventry NN11 135 B3
Wilbarston LE16 34 D5
Wollaston NN29 146 D2
Queen's Rd
Northampton NN1 159 E7
Towcester NN12 203 C6
Queen's Sq NN17 36 E5
Queens St
Culworth OX17 198 D2
Farthinghoe NN13 221 B4
Wellingborough NN8 130 A5
Queen St
Bozeat NN29 164 C2
Desborough NN14 51 B3
Earls Barton NN6 144 F5
Geddington NN14 54 A2
Irthlingborough NN9 112 E2
Kettering NN16 72 B2
Market Harborough LE16 32 A2
Middleton Cheney OX17 219 F8
Rushden NN10 132 B2
Stony Stratford MK11 229 E6
Thrapston NN14 76 E2
Weedon Bec NN7 155 A2
Queensway
Burton Latimer NN15 92 B1
Higham Ferrers NN10 132 C5
Wellingborough NN8 129 C4
Wellingborough NN8 129 D3
Queenswood Ave NN3 142 D5
Quernstone La NN4 158 E3
QUINBURY END 187 A1

QUINTON 176 B1
Quinton Green Cotts NN7 192 C7
Quinton House Sch NN5 158 B5
Quinton La NN11 184 C6
Quinton Rd NN4 175 F5
Quintonside NN4 175 F3
Quorn Cl
  Kettering NN15 92 A5
  Wellingborough NN8 129 D4
Quorn Rd NN10 132 A3
Quorn Way NN1 159 B7

R

Racecourse Rd PE9 2 D5
Racedown NN8 129 B3
Radleigh Cl NN4 159 A2
Radleigh Ct NN2 141 E1
Radnor Way NN15 92 A5
RADSTONE 222 F6
Radstone NN13 222 F6
Radstone Rd NN13 222 F2
Radstone Way NN2 141 C5
Raeburn Rd NN2 141 F2
Raeburn Sch NN2 141 F2
Raglan Cl NN10 132 D1
Raglan St NN1 159 E6
Ragsdale Ct NN14 70 E7
Ragsdale St NN14 70 E7
Ragsdale Wlk NN3 142 E6
Railport App NN6 100 B6
Railside La NN17 37 A6
Railway Cotts
  Church Brampton NN6 140 A7
  Kilsby CV23 100 A6
  Nether Heyford NN7 172 A8
Railway View NN16 72 A2
Raincliffe Cl OX17 237 C7
Rainsborough Cres NN4 158 F4
Rainsborough Gdns LE16 48 D8
Rainsbrook Ave CV22 98 E8
Rainsbrook Valley Rly* CV22 98 C6
Raisins Field Cl NN3 143 C3
Rakestone Cl 4 NN4 175 D6
Raleigh Cl
  Corby NN17 36 A8
  Rothwell NN14 70 E7
Raleigh Ct NN11 135 B5
Ramsay Cl NN9 114 C7
Randall Cl NN9 131 E8
Randall Ho NN1 159 F7
Randall Rd NN2 141 E1
Rands Way NN9 114 E5
Ranelagh Rd NN8 130 B4
Rankine Ho NN17 36 D8
Rannoch Cl NN15 91 E8
Rannoch Way NN17 21 C1
Ransome Rd NN4 159 D3
Rate's La PE8 13 F7
Rathbone Cl CV21 99 A8
Rathlin Cl NN17 36 C8
RAUNDS 114 C6
Raunds Park Inf Sch NN9 114 E6
Raunds Rd
  Chelveston NN9 133 C8
  Stanwick NN9 114 A4
Raven Dr NN15 92 A6
Ravensbank NN10 132 B4
Ravenscourt NN17 36 F8
Ravens Croft NN4 175 A7
RAVENSTHORPE 103 E1
Ravensthorpe Rd NN6 122 D5
RAVENSTONE 194 D2
Ravens Way NN3 161 C8
Rawley Cres NN5 140 A1
Rawlings Cl 2 NN11 135 D1
Rawlins Cl OX17 230 A5
Ray Cl PE8 41 F7
Raymond Cl NN29 146 E1
Raymond Rd NN5 159 A7
Raynsford Rd NN5 158 F8
Rea Cl NN4 175 C7
Rectory Cl
  Barby CV23 99 C1
  Crick NN6 100 F5
  Stanwick NN9 113 F4
  Swinford LE17 62 C4
Rectory Ct LE16 48 B6
RECTORY FARM 143 C4
Rectory Farm Ct PE8 28 D8
Rectory Farm Mews PE8 28 D8
Rectory Farm Prim Sch NN3 143 C5
Rectory Farm Rd NN3 143 D4
Rectory Gdns NN9 112 E2
Rectory Hill NN14 93 A7
Rectory La
  Barby CV23 99 C1
  Holcot NN6 126 E8
  Market Harborough LE16 32 A2
  Medbourne LE16 19 A7
  Middleton Cheney OX17 208 F1
Rectory La *continued*
  Milton Malsor NN7 174 E3
  Orlingbury NN14 110 A5
  Walgrave NN6 108 A4
  Woodford NN14 94 D6
  Yardley Hastings NN7 179 A7
Rectory Rd NN10 132 B2
Rectory Road Bsns Ctr NN10 132 B3
Rectory Way NN12 213 B8
Rectory Wlk NN15 91 F7
Redbourne Ct MK11 229 F5
Redbourn Pk NN4 160 B3
Redding Cl NN10 148 A7
Redgrave Cl NN15 90 F7
Redgrave Ct NN8 129 F8
Red Hill Cres NN29 146 D3
Redhill Way NN9 110 E1
Red House La NN6 108 E4
Redhouse Rd NN14 109 C4
Red House Rd NN3 142 B7
Red House Wharf NN7 155 C4
Redland Cl LE15 3 F5
Redland Dr NN2 141 A4
Redliech Cl LE16 32 B3
Red Lion St OX17 230 F5
Red Lodge Rd NN17 12 A1
Redmile's La PE9 1 A5
Redmoor NN12 203 B4
Red Row NN9 114 D6
Redruth Cl NN4 159 B1
Redwell Ct NN8 129 F6
Redwell Jun & Inf Sch NN8 129 E7
Redwell L Ctr NN8 129 E7
Redwell Rd NN8 129 F6
Redwing Ave NN3 142 C6
Redwood Cl NN29 147 A7
Red Wood Cl NN14 51 C2
Reedham Cl NN5 140 C1
Reedhill NN4 158 E1
Reedway NN3 142 A4
Reffield Cl NN12 203 D5
Regal Cl NN3 141 F6
Regal Ct NN10 132 C1
Regal Dr NN16 72 C6
Regency Cl NN7 155 B4
Regency Ct
  5 Daventry NN11 135 C2
  Finedon NN9 112 A5
  Rushden NN10 132 B3
Regent Cl NN15 92 A2
Regent Rd NN15 92 A2
Regents Hall MK11 229 D6
Regent St
  Desborough NN14 51 B3
  Finedon NN9 111 F4
  Kettering NN16 72 C3
  Northampton NN1 159 C6
  Wellingborough NN8 130 A5
Regent Way NN7 177 D1
Regiment Cl NN4 175 E7
Reigate Wlk NN18 36 B3
Reims Ct NN5 140 A2
Remus Gate NN13 234 A6
Rendelsham Cl NN16 72 A6
Rennishaw Way NN2 141 F3
Repton Ct NN3 142 D4
Reservoir Cl
  Irthlingborough NN9 131 E8
  Stanion NN14 37 E3
Reservoir Hos NN6 125 D5
Reservoir Rd NN16 72 B4
Resthaven Rd NN4 175 D6
Restormel Cl NN10 132 D1
Retford Ct NN3 142 F4
Retreat The
  Easton o t H PE9 1 F5
  Stony Stratford MK11 229 D5
Reynard Pk NN13 233 F5
Reynard Way NN2 141 D6
Reynolds Cl
  Kettering NN15 92 A8
  Rugby CV21 80 B1
  Wellingborough NN8 129 F7
Reynolds Rd NN18 36 E5
Reynoldston Cl NN4 160 C1
Rhodes Cl
  Daventry NN11 135 C5
  Market Harborough LE16 31 C2
Rhosili Rd NN4 160 A2
Rhymer Cl MK19 206 F4
Rhymer Ho NN2 141 D5
Ribble Cl
  Northampton NN5 140 F2
  Wellingborough NN8 129 D6
Ribblesdale Ave NN17 36 E7
Richard Cl NN15 91 C6
Richardsons La NN14 70 D2
Richardson Way NN9 114 E7
Richmond Ave NN15 91 F8
Richmond Cl NN10 132 C1
Richmond Ct NN12 203 C5
Richmond Rd
  Corby NN17 36 E6
  Towcester NN12 203 C6
Richmond St OX17 231 A5
Richmond Terr NN5 159 B6
Rickyard Rd NN3 142 E3
Rickyard Wlk NN4 175 F2
Ridding Cl NN18 36 D3
Rides Ct NN3 142 C7
Ridge Rd NN14 76 C4
Ridge The NN29 145 E7
Ridge View LE16 31 E5
Ridgeway
  Northampton NN3 160 D8
  Stony Stratford MK11 229 F4
  Wellingborough NN8 129 F7
Ridgeway Prim Sch LE16 31 F5
Ridgeway The
  Barby CV23 118 E8
  Kilsby CV23 100 A1
  Market Harborough LE16 31 F5
  Welton NN11 119 E1
Ridgeway W LE16 31 E5
Ridgmont MK19 228 E5
Ridgmont Cl MK19 228 E5
Ridgway Rd NN15 92 B8
Riding Ct NN13 233 F5
Riding Rd NN13 233 F5
Ridings The
  Brixworth NN6 106 C2
  Desborough NN14 50 E4
  Northampton, Grange Park NN4 175 E2
  Northampton NN1 159 D6
  Roade NN7 191 C4
Riding The MK19 228 D5
Ridley Ct 1 NN11 135 C2
Ridley St NN16 72 A4
Riggall Cl NN14 90 A3
Riley Cl
  Daventry NN11 134 F4
  Market Harborough LE16 31 B2
  Northampton NN3 143 C5
Riley Rd NN16 71 E4
Rillwood Ct NN3 142 E4
RINGSTEAD 95 B3
Ringstead CE Prim Sch NN14 95 B3
Ringstead Cl
  Corby NN17 36 B8
  Kettering NN15 91 F5
Ringstead Rd
  Denford NN14 95 C5
  Great Addington NN14 94 C2
Ringtail Cl NN9 131 E8
Ring The OX17 208 E4
Ring Way NN4 159 A3
Ringwell Cl NN9 112 E3
Ringwood Cl NN2 141 A5
Ripley Cl LE16 32 B3
Ripley Rd LE16 20 D1
Ripley Wlk NN18 36 C3
Ripon Cl NN4 159 A2
Risdene Ct 11 NN10 132 B2
Rise The
  Northampton NN2 141 B3
  Twyford OX17 230 A5
Ritchie Pk LE16 48 E8
Rivercrest Rd MK19 229 B6
River La PE8 28 C8
Riverside LE16 32 A4
Riverside Bsns Pk NN3 160 E7
Riverside Cl PE8 42 A4
Riverside Ct
  Kislingbury NN7 157 D4
  Market Harborough LE16 31 D2
  Weedon Bec NN7 155 B3
Riverside Dr NN7 155 B3
Riverside Ind Est LE16 32 A4
Riverside Maltings PE8 42 A6
Riverside Spinney PE8 8 A3
Riverside Way
  Islip NN14 76 B2
  Northampton NN1 159 F5
Riverside Way Ind Est NN1 159 F5
Riverstone Way NN4 158 D2
Riverview NN15 111 B8
Riverview Gdns NN14 95 C6
Riverwell NN3 143 D2
Rivetts Cl MK46 195 E4
Rixon Cl NN3 142 E1
Rixon Rd NN8 130 C7
RNIB Rushton Hall Sch NN14 52 B2
ROADE 191 E4
Roade Hill NN7 191 F1
Roade Prim Sch NN7 191 E4
Roade Sch Sports Coll NN7 191 C3
Roadins Cl NN15 91 A7
ROAD WEEDON 155 C4
Robbins Ct CV22 98 F8
Robb's La NN14 75 F6
Roberson Cl NN12 203 C4
Robert Hill Cl CV21 80 A1
Roberts Cl MK19 228 E4
Roberts Field NN7 156 B1
Robert's La PE8 42 F2
Robert Smyth Sch The LE16 31 E5
Robertson Cl CV23 80 A5
Roberts St
  Bozeat NN29 164 C2
  Rushden NN10 132 C2
  Wellingborough NN8 129 E4
Robert St NN1 159 D7
Robin Cl
  Kettering NN15 92 A6
  Towcester NN12 203 C3
Robinia Cl NN4 158 E3
Robin La NN8 130 A7
Robin Ride NN13 222 E1
Robins Cl NN7 192 C1
Robins Field PE8 8 A4
Robinson Cl NN16 71 F4
Robinson Dr NN13 233 D7
Robinson Ho NN3 142 E4
Robinson Rd NN10 132 C2
Robinson Way
  Kettering NN16 71 F4
  Northampton NN4 176 A6
Robinswood PE8 8 A4
Roche Cl NN11 153 C8
Rochelle Way NN5 140 A2
Rochester Cl NN15 91 F7
Rochester Gdns LE16 31 D1
Rochester Rd NN18 36 E2
Rochester Way OX17 230 B5
Roche Way NN8 129 F6
Rockcroft 3 NN4 175 D6
Rock Hill NN14 70 D7
Rockhill Rd NN6 121 A3
ROCKINGHAM 21 B4
Rockingham Castle & Gdns* LE16 21 B3
Rockingham Cl
  1 Daventry NN11 135 B4
  Thrapston NN14 76 E2
Rockingham Ct NN10 148 A8
Rockingham Hills PE8 41 E7
Rockingham Ind Est LE16 32 B3
Rockingham Mews NN17 37 A7
Rockingham Motor Speedway* NN17 22 E4
Rockingham Paddocks NN16 72 B6
Rockingham Prim Sch NN17 37 A8
Rockingham Rd
  Caldecott LE16 21 B6
  Corby, Great Oakley NN14 53 A3
  Corby NN17 21 E2
  Cottingham LE16 20 E2
  Gretton LE16, NN17 21 E7
  Kettering NN16 72 A5
  Market Harborough LE16 32 B4
  Northampton NN4 159 C2
Rockleigh Cl NN9 112 A5
Rock Rd
  Finedon NN9 112 A5
  Oundle PE8 41 F6
Rock St NN8 129 F5
Roderick Ct 9 NN11 135 B4
Roderick Way 7 NN11 135 B4
Rodewell Ho NN14 70 D7
Rodney Cl NN11 135 E1
Rodney Dr NN17 36 B8
Roe Rd NN1 160 A8
Rokeby Inf Sch CV22 98 A8
Rokeby Jun Sch CV22 98 A8
Rokeby Wlk NN5 140 D1
Roland Way NN10 132 B6
Rolfe Cres NN7 156 B1
Rolleston Cl LE16 32 A3
Roman Cl
  Northampton NN4 175 F5
  Weldon NN17 38 B8
Roman Dr PE8 8 D2
Roman Way
  Brackley NN13 234 A7
  Daventry NN11 135 C5
  Desborough NN14 51 B2
  Higham Ferrers NN10 132 B7
  Irchester NN29 147 B7
  Market Harborough LE16 31 E4
  Northampton NN4 175 E4
  Raunds NN9 114 E6
  Thrapston NN14 76 E3
Romany Rd NN2 141 E2
Romney Rd NN18 36 E5
Romulus Cl NN4 175 F5
Romulus Way NN13 234 A6
Rookery Farm* NN12 191 B1
Rookery La
  Northampton NN2 141 A5
  Stoke Bruerne NN12 191 B1
Rookery The NN4 175 E3
Rookwell Dr LE16 31 F1
Roper Cl CV21 99 A8
Rose Ave
  Rushden NN10 131 F1
  Weldon NN17 38 B8
Rosebay Rd NN14 51 A5
Rosebery Ave NN5 158 F6
Rosebery St
  Burton Latimer NN15 92 B1
  Kettering NN16 72 C2
  Ringstead NN14 95 B3
Rose Cl
  Broughton NN14 90 B5
  Corby NN18 36 E2
  Hartwell NN7 192 E2
  Rothwell NN14 70 E6
Rose Cotts NN14 113 B7
Rose Ct
  Irchester NN29 147 B8
  Olney MK46 195 F3
  Weldon NN17 38 B8
Rose Dale LE17 45 A4
Rosedale Ave NN17 36 E6
Rosedale Rd NN2 141 D3
Rose Dr NN13 233 D8
Rose Hall La OX17 220 A8
Rose Hill NN9 112 A5
Rose Hill Way NN14 89 C5
Roseholme Rd NN1 160 A8
Rose La MK19 206 E6
Rosemoor Cl LE16 32 B3
Rosemoor Dr NN4 175 C7
Rosemount Dr NN15 91 C7
Rosenella Cl 3 NN4 158 F3
Rose Paddock NN14 94 D7
Roses Cl NN29 146 C3
Rose Terr NN14 94 D7
Rosette Cl NN5 158 C8
Rosewood Ave CV22 98 A8
Rosewood Cl NN11 135 C5
Rosewood Ct NN8 130 C3
Rosewood Pl NN16 72 C4
Rosgill Pl NN3 142 B2
Rossendale Dr NN15 92 A5
Rossetti Rd NN18 36 E5
Rossiter Ho NN13 233 E6
Ross Rd NN5 158 E6
Rotherhithe Cl 9 NN4 158 F2
ROTHERSTHORPE 174 A7
Rothersthorpe Ave NN4 159 A3
Rothersthorpe CE Prim Sch NN7 174 A6
Rothersthorpe Cres NN4 159 A3
Rothersthorpe Rd
  Kislingbury NN7 157 E2
  Northampton NN4 159 A3
Rothesay Rd NN2 141 F2
Rothesay Terr NN2 141 F2
ROTHWELL 70 D8
Rothwell Grange Cotts NN16 71 B5
Rothwell Grange Ct NN16 71 B5
Rothwell Jun Sch NN14 70 D7
Rothwell Rd
  Desborough NN14 51 A2
  Harrington NN6 69 B5
  Kettering NN16 71 D4
  Kettering NN16 71 F3
Rothwell Victoria Inf Sch NN14 70 D7
Rotten Row NN29 146 D2
Rotton Row NN9 114 D7
Roughton Cl NN15 91 B6
Round Cl NN11 119 E1
Roundel The NN6 143 B6
Roundhill Cl LE16 32 B2
Roundhill Rd NN15 91 C8
ROUND SPINNEY 142 E7
Round The NN14 89 B4
Roundtown OX17 237 C7
Roundway The NN11 135 D6
Roundwood Way NN5 157 F8
Roveley Ct MK11 229 F5
Rowallen Way 2 NN11 135 A4
Rowan Ave
  Market Harborough LE16 31 E1
  Mawsley Village NN14 89 B4
  Northampton NN3 142 C5
Rowan Cl
  Brackley NN13 222 F1
  Northampton NN4 175 E2
  Towcester NN12 203 B4
  Wellingborough NN8 129 E5
Rowan Ct NN17 21 E1
Rowan Gate Prim Sch NN8 130 B6
Rowans The NN11 135 C4
Rowan Way NN11 184 B6
Rowe Cl CV21 99 C8
Rowell Way PE8 42 B4
Rowlandson Cl NN3 142 E1
Rowlett Cl NN10 132 C5
Rowlett Com Prim Sch NN17 37 B6
Rowlett Rd NN17 36 D8
Rowley Way NN2 141 E6
Rowtree Rd NN4 175 B6
Roxton Cl NN15 92 A5
Royal Cl NN11 135 B3
Royal Gdns NN14 50 F2
Royal Oak Ind Est NN11 134 F3
Royal Oak La OX17 220 A8
Royal Oak Way N NN11 134 F3
Royal Oak Way S NN11 134 F2
Royal Star Dr NN11 135 A4
Royal Terr NN1 159 C7
Royce Cl NN17 21 F1
Rubens Wlk NN18 36 E5
Rubicon Ho NN1 159 C7
Ruddington Cl NN3 160 E7
Rudge Mews NN5 157 F8
Rudgeway NN13 233 F2
Rufford Ave NN3 160 E7
Rufford Cl NN15 92 A5
Rufford Wlk NN18 36 C6
RUGBY 99 A7
Rugby Cl LE16 31 D2
Rugby Rd
  Barby CV23 99 C1
  Kilsby CV21, CV23 99 E5
  Lilbourne CV23 80 F6
  South Kilworth LE17 62 E6
  Swinford LE17 62 B3
Ruins The NN12 203 C6
Runnell La PE8 15 F5
Runneymede Gdns 5 NN3 142 F1
Rupert Rd LE16 31 E1
Rush Cl NN7 192 E2

RUSHDEN ... 132 E2
Rushden Com Coll The
NN10 ... 132 A4
Rushden Hospl NN10 ... 148 B8
Rushden Rd
Newton Bromswold
NN10 ... 149 C7
Wymington NN10 ... 148 A6
Rushden Station Transport Mus*
NN10 ... 132 B3
Rushes La LE16 ... 30 F3
Rushes The NN15 ... 111 B8
Rushmere Ave NN1 ... 160 B6
Rushmere Cl
Islip NN14 ... 76 B3
Raunds NN9 ... 114 C5
Rushmere Cres NN1 ... 160 B6
Rushmere Rd NN1 ... 160 B5
Rushmere Way
Northampton NN1 ... 160 B6
Rushden NN10 ... 132 B4
Rushmills NN4 ... 160 B3
RUSHTON ... 52 C2
Rushton Prim Sch
NN14 ... 52 C2
Rushton Rd
Desborough NN14 ... 51 C3
Rothwell NN14 ... 70 E8
Wilbarston LE16 ... 34 C4
Rushton Triangular Lo*
NN14 ... 52 A2
Rushwell Cl NN14 ... 94 B3
Rushy End NN4 ... 175 B6
Ruskin Ave NN8 ... 129 C4
Ruskin Jun & Inf Sch
NN8 ... 129 C3
Ruskin Rd
Daventry NN11 ... 153 C8
Northampton NN2 ... 141 C4
Russell Ct NN10 ... 132 B2
Russell Hill PE8 ... 8 A6
Russell Rise NN7 ... 155 E5
Russell Sq NN3 ... 142 C6
Russell St
Kettering NN16 ... 72 C2
Stony Stratford MK11 ... 229 D5
Russell Street Sch
MK11 ... 229 D5
Russell Way NN10 ... 132 B6
Russet Dr NN3 ... 143 A2
Russett Cl LE16 ... 31 F5
Rutherford Ct NN17 ... 22 B1
Rutherford Dr NN8 ... 129 A5
Rutherford Way NN11 ... 134 F4
Rutherglen Rd NN17 ... 36 F7
Ruth Gdns NN16 ... 72 E3
Rutland Cl NN17 ... 36 B7
Rutland Ct NN14 ... 50 F4
Rutland St NN16 ... 72 C3
Rutland Wlk
Market Harborough
LE16 ... 31 F5
Northampton NN3 ... 142 B7
Rycroft Cl NN8 ... 129 D5
Rydal NN8 ... 129 B3
Rydal Mount NN3 ... 142 C3
Rydalside
Kettering NN15 ... 72 D1
Northampton NN4 ... 158 F3
Ryder Ct NN18 ... 52 F8
Ryder View NN8 ... 129 C7
Ryeburn Way NN8 ... 129 E5
Ryebury Hill NN8 ... 111 E2
Rye Cl
Burton Latimer NN15 ... 92 C2
Rushden NN10 ... 148 C8
Ryefields NN6 ... 124 B8
Ryehill Cl
Irthlingborough NN9 ... 131 E8
Isham NN14 ... 91 E1
Long Buckby NN6 ... 121 A3
Northampton NN5 ... 140 C2
Ryehill Ct NN5 ... 140 C2
Ryehill Rd NN3 ... 142 F3
Ryeland MK11 ... 229 E6
Ryeland Rd NN5 ... 158 A8
Ryeland Way NN5 ... 140 A1
Ryland Rd
Moulton NN3 ... 142 C8
Northampton NN2 ... 141 E2
Rylands Cl LE16 ... 32 B3
Ryle Dr NN8 ... 129 A4
Rylstone The NN8 ... 129 B4
Ryngwell Cl NN6 ... 106 B1

S

Sackville St
Kettering NN16 ... 72 A4
Raunds NN9 ... 114 D6
Thrapston NN14 ... 76 D2
Sacrewell Farm & Ctry Ctr* PE8 ... 8 B5
Saddleback Rd NN5 ... 158 D6
Saddlers Sq NN3 ... 142 F6
Saddlers The NN4 ... 175 F3
Saddlers Way NN9 ... 114 B5
Saffron Cl NN4 ... 175 D5
Saffron Rd NN10 ... 132 B6
Sage Cl NN3 ... 142 E4
Saimon Cl NN13 ... 233 E8
St Alban's Cl
Kettering NN15 ... 73 A1
Northampton NN3 ... 142 B3
St Albans Pl NN29 ... 146 D2
St Alban's Rd NN3 ... 142 B3
St Amandas Cl NN15 ... 72 F2
St Andrews CE Prim Sch
NN3 ... 143 C2
St Andrew's CE Prim Sch
NN16 ... 72 A4
St Andrews Cl
Broughton NN14 ... 90 B4
Great Easton LE16 ... 20 D7
St Andrew's Cl NN14 ... 77 D3
St Andrews Cres
Rugby CV22 ... 98 A8
Wellingborough NN8 ... 129 E2
St Andrews Ct NN1 ... 159 C6
St Andrew's Ct NN14 ... 90 B4
St Andrews Dr NN11 ... 135 E3
St Andrew's Ho 9
NN1 ... 159 F6
St Andrew's Hospl
NN1 ... 159 F6
St Andrews La NN14 ... 77 D4
St Andrew's La NN14 ... 93 A7
St Andrew's Rd
East Haddon NN6 ... 122 D5
Northampton NN2 ... 159 B7
St Andrew's St
Kettering NN16 ... 72 B3
Northampton NN1 ... 159 C6
St Andrews Way NN14 ... 90 B4
St Andrew's Wlk NN17 ... 37 B6
St Annes Cl
Brackley NN13 ... 233 D8
Daventry NN11 ... 153 C8
St Anne's Rd NN15 ... 73 A1
St Ann's Ct PE8 ... 41 F5
St Anthonys Cl NN11 ... 153 B8
St Anthony's Hill NN14 ... 51 A2
St Anthony's Rd NN15 ... 72 F1
St Augustine's Cl NN15 ... 73 A1
St Augustin Way
NN11 ... 135 D1
St Barnabas CE Sch
NN8 ... 129 F4
St Barnabas Cl NN15 ... 73 A1
St Barnabas Ho 10
NN1 ... 159 C6
St Barnabas St NN8 ... 129 F4
St Bartholemews Ho 5
NN1 ... 159 C6
St Bartholomew's Cl
NN15 ... 73 A1
St Benedicts Mount
NN4 ... 158 E2
St Bernards Ct NN15 ... 72 F1
St Botolphs Gn PE8 ... 28 E7
St Botolph's Rd NN15 ... 91 F7
St Brendan's RC Inf Sch
NN18 ... 36 B6
St Catharine's Rd
NN15 ... 73 A1
St Catherines Cl
NN11 ... 153 B8
St Cecilia's Cl NN15 ... 72 F1
St Chad's Cl NN15 ... 73 A1
St Christopher's Cl
NN15 ... 73 A1
St Christopher's Dr
PE8 ... 42 B4
St Christopher's Wlk
NN3 ... 160 B7
St Clements Ct NN15 ... 91 B7
St Crispin Ave NN8 ... 129 F2
St Crispin Cl NN15 ... 92 C3
St Crispin Cres NN5 ... 157 F8
St Crispin Dr NN5 ... 158 A7
St Crispin Rd NN6 ... 144 F4
St Davids Cl NN6 ... 106 B1
St David's Cl NN15 ... 72 F1
St David's Ct NN13 ... 234 A8
St Davids RC Mid Sch
NN2 ... 141 C3
St David's Rd
Brixworth NN6 ... 106 A1
Northampton NN2 ... 141 C2
Rushden NN10 ... 131 D3
St Dunstan's Cl NN15 ... 91 F8
St Dunstans Rise NN4 ... 158 E1
St Edmunds Cl NN11 ... 153 C7
St Edmund's Hospl
NN1 ... 159 E7
St Edmund's Rd NN1 ... 159 E6
St Edmund's St NN1 ... 159 E6
St Edward's RC Prim Sch
NN15 ... 91 E7
St Emilion Cl NN5 ... 139 F1
St Francis Ave NN5 ... 159 A8
St Francis' Cl NN15 ... 73 A1
St Georges Ave CV22 ... 98 A8
St George's Ave NN2 ... 159 D8
St Georges Cl NN12 ... 203 C5
St Georges Ho 2
NN1 ... 159 C6
St George's Pl NN2 ... 159 C8
St George's St NN1 ... 159 C7
St George's Way
NN10 ... 131 F3
St Giles' Cl NN15 ... 73 A1
St Giles Mews MK11 ... 229 D6
St Giles's Cl NN14 ... 51 A3
St Giles' Sq NN1 ... 159 D5
St Giles' St NN1 ... 159 D6
St Giles' Terr NN1 ... 159 D6
St Gregory's RC Prim Sch
NN3 ... 142 D3
St Gregory's Rd NN3 ... 142 D3
St Helens Cl NN6 ... 84 D4
St Hilda's Cl NN11 ... 153 C8
St Hughes Cl NN11 ... 153 C8
St James' CE Prim Sch
NN5 ... 159 A7
St James Cl
2 Daventry NN11 ... 135 C1
Hanslope MK19 ... 207 A2
St James' Cl
Kettering NN15 ... 92 A8
Rushden NN10 ... 132 C4
St James' Cres NN14 ... 76 E2
ST JAMES' END ... 159 A5
St James Inf Sch
NN11 ... 135 C1
St James' Lake Nature Reserve* NN13 ... 233 E6
St James' Mill Rd
NN5 ... 159 A4
St James Mill Rd E
NN1 ... 159 B4
St James' Park Rd
NN5 ... 159 A6
St James Rd
Brackley NN13 ... 233 F5
Corby NN18 ... 37 A6
St James' Rd NN5 ... 159 A5
St James Ret Pk NN1 ... 159 B5
St James St NN11 ... 135 C1
St Johns Ave CV22 ... 98 E8
St John's Ave NN2 ... 141 C6
St Johns Cl
Daventry NN11 ... 153 B8
Rothersthorpe NN7 ... 174 A6
St Johns Ct NN1 ... 159 D5
St John's Ho
8 Northampton NN1 ... 159 C6
3 Wellingborough
NN8 ... 129 F5
St John's La MK19 ... 228 B4
St John's Pl NN17 ... 37 B6
St Johns Rd NN12 ... 189 E4
St John's Rd NN15 ... 91 F8
St John's Sq NN11 ... 135 C2
St John's St
Northampton NN1 ... 159 D5
Wellingborough NN8 ... 129 F5
St John's Terr NN1 ... 159 D5
St John's Way NN7 ... 177 A2
St John's Wlk NN3 ... 142 D1
St Josephs Cl MK46 ... 195 F4
St Joseph's Cl NN15 ... 73 A1
St Joseph's RC Prim Sch
LE16 ... 31 E3
St Julien Cl NN5 ... 140 A2
St Katharine's Way
NN29 ... 131 B1
St Katherine's Ct 25
NN1 ... 159 C6
St Katherine's Sq 27
NN1 ... 159 C6
St Katherine's St 2
NN1 ... 159 C5
St Laurence Way NN9 ... 113 F4
St Lawrence CE Jun Sch
NN12 ... 203 C5
St Lawrence CE Lower Sch
NN10 ... 148 A5
St Lawrence Ct 12
NN1 ... 159 E6
St Lawrence Ho 3
NN1 ... 159 C6
St Lawrence Rd NN12 ... 203 C5
St Lawrence Rd S
NN12 ... 203 C4
St Lawrence Wlk
NN10 ... 148 B5
St Leonards Cl CV47 ... 166 D8
St Leonard's Cl NN15 ... 72 F1
St Leonards Ct NN4 ... 159 C3
St Leonard's Rd NN4 ... 159 C3
St Loys CE Prim Sch
NN12 ... 200 B2
St Luke's CE Prim Sch
NN5 ... 158 C6
St Lukes Cl
Northampton NN5 ... 157 F8
Spratton NN6 ... 105 B1
St Luke's Cl NN15 ... 92 A8
St Luke's Ho 12 NN1 ... 159 C6
St Luke's Hospl LE16 ... 31 D5
St Luke's Rd NN18 ... 37 A5
St Magdalenes Rd
NN15 ... 72 F2
St Margarets Ave
NN10 ... 132 A1
St Margaret's Gdns 3
NN5 ... 140 F1
St Mark's Cl
Kettering NN15 ... 73 A1
Rushden NN10 ... 131 E2
St Mark's Cres NN2 ... 141 B6
St Marks Ho 7 NN1 ... 159 C6
St Mark's Rd NN18 ... 37 A5
St Martins Cl NN2 ... 141 C4
St Martins Ho 1 NN1 ... 159 C6
St Martins Yd 3 LE16 ... 31 E3
St Martyn's Way NN7 ... 155 B3
St Mary & St Giles CE Jun Sch MK11 ... 229 E6
St Mary's Ave
Finedon NN9 ... 111 F5
Rushden NN10 ... 132 B1
Stony Stratford MK11 ... 229 E6
St Mary's CE Prim Sch
Burton Latimer NN15 ... 92 C2
Kettering NN16 ... 72 C2
St Marys Cl
Thrapston NN14 ... 76 F3
Woodnewton PE8 ... 14 E2
St Mary's Cl
Nassington PE8 ... 15 E5
Priors Hardwick CV47 ... 166 A5
St Marys Ct NN7 ... 173 F2
St Mary's Ct
Finedon NN9 ... 111 E5
Market Harborough
LE16 ... 32 A4
22 Northampton NN1 ... 159 C6
St Marys Hill PE8 ... 14 E2
St Mary's Hospl NN15 ... 72 C1
St Mary's Paddock
NN8 ... 130 C4
St Mary's Pl LE16 ... 31 F3
St Mary's RC Prim Sch
Aston le W NN11 ... 182 F2
Northampton NN5 ... 140 F1
St Marys Rd NN29 ... 146 E2
St Mary's Rd
Bozeat NN29 ... 164 D2
Kettering NN15 ... 72 C1
Market Harborough LE16 ... 31 F3
St Mary's St NN1 ... 159 C6
St Mary's Way
Nassington PE8 ... 15 E5
Roade NN7 ... 191 D5
Weedon Bec NN7 ... 155 B3
St Matthew's Par NN2 ... 141 F1
St Matthew's Rd NN15 ... 73 A1
St Matthew's Sch
NN3 ... 142 A1
St Michael's Ave NN1 ... 159 E7
St Michael's Ct NN7 ... 205 F8
St Michaels Gdns
NN15 ... 91 C8
St Michael's La NN29 ... 146 D2
St Michael's Mount
NN1 ... 159 E7
St Michael's Rd
Kettering NN15 ... 91 C8
Northampton NN1 ... 159 D6
St Nicholas Cl
Kettering NN15 ... 72 F2
Market Harborough LE16 ... 31 F2
St Nicholas Ct NN29 ... 145 E6
St Nicholas Rd NN29 ... 145 D6
St Nicholas Way
Islip NN14 ... 76 B3
Market Harborough LE16 ... 31 F2
St Oswald's Cl NN15 ... 91 F8
St Osyths La PE8 ... 42 A5
St Patrick's RC Prim Sch
NN18 ... 36 D4
St Patrick St 11 NN1 ... 159 C7
St Paul's Ct
Kettering NN15 ... 72 B1
Stony Stratford MK11 ... 229 D6
St Pauls Gdns NN14 ... 76 D2
St Paul's Rd NN2 ... 159 C8
St Paul's Terr NN2 ... 159 C8
St Peter's Ave
Kettering NN16 ... 72 C1
Kettering NN16 ... 72 C2
Rushden NN10 ... 131 F3
St Peter's CE Jun Sch
NN9 ... 114 E6
St Peters Cl NN11 ... 153 B8
St Peter's Cl NN14 ... 37 F2
St Peters Ct NN9 ... 114 D6
St Peter's Gate NN13 ... 234 A7
St Peter's Gdns NN3 ... 142 D1
St Peter's Ho 20 NN1 ... 159 C6
St Peter's Ind Sch
NN3 ... 143 A3
St Peter's Mews 12
NN16 ... 72 C2
St Peters Rd PE8 ... 41 F7
St Peter's Rd NN13 ... 233 F8
St Peter's Sch NN15 ... 91 B8
St Peters Sq 12 NN1 ... 159 C5
St Peter's St NN1 ... 159 B5
St Peters's Way NN9 ... 112 F2
St Peters Way NN7 ... 161 F6
St Peter's Way
Corby NN17 ... 37 A6
Northampton NN1 ... 159 C5
Weedon Bec NN7 ... 155 B3
St Peters Wlk 5 NN1 ... 159 C5
St Philip's Cl NN15 ... 73 A1
St Rochus Dr NN8 ... 130 A1
St Rumbolds Dr OX17 ... 231 A5
St Saviour's Rd NN15 ... 73 A1
St Simon's Cl NN15 ... 73 A1
St Stephens Ho 9
NN1 ... 159 C6
St Stephen's Rd NN15 ... 73 A1
St Swithins Cl NN15 ... 72 F2
St Theresa's Cl NN15 ... 72 F1
St Thomas Ho NN1 ... 159 D6
St Thomas More RC Prim Sch NN16 ... 71 F1
St Thomas Rd NN7 ... 161 D3
St Valentine's Cl NN15 ... 72 F1
St Vincents Ave NN15 ... 72 F2
St Wilfrids Rd PE8 ... 41 F7
Salcey Ave NN7 ... 192 D2
Salcey Cl
2 Daventry NN11 ... 135 B4
Hartwell NN7 ... 192 E2
Kettering NN15 ... 92 A5
Salcey Forest Trail*
NN7 ... 192 F4
Salcey Forest Trail (Rose Copse)* NN7 ... 193 B2
SALCEY GREEN ... 207 B7
Salcey Rise NN7 ... 177 B1
Salcey St NN4 ... 159 C2
Salcombe Rd NN18 ... 36 E4
Salem Cl NN6 ... 121 A3
Salem La 9 NN8 ... 130 A5
Salen Cl NN15 ... 92 B5
Salford Cl NN6 ... 64 E6
Salisbury Rd NN8 ... 130 C5
Salisbury St
Kettering NN16 ... 72 C4
Northampton NN2 ... 159 C8
Salisbury Wlk NN18 ... 36 E1
Sallow Ave NN3 ... 143 C3
Sallow Rd NN17 ... 22 E1
Salmons La OX17 ... 220 B8
Salthouse Rd NN4 ... 160 C2
Salt Pikes NN6 ... 125 B8
Saltwell Sq 5 NN3 ... 143 C2
Samuel Pl NN17 ... 37 A8
Samuels Cl NN9 ... 113 F3
Samwell Way NN4 ... 158 C1
Sandby Rd NN18 ... 36 E4
Sanders Cl
Braunston NN11 ... 118 B1
Wellingborough NN8 ... 111 B1
Sanders La NN12 ... 217 D3
Sanders Lodge Ind Est
NN10 ... 131 D3
Sanderson Cl NN15 ... 91 A8
Sanders Rd NN8 ... 111 B1
Sanders Terr NN6 ... 121 B4
Sandfield Cl NN3 ... 142 B6
Sandhill Rd 2 NN5 ... 159 A6
Sandhills NN6 ... 105 A1
Sandhills Cl NN2 ... 141 B6
Sandhills Rd NN2 ... 141 B6
Sandhurst Cl NN4 ... 175 B8
Sandiland Rd NN3 ... 142 B2
Sandlands Ave NN14 ... 55 F7
Sandlands Cl NN14 ... 55 F7
Sandover NN4 ... 175 D6
Sandown Cl NN18 ... 36 E1
Sandpiper Cl NN15 ... 92 A2
Sandpiper La NN8 ... 130 A7
Sandringham Cl
Brackley NN13 ... 233 E7
Northampton NN1 ... 160 B7
Rushden NN10 ... 132 A1
Towcester NN12 ... 203 C4
Wellingborough NN8 ... 129 E2
Sandringham Ct NN15 ... 91 D5
Sandringham Rd
Kings Sutton OX17 ... 230 F5
Northampton NN1 ... 160 A7
Sandringham Way
LE16 ... 32 B3
Sandringham Wlk
NN18 ... 36 E2
Sands Cl NN12 ... 172 D1
Sandy Cl NN8 ... 129 F6
Sandy Hill La NN3 ... 126 E2
Sandyhome Rd NN12 ... 203 C5
Sandy La
Church Brampton
NN6 ... 140 D8
Harpole NN7 ... 157 E7
Northampton NN5 ... 139 F2
Saneco La NN6 ... 106 B3
Sansom Ct NN3 ... 142 D4
Sansome Cl NN7 ... 177 B3
Saplings The NN16 ... 72 C6
Sapphire Cl NN15 ... 72 C1
Sarek Pk NN4 ... 174 F7
Sargeants La NN4 ... 175 C4
Sargent Rd NN18 ... 36 E4
Sarjeant Ct NN14 ... 70 D7
Sarrington Rd NN17 ... 36 F8
Sartoris Rd NN10 ... 131 F2
Saruman La NN3 ... 143 B6
Sassoon Cl NN8 ... 129 C6
Sassoon Mews NN8 ... 129 B6
Saunders Cl NN16 ... 72 B1
Savill Cl NN4 ... 175 C7
Sawyers Cres NN9 ... 133 B8
Saxby Cres NN8 ... 130 C4
Saxilby Cl NN18 ... 36 C4
Saxon Acre NN13 ... 233 F7
Saxon Ave NN4 ... 175 E3
Saxon Cl
Desborough NN14 ... 51 A3
Higham Ferrers NN10 ... 132 B7
Market Harborough LE16 ... 31 F4
Saxon Dale NN16 ... 72 C6
Saxon Ho NN6 ... 106 B2
Saxon Hts NN6 ... 125 B8
Saxonlea Cl NN10 ... 131 E3
Saxon Rise
Earls Barton NN6 ... 144 E3
Irchester NN29 ... 147 C8
Northampton NN5 ... 158 B7
Saxon St NN3 ... 142 B1
Saxon Way NN9 ... 114 E6
Saxon Way E NN18 ... 53 A8
Saxon Way W NN18 ... 52 F8
Sayers Cl NN12 ... 214 D3
SCALDWELL ... 106 F6
Scaldwell Rd
Brixworth NN6 ... 106 D4
Old NN6 ... 107 C7
Scapa Rd NN17 ... 36 C8
Scarborough St NN9 ... 112 E2
Scarborough Wlk
NN18 ... 36 B4
Scarletwell St NN1 ... 159 B6
Scarplands The NN5 ... 158 C6
Scharpwell NN9 ... 112 E3
Scholars Ct NN1 ... 159 D5
Scholars Row NN14 ... 89 B4

School Cl
Braunston NN11 118 D1
Greens Norton NN12 202 D8
Yelvertoft NN6 82 A4
School End OX17 237 C7
School Farm Yd LE16 18 B3
School Gdns CV21 80 A1
School Hill
Irchester NN29 147 B8
Middleton LE16 35 C8
Newnham NN11 153 D4
School La
Abthorpe NN12 202 A2
Adstone NN12 186 B3
Badby NN11 152 F3
Barrowden LE15 3 F5
Braybrooke LE16 49 F5
Bythorn PE28 97 D4
Castlethorpe MK19 218 F5
Cottingham LE16 20 C1
Denford NN14 95 C6
Elton PE8 28 D8
Evenley NN13 233 F2
Everdon NN11 170 A8
Eydon NN11 184 C1
Greens Norton NN12 202 D8
Hannington NN6 108 C2
Harpole NN7 157 B6
Hartwell NN7 192 D2
Higham Ferrers NN10 132 B7
Husbands Bosworth LE17 45 E5
Irchester NN29 147 A8
Islip NN14 76 B2
Kettering NN16 72 B2
Kislingbury NN7 157 D4
Little Harrowden NN9 110 C4
Lubenham LE16 30 F3
Market Harborough LE16 31 E3
Morcott LE15 3 A6
Moulton NN3 126 C1
Naseby NN6 85 B8
Northampton NN4 175 E3
Priors Marston CV47 166 D8
Quinton NN7 176 B1
Rothwell NN14 70 D7
Scaldwell NN6 106 F6
Swinford LE17 62 B4
Titchmarsh NN14 77 C4
Wappenham NN12 213 B8
Warmington PE8 28 B3
Weldon NN17 38 B8
Wilbarston LE16 34 C5
Yardley Gobion NN12 217 E6
Yelvertoft NN6 82 B4
School Pl NN18 36 D5
School Rd
Gretton NN17 10 B1
Irchester NN29 147 A8
Mawsley Village NN14 89 B4
Pattishall NN12 188 F8
Spratton NN6 105 B1
School St
Daventry NN11 135 A2
Rugby CV21 80 A1
Sulgrave OX17 210 F7
Woodford Halse NN11 184 C6
School Wlk NN8 130 A1
Scirocco Cl NN3 141 E6
Scoborough Rd LE16, LE17 30 A1
Scotgate Dr NN17 10 F7
Scotia Cl NN4 160 C2
Scotland End LE16 31 F1
Scotland Rd LE16 32 A2
Scotland St NN16 72 C3
Scotney Cl 1 NN4 175 C8
Scotney Way NN14 76 E2
Scots Mere NN9 112 D3
Scott Ave NN14 70 E7
Scott Cl
Daventry NN11 135 C4
Market Harborough LE16 31 E5
Ravensthorpe NN6 103 D1
Scotter Wlk NN18 36 C4
Scott Rd
Corby NN17 37 A6
Kettering NN16 72 C5
Wellingborough NN8 129 C3
Scotts La LE16 34 C5
Scriveners La NN12 216 A8
Scrivens Hill NN11 184 D6
Scully Cl 8 NN4 175 E7
Scythe Rd NN11 135 C6
Seaford Wlk NN18 36 B5
Seagrave Ct NN3 143 B5
Seagrave St NN15 91 C8
Sears Cl NN7 155 E6
Sears Ho NN1 159 F7
Seaton Cres NN18 36 E4
Seaton Dr NN3 142 F1
Seaton Rd
Barrowden LE15 3 C4
Harringworth NN17 10 E8
Second Ave NN8 129 D3
Second Drift PE9 2 D8
Second La NN5 158 F6
Second St NN13 238 E6
Sedbergh Rd NN18 36 C4
Sedge Cl NN14 76 C1
Sedgemoor Ct NN11 135 C6
Sedgemoor Way NN11 135 C6
Sedgwick Ct NN3 142 F3
Sedlescombe Pk CV22 98 A8
Seedfield Cl NN3 142 E1
Selby Cl LE16 48 E8
Selby Ct NN15 91 F8
Selby Gdns NN29 164 C2
Selby Wlk NN18 36 C4
Selsey Rd NN18 36 B5
Selston Wlk NN3 160 D7
Selwyn Cl NN11 153 C7
SEMILONG 159 D8
Semilong Ho 4 NN2 159 C7
Semilong Rd NN2 159 C8
Senna Dr NN12 203 C8
Sentinel Rd NN4 158 E1
Sentry Cl 6 NN4 175 E7
Senwick Dr NN8 130 C4
Senwick Rd NN8 130 C4
Setchells Yd PE8 41 F5
Settlers Fields NN15 91 A7
Seven Sisters Cl NN13 221 B4
Severn Cl NN8 129 C6
Severn Ct NN15 92 B2
Severn Dr NN5 140 F2
Severn Ho PE8 42 A6
Severn The NN11 135 A1
Severn Way NN16 72 A5
Severn Wlk NN17 21 C1
Sewter Gdns PE8 15 E6
Sexton Cl NN11 135 B3
Seymour Pl PE8 41 E7
Seymour St NN5 159 A6
Shackleton Cl NN14 70 E7
Shackleton Dr NN11 135 C5
Shadowfax Dr NN3 143 C5
Shaftesbury Ho NN8 130 A3
Shaftesbury Rd NN18 36 B6
Shaftesbury St NN16 72 C2
Shakespeare Ave NN11 135 B2
Shakespeare Dr NN15 92 A2
Shakespeare Ho 2 NN1 159 E7
Shakespeare Rd
Kettering NN16 72 B5
Northampton NN1 159 E7
Rushden NN10 131 E2
Wellingborough NN8 129 C4
Shakespeare Way NN17 36 D8
Shale End NN5 140 A3
Shannon Cl NN10 132 D3
Shannon Ct NN18 36 E4
Shannon Way NN15 92 B2
Shap Gn NN3 142 C4
Shard Cl NN4 175 D6
Sharman Cl NN11 135 C5
Sharman Rd
Northampton NN5 159 A5
Wellingborough NN8 129 F4
Sharmans Cl NN7 162 A6
Sharman Way NN14 70 F7
Sharpes La NN6 121 B4
Sharplands NN7 163 D5
Sharrow Pl 7 NN3 143 D2
Sharwood Terr NN29 147 B8
Shatterstone 2 NN4 175 D6
Shaw Cl NN8 129 B5
Shawell Rd LE17 62 A4
Shaw The MK18 227 F1
Sheaf Cl NN5 140 B2
Sheaf St NN11 135 C1
Shearwater La NN8 130 A7
Shedfield Way NN4 175 C6
Sheep St
Kettering NN16 72 B1
Northampton NN1 159 C6
Wellingborough NN8 130 A4
Sheerwater Dr NN3 143 D3
Sheffield Ct NN9 114 C5
Sheffield Way NN6 144 E3
Sheffield Wlk NN18 36 B4
Sheila Pl NN16 72 E4
Sheldons La NN6 108 A5
SHELFLEYS 174 E8
Shelford Cl NN3 143 B5
Shelland Cl LE16 32 C2
Shelley Cl
Daventry NN11 135 B2
Towcester NN12 203 B5
Shelleycotes Rd NN6 106 A1
Shelley Dr
Corby NN17 21 D1
Higham Ferrers NN10 132 B5
Shelley Rd
Kettering NN16 72 C5
Wellingborough NN8 129 B4
Shelley St NN2 141 F1
Shelmerdine Rise NN9 114 D6
Shelsley Dr NN3 141 F4
Shelton Ct
Corby NN17 22 E2
Wollaston NN29 146 D2
Shelton Rd
Corby NN17 22 E2
Raunds NN9 114 E4
Shepherd Cl NN2 141 A5
Shepherds Hill NN29 146 F1
Shepherds Wlk
Bugbrooke NN7 173 A8
Harpole NN7 157 C6
Sheppard Way NN12 213 B8
Shepperton Cl
Castlethorpe MK19 218 F5
Northampton NN3 143 C2
Sheppey La NN7 177 B3
Shepton Ct NN18 36 A6
Sheraton Cl NN3 142 C2
Sheraton Mews NN3 142 C2
Sherborne Way NN14 76 E2
Sherborne Wlk NN18 36 A6
Sheriff Ho NN9 112 E1
Sheriff Rd NN1 159 F7
Sherrard Rd LE16 31 E5
Sherwood Ave NN2 140 F6
Sherwood Cl NN17 36 E8
Sherwood Dr
Daventry NN11 135 B4
Kettering NN15 91 F5
Shetland Way NN17 21 C1
Shieling Ct NN18 36 A1
Ship La PE8 41 F4
Shipton Way NN10 131 C3
Shire Pl NN3 143 C5
Shire Rd NN17 21 C1
Shires Bsns Pk The NN13 234 A6
Shires Rd NN13 234 A6
Shirley Rd NN10 132 B3
Shoal Creek NN4 175 C5
Shoe Maker Cl NN12 188 F7
Shoemakers Ct NN10 132 B3
Shop La NN7 179 B6
Shoreham Ct NN18 36 B5
Short Cl PE8 28 B3
Short La
Cogenhoe NN7 162 A6
Thorpe Malsor NN14 71 B3
Wellingborough NN8 129 F5
Shortlands Cl NN13 211 F3
Shortlands The NN9 113 B5
Short Massey MK46 195 E5
Short Stocks NN10 132 D2
Shortwoods Cl NN9 114 D5
SHOTLEY 11 B7
Shotwell Mill La NN14 70 D8
Showsley Rd NN12 204 D8
Shrewsbury Ave LE16 32 B2
Shropshire Cl LE16 31 E4
Shropshire Pl LE16 31 E4
Shrubberies The NN14 94 D7
Shrubfield Gr NN17 36 F8
Shuckburgh Cres CV22 98 D8
Shuckburgh Rd CV47 166 D8
Shurville Cl NN6 144 F3
SHUTLANGER 204 D8
Shutlanger Rd NN12 190 F1
SIBBERTOFT 46 F2
Sibbertoft Rd
Clipston LE16 47 E1
Husbands Bosworth LE17 45 F2
Marston Trussell LE16 47 B6
Sibley Rd NN9 112 B4
SIBSON 16 F8
Siddeley Way NN11 134 F3
Siddons Cl PE8 41 E7
Siddons Way NN3 126 D1
Sidebrook Ct NN3 142 F5
Sidegate La NN8 130 F8
Sidings Ind Ctr The NN13 234 A8
Sidings The NN9 131 D8
Sidlaw Ct MK11 229 F4
Sidmouth Wlk NN18 36 F4
Sidney Rd
Rugby CV22 98 D8
Woodford Halse NN11 184 C6
Silkweavers Mews NN14 70 D7
Sillswood MK46 195 E4
Silverdale Gr NN10 131 E2
Silverdale Rd NN3 142 D2
Silver St N OX17 208 E4
Silver St
Abthorpe NN12 201 F2
Brixworth NN6 106 B3
Broughton NN14 90 A5
Chacombe OX17 208 E4
Kettering NN16 72 B2
Northampton NN1 159 C6
Stony Stratford MK11 229 D5
Walgrave NN6 108 A5
Wellingborough NN8 130 A4
SILVERSTONE 214 D4
Silverstone CE Jun Sch NN12 214 D4
Silverstone Cl NN2 141 D5
Silverstone Inf Sch NN12 214 D5
Silverstone Motor Racing Circuit* NN12 225 E8
Silverstone Tech Pk NN12 214 E2
Silverwood Ct NN15 91 C8
Silverwood Rd NN15 91 C8
Simborough Way LE16 32 B3
Simon de Senlis Ct NN1 159 D7
Simon de Senlis Prim Sch NN4 175 B8
Simon's Wlk
17 Northampton NN1 159 C6
Pattishall NN12 172 D1
Simpson Ave NN10 132 C7
Simpson Barracks NN4 175 D6
Sinclair Dr NN8 129 B6
Sir Christopher Hatton Sch NN8 130 A6
Sir Georges La OX17 230 A4
Sir John Brown Ct NN16 72 A2
Sir John Pascoe Way NN5 158 C8
Sissinghurst Dr NN14 76 F2
Siward View NN5 140 D2
Six Cotts MK18 226 E5
Sixth St NN13 238 E7
Six Willows NN9 110 B3
Skagerrak Cl NN18 36 A2
Skawle Ct NN3 142 F3
Skeffington Cl NN14 54 A2
Skegness Wlk NN18 36 C4
Skelton Wlk 4 NN3 142 C4
Sketty Cl NN4 160 C1
Skiddaw Wlk NN3 142 C4
Skinner Ave NN5 158 D5
Skinner's Hill NN10 132 B2
Skin Yard La NN6 121 B4
Skippon Cl LE16 31 D2
Skippons Ct NN6 85 B8
Skipton Cl
Corby NN18 36 B4
Northampton NN4 175 B7
Skittle Alley OX17 237 C7
Skye Rd NN17 36 B8
Slade Cl NN14 54 B3
Slade Cres NN15 91 B7
Slade Hill NN13 234 D1
Slade Ho NN11 153 C8
Slade Leas OX17 220 B8
Sladeswell Ct 1 NN3 161 A8
Slade The
Daventry NN11 153 C8
Silverstone NN12 214 E5
Slade Valley Ave NN14 70 F7
SLAPTON 201 D2
Slapton Pre Prep Sch NN12 201 E2
Slate Drift PE9 1 E3
Slaters Cl NN10 132 D2
Slawston Rd
Medbourne LE16 18 E7
Welham LE16 17 F6
Slim Cl NN15 72 F1
Slips The NN9 110 E2
Slip The NN6 106 C2
SLIPTON 75 A3
Slipton La
Slipton NN14 75 A3
Sudborough NN14 56 C1
Sloe La NN14 89 C5
Smart's Cl NN13 233 D8
Smarts Est CV23 100 A3
Smith Cl NN7 177 A1
Smith Ct NN9 114 D5
Smitherway NN7 173 A8
Smithfield Pl NN9 114 D6
Smithland Ct NN12 202 D8
Smiths Ct NN4 159 D4
Smith St NN6 105 A1
Smiths Yd NN9 110 B3
Smithy The
Deanshanger MK19 228 E4
Northampton NN3 142 D1
Rushden NN10 132 B1
Smyth Cl LE16 31 E5
Smyth Ct NN3 142 E3
Snetterton Cl NN3 141 F4
Snowbell Sq 1 NN3 143 C2
Snowshill Cl 4 NN11 135 B7
Soane Cl NN8 129 F8
Soar Gn NN17 21 C1
Solly's Way NN12 203 C5
Somerford Rd NN8 129 E6
Somerset St NN1 159 E7
Somerton Ct NN18 36 A6
Somerville Ct OX17 230 D3
Somerville Rd
Brackley NN13 233 D8
Daventry NN11 153 B8
Sondes Cl PE8 41 E7
Sondes Rd NN17 22 E2
Sopwith Way NN11 135 B5
Sorrel Cl
Isham NN14 91 F1
Northampton NN4 175 E5
Sorrels The NN14 91 F1
Sotheby Rise NN3 143 D3
Soudan Ave NN13 233 E8
SOULDERN 237 E3
Sourton Pl NN11 135 D6
Southall Rd NN17 37 B6
Southampton Rd NN4 159 C3
Southam Rd CV47 166 D7
South Ave NN15 92 B3
South Bank NN13 234 B7
South Bridge Cl PE8 41 F4
Southbrook NN18 36 B3
Southbrook Jun & Inf Schs NN11 135 E1
South Cl
Braunston NN11 118 D1
Greatworth OX17 210 D1
Long Buckby NN6 121 B3
Rushden NN10 132 C1
South Copse NN4 175 B7
Southcourt NN3 142 C7
Southcrest NN4 158 F1
South End Jun & Inf Schs NN10 148 B8
Southfield Ave NN4 159 D3
Southfield Ct NN13 233 E6
Southfield Dr NN15 91 F4
Southfield Prim Sch NN13 233 E6
Southfield Rd
Gretton NN17 10 C1
Northampton NN5 158 B6
SOUTHFIELDS 143 A7
Southfields NN10 132 C1
Southfield Sch for Girls NN15 91 C7
South Fields Dr NN6 101 A5
South Folds Rd NN18 35 F1
Southgate Dr
Kettering NN15 72 D2
Towcester NN12 203 D5
South Gr NN10 148 B5
South Holme Ct NN3 142 E5
SOUTH KILWORTH 63 D8
South Kilworth CE Prim Sch LE17 63 C8
South Kilworth Rd NN6 64 B5
Southlands NN15 72 B1
Southleigh Gr LE16 31 D4
SOUTH LUFFENHAM 3 D8
South March NN11 153 D8
South Meadow View NN5 158 A6
South Oval NN5 140 F1
South Paddock Ct NN3 142 F4
South Pk NN10 132 B1
South Pl NN11 135 B1
South Portway Cl NN3 142 F6
South Priors Ct NN3 143 A3
South Rd
Clifton u D CV23 80 A5
Corby NN17 37 B6
Oundle PE8 42 A4
South St
Castlethorpe MK19 218 F5
Isham NN14 110 F8
Northampton NN1 159 F6
Weedon Bec NN7 155 C3
Wollaston NN29 146 D2
Woodford Halse NN11 184 C6
South Terr
Greens Norton NN12 202 E8
Northampton NN1 159 F6
South Vale NN7 179 A5
South View
Brixworth NN6 106 B1
Harpole NN7 157 E5
Nether Heyford NN7 156 B1
Roade NN7 191 D4
Whilton NN11 137 C6
South Way NN11 135 D1
SOUTHWICK 26 B5
Southwick Hall* PE8 26 C5
Southwood Hill NN4 159 A3
Southwood Ho NN8 130 A3
Sovereign Ct
Northampton NN3 142 F6
Rushden NN10 132 B3
Sovereign Pk LE16 31 F1
Sovereigns Ct NN16 72 C6
Sower Leys Rd NN18 36 C4
Spalding Rd NN18 36 C4
Spanslade Rd NN3 143 A1
Sparke Cl NN8 129 D7
Spartan Cl NN4 175 F5
Spectacle La NN3 125 F1
Speedwell Rd NN14 51 A4
Speke Dr NN11 135 C5
Spelhoe St NN3 142 F6
Spencelayh Cl NN8 129 F7
Spencer Bridge Rd NN5 159 A7
Spencer Cl
Bugbrooke NN7 173 A8
Chapel Brampton NN6 124 D1
Earls Barton NN6 144 F4
Evenley NN13 233 F2
Spencer Ct
Corby NN17 36 E5
Rushden NN10 132 A3
West Haddon NN6 102 C4
Spencer Gdns
Bozeat NN29 164 D2
Brackley NN13 233 E6
Spencer Haven NN5 159 A7
Spencer Par
Northampton NN1 159 D6
Stanwick NN9 113 F3
Spencer Rd
Irthlingborough NN9 112 E1
Long Buckby NN6 121 B3
Northampton NN1 159 E7
Rushden NN10 132 A3
Stanion NN14 37 E3
Wellingborough NN8 130 A1
Spencer St
Burton Latimer NN15 92 B2
Kettering NN16 72 B4
Market Harborough LE16 31 D3
Northampton NN5 159 A5
Raunds NN9 114 E6
Ringstead NN14 95 B3
Rothwell NN14 70 D8
Spencer Wlk NN18 36 E5
Spendlove Dr NN17 10 C1
Spenfield Ct NN3 142 F3
Spenser Cres NN11 135 A3
Spens Ho NN2 141 D5
Spey Cl NN8 129 C6
Spiers Dr NN13 233 D7
Spilsby Cl NN18 36 C4
Spinners Cotts OX17 210 F7
Spinney Bank OX17 230 F5
Spinney Cl
Boughton NN2 141 C7
Market Harborough LE16 31 C3
Rushden NN10 131 F2

Spinney Cl *continued*
Thrapston NN14 .... 76 D1
Towcester NN12 .... 203 C3
Warmington PE8 .... 28 B2
Spinney Dr
Kettering NN15 .... 91 D7
Northampton NN4 .... 175 C4
Spinney Gr NN17 .... 36 E7
SPINNEY HILL 142 A3
Spinney Hill NN11 ...... 118 D1
Spinney Hill Cres
NN3 .... 142 A4
Spinney Hill Rd
Northampton NN3 .... 142 A4
Olney MK46 .... 195 E3
Spinney La
Kettering NN15 .... 91 D7
Wellingborough NN8 ..... 129 C2
Spinney Rd
Burton Latimer NN15 ...... 92 C3
Irthlingborough NN15 ..... 112 F2
Rushden NN10 .... 131 F1
Weldon NN17 .... 38 C7
Spinney Rise
Daventry NN11 .... 135 C1
Denford NN14 .... 95 C6
Spinney St NN9 .... 114 D6
Spinney Terr [8] NN9 ..... 112 F2
Spinney The NN4 .... 175 E2
Spinney Way NN3 .... 142 A5
Sponne House Sh Ctr
NN12 .... 203 C6
Sponne Sch Tech Coll
NN12 .... 203 B6
Sponnes Rd NN12 ...... 203 C5
Spotted Cow La
NN11 .... 136 D5
SPRATTON 105 C1
Spratton CE Prim Sch
NN6 .... 105 B1
Spratton Hall Sch
NN6 .... 105 B1
Spratton Rd NN6 .... 106 A2
Spring Bank LE16 .... 18 F7
Springbanks Way [2]
NN4 .... 175 B8
Spring Cl
Boughton NN2 .... 125 C1
Brackley NN13 .... 233 F7
Daventry NN11 .... 153 C8
Hollowell NN6 .... 104 B4
Irthlingborough NN9 ..... 112 F2
Kilsby CV23 .... 100 A2
Springer Straight [1]
NN4 .... 158 F3
Springfield
Flore NN7 .... 155 E5
Northampton NN4 .... 175 E7
Springfield Ave NN14 ..... 76 E3
Springfield Cl NN15 .... 91 C7
Springfield Ct
[1] Market Harborough
LE16 .... 31 F2
Northampton NN3 .... 142 F3
Springfield Gdns
MK19 .... 228 E4
Springfield Gr NN17 ...... 36 F8
Springfield Rd
Kettering NN15 .... 91 C7
Olney MK46 .... 195 F4
Oundle PE8 .... 41 F7
Rushden NN10 .... 148 D8
Walgrave NN6 .... 107 F5
Wilbarston LE16 .... 34 C4
Springfields NN12 .... 203 B5
Springfield St LE16 .... 31 F2
Springfield Way
NN13 .... 233 E8
Spring Gdns
Burton Latimer NN15 ...... 92 C3
Earls Barton NN6 .... 144 F4
Higham Ferrers NN10 ..... 132 B6
Northampton NN1 .... 159 D5
Rothwell NN14 .... 70 D7
Towcester NN12 .... 203 D5
Wellingborough NN8 ..... 129 F4
Springhill Gdns LE16 ...... 31 C2
Springhill Hos CV22 .... 98 C8
Spring Ho [2] NN8 .... 129 F4
Spring La
Alderton NN12 .... 204 F2
Flore NN7 .... 155 E5
Northampton NN1 .... 159 B6
Olney MK46 .... 195 F3
[8] Wellingborough
NN8 .... 130 A4
Spring Lane Prim Sch
NN1 .... 159 B6
SPRING PARK 141 A5
Spring Rise NN15 .... 91 C7
Spring St [4] NN9 .... 112 F2
Springs The
Northampton NN4 .... 159 A3
Swinford LE17 .... 62 C4
Spring Terr
Irthlingborough NN9 ..... 112 F2
Medbourne LE16 .... 19 A6
Springwell Cl NN4 .... 175 F3
Springwood Ct NN3 ...... 142 F5
Spruce Ct
Kettering NN16 .... 72 C4
Northampton NN3 .... 142 E3
Spurlings PE8 .... 41 F5
Spyglass Hill NN4 .... 175 B6
Square The
Aynho OX17 .... 237 C7
Earls Barton NN6 .... 144 E4
Greatworth OX17 .... 210 E1
Square The *continued*
Holdenby NN6 .... 123 D4
Kings Sutton OX17 .... 230 F5
Market Harborough LE16 ... 31 E3
Moreton Pinkney NN11 ... 199 C7
Northampton NN4 .... 175 F3
Pitsford NN6 .... 125 C4
Raunds NN9 .... 114 D6
South Luffenham LE15 .... 3 D8
Thorpe Malsor NN14 .... 71 B3
Welford NN6 .... 64 E6
Yardley Hastings NN7 .... 179 A6
Squire Cl NN18 .... 36 A4
Squires Wlk NN3 .... 142 B3
Squirrel Cl NN4 .... 175 F2
Squirrel La NN5 .... 158 C7
Stable Ct
Brackley NN13 .... 233 F7
[4] Northampton NN2 .... 141 C3
Pitsford NN6 .... 125 D4
Stablegate Way LE16 ..... 32 A3
Stable Hill NN14 .... 55 F7
Stable Mews NN29 ...... 147 D1
Stables La NN6 .... 140 B8
Stables The PE8 .... 8 A3
Stable Yd
Loddington NN14 .... 70 C1
Thenford OX17 .... 220 E8
Stadtpeine Cl NN17 .... 36 C7
Staffa Wlk NN17 .... 36 B8
Stafford Cl NN11 .... 135 D5
Stafford Pl NN3 .... 141 F7
Stafford Rd NN17 .... 22 C8
Staffords La NN6 .... 102 B4
Stagshaw Cl [2] NN4 .... 175 C8
Staines Cl NN5 .... 158 E6
Stalbridge Wlk NN18 ...... 36 A6
Stamford Cl LE16 .... 31 E2
Stamford La PE8 .... 28 B3
Stamford Rd
Corby NN14, NN18,
NN17 .... 37 E4
Deenethorpe NN17 .... 23 E2
Duddington PE9 .... 5 C7
Easton o t H PE9 .... 2 B5
Geddington, Little Oakley
NN14 .... 54 B5
Geddington NN14 .... 54 A1
Kettering NN16 .... 72 E5
Ketton PE9 .... 1 C8
South Luffenham LE15 .... 3 D7
Weldon NN17 .... 38 A6
Stamford Wlk NN18 .... 36 C4
Stanbridge Ct MK11 ..... 229 F5
Standens Barn Prim Sch
NN3 .... 160 F8
Standens Barn Rd
NN3 .... 142 F1
Standing Stones NN3 .... 143 B3
Standside NN5 .... 158 F6
Stanfield Rd NN5 .... 158 C6
Stanford Cl NN6 .... 84 A5
Stanford Hall* LE17 .... 62 F3
STANFORD ON AVON 62 F2
Stanford Rd
Cold Ashby NN6 .... 84 A5
Swinford LE17 .... 62 D3
Stanford Way NN4 .... 175 C8
Stanhill Row NN12 .... 201 F1
Stanhope Rd NN2 .... 141 D1
Stanier Cl NN16 .... 72 A3
Stanier Rd NN17 .... 21 F1
STANION 37 F2
Stanion CE Prim Sch
NN14 .... 37 E3
Stanion La
Corby NN18 .... 37 B6
Corby NN18 .... 37 D5
Stanion Rd NN14 .... 38 C1
Stanley Boddington Ct
NN15 .... 91 C8
Stanley Ct MK46 .... 195 F3
Stanley Mews [5] NN8 .... 130 B5
Stanley Rd
Northampton NN5 .... 159 A6
Wellingborough NN8 ..... 130 B5
Stanley St
Northampton NN2 .... 159 C8
Rothwell NN14 .... 70 E7
Stanley Way NN11 .... 135 C5
Stannard Way NN6 .... 106 B2
Stanton Ave NN3 .... 142 A4
Stanton Cl
Desborough NN14 .... 51 B4
Wellingborough NN8 ..... 111 B1
Stanway Cl LE16 .... 32 A3
Stanwell Cl OX17 .... 209 A1
Stanwell Dr OX17 .... 209 A1
Stanwell Lea OX17 ...... 209 A2
Stanwell Way NN8 .... 129 C3
STANWICK 113 E4
Stanwick Prim Sch
NN9 .... 114 A3
Stanwick Rd
Higham Ferrers
NN10 .... 132 C8
Raunds NN9 .... 114 B4
Star Cnr CV23 .... 99 C1
Starmers La NN7 .... 157 D4
Starmer's Yd NN5 .... 158 C7
Starvold Cl NN6 .... 105 A1
Station Cl
Daventry NN11 .... 135 D2
Ecton NN3 .... 143 C1
Long Buckby NN6 .... 121 B3
Station Cotts NN18 .... 53 D7
Station Ct NN11 .... 184 C6
Station Gdns NN11 ..... 184 C6
Station Mews NN3 ...... 143 C2
Station Rd
Aynho OX15, OX17 .... 237 A6
Blisworth NN7 .... 174 B2
Brixworth NN6 .... 106 A4
Burton Latimer NN15 ...... 92 A2
Castlethorpe MK19 .... 218 F5
Clifton OX17 .... 236 F5
Cogenhoe NN7 .... 161 E6
Corby NN17 .... 37 A6
Cottesbrooke NN6 .... 105 A7
Desborough NN14 .... 51 A4
Earls Barton NN6 .... 144 E3
Earls Barton NN6 .... 144 F1
Finedon NN9 .... 111 D6
Great Bowden LE16 .... 32 A6
Gretton NN17 .... 10 B1
Helmdon NN13 .... 211 F4
Husbands Bosworth
LE17 .... 45 D3
Irchester MK44 .... 147 C8
Irthlingborough NN9 ..... 113 A2
Kettering NN15 .... 72 B1
Ketton PE9 .... 1 A5
King's Cliffe PE8 .... 13 F7
Lilbourne CV23 .... 81 A7
Little Houghton NN7 ..... 161 C5
Long Buckby NN6 .... 121 A2
Morcott LE15 .... 3 B6
Nassington PE8 .... 15 F5
Northampton NN3 .... 143 C1
North Kilworth LE17 .... 45 A4
Oundle PE8 .... 42 A6
Raunds NN9 .... 115 B7
Ringstead NN14 .... 94 F2
Rushden NN10 .... 132 A3
Rushton NN14 .... 52 C2
Theddingworth LE17 .... 46 D8
Watford NN6 .... 120 C5
Welton NN11 .... 119 E1
West Haddon NN6 .... 102 B4
Woodford Halse NN11 .... 184 C6
Station Yard Ind Est
OX17 .... 230 A2
Stavanger Cl NN18 .... 36 A2
Staveley Way NN6 ...... 106 C3
STAVERTON 152 C7
Staverton CE Prim Sch
NN11 .... 152 C7
Staverton Leys CV22 ...... 98 A7
Staverton Rd NN11 ...... 135 B1
Steadfold La PE9 .... 1 C8
Steane View NN13 ...... 233 D7
Steel Cl NN14 .... 76 D1
Steele Rd NN8 .... 129 D4
Steel Rd NN17 .... 22 E2
Steene St NN5 .... 159 A6
Stefen Way NN11 .... 153 B7
Stenhouse Cl NN6 ...... 121 D4
Stenson St NN5 .... 159 A6
Stent Mews NN4 .... 175 F8
Stephen Bennett Cl
NN5 .... 158 C8
Stephenson Cl NN11 ..... 134 F4
Stephenson Ct
Kilsby CV23 .... 99 F2
Roade NN7 .... 191 C4
Stephenson Way NN17 .... 37 A8
Sterling Bsns Pk NN4 ... 160 C2
Sterling Ct NN14 .... 70 C1
Sterndale Cl NN14 .... 50 E4
Stevens Ct NN6 .... 144 F5
Stevenson St NN4 .... 159 C2
Stevens St LE16 .... 31 D3
Stewart Cl NN3 .... 126 B2
Stewart Dr NN12 .... 214 D4
Stewarts Rd NN8 .... 130 B8
Steyning Cl NN18 .... 36 A5
STIBBINGTON 8 D2
Stilebrook Rd MK46 ..... 195 F6
Stile Cl NN11 .... 135 A2
Stimpson Ave NN1 .... 159 F7
Stimpson Avenue Prim
Sch NN1 .... 159 F7
Stinford Leys LE16 .... 32 B3
Stirling Cl NN18 .... 36 E2
Stirling St NN5 .... 158 F6
Stirrup Ho NN5 .... 159 B5
Stitchman Ho [8] NN5 ... 159 A6
Stockbridge Rd NN17 ..... 22 A1
Stocken Cl MK46 .... 195 E4
Stockerston La LE16 ...... 20 D8
Stockholme Cl NN18 ...... 36 A2
Stocking Cl NN7 .... 192 D1
Stocking Green Cl
MK19 .... 207 A3
Stockley St [6] NN1 ..... 159 E6
Stockmead Rd NN3 ...... 161 A8
Stocks Gn PE8 .... 28 C8
Stocks Hill
Finedon NN9 .... 111 E4
[8] Moulton NN3 .... 126 C1
Silverstone NN12 .... 214 D5
Stock's Hill PE9 .... 1 A5
Stock's La NN17 .... 37 B6
Stocks The MK19 .... 218 E2
Stockwell Ave NN4 ...... 175 D5
Stockwell Cl LE16 .... 32 B3
Stockwell La
Hellidon NN11 .... 151 D1
Sulgrave OX17 .... 210 F8
Stockwell Rd NN7 .... 174 F4
Stockwell Way NN7 ...... 174 F4
Stockwood Dr NN17 .... 21 F1
STOKE ALBANY 34 A4
Stoke Albany Rd LE16 .... 18 E1
STOKE BRUERNE 205 B8
Stoke Bruerne CE Prim
Sch NN12 .... 205 A8
STOKE DOYLE 41 C1
Stoke Doyle Rd PE8 .... 41 D4
Stoke Firs Cl NN4 .... 175 F6
Stoke Hill
Oundle PE8 .... 41 F5
Stoke Albany LE16 .... 34 A4
Stoke Rd
Ashton NN7 .... 205 E8
Blisworth NN7 .... 190 E4
Desborough NN14 .... 51 A7
Lyddington LE15 .... 9 C7
Stokes Rd NN18 .... 36 D4
Stonebridge Ct NN3 ..... 142 F3
Stone Circle Rd NN3 ..... 142 E7
Stone Cl
Wellingborough NN8 ..... 129 F8
Wollaston NN29 .... 146 D2
Stone Hill Ct NN3 .... 142 E4
Stonehill Way NN6 ...... 125 B8
Stonehouse Ct CV23 ...... 81 A6
Stone House Mews
NN6 .... 84 E4
Stonehurst Cl NN7 ...... 192 C1
Stonelea Rd NN6 .... 127 D3
Stoneleigh Chase
NN5 .... 140 D1
Stonemasons Cl
MK46 .... 195 F3
Stone Pit Cl MK46 .... 195 E3
Stonepit Dr LE16 .... 20 D1
Stoneway
Badby NN11 .... 152 F2
Hartwell NN7 .... 192 E2
Stone Way NN5 .... 158 B7
Stonewold Cl NN2 ...... 141 A4
Stoney Fields NN14 .... 89 B4
Stoneyhurst NN4 .... 158 F3
Stoney Piece Cl NN29 ... 164 C2
Stony Hill NN12 .... 216 C8
STONY STRATFORD 229 E5
Stony Stratford Nature
Reserve* MK11 .... 229 D7
Stook The NN11 .... 135 C6
Storefield Cotts NN14 .... 53 A4
Stornoway Rd NN17 .... 21 C1
Stotfold Ct MK11 .... 229 E4
Stourhead Dr NN4 ...... 175 C7
Stour Rd
Corby NN17 .... 21 D1
Northampton NN5 .... 158 F6
Stour The NN11 .... 153 A8
Stourton Cl NN8 .... 129 D1
Stow Cl NN8 .... 129 D1
Stowe Wlk NN3 .... 141 F5
Stradlers Cl NN4 .... 175 E5
Stratfield Way NN15 ...... 91 D5
Stratford Arc MK11 ..... 229 D5
Stratford Dr NN4 .... 175 D6
Stratford Rd
Cosgrove MK19 .... 218 D1
Deanshanger MK19 ...... 228 F4
Roade NN7 .... 191 C3
Stony Stratford MK12 .... 229 F6
Strathay Wlk NN17 .... 21 C1
Strath Cl CV21 .... 99 A7
Stratton Cl
Market Harborough
LE16 .... 31 D1
Northampton NN3 .... 160 D7
Stratton Dr NN13 .... 233 D7
Strawberry Hill NN3 ..... 143 C3
Strawberry Hill Cotts
MK44 .... 149 F2
Straws Cl NN9 .... 112 E1
Stream Bank Cl NN8 .... 129 D4
Streambank Rd NN3 ..... 142 E6
Streatfield Rd NN5 ...... 159 A8
Streather Ct NN9 .... 114 C5
Streather Dr NN17 .... 36 E7
Streeton Way NN6 ...... 144 E5
Street The LE15 .... 3 E8
Strelley Ave NN3 .... 160 F8
Stringer's Hill NN14 ...... 90 F2
STRIXTON 164 C8
Strixton Manor Bsns Ctr
NN29 .... 164 C8
Strode Rd NN8 .... 130 B5
Stronglands Ct PE8 .... 41 F6
Stuart Cl
Kettering NN16 .... 72 C2
Northampton NN4 .... 174 F7
Stuart Cres LE16 .... 30 F7
Stuart Rd
Brackley NN13 .... 233 E8
Corby NN17 .... 36 F6
Market Harborough LE16 ... 31 E2
Stubbing End NN18 .... 53 B8
Stubble Cl NN2 .... 141 A6
Stubbs Cl NN8 .... 129 F7
Stubbs La NN15 .... 92 A8
Stubbs Rd NN11 .... 170 B7
STUCHBURY 211 A5
Studfall Ave NN17 .... 36 E8
Studfall Ct NN17 .... 36 E7
Studfall Inf Sch NN17 .... 36 E8
Studfall Jun Sch NN17 .... 36 D8
Stud Farm Cl OX17 ...... 196 E1
Studland Rd NN2 .... 141 B1
Sturdee Cl NN11 .... 135 D1
Sturgess Ct NN15 .... 92 C2
Sturminster Way NN18 .... 36 A6
Sturton Wlk NN18 .... 36 C4
Styles Pl NN6 .... 82 B3
SUDBOROUGH 56 C1
Sudborough Rd
Brigstock NN14 .... 56 A4
Sudborough Rd *continued*
Slipton NN14 .... 75 A6
Suffolk Pl NN15 .... 91 D6
SULBY 65 B8
Sulby Hall Old Dr NN6 .... 46 B1
Sulby Rd
Northampton NN3 .... 142 E6
Welford NN6 .... 65 A8
Sulehay Rd PE8 .... 7 C1
SULGRAVE 210 F8
Sulgrave Dr NN17 .... 36 C7
Sulgrave Manor*
OX17 .... 211 A8
Sulgrave Rd
Culworth OX17 .... 198 D1
Northampton NN5 .... 158 F7
Summerfield Rd NN15 .... 91 C8
Summerfields NN4 ...... 158 E2
Summerhouse Rd
NN3 .... 142 A6
Summerlee Mews
NN9 .... 111 F4
Summerlee Rd NN9 ...... 111 F4
Summer Leys Nature
Res* NN29 .... 145 F4
Summers Cl OX17 .... 230 A5
Summers Way LE16 .... 31 D2
Summit Rise NN4 .... 175 D7
Sunderland St NN5 ..... 159 A6
Sundew Ct NN4 .... 158 D1
Sun Hill NN14 .... 70 C7
Sunley Ct NN15 .... 91 C8
Sunningdale Cl NN2 ..... 141 E2
Sunningdale Dr
Daventry NN11 .... 135 E3
Rushden NN10 .... 148 D8
Sunny Bank
Arthingworth LE16 .... 68 C7
Holcot NN6 .... 126 E8
SUNNYSIDE 141 D5
Sunnyside
Ecton NN6 .... 143 F4
Northampton NN4 .... 175 E6
Woodford NN14 .... 94 D7
Sunny Side NN6 .... 144 D4
Sunnyside Prim Sch
NN2 .... 141 D6
Sunny View NN7 .... 179 B6
Sunset Ct NN3 .... 143 A2
Sun Yd NN12 .... 203 D5
Surfleet Cl NN18 .... 36 C4
Surrey Cl NN17 .... 36 C6
Surrey Rd NN15 .... 91 D6
Surtees Way NN12 ...... 203 C7
Sussex Cl NN5 .... 158 C6
Sussex Ct [6] NN1 .... 159 C6
Sussex Pl NN10 .... 132 B4
Sussex Rd NN15 .... 91 C6
Sutcliffe Rd PE8 .... 7 D8
Sutherland Rd NN18 ...... 36 D4
SUTTON 8 F2
Sutton Acre NN7 .... 155 E5
SUTTON BASSETT 18 A1
Sutton Cl
Aston le W NN11 .... 182 F3
Northampton NN2 .... 141 D6
Sutton Ct LE16 .... 31 E1
Sutton Heath Rd PE5, PE8,
PE9 .... 8 D6
Sutton Rd
Great Bowden LE16 .... 32 B6
Oundle PE8 .... 42 B4
Sutton Bassett LE16 .... 32 E7
Weston by W LE16 .... 18 B3
Sutton St NN7 .... 155 F5
Sutton's Wlk NN12 ...... 188 F7
Swain Ct NN3 .... 142 E3
Swale Cl
Corby NN17 .... 21 D1
Roade NN7 .... 191 C3
Swale Dr
Northampton NN5 .... 140 F3
Wellingborough NN8 ..... 129 C6
Swallow Cl
Brackley NN13 .... 222 E1
Kettering NN15 .... 92 B6
Northampton NN4 .... 175 A7
Swallow Dr NN10 .... 132 B5
Swanage Ct NN18 .... 36 A6
Swan Ave NN14 .... 55 E8
Swan Cl
Brackley NN13 .... 222 D2
Burton Latimer NN15 ...... 92 A2
Hinton NN11 .... 184 B6
Middleton Cheney
OX17 .... 219 F8
Thrapston NN14 .... 76 D3
Swan Ct NN6 .... 87 D1
Swanhill PE8 .... 8 A4
Swann Dale NN11 .... 135 D1
Swann Dale Cl NN11 ..... 135 D1
Swansea Cres NN5 ...... 159 A7
Swansea Rd NN5 .... 159 A8
Swansgate Ctr The [9]
NN8 .... 130 A4
Swans La [6] NN8 .... 130 A4
Swanspool Ct NN8 ...... 130 A4
Swanspool Par NN8 ..... 130 A3
Swan St NN1 .... 159 D5
Swans Way NN10 .... 132 C8
Swan Terr MK11 .... 229 D5
Swan Valley Way
NN4 .... 174 C8
Swedish Hos NN7 .... 139 D4
Sweetacre Cl NN7 ...... 163 D4

Swift Cl NN4 175 F3
Swift Way NN13 222 E1
Swinburne Cl NN16 72 C6
Swinburne Rd NN8 129 B4
Swinfen's Yd MK11 229 D5
SWINFORD 62 C3
Swinford CE Prim Sch LE17 62 B4
Swinford Cnr LE17 62 A8
Swinford Hollow NN3 161 A8
Swinford Rd LE17 62 A8
Swingbridge St LE16 30 E8
Swinnertons La NN6 82 B4
Swinneyford Rd NN12 203 C5
Swyncombe Gn NN7 192 C1
Sycamore Ave NN11 184 B6
Sycamore Cl
Corby NN17 21 E1
Daventry NN11 135 C5
Kettering NN16 72 D4
Rushden NN10 132 C2
Towcester NN12 203 C4
Sycamore Dr
Desborough NN14 51 D2
Sywell NN6 143 D8
Sycamore Rd
Greens Norton NN12 202 E8
Northampton NN5 158 C7
Sycamores The LE17 63 D8
Sycamore Yd NN12 187 B1
Sydenham Cl OX17 230 B4
Sydney St NN16 72 D2
Syers Green Cl NN6 121 A4
Syers Green La NN6 121 A4
Sykes Ct NN17 37 A8
Syke The NN14 55 F7
Syles Cl NN6 102 B5
Sylmond Gdns NN10 148 A7
Sylvanus Ho NN8 129 D5
Symington St NN5 159 A7
Symington Way LE16 31 E3
SYRESHAM 224 B8
Syresham St James CE Prim Sch NN13 224 C7
Syresham Way NN2 141 C5
SYWELL 127 D3
Sywell Airport Bsns Pk NN6 127 F4
Sywell Ave NN8 129 D6
Sywell CE Prim Sch NN6 127 D3
Sywell Ctry Pk* NN6 144 A7
Sywell Rd
Holcot NN6 126 F8
Mears Ashby NN6 128 A1
Overstone NN6 127 B1
Wellingborough NN8 129 C6
Sywell Way NN8 129 D6

T

Taborley Cl NN3 142 E1
Tadcaster Cl NN11 135 C6
Taggies Yd NN14 109 F5
Tailby Ave NN16 72 A5
Tainty Cl NN9 111 E5
Talan Rise NN3 143 C5
Talavera Cl NN11 135 B1
Talavera Way NN3 142 D6
Talbot Rd
Northampton NN1 159 E7
Rushden NN10 131 F1
Wellingborough NN8 130 C5
Talbot Rd N NN8 130 C5
Talbots Hyde MK46 195 E4
Talbot Yd LE16 31 E3
Tall Trees Cl NN4 174 F8
Tallyfield End NN4 158 E3
Tally-Ho Cotts PE8 60 E7
Tamar Cl NN5 140 E2
Tamar Gn NN17 21 D1
Tamarisk Dr NN3 142 C6
Tamar Sq NN11 135 A1
Tancred Cl [1] NN4 175 E7
Taney Ct PE8 42 A5
Tanfield La NN1 160 C5
Tanfields Gr NN17 36 E8
Tanglewood NN4 175 D4
Tanner's La NN16 72 B2
Tanner St NN1 159 C5
Tannery The LE15 4 A5
Tann Rd NN9 111 F5
Tanser Cott LE17 63 C8
TANSOR 27 D2
Tansor Cl NN17 36 B8
Tansy Cl NN4 158 D1
Tantree Way NN6 106 C2
Tapeley Gdns NN4 175 D7
Taper Way NN11 135 B3
Tarn Croft NN3 142 B3
Tarragon Way NN4 175 D6
Tarrant Cl NN3 126 D1
Tarrant Way NN3 126 D1
Tarrys End NN6 82 B4
Tasman Way NN14 70 E6
Tate Gr NN4 175 F7
TATHALL END 207 D2
Tattersall Cl NN3 142 A5
Taunton Ave
Corby NN18 36 B6
Northampton NN3 160 C7
Tavern La [1] NN11 135 C1
Tavern Wlk NN18 36 A4
Tavistock Cl [3] NN3 143 D2
Tavistock Rd NN15 92 A5
Tavistock Sq NN18 36 F4
Tay Cl NN17 21 D1
Taylor Ave NN3 142 C1
Taylor Cl NN8 129 C7
Taylors Gn PE8 28 B2
Teal Cl
Burton Latimer NN15 91 F2
Daventry NN11 135 C4
Higham Ferrers NN10 132 C8
Northampton NN4 174 E8
Teal La NN8 130 B7
Teasel Cl NN10 148 C7
Teasel Dr NN14 51 A4
Tebbitt Cl NN6 121 B4
Tebbutt Cl NN14 70 F7
Tebbutt's Yd NN6 144 E4
Tees Cl NN8 129 C6
Teesdale NN3 142 F6
Teesdale Rd NN17 36 D7
TEETON 104 D1
Teeton La NN6 104 E3
Teeton Rd
Guilsborough NN6 103 F5
Ravensthorpe NN6 103 E1
Telfords La NN17 37 A8
Telford Way
Kettering NN16 71 F4
Northampton NN5 158 D4
Temperance Terr MK11 229 C6
Templar Dr NN2 141 A4
Templar Rd NN15 72 F1
Temple Bar [21] NN1 159 C7
Temple Ct NN10 132 B7
Tenbury Way NN14 70 F7
Tenby Rd NN5 159 A8
Ten Cotts
Church Brampton NN6 140 B8
Wormleighton CV47 181 B8
Tenlands OX17 219 F8
Tennyson Cl
[3] Northampton NN5 158 F8
Towcester NN12 203 B5
Tennyson Dr NN17 36 D8
Tennyson Rd
Daventry NN11 135 B3
Kettering NN16 72 B2
Rothwell NN14 70 C7
Rushden NN10 131 F2
Wellingborough NN8 129 D3
Tennyson Road Inf Sch NN10 131 F2
Ten Pines NN3 142 F7
Tenter Cl NN10 132 B5
Tenter La NN9 111 F5
Tenter Rd NN3 141 F7
Tentsmuir Cl NN16 72 A6
Terrace The NN13 224 C5
Terrington Cl NN13 233 E7
Test Gn NN17 21 D1
Tettenhall Cl NN18 36 A1
Teviot Cl
Corby NN17 21 D1
Northampton NN5 140 E2
Tewkesbury Cl
Northampton NN4 159 A1
Wellingborough NN8 129 D6
Tewkesbury Dr NN10 148 D8
TEW'S END 216 C8
Tews End La NN12 216 C8
Thackers Cl PE8 8 A4
Thames Ct NN15 92 B2
Thames Rd
Daventry NN11 135 A1
Northampton NN4 175 C7
Wellingborough NN8 129 C6
Thames Rise NN16 72 A4
Thames Wlk NN17 21 D1
Thatch Meadow Dr LE16 32 B3
Thatchwell Ct NN3 160 F8
THE ARBOURS 142 C3
Theatre Ct NN1 159 D5
Thebwell Rd [3] NN3 142 F1
THEDDINGWORTH 46 C8
Theddingworth Rd
Husbands Bosworth LE17 46 A6
Lubenham LE16 30 C2
Marston Trussell LE16 47 B8
THENFORD 220 E8
Thenford Rd OX17 209 D1
Thenford St NN1 159 E6
Thetford Cl NN18 36 B1
Third Ave NN8 129 D3
Third St NN13 238 E6
Thirlestane Cres NN4 159 B3
Thirlestane Rd NN4 159 B3
Thirlmere NN8 129 C5
Thirlmere Ave NN3 142 C3
Thirlmere Cl
Daventry NN11 135 A2
Kettering NN16 71 E3
Thirlmere Flats NN16 71 E3
Thirsk Rd NN18 36 C5
Thistle Ct [3] NN4 159 A3
Thistle Dr NN14 51 A5
Thistleholme Cl NN2 141 E3
Thoday Cl NN14 90 A3
Thomas Becket RC Sch NN3 142 B5
Thomas Chapman Gr NN4 159 C4
Thomas Cl
Byfield NN11 183 D6
Thomas Cl *continued*
Corby NN18 36 D4
Crick NN6 101 A6
Thomas Crewe Cl NN13 233 F7
Thomas Flawn Rd NN9 131 D8
Thomas Rd NN15 91 C7
Thomas Rippin Cl NN14 54 A2
Thomas St
Northampton NN1 159 D7
Wellingborough NN8 130 B5
Thomas Webb Cl [10] NN11 135 C2
Thompson Cl NN5 158 A6
Thompson Way NN15 90 F8
Thorburn Rd NN3 160 E8
Thoresby Ct NN18 36 C5
Thornapple Cl NN3 143 C4
Thornborough Cl LE16 32 A2
Thornbridge Cl NN10 132 A1
THORNBY 84 E4
Thornby Dr NN2 141 B3
Thornby Rd
Cold Ashby NN6 84 B5
Naseby NN6 85 B8
Thorn Cl NN16 72 B6
Thorne Ct NN18 36 C5
Thornfield NN3 143 C4
Thorngate St NN16 72 C2
THORNHAUGH 7 F5
Thornhill OX17 208 F4
Thorn Hill NN4 159 A3
Thornlea Croft MK46 195 F3
THORNTON 235 C4
Thornton Cl
Crick NN6 101 A6
Flore NN7 155 F5
Newnham NN11 153 D3
Thornton Coll MK17 235 C5
Thornton Park Farm MK17 235 D4
Thornton Rd
Northampton NN2 141 B1
Thornton MK17 235 F2
Thoroughsale Rd NN17 36 E7
THORPE BY WATER 10 A6
Thorpe Cl
Banbury OX16 219 A6
Wellingborough NN8 129 C5
Thorpe Ct NN14 77 C7
Thorpe Dr OX16 219 A6
THORPE LANGTON 17 A5
Thorpe Langton Rd LE16 17 D6
THORPE MALSOR 71 B3
THORPE MANDEVILLE 210 B7
Thorpe Rd
Chacombe OX17 208 E4
Earls Barton NN6 144 E2
Lyddington LE15 9 D6
Northampton NN4 159 C3
Thorpe Waterville NN14 77 A8
Upper Wardington OX17 208 F8
Thorpe St NN9 114 D5
THORPE UNDERWOOD 69 C7
Thorpeville NN3 142 D7
THORPE WATERVILLE 77 C8
Thorplands Prim Sch NN3 142 E5
Thor Wlk NN18 36 A2
THRAPSTON 76 E1
Thrapston Prim Sch NN14 76 D1
Thrapston Rd
Finedon NN9, NN14 93 C2
Woodford NN14 94 D8
Three Shires Hospl NN1 159 F5
Thrift Mews [13] NN1 159 F6
Thrift St
Higham Ferrers NN10 132 B5
Irchester NN29 147 A7
Wollaston NN29 146 D2
Thrupp Bridge NN4 176 A6
Thrush La NN8 130 B6
Thruxton Dr NN3 141 F4
Thurburn Cl NN14 90 B5
THURNING 60 D2
Thurning Rd PE8, PE28 79 F7
Thursby Rd NN1 160 B7
Thurso Wlk NN17 21 D1
Thurspit Pl [8] NN3 143 D2
Thurston Dr NN15 91 A8
Thyme Ct NN3 142 E3
Tibbs Way NN7 173 A6
Tideswell Cl
Desborough NN14 50 E4
Northampton NN4 174 F8
Tiffany Gdns NN4 175 C6
TIFFIELD 189 D4
Tiffield CE Prim Sch NN12 189 D3
Tiffield Rd NN7 189 E8
Tilbury Rd NN6 122 C5
Tilbury Rise NN6 122 C5
Tilley Hill Cl PE8 41 E7
Timken Ho [3] NN11 135 A4
Timken Lo NN11 135 A4
Timken Way NN11 135 A4
Timor Ct MK11 229 D6
Timpson Cl NN16 72 C5
Timson Cl LE16 31 D5
Tingdene Rd NN9 111 F5
Tinkers Cres NN6 128 B2
Tinsley Cl NN3 143 B3
Tintagel Cl NN10 132 D1
Tintern Ave NN5 159 A7
Tintern Ct NN15 91 F8
Tippings La LE15 3 F5
Tiptoe Cl NN3 143 C3
TITCHMARSH 77 D4
Titchmarsh CE Prim Sch NN14 77 C4
Tithe Barn Cl NN9 114 E7
Tithe Barn Rd NN8 130 A4
Tithe Barn Way NN4 174 B8
Tithe Cl
Holcot NN6 126 E8
Ringstead NN14 95 A3
Tithe La OX15, OX17 236 C6
Tithe Rd NN7 155 A2
Tithe Way NN7 191 D5
Titley Bawk Ave NN6 144 F6
Titty Ho NN9 114 C5
Tiverton Ave NN2 141 C7
TIXOVER 4 E5
Tixover Grange PE9 4 F8
Todd's Hill PE9 5 B6
Todmorden Cl NN18 36 C5
Tofts Cl NN14 77 D4
Tollbar NN10 132 B5
Toll Bar La PE28 97 B4
Toll Bar Rd NN14 76 B2
Toller Pl NN15 91 F6
Toller St NN16 72 C3
Tollgate Cl NN2 141 B2
Tollgate Pl NN18 37 B6
Tollgate Way NN5 158 D6
Tompson Cl NN11 118 C1
Toms Cl
Northampton NN4 175 C3
Theddingworth LE17 46 D8
Tonmead Rd NN3 142 E3
Top Cl NN14 76 F3
Top Dysons NN14 92 F7
Top End
Little Addington NN14 113 B7
Pytchley NN14 90 F2
Top Farm Ct NN11 184 B6
Top Farm La NN29 145 E7
Top Lo NN17 5 A1
Top Station Rd NN13 234 A8
Top Station Road Ind Est NN13 234 A8
Topwell Ct NN3 143 A1
Top Yard Farm LE16 31 F6
Torch Way LE16 48 F8
Tordoff Pl NN16 72 B2
Torksey Cl NN18 36 A1
Torridge Cl NN16 71 F4
Torridon Cl NN17 21 C1
Torrington Cres NN8 129 D6
Torrington Gn NN8 129 E6
Torrington Rd NN8 129 E6
Torville Cres NN15 91 A8
Totnes Cl NN18 36 F4
Toulouse Cl [11] NN4 175 E7
Touraine Cl NN5 139 F2
Tove La NN12 203 A6
Tovey Dr NN11 135 D1
TOWCESTER 203 B3
Towcester Cl NN18 36 E1
Towcester Dr NN12 217 B3
Towcester Inf Sch NN12 203 C5
Towcester Rd
Blisworth NN7 190 B6
Greens Norton NN12 188 E1
Litchborough NN12 171 C1
Milton Malsor NN7 174 E5
Northampton NN4 159 B2
Old Stratford MK19 229 B7
Silverstone NN12 214 E4
Towcester NN12 203 A8
Whittlebury NN12 215 C5
Tower Cl NN9 112 A4
Tower Ct
Lubenham LE16 30 F3
Northampton NN6 143 B7
Wollaston NN29 146 F3
Tower Field Sq NN3 143 A6
Tower Hill Cl NN4 158 E3
Tower Hill Rd NN18 36 A4
Tower Sq NN5 158 F6
Tower St NN1 159 C6
Town Cl NN9 110 C3
Town Cnr NN5 158 F6
Townley Way NN6 144 E5
Townsend
Hinton NN11 184 B6
Maidford NN12 186 D6
Towns End NN6 121 C4
Townsend Cl
Hanging Houghton NN6 106 C8
Wellingborough NN8 129 F4
Townsend Ct PE8 39 E7
Townsend La
Thorpe Mandeville OX17 209 F6
Upper Boddington NN11 182 B8
Townsend Leys NN10 132 B8
Townsend Rd NN6 107 F5
Townson Cl NN6 107 D7
Townwell La NN29 147 B8
Towrise OX17 210 F8
Towton Ct NN4 159 A1
Trafalgar Rd NN16 72 A2
Trafalgar Rd Ind Est NN16 72 A2
Trafalgar Way NN11 135 D1
Trafford Rd NN10 132 D2
Trailli La NN14 94 D6
Treen Cl NN14 76 F2
Treetops NN3 143 A5
Trefoil Cl NN10 148 C7
Trelawney NN8 129 B5
Trenery Way NN4 159 D4
Trengothal Ct NN13 223 D4
Trent Cl
Northampton NN5 140 F2
Wellingborough NN8 129 C6
Trent Cres NN15 92 B1
Trentham Cl NN4 175 C7
Trent Ho PE8 42 A6
Trent Rd
Corby NN17 21 D1
Kettering NN16 72 A5
Wittering PE8 7 D8
Trent Wlk NN11 135 A1
Tresham Gn NN5 140 D1
Tresham Inst
Corby NN17 36 E6
Kettering NN15 72 C1
Kettering NN15 91 D8
Tresham Inst (Wellingborough Campus) NN8 130 A5
Tresham St
Kettering NN16 72 C3
Rothwell NN14 70 D7
Trevithick Rd NN17 37 C8
Trevor Cl NN5 158 E7
Trevor Cres NN5 158 E7
Trimley Cl NN3 160 D6
Trinity Ave NN2 141 D1
Trinity CE Lower Sch NN14 76 F8
Trinity Cl
Daventry NN11 153 B8
Old Stratford MK19 229 B7
Trinity Ct NN14 70 C6
Trinity Ctr NN8 129 A7
Trinity Rd NN14 70 C6
Trinity Way OX17 230 D3
Trinity Wlk NN18 36 E4
Triumph Gdns NN5 139 F1
Trojan Ctr NN8 130 B8
Tromso Cl NN18 36 A2
Troon Cres NN8 129 C7
Troutbeck Wlk NN3 142 C4
Trussell Rd NN3 143 C1
Tudely Cl NN4 175 F7
Tudor Ct [4] NN16 72 C2
Tudor Gdns MK11 229 E4
Tudor Rd NN1, NN2 142 A2
Tudor Way
Brackley NN13 233 E8
Wellingborough NN8 129 E7
Tudor Wlk NN10 132 C3
Tulbrook Stones OX17 220 B7
Tulip Dr NN10 148 B7
Tungstone Way LE16 31 E1
Tunnel Hill Cotts NN4 159 A2
Tunwell La NN17 37 B7
Turnberry Ct NN8 129 C7
Turnberry La NN4 175 C5
Turnbrook Cl NN9 112 E3
Turnells Mill La NN8 130 A1
Turner Cl
Kettering NN15 92 A8
Rugby CV21 99 B8
Turner Rd
Corby NN18 36 E5
Wellingborough NN8 129 F7
Turners Ct NN4 175 D7
Turners Farm Cl NN6 108 C2
Turner St NN1 159 F7
Turners Yd PE8 41 F5
Turn Furlong NN2 141 A5
Turnpike Cl LE16 31 D5
Turvins Mdw CV47 166 D8
TURWESTON 234 C8
Turweston Manor NN13 234 C8
Turweston Rd NN13 223 A1
Tweed Cl
Burton Latimer NN15 92 B2
Daventry NN11 153 A8
Tweed Rd NN5 158 E6
Twickenham Ct [5] NN18 36 B5
Twigden Rd NN7 157 D3
Twistle The NN11 183 C7
Twitch Hill NN12 204 D8
TWYFORD 230 B5
Twyford Ave
Raunds NN9 114 C7
Twyford OX17 230 A6
Twyford Cl [7] NN3 161 A8
Twyford Gdns OX17 230 A6
Twyford Gr OX17 230 A6
Twyford Rd OX17 230 C7
TWYWELL 75 A1
Twywell Hills & Dales Nature Res* NN14 93 F8
Tyebeck Ct NN2 141 B3
Tyes Ct NN3 142 F5
Tyler Way NN14 76 E1
Tymecrosse Gdns LE16 31 D5
Tynan Cl NN15 92 A8
Tyne Cl NN8 129 C6

Tyne Rd
Corby NN17 21 D1
Daventry NN11 153 A8
Northampton NN5 158 E6
Tyringham Cl NN3 142 D1
Tyrrell Way NN12 203 C8
Tyson Ctyd NN18 37 E7
Tythings The OX17 208 F2

U

Uist Wlk NN17 21 C1
Ullswater Cl
Higham Ferrers NN10 132 B8
Wellingborough NN8 129 C5
Ullswater Rd NN16 71 E2
Underbank La NN3 142 C6
Underwood Rd NN14 70 C7
Union St
Desborough NN14 51 B3
Finedon NN9 112 A5
Kettering NN16 72 A3
Unity Cl NN29 146 C3
Unity Coll NN2 141 D1
Unity St NN14 51 A2
Univ Coll Northampton NN2 141 D1
Univ of Leicester (Northampton Ctr) NN2 159 C8
Upland Rd NN3 142 C2
UPPER ASTROP 231 C7
Upper Astrop Rd OX17 231 A5
Upper Bath St NN1 159 C6
UPPER BENEFIELD 39 F7
UPPER BODDINGTON 182 D8
UPPER CATESBY 151 F4
Upper Cross St 18 NN1 159 C6
Upper Dane NN14 50 E3
Upperfield Gr NN17 36 E8
Upper George St NN10 132 C7
Upper Glen Ave NN7 174 B2
Upper Gn NN11 199 D7
Upper Green Pl LE16 32 A6
UPPER HARLESTONE 139 D4
Upper Havelock St 7 NN8 130 A5
UPPER HEYFORD 156 D3
Upper Higham La NN10 133 C3
Upper High St NN7 157 C7
Upper Kings Ave NN10 132 C7
Upper Mounts NN1 159 D6
Upper Park Ave NN10 131 F1
Upper Priory St 7 NN1 159 C7
Upper Queen St NN10 132 C3
Upper St NN16 72 A2
Upper Steeping NN14 51 B2
UPPER STOWE 171 E6
Upper Thrift St NN1 159 F6
UPPER WARDINGTON 196 F1
UPPER WEEDON 155 A2
Uppingham Rd
Caldecott LE16 9 B2
Corby NN17 36 A7
Medbourne LE16 19 A8
Uppingham St NN1 159 B7
UPTON 158 C5
Upton Cl NN2 141 D6
Upton Way NN4, NN5 158 D3
Usher Ho NN2 141 C5

V

Vale Cl CV21 99 A8
Valentine Way NN3 143 C3
Vale St NN16 72 A3
Vale The NN1 141 F1
Valley Cl NN13 234 A8
Valley Cres
Brackley NN13 234 A8
Northampton NN3 143 B1
Valley End NN12 172 D1
Valley Rd
Brackley NN13 234 A8
Northampton NN3 143 B1
Wellingborough NN8 129 F1
Weston by W LE16 18 B3
Valley Rise
Brackley NN13 233 F8
Desborough NN14 51 B2
Valley Way LE16 32 B4
Valley Wlk NN16 72 E2
Vancouver Cl NN18 36 B2
Vantage Mdw NN3 143 D3
Vara Cl NN18 36 B2
Vardon Cl NN8 129 C7
Varley Cl NN8 129 E8
Vaughan Cl LE16 48 E8
Vaux Rd NN8 111 A1
Velbert Ho NN17 21 E1
Velocette Way NN5 140 A1
Venture Cl NN17 22 F1
Verdant Vale 1 NN4 175 D6
Vermont Standing 3 NN16 72 C3
Vernier Cl NN11 135 A3
Vernon Ave CV22 98 E8
Vernon Cl NN11 153 E8
Vernon Ct NN16 71 F5
Vernon Ct 10 NN1 159 F6
Vernon Rd NN12 203 D5
Vernon St NN1 159 F6
Vernon Terr NN1 159 F6
Vernon Terrace Prim Sch NN1 159 F6
Vernon Wlk 7 NN1 159 F6
Verwood Cl NN3 142 F5
Veteran Cl NN4 175 E7
Vian Way NN17 36 B8
Vicarage Cl
Hackleton NN7 177 A3
Northampton NN2 141 A3
Wellingborough NN8 129 D6
Whittlebury NN12 215 C5
Yardley Gobion NN12 217 E6
Vicarage Ct MK19 207 B2
Vicarage Farm Rd NN8 129 D6
Vicarage Hill NN11 153 A2
Vicarage La
Denton NN7 178 B8
East Haddon NN6 122 D5
Mears Ashby NN6 128 B2
Northampton NN2 141 B3
Podington NN29 147 E2
Priors Marston CV47 166 E8
Vicarage Rd
Northampton NN5 159 A7
Rushden NN10 132 C3
Stony Stratford MK11 229 D6
Vicarage Rise NN12 200 C3
Vicarage Wlk MK11 229 D6
Vicar La NN11 135 D2
Viceroy Cl NN9 114 E6
Vickers Cl NN14 70 F7
Victoria Ave LE16 31 D5
Victoria Bsns Pk NN5 159 B6
Victoria Cl
Earls Barton NN6 144 E5
Rushden NN10 132 B3
West Haddon NN6 102 C5
Victoria Ct
10 Kettering NN16 72 C2
Rothwell NN14 70 D7
Rushden NN10 132 B3
Woodford NN14 94 C7
Victoria Gdns NN1 159 D5
Victoria Ho NN1 159 E6
Victoria Pk NN8 130 B2
Victoria Prim Sch NN8 130 B6
Victoria Prom NN1 159 D5
Victoria Rd
Cogenhoe NN7 161 E5
Finedon NN9 111 F5
Northampton NN1 159 E6
Oundle PE8 42 A6
Rushden NN10 132 B3
Wellingborough NN8 130 B4
Victoria St
Burton Latimer NN15 92 B2
Desborough NN14 51 A3
Earls Barton NN6 144 F5
Irthlingborough NN9 112 E1
Kettering NN16 72 B2
Northampton NN1 159 D6
Vienne Cl NN5 157 F8
Viking Cl NN16 72 C6
Viking Way NN18 36 B1
Villa Gdns NN15 92 B1
Villagers Cl NN4 175 E5
Villa La NN9 113 F3
Villa Rise NN10 132 B7
Villa Way NN4 175 F5
Vincent Cl NN5 157 F8
Vinco Terr PE8 28 D8
Vine Cl PE8 42 A5
Vine Hill Cl NN10 132 A6
Vine Hill Dr NN10 132 B6
Violet Cl NN18 36 D2
Violet La
Creaton NN6 104 F4
Rothwell NN14, NN16 71 C6
Viscount Rd NN3 143 C6
Vislok Cl LE16 31 E1
Vivian Rd NN8 130 B5
Vokes Cl NN3 143 A1
Volunteer Cl NN4 175 E6
Vulcan Cl NN11 135 A3
Vyse Rd NN2 141 C8

W

Wadcroft 3 NN16 72 B2
Wadd Close La NN11 137 D6
Wade Meadow Ct NN3 142 F4
WADENHOE 58 A4
Wadenhoe La PE8 57 F4
Wadenhoe Rd NN14 57 E1
Wades Cl PE8 14 F1
Wadham Ct NN11 153 C7
Waggoners Way NN7 173 A7
Wagstaff Way MK46 195 F3
Wagtail Cl NN3 142 C7
Waingrove NN3 143 B4
Wainwright Ave NN14 76 D1
Wake Cl NN8 130 A1
Wakefield NN8 129 C4
Wakefield Dr NN6 64 D5
Wakefield Rd NN2 141 D4
Wakefield Way NN7 156 C1
Wakehurst Dr NN4 175 C7
WAKERLEY 4 A3
Wakerley Cl PE8 41 D5
Wakerley Great Wood Forest Trail* LE15 4 C2
Wakerley Great Wood Orienteering Course* LE15 4 B2
Wakerley Rd
Barrowden LE15 4 A4
Harringworth NN17 10 F7
Wake Way NN4 175 F3
Walcot Cl PE8 41 E7
Walcote Rd LE17 63 C8
Walcot Rd LE16 31 E2
WALES 230 F5
Wales St
Kings Sutton OX17 230 F5
Rothwell NN14 70 C7
Walford Pl CV22 98 F8
WALGRAVE 108 B5
Walgrave Cl NN3 161 B8
Walgrave Prim Sch NN6 108 A5
Walgrave Rd
Holcot NN6 107 E1
Old NN6 107 E6
Walgrave NN6 108 B4
Walker Dr NN12 203 C8
Walkers Acre NN6 108 A5
Walkers Field PE8 13 F8
Walkers La NN6 140 B8
Walker's La 5 NN16 72 B2
Walker Sq NN8 129 C7
Walkers Way NN4 175 E5
Walker's Way NN9 111 F4
Walks The PE9 1 D2
Walk The NN6 124 B8
Wallace Gdns NN2 141 F2
Wallace Rd NN2 141 F2
Wallace Terr NN2 141 F2
Wallbeck Cl NN2 141 C4
Walledwell Ct 4 NN3 142 F1
Wallingford End 6 NN3 161 A8
Wallis Cl NN8 129 A4
Wallis Cres NN15 91 C8
Wallis Rd NN15 91 C8
Wallwin Cl NN7 191 C4
Walmer Cl NN10 132 D1
Walnut Cl
Brackley NN13 222 F1
Braunston NN11 118 D2
Clifton OX15 236 E4
Culworth OX17 198 D2
Silverstone NN12 214 D4
Weldon NN17 38 B8
Walnut Cres NN16 72 D4
Walnut Gdns OX17 181 D1
Walnut Gr NN3 142 C1
Walnut Tree Cl NN14 94 D6
Walnut Tree Ct NN10 132 B7
Walsingham Ave NN15 91 F8
Waltham Cl NN17 36 D8
Waltham Gdns OX16 219 A6
Walton Ave OX17 230 B5
Walton Heath Way NN2 141 E3
Walton Pl NN18 36 B6
Wansell Rd NN17 37 F8
WANSFORD 8 B4
Wansford Pl NN17 36 B8
Wansford Rd
Elton PE8 16 E3
Yarwell PE8 7 F2
Wansford Sta* PE8 16 E8
Wansford Wlk NN3 142 E6
Wantage Cl
Hackleton NN7 177 B3
Moulton NN3 126 E1
Wantage Pl NN29 147 B8
Wantage Rd
Irchester NN29 147 B8
Northampton NN1 160 A8
WAPPENHAM 213 A8
Wappenham Rd
Abthorpe NN12 201 F1
Helmdon NN13 212 A5
Syresham NN13 213 C2
Wardens Lo 2 NN11 135 C2
WARDINGTON 196 D2
Wardington Rd OX17 208 D6
Wardle Ct NN16 72 B3
Wardle's Cl NN7 138 C7
Wardlow Cl NN4 174 F8
Ward Rd NN13 234 A5
Wards La NN6 82 C3
Wareham Gn NN18 36 B6
Warehouse The LE16 31 D4
Wareing La NN7 178 B8
Ware Orch CV23 99 C2
Ware Rd CV23 99 C2
WARKTON 73 A4
Warkton La NN15, NN16 73 B2
Warkton Way NN17 36 B8
WARKWORTH 219 D5
Warkworth Rd OX17 219 E7
WARMINGTON 28 C3
Warmington Sch PE8 28 B3
Warminster Cl NN18 36 A7
WARMONDS HILL 132 A6
Warmonds Hill NN10 132 B5
Warners Hill NN29 164 D2
Warnham NN8 129 B5
Warren Bridge PE8 41 E5
Warren Cl NN29 147 C7
Warren End
Desborough NN14 51 B4
Mawsley Village NN14 89 A4
Warren Hill NN16 71 E3
Warren La
Bythorn PE28 97 D4
Clopton NN14 78 F1
Warren Rd
Northampton NN5 158 F7
Stanion NN14 37 E3
Wothorpe PE9 2 E7
Yardley Gobion NN12 217 F6
Warrens Cl NN9 112 F2
Warren The
Northampton NN4 175 F8
Thorpe Mandeville OX17 210 A6
Warren Yd MK12 229 F6
WARRINGTON 180 B1
Warrington Rd MK46 195 F5
Warth Park Way NN9 114 B7
Wartnaby St LE16 31 D3
Warwick Ave NN14 37 E3
Warwick Cl
Market Harborough LE16 31 F5
Northampton NN5 158 B8
Raunds NN9 114 D5
Warwick Ct
Daventry NN11 135 B1
Kettering NN15 91 F8
Warwick Gdns NN14 76 F2
Warwick Ho NN5 158 F7
Warwick Prim Sch NN8 129 F1
Warwick Rd
Hanslope MK19 207 A3
Upper Boddington NN11 182 C7
Wellingborough NN8 130 A2
Warwick St NN11 135 B1
Warwick Way NN17 36 C6
Washbrook Cl NN3 143 B1
Washbrook La NN6 143 F5
Washbrook Rd NN10 132 A3
Washingley La PE7 44 F6
Washington Ct NN14 76 E3
Washington Sq NN16 72 D3
Washington St NN2 141 C3
Washle Dr OX17 220 B7
Water Cl MK19 229 B7
Waterfall Way LE16 18 F6
Waterfield Pl LE16 31 E5
Waterhouse Gdns NN15 92 A7
Watering La NN4 175 C3
Water La
Adderbury OX17 230 A3
Bradden NN12 201 F5
Chelveston NN9 133 B8
Cottingham LE16 35 D8
Northampton NN4 175 E6
Shutlanger NN12 204 D8
Towcester NN12 203 C5
Weldon NN17 38 A8
Waterlee Furlong NN6 106 C1
Waterloo NN11 135 C1
Waterloo Way NN9 131 D8
Waterlow Bridge NN9 111 F5
Water Meadow Cl NN18 36 B1
Watermeadow Dr NN3 142 F6
Watermill Cl NN14 51 D3
Waterpike NN6 106 C2
Waterpump Ct NN3 142 F5
Waters Edge PE8 16 B8
Waterside Way NN4 160 B4
Waters La OX17 209 B1
Watersmeet NN1 160 C6
Water St NN16 72 C2
Watervill Way NN14 113 B8
Waterworks Way LE17 45 F5
Watery La
Brackley NN13 234 A7
Nether Heyford NN7 156 C2
WATFORD 120 C6
Watford Rd
Crick NN6 101 A2
West Haddon NN6 102 B3
Watkin Ct NN1 159 D7
Watkin Terr NN1 159 D7
Watling St E
Pattishall NN12 188 D8
Towcester NN12 203 C6
Watling St W
Pattishall NN12 188 D8
Towcester NN12 203 C6
Watling St
Kilsby CV23 100 A3
Potterspury NN12 217 D3
Weedon Bec NN7 155 C4
Watson Ave LE16 48 D8
Watson Cl
Corby NN17 21 E2
Oundle PE8 41 E7
Wellingborough NN8 129 C7
Watson Rd NN6 121 B2
Watts Cl MK19 207 A3
Watts La CV21 99 B8
Watts Way NN6 121 C3
Wavell Cl NN15 72 E1
Waveney Cl NN11 153 A8
Waveney Way NN5 140 F1
Waver Cl NN18 36 D3
Waverley Ave NN17 37 A6
Waverley Cl OX17 230 F5
Waverley Rd
Kettering NN15 91 D8
Northampton NN2 141 E1
Waverley Rd *continued*
Rugby CV21 80 A1
Waynflete Ave NN13 233 E7
Waynflete Cl NN13 233 E7
Waypost Ct NN3 142 F3
Wayside Acres 3 NN4 175 B8
Weares Cl LE15 3 B5
Weaver Cl NN16 72 B6
Weavers End MK19 207 B2
Weavers Rd NN8 129 D4
Weavers Sch NN8 129 D4
Weavers The NN4 175 C6
Webb Cl PE8 42 B5
Webb Rd NN9 114 C7
Webbs Factory NN2 141 D1
Webbs La NN6 127 D3
Webster Cl NN9 114 D7
Weddell Way NN4 160 C2
Wedgwood Cl NN14 50 F3
Wedmore Cl NN5 158 D7
Wedmore Ct NN18 36 B6
WEEDON BEC 155 A3
Weedon Bec Prim Sch NN7 155 B3
Weedon La NN11 136 C4
WEEDON LOIS 200 C2
Weedon Rd
Farthingstone NN12 170 F3
Kislingbury NN7 157 D5
Nether Heyford NN7 156 B2
Newnham NN11 153 E4
Northampton NN5 158 D5
WEEKLEY 72 F6
Weekley Glebe Rd NN16 72 D5
Weekley Wood La NN16 72 E6
Weekly Cl NN14 113 B8
Weggs Farm Rd NN5 139 F1
Weighbridge Way NN9 114 C5
Weinahr Cl LE16 34 C5
Weir Cl NN8 129 F7
Weir The 14 NN11 135 B7
Welbeck Ct
Corby NN18 36 C5
Kettering NN15 91 F8
Welbourne Cl NN9 114 C6
WELDON 38 C8
Weldon CE Prim Sch NN17 38 A8
Weldon Cl NN8 129 D7
Weldon North Ind Est NN17 22 F1
Weldon Rd NN17 37 C7
Weldon St 2 NN16 72 C3
WELFORD 64 E5
Welford Ave NN9 113 B5
Welford Cl NN9 113 B5
Welford Gr NN17 36 C7
Welford Rd
Husbands Bosworth LE17 45 E3
Northampton NN2 141 B4
Sibbertoft LE16 46 D2
South Kilworth LE17 63 D7
Spratton NN6 124 A8
Thornby NN6 84 D4
Welford NN6 64 E7
Welford Sibbertoft & Sulby Endowed Sch NN6 64 E5
WELHAM 17 E5
Welham La
Great Bowden LE16 32 C8
Welham LE16 17 E8
Welham Rd
Great Bowden LE16 32 B8
Thorpe Langton LE16 17 B5
Welham LE16 18 A8
Weston by W LE16 18 A4
Welland Ave LE16 30 E7
Welland Bsns Pk LE16 32 B4
Welland Cl
Caldecott LE16 21 C8
Daventry NN11 152 F8
Gretton NN17 22 B8
Raunds NN9 114 C7
Welland Ct
Burton Latimer NN15 92 B2
Desborough NN14 51 A3
3 Market Harborough LE16 31 F2
Market Harborough LE16 32 A4
Welland Gn NN5 140 F2
Welland Mdws PE9 4 F8
Welland Park Com Coll LE16 31 E2
Welland Park Rd LE16 31 E2
Welland Rd NN16 72 A5
Welland Rise LE16 46 F2
Welland Vale Rd NN17 21 E1
Welland View Rd LE16 20 D1
Welland Way NN5 141 A2
Welland Wlk NN5 140 F2
Well Hill Cl NN6 100 F5
WELLINGBOROUGH 130 D6
Wellingborough Jun Sch NN8 130 B3
Wellingborough Rd
Broughton NN14 90 B3
Earls Barton NN6 144 F6
Finedon NN9 111 F4

Wellingborough Rd *continued*
Great Harrowden NN9 110 E1
Irthlingborough NN9 131 C8
Isham NN14 110 F8
Little Harrowden NN9 110 B3
Mears Ashby NN6 128 C2
Northampton, Cottarville NN3 142 E1
Northampton NN1 159 F6
Olney MK46 195 F5
Rushden NN10 131 F3
Sywell NN6 127 F4
Wellingborough NN8 111 E1
Wellingborough Sch
Wellingborough NN8 130 B3
Wellingborough NN8 130 B4
Wellingborough Sta NN8 130 C5
Wellington Pl 18 NN1 159 C7
Wellington Rd NN9 114 C5
Wellington St
Kettering NN16 72 C3
Northampton NN1 159 D6
Wellington Terr NN14 76 B2
Wellington Wks 1 NN16 72 C3
Well La
Barnwell PE8 59 B7
Everdon NN11 170 A8
Guilsborough NN6 103 F6
Rothwell NN14 70 D7
Staverton NN11 152 B7
Welton NN11 119 E1
Wells Cl
Husbands Bosworth LE17 45 E5
Kettering NN15 90 F8
Wells Ct NN3 142 C8
Wells Gn NN18 36 B6
Wellspring NN7 190 D7
Well St NN9 111 F5
Wells The NN9 111 F5
Well Yd NN2 141 B3
Welsh Rd
Aston le W NN11 182 C8
Chipping Warden OX17 197 C6
WELTON 119 E1
Welton CE Prim Sch NN11 119 E1
Welton La NN11 135 D6
Welton Pk NN11 119 E1
Welton Pl CV22 98 D8
Welton Rd
Braunston NN11 118 D1
Daventry NN11 135 C3
Wenlock Way NN5 140 D1
Wensleydale NN2 140 F5
Wensleydale Pk NN17 36 D8
Wentin Cl NN18 36 C1
Wentworth Ave NN8 129 C7
Wentworth Cl NN11 135 E3
Wentworth Cotts MK18 227 A5
Wentworth Dr PE8 41 E7
Wentworth Rd
Finedon NN9 112 A5
Rushden NN10 132 A2
Wentworth Way
Northampton NN2 141 E3
Stoke Bruerne NN12 204 F8
Weskers Cl LE16 67 A7
Wesley Ct NN9 114 D6
Wesley Pl OX17 208 E4
Wesley Rd CV21 99 A8
Wessex Cl NN16 72 B6
Wessex Way NN3 142 B1
West Ave NN15 92 B3
West Bank NN3 142 E6
Westbrook NN8 129 B4
West Brook
Blisworth NN7 190 D8
Newnham NN11 153 D4
WESTBURY 234 F4
Westbury Cl NN5 158 D7
Westbury Mill NN13 234 F4
Westbury Wlk NN18 36 B6
West Cotton Cl NN4 159 C4
Westcott Way
Corby NN18 36 D5
Northampton NN3 160 E7
West Cres NN10 131 E2
West Ct NN11 135 C1
West End
Bugbrooke NN7 172 E7
Scaldwell NN6 106 F5
Silverstone NN12 214 C4
Welford NN6 64 D4
West Haddon NN6 102 B4
Westerburgh Sq NN11 153 C8
Westerdale NN2 140 F5
Western Ave
Daventry NN11 153 B8
Easton o t H PE9 1 F5
Market Harborough LE16 31 D1
Nether Heyford NN7 156 B1
Western Cl NN11 135 B2
Western Dr MK19 207 A3
Western View NN1 159 B5
Western Way NN8 129 D3
West Farm Cl NN6 108 C3
West Farm Dr LE15 3 E5
WEST FARNDON 183 F3
Westfield Ave
Deanshanger MK19 228 D5
Raunds NN9 114 B4
Rushden NN10 131 F2
Westfield Barns CV47 166 D7
Westfield Cl LE16 31 C3
Westfield Cres NN6 64 E6
Westfield Ct NN6 102 C4
Westfield Ctr NN13 233 E8
Westfield Dr NN9 114 B4
Westfield Ho 8 NN16 72 B2
Westfield Pl NN10 131 F2
Westfield Rd
Northampton, Duston NN5 158 B8
Northampton NN5 158 F6
Wellingborough NN8 129 E4
Westfields
Little Harrowden NN9 110 B3
Wellingborough NN8 130 D3
West Fields PE9 1 F5
Westfields Ave NN10 132 B5
Westfields Rd NN17 36 E8
Westfields St NN10 132 B5
Westfields Terr NN10 132 B5
West Furlong NN15 71 F1
Westgate La LE16 30 E3
Westgate Rd NN5 158 D6
West Glebe Rd NN17 36 F7
WEST HADDON 102 C4
West Haddon Endowed CE Prim Sch NN6 102 B4
West Haddon Rd
Cold Ashby NN6 84 A5
Crick NN6 101 B6
Guilsborough NN6 103 D7
Ravensthorpe NN6 103 C1
Watford NN6 120 D7
Westhaven PE9 2 A5
Westhill Ave NN13 233 E7
Westhill Cl
Brackley NN13 233 E7
Kettering NN15 71 F1
Westhill Dr NN15 71 F1
Westhill Gdns NN13 233 D7
WESTHORP 183 C7
Westhorp OX17 210 E2
Westhorpe
Ashley LE16 18 E2
Sibbertoft LE16 46 F2
Westhorpe La NN11 183 C7
Westhorpe Mews NN11 183 C6
Westland Cl LE16 30 E3
Westlea Rd NN6 127 D3
Westleigh Cl NN1 159 F8
Westleigh Pk NN3 141 E6
Westleigh Rd NN15 92 B8
Westley Cl NN15 92 B1
West Leys Ct NN3 142 C7
West Lodge Rural Ctr* NN14 51 C6
West March NN11 153 D7
Westmead Ct NN3 142 F1
West Mill PE9 1 F4
Westminster Cl NN13 234 A7
Westminster Cres NN13 234 A7
Westminster Croft NN13 233 F7
Westminster Dr NN15 91 F7
Westminster Rd
Brackley NN13 233 F6
Wellingborough NN8 129 E7
Westminster Wlk NN18 36 C4
Westmoreland Cl PE8 15 E5
Westmorland Dr NN14 51 C4
WESTON 200 A2
WESTON BY WELLAND 18 A3
Westone Ave NN3 142 E1
WESTON FAVELL 160 E8
Weston Favell CE Prim Sch NN3 142 D1
Weston Favell Ctr NN3 142 F2
Weston Favell Sch NN3 142 D3
Weston Mill La NN3 160 E6
Weston Rd
Ashley LE16 18 D3
Olney MK46 195 D3
Ravenstone MK46 194 E2
Sulgrave OX17 211 A8
Sutton Bassett LE16 18 A2
Welham LE16 17 F5
WESTON UNDERWOOD 195 A2
Westonville PE9 1 D2
Weston Way NN3 160 C8
Weston Wlk NN18 36 C6
West Oval NN5 140 F1
Westover Rd NN15 71 F1
West Paddock Ct NN3 142 F4
West Priors Ct NN3 143 A4
West Ridge NN2 141 D3
West Rising NN4 175 D7
West Side Rise MK46 195 F4
West St
Broughton NN14 90 A5
Earls Barton NN6 144 E4
Easton o t H PE9 2 A5
Ecton NN6 143 F4
Geddington NN14 54 A3
Kettering NN16 72 B1
King's Cliffe PE8 13 E7
West St *continued*
Long Buckby NN6 121 A4
Moulton NN3 126 C1
Northampton NN1 159 F6
Olney MK46 195 F4
Oundle PE8 41 F5
Raunds NN9 114 D6
Rushden NN10 132 B2
Stanwick NN9 113 E3
Weedon Bec NN7 155 B3
Welford NN6 64 E6
Wellingborough NN8 129 F4
Woodford NN14 94 C7
West View
Corby NN17 37 B7
Daventry NN11 135 B1
Westvilla Cotts NN8 129 F4
West Villa Rd NN8 129 F4
Westway NN15 71 F1
West Way
Earls Barton NN6 144 D5
Weedon Bec NN7 155 B3
Westway The NN11 153 D8
Westwood Rd CV22 98 F7
Westwood Way NN3 142 D1
Westwood Wlk NN18 36 C5
Wetenhall Rd NN9 114 A4
Wetheral Cl NN3 142 C4
Weymouth Cl NN18 36 B6
Whaddon Cl NN4 158 E1
Whaddon Field NN6 106 C1
Whalley Gr NN7 161 F6
Wharf Cl MK19 229 B7
Wharfedale Rd NN17 21 E1
Wharfe Gn NN5 140 F2
Wharf La
Old Stratford MK19 229 C7
Souldern OX27 237 B4
Wharf Rd NN10 132 B6
Wharton Cl NN8 129 F5
Wheat Cl NN11 135 C6
Wheatcroft Gdns NN10 132 C2
Wheatens Cl NN6 125 C8
Wheatfield Dr NN15 92 C2
Wheatfield Gdns NN3 142 B1
Wheatfield Rd NN3 142 B1
Wheatfield Rd N NN3 142 B2
Wheatfield Rd S NN3 142 B1
Wheatfield Terr NN3 142 B1
Wheatley Ave NN17 36 F6
Wheeler's Rise NN13 238 C8
Wheel La LE15 3 F5
Wheelwright Cl NN9 114 E7
Wheelwright Ho NN14 70 D7
Wheelwrights Way MK19 229 C7
Wheelwrights Yd NN29 164 D2
Whernside NN8 129 D6
Whernside Way NN5 158 C8
WHILTON 137 D6
Whilton Lo NN11 136 D8
WHILTON LOCKS 136 F6
Whilton Mill* NN11 137 C6
Whilton Rd
Great Brington NN7 138 C7
Northampton NN2 141 D4
Whistlefield Cotts NN6 143 C7
Whistlets Cl NN4 158 D1
WHISTON 162 D6
Whiston Rd
Cogenhoe NN7 162 C6
Denton NN7 162 B2
Northampton NN2 141 D4
Whitby Cl NN15 91 F8
Whitecroft Gdns NN11 184 B7
White Delves NN8 129 E7
White Doe Dr NN3 142 C7
Whitefield Rd NN5 140 C1
Whitefield Way NN9 114 C7
Whiteford Dr NN15 91 C7
Whitefriars NN10 131 F1
Whitefriars Jun & Inf Schs NN10 147 F8
Whitegates NN4 158 D1
Whiteheart Cl NN3 143 B2
Whitehill MK46 195 E5
Whitehill Rd NN14 50 E3
WHITE HILLS 141 B6
White Hills Cres NN2 141 B6
Whitehills Prim Sch NN2 141 A6
White Hills Way NN2 141 B6
White Horse Yd
Stony Stratford MK11 229 D5
Towcester NN12 203 C6
White House Ct NN10 132 C1
White House Ind Est NN6 144 D6
Whiteland Rd NN3 142 C2
Whiteman La NN14 70 C7
White Post Ct NN17 21 E2
Whitesands Way NN4 158 C2
Whites Rise NN9 112 E1
Whitethorns Cl LE17 62 B3
White Way NN6 144 E5
WHITFIELD 223 E3
Whitfield Way NN2 141 D5
Whiting Ct NN3 142 C8
Whitmees Cl MK46 195 E4
Whitmore Ct NN12 214 D5
Whitney Cl NN9 114 C5
Whitney Rd NN15 92 B1
Whitsundale Cl NN9 111 F4
Whittall St OX17 230 F5
Whittam Cl NN9 114 C7
Whittemore Rd NN10 132 D3
WHITTLEBURY 215 C4
Whittlebury CE Prim Sch NN12 215 C4
Whittlebury Cl NN2 141 D5
Whittlebury Ct NN12 215 C5
Whittlebury Rd NN12 214 E5
Whittle Cl
Daventry NN11 135 A5
Wellingborough NN8 129 B6
Whittle Rd NN17 37 B8
Whittles Cross NN4 176 A6
Whittlesea Terr NN14 94 D6
Whitton Cl OX17 210 E2
Whittons La NN12 203 C6
Whitwell Cl PE8 41 E5
Whitworth Ave NN17 37 A8
Whitworth Cres NN6 144 E5
Whitworth Rd
Northampton NN1 159 F7
Wellingborough NN8 130 C5
Whitworth Way
Irthlingborough NN9 131 E8
Wellingborough NN8 130 B2
Whytewell Rd NN8 129 F6
Wick Cl NN18 36 D3
WICKEN 228 A3
Wicken Park Rd MK19 228 B1
Wicken Rd MK18 227 E1
Wickery Dene NN4 176 A6
Wicksteed Cl NN15 91 C6
Wicksteed L Pk* NN15 91 D6
Wiggins Cl CV21 99 B8
WIGSTHORPE 59 B2
Wigston Rd 3 CV21 80 A1
WILBARSTON 34 D5
Wilbarston CE Prim Sch LE16 34 C5
Wilbarston Rd LE16 34 B4
Wilberforce St 3 NN1 159 E6
WILBY 129 A1
Wilby CE Prim Sch NN8 129 B1
Wilby Cl NN17 36 B8
Wilbye Grange NN8 129 D2
Wilby La NN29 145 D6
Wilby Park Mobile Home Pk NN8 129 C2
Wilby Rd NN6 128 D2
Wilby St NN1 159 F6
Wilby Way NN8 129 D1
Wilce Ave NN8 130 A1
Wildacre Rd NN10 131 E2
Wild Cherry Cl NN11 184 B6
Wildern La NN4 175 C5
Wilford Ave NN3 160 F8
Wilkie Cl NN15 90 F8
Wilkie Rd NN8 129 F8
Wilks Wlk NN4 175 E3
Willetts Cl NN17 36 E8
Willey Ct MK11 229 F4
William Rd NN6 121 B3
Williams Cl MK19 206 F3
WILLIAMSCOT 208 C8
Williamscot Hill OX17 208 B6
Williamscot Road Ind Ctr OX17 196 A1
William St
Burton Latimer NN15 92 B2
Finedon NN9 112 A4
Kettering NN16 72 B4
Northampton NN1 159 D7
William Steele Way NN10 132 C5
Williams Terr NN11 135 B2
Williams Way
Higham Ferrers NN10 132 B5
Northampton NN4 175 E3
William's Way NN29 146 E1
William Trigg Cl NN9 131 E8
Willis Way NN12 203 C5
Williton Cl NN3 160 D7
Willmott Rd NN10 148 C8
WILLOUGHBY 117 C3
Willoughby Cl NN11 135 B3
Willoughby Pl CV22 98 D7
Willoughby Rd LE15 3 A6
Willoughby Way NN7 177 A1
Willowbrook Apartments The NN8 130 B4
Willowbrook East Ind Est NN17 22 E2
Willow Brook Rd NN17 36 C8
Willow Brook Sq NN3 143 D2
Willow Cl
Desborough NN14 51 C3
Hinton NN11 184 A6
Spratton NN6 124 A8
Towcester NN12 203 C3
Willow Cres
Great Houghton NN4 160 F2
Market Harborough LE16 31 C2
Willow Ct NN1 160 A7
Willow Gr MK19 229 B6
Willow Herb Cl NN10 148 C7
Willow Herb Wlk NN14 51 A4
Willow La
Great Houghton NN4 160 E2
King's Cliffe PE8 13 F7
Stanion NN14 37 F2
Stony Stratford MK11 229 C5
Willow Rd
Brackley NN13 234 A6
Kettering NN15 72 C1
Willow Rise NN3 161 B8
Willows Hill NN12 201 F5
Willows The
Daventry NN11 135 C3
Kings Sutton OX17 231 A6
Little Harrowden NN9 110 B3
Silverstone NN12 214 C5
Thrapston NN14 76 C1
Willow Tree Gdns CV21 99 A8
Willow View NN7 157 C3
Wills Cl NN6 103 E7
Willson Cl LE16 32 A3
Wilmington Wlk 1 NN18 36 B5
Wilson Cl NN11 135 A4
Wilson Cres NN9 112 E1
Wilson Rd 5 NN10 132 A2
Wilson Terr NN16 72 B4
Wilson Way NN6 144 E3
Wilton Cl NN14 51 A2
Wilton Rd NN15 91 F8
Wimbledon St NN5 159 A6
Wimborne Cl NN3 143 D3
Wimborne Pl NN11 135 C5
Wimborne Wlk NN18 36 A7
Wimpole NN8 129 C4
Wimpole Ho 5 NN11 135 B7
Wincanton Ct NN18 36 B6
Wincely Cl NN11 135 C6
Winchester Cl NN4 159 C1
Winchester House Sch NN13 233 F7
Winchester Rd
Northampton NN4 159 C1
Rushden NN10 132 C1
Winchilsea Dr NN17 10 B1
Windermere Cl NN11 135 B2
Windermere Dr
Higham Ferrers NN10 132 B8
Wellingborough NN8 129 C6
Windermere Rd NN16 71 F2
Windermere Way NN3 142 C4
Windflower Pl 2 NN3 143 D2
Windgate Way PE8 8 A6
Windingbrook La NN4 175 C5
Winding Way NN14 76 E2
Windmill Ave
Blisworth NN7 190 E7
Kettering NN15, NN16 72 D2
Raunds NN9 114 D6
Windmill Banks NN10 132 C7
Windmill Bsns Ctr 7 NN10 132 A2
Windmill Cl
Cottingham LE16 20 D1
Wellingborough NN8 129 E2
Wollaston NN29 146 E2
Windmill Cotts NN15 92 D4
Windmill Ct NN16 72 D3
Windmill Gdns NN11 152 C7
Windmill Glade NN6 106 A1
Windmill Gr NN9 114 D6
Windmill La
Denton NN7 178 B8
Raunds NN9 114 D7
Staverton NN11 152 C7
Windmill Prim Sch NN9 114 C7
Windmill Rd
Irthlingborough NN9 112 E1
Rushden NN10 132 A2
Windmill Rise LE16 20 D1
Windmill Terr NN2 141 D4
Windmill Way
Greens Norton NN12 202 D8
Lyddington LE15 9 D6
Windmill Wlk NN15 72 D1
Windrush Rd NN4 175 F8
Windrush Way NN5 141 A2
Windsor Ave NN14 50 F2
Windsor Cl
Daventry NN11 135 B1
Kings Sutton OX17 230 F6
Long Buckby NN6 121 B3
Towcester NN12 203 B4
Weedon Bec NN7 155 B4
Wilbarston LE16 34 C4
Windsor Cres NN5 158 E6
Windsor Ct
Market Harborough LE16 31 D4
Northampton NN3 143 C2
Windsor Dr
Brackley NN13 233 E8
Thrapston NN14 76 E2
Windsor Gdns NN16 72 A2
Windsor Ho NN5 158 C8
Windsor Pl NN17 36 E5
Windsor Rd
Rushden NN10 132 C3
Wellingborough NN8 129 F1
Windyridge NN2 141 D3
Winemar Cl MK19 207 A3
Wingate Cl NN15 72 E1
Wing Rd LE15 3 A6
Winnington Cl NN3 143 C5
Winsford Way NN3 160 D7
Winsland Ct NN6 126 E8
Winstanley Rd NN8 130 B5
Winston Cl
Nether Heyford NN7 156 B1

Winston Cl *continued*
Northampton NN3 142 C5
Woodford Halse NN11 184 D5
Winston Cres NN13 233 F6
Winston Dr NN14 91 D1
Winter Bourne Ct NN18 36 B6
Winterburn Ct NN16 71 E3
Winthorpe Way NN18 36 C6
WINWICK 102 B8
Winwick Rd PE28 61 D1
Winwood Cl MK19 228 E5
Wire La LE16 19 D2
Wisley Cl NN4 175 C7
Wisteria Cl NN10 148 B7
Wisteria Way NN3 160 C6
Witham Gn NN5 140 E2
Witham Ho NN2 141 E1
Witham The NN11 134 F1
Witham Way NN5 140 F1
Witham Wlk NN5 140 F2
Witheys The NN4 175 F2
WITTERING 7 D8
Wittlich Rd NN8 130 B6
Witton Rd NN5 158 C8
Woburn Cl LE16 32 A3
Woburn Ct NN10 148 A8
Woburn Gate NN3 143 D3
Wodhams Dr NN13 222 E1
Wold Farm Ind Pk NN6 107 D7
Wold Rd NN15 92 E2
Wolfe Cl NN15 72 F1
WOLLASTON 146 F2
Wollaston Com Prim Sch NN29 146 D2
Wollaston Mus* NN29 146 D2
Wollaston Rd
Bozeat NN29 164 C5
Irchester NN29 146 F6
Wollaston Sch NN29 146 E2
Wollaton Gdns [2] NN3 160 F8
Wollongong Ho NN17 36 F8
Wolsey Cl NN6 101 A6
Wolverton Rd MK11 229 E6
Wood Avens Cl NN4 158 E1
Woodbine Cotts NN6 108 A5
Woodborough Gdns [5] NN3 160 F8
Woodbreach Dr LE16 32 B3
WOOD BURCOTE 203 C2
Woodcock St NN15 92 D3
Woodcote Ave NN3 142 A5
Woodcroft Cl NN12 203 C3
Woodcroft Way NN15 91 C8
WOODEND 200 F7
WOODEND GREEN 200 E6
Woodfield PE9 1 D1
Woodfield Gr NN17 36 E7
WOODFORD 94 C6
Woodford CE Prim Sch NN14 94 D6
Woodford Chase NN6 127 C2
Woodford Cl NN15 91 F5
Woodford Glebe NN6 64 E5
WOODFORD HALSE 184 C6
Woodford Halse CE Sch NN11 184 D6
Woodford La NN14 75 E6
Woodford Rd
Byfield NN11 183 D7
Eydon NN11 184 B2
Great Addington NN14 94 C1
Little Addington NN14 94 C3
Woodford St [7] NN1 159 E6
Woodford Wlk [9] NN1 159 E6
Woodgate LE16 30 E8
Woodgate Cl LE16 32 B2
Woodgate Rd NN4 175 F6
WOOD GREEN 224 F1
Woodhall Cl NN4 158 D1
Wood Hill NN1 159 D5
Woodhill Rd NN5 140 C1
Wood La
Hartwell NN7 192 E2
King's Cliffe PE8 13 E7
Oundle PE8 41 D4
Weston Underwood MK46 195 A2
Woodland Ave
Kettering NN15 92 A5
Northampton NN3 142 A1
Overstone NN6 127 B1
Woodland Cl NN5 140 B1
Woodland Dr NN15 92 C4
Woodland Hospl The NN16 71 B5
Woodland Rd NN10 132 A3
Woodlands NN4 175 E1
Woodlands Ave NN17 21 F1
Woodlands Cl NN14 55 F7
Woodlands Ct
[1] Kettering NN16 72 C4
Watford NN6 120 C6
Woodlands Grange NN6 145 A4
Woodlands La NN18 53 C8
Woodlands Mews NN14 55 F7
Woodlands Rd
Irchester NN29 147 A7
Weldon NN17 38 C7
Woodlands The
Geddington NN14 54 B3
Market Harborough LE16 31 C4
Silverstone NN12 214 D4
Stanwick NN9 114 A3
Staverton NN11 152 B7
Woodland View Prim Sch NN4 175 E3
Woodland Wlk NN3 143 B6
Woodleigh Pl NN17 36 E6
Woodley Chase NN5 140 B1
Woodmans Cl MK19 228 E4
WOODNEWTON 14 F2
Woodnewton Inf Sch NN17 36 C8
Woodnewton Rd PE8 15 D4
Woodnewton Way NN17 36 C7
Woodpecker Cl NN13 222 D1
Woodpecker Way NN4 174 F7
Wood Rd PE8 13 F7
Woodroffe Rd PE8 7 D8
Woodrush Way NN3 142 C7
Woods Ct
Brackley NN13 233 D7
Rushden NN10 132 B3
Woodsfield NN6 106 A2
Woodside
Stony Stratford MK11 229 E6
Sywell NN6 127 D1
Woodside Ave NN3 142 D4
Woodside Cres NN3 142 D4
Woodside Gn NN5 140 F1
Woodside Pk NN17 38 C7
Woodside Way NN5 140 F1
Woodside Wlk NN5 140 E1
Woods La NN12 217 E3
Wood St
Corby NN17 36 E6
Geddington NN14 54 B3
Higham Ferrers NN10 132 C5
Kettering NN16 72 C4
Northampton NN1 159 D6
Wellingborough NN8 129 F4
Woodstock [12] NN1 159 F6
Woodstock Cl NN8 129 E7
Woodvale Prim Sch NN3 143 A5
Woodville Cres NN12 217 E6
Woodward Cl NN11 135 E1
WOODWELL 94 A8
Woodwell Cotts NN14 94 A8
Woodwell Hill NN14 50 F2
Woodyard Cl NN14 55 F8
Woodyard The NN7 163 A3
Wooldale Rd NN4 175 E4
Woolmans MK11 229 F4
Woolmonger St [4] NN1 159 C5
Woolrich Gdns MK11 229 E5
Woolscott Rd CV23 117 C4
Woolston Ct NN17 10 C1
WOOTTON 175 F5
Wootton Brook Cl NN4 175 C6
Wootton Ct NN12 203 D5
WOOTTON HALL 175 C8
Wootton Hall Pk NN7 175 D8
Wootton Hill Farm NN4 174 F8
Wootton Hope Dr NN4 175 F6
Wootton Prim Sch NN4 175 E6
Wootton Rd NN7 176 A2
Wootton Trad Est NN4 175 F6
Worcester Cl
Corby NN18 36 E1
Northampton NN3 143 B2
West Haddon NN6 102 C5
Worcester Dr LE16 31 E5
Worcester Way NN11 153 C7
Wordsworth Ave NN17 21 D1
Wordsworth Cl
Brackley NN13 222 F1
Towcester NN12 203 B5
Wordsworth Rd
Daventry NN11 135 B3
Kettering NN16 72 C5
Wellingborough NN8 129 B3
Worksop Gdns NN18 36 B6
Works The [8] NN1 159 E6
WORMLEIGHTON 181 B8
Wormleighton Way NN14 54 A3
Worthing Rd NN18 36 B5
WOTHORPE 2 D8
Wothorpe Hill PE9 2 C7
Wothorpe Villas PE9 2 D8
Wrekin Cl NN4 158 E3
Wrenbury Rd NN5 140 A1
Wren Cl
Brackley NN13 222 D1
Corby NN18 36 E3
Kettering NN15 92 A6
Northampton NN4 175 F3
Towcester NN12 203 C3
Wrendyke Cl LE15 3 A6
Wrenn Sch
Wellingborough NN8 130 A3
Wellingborough NN8 130 B3
Wren Spinney Com Specl Sch NN15 71 F1
Wrightons Hill NN13 211 F4
Wright Rd NN6 121 B3
Wroe Cl NN18 36 C1
Wroe The NN10 132 B7
Wyatt St NN16 72 C2
Wyatt Way PE8 41 E6
Wychwood Cl NN5 140 A1
Wyckley Cl NN9 112 E3
Wycliffe Rd NN1 160 A6
Wye Cl NN8 129 C6
Wye The NN11 153 A8
Wykeham Rd NN10 132 C7
Wyman Cl NN29 164 D2
Wymersley Cl NN4 160 F2
WYMINGTON 148 B5
Wymington Pk NN10 132 B1
Wymington Rd
Podington NN29 147 E3
Rushden NN10 148 B8
Wyndham Way NN16 71 E4
Wysall Rd NN3 143 B5

Y

Yaffle Cres NN14 51 B4
Yardley Cl NN17 21 D1
Yardley Dr NN2 141 D6
YARDLEY GOBION 217 E5
Yardley Gobion CE Prim Sch NN12 217 E6
YARDLEY HASTINGS 179 B6
Yardley Hastings Prim Sch NN7 179 A7
Yardley Rd
Cosgrove MK19 218 D2
Grendon NN7 163 D4
Olney MK46 195 F5
Yardley Gobion NN12 217 F4
Yarrow NN8 129 B3
Yarrow Cl NN10 148 C7
Yarrow Ho NN2 141 C5
YARWELL 16 A8
Yarwell Ct NN15 91 C6
Yarwell Junc* PE8 16 B7
Yarwell Rd PE8 8 A3
Yarwell Sq NN4 158 F2
Yateley Dr NN15 92 A5
YELDEN 133 F3
Yelden Cl NN10 131 F2
Yeldon Ct NN8 111 B1
YELVERTOFT 82 C4
Yelvertoft Prim Sch NN6 82 B4
Yelvertoft Rd
Crick NN6 101 A8
Lilbourne CV23 81 D6
Northampton NN2 141 C3
West Haddon NN6 102 B5
Yeoman Cl NN14 95 A3
Yeoman Dr NN2 141 B5
Yeoman Mdw NN4 174 F8
Yeomanry Cl NN11 135 B1
Yeomanry Ct LE16 31 E3
Yeomanry Way NN11 135 B1
Yeomans Cl NN13 234 A8
Yeomans Ct NN15 92 C2
Yew Cl NN17 21 E1
Yew Tree Cl
Kettering NN15 91 C8
Middleton Cheney OX17 220 A8
Yewtree Ct NN3 142 D5
Yew Tree Gdns NN7 155 F5
Yew Tree Gr NN11 153 B8
Yew Tree La NN6 124 B8
Yew Tree Rise NN13 238 D8
York Ave NN7 161 F6
York Cl
Higham Ferrers NN10 132 C7
Towcester NN12 203 C4
York Ct NN12 203 C5
York Dr NN13 233 E8
Yorke Cl NN9 111 E5
York Ho NN1 159 F6
York Rd
Corby NN18 36 C5
Higham Ferrers NN10 132 C7
Kettering NN16 72 B2
Northampton NN1 159 E6
Rushden NN10 132 C1
Stony Stratford MK11 229 D5
Wellingborough NN8 130 B5
Wollaston NN29 146 D3
York Ride NN7 155 B4
York St LE16 31 F3
York Way NN9 114 C7

Zion Hill NN6 108 A5

Addresses

Name and Address	Telephone	Page	Grid reference

Using the Ordnance Survey National Grid

Any feature in this atlas can be given a unique reference to help you find the same feature on other Ordnance Survey maps of the area, or to help someone else locate you if they do not have a Street Atlas.

The grid squares in this atlas match the Ordnance Survey National Grid and are at 500 metre intervals. The small figures at the bottom and sides of every other grid line are the National Grid kilometre values (**00** to **99** km) and are repeated across the country every 100 km (see left).

To give a unique National Grid reference you need to locate where in the country you are. The country is divided into 100 km squares with each square given a unique two-letter reference. Use the administrative map to determine in which 100 km square a particular page of this atlas falls.

The bold letters and numbers between each grid line (**A** to **F**, **1** to **8**) are for use within a specific Street Atlas only, and when used with the page number, are a convenient way of referencing these grid squares.

Example *The railway bridge over DARLEY GREEN RD in grid square B1*

Step 1: Identify the two-letter reference, in this example the page is in **SP**

Step 2: Identify the 1 km square in which the railway bridge falls. Use the figures in the southwest corner of this square: Eastings **17**, Northings **74**. This gives a unique reference: **SP 17 74**, accurate to 1 km.

Step 3: To give a more precise reference accurate to 100 m you need to estimate how many tenths along and how many tenths up this 1 km square the feature is (to help with this the 1 km square is divided into four 500 m squares). This makes the bridge about **8** tenths along and about **1** tenth up from the southwest corner.

This gives a unique reference: **SP 178 741**, accurate to 100 m.

Eastings (read from left to right along the bottom) come before Northings (read from bottom to top). If you have trouble remembering say to yourself Along the hall, THEN up the stairs !

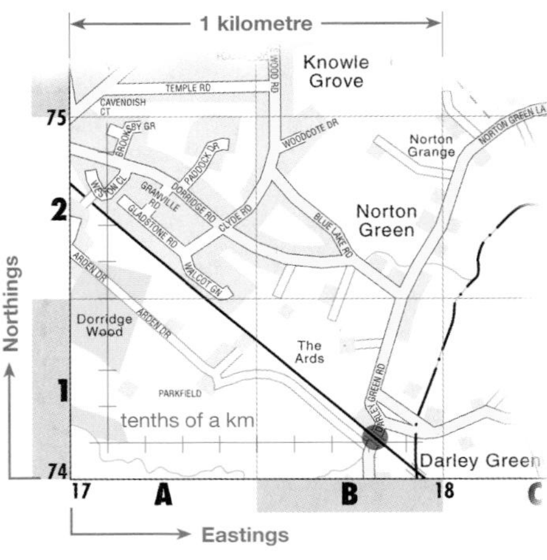